International Business – European Edition

International Business – European Edition

Michael Czinkota
Ilkka Ronkainen
Michael Moffett
Svetla Marinova
Marin Marinov

A John Wiley and Sons, Ltd, Publication

Authorized adaptation of the seventh edition by Michael R. Czinkota, Ilkka A. Ronkainen and Michael H. Moffett, *International Business*, (ISBN 0-324-22532-6), published by South-Western, part of the Thomson Corporation. Copyright © 2005 by South-Western, part of the Thomson Corporation. All rights Reserved. Used by permission.

This edition Copyright © 2009 John Wiley & Sons, Ltd
                 The Atrium, Southern Gate, Chichester,
                 West Sussex PO19 8SQ, England
                 Telephone +44 (0) 1243 779777

Email (for orders and customer service enquiries): cs-books@wiley.com
Visit our Home Page on www.wiley.com

Other Wiley Editorial Offices

John Wiley & Sons Inc., 111 River Street, Hoboken, NJ 07030, USA

Jossey-Bass, 989 Market Street, San Francisco, CA 94103-1741, USA

Wiley-VCH Verlag GmbH, Boschstr. 12, D-69469 Weinheim, Germany

John Wiley & Sons Australia Ltd, 42 McDougall Street, Milton, Queensland 4064, Australia

John Wiley & Sons (Asia) Pte Ltd, 2 Clementi Loop #02-01, Jin Xing Distripark, Singapore 129809

John Wiley & Sons Canada Ltd, 6045 Freemont Blvd, Mississauga, ONT, L5R 4J3

Wiley also publishes its books in a variety of electronic formats. Some content that appears in print may not be available in electronic books.

Library of Congress Cataloging-in-Publication Data

International business/Michael R. Czinkota ... [et al.]. – European ed.
    p. cm.
Includes bibliographical references and index.
ISBN 978-0-470-51029-2 (pbk.)
   1. International trade. 2. International finance. 3. Investments, Foreign. 4. International business enterprises.
I. Czinkota, Michael R.
HF1379.C94 2009
658′.049–dc22
                                    2008036184

A catalogue record for this book is available from the British Library

ISBN: 978-0-470-51029-2

Typeset in Sabon-Roman by Thomson Digital

Printed and bound in Spain by Grafos SA, Barcelona

CONTENTS

PART 6 CASE STUDIES 441

ABOUT THE AUTHORS

Michael R. Czinkota is on the faculty of marketing and international business at Georgetown University and the University of Birmingham in the United Kingdom. He served in the US government as Deputy Assistant Secretary of Commerce for international trade. He was also the head of the US delegation to the OECD Industry Committee in Paris and the Senior Trade Adviser for Export Controls. Dr Czinkota has been a partner in a trading company and in an advertising agency. He serves as adviser to the United Nations' and World Trade Organization's Executive Forum on National Export Strategies.

He was listed as one of the three most published contributors to international business research in the *Journal of International Business Studies*. He has received the Lifetime Contribution Award from the American Marketing Association and was named a Distinguished Fellow of the Academy of Marketing Science. He holds honorary degrees from the Universidad Pontificia Madre y Maestra in the Dominican Republic and the Universidad del Pacifico in Lima, Peru.

Dr Czinkota was born and raised in Germany and educated in Austria, Scotland, Spain and the United States. He studied law and business administration at the University of Erlangen-Nürnberg and holds and MBA in international business and a PhD in logistics from Ohio State University.

Ilkka A. Ronkainen is a member of the faculty of marketing and international business at the School of Business Adminstration at Georgetown University. He also serves as docent of international marketing at the Helsinki School of Economics. Dr Ronkainen has consulted to a wide range of US and international institutions, such as IBM and the Rand Corporation. He also maintains close relations with a number of Finnish companies and their internationalization and educational efforts.

Dr Ronkainen has published extensively in academic journals and the trade press. He is also on the review boards of the *Journal of Business Research, International Marketing Review* and *Journal of International Business Studies*. He has previously served as the North American co-ordinator for the European Marketing Academy and was a member of the board of the Washington International Trade Association.

Michael H. Moffett is Associate Professor of International Finance at the Thunderbird School of Global Management. He has served as an executive education consultant to numerous global companies and organizations, including BP (UK), ExxonMobil (USA), IBM (USA), Kimberly-Clarke (USA), Kelloggs (USA), Mattel (USA), Statoil (Norway), the East Asiatic Company (Denmark), Brasil Telecom (Brazil), Vitro de Mexico (Mexico), McDonald's (USA), Delphi (USA), Woodward Governor (USA), Briggs & Stratton (USA), SK (Korea), Phelps Dodge (USA), Texaco (USA), Chrysler LLC (USA), Legrand (France), Teleflex (USA/France), Engelhard (USA), EDS (USA), General Motors (USA), Dow Chemical (USA), Pfizer (USA), Textron (USA), Smith International (USA), Standard Bank (South Africa) and Ranbaxy (India).

Professor Moffett has authored, co-authored or contributed to numerous books, articles, periodicals and collected works. His articles have appeared in the *Journal of Financial and Quantitative Analysis, Journal of Applied Corporate Finance, Journal of International Money and Finance, Journal of International Financial Management and Accounting, Contemporary Policy Issues, Brookings Discussion Papers in International Economics* and others. He has contributed to a number of collected works including the *Handbook of Modern Finance, International Accounting and Finance Handbook* and *Encyclopedia of International Business*. He is also co-author of two books on multinational financial management with David Eiteman and Arthur Stonehill, *Multinational Business Finance* (10th edition) and *Fundamentals of Multinational Finance* (3rd edition).

Svetla T. Marinova is on the faculty of marketing and international business of the Birmingham Business School at the University of Birmingham, Business School. Dr Marinova graduated from the University of Economics in Varna, Bulgaria, holds an MBA from the University of Warwick (UK) and a PhD from Copenhagen Business School, (Denmark). She has held academic posts at Copenhagen Business School, University of Groningen (The Netherlands), University of Gloucestershire (UK), teaching international marketing and international business. Currently, Dr Marinova is Director of the highly successful MSc in International Business programme at the University of Birmingham.

Svetla Marinova's background is in economics, international business and marketing. She has been guest professor at a number of universities around the world, including Vienna University of Economics (Austria), University of Umeå (Sweden), FUMEC (Brazil) and University of Colorado (USA). She has enjoyed working with students from all over the world on international bachelors, masters and executive programmes.

Dr Marinova's publications have appeared in a number of academic journals, including *European Journal of Marketing, European Management Journal, International Marketing Review, Advances of International Marketing, Journal of Euromarketing* and *Thunderbird International Business Review*. She has co-authored a book on *Foreign Direct Investment in Central and Eastern Europe,* with Marin A. Marinov.

She works with multinational and small and medium-sized companies on their internationalization strategies in emerging economies and Europe.

Marin Marinov is Professor of International Business and Management at the University of Gloucestershire. He has held a number of professorial appointments all over the world, including the University of Southern Denmark and Copenhagen Business School (Denmark), University of Witten-Herdecke (Germany), University of Colorado at Colorado Springs (USA), University of Vaasa (Finland), University of Umeå (Sweden), Rennes Business School (France) and University of Hanan (China).

Dr Marinov graduated and developed his doctoral thesis in Bulgaria before starting his international academic career. His teaching and research interests include international business and management; in more specific terms, emerging markets, internationalization, marketization of emerging and transition economies, and foreign direct investment.

Marin Marinov has authored the following books: *Internationalisation in Central and Eastern Europe, Marketing in the Emerging Markets of Central and Eastern Europe, Marketing in the Emerging Markets of Latin America* and *Marketing in the Emerging Markets of Islamic Countries.* He has also co-authored with Svetla T. Marinova the book *Foreign Direct Investment in Central and Eastern Europe.* Dr Marinov has published a number of papers in academic journals, including *European Journal of Marketing, Journal of Marketing Management, International Marketing Review, Thunderbird International Business Review* and *Advances in International Marketing,* among others. He serves as review editor of the new *Journal of Islamic Marketing* and is on the editorial board of several academic journals.

PREFACE

This is the first European edition of *International Business*. It is based on the 7th edition of the widely respected text by Michael Czinkota, Ilkka Ronkainen and Michael Moffett.

The textbook is unique in its approach to international business as it provides insights at the forefront of global thinking from the perspective of the multinational corporation as well as that of the small international start-up firm. The book presents an exclusive theoretical base that can be associated with the managerial challenges faced by business people at the vanguard of international business operations and strategy. It will help the reader understand the complex interplay between international institutions, national governments, corporate governance and markets that affects the achievement of corporate objectives in the international marketplace. The book addresses the specificities of various markets with a special focus on European business activities and environment. The improvements in pedagogy, presentation and illustrative material writing continue to make this a valuable book to be used in teaching and learning.

The experience of Michael Czinkota, Ilkka Ronkainen and Michael Moffett in teaching managers and advising companies, both large and small, allows them to share with the reader the realities of the battle in the international business arena. Due to their ongoing policy work with both national and international organizations, they are able to give the reader a first-hand perspective of government activities in international business.

Svetla Marinova and Marin Marinov, both from the UK, have built upon this excellent foundation in this new updated European edition. They have added European examples and case studies throughout. They have retained the global focus and coverage of the previous edition, and the many cases and examples cover the US, China, India, as well as other emerging economies such as Brazil and Russia. Their overall focus has been to update the perspective of the book to make it more relevant to the European business reality, and to introduce new examples that show the diversity within Europe and the rest of the world. They have invigorated the debate on controversial issues in international business, suggesting that international business phenomena are multifaceted and viewpoints can differ. Lastly they have made the original book more concise, by condensing it to 14 chapters that will fit better with the length of the majority of European courses. The European edition therefore covers the relevant international business topics in a logical and concise manner.

Today, change happens at breakneck speed. Keeping on top of the evolving world of international issues and their impact on international business is difficult. In this book, the topics of transparency and governance are covered thoroughly to echo the changing times in which we live. Multinational corporate issues, together with co-operative modes of market development, are presented in the context of international business entry and strategic planning. Countertrade is covered in conjunction with multinational financial management. Controversies in international business, including the role of international institutions, such as the World Trade Organization, the World Bank, and the International Monetary Fund, are fully addressed. There is an extended discussion on the pro- and anti-globalization movements and arguments. Also presented are some of the areas of friction in international business and development, such as payment for intellectual property rights, distribution of patented medication to poor countries, and development of genetically engineered foods. Issues of bribery and corruption are addressed, as well as the benefits of good governance; in-depth attention is paid to the role of culture, policies and politics. The dimension of ethics, social responsibility and diversity are fully reflected through examples and vignettes.

TOPIC COVERAGE AND ORGANIZATION

The first European Edition of *International Business* is organized into six parts, containing 14 chapters. The sixth part has extended Case Studies exclusively. The order of the chapters in the first five parts allows the text to flow logically from introductory material, to the international environment, and on to marketing and financial considerations in the international marketplace.

Part 1 deals with the *International Business Environment*. Chapter 1 provides an overview of the key issues facing international business today. It has an extended section on the pros and cons of globalization and fully addresses the complexities of the issues surrounding it. It also covers the migration of manufacturing from developed nations to developing countries, discusses the highly charged issue of international sweatshops for the sake of low prices and also reflects some of the political divisiveness that affects trade issues, such as the rift between the US and Europe.

Chapter 2 covers theories of trade and investment and provides a directed path through centuries of thought on why and how trade and investment across borders occurs. It covers the international trade discussions in the Doha round and difficulties within trading blocs, such as NAFTA, are discussed, as are new efforts aimed at export promotion.

Chapter 3 focuses on culture, emphasizing not only the importance of preparing for differences, but also how culture can be used as a competitive tool. The intent of this chapter is to analyse the concept of culture and its various elements and then to provide suggestions for not only meeting the cultural challenge but also making it a basis of obtaining and maintaining a competitive advantage.

Chapter 4 looks at the political and legal environment. Substantial coverage is given to the issue of terrorism and its effect on world business. There is an additional focus on Africa and the prevailing corruption and lack of transparency that have made economic progress difficult. The chapter stresses the international need for managerial and corporate virtue, vision and veracity if the market force model is to be accepted around the globe.

Part 2 covers *International Business and Markets* with three chapters on financial markets, economic integration and emerging markets. Chapter 5 provides a detailed explanation of the structure and functions of the foreign currency markets, the international money markets and the international securities markets.

Chapter 6 begins with an explanation of the various levels of economic integration. The level of integration defines the nature and degree of economic links among countries. The major arguments both for and against economic integration are reviewed. Then, the European Union, the North American Free Trade Agreement, the Asia-Pacific Economic Co-operation and other economic alliances are discussed. Finally, possible strategic moves by international managers in response to integration are outlined.

Chapter 7 addresses major societal, economic and ideological shifts that take place in the global economy. The focus is on the changing economies of: Asia, particularly China, India, Pakistan; Latin America, specifically, Brazil, Argentina, Chile; and Africa, notably Morocco, South Africa and Nigeria. These nations are called *emerging economies*, because they are gradually becoming integrated into the global marketplace. The second type of changing economies are the *transition economies* – found in Eastern Europe, the former Soviet Union and other formerly socialist states. Transition economies have experienced a shift in economic thinking from central planning to a market-based model. Finally, the lesser-developed markets of Africa, Latin America and some of Asia, characterized by lack of economic freedom and transparency, are discussed.

Part 3 looks at *International Business Strategy*. Chapter 8 is concerned with firms preparing to enter international markets and companies expanding their current international activities. Initial emphasis is placed on export activities with a focus on the role of management in starting up international operations and a description of the basic stimuli for international activities. Entry modes for the international arena are highlighted and the problems and benefits of each mode are discussed. The role of facilitators and intermediaries in international business is described. Finally, alternatives that involve a local presence by the firm are presented.

Chapter 9 combines the topics of strategic planning, organization, implementation and control. Global strategy focuses on leveraging resources across markets. This means taking advantage of converging market trends by maximizing economies of scale or concentrating activities where they can be carried out most effectively. Large companies regularly have extensive operations worldwide, and many new companies transcend nationality almost entirely by making their operations virtual. Organizational structures need to reflect changes in the environment and companies' adjustment to these changes. The implementation of global strategy is discussed using centres of excellence and management of global knowledge networks as examples.

Part 4 focuses on *International Business Operations* including marketing, logistics and supply-chain management, financial management, international human resource management and corporate governance, accounting and taxation. Chapter 10 looks at how environmental differences generate new challenges for the international marketing manager, before focusing on the importance of logistics and supply-chain management as crucial tools for competitiveness in the international business arena. Chapter 11 considers multinational financial management and compares stockholder wealth maximization in the US and the UK with corporate wealth maximization in continental Europe and Japan. There is a discussion of countertrade, import–export financing, and the management of currency exposures and cash flows. Chapter 12 examines the management of human resources in international business, in particular the importance of the expatriate phenomenon, from two points of view: first that of the manager and then that of the worker. Chapter 13 centres on the critical topics of corporate governance, shareholder rights and transparency, all of which are so much at the forefront now in the international business world. The discussion details both the theory and the reality of how corporate governance provides accountability to shareholders and enumerates the diverse principles and practices employed across countries.

Part 5 looks at the future in terms of emerging issues in international business. Chapter 14 analyses the international business environment by looking at political, financial, societal and technological conditions of change and by providing a glimpse of possible future developments as envisioned by an international panel of experts. The chapter now also covers the concept of knowledge in international business, including organizational approaches to cross-border knowledge exchanges. The chapter ends with an overview of careers in international business, focusing on further training, opportunities for women and employment in different-sized companies as well as self-employment options.

Part 6 comprises a repository of global case studies to encourage in-depth discussion of the material covered and to extend students' understanding of the theory and application of the knowledge gained. The cases cover key international business issues from diverse countries such as Turkey, China, Poland, Bolivia, Germany and Russia. Challenging questions accompany each case and full teaching notes are available in the Instructor's Manual on the book companion web site.

DISTINGUISHING PEDAGOGICAL FEATURES

Contemporary Realism

Each chapter offers a number of Focus on Issues boxes that describe contemporary business situations. These include Politics, Ethics, e-Business, Culture and Entrepreneurship. These boxes are intended to serve as reinforcing examples or mini-case studies. As such they will assist the instructor in stimulating class discussion and aid the student in understanding the text material.

Chapter Summary and Review Questions

Each chapter closes with a chapter summary of key points that students should retain, organized by learning objective. The discussion questions are a complementary learning tool that will enable students to check their understanding of key issues, to think beyond basic concepts, and to determine areas that require further study. All these tools help students discriminate between main and supporting points and provide mechanisms for classroom activity or personal review.

Internet Exercises

At the end of each chapter, students are asked to explore the web to research topics related to material in that chapter. This hands-on experience helps to develop Internet, research and business skills.

Take a Stand

These end-of-chapter exercises ask students to read brief outlines of relevant situations in which differing standpoints can be applied. Discussion questions then challenge students to make an educated assessment and argue the case in the way they see it. These exercises can be used as homework assignments, for personal assessment or for classroom discussion.

COMPREHENSIVE LEARNING PACKAGE

This text is supported by an enlivened set of instructor and student resources. These include all the core resources such as the Instructor's Manual, Test Bank and PowerPoint slides. Both the instructor and student companion web sites are available at www.wileyeurope.com/college/czinkota.

INSTRUCTOR COMPANION WEB SITE

Instructor's Manual

The in-depth Instructor's Manual includes the following:

- General suggestions for teaching
- Group project ideas
- Guide to Focus on Issues boxes
- Suggested answers and notes on the end-of-chapter questions
- Suggestions and notes for Internet Exercises
- Discussion points and notes for the Take a Stand questions
- Detailed answers and notes on all case study discussion questions

Test Bank

Fully revised for this European edition, this Test Bank consists of more than 2000 true/false questions, multiple-choice questions, short answer and essay questions. The questions are also available in Blackboard and WebCT course packages from the instructor companion web site.

PowerPoint Lecture Presentations

The lectures provide outlines for every chapter, graphics of the illustrations from the text and additional examples providing instructors with a number of learning opportunities for students.

Student Companion web site

Students can access online quizzes for every chapter, with automatic feedback on how they scored. They can also access an online version of the glossary and links to relevant web sites for their own study.

GLOBAL MARKET POTENTIAL SYSTEM ONLINE (GMPSO©)
http://www.gmpso2.com

Available for use with Czinkota's *International Business*

GMPSO software, addresses one of the most important challenges faced by international business faculty and practitioners alike. GMPSO brings the real world of business in the classroom or training environment by providing the platform needed to support users in their roles as managers and decision makers in a global setting.

How does GMPSO Work?

GMMSO guides users through a systematic and integrative process for gathering, evaluating and entering data for a chosen company into the GMPSO online system. Users are provided with helpful tools such as step-by-step instructions, user guide, targeted internet resources, case examples and a glossary.

GMPSO is free for instructors adopting Czinkota's *International Business*. Access for students is available at specially discounted rates. For more information please email highereducation@wiley.com

ACKNOWLEDGEMENTS

We are grateful to the following reviewers for their input to the development of the European edition:

- Amelia Au-Yeung, Kingston Business School
- David Boughey, University of West England
- Erik Bruijn, University of Twente
- Caroline Burr, University of Bournemouth
- Howard Cox, University of Worcester
- Leif Enarsson, Handelshogskolan Goteborg
- Grahame Fallon, University of Northampton
- Theo Haupt, Cape Peninsula University of Technology
- Debra Johnson, University of Hull
- Martin de Jong, Delft University of Technology
- Vince Kane, University of Brighton
- Levin Lance, University of Johannesburg
- Val Lencioni, University of Middlesex
- George Lodorfos, Leeds Metropolitan University
- David Long, University of Canterbury
- Lorraine Mckechnie, Glasgow Caledonian University
- Alex Muresan, London Metropolitan University
- Nicholas Perdikis, University of Abersytwyth
- David Pollard, Leeds Metropolitan University
- Helen Rogers, University of Manchester
- Diane Rushton, Sheffield Hallam University
- Lorna Uden, University of Staffordshire
- Guglielmo Volpe, London Metropolitan University
- Alec Wersun, Glasgow Caledonian University

EUROPEAN EDITION AUTHORS' ACKNOWLEDGEMENTS

Many thanks to those faculty members who helped us by providing challenging comments and questions. Several individuals, in particular, have given us insights into the development of the book. Special thanks are extended to Professor Klaus Macharzina, from the University of Hohenheim, and Dr. Maja Macovec-Brencic from the University of Ljubljana.

We are much indebted to the editorial team at John Wiley & Sons, Ltd who have been supportive and helpful throughout the process despite its ups and downs. The commitment and persistence of Deborah Egleton and Sarah Booth have brought this project to a successful completion. Claire Jardine, Anneli Mockett and Céline Durand have worked hard on the publication.

We are grateful to our children, Della-Maria and Vassil, who have been patient and tolerated the long hours and weekends spent on this text.

PART 1

INTERNATIONAL BUSINESS ENVIRONMENT

Part 1 sets the stage by introducing the nature of international business and demonstrating the need to participate in international activities.

The globalization of business sets challenges and brings new opportunities and threats to governments, firms and individuals. These are linked with finding how to compete successfully in the global marketplace of today and tomorrow.

In order to succeed in international business, one needs to be able to manage variations among cultures. This in turn requires an understanding of cultural differences in language, religion, values, customs and education, so that one can develop cross-cultural competence. Chapter 3 on culture addresses these dimensions.

This part also highlights the policy issues surrounding the corporate decision maker and discusses the effect of politics and laws on business, together with the agreements, treaties and laws that govern the relationships between home and host countries.

CHAPTER

1

The Nature of International Business

LEARNING OBJECTIVES

- To discuss and evaluate the nature and impact of globalization.
- To understand the nature of international business.
- To learn the definition of international business.
- To realize the significance of international business.
- To recognize the growth of global linkages today.
- To appreciate the opportunities and challenges offered by international business.

GLOBALIZATION: OPPORTUNITY OR THREAT?

Globalization of business is seen by many as creating wealth that benefits nations and individuals worldwide. Peter Woicke, of the World Bank, credits globalization with providing the essential ingredients of success to entrepreneurs and corporations in developing regions. A multinational firm brings a reliable electricity source to local farmers, manufacturers and businesses by building a hydroelectric dam in Uganda. A banana grower in Ecuador expands his agribusiness into Russia and China, allowing him

© Getty Images. Reproduced with permission.

to channel profits to protect a local tropical rain forest. A Bulgarian manufacturing firm making hydraulic equipment expands its business via exporting worldwide. World Bank loans support a network of entrepreneurs in Eastern Europe and upgrade bank services in Latin America. 'Globalization', Woicke concludes, 'can help would-be industrialists change the labels of their countries from developing to developed'.

However, entry into the world economy also causes its share of problems. Critics of globalization believe that international business mainly increases the wealth of multinational corporations (MNCs) and investors at the expense of the poor. They say that it supports dictators, fails to relieve the massive debts of developing countries, spoils the environment and causes terrorism. There are growing protests over labour exploitation and the export of jobs and questions have been raised about the value and morality of the trade precepts guiding the world. In what seems to have quickly become a tradition, opponents of globalization regularly disrupt the meetings of the World Trade Organization (WTO). Protestors, police and policy makers also encounter ongoing clashes at meetings of the International Monetary Fund (IMF) and the World Bank.

The 2005 G8 summit was held in Scotland. It focused on the issues of global climate change, the lack of economic development in Africa, counter-terrorism, non-proliferation and reform in the Middle East. Breaking with historical tradition, the British government allowed non-governmental organizations to play a key role in deliberations, perhaps prompted by the public pressure of the Make Poverty History movement and Live 8. The summit continued the trend of including the developing world in talks. The leaders of seven African nations attended, as well as the five leading developing countries: China, India, Brazil, Mexico and South Africa. Nevertheless, many demonstrations were organized, such as the ones against Shell, the limits of Gordon Brown's debt cancellation proposal and the non-violent blockade of the Royal Navy submarine base of Faslane. In fact, the summit was overshadowed by the vicious bomb attacks in London on the second day of the conference that killed many people of different nationalities and faiths. The 2006 G8 summit held in Russia made important decisions on the priority topics of international energy security, the fight against dangerous infectious diseases and the development of education.

Proponents of globalization believe it is simplistic to blame globalization for worldwide poverty. The causes of poverty are numerous and complex, including war, disease (such as the African AIDS pandemic), corruption, illiteracy and lawlessness. However, as a result of protests, many international firms and organizations have begun to revise some of their practices, suggesting that a middle ground might be found.

In 2003, the IMF released a report stating that countries that follow IMF suggestions often suffer a 'collapse in growth rates and significant financial crises', and admitted it was considering changes in its practices. Since the protests began, the World Bank has also made changes to the way it operates by shifting its focus away from government loans to micro-credit schemes and increasing the input from locals in the countries it is trying to help. As the worldwide process of adjustment to globalization continues, the negotiations between those who benefit from it and those who lose out will continue. The WTO reports from 2006 to 2007 have recognized the growing role of developing countries not only in the Doha negotiations but also in the Dispute Settlement process and in all facets of WTO activity. Today, the real dynamism in trade development is found in the developing world. Reflecting this power, negotiating groups such as the G-22, the G-33, the G-20 and the G-90 have emerged to play an important role in globalization.

The establishment of the Group of 22 (G-22), also known as the Willard Group, was announced by President Clinton and the leaders of APEC countries at their meeting in Vancouver, Canada, in November 1997, aimed at advancing the reform of the global financial system. The G-22 comprised finance ministers and central bank governors from the G-7 industrial countries and 15 other nations, namely Argentina, Australia, Brazil, China, Hong Kong SAR, India, Indonesia, Korea, Malaysia, Mexico, Poland, Russia, Singapore, South Africa and Thailand. The G-22 was superseded first by the Group of 33 (G-33) and then by the Group of 20 (G-20). The formation of the G-33 and its seminars on the international financial issues were carried out at the proposals of the finance ministers and central bank governors of the G-7. The first G-33 meeting was hosted by Germany in Bonn on 11 March 1999. The G-33 consisted of the finance ministers and central bank governors of Argentina, Australia, Belgium, Brazil, Canada, Chile, China, Côte d'Ivoire, Egypt, France, Germany, Hong Kong SAR, India, Indonesia, Italy, Japan, Korea, Malaysia, Mexico, Morocco, the Netherlands, Poland, Russia, Saudi Arabia, Singapore, South Africa, Spain, Sweden, Switzerland, Thailand, Turkey, the United Kingdom and the United States. Replacing the G-33, the G-20 was formed as a new forum for co-operation and consultation on challenging matters pertaining to the international financial system addressing, reviewing and promoting financial debates among key industrial and emerging market countries. The membership of the G-20 comprises the finance ministers and central bank governors of Argentina, Australia, Brazil, Canada, China, France, Germany, India, Indonesia, Italy, Japan, Korea, Mexico, Russia, Saudi Arabia, South Africa, Turkey, the United Kingdom and the United States.

The Group of 90 (G-90) is an international trade alliance between the poorest and least developed countries associated with the WTO. The G-90 was established at the WTO's Ministerial Conference in Cancun, Mexico, in September 2003. Representatives of G-90 consist of trade ministers from African, Caribbean and Pacific states, including trade ministers from the least developed countries in the world.

Sources: Simon English, 'IMF Says its Policies Seldom Work', *The Daily Telegraph*, 20 March 2003, 31; 'Globalization and Its Critics', *The Economist*, 27 September 2001, www.economist.com, accessed 4 February 2002; Dan Ackman, 'Davos Go Home', 4 February 2002, www.forbes.com; 'Going Global', *The Economist Global Agenda*, 1 February 2002; Paul Blustein, 'A Quiet Round in Qatar?' *Washington Post*, 30 January 2001, E1; World Trade Organization, Annual Report 2006, WTO Publications, Lausanne, Switzerland; Jeffrey Sachs, 'Spirit of London a Lesson for the World', *Financial Times*, 6 July 2005, www.ft.com, accessed 29 December 2006; Caroline Daniel, 'G8 diary from St Petersburg', *Financial Times*, 14 July 2006, www.ft.com, accessed 29 December 2006.

GLOBALIZATION: MAKE YOUR CHOICE

The Anti-Globalization View

The possibility that international trade and investment might be economically damaging the interests of poorer and less developed nations or that they might erode democratic controls has not been adequately addressed. As an ideology, globalization connotes free international business; it assists the realizations of the benefits of free trade thus facilitating the development of comparative advantage and international division of labour. It also enhances efficiency and productivity. Because of these assumptions, globalization is widely perceived as positive and taken for granted, occurring with little external intervention.

However, there is also another side of the coin often referred to as the 'Janus face' of globalization. Some argue that globalization has been engineered by corporate elites to serve their interests. Their global activities have successfully conveyed the impression that globalization is not only inevitable but also has been a great success.

Even ignoring for the moment its distributional effects, globalization has been marked by substantial declines in rates of output and investment growth. Under the new regime of enhanced financial mobility and power, with greater volatility of financial markets and increased risk, real interest rates have risen substantially. Globalization has helped keep wages down, while increasing real interest rates. The income of the rich has increased and stock market values have risen rapidly. But it is a different story for the majority of players in the global marketplace. Income inequality rose markedly both within and between countries. The gap in incomes between 20% of the world's population in the richest and poorest countries has risen from 30 to 1 in 1960 to 112 to 1 in 2005. Some 3 billion people, almost half the world's population, live on less than US$2 a day; more than 800 million people suffer from malnutrition. In developing countries, unemployment and underemployment are rampant and massive poverty exists side-by-side with growing elite affluence. More than 100 million people a year attempt to find asylum or employment in the richer countries, some of them successfully, as governments of developing economies allow virtually unrestricted capital flight and seek no options but to attract foreign investment that hardly helps the fight against unemployment.

The globalization of recent decades has not been a democratic choice by the peoples of the world. Rather, the process has been business driven, by corporate strategies and tactics for their own benefit. Governments have helped, by incremental policy actions and by larger actions that were often taken in secret using classified information, without national debate and discussion of where the entire process was taking the community at large. In the case of some major actions advancing the globalization process, such as passing the North American Free Trade Agreement (NAFTA) or joining the European Monetary Union (EMU), the public has been subjected to massive propaganda campaigns by the interested political or business-media elites. Global businesses have also launched a powerful effort to dominate governments by limiting their ability to serve ordinary citizens.

Proponents of globalization and free trade argue that they support economic growth. However, no country, past or present, has experienced sustained economic growth and moved from economic backwardness to modernity without government protectionism on a large-scale and enormous subsidization of domestic industries. The governments and institutions bargaining on behalf of the multinational corporations today, through the IMF, World Bank, WTO and NAFTA, have been able to remove these modes of protection from less developed countries. This threatens them with extensive takeovers by global giants, integration into foreign economic systems as 'branch plant economies' and preservation in a state of dependence and underdevelopment.

The Pro-Globalization View

Globalization processes were laid upon the foundations of the political and economic integration between the US, Western Europe and Japan after the Second World War. Technological achievements lowered the costs of transportation and communication, as the air freight fleet was converted from propeller to jet and new container shipping techniques became the norm. Computing and telecommunications brought about a speed and information boom. Markets became more easily accessible and this allowed a greater range of products to be involved in international trade. Tariff barriers that were rather high during the Great Depression became much lower as a result of the negotiations within the General Agreement on Tariffs and Trade (GATT). The Cold War and its geopolitical considerations strengthened the aspirations of the Western market economies for economic integration. However, regulations limiting the flow of financial capital across national borders were still in place until recently.

National political priorities have underpinned and determined the extent of international economic integration throughout history. For example, Britain adopted free trade and allowed free capital flows, which helped the growth of the British Empire and increased the dynamism of international integration in the nineteenth century. After the Second World War the institutional framework for global trade, the World Trade Organization, evolved. Regional frameworks and agreements, such as the North American Free Trade Agreement and the European Union enlargement, have also promoted trade and integration. Government restrictions on international capital flows have generally declined and legal frameworks and accounting rules have improved, in part through international co-operation.

Presently, new technologies have become a major pillar supporting global economic integration. Economic incentives for increased innovation have led to a much faster rate of technological progress. The increase of market access and size has provided a fertile ground for the commercialization of innovation and consumer demand for novelty products has spurred innovation and dramatically reduced product life cycle (PLC). Dramatic improvements in logistics and supply-chain management, made possible by advances in communication and computer technologies, have significantly reduced the costs of co-ordinating production among globally distributed suppliers.

The expansion of international trade and the development of services have broadened the spectrum of goods that countries can offer internationally. Particularly striking is the extent to which information and communication technologies now facilitate active international trade in a wide range of services, from call centre operations to sophisticated financial, legal, medical and engineering services.

The emergence of Brazil, Russia, India and China (the BRICs) as economic challengers to the leading world economies and the rise of the former communist-bloc countries implies that companies from all over the world have become involved in the global economy. The developed industrial economies and the emerging-market economies are rapidly becoming more integrated and interdependent. Production processes are becoming geographically fragmented to an unprecedented degree. Specialization of production has allowed companies to introduce discrete production steps and perform each step in locations that allow them to minimize costs.

The globalization of business today has been grounded in mature and emerging international capital markets. Moreover, capital flows have been diversified and investors hold diverse portfolios. The volume of foreign direct investment has grown substantially supported by market liberalization and global standardization.

Sources: Herman, E. (1999) 'The Threat of Globalization' *New Politics*, Winter, 7(2); Bernanke, B. (2006) Speech at a symposium of the Federal Reserve Bank in Jackson Hole, Wyoming, USA; Eden, L. and Lenway, S. (2001) 'Introduction to the Symposium Multinationals: The Janus Face of Globalization', *Journal of International Business Studies*, **32**(3), 383–400; *Africa Insight* (2001), 30(3–4), 19–37; 'Globalization is a Reverse Gear for Africa' (2002), Kampala: Uganda Martyrs University.

A THEORETICAL VIEWPOINT

Unbundling Globalization

Globalization describes the increased mobility of goods, services, labour, technology and capital throughout the world. In-depth analysis of globalization shows that the globalization process evolves over time, thus creating new challenges to policy makers and companies. Professor Richard Baldwin from the Graduate Institute of International Studies in Geneva, Switzerland[1], suggests that the dynamic changes of globalization in recent years have led to new phenomena, which are re-shaping the international business landscape.

The initial processes that have characterized globalization include:

- *Industrialization/Deindustrialization.* The 'North' (Western Europe and the US) industrialized while the 'South' (especially India and China) deindustrialized. In the second wave, the South (East Asia) industrialized while the North deindustrialized.
- *International divergence/convergence.* The first wave saw North and South incomes diverge massively, while the second wave witnessed a convergence, at least between the North and the industrializing South.
- *Trade.* International trade in goods and factors exploded in the first wave. The second wave was marked by a return of trade and capital flows to levels that have recently topped even those seen in Victorian England.
- *Growth Take-off.* The first wave began in the UK and spread to Western Europe and the US around the middle of the nineteenth century. The income convergence in the second wave is linked to spectacular growth in the industrializing South and a moderate slowdown in the North.
- *Urbanization.* The first globalization wave was accompanied by a rapid and historically unprecedented urbanization in the North. Northern urbanization continued during the second wave but cities grew even more rapidly in the South.
- *Internal divergence.* During the second wave, inequality in incomes and/or unemployment outcomes increased in the North. The industrialization process in some developing nations during the late twentieth century was even more revolutionary, with income growth rates rising faster than ever before.

More recent globalization processes have led to:

- *Unpredictability.* The winners and losers from globalization are much harder to predict. When the main barrier is the cost of exchanging information and co-ordinating production across distances (trading ideas), it is difficult to identify winning and losing tasks.
- *Suddenness.* Cheap communication costs line up with new management technology and a new task can be offshored very quickly to a lower cost location. No jobs are safe in the developed world any longer.

Individuals Not Firms, Sectors or Skill Groups

Globalization can be thought of as an unbundling of things. Roughly speaking, the first unbundling meant that it became economical to locate factories far from consumers. The second unbundling meant that it became economical to 'unpackage' the factories and locate various production stages far from each other.

In the first unbundling, one can view firms as black-box bundles of tasks because firm-against-firm competition was globalization's finest level of resolution. The new paradigm of the second unbundling suggests that globalization has been forcing international competition at the level of tasks within firms.

The Need for International Business

You are about to begin an exciting, important and necessary task: the exploration of international business. International business is exciting because it combines the science and the art of business with many other disciplines, such as economics, anthropology, geography, history, culture studies, jurisprudence, statistics and demography. International business is important and necessary because economic isolationism has become impossible. Failure to become a part of the global market assures a nation of declining economic influence and a deteriorating standard of living for its citizens. Successful participation in international business, however, holds the promise of improved quality of life and a better society, even leading, some believe, to a more peaceful world.

On an individual level, most students are likely to become involved with international business enterprises during their careers. Manufacturing firms, as well as service companies such as banks, insurance or consulting firms are going global. Artwork, films and music are already widely exposed to the international market. Many of the future professional colleagues and competitors of today's students will come from around the world. In an era of open borders, niche marketing, instant communications and virtually free ways of reaching millions of people, an unprecedented opportunity emerges for individuals to enter the international business arena. Start-up firms can challenge the existing, long-dominant, large competition. Speed, creativity and innovation have often become more important to international success than size. Understanding international business is therefore crucial in preparing for the opportunities, challenges and requirements of a future career.

International business offers companies new markets. Since the 1950s, the growth of international trade and investment has been substantially larger than the growth of domestic economies. Technology continues to increase the reach and the ease of conducting international business, pointing to even larger growth potential in the future. A combination of domestic and international business, therefore, presents more opportunities for expansion, growth and income than domestic business alone. International business causes the flow of ideas, services and capital across the world. As a result, innovations can be developed and disseminated more rapidly, human capital can be used better and financing can take place more quickly. International business also offers consumers new options. It can permit the acquisition of a wider variety of products, both in terms of quantity and quality, and do so at reduced prices through international competition. International business facilitates the mobility of factors of production – except land – and provides challenging employment opportunities to individuals with professional and entrepreneurial skills. At the same time, international business reallocates resources, makes preferential choices and shifts activities on a global level. It also opens up markets to competition, which in many instances has been unexpected and difficult to cope with.

As a result, international business activities do not benefit everyone to the same degree. Just like Janus, the two-faced god of the Romans, international business can bring benefits and opportunity to some, while delivering drawbacks and problems to others. The international firm and its managers, as well as the consumers of international products and services, need to understand how to make globalization work for them, as well as think about how to ensure that these benefits are afforded to a wide variety of people and countries. Therefore, both as an opportunity and a challenge, international business is of vital concern to countries, companies and individuals.

A Definition of International Business

International business consists of transactions that are devised and carried out across national borders to satisfy the objectives of individuals, companies and organizations. These transactions take on various forms, which are often interrelated. Primary types of international business are export-import trade and direct foreign investment. The latter is carried out in varied forms, including wholly owned subsidiaries and joint ventures. Additional types of international business are licensing, franchising and management contracts.

F⬤CUS ON

GLOBALIZATION

Globalization and Consumption: African Perspective

Globalization and consumption are regarded as the most important business topics of today, reminding us of the fact that in the contemporary world consumers determine the success of business operations. Agricultural producers in sub-Saharan African countries comprise more than 60% of all producers in the region. Yet, stagnant production has relegated many of the African poor to the status of consumers of imported foodstuffs. Moreover, African markets have also become major importers of manufactured items.

Globalization has led to unemployment caused by privatization and the implementation of the Structural Adjustment Programme. The divide between the majority of Africans who live in rural areas and the rest of the world is widening. Moreover, globalization makes African governments vulnerable to external pressure to democratize because of their crucial dependences on foreign capital, both as humanitarian aid and foreign direct investment. Benin, Ghana, Malawi, Somalia, Zambia and many other countries are examples of such 'choiceless democracies'.

Generally speaking, globalization is mostly disadvantageous for African countries. The ability of investment capital to seek out the most efficient markets, and for producers and consumers to access the most competitive resources and products, exposes and worsens existing structural weaknesses in African countries. Exacerbated by globalization, corruption is a serious problem that has spread freely throughout the continent. Due to policies of unrestricted access to natural endowments many companies, including some with illegal operations, are draining Africa of its resources. Increased capital mobility carries the risk of destabilizing capital flows and has heightened exchange rate volatility.

Many local businesses are destroyed because of globalization, thus curbing the creativity and innovativeness of Africans. The benefits of globalization have been enjoyed by a few privileged Africans who are able to catch up with its speed under the leadership of well-established international organizations.

Moreover, there is also biased reporting on African issues by the Western media depicting Africa as providing inappropriate conditions for ethical consumption. Improved information technology has led to increased consumption of uncensored information that is detrimental to African values and morals. The media has also created superior images of Westerners while the younger African generations are made to think that Africa has been a failure.

Sources: Africa Insight (2001), 30(3–4), 19–37; 'Globalization is a Reverse Gear for Africa' (2002), Kampala: Uganda Martyrs University.

The definition of international business focuses on transactions. The use of this term recognizes that doing business internationally is an activity, not merely a passive observation. Closely linked to activity is the term 'satisfaction'. It is crucial that the participants in international business are satisfied. Only if they feel they are better off after the transaction than they were before, will individual business transactions develop into a business relationship. The fact that the transactions are *across national borders* highlights a key difference between domestic and international business. The international executive is subject to a new set of macro-environmental factors, to different constraints and to quite frequent conflicts resulting from different laws, cultures and societies. The basic principles of business are still relevant, but their application, complexity and intensity vary substantially.

Subject to constant change, international business is as much an art as a science. Yet success in the art of business depends on a firm grounding in its scientific aspects. Individual consumers, policymakers and business executives with an understanding of both aspects will be able to incorporate international business considerations into their thinking and planning. They will be able to consider international issues and repercussions and make decisions related to questions such as the following:

- How will our idea, good or service fit into the international market?
- Should we enter the market through trade or through investment?
- Should we obtain our supplies domestically or from abroad?
- What product adjustments are necessary to be responsive to local conditions?
- What threats from global competition should be expected and how can these threats be counteracted?

When management integrates these issues into each decision, international markets can provide growth, profit and needs satisfaction not available to those firms that limit their activities to the domestic marketplace. The purpose of this book is to aid in this decision process.

A Brief History

Ever since the first national borders were formed, international business has been conducted by nations and individuals. In many instances, international business itself has been a major force in shaping borders and changing world history.

As an example, international business played a vital role in the formation and decline of the Roman Empire, whose impact on thought, knowledge and development can still be felt today. Although we read about the marching of the Roman legions, it was not through military might that the empire came about. The Romans used the pax Romana or Roman peace, as a major stimulus. This ensured that merchants were able to travel safely and rapidly on roads built, maintained and protected by the Roman legions and their affiliated troops. A second stimulus was the use of common coinage, which simplified business transactions and made them comparable throughout the empire. In addition, Rome developed a systematic law (code law), central market locations through the founding of cities and an effective communication system; all of these actions contributed to the functioning of the marketplace and a reduction of business uncertainty.

International business flourished within the empire and the improved standard of living within the empire became apparent to those outside. Soon city-nations and tribes that were not part of the empire decided to join as allies. They agreed to pay tribute and taxes because the benefits were greater than the drawbacks.

Thus, the immense growth of the Roman Empire occurred mainly through the linkages of business. Of course, preserving this favourable environment required substantial effort. When pirates threatened the seaways, for example, Pompeius sent out a large fleet to subdue them. Once this was accomplished, the cost of international distribution within the empire dropped substantially because fewer shipments were lost at sea. Goods could be made available at lower prices, which in turn translated into larger demand and greater, more widely available benefits.

The fact that international business was one of the primary factors that held the empire together can also be seen in the decline of Rome. When 'barbaric' tribes overran the empire, again it was not mainly through war and prolonged battles that Rome had lost ground. Rather, outside tribes were attacking an empire that was already substantially weakened at its foundations because of infighting and increasing decadence. The Roman peace was no longer enforced, the use and acceptance of the common coinage had declined and communications no longer worked as well. Therefore, affiliation with the empire no longer offered the benefits of the past. Former allies, who no longer saw any benefits in their association with Rome, willingly co-operated with invaders rather than face prolonged battles.

Similar patterns also can be seen in later eras. The British Empire grew mainly through its effective international business policy, which provided for efficient transportation, intensive trade and an insistence on open markets.[2] Initially British merchants sent out ships to trade with North America and the West Indies, where the empire had established a network of colonies, following on from the permanent settlement of Virginia in 1607 and the acquisition of Barbados in 1625. Later trade occurred in Asian waters. This was mainly based around the activities of the East India Company, a large joint-stock company based in London. More recently, the United States developed a world leadership position largely due to its championship of market-based business transactions in the Western world; the broad flow of ideas, goods and services across national borders; and an encouragement of international communication and transportation. Some say that the period from 1945 to 1990 for Western countries and since then, for the world, has been characterized by a pax Americana, an American sponsored and enforced peace.

The importance of international business has not always persisted, however. For example, in 1896, the Empress Dowager Tz'u-hsi, in order to finance the renovation of the summer palace, impounded government funds that had been designated for Chinese shipping and its navy. As a result, China's participation in world trade almost came to a halt. In the subsequent decades, China operated in almost total isolation, without any transfer of knowledge from the outside, without major inflow of goods and without the innovation and productivity increases that result from exposure to international business.

Withholding the benefits of international business has also long been a tool of national policy. The use of economic coercion by nations or groups of nations, for example, can be traced back to the time of the Greek city-states and the Peloponnesian War. In the Napoleonic Wars, combatants used naval blockades to achieve their goal of 'bringing about commercial ruin and shortage of food by dislocating trade'.[3] Similarly, during the Civil War period in the United States, the North consistently pursued a strategy of denying international business opportunities to the South in order to deprive it of needed export revenues.

The importance of international business linkages was highlighted during the 1930s. At that time, the Smoot-Hawley Act raised import duties to reduce the volume of goods coming into the United States. The act was passed in the hope that it would restore domestic employment. The result, however, was retaliation by most trading partners. The ensuing worldwide depression and the collapse of the world financial system were instrumental in bringing about the events that led to the Second World War.

World trade and investment have assumed a heretofore unknown importance to the global community. In past centuries, trade was conducted internationally but not at the level or with the impact on nations, firms and individuals that it has recently achieved. In the past 30 years alone, the volume of international trade in goods and services has expanded from US$200 billion to more than US$7.5 trillion.[4] As Figure 1.1 shows, during almost all that time, the growth in the value of trade has greatly exceeded the level of overall world output growth.

The sales of foreign affiliates of multinational corporations are now twice as high as global exports.[5] As Table 1.1 shows, many of these corporations have their origins in developing economies as well. Nonetheless, foreign direct investment is highly selective. In 2001, global foreign direct investment (FDI) inflows reached US$735 billion; while developed countries received US$503 billion or about 68% of those inflows, the 49 least developed countries received less than 1%.[6] Individuals and firms have come to recognize that they are competing not only domestically but also in a global marketplace. As a result, the international market has taken on a new dynamic, characterized by major change.

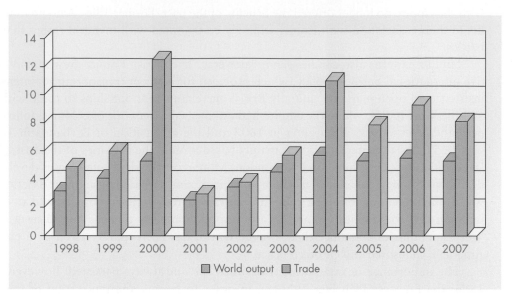

Figure 1.1: Growth of world output and trade, 1998–2007.

Sources: UN World Economic and Social Survey 2003, New York; World Economic Outlook, Washington, DC: IMF, 2006, www.imf.org.

Global Links Today

International business has forged a network of global links around the world that binds all countries, institutions and individuals much closer than ever before. These links tie together trade, financial markets, technology and living standards in an unprecedented way. A freeze in Brazil and its effect on coffee production would be felt around the world. The sudden decline in the Mexican peso affected financial markets in the United States and reverberated throughout Europe and beyond. The economic turmoil in Asia, followed by the one in Russia, influenced stock markets, investments and trade flows in all corners of the Earth. The introduction of the European monetary union and its common currency, the euro (€), has changed the landscape of financial transactions and markets in the world. The euro has helped to establish more balanced global monetary relations. Thanks to the euro, the EU financial and commercial role in the world has been re-asserted. The size of the EU market and its position as the world's main economic power has turned the euro into a world currency of trade, investment and reserve alongside the US dollar.

Countries with close economic, commercial and financial ties with the European Union have been directly affected by the launch of the euro. On 1 January 1999 the 11 EMU member states constituted 290 million inhabitants, had 19.4% of world GDP (cf. 19.6% for the US and 7.7% for Japan) and 18.6% of world trade (cf. 16.6% for the US and 8.2% for Japan). The European EMU has grown since its birth to include 13 members in 2007.

The international business linkages have also become more intense on an individual level. Communication has built new international bridges, be it through music or the watching of international programmes transmitted by the BBC, EuroNews, Deutsche Welle or CNN (www.bbc.co.uk; www.euronews.net; www.dw-world.de; www.cnn.com). New products have attained international appeal and encouraged similar activities around the world – cosmopolitan consumers wear jeans; eat hamburgers, chocolate, pizzas, noodles and sushi; drink coffee, beer, wine and tea but preserve their taste and liking for locally sourced food and drinks. Transportation links let individuals from different countries see and meet each other with unprecedented ease. Yet, political interests and economic boundaries still divide people and complicate the conduct of international

Ranking by Foreign Assets	Corporation	Home Economy	Industry	Assets Foreign	Assets Total	Sales Foreign	Sales Total	Employment Foreign	Employment Total
1	Hutchison Whampoa	Hong Kong, China	Diversified	67 638	84 162	11 426	23 080	150 687	182 000
2	Petronas Nasional Bhd	Malaysia	Petroleum expl./ref./distr.	22 647	62 915	10 567	36 065	4016	33 944
3	Singtel	Singapore	Telecommunications	18 641	21 626	5396	7722	8676	19 155
4	Samsung Corporation	Korea, Republic of	Electrical and electronic equip.	14 609	66 665	61 524	79 184	21 259	61 899
5	CITIC Group	China	Diversified	14 452	84 744	1746	6413	15 915	93 323
6	Cemex	Mexico	Non-metallic mineral products	13 323	17 188	5412	8059	16 822	26 679
7	LG Electronics	Korea, Republic of	Electrical and electronic equip.	10 420	28 903	36 082	41 782	32 000	41 923
8	China Ocean Shipping	China	Shipping	9024	14 994	4825	11 293	4230	70 474
9	Petroleós de Venezuela	Venezuela	Petroleum expl./ref./distr.	8868	55 355	25 551	46 589	5157	33 998
10	Jardine Matheson Holdings	Hong Kong, China	Diversified	7141	10 555	5830	8988	57 895	110 000
11	Formosa Plastic Group	Taiwan	Industrial chemicals	6968	58 023	6995	37 738	61 626	82 380
12	Petroleo Brasileiro	Brazil	Petroleum expl./ref./distr.	6221	63 270	11 082	52 109	6196	52 037
13	Hyundai Motor Company	Korea, Republic of	Motor vehicles	5899	56 387	15 245	51 300	4954	53 218
14	Flextronics International	Singapore	Electrical and electronic equip.	5862	11 130	8181	16 085	8958	92 000
15	Capitaland	Singapore	Real Estate	5231	10 545	1536	2328	5277	10 668
16	Sasol	South Africa	Industrial chemicals	4902	12 998	5541	10 684	5841	31 100
17	Telmex	Mexico	Telecommunications	4734	22 710	1415	12 444	15 616	76 386
18	América Móvil	Mexico	Telecommunications	4448	17 277	5684	11 962	13 949	23 303
19	China State Construction Engineering Corp.	China	Construction	4357	11 130	2513	11 216	21 456	130 813
20	Hon Hai Precision Industries	Taiwan	Electrical and electronic equip.	4355	9505	7730	16 969	140 518	166 509
21	Shangri-La Asia	Hong Kong, China	Hotels and motels	4209	5208	571	726	14 013	18 100
22	New World Development	Hong Kong, China	Diversified	4202	15 567	891	2865	12 687	47 000
23	Sappi	South Africa	Paper	4187	6150	4351	4762	8936	16 010
24	China National Petroleum Corp.	China	Petroleum expl./ref./distr.	4060	110 393	5218	68 952	22 000	1 167 129
25	Companhia Vale do Rio Doce	Brazil	Mining and quarrying	4025	16 382	9395	10 380	2736	36 176

Source: UNCTAD World Investment Report 2006: Transnational Corporations and Export Competitiveness, Table 5

Table 1.1: The top 25 nonfinancial transnational corporations from developing economies, ranked by foreign assets (millions of dollars and number of employees).

business. Common cultural pressures result in similar social phenomena and behaviour – for example, traditional family values are changing, more dual-income families are emerging around the world, which leads to more frequent, but also more stressful, shopping.[7] Yet, in traditional, less developed societies, individuals are restrained in their communication exchanges due to a lack of basic infrastructure, availability of communication channels and affordability limitations.

International business has also brought a global reorientation in production strategies. Only a few decades ago, for example, it would have been thought impossible to produce parts for a car in more than one country, assemble it in another and sell it in yet other countries around the world.

Ingredient	Country of Origin
Sesame seeds	Mexico
Pickles	Germany
Special sauce	Germany
Bun	Russia
Onions	United States
Beef patties	Hungary
Cheese	Poland
Lettuce	Ukraine

Source: Thomas Goetz & McDonald's Corporation.

Table 1.2: The global components of a Big Mac in the Ukraine.

Today, such global strategies, coupled with production and distribution sharing, are common. Consumers, union leaders, policy makers and sometimes even the firms themselves are finding it increasingly difficult to define where a particular product was made, because subcomponents may come from many different nations. As the Focus on Politics on page 16 explains, the lack of such information may make the tools of the international business activist – such as boycotts – much blunter than ever before. Firms are also linked to each other through global supply agreements and joint undertakings in research and development. Table 1.2 gives an example of how such links result in a final consumer product.

EAT LOCALLY, SPEND GLOBALLY

Every three hours a new McDonald's opens somewhere on the Earth. The menu varies somewhat from country to country – noodles in the Philippines, chips with mayonnaise in the Netherlands – but there's one constant: the Big Mac, a towering illustration of the glocal economy at work. Whereas every Big Mac in the USA is made from domestic ingredients (except for the sesame seeds), a Big Mac elsewhere in the world uses ingredients from a variety of local and international suppliers. With over 21 000 restaurants in over a hundred countries, McDonald's relies on its overseas operations to generate half its $32 billion in sales. Table 1.2 provides a look at what goes into a Ukrainian Big Mac – and where it comes from.

In addition to the production of goods, service firms are increasingly part of the international scene. Consulting firms, insurance companies, software firms and universities are participating to a growing degree in the international marketplace. Firms and governments are recognizing production's worldwide effects on the environment common to all. For example, high sulphur emissions in one area may cause acid rain in another. Pollution in one country may result in water contamination in another. Service activities can have cross-national impacts as well. For example, weaknesses in some currencies, due to problems in a country's banking sector, can quickly spill over and affect the currency values of other nations. The deregulation of some service industries, such as air transport or telephony can thoroughly affect the structure of these industries around the world.

All these changes have affected the international financial position of countries and the ownership of economic activities. For example, the United States, after having been a net creditor to the world for many decades, has been a world debtor since 1985. This means that the United States owes more to foreign institutions and individuals than to US entities. The shifts in financial flows have had major effects on international direct investment into plants as well. US foreign direct investment (FDI) in 2002 had a market value of more than US$2.3 trillion; foreign direct investment in the United

States had grown to US$2.8 trillion.[8] FDI has been a cornerstone of the powerful US–EU economic relationships. There is no larger bilateral transfer of capital in the world. Half of the world's total FDI originates from the US and the bulk of it pours into Europe while EU nations put two-thirds of their annual FDI into the United States. The US Department of Commerce reported that, in 2005 alone, US$326 billion of FDI was conducted by the US and EU. More than 1.1 million of the workers in the US chemical, computer and transportation industries work for foreign owners.[9] The opening of plants abroad increasingly takes the place of trade.

All of these developments make everyone more and more dependent on each another.

This interdependence, however, is not stable. On an ongoing basis, realignments take place on both micro and macro levels that make past orientations at least partially obsolete. For example, for its first 200 years, the United States looked to Europe for markets and sources of supply. Despite the maintenance of this orientation by many individuals, firms and policy makers, the reality of trade relationships has changed.

At the same time, entirely new areas for international business activities have opened up. The East–West juxtaposition had for more than 40 years effectively separated the 'Western' economies from the centrally planned ones in Central and Eastern Europe. The lifting of the Iron Curtain and the EU enlargement presented new opportunities for trade and investment.

The Open Door and Going Abroad Policies of China and the country's membership of the WTO since 2001 significantly opened up the Chinese market to foreign firms. As the Chinese market develops, foreign trade opportunities have grown, particularly in sectors such as consumer goods, environmental protection, healthcare, education and training and financial services.

Concurrently, an increasing regionalization is taking place around the world, resulting in the split up of countries in some areas of the world and the development of country and trading blocs in others. Over time, firms may find that the free flow of goods, services and capital encounters new impediments as regions become more inward looking. This powerful flow of capital is facing its first serious threat in decades. Fear of outside ownership has prompted discussions about the proper balance between economic openness and national security. Recent takeover bids by Enel, EON AG and the Chinese National Offshore Oil Corporation sparked public concern in the USA that vital domestic industries could be controlled by foreign – and potentially hostile – companies or governments. In particular, the recent purchase by Dubai Ports World of the British maritime giant P&O, which manages major American ports, caused a political firestorm in the US.[10] Such trends are also evident in developed countries worldwide.

Not only is the environment changing, but also the pace of change is accelerating. Atari's Pong was first introduced in the early 1980s; today, action games and movies are made with computerized humans. The first office computers emerged in the mid-1980s; today, home computers have become commonplace. E-mail was introduced to a mass market only in the 1990s; today, many students hardly ever send personal notes using a stamp and an envelope.[11]

These changes and the speed with which they come about significantly affect countries, corporations and individuals. For example, the relative participation of countries in world trade is shifting. Over the past decades, in a world of rapidly growing trade, the market share of Western Europe in trade has been declining. For the United States, the export share has declined while the import share has increased. Concurrent with these shifts, the global market shares of Japan, Southeast Asian countries and China have increased.

The composition of trade has also been changing. For example, from the 1960s to the 1990s, the trade role of primary commodities has declined precipitously while the importance of manufactured goods has increased. This change has meant that those countries and workers specializing in commodities such as *caoutchouc* (rubber plantations) or mining were likely to fall behind those who embarked on strengthening their manufacturing sector. With sharply declining world market prices for commodities and rising prices for manufactured goods, commodity producers were increasingly unable to catch up.

F○CUS ON

POLITICS   ## Consumers Get Political (1)

Using economic levers to reward friends and punish foes is nothing new in American foreign politics. But with the US and Allied Forces-led Operation Iraqi Freedom, consumers' purchasing decisions are becoming a form of political protest. A poll directed by Supermarket Guru, a leading analyser of consumer and marketing trends, notes that 71% of Americans agree that political disagreements should carry over to the trade arena, while 73% believe US consumers should boycott French- and German-made goods.

American consumers exercising 'purchasing protests' can easily find Californian, Australian, Spanish, Portuguese and Chilean products as substitutes for French champagne. Danish and British cheeses are fine surrogates for French varieties and perceived 'American' and 'Japanese' luxury cars may well be on par with 'German' Mercedes-Benz and BMW.

But before US customers become gung-ho about anti-French and German purchases, maybe a little research would be useful. If they're to bypass the bottled water of Perrier, Vittel and Evian, maybe a closer look at household tap water would be interesting: it may well be purified by Culligan, a 65-year-old French water-treatment firm. Although RCA stands for Radio Corporation of America, it's actually owned by the France-based Thales Group, 33% of which is owned by the French government. US Consumers aren't tempted to buy Renault, Citroën or Peugeot cars because these are not exported to the United States any more, but what about those purchases of 'Japanese' Nissans? Renault holds 44.4% of Nissan's equity. Once American consumers buy those Nissans, what about the tyres? Of course, Michelins will be avoided and B.F. Goodrich and Uniroyal 'patriotic purchases' will be made. But, wait a minute. Haven't both those firms been acquired by French companies? Let's assume people will be tired of driving and opt to fly. Air France may surely be avoided, but how often will the distinction between an Airbus A300 and a Boeing 737 be made? After all, the French have a major stake in EADS, the parent firm of Airbus.

Not only will US consumers have difficulty finding the 'right' goods to boycott, American-owned firms also run the risk of being wrongly identified. Take Grey Poupon, for example. Its name and advertisement models may have a French flair, but the mustard has been made in the United States since 1946 by Kraft Foods, a US firm. What about the 'All-American' Dannon versus Yoplait, 'France's c'est si bon' yoghurt? Some consumers may be shocked to learn that Yoplait is made by American food giant General Mills, while Dannon is made by a subsidiary of Groupe Danone of France. The maker of French's mustard, US-owned Reckitt Benckiser, took no chances and issued a press release: 'For the record, French's would like to say there's nothing more American than French's mustard'.

Sources: Caroline Mayer, 'Identity Crisis in Aisle 7', *The Washington Post*, 2 April 2003, E1; 'Consumers Support a Boycott of French-Made Products', *PR Newswire Association*, 17 March 2003.

F○CUS ON

POLITICS   ## Consumers Get Political (2)

Research carried out by GMI shows that the US foreign policy in the last few years has brought many problems for US companies in foreign markets. GMI was founded by Rob Monster in Issaquah, WA, USA, and received the Best Companies to Work For Award from *CEO Magazine* in 2005. The company surveyed

8000 international consumers. Findings show that a third of all consumers in Canada, China, France, Germany, Japan, Russia and the United Kingdom associated all US products and brands with the 'war on terror' and the occupation of Iraq. Brands closely identified with the USA, such as McDonald's Marlboro cigarettes, AOL, American Airlines and Coca-Cola have been targeted by consumers opposing the US foreign policy.

Twenty per cent of respondents in Europe and Canada said they consciously avoided buying US products as a protest against those policies. High profile business figures such as Kevin Roberts, chief executive of Saatchi & Saatchi, stated that he believed consumers in Europe and Asia were becoming increasingly resistant to having 'brand America rammed down their throats'. Simon Anholt, the author of *Brand America* has also predicted a consumer backlash against US foreign policy, which might have grave consequences for the international market share of US companies. Allyson Stewart-Allen, co-author of *Working with Americans*, argues that US companies are seen as arrogant and aggressive, imposing their way of doing business in international markets and killing smaller domestic competitors. She suggests that 'US companies abroad now need to focus on adding yet more value and repositioning their brands to consumers in the intensely competitive global village in which they compete. The more aligned they are with those customers – regardless of their US-created DNA – they'll win'. US companies need to focus on alignment with international markets and embrace their market differences and idiosyncrasies.

Companies that appear less American, such as Visa, Kodak, Kleenex or Gillette and those that are clear market leaders, such as Microsoft, Heinz and Disney, attract a more favourable consumer response. Problem US brands include Marlboro, Exxon-Mobil, AOL, American, Chevron Texaco, United Airlines, Budweiser, Chrysler, Barbie Doll, Starbucks and General Motors among others.

Many consumers in Europe believe that the war in Iraq was motivated by a desire to control oil supplies, while only 15% believed it was related to terrorism. Nearly two thirds of European and Canadian consumers also said they believe that US foreign policy is guided primarily by self-interest and empire-building, while only 17% believe that the defence of freedom and democracy is its guiding principle.

Source: Based on J. Lobe (2004) US Businesses Overseas Threatened by Rising Anti-Americanism, OneWorld.net, 29 December; www.gmimr.com.

More recently, there has been a shift of manufacturing to new nations. In the mid-1800s, manufacturing accounted for about 17% of employment in the United States. This proportion grew to almost 30% in the 1960s, only to decline at a rising rate thereafter. At the beginning of the new millennium, US manufacturing employment, at 14.8%, had decreased below the levels of when it was first officially measured. In the past 30 years, German manufacturing employment dropped by more than 13% points, while in Japan the decrease was 6.5%. A total of 3.03 million workers were employed in manufacturing in the third quarter of 2006 in the United Kingdom, a drop of more than 77 000 from the same time period in 2005. All these shifts in employment reflect a transfer of manufacturing away from the industrialized nations toward the emerging economies. During the times of decline in the United States, the United Kingdom, Germany and Japan, the proportion of manufacturing of GNP has more than doubled in many emerging economies such as Malaysia, Thailand and Indonesia.[12]

Increasingly, substantial shifts are also occurring in the area of services trade. Activities that were confined to specific locales have become mobile and more internationalized. The global transmission of radiology charts to physicians in India may be a portent of new shifts in trade composition in the future.

The Structure of the Book

This book is intended to enable you to become a better, more successful participant in the global business place. It is written for both those who want to obtain more information about what is going on in international markets in order to be well-rounded and better educated and for those who want to translate their knowledge into successful business transactions. The text melds theory and practice to balance conceptual understanding and knowledge of day-to-day realities. The book, therefore, addresses the international concerns of both beginning internationalists and multinational corporations.

The novice international manager will need to know the answers to basic, yet important, questions: how can I find out whether demand for my product exists abroad? What must I do to get ready to market internationally? These issues are also relevant for managers in multinational corporations, but the questions they consider are often much more sophisticated. Of course, the resources available to address them are also much greater.

F CUS ON

ETHICS   Students Against Sweatshops

In November 1997, students at Georgetown, Harvard, Duke and Holy Cross universities began to look at the labels of logo merchandise in their campus bookstores to get an idea of where the clothing was made. Their goal was to find ways to improve the working conditions of people who made their caps and shirts.

In April 1998, UNITE, a union of textile workers, sponsored two workers from a Korean-owned apparel factory in the Dominican Republic for a tour of US college campuses. Kenia Rodriguez and Roselio Reyes, both college-age, described the terrible conditions at the BJ&B factory where goods featuring the logos of major American colleges such as Georgetown, Brown, Duke, Harvard and Princeton were made.

They explained that workers had to cope with rancid drinking water, locked bathrooms, sweltering conditions and intimidation. Men and women had unequal pay scales and workers were fired when they tried to start a union. None of the workers, who all worked 75 hours a week, earned more than one third of what the Dominican government considers sufficient for 'the most basic life necessities'.

In response, students at Georgetown and other universities began pressuring their administrations to adopt basic labour standards for any factories where school apparel would be made. Students wanted licensees to agree to pay workers enough to live on and disclose the locations of all of their factories. To help schools monitor factory conditions

for themselves, students formed an independent organization called the Workers Rights Consortium (WRC).

Over the next two years, students used tactics such as petitions, faculty and student government resolutions and rallies to persuade their administrations to sign on to the WRC. Some schools, such as Duke and the University of Wisconsin, held sit-ins when other tactics were not successful. At Georgetown, students occupied the office of the university's president for more than 100 hours before the administration agreed to sign on to the WRC and endorse a code of conduct that students felt was stringent enough.

Student groups across the United States continued to form and agitate for change on their campuses. As of 21 January, 2003, 112 colleges and universities in the United States had joined. WRC income in 2002–2003 was more than one million dollars: 25% from affiliate schools and 75% from grants and other nonprofit donors. The organization had eight full-time employees who conduct 10–12 investigations per year in places such as Mexico, Indonesia, the Dominican Republic and New York City. The WRC also maintains a searchable database of factory locations for all its member schools on its web site, so students can easily find out where their school's apparel is made.

In March 2003, the WRC announced a major victory at the factory where Kenia and Roselio had worked. The FEDOTRAZONAS union and the management of the BJ&B factory signed the first collective bargaining agreement in the factory's 17-year history, in part because of the WRCs efforts. The WRC continues to work to improve the conditions of factory workers who make licensed college apparel.

Sources: www.workersrights.org, accessed 26 April 2003; http://www.georgetown.edu/organizations/ solidarity/info.html, accessed 26 April 2003; Interview with Andrew Milmore, former Solidarity Committee president, 22 April, 2003 and 26 April, 2003.

Throughout this book, public policy concerns are included in discussions of business activities. In this way, you are exposed to both macro and micro issues. Part 1 of the book introduces the importance of international business and its global linkages. It presents the theoretical foundations of trade and investment and addresses the complexities of international business environment. Part 2 provides coverage of international business and markets. It explores the role of international financial markets, economic integration, and the increasing challenges of emerging markets. Part 3 focuses on international market entry and expansion with a particular emphasis on international strategic planning, organization, implementation and control. Part 4 provides coverage of international business operations and corporate governance. Part 5 presents an overview and discussion of more recent topics in international business encompassing knowledge creation, ethics and sustainability. Part 6 offers a catalogue of global case studies to encourage discussions.

We hope that upon finishing the book, you will not only have completed another academic subject but also be well versed in the theoretical, policy and strategic aspects of international business and therefore able to contribute to improved international competitiveness and a better global standard of living.

SUMMARY

International business has been conducted ever since national borders were formed and has played a major role in shaping world history. Growing in importance over the past three decades, it has shaped an environment that, due to economic linkages, today presents us with a global marketplace.

In the past three decades, world trade has expanded from US$200 billion to more than US$7.5 trillion, while international direct investment has grown to US$6.6 trillion. The growth of both has been far more rapid than the growth of most domestic economies. As a result, nations are much more affected by international business than in the past. Global links have made possible investment strategies and business alternatives that offer tremendous opportunities. Yet these changes and the speed of change can also represent threats to nations, firms and individuals.

Over the past 30 years, the dominance of the US international trade position has gradually eroded. New participants in international business compete fiercely for world market share. Individuals, corporations and policymakers around the globe have awakened to the fact that international business is a major imperative and offers opportunities for future growth and prosperity. International business provides access to new customers, affords economies of scale and permits the honing of competitive skills. Performing well in global markets is the key to improved standards of living, higher profits and better wages. Knowledge about international business is therefore important to everyone, whether it is used to compete with foreign firms or simply to understand the world around us.

QUESTIONS FOR DISCUSSION

1. What will be the future of international business? How can globalization and anti-globalization trends have an impact on international business?
2. Does increased international business mean increased risk?
3. Is it beneficial for nations to become dependent on one another?
4. Discuss the reasons for the increase in Chinese world trade market share.
5. How do European companies compete internationally?
6. Why do small and medium-sized European companies engage in international business?
7. Why do firms from countries such as Slovenia and Denmark seek greater presence on international markets?

INTERNET EXERCISE

1. Using World Trade Organization data (shown on the International Trade page of its web site, www.wto.org, determine the following information: (a) the fastest growing traders; (b) the top ten exporters and importers in world merchandise trade; and (c) the top ten exporters or importers of commercial services.

TAKE A STAND

The term 'globalization' describes the increased mobility of goods, services, labour, technology and capital throughout the world. Although globalization is not a new development, its pace has increased with the advent of new technologies that make it easier for people to travel, communicate and do business internationally.

FOR DISCUSSION

Recent anti-globalization protests have revealed significant differences between businesses and the public in terms of how they view globalization and its effects. Some point out that globalization brings modern medicines, Western communications technology and better education and jobs for women. Others feel that globalization leads to cultural homogenization and are concerned about its effects on human rights and the environment. Can globalization be doing more harm than good?

CHAPTER

2

Theory of Trade and Investment

- The Age of Mercantilism
- Classical Trade Theory
- Factor Proportions Trade Theory
- International Investment and Product Cycle Theory
- The New Trade Theory: Strategic Trade
- The Theory of International Investment

LEARNING OBJECTIVES

- To understand the traditional arguments of how and why international trade improves the welfare of all countries.

- To review the history and compare the implications of trade theory from the original work of Adam Smith to the contemporary theories of Michael Porter.

- To examine the criticisms of classical trade theory and examine alternative viewpoints of which business and economic forces determine trade patterns between countries.

- To explore the similarities and distinctions between international trade and international investment.

GLOBAL OUTSOURCING: COMPARATIVE ADVANTAGE TODAY

Comparative advantage is still a relevant theory to explain why particular countries are most suitable for exports of goods and services that support the global supply chain of both multinational corporations (MNCs) and domestic firms. The comparative advantage of the twenty-first century is one that is based more on services and their cross-border facilitation by telecommunications and the Internet. The source of a nation's comparative advantage, however, is still created from the mixture of its own labour skills, access to capital and technology. Table 2.1 provides a sample of the many recent global outsourcing ventures.

For example, India has developed a highly efficient and low-cost software industry. This industry supplies not only the creation of custom software, but also call centres for customer support and other information technology services. The Indian software industry is composed of both subsidiaries of MNCs and independent companies.

If you own a Compaq computer and call the customer support centre number for help, you are likely to reach a call centre in India. Answering your call will be a knowledgeable Indian software engineer or programmer who will 'walk' you through your problem. India has a large number of well-educated, English-speaking, technical experts who are paid only a fraction of the salary and overhead earned by their Western counterparts. The overcapacity and low cost of international telecommunication networks today further enhances the comparative advantage of an Indian location.

Country/Region	Specialism
China	Chemical, mechanical and petroleum engineering services; business and product development centres for companies such as GE
Costa Rica	Call centres for Spanish-speaking consumers in many industrial markets; Accenture has IT support and back-office operations call centres
Eastern Europe	American IT service providers operate call centres for customer and business support in Hungary, Poland and the Czech Republic; Romanian and Bulgarian centres for German-speaking IT customers in Europe
India	Software engineering and support; call centres for all types of computer and telecom services; medical analysis and consultative services; Indian companies such as Tata, Infosys and Wipro are already global leaders in IT design, implementation and support
Mexico	Automotive engineering and electronic-sector services
Philippines	Financial and accounting services; architecture services; telemarketing and graphic arts
Russia	Software and engineering services; R&D centres for Boeing, Intel, Motorola and Nortel
South Africa	Call- and user-support services for French, English and German-speaking consumers throughout Europe

Table 2.1: Examples of global outsourcing of comparative advantage in intellectual skills.

As illustrated by Table 2.1, the extent of global outsourcing is already reaching out to every corner of the globe. From financial back-offices in Manila, to information technology engineers in Hungary, modern telecommunications now take business activities to labour, rather than labour migrating to the places of business.

Source: Abstracted from 'Is Your Job Next', *Business Week*, 3 February 2003.

INTRODUCTION

The debates, costs, benefits and dilemmas of international trade have in many ways not changed significantly from the time when Marco Polo crossed the barren wastelands of Eurasia to the time of the expansion of US and Canadian firms across the Rio Grande into Mexico under the North American Free Trade Agreement (NAFTA). At the heart of the issue is what the gains – and the risks – are to the firm and the country as a result of a seller from one country servicing the needs of a buyer in a different country. If a Spanish firm wants to sell its product to the enormous market of mainland China, whether it produces at home and ships the product from Cadiz to Shanghai (international trade) or actually builds a factory in Shanghai (international investment), the goal is still the same: to sell a product for profit in the foreign market.

This chapter provides a directed path through centuries of thought on why and how trade and investment across borders occurs. Although theories and theorists come and go with time, a few basic questions have dominated this intellectual adventure:

* Why do countries trade?
* Do countries trade or do firms trade?
* Do the elements that give rise to the competitiveness of a firm, an industry or a country as a whole, arise from some inherent endowment of the country itself or do they change with time and circumstance?
* Once identified, can these sources of competitiveness be manipulated or managed by firms or governments to the benefit of the traders?

International trade is expected to improve the productivity of industry and the welfare of consumers. Let us look at how and why we still seek the exotic silks of the Far East and the telecommunication-linked call centres of Manila.

THE AGE OF MERCANTILISM

The evolution of trade into the form we see today reflects three events: the collapse of feudal society, the emergence of the mercantilist philosophy and the life cycle of the colonial systems of the European nation-states. Feudal society was a state of autarky, a society that did not trade because all of its needs were met internally. The feudal estate was self-sufficient, although hardly 'sufficient' in more modern terms, given the limits of providing entirely for oneself. Needs literally were only those of food and shelter and all available human labour was devoted to the task of fulfilling those basic needs. As merchants began meeting in the marketplace, and as travellers began exchanging goods from faraway places at the water's edge, the attractiveness of trade became evident.

In the centuries leading up to the Industrial Revolution, international commerce was largely conducted under the authority of governments. The goals of trade were, therefore, the goals of governments. As early as 1500 the benefits of trade were clearly established in Europe, as nation-states expanded their influence across the globe in the creation of colonial systems. To maintain and expand their control over these colonial possessions, the European nations needed fleets, armies, food and all the other resources the nations could muster. They needed wealth. Trade was therefore conducted to fill the governments' treasuries, at minimum expense to themselves but to the detriment of their captive trade partners. Although colonialism normally is associated with the exploitation of those captive societies, it went hand in hand with the evolving exchange of goods among the European countries themselves, called mercantilism.

Mercantilism mixed exchange through trade with accumulation of wealth. Since government controlled the patterns of commerce, it identified strength with the accumulation of *specie* (gold and silver) and maintained a general policy of exports dominating imports. Trade across borders – exports – was considered preferable to domestic trade because exports would earn gold. Import duties, tariffs, subsidization of exports and outright restriction on the importation of many goods were used to maximize the gains from exports over the costs of imports. Laws were passed making it illegal to take gold or silver out of the country, even if such specie was needed to purchase imports to produce their own goods for sale. This was one-way trade; the trade of greed and power.

The demise of mercantilism was inevitable given class structure and the distribution of society's product. As the Industrial Revolution introduced the benefits of mass production, lowering prices and increasing the supplies of goods to all, the exploitation of colonies and trading partners came to an end. However, governments still exercise considerable power and influence on the conduct of trade.

CLASSICAL TRADE THEORY

The question of why countries trade has proven difficult to answer. Since the second half of the eighteenth century, academicians have tried to understand not only the motivations and benefits of international trade, but also why some countries grow faster and wealthier than others through trade. Figure 2.1 provides an overview of the evolutionary path of trade theory since the fall of mercantilism. Although somewhat simplified, it shows the line of development of the major theories put forward over the past two centuries. It also serves as an early indication of the path of modern theory: the shifting focus from the country to the firm, from cost of production to the market as a whole and from the perfect to the imperfect.

The Theory of Absolute Advantage

Generally considered the father of economics, Adam Smith published *The Wealth of Nations* in 1776 in London. In this book, Smith attempted to explain the process by which markets and production actually operate in society. Smith's two main areas of contribution, absolute advantage and the division of labour were fundamental to trade theory.

Production, the creation of a product for exchange, always requires the use of society's primary element of value, human labour. Smith noted that some countries, owing to the skills of their workers or the quality of their natural resources, could produce the same products as others with fewer labour-hours. He termed this efficiency absolute advantage.

Adam Smith observed the production processes of the early stages of the Industrial Revolution in England and recognized the fundamental changes that were occurring in production. In previous

The Theory of Absolute Advantage
Adam Smith

Each country should specialize in the production and export of that good which it produces most efficiently, that is, with the fewest labour-hours.

↓

The Theory of Comparative Advantage
David Ricardo

Even if one country was most efficient in the production of two products, it must be relatively more efficient in the production of one good. It should then specialize in the production and export of that good in exchange for the importation of the other good.

↓

The Theory of Factor Proportions
Eli Heckscher and Bertil Ohlin

A country that is relatively labour abundant (capital abundant) should specialize in the production and export of that product which is relatively labour intensive (capital intensive).

The Leontief Paradox
Wassily Leontief

The test of the factor proportions theory which resulted in the unexpected finding that the United States was actually exporting products that were relatively labour intensive, rather than the capital intensive products that a relatively capital abundant country should, according to the theory.

Overlapping Product Ranges Theory
Staffan Burenstam Linder

The type, complexity, and diversity of product demands of a country increase as the country's income increases. International trade patterns would follow this principle, so that countries of similar income per capita levels will trade most intensively having overlapping product demands.

Product Cycle Theory
Raymond Vernon

The country that possesses comparative advantage in the production and export of an individual product changes over time as the technology of the product's manufacture matures.

Imperfect Markets and Strategic Trade
Paul Krugman

Theories that explain changing trade patterns, including intra-industry trade, based on the imperfection of both factor markets and product markets.

The Competitive Advantage of Nations
Michael Porter

A nation's competitiveness depends on the capacity of its industry to innovate and upgrade. Companies gain competitive advantage because of pressure and challenge. Companies benefit from having strong domestic rivals, aggressive home-based suppliers, and demanding local customers. Competitive advantage is also established through geographic "clusters" or concentrations of companies in different parts of same industry.

Figure 2.1: The evolution of trade theory.

states of society, a worker performed all stages of a production process, with resulting output that was little more than sufficient for the worker's own needs. The factories of the industrializing world were, however, separating the production process into distinct stages – in which each stage would be performed exclusively by one individual – known as the division of labour. This specialization increased the production of workers and industries. Smith's pin factory analogy has long been considered the recognition of one of the most significant principles of the industrial age.

To take an example, therefore, from a very trifling manufacture; but one in which the division of labour has been very often taken notice of, the trade of the pin maker; a workman not educated to this business . . . could scarce, perhaps, with his utmost industry, make one pin in a day and certainly could not make twenty. But in a way in which this business is now carried on, not only the whole work is a peculiar trade, but it is divided into a number of branches, of which the greater part are likewise peculiar trades. One man draws out the wire, another straights it, a third cuts it, a fourth points it, a fifth grinds it at the top for receiving the head: to make the head requires two or three distinct operations; to put it on is a peculiar business. . . . I have seen a small manufactory of this kind where ten men only were employed and where some of them consequently performed two or three distinct operations. But though they were very poor and therefore but indifferently accommodated with the necessary machine, they could, when they exerted themselves, make among them about twelve pounds of pins in a day. There are in a pound upwards of four thousand pins of a middling size.[1]

Adam Smith then extended his division of labour in the production process to a division of labour and specialized product across countries. Each country would specialize in a product for which it was uniquely suited. More would be produced for less. Thus, by each country specializing in products for which it possessed absolute advantage, countries could produce more in total and exchange products – trade – for goods that were cheaper in price than those produced at home.

The Theory of Comparative Advantage

Although Smith's work was instrumental in the development of economic theories about trade and production, it did not answer some fundamental questions about trade. First, Smith's trade relied on a country possessing absolute advantage in production, but did not explain what gave rise to the production advantages. Second, if a country did not possess absolute advantage in any product, could it (or would it) trade?

David Ricardo, in his 1819 work entitled *On the Principles of Political Economy and Taxation*, sought to take the basic ideas set down by Smith a few steps further. Ricardo noted that even if a country possessed absolute advantage in the production of two products, it still must be relatively more efficient than the other country in one good's production than the other. Ricardo termed this the comparative advantage. Each country would then possess comparative advantage in the production of one of the two products and both countries would then benefit by specializing completely in one product and trading for the other.

A Numerical Example of Classical Trade

To understand fully the theories of absolute advantage and comparative advantage, consider the following example. Two countries, France and England, produce only two products, wheat and cloth (or beer and pizza, guns and butter and so forth). The relative efficiency of each country in the production of the two products is measured by comparing the number of labour-hours needed to produce one unit of each product. Table 2.2 provides an efficiency comparison of the two countries.

England is obviously more efficient in the production of wheat. Whereas it takes France four labour-hours to produce one unit of wheat, it takes England only two hours to produce the same unit of wheat. France takes twice as many labour-hours to produce the same output. England has absolute advantage in the production of wheat. France needs two labour-hours to produce a unit of cloth that it takes England four labour-hours to produce. England therefore requires two more labour-hours than France to produce the same unit of cloth. France has absolute advantage in the production of cloth. The two countries are exactly opposite in relative efficiency of production.

David Ricardo took the logic of absolute advantages in production one step further to explain how countries could exploit their own advantages and gain from international trade. Comparative advantage, according to Ricardo, was based on what was given up or traded off in producing one product instead of the other. In this numerical example England needs only two-fourths as many labour-hours to produce a unit of wheat as France, whereas France needs only two-fourths as many

Country	Wheat	Cloth
England	2	4
France	4	2

- England has absolute advantage in the production of wheat. It requires fewer labour-hours (2 being less than 4) for England to produce one unit of wheat.
- France has absolute advantage in the production of cloth. It requires fewer labour-hours (2 being less than 4) for France to produce one unit of cloth.
- England has comparative advantage in the production of wheat. If England produces one unit of wheat, it is forgoing the production of 2/4 (0.50) of a unit of cloth. If France produces one unit of wheat, it is forgoing the production of 4/2 (2.00) of a unit of cloth. England therefore has the lower opportunity cost of producing wheat.
- France has comparative advantage in the production of cloth. If England produces one unit of cloth, it is forgoing the production of 4/2 (2.00) of a unit of wheat. If France produces one unit of cloth, it is forgoing the production of 2/4 (0.50) of a unit of wheat. France therefore has the lower opportunity cost of producing cloth.

*a*Labour-hours per unit of output.

Table 2.2: Absolute advantage and comparative advantage*a*.

labour-hours to produce a unit of cloth. England therefore has comparative advantage in the production of wheat, whereas France has comparative advantage in the production of cloth. A country cannot possess comparative advantage in the production of both products, so each country has an economic role to play in international trade.

National Production Possibilities

If the total labour-hours available for production within a nation were devoted to the full production of either product, wheat or cloth, the production possibilities frontiers of each country can be constructed. Assuming both countries possess the same number of labour-hours, for example 100, the production possibilities frontiers for each country can be plotted on a graph, as in Figure 2.2. If England devotes all labour-hours (100) to the production of wheat (which requires 2 labour-hours per unit produced), it can produce a maximum of 50 units of wheat. If England devotes all labour to the production of cloth instead, the same 100 labour-hours can produce a maximum of 25 units of cloth (100 labour-hours/ 4 hours per unit of cloth). If England did not trade with any other country, it could only consume the products that it produced itself. England would therefore probably produce and consume some combination of wheat and cloth such as point A in Figure 2.2 (15 units of cloth, 20 units of wheat).

France's production possibilities frontier is constructed in the same way. If France devotes all 100 labour-hours to the production of wheat, it can produce a maximum of 25 units (100 labour-hours/4 hours per unit of wheat). If France devotes all 100 labour-hours to cloth, the same 100 labour-hours can produce a maximum of 50 units of cloth (100 labour-hours/2 hours per unit of cloth). If France did not trade with other countries, it would produce and consume a combination such as point D in Figure 2.2 (20 units of cloth, 15 units of wheat).

These frontiers depict what each country could produce in isolation – without trade (sometimes referred to as autarky). The slope of the production possibility frontier of a nation is a measure of how one product is traded off in production with the other (moving up the frontier, England is choosing to produce more wheat and less cloth). The slope of the frontier reflects the 'trade-off' of producing one product over the other; the trade-offs represent prices or opportunity costs. Opportunity cost is the forgone value of a factor of production in its next-best use. If England chooses to produce more units of wheat (in fact, produce only wheat), moving from point A to point B along the production possibilities frontier, it is giving up producing cloth to produce only wheat. The 'cost' of the additional wheat is the loss of cloth. The slope of the production possibilities frontier is the ratio of product prices

England

1. Initially produces and consumes at point A.
2. England chooses to specialize in the production of wheat and shifts production from point A to point B.
3. England now exports the unwanted wheat (30 units) in exchange for imports of cloth (30 units) from France.
4. England is now consuming at point C, where it is consuming the same amount of wheat but 15 more units of cloth than at original point A.

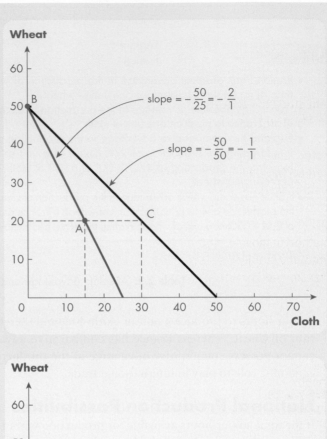

France

1. Initially produces and consumes at point D.
2. France chooses to specialize in the production of cloth and shifts production from point D to point E.
3. France now exports the unwanted cloth (30 units) in exchange for imports of wheat (30 units) from England.
4. France is now consuming at point F, where it is consuming the same amount of cloth but 15 more units of wheat than at original point D.

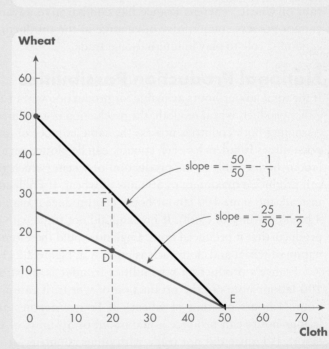

Figure 2.2: Production possibility frontiers, specialization of production and the benefits of trade.

(opportunity costs). The slope of the production possibilities frontier for England is −50/25, or −2.00. The slope of the production possibilities frontier for France is flatter, −25/50, or −0.50.

The relative prices of products also provide an alternative way of seeing comparative advantage. The flatter slope of the French production possibilities frontier means that to produce more wheat (move up the frontier), France would have to give up the production of relatively more units of cloth than would England, with its steeper sloped production possibilities frontier. But, as the following Focus on Ethics describes, prices do not always tell the whole story.

FOCUS ON

ETHICS   Over- and Under-Invoicing

A recent study raises questions about the legitimacy of the invoicing practices of many importers and exporters operating in the United States. The study estimated that multinational enterprises (MNEs) avoided US$45 billion in US taxes in the year 2000. Import transactions were examined for over-invoicing the use of a transfer price to pay more than what is typical for that product or service. Over-invoicing is one method of moving funds out of the United States and into the subject country. Export transactions were examined for under-invoicing, the use of a lower than normal export price to also reposition profits outside the United States.

The study examined approximately 15 000 import commodity-code categories and 8000 export commodity codes to determine the average selling prices – import and export – to determine implied prices. The study first calculated the median price, lower export quartile price and upper import quartile price by bilateral transfers (between the United States and nearly 230 individual countries). The following is a sample of some of the more suspicious results.

Overpriced Imports

Item	From	Unit Price (US$)
Sunflower seeds	France	5519/kg
Toothbrushes	UK	5655/unit
Hacksaw blades	Germany	5485/unit
Razor blades	India	461/unit
Vinegar	Canada	5430/litre
Flashlights	Japan	5000/unit
Sawdust	UK	642/kg
Iron/steel ladders	Slovenia	15 852/unit
Inkjet printers	Colombia	179 000/unit
Lard	Canada	484/kg
Hypodermic syringes	Switzerland	2306/unit

Underpriced Imports

Item	To	Unit Price (US$)
Truck caps	Mexico	4.09/unit
Turbojet engines	Romania	10 000/unit
Cameras (SLRs)	Mexico	3.30/unit
Soybeans	Netherlands	1.58/tonne
ATM machines	Salvador	35.93/unit
Bulldozers	Mexico	527.94/unit
Rocket launchers	Bolivia	40.00/unit
Toilets, porcelain	Hong Kong	1.08/unit
Prefabricated bldgs	St. Lucia	0.82/unit
Video projectors	Malta	28.71/unit
Radial tyres (bus)	UK	8.46/unit

Source: Simon Pak and John Zdanowicz (2001) 'US Trade With The World: An Estimate of 2000 Lost US Federal Income Tax Revenues Due to Over-Invoiced Imports and Under-Invoiced Exports', Florida International University, 1 November 2001, unpublished.

The Gains from International Trade

Continuing with Figure 2.2, if England were originally not trading with France (the only other country) and it was producing at its own maximum possibilities (on the frontier and not inside the line), it would be producing at point A. Since it was not trading with another country, whatever it was producing it must also be consuming. So England could be said to be consuming at point A as well. Therefore, without trade, you consume what you produce.

If, however, England recognized that it has comparative advantage in the production of wheat, it should move production from point A to point B. England should specialize completely in the product it produces best. It does not want to consume only wheat, however, so it would take the wheat it has produced and trade with France. For example, England may only want to consume 20 units of wheat, as it did at point A. It is now producing 50 units and therefore has 30 units of wheat it can export to France. If England could export 30 units of wheat in exchange for imports of 30 units of cloth (a 1 : 1 ratio of prices), England would clearly be better off than before. The new consumption point would be point C, where it is consuming the same amount of wheat as point A, but is now consuming 30 units of cloth instead of just 15. More is better; England has benefited from international trade.

France, following the same principle of completely specializing in the product of its comparative production advantage, moves production from point D to point E, producing 50 units of cloth. If France now exported the unwanted cloth, for example 30 units, and exchanged the cloth with England for imports of 30 units of wheat (note that England's exports are France's imports), France too is better off as a result of international trade. Each country would do what it does best, exclusively and then trade for the other product.

But at what prices do the two countries trade? Since each country's production possibilities frontier has a different slope (different relative product prices), the two countries can determine a set of prices between the two domestic prices. In the above example, England's price ratio was $-2 : 1$, while France's domestic price was $-1 : 2$. Trading 30 units of wheat for 30 units of cloth is a price ratio of $-1 : 1$, a slope or set of prices between the two domestic price ratios. The dashed line in Figure 2.2 illustrates this set of trade prices.

Are both countries better off as a result of trade? Yes. The final step to understanding the benefits of classical trade is to note that the point where a country produces (point B for England and point E for France in Figure 2.2) and the point where it consumes are now different. This allows each country to consume beyond its own production possibilities frontier. Society's welfare, which is normally measured in its ability to consume more wheat, cloth or any other goods or services, is increased through trade.

Concluding Points about Classical Trade Theory

Classical trade theory contributed much to the understanding of how production and trade operates in the world economy. All economic theories are often criticized for being unrealistic or out of date. However, the purpose of a theory is to simplify reality so that the basic elements of the logic can be seen and several of these simplifications have continued to provide insight in understanding international business.

- *Division of Labour:* Adam Smith's explanation of how industrial societies can increase output using the same labour-hours as in pre-industrial society is fundamental to our thinking even today. Smith extended this specialization of the efforts of a worker to the specialization of a nation.
- *Comparative Advantage:* David Ricardo's extension of Smith's work explained for the first time how countries that seemingly had no obvious reason for trade could individually specialize in producing what they did best and trade for products they did not produce.

- *Gains from Trade:* The theory of comparative advantage argued that nations could improve the welfare of their populations through international trade. A nation could actually achieve consumption levels beyond what it could produce by itself. To this day this is one of the fundamental principles underlying the arguments for all countries to strive to expand and 'free' world trade.

FACTOR PROPORTIONS TRADE THEORY

Trade theory changed drastically in the first half of the twentieth century. The theory developed by the Swedish economist Eli Heckscher and later expanded by his former student Bertil Ohlin formed the theory of international trade that is still widely accepted today; factor proportions theory.

Factor Intensity in Production

The Heckscher-Ohlin theory considered two factors of production, labour and capital. Technology determines the way they combine to form a good. Different goods required different proportions of the two factors of production.

Figure 2.3 illustrates what it means to describe a good by its factor proportions. The production of one unit of good X requires 4 units of labour and 1 unit of capital. At the same time, to produce 1 unit of good Y requires 4 units of labour and 2 units of capital. Good X therefore requires more units of labour per unit of capital (4 to 1) relative to Y (4 to 2). X is therefore classified as a relatively labour-intensive product and Y is relatively capital intensive. These factor intensities or proportions are truly relative and are determined only on the basis of what product X requires relative to product Y and not to the specific numbers of labour to capital.

It is easy to see how the factor proportions of production differ substantially across goods. For example, the manufacturing of leather footwear is still a relatively labour-intensive process, even with

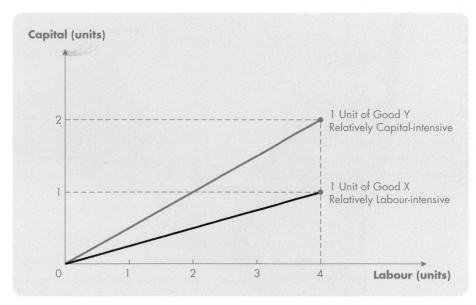

Figure 2.3: Factor proportions in production.

Current Account Balances as a Percentage of Gross Domestics Product

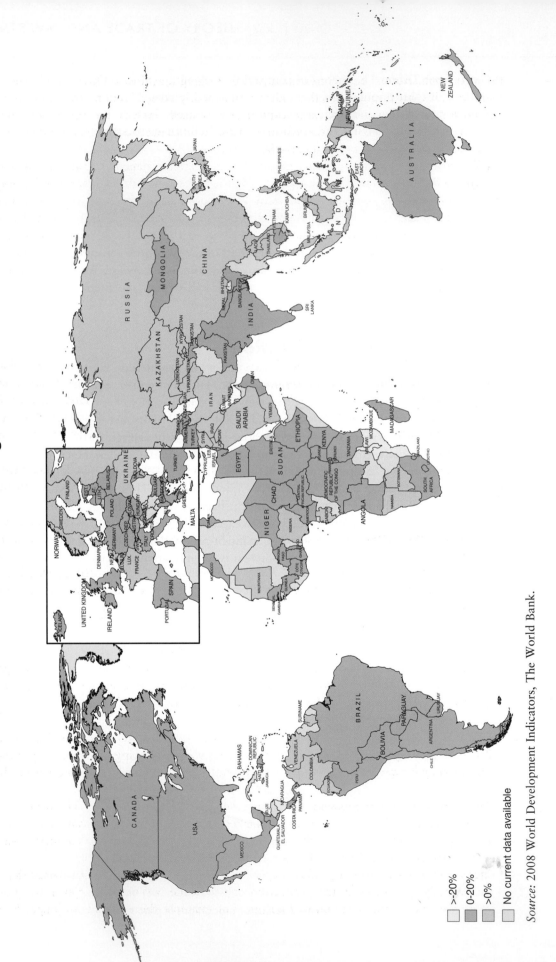

>-20%

0-20%

>0%

No current data available

Source: 2008 World Development Indicators, The World Bank.

the most sophisticated leather treatment and patterning machinery. Other goods, such as computer memory chips, however, although requiring some highly skilled labour, require massive quantities of capital for production. These large capital requirements include the enormous sums needed for research and development and the manufacturing facilities needed for clean production to ensure the extremely high quality demanded in the industry.

According to factor proportions theory, factor intensities depend on the state of technology – the current method of manufacturing a good. The theory assumed that the same technology of production would be used for the same goods in all countries. It is not, therefore, differences in the efficiency of production that determine trade between countries, as in classical theory. Classical theory implicitly assumed that technology or the productivity of labour is different across countries. Otherwise, there would be no logical explanation why one country requires more units of labour to produce a unit of output than another country. Factor proportions theory assumes no such productivity differences.

Factor Endowments, Factor Prices and Comparative Advantage

If there is no difference in technology or productivity of factors across countries, what then determines comparative advantage in production and export? The answer is that factor prices determine cost differences. And these prices are determined by the endowments of labour and capital the country possesses. The theory assumes that labour and capital are immobile; factors cannot move across borders. Therefore, the country's endowment determines the relative costs of labour and capital as compared with other countries.

Using these assumptions, factor proportions theory states that a country should specialize in the production and export of those products that use intensively its relatively abundant factor.

- A country that is relatively labour abundant should specialize in the production of relatively labour-intensive goods. It should then export those labour-intensive goods in exchange for capital-intensive goods.
- A country that is relatively capital abundant should specialize in the production of relatively capital-intensive goods. It should then export those capital-intensive goods in exchange for labour-intensive goods.

Assumptions of the Factor Proportions Theory

The increasing level of theoretical complexity of the factor proportions theory, as compared with the classical trade theory, increased the number of assumptions necessary for the theory to 'hold'. It is important to take a last look at the assumptions before proceeding further.

- The theory assumed two countries, two products and two factors of production, the so-called $2 \times 2 \times 2$ assumption. Note that if both countries were producing all of the output they could and trading only between themselves (only two countries), both countries would have to have balances in trade!
- The markets for the inputs and the outputs were perfectly competitive. The factors of production, labour and capital were exchanged in markets that paid them only what they were worth. Similarly, the trade of the outputs (the international trade between the two countries) was competitive so that one country had no market power over the other.
- Increasing production of a product experiences diminishing returns. This meant that as a country increasingly specialized in the production of one of the two outputs, it eventually would require more and more inputs per unit of output. For example there would no longer be the constant

'labour-hours per unit of output' as assumed under the classical theory. Production possibilities frontiers would no longer be straight lines but concave. The result was that complete specialization would no longer occur under factor proportions theory.

• Both countries were using identical technologies. Each product was produced in the same way in both countries. This meant the only way that a good could be produced more cheaply in one country than in the other was if the factors of production used (labour and capital) were cheaper.

Although a number of additional technical assumptions were necessary, these four highlight the very specialized set of conditions needed to explain international trade with factor proportions theory. Much of the trade theory developed since has focused on how trade changes when one or more of these assumptions are not found in the real world.

The Leontief Paradox

One of the most famous tests of any economic or business theory occurred in 1950, when economist Wassily Leontief tested whether the factor proportions theory could be used to explain the types of goods the United States imported and exported. Leontief's premise was the following.

> A widely shared view on the nature of the trade between the United States and the rest of the world is derived from what appears to be a common sense assumption; that the US has a comparative advantage in the production of commodities that require for their manufacture large quantities of capital and relatively small amounts of labour. The US's economic relationships with other countries are supposed to be based mainly on the export of such 'capital intensive' goods in exchange for forgoing products which – if America were to make them at home – would require little capital but large quantities of American labour. Since the United States possesses a relatively large amount of capital – so goes this oft-repeated argument – and a comparatively small amount of labour, direct domestic production of such 'labour intensive' products would be uneconomical; the US can much more advantageously obtain them from abroad in exchange for its capital intensive products.[2]

Leontief first had to devise a method to determine the relative amounts of labour and capital in a good. His solution, known as input–output analysis, was an accomplishment on its own. Input–output analysis is a technique of decomposing a good into the values and quantities of the labour, capital and other potential factors employed in the good's manufacture. Leontief then used this methodology to analyse the labour and capital content of all US merchandise imports and exports. The hypothesis was relatively straightforward: US exports should be relatively capital intensive (use more units of capital relative to labour) than US imports. Leontief's results were, however, a bit of a shock.

Leontief found that the products that US firms exported were relatively more labour intensive than the products the United States imported.[3] It seemed that if the factor proportions theory was true, the United States is a relatively labour-abundant country! Alternatively, the theory could be wrong. Neither interpretation of the results was acceptable to many in the field of international trade.

A variety of explanations and continuing studies have attempted to solve what has become known as the Leontief Paradox. At first, it was thought to have been simply a result of the specific year (1947) of the data. However, the same results were found with different years and data sets. Second, it was noted that Leontief did not really analyse the labour and capital contents of imports but rather the labour and capital contents of the domestic equivalents of these imports. It was possible that the United States was actually producing the products in a more capital-intensive fashion than were the countries from which it also imported the manufactured goods.[4] Finally, the debate turned to the need to distinguish different types of labour and capital. For example, several studies attempted to separate labour factors into skilled labour and unskilled labour. These studies have continued to show results more consistent with what the factor proportions theory would predict for country trade patterns.

Linder's Overlapping Product Ranges Theory

The difficulties in empirically validating the factor proportions theory led many in the 1960s and 1970s to search for new explanations of the determinants of trade between countries. The work of Staffan Burenstam Linder focused not on the production or supply side, but instead on the preferences of consumers – the demand side. Linder acknowledged that in the natural resource-based industries, trade was indeed determined by relative costs of production and factor endowments.

However, Linder argued, trade in manufactured goods was dictated not by cost concerns but rather by the similarity in product demands across countries. Linder's theory was a significant departure from previous theory and was based on two principles:

- As income or more precisely per capita income rises, the complexity and quality level of the products demanded by the country's residents also rises. The total range of product sophistication demanded by a country's residents is largely determined by its level of income.
- The entrepreneurs directing the firms that produce society's needs are more knowledgeable about their own domestic market than about foreign markets. An entrepreneur could not be expected to serve effectively a foreign market that is significantly different from the domestic market, because competitiveness comes from experience. A logical pattern would be for an entrepreneur to gain success and market share at home first then expand to foreign markets that are similar in their demands or tastes.

International trade in manufactured goods would then be influenced by similarity of demands. The countries that would see the most intensive trade are those with similar per-capita income levels, because they would possess a greater likelihood of overlapping product demands.

So where does trade come in? According to Linder, the overlapping ranges of product sophistication represent the products that entrepreneurs would know well from their home markets and could therefore potentially export and compete with in foreign markets. For example, the United States and Canada have almost parallel sophistication ranges, implying they would have a lot of common ground, overlapping product ranges, for intensive international trade and competition. They are quite similar in their per capita income levels. But Mexico and the United States or Mexico and Canada, would not. Mexico has a significantly different product sophistication range as a result of a different per capita income level.

The overlapping product ranges described by Linder would today be termed market segments. Not only was Linder's work instrumental in extending trade theory beyond cost considerations, but it also found a place in the field of international marketing. As illustrated in the theories following the work of Linder over the next few decades, many of the questions that his work raised were the focus of considerable attention.

INTERNATIONAL INVESTMENT AND PRODUCT CYCLE THEORY

A very different path was taken by Raymond Vernon in 1966 concerning what is now termed product cycle theory. Diverging significantly from traditional approaches, Vernon focused on the product (rather than the country and the technology of its manufacture), not its factor proportions. Most striking was the appreciation of the role of information, knowledge and the costs and power that go hand in hand with knowledge: '. . . we abandon the powerful simplifying notion that knowledge is a universal free good and introduce it as an independent variable in the decision to trade or to invest'.

Using many of the same basic tools and assumptions of factor proportions theory, Vernon added two technology-based premises to the factor-cost emphasis of existing theory:

- Technical innovations leading to new and profitable products require large quantities of capital and highly skilled labour. These factors of production are predominantly available in highly industrialized capital-intensive countries.
- These same technical innovations, both the product itself and more importantly the methods for its manufacture, go through three stages of maturation as the product becomes increasingly commercialized. As the manufacturing process becomes more standardized and low-skill labour-intensive, the comparative advantage in its production and export shifts across countries. And as the following Focus on Politics describes, even accurately tracking exports and imports is sometimes daunting.

The Stages of the Product Cycle

Product cycle theory is both supply-side (cost of production) and demand-side (income levels of consumers) in its orientation. Each of these three stages that Vernon described combines differing elements of each.

- *Stage I: The New Product.* Innovation requires highly skilled labour and large quantities of capital for research and development. The product will normally be most effectively designed and initially manufactured near the parent firm and therefore in a highly industrialized market due to the need for proximity to information and the need for communication among the many different skilled-labour components required.

  In this development stage, the product is non-standardized. The production process requires a high degree of flexibility (meaning continued use of highly skilled labour). Costs of production are therefore quite high. The innovator at this stage is a monopolist and therefore enjoys all of the benefits of monopoly power, including the high profit margins required to repay the high development costs and expensive production process. Price elasticity of demand at this stage is low; high-income consumers buy it regardless of cost.

- *Stage II: The Maturing Product.* As production expands, its process becomes increasingly standardized. The need for flexibility in design and manufacturing declines and therefore the demand for highly skilled labour declines. The innovating country increases its sales to other countries. Competitors with slight variations develop, putting downward pressure on prices and profit margins. Production costs are an increasing concern.

  As competitors increase, as well as their pressures on price, the innovating firm faces critical decisions on how to maintain market share. Vernon argues that the firm faces a critical decision at this stage: either to lose market share to foreign-based manufacturers using lower-cost labour or to invest abroad to maintain its market share by exploiting the comparative advantages of factor costs in other countries. This is one of the first theoretical explanations of how trade and investment become increasingly intertwined.

- *Stage III: The Standardized Product.* In this final stage, the product is completely standardized in its manufacture. Thus, with access to capital on world capital markets, the country of production is simply the one with the cheapest unskilled labour. Profit margins are thin and competition is fierce. The product has largely run its course in terms of profitability for the innovating firm.

The country of comparative advantage has therefore shifted as the technology of the product's manufacture has matured. The same product shifts in its location of production. The country possessing the product during that stage enjoys the benefits of net trade surpluses. But such advantages are fleeting, according to Vernon. As knowledge and technology continually change, so does the country of that product's comparative advantage.

F○CUS ON

When the Numbers Don't Add Up

The international trade statistics between countries, as reported by each, often do not match. As part of the continuing co-operation between the North American Free Trade Agreement (NAFTA) countries, the US Department of Commerce recently concluded a study into the differences among the official trade statistics released by the United States, Mexico and Canada in 1998 and 1999. The significance of these differences is compounded by the importance of trade among the three countries: 30% of all US merchandise trade is with Canada and Mexico; 80% of Mexico's merchandise and service trade is with the United States and Canada.

The primary sources of the discrepancy in statistics include *geographic coverage, partner country attribution, non-filing of US exports* and *low-value transactions*. An example of *geographic coverage* would be that the United States considers Puerto Rico and the US Virgin Islands as part of the United States for reporting reasons, whereas Mexico regards them as separate trading partners. *Partner country attribution* occurs, for example, in Mexico, where the import entry form allows for the reporting of only a single country of origin. As a result, some imports are misattributed to the United States.

For more details on the study of trade statistics discrepancies see www.census.gov/foreign-trade/.

Trade Implications of the Product Cycle

Product cycle theory shows how specific products were first produced and exported from one country but, through product and competitive evolution, shifted their location of production and export to other countries over time. Figure 2.4 illustrates the trade patterns that Vernon visualized as resulting from the maturing stages of a specific product cycle. As the product and the market for the product mature and change, the countries of its production and export shift.

Let us look at an example of a product initially designed and manufactured in the UK. In its early stages (from time t_0 to t_1), the UK is the only country producing and consuming the product. Production is highly capital-intensive and skilled-labour-intensive at this time. At time t_1 the UK begins exporting the product to Other Advanced Countries, as Vernon classified them. These countries possess the income to purchase the product in its still New Product Stage, in which it was relatively highly priced. These Other Advanced Countries also commerce their own production at time t_1 but continue to be net importers. A few exports, however, do find their way to the Less Developed Countries at this time as well.

As the product moves into the second stage, the Maturing Product Stage, production capability expands rapidly in the Other Advanced Countries. Competitive variations begin to appear as the basic technology of the product becomes more widely known and the need for skilled labour in its production declines. These countries eventually also become net exporters of the product near the end of the stage (time t_3). At time t_2 the Less Developed Countries begin their own production, although they continue to be net importers. Meanwhile, the lower cost of production from these growing competitors turns the UK into a net importer by time t_4. The competitive advantage for production and export is clearly shifting across countries at this time.

The third and final stage, the Standardized Product Stage, sees the comparative advantage of production and export now shifting to the Less Developed Countries. The product is now a relatively mass-produced product that can be made with increasingly less-skilled labour. The UK continues to reduce domestic production and increase imports. The Other Advanced Countries

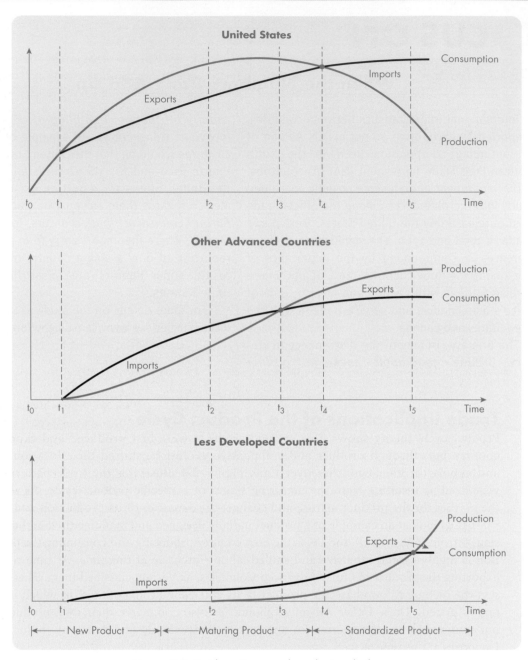

Figure 2.4: Trade patterns and product cycle theory.

Source: Raymond Vernon (1966) 'International investment and international trade in the product cycle', *Quarterly Journal of Economics*, May, 199. Reproduced with permission of MIT Press – Journals in the format Textbook via Copyright Clearance Center.

continue to produce and export, although exports peak as the Less Developed Countries expand production and become net exporters themselves. The product has run its course or life cycle in reaching time t_5.

A final point: note that throughout this product cycle, the countries of production, consumption, export and import are identified by their labour and capital levels, not firms. Vernon noted that it could very well be the same firms that are moving production from the UK to Other Advanced Countries to Less Developed Countries. The shifting location of production was instrumental in the changing patterns of trade but not necessarily in the loss of market share, profitability or competitiveness of the firms. The country of comparative advantage could change.

Although interesting in its own right for increasing emphasis on technology's impact on product costs, product cycle theory was most important because it explained international investment. Not only did the theory recognize the mobility of capital across countries (breaking the traditional assumption of factor immobility), it shifted the focus from the country to the product. This made it important to match the product by its maturity stage with its production location to examine competitiveness.

Product cycle theory has many limitations. It is obviously most appropriate for technology-based products. These are the products that are most likely to experience the changes in production process as they grow and mature. Other products, either resource-based (such as minerals and other commodities) or services (which employ capital but mostly in the form of human capital), are not so easily characterized by stages of maturity. And product cycle theory is most relevant to products that eventually fall victim to mass production and therefore cheap labour forces. But, all things considered, product cycle theory served to breach a wide gap between the trade theories of old and the intellectual challenges of a new, more globally competitive market in which capital, technology, information and firms themselves were more mobile.

THE NEW TRADE THEORY: STRATEGIC TRADE

Global trade developments in the 1980s and 1990s led to much criticism of the existing theories of trade. First, although there was rapid growth in trade, much of it was not explained by current theory. Second, the massive size of the merchandise trade deficit of the United States – and the associated decline of many US firms in terms of international competitiveness – served as something of a country-sized lab experiment demonstrating what some critics termed the 'bankruptcy of trade theory'. Academics and policy makers alike looked for new explanations.

Two new contributions to trade theory were met with great interest. Paul Krugman, along with several colleagues, developed a theory of how trade is altered when markets are not perfectly competitive or when production of specific products possesses economies of scale. A second and very influential development was the growing work of Michael Porter, who examined the competitiveness of industries on a global basis, rather than relying on country-specific factors to determine competitiveness.

Economies of Scale and Imperfect Competition

Paul Krugman's theoretical developments once again focused on cost of production and how cost and price drive international trade. Using theoretical developments from microeconomics and market structure analysis, Krugman focused on two types of economics of scale, internal economies of scale and external economies of scale.[5]

According to the government, Chinese mobile phone usage reached 200 million subscribers in 2002. As domestic spending grows, China will be able to sustain its economic growth and as a result be less dependent upon exports. This growing Chinese economy also helps China's trade partners.

Internal Economies of Scale
When the cost per unit of output depends on the size of an individual firm, the larger the firm the greater the scale benefits and the lower the cost per unit. A firm possessing internal economies of scale could potentially monopolize an industry (creating an imperfect market),

both domestically and internationally. If the firm produces more, lowering the cost per unit, it can lower the market price and sell more products, because it *sets* market prices.

The link between dominating a domestic industry and influencing international trade comes from taking this assumption of imperfect markets back to the original concept of comparative advantage. For this firm to expand sufficiently to enjoy its economies of scale, it must take resources away from other domestic industries in order to expand. A country then sees its own range of products in which it specializes narrowing, providing an opportunity for other countries to specialize in these so-called abandoned product ranges. Countries again search out and exploit comparative advantage.

A particularly powerful implication of internal economies of scale is that it provides an explanation of intra-industry trade, one area in which traditional trade theory had indeed seemed bankrupt. Intra-industry trade is when a country seemingly imports and exports the same product, an idea that is obviously inconsistent with any of the trade theories put forward in the past three centuries. According to Krugman, internal economies of scale may lead a firm to specialize in a narrow product line (to produce the volume necessary for economies of scale cost benefits); other firms in other countries may produce products that are similarly narrow, yet extremely similar, known as product differentiation. If consumers in either country wish to buy both products, they will be importing and exporting products that are, for all intents and purposes, the same.[6]

Intra-industry trade has been studied in detail in the past decade. Intra-industry trade is measured with the Grubel-Lloyd Index, the ratio of imports and exports of the same product occurring between two trading nations. It is calculated as follows:

$$\text{Intra-Industry Trade Index}_i = \frac{|X_i - M_i|}{(X_i + M_i)}$$

where i is the product category and $|X-M|$ is the absolute value of net exports of that product (exports − imports). For example, if Sweden imports 100 heavy machines for its forest products industry from Finland and at the same time exports to Finland 80 of the same type of equipment, the intra-industry trade (IIT) index would be:

$$\text{IIT} = \frac{|80 - 100|}{(80 + 100)} = 1 - 0.1111 = 0.89$$

The closer the index value is to 1, the higher the level of intra-industry trade in that product category. The closer the index is to 0, the more one-way the trade is between the countries, as traditional trade theory would predict.

Intra-industry trade is now thought to compose roughly 25% of global trade. And to its credit, intra-industry trade is increasingly viewed as having additive benefits to the fundamental benefits of comparative advantage. Intra-industry trade does allow some industrial segments in some countries to deepen their specialization while simultaneously allowing greater breadth of choices and commensurate benefits to consumers. Of course, one potentially disturbing characteristic of the growth in intra-industry trade is the potential for trade of all kinds to continue to expand in breadth and depth between the most industrialized countries (those producing the majority of the more complex manufactured goods) while those less industrialized nations do not see this added boost to trade growth.

External Economies of Scale

When the cost per unit of output depends on the size of an industry, and not the size of the individual firm, the industry of that country may produce at lower costs than the same industry that is smaller in size in other countries. A country can potentially dominate world markets in a particular product, not because it has one massive firm producing enormous quantities (for example, Boeing), but rather because it has many small firms that interact to create a large, competitive, critical mass (e.g., semi-conductors in Penang, Malaysia). No one firm needs to be all that large, but several small firms in total may create such a competitive industry so that firms in other countries can never break into the industry on a competitive basis.[7]

Unlike internal economies of scale, external economies of scale may not necessarily lead to imperfect markets, but they may result in an industry maintaining its dominance in its field in world markets. This provides an explanation as to why all industries do not necessarily always move to the country with the lowest-cost energy, resources or labour. What gives rise to this critical mass of small firms and their interrelationships is a much more complex question. The work of Michael Porter provides a partial explanation of how these critical masses are sustained.

Strategic Trade

Often criticized as being simplistic or naive, trade theory in recent years has, in the words of one critic, grown up. One fundamental assumption that both classical and modern trade theories have not been willing to stray far from is the inefficiencies introduced with governmental involvement in trade. Economic theory, however, has long recognized that government can play a beneficial role when markets are not purely competitive. This theory has now been expanded to government's role in international trade as well. This growing stream of thought is termed strategic trade. There are (at least) four specific circumstances involving imperfect competition in which strategic trade may apply, which we denote as *price*, *cost*, *repetition* and *externalities*.

Price

A foreign firm that enjoys significant international market power – monopolistic power – has the ability to both restrict the quantity of consumption and demand higher prices. One method by which a domestic government may thwart that monopolistic power is to impose import duties or tariffs on the imported products. The monopolist, not wishing to allow the price of the product to rise too high in the target market, will often absorb some portion of the tariff. The result is roughly the same amount of product imported and at relatively the same price to the customer, but the excessive profits (economic rent in economic theory) have been partly shifted from the monopolist to the domestic government. Governments have long fought the power of global petrochemical companies with these types of import duties.

Cost

Although much has been made in recent years about the benefits of 'small and flexible', some industries are still dominated by the firms that can gain massive productive size – scale economies. As the firm's size increases, its per unit cost of production falls, allowing it a significant cost advantage in competition. Governments wishing for specific firms to gain this stature may choose to protect the domestic market against foreign competition to provide a home market of size for the company's growth and maturity. This strategic trade theory is actually quite similar to the traditional arguments for the protection of infant industries, though this is a protection whose benefits accrue to firms in adolescence rather than childhood!

Repetition

Some firms in some industries have inherent competitive advantages, often efficiency based, from simply having produced repetitively for years. Sometimes referred to as 'learning-by-doing', these firms may achieve competitive cost advantages from producing not only more units (as in the scale economies described above) but also from producing more units *over time*. A government that wishes to promote these efficiency gains by domestic firms can help the firm move down the learning curve faster by protecting the domestic market from foreign competitors. Again similar in nature to the infant industry argument, the idea is not only to allow the firm to produce more, but also to produce more cumulatively over time to gain competitive knowledge from the actual process itself.

Externalities

The fourth and final category of strategic trade involves those market failures in which the costs or benefits of the business process are not borne or captured by the firm itself. If, for example, the government believes that the future of business is in specific knowledge-based industries, it may be willing to subsidize the education of workers for that industry, protect that industry from foreign competition or even aid the industry in overcoming the costs of environmental protection in order to promote the industry's development. This argument is similar to those used by governments in the 1970s and 1980s to support the development of certain industries in their countries (for example, microelectronics in Japan and steel in Korea), which was then referred to as industrial policy. In fact, this strategic trade argument could be used in support of Michael Porter's cluster theory, in which society and industry would reap the benefits of reaching critical mass in experience and interactions through promotion and protection.

Although the arguments by proponents of strategic trade are often seductive, critics charge that these theories play more to emotion than rational thought. Industries do not often learn by doing or reduce costs through scale and governments are infamous for their inability to effectively protect (and unprotect, when the time comes) in order to promote industrial development and growth. Protection and state-supported monopolists are often some of the world's least efficient rather than most efficient. And as always, there is no assurance that foreign governments themselves will not react and retaliate, again undermining the potentially rational policies put into place in isolation. A final note of caution about strategic trade goes back to the very origins of trade theory: many of the benefits of international trade accrue to those who successfully divorce the politic from the economic.

The Competitive Advantage of Nations

The focus of early trade theory was on the country or nation and its inherent, natural or endowment characteristics that might give rise to increasing competitiveness. As trade theory evolved, it shifted its focus to the industry and product level, leaving the national-level competitiveness question somewhat behind. Recently, many have turned their attention to the question of how countries, governments and even private industry can alter the conditions within a country to aid the competitiveness of its firms.

The leader in this area of research has been Michael Porter of Harvard. As he states:

National prosperity is created, not inherited. It does not grow out of a country's natural endowments, its labour pool, its interest rates or its currency's values, as classical economics insists.

A nation's competitiveness depends on the capacity of its industry to innovate and upgrade. Companies gain advantage against the world's best competitors because of pressure and challenge. They benefit from having strong domestic rivals, aggressive home-based suppliers and demanding local customers.

In a world of increasingly global competition, nations have become more, not less, important. As the basis of competition has shifted more and more to the creation and assimilation of knowledge, the role of the nation has grown. Competitive advantage is created and sustained through a highly localized process. Differences in national values, culture, economic structures, institutions and histories all contribute to competitive success. There are striking differences in the patterns of competitiveness in every country; no nation can or will be competitive in every, or even most industries. Ultimately, nations succeed in particular industries because their home environment is most forward-looking, dynamic and challenging.[8]

Porter argues that innovation is what drives and sustains competitiveness. A firm must avail itself of all dimensions of competition, which he categorized into four major components of 'the diamond of national advantage':

- *Factor Conditions:* The appropriateness of the nation's factors of production to compete successfully in a specific industry. Porter notes that although these factor conditions are very important in the determination of trade, they are not the only source of competitiveness as suggested by the classical or factor proportions theories of trade. Most importantly for Porter, it is the ability of a nation continually to create, upgrade and deploy its factors (such as skilled labour) that is crucial, not the initial endowment.
- *Demand Conditions:* The degree of health and competition the firm must face in its original home market. Firms that can survive and flourish in highly competitive and demanding local markets are much more likely to gain the competitive edge. Porter notes that it is the character of the market and not its size that is paramount in promoting the continual competitiveness of the firm. And Porter takes 'character' to mean demanding customers.
- *Related and Supporting Industries:* The competitiveness of all related industries and suppliers to the firm. A firm that is operating within a mass of related firms and industries gains and maintains advantages through close working relationships, proximity to suppliers and timeliness of product and information flows. The constant and close interaction is successful if it occurs not only in terms of physical proximity but also through the willingness of firms to work at it.
- *Firm Strategy, Structure and Rivalry:* The conditions in the home-nation that either hinder or aid in the firm's creation and sustaining of international competitiveness. Porter notes that no single managerial, ownership or operational strategy is universally appropriate. It depends on the fit and flexibility of what works for that industry in that country at that time.

These four points, as illustrated in Figure 2.5, constitute what nations and firms must strive to 'create and sustain through a highly localized process' to ensure their success.

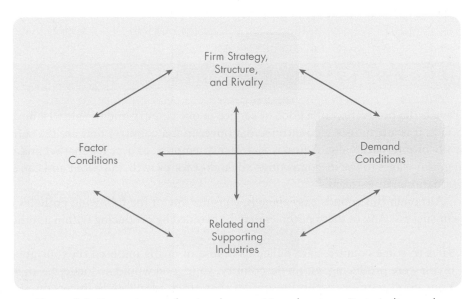

Figure 2.5: Determinants of national competitive advantage: Porter's diamond.

Porter's emphasis on innovation as the source of competitiveness reflects an increased focus on the industry and product that we have seen in the past three decades. The acknowledgment that the nation is 'more, not less, important' is to many eyes a welcome return to a positive role for government and even national-level private industry in encouraging international competitiveness. Including factor conditions as a cost component, demand conditions as a motivator of firm actions and competitiveness all combine to include the elements of classical, factor proportions, product cycle and imperfect competition theories in a pragmatic approach to the challenges that the global markets of the twenty-first century present to the firms of today.

Clusters and the New Economics

Michael Porter added an additional theoretical development to the concept of competitive advantage; that of competitive clusters.[9] Clusters, according to Porter, are 'critical masses – in one place – of unusual competitive success in particular fields'. Examples often cited are leather fashion product manufacturing in northern Italy, wine in California in the United States or semiconductors on the Penang Peninsula in Malaysia. These geographic concentrations of competitive excellence seemingly fly in the face of modern thought on the mobility of capital and knowledge.

Porter's theoretical argument was based on his assertion that significant advantages accrue to companies from being in proximity to complementary products and services – within reach of all the suppliers and partners in the product value chain. The premise was quite simple: competitive advantages are gained through interconnected companies and institutions locally, not through the scale and scope of the firms themselves. Cluster theory suggests that competition is altered in at least three ways when clusters form successfully: (1) by increasing the productivity of the companies based in the area; (2) by driving and supporting the momentum of innovation in the area; and (3) by stimulating the creation of new companies and new configurations of business in the area. In effect, the cluster itself acts as an extended family or single firm, but flexibly and efficiently. Interestingly, the cluster's competitive sustainability is assured by the second change – the momentum gains to innovation – which is consistent with Porter's earlier work on what drives competitive advantage of the individual firm through time.

The writing of Porter and others has continued to be instrumental in the thinking of both business and government when approaching trade policy. Many, although supporting much of the findings of Porter's theories, see the true insights as being related to the complex relationships between knowledge and how knowledge is developed, shared and transmitted within industries over time.

THE THEORY OF INTERNATIONAL INVESTMENT

Trade is the production of a good or service in one country and its sale to a buyer in another country. In fact, it is a firm (not a country) and a buyer (not a country) that are the subjects of trade, domestically or internationally. A firm is therefore attempting to access a market and its buyers. The producing firm wants to use its competitive advantage for growth and profit and can also reach this goal by international investment.[9]

Although this sounds easy enough, consider any of the following potholes on the road to investment success. Any of these potholes may be avoided by producing within another country:

- Sales to some countries are difficult because of tariffs imposed on your good when it is entering. If you were producing within the country, your good would no longer be an import.
- Your good requires natural resources that are available only in certain areas of the world. It is therefore imperative that you have access to the natural resources. You can buy them from that

country and bring them to your production process (import) or simply take the production to them.

- Competition is constantly pushing you to improve efficiency and decrease the costs of producing your good. You therefore may want to produce where it will be cheaper – cheaper capital, cheaper energy, cheaper natural resources or cheaper labour. Many of these factors are still not mobile and therefore you will go to them instead of bringing them to you.

There are thousands of reasons why a firm may want to produce in another country and not necessarily in the country that is cheapest for production or the country where the final good is sold.

The subject of international investment arises from one basic idea: the mobility of capital. Although many of the traditional trade theories assumed the immobility of the factors of production, it is the movement of capital that has allowed foreign direct investments across the globe. If there is a competitive advantage to be gained, capital can and will get there.

The Foreign Direct Investment Decision

Consider a firm that wants to exploit its competitive advantage by accessing foreign markets as illustrated in the decision-sequence tree of Figure 2.6.

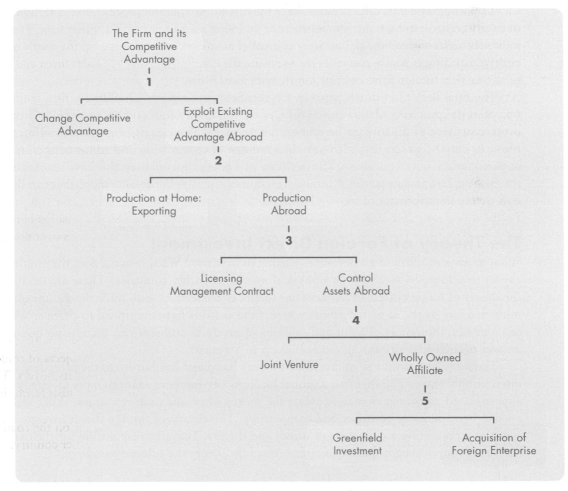

Figure 2.6: The foreign direct investment decision sequence.

Source: Adapted from Gunter Dufey and R. Mirus, 'Foreign direct investment: theory and strategic considerations', unpublished, University of Michigan, May 1985. Reproduced by permission of Gunter Dufey.

The first choice is whether to exploit the existing competitive advantage in new foreign markets or to concentrate resources in the development of new competitive advantages in the domestic market. Although many firms may choose to do both as resources allow, more and more firms are choosing to go international as at least part of their expansion strategies.

Second, should the firm produce at home and export to the foreign markets or produce abroad? The firm will choose the path that allows it to access the resources and markets it needs to exploit its existing competitive advantage. But it will also consider two additional dimensions of each foreign investment decision: (1) the degree of control over assets, technology, information and operations; and (2) the magnitude of capital that the firm must risk. Each decision increases the firm's control at the cost of increased capital outlays.

After choosing to produce abroad, the firm must decide how. The distinctions among different kinds of foreign direct investment (branch 3 and downward in Figure 2.6), licensing agreements to greenfield construction (building a new facility from the ground up), vary by degrees of ownership. The licensing management contract is by far the simplest and cheapest way to produce abroad. Another firm is licensed to produce the product, but with your firm's technology and know-how. The question is whether the reduced capital investment of simply licensing the product to another manufacturer is worth the risk of loss of control over the product and technology.

The firm that wants direct control over the foreign production process next determines the degree of equity control: to own the firm outright or as a joint investment with another firm. Trade-offs with joint ventures continue the debate over control of assets and other sources of the firm's original competitive advantage. Many countries try to ensure the continued growth of local firms and investors by requiring that foreign firms operate jointly with local firms.

The final decision branch between a 'greenfield investment' – building a firm from the ground up – and the purchase of an existing firm, is often a question of cost. A greenfield investment is the most expensive of all foreign investment alternatives. The acquisition of an existing firm is often lower in initial cost but may also contain a number of customizing and adjustment costs that are not apparent at the initial purchase. The purchase of a going concern may also have substantial benefits if the existing business possesses substantial customer and supplier relationships that can be used by the new owner in the pursuit of its own business.

The Theory of Foreign Direct Investment

What motivates a firm to go beyond exporting or licensing? What benefits does the multinational firm expect to achieve by establishing a physical presence in other countries? These are the questions that the theory of foreign direct investment has sought to answer. As with trade theory, the questions have remained largely the same over time, whereas the answers have continued to change. With hundreds of countries, thousands of firms and millions of products and services, there is no question that the answer to such an enormous question is likely to get messy.

The following overview of investment theory has many similarities to the preceding discussion of international trade. The theme is a global business environment that attempts to satisfy increasingly sophisticated consumer demands, while the means of production, resources, skills and technology needed become more complex and competitive. The theory of foreign direct investment is indeed eclectic, representing a collection of forces and drivers. The man responsible for the majority of the theoretical development, John Dunning, termed the theory the eclectic paradigm.

Firms as Seekers

A firm that expands across borders may be seeking any of a number of specific sources of profit or opportunity.

- *Seeking Resources:* There is no question that much of the initial foreign direct investment of the eighteenth and nineteenth centuries was the result of firms seeking unique and valuable natural resources for their products. Whether it be the copper resources of Chile, the linseed oils of Indonesia or the petroleum resources spanning the Middle East, firms establishing permanent presences around the world are seeking access to the resources at the core of their business.
- *Seeking Factor Advantages:* The resources needed for production are often combined with other advantages that are inherent in the country of production. The same low-cost labour at the heart of classical trade theory provides incentives for firms to move production to countries possessing these factor advantages. As noted by Vernon's product cycle, the same firms may move their own production to locations of factor advantages as the products and markets mature.
- *Seeking Knowledge:* Firms may attempt to acquire other firms in other countries for the technical or competitive skills they possess. Alternatively, companies may locate in and around centres of industrial enterprise unique to their specific industry, such as the footwear industry of Milan or the semiconductor industry of the Silicon Valley of California.
- *Seeking Security:* Firms continue to move internationally as they seek political stability or security. For example, Mexico has experienced a significant increase in foreign direct investment as a result of the tacit support of the United States, Canada and Mexico itself as reflected by the North American Free Trade Agreement.
- *Seeking Markets:* Not the least of the motivations, the ability to gain and maintain access to markets is of paramount importance to multinational firms. Whether following the principles of Linder, in which firms learn from their domestic market and use that information to go international, or the principles of Porter, which emphasize the character of the domestic market as dictating international competitiveness, foreign market access is necessary.

Firms as Exploiters of Imperfections

Much of the investment theory developed in the past three decades has focused on the efforts of multinational firms to exploit the imperfections in factor and product markets created by governments. The work of Hymer, Kindleberger and Caves noted that many of the policies of governments create imperfections. These market imperfections cover the entire range of supply and demand of the market: trade policy (tariffs and quotas), tax policies and incentives, preferential purchasing arrangements established by governments themselves and financial restrictions on the access of foreign firms to domestic capital markets.

- *Imperfections in Access:* Many of the world's developing countries have long sought to create domestic industry by restricting imports of competitive products in order to allow smaller, less competitive domestic firms to grow and prosper – so-called import substitution policies. Multinational firms have sought to maintain their access to these markets by establishing their own productive presence within the country, effectively bypassing the tariff restriction.
- *Imperfections in Factor Mobility:* Other multinational firms have exploited the same sources of comparative advantage identified throughout this chapter – the low-cost resources or factors often located in less developed countries or countries with restrictions on the mobility of labour and capital. However, combining the mobility of capital with the immobility of low-cost labour has characterized much of the foreign direct investment seen throughout the developing world over the past 50 years.
- *Imperfections in Management:* The ability of multinational firms to exploit successfully or at least manage these imperfections still relies on their ability to gain an 'advantage'. Market advantages or powers are seen in international markets just as in domestic markets: cost advantages, economies of scale and scope, product differentiation, managerial or marketing technique and knowledge, financial resources and strength.

All these imperfections are the things of which competitive dreams are made. The multinational firm needs to find these in some form or another to justify the added complexities and costs of international investments.

Firms as Internalizers

The questions that have plagued the field of foreign direct investment are: why can't all of the advantages and imperfections mentioned be achieved through management contracts or licensing agreements (the option available to the international investor at Step 3 in Figure 2.6)? Why is it necessary for *the firm itself* to establish a physical presence in the country? What pushes the multinational firm further down the investment decision tree?

The research of Buckley and Casson and Dunning has attempted to answer these questions by focusing on non-transferable sources of competitive advantage – proprietary information possessed by the firm and its people. Many advantages that firms possess centre around their hands-on knowledge of producing a good or providing a service. By establishing their own multinational operations they can internalize the production, thus keeping confidential the information that is at the core of the firm's competitiveness. Internalization is preferable to the use of arm's-length arrangements such as management contracts or licensing agreements. They either do not allow the effective transmission of the knowledge or represent too serious a threat to the loss of the knowledge to allow the firm to achieve successfully the hoped-for benefits of international investment.

SUMMARY

The theory of international trade has changed drastically from that first put forward by Adam Smith. The classical theories of Adam Smith and David Ricardo focused on the abilities of countries to produce goods more cheaply than other countries. The earliest production and trade theories saw labour as the major factor expense that went into any product. If a country could pay that labour less and if that labour could produce more physically than labour in other countries, the country might obtain an absolute or comparative advantage in trade.

Subsequent theoretical development led to a more detailed understanding of production and its costs. Factors of production are now believed to include labour (skilled and unskilled), capital, natural resources and other potentially significant commodities that are difficult to reproduce or replace, such as energy. Technology, once assumed to be the same across all countries, is now seen as one of the premier driving forces in determining who holds the competitive edge or advantage. International trade is now seen as a complex combination of thousands of products, technologies and firms that are constantly innovating to either keep up with or get ahead of the competition.

Modern trade theory has looked beyond production cost to analyse how the demands of the marketplace alter who trades with whom and which firms survive domestically and internationally. The abilities of firms to adapt to foreign markets, both in the demands and the competitors that form the foreign markets, have required much of international trade and investment theory to search out new and innovative approaches to what determines success and failure.

Finally, as world economies grew and the magnitude of world trade increased, the simplistic ideas that guided international trade and investment theory have had to grow with them. The choices that many firms face today require them to move their capital, technology and know-how directly to countries that possess other unique factors or market advantages that will help them keep pace with market demands. Even then, world business conditions constitute changing fortunes.

QUESTIONS FOR DISCUSSION

1. According to the theory of comparative advantage as explained by Ricardo, why is trade always possible between two countries, even when one is absolutely inefficient compared to the other?

2. The factor proportions theory of international trade assumes that all countries produce the same product the same way. Would international competition cause or prevent this from happening?

3. What, in your opinion, were the constructive impacts on trade theory resulting from the empirical research of Wassily Leontief?

4. Product cycle theory has always been a very 'attractive theory' to many students. Why do you think that is?

5. Many trade theorists argue that the primary contribution of Michael Porter has been to re-popularize old ideas, in new, more applicable ways. To what degree do you think Porter's ideas are new or old?

6. How would you analyse the statement that 'international investment is simply a modern extension of classical trade'?

7. How can a crisis in Russia have an impact on jobs and profits in the European Union?

INTERNET EXERCISES

1. The differences across multinational firms are striking. Using a sample of firms, such as those listed here, pull from their individual web pages the proportions of their incomes that are earned outside their country of incorporation.

Walt Disney	www.disney.com/
Nestlé S.A.	www.nestle.com/
Intel	www.intel.com/
DaimlerChrysler	www.daimlerchrysler.com/
Mitsubishi Motors	www.mitsubishi-motors.com/

Also note the way in which international business is now conducted via the Internet. Several of the above home pages allow the user to choose the language of the presentation viewed. Others, like DaimlerChrysler, report financial results in two different accounting frameworks, those used in Germany and the Generally Accepted Accounting Practices (GAAP) used in the United States.

2. There is no hotter topic in business today than corporate governance, the way in which firms are controlled by management and ownership across countries. Use the following web sites to view recent research, current events and news items and other information related to the relationships between a business and its stakeholders.

Corporate Governance Net	www.corpgov.net/
Corporate Governance Research	www.irrc.org/

TAKE A STAND

Many multinational companies are now following a very similar strategy of moving their manufacturing facilities out of large, industrialized countries such as the UK and Germany and relocating them to countries in which labour is much cheaper, such as mainland China. This is, however, very controversial given slow economic growth and growing unemployment in the industrial countries.

According to most theories of international trade, once the technology of an industry has matured and countries have deregulated their economies sufficiently to allow capital to flow across borders relatively freely, companies in industries that can use lower-cost labour – assuming sufficient skills are available – should move their manufacturing to those lower-labour-cost countries. The competitive strategy argument is that if one company does not and another does, the first will be unable to compete in the future.

FOR DISCUSSION

1. Multinationals should not continue to move their manufacturing out of industrial countries. They are contributing to rising unemployment, undermining the economies of countries like the UK and Germany and simply serving as devices to exploit cheap labour in developing countries.

2. Multinationals must continue to take whatever actions are necessary, including moving manufacturing to lower-cost countries, to remain competitive. The people, the workers and the economies of countries such as the UK and Germany cannot artificially protect their economies from global competition; it only serves to create countries of lesser and lesser competitiveness in the coming years.

CHAPTER
3
Culture

- Culture Defined
- The Elements of Culture
- Sources of Cultural Knowledge
- Cultural Analysis
- The Training Challenge
- Making Culture Work for Business Success

LEARNING OBJECTIVES

- To define and demonstrate the effect of culture's various dimensions on business.
- To examine ways in which cultural knowledge can be acquired and individuals and organizations prepared for cross-cultural interaction.
- To illustrate ways in which cultural risk poses a challenge to the effective conduct of business communications and transactions.
- To suggest ways in which businesses act as change agents in the diverse cultural environments in which they operate.

IS THERE A EUROPEAN IDENTITY?

The question about the cultural borders and unity of Europe has raised a heated debate. Europe does not have the integrative historical processes and common language that have shaped the American culture and the sense of being part of it. The European cultural identity has been influenced by political values and behaviours in the culturally diverse European states. The differences between Western, Central and Eastern Europe, and their cultural borders associated with the European Union (EU) enlargement process, have only added new perspectives to the culture debate.

It has been suggested that there seems to be a divide, from a cultural point of view, between Western and Eastern parts of Europe, a great 'schism', forged by history. This can be dated back to the separation of Christianity into its Roman and Byzantine versions, and it has even deepened since the end of the Second World War. Thus it is argued that there are two distinct cultural communities in modern Europe that have a deep historical embeddedness, namely, the Euro-Atlantic Community and the Euro-Asian Community (the West and the East, respectively).

Research by the International Social Survey Program (ISSP) suggests that this is a rather simplistic explanation of contemporary European culture, omitting thousands of years of history. Using cross-country data for language, religion and popular culture, the study shows that a pan-European cosmopolitan culture exists across Europe. Parallel with this cosmopolitan European culture there exist national cultures with differences reflecting not only the links with the Roman and Byzantine empires, but also to the Austro-Hungarian, Russian and Ottoman empires, as well as cultural traits embedded in the Celtic, Slavonic, Gaelic, Arian, Anglo-Saxon and Latin ethnicities. Although the differences between the national cultures of the EU states are considerable, there are unifying cultural norms and aspirations for a better future and peaceful European co-existence. Research results reveal that the cultural proximity between the first six member states of the EU and the 2004 new entrants is much greater than the one between the original six EEC countries and the post-six entrants that formed the EU-15.

Similarly, it has been argued that the Eastward enlargement of the EU can increase the speed of European integration from a cultural perspective. The belief is that the citizens of the new member states are moving towards what is calls the 2 ± 1 configuration of Europe where Europeans who wish to participate fully in mobility opportunities should be able to communicate with an all-European continental culture. They also have to be integrated into the national culture of the state in which they are citizens/residents and will maintain the vital differences in the so-called 'mentalités' that differentiate intra-European national cultures. Hence, all socially mobile Europeans will exist and perform in two complementary cultural worlds. When Europeans come from states with a higher cultural similarity to the continental norm, these EU citizens will be members of a single cultural world $(2-1)$. Europeans who live in countries promoting 'state' or 'regional' cultures may need to be fully familiar with three cultural worlds $(2+1)$. For instance, this can be translated in language skills, where bilingual or trilingual socially mobile citizens are becoming a European standard. According to the ISSP survey results with three core member-states of the EEC (West Germany, Italy and Netherlands), six members of the expanded EU (Austria, Ireland, UK, Spain, Sweden and East Germany) and seven new members of the EU (Poland, Latvia, Czech Republic, Slovakia, Slovenia, Bulgaria and Hungary), all those who wish to be part of integrated Europe know/learn or aspire to speak several European languages.

Religion, value systems, traditions and other fields of culture such as film, music and popular culture, are also affected. Mobile EU citizens are more appreciative of differences and are more willing to embrace diversity in culture dimensions across Europe. National institutional shifts support the move in cultural norms toward the European standard. The data of the ISSP study show that there is a common sense of cosmopolitanism, multilingualism and secularism among the original member-states and the new EU member-states. Business transactions, political links and exchanges, cultural exchanges and institutional support structures foster the emergence of a cultural configuration representing a common European cultural sphere.

Sources: Urbán, A. (2003) 'EU Enlargement, EU Identity, Culture and National Identity in the Eastern Regions', *European Integration Studies*, Miskolc, 2(2), 45–51; Huntington, S. (1996) *Clash of Civilizations and the Remaking or World Order*. Simon and Schuster, New York; www.icpsr.umrich.edu; Laitin D. (1997) 'The Cultural Identities of a European State', *Politics and Society*, 25(3), 277–302.

INTRODUCTION

The ever-increasing degree of globalization, the opening of new markets and the intensifying competition have allowed and sometimes forced businesses to expand their operations. The challenge for managers is to handle the different values, attitudes and behaviour that govern human interaction. First, managers must ensure smooth interaction of the business with its different constituents and second, they must assist others to implement programmes within and across markets. It is no longer feasible to think of markets and operations in terms of domestic and international. Because the separation is no longer distinguishable, the necessity of culturally sensitive management and personnel is paramount.

As firms expand their operations across borders, they acquire new customers and new partners in new environments. Two distinct tasks become necessary: first, to understand cultural differences and the ways they manifest themselves and, second, to determine similarities across cultures and exploit them in strategy formulation. Success in new markets is very much a function of cultural adaptability: patience, flexibility and appreciation of others' beliefs.[1]

Recognition of different approaches may lead to establishing best practice; that is, a new way of doing things applicable throughout the firm. Ideally, this means that successful ideas can be transferred across borders for efficiency and adjusted to local conditions for effectiveness. Take the case of Nestlé. In one of his regular trips to company headquarters in Switzerland, the general manager of Nestlé Thailand was briefed on a summer coffee promotion from the Greek subsidiary, a cold coffee concoction called the Nescafe Shake. The Thai Group swiftly adopted and adapted the idea. It designed plastic containers to mix the drink and invented a dance, the Shake, to popularize the activity.[2]

To take advantage of the global marketplace, companies need to have or gain a thorough understanding of market behaviour, especially in terms of similarities. For example, no other group of emerging markets in the world has as much in common as those in Latin America. Some of them share a Spanish language and heritage; the Portuguese language and heritage are close enough to allow Brazilians and their neighbours to communicate easily. The Southern Florida melting pot, where Latin Americans of all backgrounds mix in a blend of Hispanic cultures, is in itself a picture of what Latin America can be. Tapping into the region's cultural affinities through a network-scale approach (e.g. regional hubs for production and pan-Latin brands) is not only possible but advisable.[3]

Cultural competence must be recognized as a key management skill. Cultural inflexibility can easily jeopardize millions of currency units (euros, US dollars, pound sterling, etc.) through wasted negotiations;

lost purchases, sales and contracts; and poor customer relations. Furthermore, the internal efficiency of a multinational corporation may be weakened if managers and workers are not 'on the same wavelength'. The tendency for Western managers is to be open and informal, but in some cultural settings that may be inappropriate. Cultural risk is just as real as commercial or political risk in the international business arena.

The intent of this chapter is to analyse the concept of culture and its various elements and then to provide suggestions for not only meeting the cultural challenge but making it a base of obtaining and maintaining a competitive advantage.

CULTURE DEFINED

Culture gives an individual an anchoring point, an identity, as well as codes of conduct. Of the more than 160 definitions of culture analysed by Kroeber and Kluckhohn, some conceive culture as separating humans from nonhumans, some define it as communicable knowledge and some as the sum of historical achievements produced by the social life of humans.[4] All of the definitions have common elements: culture is learned, shared and transmitted from one generation to the next. Culture consists of patterns of interrelated and interdependent characteristics, providing mindset, directions and guidance in all phases of human problem solving. It is shared by members of groups, societies, regions and nations, defining their commonalities and differences. Culture is primarily passed on from parents to their children but also transmitted by social organizations, special interest groups, the government, schools and churches. Common ways of thinking and behaving that are developed are then reinforced through social pressure. Culture is dynamic in time and develops through interactions among groups of people, societies, regions and nations. Culture exists both explicitly and implicitly as including conscious and unconscious values, attitudes, symbols and characteristics of human behaviour. Geert Hofstede calls this the 'collective programming of the mind'.[5] Culture is also multidimensional, consisting of a number of common elements that are interdependent. Changes occurring in one of the dimensions will affect the others as well.

For the purposes of this text, culture is defined as an *integrated system of learned behaviour patterns that are characteristic of the members of any society*. It includes everything that a group thinks, says, does and makes – its customs, language, material artefacts and shared systems of attitudes and feelings.[6] The definition, therefore, encompasses a wide variety of elements from the materialistic to the spiritual. Culture is inherently conservative, resisting change and fostering continuity. Every person is encultured into a particular culture, learning the 'right way' of doing things. Problems may arise when a person encultured in one culture has to adjust to another one. The process of acculturation – adjusting and adapting to a specific culture other than one's own – is one of the keys to success in international operations.

Edward Hall has studied the effects of culture on business and makes a distinction between high- and low-context cultures.[7] In countries with high-context cultures, such as Japan and Saudi Arabia, context is at least as important as what is actually said. The speaker and the listener rely on a common understanding of the context and what is not being said can carry more meaning than what is said. In low-context cultures, however, most of the information is contained explicitly in the words. North American and many European cultures such as German and Scandinavian engage in low-context communications. Unless one is aware of this basic difference, messages and intentions can easily be misunderstood. As an example, performance appraisals are typically a human resources function. If performance appraisals are to be centrally guided or conducted in a multinational corporation, those involved must be acutely aware of cultural nuances. One of the interesting differences is that the Anglo-Saxon system emphasizes the individual's development, whereas the Japanese system focuses on the group within which the individual works. In the United States, criticism is more direct and recorded formally, whereas in Japan it is more subtle and verbal.

F○CUS ON

Protecting Mozzarella

If European negotiators in the World Trade Organization get their way, food names associated with specific regions – Parma ham from Italy, Stilton cheese from the United Kingdom and Marsala wine from Italy – would be reserved solely for companies located in the respective regions; that is, through so-called geographic indications. EU officials argue that mozzarella, for example, is made according to exacting standards only in that particular part of Italy.

EU Trade Commissioner Pascal Lamy summarized the European point of view in this way: 'Geographical indications offer the best protection to quality products which are sold by relying on their origin and reputation and other special characteristics linked to such an origin. They reward investment in quality by our producers. Abuses in other countries undermine the heritage of EU products and create confusion among consumers.' Furthermore, Europeans fear that they may not be able to use their own names selling abroad in the future. A company in Canada, for example, could trademark a product named for a European place, preventing the rightful European originator from selling its goods in that market. The European Union has adopted geographic-indication laws governing 600 products sold inside the EU. Most recently, a ruling was issued that only Greek companies (which use goat's milk and specific production methods) can sell Feta cheese inside the EU. Now the EU wants to expand such a list worldwide and establish a multilateral register to police it.

For many outside of the EU, the European idea is bald-faced protectionism and has no merit in protecting cultural values. 'This does not speak of free trade; it is about making a monopoly of trade,' said Sergio Marchi, Canada's ambassador to the WTO. 'It is even hard to calculate the cost and confusion of administering such a thing.' Others argue that the EU is merely trying to cover up for inefficient production practices. Some even make the argument that multinational companies are the ones who have built up the value of the product names on the list – not the small producers in the regions in question.

The debate is still in its early stages. It is not clear how many names the EU will eventually want to have on the list, especially with the expansion of the EU to 10 new countries in 2004 and 2 more in 2007. The definition of geographic indications is not altogether clear in that some countries want to protect the adjectives found on product labels (such as 'tawny' or 'ruby' to describe Portuguese port wine). Other countries have their own lists as well; for example India wants basmati rice to be protected even though 'basmati' is not a place name.

Sources: 'WTO Talks: EU Steps Up Bid for Better Protection of Regional Quality Products', *EU Institutions Press Releases*, 28 August 2003, DN:IP/03/1178; 'Ham and Cheese: Italy Wins EU Case', *CNN.com*, 20 May 2003; 'Europe Says, "That Cheese is No Cheddar!"' *The Wall Street Journal*, 13 February 2003, B1; and 'USTR Supports Geographic Indications for Drinks' (2003) *Gourmet News*, January, 3.

Hans Gullestrup[8] emphasizes the *relative* nature of culture. When speaking of the relativity of cultures, he refers to 'national culture' or 'macro culture'. Individuals might consider themselves to be representatives of different layers of culture within the category of macro culture. For example, a Finn can see him/herself as a citizen of Northern Europe, a European, as a 'Lapp' or even a 'Saami'. In this way we can talk about cultural units and a cultural hierarchy within a specific category of culture. The complexity of cross-cultural relations is also caused by the fact that people are not only to be considered as members of one category of culture, but also of many different cultural categories at the same time. This can be referred to as the co-incidence of cultures. Gullestrup also identifies horizontal, vertical and dynamic cultural dimensions and defines the concept of hierarchy of cultures and subcultures.

Few cultures today are as homogeneous as those of Japan or Saudi Arabia. Elsewhere intra-cultural differences based on nationality, religion, race, or geographic areas have resulted in the emergence of distinct subcultures. The international manager's task is to distinguish relevant cross-cultural and intra-cultural differences and then to isolate potential opportunities and problems. Good examples are the Indian subculture in Britain and the Flemish and the Walloons in Belgium. On the other hand, borrowing and interaction among national cultures may narrow gaps between cultures. Here the international business entity acts as a change agent by introducing new products or ideas and practices. Although this may only shift consumption from one product brand to another, it may also lead to massive social change in the manner of consumption, the type of products consumed and social organization. Consider, for example, that the international portion of Kentucky Fried Chicken's (KFC) annual sales has grown substantially. In markets such as China and Taiwan, companies such as KFC, McDonald's and other fast food entities dramatically changed eating habits, especially of the younger generation.

The example of KFC in India illustrates the difficulties that companies may have in entering culturally complex markets. Even though the company opened its outlets in two of India's most cosmopolitan cities (Bangalore and New Delhi), it found itself the target of protests by a wide range of opponents. KFC could have alleviated or eliminated some of the anti-Western passions by tailoring its activities to the local conditions. First, rather than opting for more direct control, KFC should have

© Getty Images. Reproduced with permission.

allied itself with local partners for advice and support. Second, KFC should have tried to appear more Indian rather than using high-profile advertising with Western ideas. Indians are ambivalent toward foreign culture and its ideas may not always work well there. Finally, KFC should have planned for competition, which came from small restaurants with political clout at the local level.[9]

Many governments have taken action to protect their culture-specific industries. A specific example is provided in the earlier Focus on Politics, which highlights the European Union's attempt to protect the quality and reputation of regional and often very culture-specific products. The industry that many countries (such as Brazil, Canada, France and Indonesia) protect is entertainment, mainly cinema and music. The WTO agreement that allows restrictions on exports of US entertainment to Europe is justified by the EU as a cultural safety net intended to preserve national and regional identities.[10] In June 1998, Canada organized a meeting in Ottawa about US cultural dominance. Nineteen countries attended, including Britain, Brazil and Mexico; the United States was excluded. At issue were ways of exempting cultural goods from treaties lowering trade barriers, on the view that free trade threatened national cultures. The Ottawa meeting followed a similar gathering in Stockholm, sponsored by the United Nations, which resolved to press for special exemptions for cultural goods in the Multilateral Agreement on Investment.[11]

In many cases the commonly suggested solution of protectionism may not work. Although the EU has a rule that 40% of the television programming has to be domestic, anyone wanting an American programme can choose an appropriate channel or rent a DVD. Quotas therefore result in behaviour not intended by regulators. Companies simply cannot always abide by these regulations and control of these regulations is extremely difficult to implement. Furthermore, quotas may also lead to local productions designed to satisfy official mandates and capture subsidies that accompany them. Many emerging markets are following suit; in Cambodia, for example local TV stations are requested by the Information Ministry to show local films three times a week.[12] The Internet and satellite channels have increased the proliferation of American culture but have also allowed the spread of Bollywood films across the globe.

Popular culture is not just an American bastion. In many areas, such as pop music and musicals, Europe has developed an equally dominant position worldwide. Furthermore, no market is only an exporter of culture. Given the ethnic diversity in European markets (as in many other country markets), programming from around the world is made available. Many of the greatest successes of cultural products of the past five years in the United States were non-US; for example, television programmes such as 'Who Wants to Be a Millionaire?' and 'Weakest Link' are British concepts, and the popular cartoon Pokémon is from Japan.

The worst scenario for companies is when they are accused of pushing Western behaviours and values – along with products and promotions – into other cultures and the result is **consumer boycotts** and even destruction of property. Nestlé, McDonald's, KFC, Coca-Cola, Disney and Pepsi, for example, have all drawn the ire of anti-globalization demonstrators for being icons of globalization. Similarly, noisy boycotts and protests targeted many multinational companies in the wake of the invasion of Iraq. In the United States, those protests were aimed at French and Germans, while opponents of the war focused on British and US companies across the world.[13]

THE ELEMENTS OF CULTURE

The study of culture has led to generalizations that may apply to all cultures. Such characteristics are called **cultural universals**, which are manifestations of the total way of life of any group of people. These include such elements as bodily adornment, courtship rituals, etiquette, concepts of family, gestures, joking, mealtime customs, music, personal names, status differentiation and trade customs.[14] These activities occur across cultures, but they may be uniquely manifested in a particular society, bringing about cultural diversity. Common denominators can indeed be found across cultures, but cultures may vary dramatically in how they perform the same activities.[15] Even when a segment may be perceived to be similar across borders – as in the case of teenagers or the affluent – cultural differences make dealing with them challenging. For example, European teens resent being treated like Americans with an accent by US companies.[16]

Observation of the major cultural elements summarized in Table 3.1 suggests that these elements are both material (such as tools) and abstract (such as attitudes). The sensitivity and adaptation to these elements by an international firm depends on the firm's level of involvement in the market – for example, licensing versus direct investment – and the good or service marketed. Naturally, some goods and services or management practices require very little adjustment, while some have to be adapted dramatically.

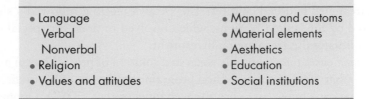

• Language	• Manners and customs
Verbal	• Material elements
Nonverbal	• Aesthetics
• Religion	• Education
• Values and attitudes	• Social institutions

Table 3.1: Elements of culture.

Language

Language has been described as the mirror of culture. Language itself is multidimensional by nature. This is true not only of the spoken word but also of what can be called the nonverbal language of international business. Messages are conveyed by the words used, by how the words are spoken (e.g., tone of voice) and through nonverbal means such as gestures, body position and eye contact.

Very often mastery of the language is required before a person is acclimatized to a culture other than his or her own. Language mastery must go beyond technical competency, because every language has words and phrases that can be readily understood only in context. For example when asked how he or she feels, the English often use the understated 'Not too bad, thank you' while Americans respond with a positive 'Great'. Such phrases are carriers of culture; they represent special ways a culture has developed to view some aspect of human existence.

Language capability serves four distinct roles in international business:[17]

- *Language aids in information gathering and evaluation.* Rather than rely completely on the opinions of others, the manager is able to see and hear personally what is going on. People are far more comfortable speaking their own language and this should be treated as an advantage. The best intelligence on a market is gathered by becoming part of the market rather than observing it from the outside. For example, local managers of a multinational corporation should be the firm's primary source of political information to assess potential risk.
- *Language provides access to local society.* Although English may be widely spoken and may even be the official company language, speaking the local language may make a dramatic difference.
- *Language capability is increasingly important in company communications, whether within the corporate family or with channel members.* Imagine the difficulties encountered by a country manager who must communicate with employees through an interpreter.
- *Language provides more than the ability to communicate.* It extends beyond mechanics to the interpretation of contexts that may influence business operations.

The manager's command of the national language(s) in a market must be greater than simple word recognition. Consider, for example how dramatically different English terms can be when used in the United Kingdom or the United States. In negotiations, for US delegates, 'tabling a proposal' means that they want to delay a decision, whereas their British counterparts understand the expression to mean that immediate action is to be taken. Other languages are not immune to this phenomenon either. Goodyear has identified five different terms for the word 'tyres' in the Spanish-speaking Americas: *cauchos* in Venezuela, *cubiertas* in Argentina, *gomas* in Puerto Rico, *neumaticos* in Chile and *llantas* in most of the other countries in the region. The company has to adjust its communications messages accordingly.[18]

The advertising campaign presented in Figure 3.1 highlights the difficulties of transferring advertising campaigns across markets. Electrolux's theme for vacuum cleaners is taken literally in the United Kingdom, but in the United States slang implications interfere with the intended message. Another example is the adaptation of an advertisement into Arabic. When this is carried out without considering that Arabic reads from right to left, the creative concept can be destroyed.

Figure 3.1: Example of an advert that transferred poorly.
Source: Electrolux.

The role of language extends beyond that of a communication medium. Linguistic diversity is often an indicator of other types of diversity. In Quebec, the French language has always been a major consideration of most francophone governments, because it is one of the clear manifestations of the province's identity *vis-à-vis* the English-speaking provinces. The Charter of the French Language states that the rights of the francophone collectivity are: (1) the right of every person to have the civil administration, semi-public agencies and business firms communicate with him or her in French; (2) the right of workers to carry on their activities in French; and (3) the right of consumers to be informed and served in French. The Bay, a major Quebec retailer, spends millions of dollars annually on translation. It has even changed its name to La Baie in appropriate areas. Similarly, in trying to battle English as the lingua franca, the French government has tried to ban the use of any foreign term or expression wherever an officially approved French equivalent (e.g. *mercatique*, not *un brainstorming;* and *jeune-pousse*, not *un start-up*) exists.[19] This applies also to web sites that bear the 'fr' designation; they have to be in the French language.

Other countries have taken similar measures. Germans have founded a society for the protection of the German language from the spread of 'Denglish'. Poland has directed that all companies selling or advertising foreign products use Polish in their advertisements. In Hong Kong, the Chinese government is promoting the use of Cantonese rather than English as the language of commerce, whereas some people in India – with its 800 dialects – scorn the use of English as a *lingua franca* because it is a reminder of British colonialism.[20]

Despite the fact that English is encountered daily by those on the Internet, the 'e' in e-Business does not translate into English. In a survey, European users highlighted the need to bridge the language gap. One-third of the senior managers said they will not tolerate English online, while less than 20% of German middle managers and less than 50% of French ones believe they can use English well. Being forced to use non-localized content was perceived to have a negative impact on productivity among 75% of those surveyed.[21] A truly global portal works only if the online functions are provided in a multilingual and multicultural format.

Dealing with language invariably requires local assistance. A good local advertising agency and a good local market research firm can prevent many problems. When translation is required, as when communicating with suppliers or customers, care should be taken in selecting the translator. The old saying, 'If you want to kill a message, translate it', is true in that what needs to be conveyed is a feeling, which may require dramatically different terms than is achieved through a purely technical, literal translation. In this context, translation software can generate a rough translation (it is 85% accurate), which then can be proofread and edited.[22] To make sure, the simplest method of control is back translation – translating a foreign language version back to the original language by a different person than the one who made the first translation. This approach may be able to detect only omissions and blunders, however. To assess the quality of the translation, a complete evaluation with testing of the message's impact is necessary.[23] A significant benefit of the Internet is accessibility to translation services worldwide to secure best quality and price.

Language also has to be understood in the historic context. Nokia launched an advertising campaign in Germany for the interchangeable covers for its portable phones using a theme '*Jedem das Seine*' ('to each his own'). The campaign was withdrawn after the American Jewish Congress pointed out that the same slogan was found on the entry portal to Buchenwald, a Nazi-era concentration camp.[24] The Indian division of Cadbury-Schweppes incensed Hindu society by running an advertisement comparing its Temptations chocolate to war-torn Kashmir. The ad carried a tagline: 'I'm good. I'm tempting. I'm too good to share. What am I? Cadbury's Temptations or Kashmir?' The ad also featured a map of Kashmir to highlight the point. To add insult to injury, the ad appeared on 15 August, Indian Independence Day.[25]

Nonverbal Language

Managers also must analyse and become familiar with the hidden language of foreign cultures.[26] Five key topics – time, space, material possessions, friendship patterns and business agreements – offer a starting point from which managers can begin to acquire the understanding necessary to do business in foreign countries. In many parts of the world, time is flexible and not seen as a limited commodity; people come late to appointments or may not come at all. In Hong Kong, for example it is futile to set exact meeting times, because getting from one place to another may take minutes or hours depending on the traffic situation. Showing indignation or impatience at such behaviour would astonish an Arab, Latin American, or Asian. Understanding national and cultural differences in the concept of time is critical for an international business manager.

In some countries, extended social acquaintance and the establishment of appropriate personal rapport are essential to conducting business. The feeling is that one should know one's business partner on a personal level before transactions can occur. Therefore, rushing straight to business will not be rewarded, because deals are made on the basis of not only the best product or price but also the entity or person deemed most trustworthy. Contracts may be bound on handshakes, not lengthy and complex agreements – a fact that makes some, especially Western, businesspeople uneasy.

Individuals vary in the amount of space they want separating them from others. Arabs and Latin Americans like to stand close to people when they talk. If a British person, who may not be comfortable at such close range, backs away from an Arab, this might incorrectly be taken as a negative reaction.

International body language must be included in the nonverbal language of international business. For example, an American manager may, after successful completion of negotiations, impulsively give a finger-and-thumb OK sign. In southern France, the manager would have indicated that the sale was worthless and, in Japan, that a little bribe had been requested; the gesture would be grossly insulting to Brazilians. An interesting exercise is to compare and contrast the conversation styles of different nationalities. Northern Europeans are quite reserved in using their hands and maintain a good amount of personal space, whereas southern Europeans involve their bodies to a far greater degree in making a point.

Religion

In most cultures, people find in religion a reason for being and legitimacy in the belief that they are of a larger context. To define religion requires the inclusion of the supernatural and the existence of a higher power. Religion defines the ideals for life, which in turn are reflected in the values and attitudes of societies and individuals. Such values and attitudes shape the behaviour and practices of institutions and members of cultures.

Religion has an impact on international business that is seen in a culture's values and attitudes toward entrepreneurship, consumption and social organization. The impact will vary depending on the strength of the dominant religious tenets. Although the impact of religion may be indirect in Protestant northern Europe, its impact in countries where Islamic fundamentalism is on the rise may be profound.

Religion provides the basis for transcultural similarities under shared beliefs and behaviour. The impact of these similarities will be assessed in terms of the dominant religions of the world, Christianity, Islam, Hinduism, Buddhism and Confucianism. Other religions may have smaller numbers of followers, such as in the case of Judaism with 14 million followers around the world, but their impact is still significant due to the centuries they have influenced world history. Although some countries may officially have secularism as a state belief (e.g., China, Vietnam, North Korea and Cuba), traditional religious beliefs still remain a powerful force in shaping behaviour. Some Western democracies such as France have been recently trying to emphasize the importance of secular principles in public life, more specifically in education and healthcare. This is in reaction to increased pressure from Islamic fundamentalism.

International managers must be aware of the differences not only among the major religions but also within them. The impact of these divisions may range from hostility, as in Sri Lanka, to barely perceptible historic suspicion, as in many European countries where Protestant and Catholic are the main divisions. With some religions, such as Hinduism, people may be divided into groups, which determines their status and to a large extent their ability to consume.

Christianity has the largest following among world religions, with more than 2 billion people.[27] Although there are many sub-groups within Christianity, the major divisions are between Catholicism, Protestantism and Christian Orthodox. A prominent difference between Catholicism and Protestantism is the attitude toward making money. Whereas Catholicism has questioned it, the Protestant ethic has emphasized the importance of work and the accumulation of wealth for the glory of God. At the same time, frugality was emphasized and the residual accumulation of wealth from hard work formed the basis for investment. It has been proposed that the work ethic is responsible for the development of capitalism in the Western world and the rise of predominantly Protestant countries into world economic leadership in the twentieth century.[28]

Major holidays are often tied to religion. Holidays are observed differently from one culture to the next, to the extent that the same holiday may have different connotations. Christian cultures observe Christmas and exchange gifts on either December 24 or December 25. Similar traditions exist in countries such as Russia but Christmas there is celebrated on January 7. The Dutch exchange gifts on St. Nicholas Day, December 6. Tandy Corporation, in its first year in the Netherlands, targeted its major Christmas promotion for the third week of December with less than satisfactory results. The international manager must see to it that local holidays, such as Mexico's Dìa De Los Muertos (31 October to 2 November), are taken into account in scheduling events ranging from fact-finding missions to marketing programmes and in preparing local work schedules.

Islam, which reaches from the west coast of Africa to the Philippines and across a broad band that includes Tanzania, central Asia, western China, India and Malaysia, has more than 1.2 billion followers.[29] Islam is also a significant minority religion in many parts of the world, including Europe. Islam has a pervasive role in the life of its followers, referred to as Muslims, through the Shariah (law of Islam). This is most obvious in the five stated daily periods of prayer, fasting during the holy month of Ramadan and the pilgrimage to Mecca, Islam's holy city. Although Islam is supportive of entrepreneurship, it nevertheless strongly discourages acts that may be interpreted as exploitation. Islam is also absent of discrimination, except against those outside the religion. Some have argued that Islam's basic fatalism (that is, nothing happens without the

Religions of the World – A Part of Culture

ATHEIST

BUDDHISM

CHRISTIAN, OTHER

CHRISTIAN, ROMAN CATHOLIC

HINDU

INDIGENUOUS

JUDAISM

MUSLIM

ORTHODOX, NOT MAJOR SECTS

CONFUCIAN

OTHER
(UNSPECIFIED)

NO CURRENT DATA AVAILABLE

Source: The World Factbook 2008.

will of Allah) and traditionalism have deterred economic development in countries observing the religion.

The role of women in business is tied to religion, especially in the Middle East, where women do not function as they do in the West. This affects the conduct of business in various ways; for example, the firm may be limited in its use of female managers or personnel in these markets and women's roles as consumers and influencers in the consumption process may be different. Access to women in Islamic countries may only be possible through the use of female sales personnel, direct marketing and women's specialty shops.[30] Religion affects goods and services, as well. When beef or poultry is exported to an Islamic country, the animal must be killed in the 'halal' method and certified appropriately. Recognition of religious restrictions on products (e.g., alcoholic beverages) can reveal opportunities, as evidenced by successful launches of several non-alcoholic beverages in the Middle East. Other restrictions may call for innovative solutions. A challenge for the Swedish firm that had the primary responsibility for building a traffic system to Mecca was that non-Muslims are not allowed access to the city. The solution was to use closed-circuit television to supervise the work. Given that Islam considers interest payments to be usury, bankers and Muslim scholars have worked to create interest-free banking that relies on lease agreements, mutual funds and other methods to avoid paying interest.[31]

Hinduism has 860 million followers, mainly in India, Nepal, Malaysia, Guyana, Suriname and Sri Lanka. In addition to being a religion it is also a way of life predicated on the caste, or class, to which one is born. Although the caste system has produced social stability, its impact on business can be quite negative. For example, if it is difficult to rise above one's caste, individual effort is hampered. Problems in workforce integration and co-ordination may become quite severe. Furthermore, the drive for business success may not be important if followers place value mostly on spiritual rather than materialistic achievement.

The family is an important element of Hindu society, with extended families being a norm. The extended family structure affects the purchasing power and consumption of Hindu families and market researchers, in particular, must take this into account in assessing market potential and consumption patterns.

Buddhism, which extends its influence throughout Asia from Sri Lanka to Japan, has 360 million followers. Although it is an offspring of Hinduism, it has no caste system. Life is seen as filled with suffering, with achieving nirvana – a spiritual state marked by an absence of desire – as the solution. The emphasis in Buddhism is on spiritual achievement rather than worldly goods.

Confucianism has over 150 million followers throughout Asia, especially among the Chinese and has been characterized as a code of conduct rather than a religion. However, its teachings, which stress loyalty and relationships, have been broadly adopted. Loyalty to central authority and placing the good of a group before that of the individual may explain the economic success of Japan, South Korea, Singapore and the Republic of China. It also has led to cultural misunderstandings: Western societies often perceive the subordination of the individual to the common good as a violation of human rights. The emphasis on relationships is very evident in developing business ties in Asia. Preparation may take years before understanding is reached and actual business transactions can take place.

Values and Attitudes

Values are shared beliefs or group norms that have been internalized by individuals.[32] Attitudes are evaluations of alternatives based on these values. Differences in cultural values affect the way planning is executed, decisions are made, strategy is implemented and personnel are evaluated. Table 3.2 provides examples of how US values differ from other values around the world and how this, in turn, affects management functions. These cultural values have to be accommodated or used in the management of business functions.

Value of US Culture	Alternative Value	Management Functions Affected
The individual can influence the future (where there is a will there is a way).	Life follows a preordained course and human action is determined by the will of God.	Planning and scheduling
We must work hard to accomplish our objectives (Protestant ethic).	Hard work is not the only prerequisite for success. Wisdom, luck and time are also required.	Motivation and reward system
Commitments should be honoured (people will do what they say they will do).	Conflicting request or an agreement may only signify intention and have little or no relationship to the capacity of performance.	Negotiating and bargaining
One should effectively use one's time (time is money that can be saved or wasted).	Schedules are important but only in relation to other priorities.	Long- and short-range planning
A primary obligation of an employee is to the organization.	The individual employee has a primary obligation to his or her family and friends.	Loyalty, commitment and motivation
The best-qualified persons should be given the positions available.	Family considerations, friendship and other considerations should determine employment practices.	Employment, promotions, recruiting, selection and reward
Intuitive aspects of decision making should be reduced and efforts should be devoted to gathering relevant information.	Decisions are expressions of wisdom by the person in authority and any questioning would imply a lack of confidence in his or her judgement.	Decision-making process
Data should be accurate.	Accurate data are not as highly valued.	Record keeping
Company information should be available to anyone who needs it within the organization.	Withholding information to gain or maintain power is acceptable.	Organization communication, managerial style
Each person is expected to have an opinion and to express it freely even if that view does not agree with his or her colleagues.	Deference is to be given to persons in power or authority and to offer judgement that is not in support of the ideas of one's superiors is unthinkable.	Communications, organizational relations
A person is expected to do whatever is necessary to get the job done (one must be willing to get one's hands dirty).	Various kinds of work are accorded low or high status and some work may be below one's 'dignity' or place in the organization.	Assignment of tasks, performance and organizational effectiveness
Change is considered an improvement and a dynamic reality.	Tradition is revered and the power of the ruling group is founded on the continuation of a stable structure.	Planning, morale and organizational development

Source: Adapted from Philip R. Harris and Robert T. Moran (1996) *Managing Cultural Differences*, Gulf Publishing, Houston, TX, Table 4.1.

Table 3.2: Effect of value differences on management practice.

The more rooted values and attitudes are in central beliefs (such as religion), the more cautiously one has to move. Attitude toward change is basically positive in industrialized countries, as is one's ability to improve one's lot in life; in tradition-bound societies, however, change is viewed with suspicion – especially when it comes from a foreign entity.

The Japanese culture raises an almost invisible – yet often unscalable – wall against all *gaijin* (foreigners). Many middle-aged bureaucrats and company officials believe that buying foreign products is unpatriotic. The resistance is not so much to foreign products as to those who produce and market them. Similarly, foreign-based corporations have had difficulty hiring university graduates or mid-career personnel because of bias against foreign employers. Even under such adverse conditions, business success can come through tenacity, patience and drive.

Cultural attitudes are not always a deterrent to foreign business practices or foreign goods. Japanese youth, for instance, display extremely positive attitudes toward Western goods, from popular music to Nike trainers to Louis Vuitton haute couture to Starbuck's lattes. Even in Japan's faltering economy, global brands are able to charge premium prices if they tap into cultural attitudes that revere imported goods. Similarly, attitudes of Western youth toward Japanese 'cool' have increased the popularity of authentic Japanese 'manga' comics and animated cartoons. Pokémon cards, Hello Kitty and Sony's tiny mini-disc players are examples of Japanese products that caught on in Europe and the United States almost as quickly as in Japan.[33]

Dealing in China and with the Chinese, the international manager needs to realize that making deals has more to do with co-operation than competition. The Chinese believe that one should build the relationship first and, if successful, transactions will follow. The relationship, or *guanxi*, is a set of favour exchanges to establish trust.[34]

A manager must be careful not to assume that success in one market using the cultural extension ensures success somewhere else. For example, although the Disneyland concept worked well in Tokyo, it had a tougher time in Paris. One of the main reasons was that while the Japanese are fond of American pop culture, Europeans are quite content with their own cultural heritage.[35]

Manners and Customs

Changes occurring in manners and customs must be carefully monitored, especially in cases that seem to indicate a narrowing of cultural differences among peoples. Phenomena such as McDonald's and Coca-Cola have met with success around the world, but this does not mean that the world is becoming Westernized. Modernization and Westernization are not at all the same, as can be seen in Saudi Arabia, for example.

Understanding manners and customs is especially important in negotiations, because interpretations based on one's own frame of reference may lead to a totally incorrect conclusion. To negotiate effectively abroad, all types of communication should be read correctly. Americans often interpret inaction and silence as negative signs. As a result, Japanese executives tend to expect that their silence can get Americans to lower prices or sweeten a deal. Even a simple agreement may take days to negotiate in the Middle East because the Arab party may want to talk about unrelated issues or do something else for a while. The aggressive style of Russian negotiators and their usual last-minute change requests may cause astonishment and concern on the part of ill-prepared negotiators. Some of the potential ways in which negotiators may not be prepared include: (1) insufficient understanding of different ways of thinking; (2) insufficient attention to the necessity to save face; (3) insufficient knowledge and appreciation of the host country – its history, culture, government and image of foreigners; (4) insufficient recognition of the decision-making process and the role of personal relations and personalities; and (5) insufficient allocation of time for negotiations.[36]

Gift-giving is one area where preparation and sensitivity are called for. Table 3.3 provides examples of what and when to give. Gifts are an important part of relationship management during visits or recognizing partners during holidays. Care should be taken how the gift is wrapped; that is, in appropriately coloured paper. If delivered in person, the actual giving has to be executed correctly; for example in China, by extending the gift to the recipient using both hands.[37]

Managers must be concerned with differences in the ways products are used. General Foods' Tang is positioned as a breakfast drink in the United States; in France, where fruit juices and drinks

	China	India	Japan	Mexico	Saudi Arabia
	Chinese New Year (January or February)	Hindu Diwali Festival (October or November)	Oseibo (January 1)	Christmas/New Year	Id al-Fitr (December or January)
Recommended	Modest gifts such as coffee table books, ties, pens	Sweets, nuts and fruit; elephant carvings; candleholders	Scotch, brandy Americana, round fruit such as melons	Desk clocks, fine pens, gold lighters	Fine compasses to determine direction for prayer, cashmere
To be avoided	Clocks, anything from Taiwan	Leather objects, snake images	Gifts that come in sets of four or nine	Sterling silver items, logo gifts, food baskets	Pork and pigskin, alcoholic drinks

Source: Kate Murphy, 'Gifts Without Gaffes for Global Clients', *Business Week*, 6 December, 1999, 153.

Table 3.3: When and what to give as gifts.

are not usually consumed at breakfast, Tang is positioned as refreshment. To challenge powdered-soup domination in Argentina, Campbell markets its products as 'the real soup', stressing its list of fresh ingredients. In Poland, where most soup consumed is homemade, Campbell promotes to mothers looking for convenience. The questions that the international manager has to ask are: 'What are we selling?' 'What are the benefits we are providing?' and 'Who or what are we competing against?' Care should be taken not to assume cross-border similarities even if many of the indicators converge. For example a jam producer noted that the Brazilian market seemed to hold significant potential because per capita jelly and jam consumption was one-tenth that of Argentina, clearly a difference not justified by obvious factors. However, Argentines consume jam at tea time, a custom that does not exist in Brazil. Furthermore, Argentina's climate and soil favour growing wheat, leading it to consume three times the bread that Brazil does.[38]

Approaches that would not be considered in Europe or the United States might be recommended in other regions; for example, when Conrad Hotels (the international division of Hilton Hotels) experienced low initial occupancy rates at its Hong Kong facility, they brought in a *fung shui* man. These traditional 'consultants' are foretellers of future events and the unknown through occult means and are used extensively by Hong Kong businesses.[39] In Hilton's case, the *fung shui* man suggested a piece of sculpture be moved outside the hotel's lobby because one of the characters in the statue looked like it was trying to run out of the hotel. The hotel later reported a significant increase in its occupancy rate.

Meticulous research plays a major role in avoiding these types of problems. Concept tests determine the potential acceptance and proper understanding of a proposed new product. Focus groups, each consisting of 8 to 12 consumers representative of the proposed target audience, can be interviewed and their responses used as disaster checks and to fine-tune research findings. The most sensitive products, such as consumer packaged goods, require consumer usage and attitude studies as well as retail distribution studies and audits to analyse the movement of the product to retailers and eventually to households.

The adjustment to the cultural nuances of the marketplace has to be viewed as long term and may even be accomplished through trial and error. For example, US retailers have found that US-style retail outlets baffle overseas consumers with their size and warehouse-like atmosphere. Office Depot reduced the size of its Tokyo store by one-third, crammed the merchandise closer together and found that sales remained at the same level as before.[40]

Material Elements

Material culture refers to the results of technology and is directly related to how a society organizes its economic activity. It is manifested in the availability and adequacy of the basic economic, social, financial and marketing infrastructure for the international business in a market. The basic economic infrastructure consists of transportation, energy and communications systems. Social infrastructure refers to housing, health and educational systems prevailing in the country of interest. Financial infrastructure and marketing infrastructure provide the facilitating agencies for the international firm's operation in a given market – for example, banks and research firms. In some parts of the world, the international firm may have to be an integral partner in developing the various infrastructures before it can operate, whereas in others it may greatly benefit from their high level of sophistication.

The level of material culture can aid segmentation efforts if the degree of industrialization of the market is used as a basis. For companies selling industrial goods, such as General Electric, this can provide a convenient starting point. In developing countries, demand may be highest for basic energy-generating products. In fully developed markets, time-saving home appliances may be more in demand.

While infrastructure is often a good indicator of potential demand, goods sometimes discover unexpectedly rich markets due to the informal economy at work in developing nations. In Kenya, for example, where most of the country's 30 million population live on less than one euro a day, more than 770 000 people have signed up for mobile-phone service in less than two years; wireless providers are scrambling to keep up with demand. Leapfrogging older technologies, mobile phones are especially attractive to Kenya's thousands of small-time entrepreneurs – market stall owners, taxi drivers and even hustlers who sell on the pavements. For most, income goes unreported, creating an invisible wealth on the streets. Mobile phones outnumber fixed lines in Kenya, as well as in Uganda, Venezuela and Cambodia. This development is also attractive to companies, given the expense of laying land lines.

Technological advances have been the major cause of cultural change in many countries. Increasingly, consumers are seeking more diverse products as a way of satisfying their demand for a higher quality of life and more leisure time. For example, a 1999 Gallup survey in China found that 44% of the respondents were saving to buy electronic items and appliances, which was second only to saving for a rainy day.[41] With technological advancement comes also cultural convergence. Black and white television sets extensively penetrated US households more than a decade before similar levels occurred in Europe and Japan. With colour television, the lag was reduced to five years. With video cassette recorders, the difference was only three years, but this time the Europeans and Japanese led the way while the United States was concentrating on cable systems. With the compact disc, penetration rates were equal in only one year. Today, with satellite TV available around the world and the use of the Internet increasing, no lag exists.[42]

Material culture – mainly the degree to which it exists and how it is esteemed – has an impact on business decisions. Many US exporters do not understand the degree to which Americans are package conscious; for example, cans must be shiny and beautiful. In other markets, packaging problems may arise due to the lack of materials, different specifications when the material is available and immense differences in quality and consistency of printing ink, especially in developing markets. Ownership levels of television sets, radios and personal computers have an impact on the ability of media to reach target audiences.

Aesthetics

Each culture makes a clear statement concerning good taste, as expressed in the arts and in the particular symbolism of colours, form and music. What is and what is not acceptable may vary dramatically even in otherwise highly similar markets. Sex, for example is a big selling point in many countries. In an apparent attempt to preserve the purity of Japanese womanhood, however, advertisers frequently turn to blond, blue-eyed foreign models to make the point. In introducing the shower soap Fa from the European market to the North American market, Henkel extended its European advertising campaign to the new market. The main creative difference was to have the young woman in the waves don a bathing suit for the more conservative American market rather than be naked as in the German original.

Colour is often used as a mechanism for brand identification, feature reinforcement and differentiation. In international markets, colours have more symbolic value than in domestic markets. Black, for instance, is considered the colour of mourning in Europe and the United States, whereas white has the same symbolic meaning in Japan and most of the Far East. A British bank was interested in expanding its operations to Singapore and wanted to use blue and green as its identification colours. A consulting firm was quick to tell the client that green is associated with death in that country. Although the bank insisted on its original choice of colours, the green was changed to an acceptable shade.

With the global reach of the Internet, symbols used have to be tested for universal appropriateness. The e-mailbox with its red flag is baffling to users outside of the United States and Canada. Similarly, the rubbish bin on the e-mail interface may look to some like the British-styled postbox. A British software application used the owl as a help icon only to find that in some countries it was not a symbol of wisdom but of evil and insanity.[43] Another example is shown in Figure 3.2, which shows the different names for the '@' symbol used around the world.

International firms, such as McDonald's, have to take into consideration local tastes and concerns in designing their outlets. They may have a general policy of uniformity in building or office space design, but local tastes often warrant modifications. Respecting local cultural traditions may also generate goodwill toward the international marketer. For example, McDonald's painstakingly renovated a seventeenth-century building for their third outlet in Moscow.

Education

Education, either formal or informal, plays a major role in the passing on and sharing of culture. Educational levels of a culture can be assessed using literacy rates, enrolment in secondary education, or enrolment in higher education, available from secondary data sources. International firms also need to know about the qualitative aspects of education, namely, varying emphases on particular skills and the overall level of the education provided. Japan and South Korea, for example, emphasize the sciences, especially engineering, to a greater degree than Western countries.

Educational levels also affect various business functions. For example, a high level of illiteracy suggests the use of visual aids rather than printed manuals. Local recruiting for sales jobs is affected by the availability of suitably trained personnel. In some cases, international firms routinely send locally recruited personnel to headquarters for training.

The international manager may also need to overcome obstacles in recruiting a suitable sales force or support personnel. For example, the Japanese culture places a premium on loyalty and employees consider themselves members of the corporate family. If a foreign firm decides to terminate its operations in Japan, its employees may find themselves stranded in mid-career, unable to find their place in the Japanese business system. Therefore, university graduates are reluctant to join any but the largest and most well-known foreign firms.

If technology is marketed, the product's sophistication will depend on the educational level of future users. Product adaptation decisions are often influenced by the extent to which targeted customers are able to use the good or service properly.

Social Institutions

Social institutions affect the ways people relate to each other. The family unit, which in Western industrialized countries consists of parents and children, is extended in a number of cultures to

What do people around the world call the '@' symbol, so prevalent in e-mail addresses? While in the United States most say 'at', in other countries it's referred to by different, and often humorous, names associated with what the @ reminds speakers of.

DOG In Russia, the most common word for @ is *sobaka* or *sokachka*, meaning 'dog' and 'little doggie', respectively.

MONKEY In countries such as Bulgaria, Poland and Serbia, the @ symbol seems to remind speakers of a monkey with a long tail. They refer to it as *alpa* (Polish), *majmunsko* (Bulgarian) and *majmun* (Serbian). Another variation is 'ape's tail', said as *aapstert* in Afrikaans, *aperstaart* in Dutch and *apsvans* in Swedish.

SNAIL While traditional stamp and envelope mail is often referred to as 'snail mail', many speakers insert a @ into their e-mail addresses. In Korea, @ is known as *dolphaengi* and in Italian it's *chlocciola* (both literally meaning 'snail').

CAT When the Poles aren't referring to @ as a monkey, they know it as a curled up kitten (*kotek*). Similarly, Finns use the phrase *miuku mouku*.

FISH A quite creative name for the @ is *zavinac* or 'rolled up pickled herring' in Slovakia and the Czech Republic.

ELEPHANT In Denmark, you would refer to @ as *snabel* or elephant's trunk.

MOUSE In China, the word 'mouse', used in references to a computer means more than the object you click and point with. *Xiao lao shu* ('little mouse') is also used for the symbol @.

WORM In Hungary, the mental image of a *kukac* (literally 'worm') is associated with @.

Figure 3.2: Different interpretation of the '@' symbol.

Source: Reproduced with permission of David Clark Illustration.

include grandparents and other relatives. This affects consumption patterns and must be taken into account, for example when conducting market research.

The concept of kinship, or blood relations between individuals, is defined in a very broad way in societies such as those in sub-Saharan Africa. Family relations and a strong obligation to family are important factors to consider in human resource management in those regions. Understanding tribal politics in countries such as Nigeria may help the manager avoid unnecessary complications in executing business transactions.

The division of a particular population into classes is termed social stratification. Stratification ranges from the situation in northern Europe, where most people are members of the middle class, to highly stratified societies in which the higher strata control most of the buying power and decision-making positions.

An important part of the socialization process of consumers worldwide are reference groups. These groups provide the values and attitudes that influence behaviour. Primary reference groups include the family and co-workers and other intimate acquaintances, and secondary groups are social organizations where less-continuous interaction takes place, such as professional associations and trade organizations. In addition to providing socialization, reference groups develop a person's concept of self, which is manifested, for example, through the choice of products used. Reference groups also provide a baseline for compliance with group norms, giving the individual the option of conforming to or avoiding certain behaviours.

Social organization also determines the roles of managers and subordinates and how they relate to one another. In some cultures, managers and subordinates are separated explicitly and implicitly by various boundaries ranging from social class differences to separate office facilities. In others, co-operation is elicited through equality. For example, Nissan USA has no privileged parking spaces and no private dining rooms, everyone wears the same type of white coveralls and the president sits in the same room with a hundred other white-collar workers. Fitting an organizational culture to the larger context of a national culture has to be executed with care. Changes that are too dramatic may disrupt productivity or, at the minimum, arouse suspicion.

Although Western business has impersonal structures for channelling power and influence – primarily through reliance on laws and contracts – the Chinese emphasize personal relationships to obtain clout. Things can get done without this human political capital, or *guanxi*, only if one invests enormous personal energy, is willing to offend even trusted associates and is prepared to see it all melt away at a moment's notice.[44] For the Chinese, contracts form a useful agenda and a symbol of progress, but obligations come from relationships. McDonald's found this out in Beijing, where it was evicted from a central building after only two years despite having a 20-year contract. The incomer had a strong *guanxi*, whereas McDonald's had not kept its in good repair.[45]

F●CUS ON

CULTURE   National Culture – Culture in Russia

Introduction

The Russian Federation has over 150 million people and covers an area of more than 17 075 350 square kilometres. Russia is the largest country in the world. It has a rich cultural identity that has been shaped and moulded by its distinguished history and vast

geography. Russia is a vast and diverse nation that after several decades of communism continues to evolve politically and economically. With the world's largest resource of raw materials, oil and gas revenues heavily support Russia's economy. Recently, within the big cities, a consumer economy has been established. This, along with an improvement in the country's financial position has raised business and investor confidence in Russia's economic prospects. However, in order to conduct business successfully in Russia, there are a number of important issues to consider before and during business interactions.

Russian culture – key concepts and values

- **Collectivism:** Throughout its history, Russia has assumed a strong communal spirit that is still reflected in Russian business practices today. Russia's severe climatic conditions have also meant that co-operation and collaboration have been vital for survival. This sense of togetherness is one of the traits that distinguish Russians from many Westerners. Russian collectivism dates back to the peasant farmers, who lived in agricultural villages known as 'mirs' or 'obschina' and worked together in an organized and self-managed community.
- **Egalitarianism:** An important concept related to the village milieu is 'egalitarianism', the social philosophy that supports the removal of inequity and promotes an equal distribution of benefits. In Russian business terms, this equates to important strategies of equality, reciprocity and mutual advantage. Russians are very status conscious and believe in co-equals. A 'deal' is often thought of from the perspective of equally shared benefit.
- **Dusha:** The famous and enigmatic Russian soul remains central to everyday Russian behaviour. As a result, mutual liking and emotion form a strong basis when building successful business relationships with Russians.

Working practices in Russia

- The Russians' attitude to time means that a few minutes delay on their part is of little importance. However, they will expect you to be punctual. Do not expect an apology from a late Russian and do not demonstrate any kind of attitude if your business appointments begin one or two hours late. This may also be a test of your patience.
- Faxes and e-mails are the best way to communicate in Russia, because the post can often be unreliable. It is customary before making a trip to Russia to inform the prospective company of your intended business proposals and objectives.
- Paperwork and putting pen to paper is an essential part of all working practices in Russia. In general, they have little faith in unsigned documents.

- Negotiations with Russians often involve flared tempers. During negotiations and meetings, temper tantrums and walkouts often occur.
- Businessmen in Russia usually wear suits that are dark and well tailored along with good shoes. A businessman's wardrobe demonstrates the individual's image as a professional.
- Men often do not take off their jackets in negotiations.
- Women dress rather conservatively, avoiding overly flashy or gaudy outfits. Women should wear skirts rather than trousers.
- When attending dinner in a citizen's home, casual dress of slacks and a nice shirt without a tie are appropriate.

Structure and hierarchy in Russian companies

- The hierarchical structure in Russian business practices means that the decision makers higher up have authority over their subordinates. However, the nature of the collective good often encourages a flexible and democratic work ethos.
- Showing respect for seniority and recognizing the hierarchical structure is vital for establishing and maintaining strong business relationships.

Working relationships in Russia

- Personal and informal contact is a central part in doing business in Russia.
- Physical contact during business meetings, for example, a simple hand on the arm or even embracing is a positive sign. There is no word for 'privacy' in Russia; therefore the notion of social space is much closer in Russia.
- In situations of conflict try to avoid taking an official stance and remember that Russians are 'people orientated' and will respond to a more personal approach.

Business practices in Russia

- Business cards are essential. If possible, ensure that one side is printed in Russian and one side in English.
- Presentations should be straightforward and comprehensible.
- Although many principal concerns are discussed in an informal environment, final negotiations will be conducted in the office.
- Generally, when beginning a meeting, the head of the organization will open the discussion and

introductions should then be made in order of importance.

Russian business etiquette

- DO shake hands firmly when greeting and leaving your Russian partners and make direct eye contact.
- DO partake in small talk, which normally involves talk of family and personal matters, before dealing with business.
- DO take a gift that symbolizes the stature of your company and the importance of the impending business deal, preferably an item characteristic of your local area or one that displays the company logo.
- DON'T be afraid to show some emotion, the Russians won't!
- DON'T as the Russian proverb states 'hurry to reply', but 'hurry to listen'.
- DON'T praise or reward anyone in public as it may be viewed with suspicion or cause envy and jealousy. Remember the collective rules over the individual.
- DON'T stand with your hands in your pockets. This is considered rude.
- DON'T show the soles of your shoes, as this is considered impolite. They are considered dirty and should never come in contact with any type of seat (like on a subway or bus).

Russian behaviour

- Patience is an extremely important virtue among Russians; punctuality is not. Russians are known as great 'sitters' during negotiations, this demonstrates their tremendous patience.
- The USSR was officially an atheist nation in the days of communism. Now, however, participation in religion in increasing, with many citizens practising Protestantism, Islam, Russian Orthodoxy and Judaism.
- As a foreigner, you should realize that 'Final Offers' are not usually the end of the negotiations and that often the outcome will be more beneficial and attractive if you can hold out.
- There is a Russian term meaning 'connections' or 'influences'. It is extremely difficult to do business in Russia without help from a local. To help with this, gifts, money or other items are often a good idea when doing business in Russia.

- If attending dinner at a family residence, it is appropriate to bring a gift, such as a bottle of wine, dessert or a bouquet of flowers.
- When attending any formal engagements such as the theatre, it is appropriate to check your coat and other belongings at the front door of the establishment.
- Be alert and open to taking a drink or having a toast, because refusing to do so is a serious breach of etiquette.

Communications

- Russian is the official language.
- Speaking or laughing loudly in public is considered rude, as Russians are generally reserved and sombre.
- Many Russians speak English, because it is often taught from the age of 9.
- Russians are highly literate and have almost a 100% literacy rate.
- Good topics of conversation include peace, the current changes taking place in Russia and their current economic situation.

Russian Culture Quiz – true or false

1. It is considered good luck to shake hands over the threshold of the doorstep.
2. When taking flowers as a gift you must only take an odd number.
3. If you leave something behind in Russia it means you are coming back.
4. In business negotiations Russians view compromise as a sign of weakness.
5. In Russia, the 'OK' symbol with the thumb and forefinger touching in a circle means 'everything is fine'.

Answers

1. False. It is considered bad luck to shake hands over a threshold and should be done either inside or outside.
2. True. Even numbers of flowers are only given at funerals and are a sign of bad luck.
3. True. A Russian superstition that is still present today.
4. True.
5. False. The Western sign for 'OK' is considered rude in Russia.

Sources: www.communicaid.com/russian-business-culture; www.cyborlink.com/besite/russia; www.russiaprofile.org/culture.

SOURCES OF CULTURAL KNOWLEDGE

The concept of cultural knowledge is broad and multifaceted. Cultural knowledge can be defined by the way it is acquired. Objective or factual information is obtained from others through communication, research and education. Experiential knowledge, on the other hand, can be acquired only by being involved in a culture other than one's own. A summary of the types of knowledge needed by the international manager is provided in Table 3.4. Both factual and experiential information can be general or country-specific. In fact, the more a manager becomes involved in the international arena, the more he or she is able to develop a meta-knowledge; that is, ground rules that apply whether in Kuala Lumpur, Malaysia, or Asunción, Paraguay. Market-specific knowledge does not necessarily travel well; the general variables on which the information is based do.

In a survey of managers on how to acquire international expertise, they ranked eight factors in terms of their importance, as shown in Table 3.5. The managers emphasized the experiential acquisition of knowledge. Written materials played an important but supplementary role, very often providing general or country-specific information before operational decisions were made. Interestingly, many of today's international managers have pre-career experience in government, the Peace Corps, the armed forces or voluntary work. Although the survey emphasized travel, a one-time trip to New York with a stay at a very large hotel and scheduled sightseeing tours does not significantly contribute to cultural knowledge. Travel that involves meetings with company personnel, intermediaries, facilitating agents, customers and government officials, on the other hand, does contribute.

Source of Information	Type of Information	
	General	Country Specific
Objective	Examples: Impact of GDP Regional integration	Examples: Tariff barriers Government regulations
Experiential	Example: Corporate adjustment to internationalization	Examples: Product acceptance Programme appropriateness

Table 3.4: Types of international information.

Factor	Considered Critical (%)	Considered Important (%)
1. Assignments overseas	85	9
2. Business travel	83	17
3. Training programmes	28	57
4. Non-business travel	28	54
5. Reading	22	72
6. Graduate courses	13	52
7. Pre-career activities	9	50
8. Undergraduate courses	1	48

Source: Data collected by authors from 110 executives, by questionnaire, February, 2003.

Table 3.5: Managers' ranking of factors involved in acquiring international expertise.

However, from the corporate point of view, global capability is developed in more painstaking ways: foreign assignments, networking across borders and the use of multi-country, multicultural teams to develop strategies and programs. At Nestlé, for example, managers move around a region (such as Asia or Latin America) at four- or five-year intervals and may serve stints at headquarters for two to three years between such assignments. Such broad experience allows managers to pick up ideas and tools to be used in markets where they have not been used or where they have not been necessary before. In Thailand, where supermarkets are revolutionizing consumer-goods marketing, techniques perfected elsewhere in the Nestlé system are being put to effective use. The experiences then, in turn, are used to develop newly emerging markets in the same region, such as Vietnam.

Managers have a variety of sources and methods to extend their knowledge of specific cultures. Most of these sources deal with factual information that provides a necessary basis for market studies. For example, beyond the normal business literature and its anecdotal information, governments, private companies and universities publish country-specific studies. The US Department of Commerce's (www.ita.doc.gov) *Country Commercial Guides* cover more than 133 countries, while the Economist Intelligence Unit's (www.eiu.com) *Country Reports* cover 180 countries. *Culturegrams* (www.culturegrams.com), which detail the customs of people of 174 countries, are published by the Centre

Figure 3.3: An example of culture consulting.

Source: Intertrend Communications Inc.

for International and Area Studies at Brigham Young University. Many facilitating agencies – such as advertising agencies, banks, consulting firms and transportation companies – provide background information on the markets they serve for their clients. These range from Runzheimer International's (www.runzheimer.com) international reports on employee relocation and site selection for 44 countries, to the Hong Kong and Shanghai Banking Corporation's (www.hsbc.com) *Business Profile Series* for 22 countries in the Asia-Pacific region, to *World Trade* (www.worldtrademag.com) magazine's 'Put Your Best Foot Forward' series, which covers Europe, Asia, Mexico/Canada and Russia.

Specialists who advise clients on the cultural dimensions of business are available as well. Their task is not only to help avoid mistakes but also to add culture as an ingredient of success in country- or region-specific programmes. An example of such a service provider is shown in Figure 3.3.

Blunders in foreign markets that could have been avoided with factual information are generally inexcusable. A manager who travels to Taipei without first obtaining a visa and is therefore turned back has no one else to blame. Other oversights may lead to more costly mistakes. For example, Brazilians are several inches shorter than the average American, but this was not taken into account when the US store Sears erected American-height shelves that block Brazilian shoppers' view of the rest of the store.

International business success requires not only comprehensive fact finding and preparation but also an ability to understand and fully appreciate the nuances of different cultural traits and patterns. Gaining this interpretive cultural knowledge requires 'getting one's feet wet' over a sufficient length of time. Over the long run, culture can become a factor in the firm's overall success.

CULTURAL ANALYSIS

To try to understand and explain differences among and across cultures, researchers have developed checklists and models showing pertinent variables and their interaction. An example of such a model is provided in Figure 3.4. Developed by Sheth and Sethi, this model is based on the premise that all international business activity should be viewed as innovation and as producing change.[46] After all, multinational corporations introduce management practices, as well as goods and services, from one country to others, where they are perceived to be new and different. Although many question the usefulness of such models, they do bring together all or most of the relevant variables on how consumers in different cultures may perceive, evaluate and adopt new behaviours. However, any manager using such a tool should periodically cross-check its results against reality and experience.

The key variable of the model is propensity to change, which is a function of three constructs: (1) cultural lifestyle of individuals in terms of how deeply held their traditional beliefs and attitudes are and also which elements of culture are dominant; (2) change agents (such as multinational corporations and their practices) and strategic-opinion leaders (e.g., social elites); and (3) communication about the innovation from commercial sources, neutral sources (such as government) and social sources, such as friends and relatives.

It has been argued that differences in cultural lifestyle can be explained by four dimensions of culture:[47] (1) individualism ('I' consciousness versus 'we' consciousness); (2) power distance (levels of equality in society); (3) uncertainty avoidance (need for formal rules and regulations); and (4) masculinity (attitude toward achievement, roles of men and women). Figure 3.5 presents a summary of the positions of 12 countries along these dimensions. A fifth dimension has also been added to distinguish cultural differences: long-term versus short-term orientation.[48] All the high-scoring countries are Asian (e.g., China, Hong Kong, Taiwan, Japan and South Korea), while most Western countries (such as the United States and Britain) have low scores. Some have argued that this cultural dimension may explain the Japanese marketing success based on market share (rather than short-term profit) motivation in market development.

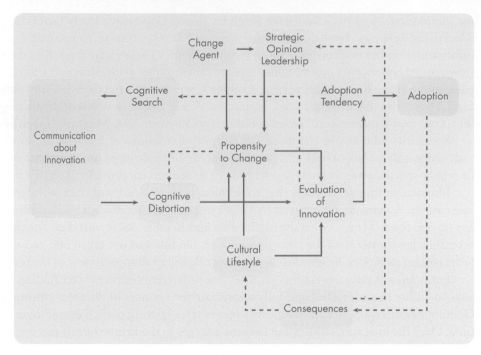

Figure 3.4: A model of cross-cultural behaviour.

Source: Jagdish N. Sheth and S. Prakash Shethi (1977) 'A Theory of Cross-Cultural Buying Behaviour', *Consumer and Industrial Buyer Behaviour*, Arch G. Woodside, Jagdish N. Sheth and Peter D. Bennett (eds), 373. Reproduced by permission of Jagdish N. Sheth and S. Prakash Sethi.

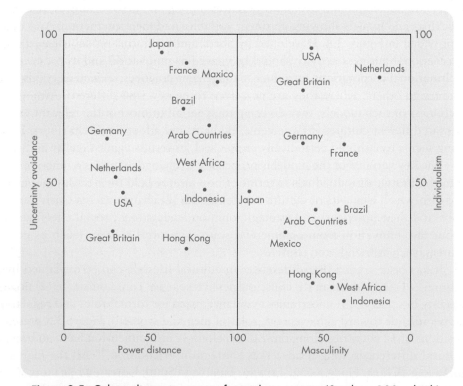

Figure 3.5: Culture dimension scores for twelve countries (0 = low; 100 = high).

Source: Data for the figure derived from Geert Hofstede, 'Management Scientists are Human' (1994) *Management Science*, 40(1), 4–13.

	Size (Million)	Cultural Characteristics				Illustrative Marketing Implications
		Power Distance	Uncertainty Avoidance	Individualism	Masculinity	
Cluster 1 Denmark, Sweden, Finland, Netherlands, Norway	37	Small	Low	High	Low	Relatively weak resistance to new products, strong consumer desire for novelty and variety, high consumer regard for 'environmentally friendly' marketers and socially conscious firms
Cluster 2 Belgium, France, Greece, Portugal, Spain, Turkey	182	Medium	Strong	Varied	Low–Medium	Appeal to consumer's status and power position, reduce perceived risk in product purchase and use, emphasize product functionality
Cluster 3 Austria, Germany, Switzerland, Italy, Great Britain, Ireland	203	Small	Medium	Medium–High	High	Preference for 'high-performance' products; use 'successful achiever' theme in advertising; desire for novelty, variety and pleasure; fairly risk-averse market

Source: Adapted from Sudhir H. Kale (1995) 'Grouping Euroconsumers: A Culture-Based Clustering Approach', *Journal of International Marketing*, 3(3), 42, with permission of Emerald Group Publishing Limited in the format Textbook via Copyright Clearance Center.

Table 3.6: Culture-based segmentation.

Knowledge of similarities along these four dimensions allows us to cluster countries and regions and establish regional and national marketing or business programmes.[49] An example is provided in Table 3.6, in which the European market is segmented along cultural lines for the development of programmes. Research has shown that the take-off point for new products (i.e., when initial sales turn into mass-market sales) is six years, on average, in Europe. However, in northern Europe new products take off almost twice as fast as they do in southern Europe.[50] Culturally, consumers in Cluster 1 are far more open to new ideas. Cluster 2, consisting of southern Europe, displays the highest uncertainty avoidance and should therefore be targeted with risk-reducing marketing programmes such as extended warranties and return privileges.[51] It is important to position the product as a continuous innovation that does not require radical changes in consumption patterns.[52] Since the United States highly regards individualism, promotional appeals should be relevant to individual empowerment. Also, in order to incorporate the lower power distance, messages should be informal and friendly. In opposite situations, marketing communications have to emphasize that the new product is socially accepted. However, if the product is imported it can sometimes utilize global or foreign cultural positioning. For example in China, individualism is often used for imported products but almost never for domestic ones.[53]

Understanding the implications of the dimensions helps businesspeople prepare for international business encounters. For example, in negotiating in Germany one can expect a counterpart who is thorough, systematic, very well prepared, but also rather dogmatic and therefore less flexible and willing to compromise. Efficiency is emphasized. In Mexico, however, the counterpart may prefer to address problems on a personal and private basis rather than on a business level. This means more emphasis on socializing and conveying one's humanity, sincerity, loyalty and friendship. Also, differences in the pace and business practices of a region have to be accepted. Boeing Airplane Company found in its annual study on world aviation safety that countries with both low individualism and substantial power distances had accident rates 2.6 times greater than those at the other end of the scale. The findings naturally have an impact on training and service operations of airlines.[54]

Communication about innovation takes place through the physical product itself (samples) or through experiencing a new company policy. If a new personnel practice, such as quality circles or flex time, is being investigated, results may be communicated in reports or through word of mouth by the participating employees. Communication content depends on the following factors: the good's or policy's relative advantage over existing alternatives; compatibility with established behavioural patterns; complexity, or the degree to which the good or process is perceived as difficult to understand and use; trialability, or the degree to which it may be experimented with without incurring major risk; and observability, which is the extent to which the consequences of the innovation are visible.

Before a good or policy is evaluated, information should be gathered about existing beliefs and circumstances. Distortion of data may occur as a result of selective attention, exposure and retention. As examples, anything foreign may be seen in a negative light, another multinational company's efforts may have failed, or the government may discourage the proposed activity. Additional information may then be sought from any of the sources or from opinion leaders in the market.

Adoption tendency refers to the likelihood that the product or process will be accepted. Examples are advertising in the People's Republic of China and equity joint ventures with Western participants in Russia, both of them unheard of a decade ago. If an innovation clears the hurdles, it may be adopted and slowly diffused into the entire market. An international manager has two basic choices: to adapt company offerings and methods to those in the market or to try to change market conditions to fit company programmes.

In Japan, a number of Western companies have run into obstructions in the Japanese distribution system, where great value is placed on established relationships; everything is done on the basis of favouring the familiar and fearing the unfamiliar. In most cases, this problem is solved by joint ventures with a major Japanese entity that has established contacts. On occasion, when the company's approach is compatible with the central beliefs of a culture, the company may be able to change existing customs rather than adjust to them. Initially, Procter & Gamble's traditional hard-selling style in television commercials jolted most Japanese viewers accustomed to more subtle approaches. Now the ads are being imitated by Japanese competitors. However, this is not to be interpreted to mean that the Japanese will adapt to Western approaches. The emphasis in Japan is still on who speaks rather than on what is spoken. That is why, for example, Japan is a market where Procter & Gamble's company name is also presented in the marketing communication for a brand, rather than only the product's brand name, which is customary in the United States and European markets.[55]

Although models such as the one in Figure 2.3 in the previous chapter may aid in strategy planning by making sure that all variables and their interlinkages are considered, any analysis is incomplete without the basic recognition of cultural differences. Adjusting to differences requires putting one's own cultural values aside. James A. Lee proposes that the natural self-reference criterion – the unconscious reference to one's own cultural values – is the root of most international business problems.[56] However, recognizing and admitting this is often quite difficult. The following analytical approach is recommended to reduce the influence of cultural bias:

1. Define the problem or goal in terms of the domestic cultural traits, habits or norms.
2. Define the problem or goal in terms of the foreign cultural traits, habits or norms. Make no value judgements.
3. Isolate the self-reference criterion influence in the problem and examine it carefully to see how it complicates the problem.
4. Redefine the problem without the self-reference criterion influence and solve for the optimum-goal situation.

This approach can be applied to product introduction. If Kellogg's Co. wants to introduce breakfast cereals into markets where breakfast is traditionally not eaten or where consumers drink very little milk, managers must consider very carefully how to instill the new habit. The traits, habits and norms concerning the importance of breakfast are quite different in the United States, France and Brazil and they have to be outlined before the product can be introduced. In France, Kellogg's commercials are aimed as much at providing nutrition lessons as they are at promoting the product. In Brazil, the company advertised on a soap opera to gain entry into the market because Brazilians often emulate the characters of these television shows.

Analytical procedures require constant monitoring of changes caused by outside events as well as the changes caused by the business entity itself. Controlling ethnocentrism – the tendency to consider one's own culture superior to others – can be achieved only by acknowledging it and properly adjusting to its possible effects in managerial decision making. The international manager needs to be prepared and able to put that preparedness to effective use.

THE TRAINING CHALLENGE

International managers face a dilemma in terms of international and intercultural competence. For example, the lack of adequate foreign language and international business skills have cost US firms lost contracts, weak negotiations and ineffectual management. A UNESCO study of 10- to 14-year-old students in nine countries placed Americans next to last in their comprehension of foreign cultures. The terrorist attacks of 11 September 2001, alerted the US government not only to the national lack of competence in foreign language skills, but also to the nation's failure to educate its population to cultural sensibilities at home and around the world.[57]

The increase in the overall international activity of firms has increased the need for cultural sensitivity training at all levels of the organization. Further, today's training must encompass not only outsiders to the firm but also interaction within the corporate family as well. However inconsequential the degree of interaction may seem, it can still cause problems if proper understanding is lacking. Consider, for example, the date written as follows: 11/12/04. A European will interpret this as the 11th of December; an American as November the 12th.

Some companies try to avoid the training problem by hiring only nationals or well-travelled individuals for their international operations. This makes sense for the management of overseas operations but will not solve the training need, especially if transfers to a culture unfamiliar to the manager are likely. International experience may not necessarily transfer from one market to another.

To foster cultural sensitivity and acceptance of new ways of doing things within the organization, management must institute internal education programmes. The programmes may include: (1) culture-specific information (data covering other countries, such as video packs and culture-grams); (2) general cultural information (values, practices and assumptions of countries other than one's own); and (3) self-specific information (identifying one's own cultural paradigm, including values, assumptions and perceptions about others).[58] One study found that Japanese employees assigned to the United States get mainly language training as preparation for the task. In addition, many companies use mentoring, whereby an individual is assigned to someone who is experienced and who spends time advising and explaining. Talks given by returnees and by visiting lecturers hired specifically for the task round out the formal part of training.[59] At Samsung, several special interest groups were formed to focus on issues such as Japanese society and business practices, the Chinese economy, changes in Europe and the US economy. In addition, groups also explore cutting-edge business issues, such as new technology and marketing strategies. And for the past few years, Samsung has been sending the brightest junior employees abroad for a year.[60]

The objective of formal training programmes is to foster the four critical characteristics of preparedness, sensitivity, patience and flexibility in managers and other personnel. The programmes vary

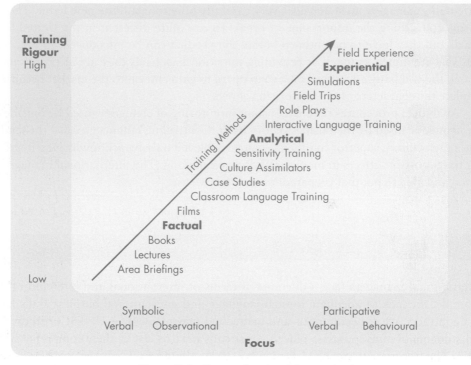

Figure 3.6: Cross-cultural training methods.

Source: J. Stewart Black and Mark Mendenhall (1991) 'A Practical but Theory-Based Framework for Selecting Cross-Cultural Training Methods', *Human Resource Management*, 28(4), 511–539. Reproduced with permission of John Wiley & Sons, Inc.

dramatically in terms of their rigour, involvement and, of course, cost.[61] A summary of the programmes is provided in Figure 3.6.

Environmental briefings and cultural-orientation are types of area studies programmes. The programmes provide factual preparation for a manager to operate in, or work with people from, a particular country. Area studies should be a basic prerequisite for other types of training programmes. Alone, area studies serve little practical purpose because they do not really get the manager's feet wet. Other, more involved, programmes contribute context in which to put facts so that they can be properly understood.

The cultural assimilator is a programme in which trainees must respond to scenarios of specific situations in a particular country. The programmes have been developed for the Arab countries, Iran, Thailand, Central America and Greece. The results of the trainees' assimilator experience are evaluated by a panel of judges. This type of programme has been used most frequently in cases of transfers abroad on short notice.

When more time is available, managers can be trained extensively in language. This may be required if an exotic language is involved. Sensitivity training focuses on enhancing a manager's flexibility in situations that are quite different from those at home. The approach is based on the assumption that understanding and accepting oneself is critical to understanding a person from another culture. While most of the methods discussed are best delivered in face-to-face settings, web-based training is becoming more popular, as seen in the following Focus on e-Business.

Finally, training may involve field experience, which exposes a manager to a different cultural environment for a limited amount of time. As the expense of placing and maintaining an expatriate is high (and, therefore, the cost of failure is high), field experience is rarely used in training. One field

FOCUS ON

E-BUSINESS   ## Online Cultural Training

The Internet can play an important role in preparing marketing people for the international marketplace. Although it cannot replace real-life interaction as an experiential tool, it does provide a number of benefits, including comparisons between cultural ways of behaving, and can provide an opportunity to develop the skills needed to interact successfully with people from other cultures. Many companies use online learning as an addition to existing instructor-led programmes. When time is at a premium (due to a fast-approaching assignment/project or to a manager's overall schedule), the role of this learning approach becomes even more critical.

Companies typically rely on the following elements in designing web-based training:

- **Detailed Scenarios:** Much of the training material consists of a detailed, realistic story that is tied into elements of the learner's background; that is, the session becomes more than a briefing, it becomes a narrated experience full of learning moments for participants. This is made possible by the ability of the web to store and circulate a lot of information instantaneously around the world.

- **Gradual Delivery:** The ability to control the flow of information to the participant supports the learning process in a number of ways. First, the participant is allowed to fit the training into his or her schedule. Second, the real-life flow of information is mimicked and a higher degree of realism is achieved.

- **Support:** A set of detailed materials is provided to the participants 24 hours a day. At any hour and at any location, participants can check their perceptions against the materials, reinforce learning from a dimly recalled lesson, or seek feedback on an important point or issue.

- **Relevant Exercises:** Participants can be provided with topical exercises and activities, the level of which can be adjusted depending upon how the participant has invested in the training.

- **Online Discussions:** Sessions can be simulcast to hundreds of participants around the world. The lack of face-to-face interaction can be remedied by having discussion groups where participants can share their experiences with each other. The pooled learning experience is stronger than one with a solitary participant.

Online cross-cultural programmes focus on preparing international managers for the host of business scenarios they will encounter overseas. Training is often specific to a location, priming managers for posts in the Asian Pacific, Latin America, the US or the Middle East. There are also online programmes that prepare international managers for repatriation into their home country. Using a range of training tools, from compelling case studies that are revealed over time to web-based activities and exercises, programmes cover such topics as intercultural adaptation, recognizing differences in communication styles, negotiation strategies and practical information on aspects of business and daily life.

Sources: Mike Bowler, 'Online Learning is Fastest Growing Segment of Higher Education,' *Knight Ridder Tribune Business News*, 17 August 2003, 1; 'On-line Learning,' Special Advertising Section, *Fortune*, 1 July 2002, S1–S19; Peter T. Burgi and Brant R. Dykehouse (2000) 'On-Line Cultural Training: The Next Phase', *International Insight*, Winter, 7–10. See also www.runzheimer.com; IOR Global Services, www.ioworld.com, accessed 6 February 2002.

experience technique that has been suggested when the training process needs to be rigorous is the host-family surrogate. This technique places a trainee (and possibly his or her family) in a domestically located family of the nationality to which they are assigned.[62]

Regardless of the degree of training, preparation and positive personal characteristics, a manager will always remain foreign. A manager should never rely on his or her own judgement when local managers can be consulted. In many instances, a manager should have an interpreter present at negotiations, especially if the manager is not completely bilingual. Overconfidence in one's language capabilities can create problems.

MAKING CULTURE WORK FOR BUSINESS SUCCESS

Culture should not be viewed as a challenge, but rather as an opportunity that can be exploited. This requires, as has been shown in this chapter, an understanding of cultural differences and their fundamental determinants. Differences can quite easily be dismissed as indicators of inferiority or viewed as approaches to be changed; however, the opposite may actually be the case. Best practice knows no one particular origin, nor should it acknowledge boundaries. The following rules serve as a summary of how culture and its appreciation may serve as a tool to ensure success:

- *Embrace local culture:* Many corporate credos include a promise to be best possible corporate citizens in every community operated in.[63] For example, in 3M's plant near Bangkok, Thailand, a Buddhist shrine, wreathed in flowers, pays homage to the spirits Thais believe took care of the land prior to the plant's construction. Showing sensitivity to local customs helps create local acceptance and builds employee morale. More important, it contributes to a deeper understanding of the market and keeps the company from inadvertently doing something to alienate constituents.
- *Build relationships:* Each country-market has its own unique set of constituents who need to be identified and nurtured. Establishing and nurturing local ties at the various stages of the market-development cycle develops relationships that can be invaluable in expansion and countering political risk. 3M started preparing to enter the China market soon after President Nixon's historic visit in 1972. For ten years, company officials visited Beijing and entertained visits of Chinese officials to company headquarters in Minneapolis-St. Paul. Such efforts paid off in 1984, when the Chinese government made 3M the first wholly owned venture in the market. Many such emerging markets require long-term commitment on the part of the company.
- *Employ locals in order to gain cultural knowledge:* The single best way to understand a market is to grow with it by developing the human resources and business partnerships along the way. Of the 7500 3M employees in Asia, fewer than ten are from the United States. In fact, of the 34 000 3M employees outside of the United States, and less than 1% are expatriates. The rest are locals who know local customs and purchasing habits of their compatriots. In every way possible, locals are made equals with their US counterparts. For example, grants are made available for 3M employees to engage in the product-development process with concepts and idea development.
- *Help employees understand you:* Employing locals will give a marketer a valuable asset in market development (i.e., in acculturation). However, these employees also need their own process of adjustment (i.e., 'corporatization') in order to be effective. At any given time, more than 30 of 3M's Asian technicians are in the United States, where they learn about the latest product and process advances while gaining insight into how the company works. Also, they are able to develop personal ties with people they may work with. Furthermore, they often contribute by infusing their

insights into company plans. Similar schemes are in place for distributors; distributor advisory councils allow intermediaries to share their views with the company.

- *Adapt products and processes to local markets:* Nowhere is commitment to local markets as evident as in product offerings. Global, regional and purely local products are called for and constant and consistent product-development efforts on a market-by-market basis are warranted to find the next global success. When the sales of 3M's famous Scotchbrite cleaning pads were languishing in China, company researchers interviewed housewives and domestic help to determine why. Traditionally, floors are scrubbed with the help of the rough shells of coconuts. 3M responded by making its cleaning pads brown and shaping them like a foot. Similarly, a big seller for 3M in China is a composite to fill tooth cavities. In the United States, dentists pack a soft material into the cavity and blast it with a special beam of light, making it as hard as enamel in a matter of seconds. In China, dentists cannot afford this technology. 3M's solution was an air-drying composite that achieved similar effects in a matter of minutes, with minimal expense.

- *Coordinate by region:* The transfer of best practice is critical, especially in areas that have cultural similarities. When 3M designers in Singapore discovered that customers used its Nomad household mats in their cars, they spread the word to their counterparts throughout Asia. The company encourages its product managers from different parts of Asia to hold regular periodic meetings and share insights and strategies. The goal of this cross-pollination is to come up with regional programmes and 'Asianize' or even globalize a product more quickly. Joint endeavours build cross-border *esprit de corps*, especially when managers may have their own markets' interests primarily at heart.[64]

SUMMARY

Culture is one of the most challenging elements of the international marketplace. This system of learned behaviour patterns characteristic of the members of a given society is constantly shaped by a set of dynamic variables: language, religion, values and attitudes, manners and customs, aesthetics, technology, education and social institutions. To cope with this system, an international manager needs both factual and interpretive knowledge of culture. To some extent, the factual knowledge can be learned; its interpretation comes only through experience.

The most complicated problems in dealing with the cultural environment stem from the fact that to truly become part of a culture, one has to live in it. Two schools of thought exist in the business world on how to deal with cultural diversity. One is that business is business the world around, following the model of Pepsi and McDonald's. In some cases, globalization is a fact of life; however, cultural differences are still far from converging.

The other school proposes that companies must tailor business approaches to individual cultures. Setting up policies and procedures in each country has been compared to an organ transplant; the critical question centres around acceptance or rejection. The major challenge to the international manager is to make sure that rejection is not a result of cultural myopia or even blindness.

The internationally successful companies all share an important quality: patience. They have not rushed into situations but rather built their operations carefully by following the most basic business principles. These principles are to know your competition, know your audience and know your customer.

QUESTIONS FOR DISCUSSION

1. Comment on the assumption, 'If people are serious about doing business with you, they will speak English'.
2. You are on your first business visit to Germany. You feel confident about your ability to speak the language (you studied German in school and have taken a refresher course) and you decide to use it. During introductions, you want to break the ice by asking 'Wie geht's?' and insisting that everyone call you by your first name. Speculate as to the reaction.
3. Q: 'What do you call a person who can speak two languages?'
   A: 'Bilingual'.
   Q: 'How about three?'
   A: 'Trilingual'.
   Q: 'Excellent. How about one?'
   A: 'Hmmmm...American or British!'
   Is this joke malicious, or is there something to be learned from it?
4. What can be learned about a culture from reading and attending to factual materials?
5. Provide examples of how the self-reference criterion might manifest itself.
6. Is any international business entity not a cultural imperialist? How else could one explain the phenomenon of multinational corporations?

INTERNET EXERCISES

1. Various companies, such as GMAC Relocation Service, are available to prepare and train international managers for the cultural challenge. Using GMAC's web site (www.gmacglobalrelocation.com), assess their role in helping the international manager.
2. Compare and contrast an international company's home pages for presentation and content; for example Coca-Cola (at www.coca-cola.com) and its Japanese version (www.cocacola.co.jp). Are the differences cultural?

TAKE A STAND

France's Ministry of Culture is worried about the threat that the United States presents, especially to French cinema. However, the threat is perceived to be broader. Hollywood is seen as the Trojan horse bringing Disneyland Paris, fast-food chains and advertising for US products ranging from clothes to rock and country music. 'The United States is not only interested in exporting movies', says Giles Jacob, the head of the Cannes Film Festival, 'but it is also exporting its way of life'. Although the United States may not make the most movies in the world, it is the only country whose movies have global reach. Of any year's top-50 grossing movies, typically 48 or 49 are made in the United State. In the European Union, US movies hold a 70% market share, up from 50% only 15 years ago. Marketing budgets for US movies easily surpass an average European movie's total budget. At the same time, overseas markets, Europe in particular, have become critical to studios as production budgets have grown.

The French government has launched an offensive against what they see as American cultural hegemony. The French convinced the European Union to decree that 40% of TV programmes be domestic. The government has also strengthened its substantial system of support, which for example taxes cinema tickets to help local film production, by extending subsidies to television.

In addition to criticism from the United States about these policies, some influential individuals in France have also spoken against this system of subsidies and quotas. Jeanne Moreau, the doyenne of French actors, argues that French film producers should stop relying on protectionism and start believing in themselves again.

FOR DISCUSSION

1. Is American culture, in your opinion, taking over the world?
2. What constructive steps can governments take to protect their own cultural heritage in areas such as film and cinema?

CHAPTER
4

Political and Legal Environment

LEARNING OBJECTIVES

● To understand the importance of the political and legal environments to the international business executive, in both the home and host countries.

● To learn how governments affect business through legislation and regulations.

● To see how the political actions of countries expose firms to international risks.

● To examine the differing laws regulating international trade found in different countries.

● To understand how international political relations, agreements and treaties can affect international business.

CORRUPTION, GUNS AND TERRORISM

In a global economy, companies transact business in emerging nations where the political and legal climates are unfamiliar and often unstable. Productive trade relationships are under constant threat when corruption, lawlessness and political turmoil reign, and yet business often continues in the face of adversity.

Before the 11 September 2001 terrorist attacks on the United States, a brisk trade of contraband goods across borders played a critical role in the fragile economies of Afghanistan and Pakistan. Electronics from Dubai, televisions from Japan and cosmetics from Iran all moved swiftly through Taliban-controlled checkpoints, selling in Pakistan at far lower prices than legally imported items. Millions of dollars in 'Islamic levies' imposed by the Taliban, along with protection money paid to powerful people in Pakistan, also facilitated the trafficking of drugs across borders, headed for black-market bazaars in Pakistan. Together, drugs and illegal contraband were estimated to be worth US$30 billion a year – half of Pakistan's official gross domestic product. Following the attacks, Afghan warlords quickly took control of border cities such as Herat on the Afghan-Iran border, sustaining the underground economy even in the face of political chaos.

As another example, Zimbabwe used to have one of the most vibrant economies in Africa. Recently, however, corruption, mismanagement and the near complete disruption of commercial farming have led to a crisis that has seen unemployment rise to over 85%. In September 2008, monthly inflation reached 16 600%, which at that time translated in nearly 2 000 000 000 000% annual inflation rate, helped by the decision to print US$230 million worth of Zimbabwean currency to pay international debts and sustain operations. Poverty is over 90% and foreign reserves are almost depleted. Consequently, more than half of the country's 12 million citizens are thought to be at risk of famine.

This economic collapse is widely blamed on government incompetence and President Robert Mugabe's controversial seizure of white-owned farms. Of the 4500 white farmers, only 600 have stayed on their farms since the programme commenced. The land was earmarked for 'redistribution' to the country's poor but an audit by a ministerial committee ascertained that less than one third of the allocated plots had actually been worked. Critics say the new farmers lack the financial backing and infrastructure needed to restore Zimbabwe's agricultural sector. In truth, Mugabe's 'land reform' has chiefly benefited idle party hacks and stalwarts, not landless peasants.

What's more, Mugabe's administration was unwilling to devalue its currency and tried to keep its official exchange rate at just Zim$55 to the US dollar, even while its real worth (parallel rate) was about Zim$811 to the US dollar. Revaluation of the Zimbabwean dollar finally took place in August 2006, and since then there have been repeated discussions and proposals regarding its further revaluation. The official exchange rate on 10 October 2008 was US$1 = Zim$184.380. The exchange rate imbalance, economists say, makes economic management impossible. Businesses are paid for their exports at the official rate, but are obliged to buy imports from abroad at the parallel rate. Over four million persons are in desperate need of food. HIV/AIDS and malnutrition kill thousands every month. The government-sponsored

2005 'Operation Murambatsvina' to clear urban slums forcibly deprived more than 18% of the population of homes or livelihoods and badly damaged the informal sector, the lifeline for many urban poor.

Aid agencies and critics partly blame food shortages on the land reform programme. The government blames a long-running drought and Mr Mugabe has accused Britain and its allies of sabotaging the economy in revenge for the redistribution programme.

Zimbabwe, formally known as Rhodesia, has a history of conflict, with white settlers dispossessing the resident population, guerrilla armies forcing the white government to submit to elections and the post-independence leadership committing atrocities in southern areas where it lacked the support of the Matabele people.

Zimbabwe has had a rocky relationship with the British Commonwealth – it was suspended after President Mugabe's controversial re-election in 2002 and later announced that it was pulling out for good.

Both Great Britain and the United States have instituted visa restrictions barring travel to their respective countries by members of Mr Mugabe's inner circle. Prominent statesmen such as the former US Secretary of State Colin Powell and the ex-British Prime Minister Tony Blair have been vocal about Zimbabwe's threat to the peace, stability and prosperity of the region.

Sources: BBC News Service http://news.bbc.co.uk/2/hi/business/2476563.stm, accessed 1 July 2003; www.zwnews .com/issuefull.cfm?ArticleI=7421, accessed 1 July 2003; 'If You Want a Mercedes, Try Heart', *The Economist,* 24 January 2002; www.economist.com; 'Dark Days for a Black Market', *Business Week Online,* 15 October 2001, www.businessweek.com; www.crisisgroup.org; www.news.bbc.co.uk, accessed 12 April 2007.

INTRODUCTION

Politics and laws play a critical role in international business. Even the best plans can go awry as a result of unexpected political or legal influences and the failure to anticipate these factors can be the undoing of an otherwise successful business venture.

Of course, a single international political and legal environment does not exist. The business executive has to be aware of political and legal factors on a variety of levels. For example, although it is useful to understand the complexities of the host country's legal system, such knowledge may not protect against sanctions imposed by the home country. The firm, therefore, has to be aware of conflicting expectations and demands in the international arena.

This chapter will examine politics and laws from the manager's point of view. The two subjects are considered together because generally laws are the result of political decisions. The chapter discussion will break down the study of the international political and legal environment into three segments: the politics and laws of the home country; those of the host country; and the bilateral and multilateral agreements, treaties and laws governing the relations among host and home countries.

THE HOME-COUNTRY PERSPECTIVE

No manager can afford to ignore the rules and regulations of the country from which he or she conducts international business transactions. Many of the laws and regulations may not specifically address international business issues, and yet they can have a major impact on a firm's opportunities abroad. Minimum-wage legislation, for example, has a bearing on the international competitiveness of a firm using production processes that are highly labour intensive.

The cost of domestic safety regulations may significantly affect the pricing policies of firms. For example, the European Commission Directives on Environmental Impact Assessment of 1985 and 1997 are the foundation stone on which environmental policies have been developed and implemented in the UK. Development Control is used in the UK as a tool of environmental protection. US legislation creating the Environmental Superfund requires payment by chemical firms based on their production volume, regardless of whether the production is sold domestically or exported. As a result, these firms are at a disadvantage internationally when exporting their commodity-type products. They are required to compete against firms that have a cost advantage because their home countries do not require payment into an environmental fund.

There are legal and regulatory measures that are clearly aimed at international business. Some may be designed to help firms in their international efforts. For example, governments may attempt to aid and protect the business efforts of domestic companies facing competition from abroad by setting standards for product content and quality.

The European Commission has introduced 10 basic principles to protect consumers, because promoting consumers' rights, prosperity and well-being are core values of the European Union and this is reflected in its laws. Membership of the European Union ensures additional protection for consumers. The details of exactly what consumer rights are in each EU country, and how consumers can apply them, vary from country to country depending on how they have implemented the EU rules in their national law. Companies doing business in the EU must comply with the EU and national consumer protection requirements and laws.

Here are the 10 basic principles of consumer protection in the European Union:

1. Buy what you want, where you want.
2. If it doesn't work, send it back.
3. High safety standards for food and other consumer goods.
4. Know what you are eating.
5. Contracts should be fair to consumers.
6. Sometimes consumers can change their mind.
7. Make it easier to compare prices.
8. Consumers should not be misled.
9. Protection while you are on holiday.
10. Effective redress for cross-border disputes.

Source: European Commission, Health and Consumer Protection Directorate-General, 20 July 2004, www.ec.europa.eu/consumers.

F CUS ON

LAW Ensuring Protection of US Exports in the European Union

American exporters of products and services are sometimes unaware that US trademark and design protection does not extend beyond the boundaries of the United States. Exporters to the European Union should either register marks and designs in individual countries or secure protection for the entire area by obtaining a 'Community Trade Mark' (CTM) or a 'Registered Community Design' (RCD).

The Office of Harmonization in the Internal Market (OHIM) is the EU agency that handles the registration process for marks and designs. EU design registration offers protection for the appearance of a product, rather than the product itself, resulting from its various features, such as lines, textures, ornamentation and patterns. A registered design also has to fulfil the requirement of being novel, although this criterion is not examined prior to registration. EU trademark protection protects any sign that could be represented graphically and which at the same time has the capacity to distinguish the trade origin of the goods it is applied to from one undertaking to another.

Although design protection can be obtained for up to 25 years, a trademark can be renewed indefinitely.

Following the European Union's decision to accede to the Madrid Protocol, the OHIM has started to accept any international application designating the European Union, as well as offering the extension of an application to the Madrid Protocol countries since 2004.

For Americans, this means that they can file an application through the US Patent and Trademark Office and then apply through the Madrid system for an extension of that protection to the European Union. The option to apply direct to the OHIM is also available.

Source: 'Ensuring Protection in the European Union: Design and Trademark Registration', US Commercial Service, US Department of Commerce, www.buyusa.gov.

F CUS ON

LAW   European Union Product Warranty Directive

EU legislation requires that exporters to any country in the European Union should provide warranty of at least two years from the delivery of goods. Sellers whose products are found not to conform to the 'contract' between the buyer and seller at the time the goods were delivered are required to replace or repair the nonconforming goods free of charge, reduce the price of the goods or release the consumer from the contract. The term 'contract' may apply to a written agreement between the seller and the buyer; warrantees as to the product's fitness for certain applications or its performance characteristics are also considered to form a 'contract' between seller and buyer. Even advertising can create liability.

However, this law cannot be applied extraterritorially. So, in practical terms, a Japanese or US exporter has the option to refuse to accept the importer's liability so long as the company is not the final seller of the good. In effect, the buyer has a maximum of six months to establish that the goods do not conform to the contract and the burden of proof is on the buyer. The two-year warrantee does not apply to perishable goods or unintended uses.

Source: EU Commission, Product Warranty Directive, www.europa.eu.int/eur-lex/en/lif/dat/1999/en_399L0044.html.

The political environment in most countries tends to provide general support for the international business efforts of firms headquartered within the country. For example, a government may work to reduce trade barriers or to increase trade opportunities through bilateral and multilateral negotiations. Such actions will affect individual firms to the extent that they improve the international climate for free trade.

Often governments also have specific rules and regulations that restrict international business. Such regulations are frequently political in nature and are based on governmental objectives that override commercial concerns. The restrictions are particularly sensitive when they address activities outside the country. Such measures challenge the territorial sovereignty of other governments and raise the issue of extraterritoriality – meaning a nation's attempt to set policy outside its territorial limits. Yet actions implying such extraterritorial reach are common, because nations often argue that their citizens and products maintain their nationality wherever they may be and they therefore continue to be subject to the rules and laws of their home country.

Three main areas of governmental activity are of major concern to the international business manager. They are embargoes or trade sanctions, export controls and the regulation of international business behaviour.

Embargoes and Sanctions

The terms embargo and sanction as used here refer to governmental actions that distort free flows of trade in goods, services or ideas for decidedly adversarial and political, rather than economic, purposes. Sanctions tend to consist of specific coercive trade measures such as the cancellation of trade financing or the prohibition of high-technology

trade, whereas embargoes are usually much broader in that they prohibit trade entirely. For example the United States imposed sanctions against some countries by prohibiting the export of weapons to them, but it initiated an embargo against Cuba when all but humanitarian trade was banned. To understand sanctions and embargoes better, it is useful to examine the auspices and legal justifications under which they are imposed.

Trade embargoes have been used quite frequently and successfully in times of war or to address specific grievances. For example in 1284, the Hansa, an association of north German merchants, believed that its members were suffering from several injustices by Norway. On learning that one of its ships had been attacked and pillaged by the Norwegians, the Hansa called an assembly of its members and resolved an economic blockade of Norway. The export of grain, flour, vegetables and beer was prohibited on pain of fines and confiscation of the goods. The blockade was a complete success. Deprived of grain from Germany, the Norwegians were unable to obtain it from England or elsewhere. As a contemporary chronicler reports: 'Then there broke out a famine so great that they were forced to make atonement'. Norway was forced to pay indemnities for the financial losses that had been caused and to grant the Hansa extensive trade privileges.[1]

Over time, economic sanctions and embargoes have become a principal tool of the foreign policy for many countries. Often, they are imposed unilaterally in the hope of changing a country's government or at least changing its policies. Reasons for the impositions have varied, ranging from the upholding of human rights to attempts to promote nuclear non-proliferation or antiterrorism.

After the First World War, the League of Nations set a precedent for the legal justification of economic sanctions by subscribing to a covenant that contained penalties or sanctions for breaching its provisions. The members of the League of Nations did not intend to use military or economic measures separately, but the success of the blockades of First World War fostered the opinion that 'the economic weapon, conceived not as an instrument of war but as a means of peaceful pressure, is the greatest discovery and most precious possession of the League'.[2] The basic idea was that economic sanctions could force countries to behave peacefully in the international community.

The idea of multilateral use of economic sanctions was again incorporated into international law under the charter of the United Nations, but greater emphasis was placed on the enforcement process.

Sanctions decided on are mandatory, even though each permanent member of the Security Council can veto efforts to impose them. The charter also allows for sanctions as enforcement actions by regional agencies, such as the Organization of American States, the Arab League and the Organization of African Unity, but only with the Security Council's authorization.

The apparent strength of the United Nations' enforcement system was soon revealed to be flawed. Stalemates in the Security Council and vetoes by permanent members often led to a shift of discussions to the General Assembly, where sanctions are not enforceable. Also, concepts such as 'peace' and 'breach of peace' were seldom perceived in the same context by all members and thus no systematic sanctioning policy developed under the United Nations.[3]

Another problem with sanctions is that frequently their unilateral imposition has not produced the desired result. Sanctions may make the obtaining of goods more difficult or expensive for the sanctioned country, but their purported objective is almost never achieved. In order to work, sanctions need to be imposed multilaterally and affect goods that are vital to the sanctioned country – goals that are clear, yet difficult to implement.

Close multinational collaboration can strengthen the sanctioning mechanism of the United Nations greatly. Economic sanctions can extend political control over foreign companies operating abroad, with or without the support of their local government.[4] When one considers that sanctions may well be the middle ground between going to war or doing nothing, their effective functioning can represent a powerful arrow in the quiver of international policy measures.

Sanctions usually mean significant loss of business to firms. One estimate claims that the economic sanctions held in place by the United States annually cost the country some US$20 billion in lost exports.[5] Due to these costs, the issue of compensating the domestic firms and industries affected by these sanctions needs to be considered. Yet, trying to impose sanctions slowly or making them less expensive to ease the burden on these firms undercuts their ultimate chance for success. The international business manager is often caught in this political web and loses business as a result. Frequently, firms try to anticipate sanctions based on their evaluations of the international political climate. Nevertheless, even when substantial precautions are taken, firms may still suffer substantial losses due to contract cancellations. However, the reputation of a supplier unable to fill a contractual obligation will be damaged much more seriously than that of an exporter who anticipates sanctions and realizes it cannot offer a transaction in the first place.[6]

There are embargoes and sanctions set forth by the US administration that are still in place. These include the embargoes to Iran, Iraq, Libya, Cuba and Sudan that still require export licences when shipping to those destinations.

Lately, there have been subtle changes of attitude by US government officials toward shipping to some of these destinations. The Office of Foreign Assets Control (OFAC) grants licences on exports if the goods are for humanitarian aid. When the goods are food, medical supplies or pharmaceuticals destined for Iraq, Cuba, Libya or Sudan, the licence process is very quick.

A recent major change in the US export policy has been with regard to shipments to Afghanistan. The original embargo against Afghanistan was always termed as 'controlled by the Taliban'. With the recent political changes in this country, OFAC has published appropriate modifications in the federal register. However, it is prudent to keep in mind that serious military actions still take place there, making shipping to this destination a significant logistics challenge.

Export Controls

Many nations have export-control systems, which are designed to deny or at least delay the acquisition of strategically important goods by adversaries. The legal basis for export controls varies in nations. For example, in Germany, armament exports are covered in the so-called War Weapons list, which is a part of the War Weapons Control Law. The exports of other goods are covered by the German Export List.

Dual-use items, which are goods useful for both military and civilian purposes, are then controlled by the Joint List of the European Union.[7] The list of products subject to the special control under the dual-use regime is quite large (covering approximately 650 products). For several categories of product (mainly nuclear materials, chemicals, micro-organisms, toxins, electronics, computers, telecommunications and information security products, sensors and lasers, navigation and avionics, marine, propulsion systems, space vehicles and related equipment), an export licence is required. However, a licence is not necessary with respect to these categories when they are moved from one EU member state to another (intra-Community movement). An automatic licence is provided for most of the products contained in these categories, in cases where the country of destination is Australia, Canada, the US, Japan, Norway, New Zealand or Switzerland. The transmission of software or technology by electronic media, fax or telephone (intangible transfers) is also subject to export controls. Exporters can apply for two types of licence, depending on the end-use and the country of final destination:

- *Individual export licence:* This may cover several consignments of a specific product to the consignee/end-user specified in the licence and is the most common one.
- *Global licence:* This allows for the export of an unlimited number of goods to one or several consignee(s) or end-user(s).

The duration of these licences may vary depending on the issuing EU member state, although normally the licence lasts for six months, which may be extended by up to three years.

The export of cultural goods is subject to the presentation of an export licence that is valid throughout the EU. Cultural goods are deemed to be archaeological objects, paintings, films, books, antiques, manuscripts, means of transportation, maps, and so on, all of which have a particular historical value. An export licence may be refused if the goods in question fall into the category of national treasures covered by the legislation of an EU member state.

Trade Controls were introduced by the UK as a result of the Export Control Act 2002, which made the trading (commonly referred to as trafficking and brokering) of goods from one overseas destination to another a licensable activity. If the export from the United Kingdom of particular goods, technology or software is subject to control, those goods, technology or software may not legally be exported without a licence. The Strategic Export Control List contains details of the goods, technology and software that are controlled. The export of other types of goods and certain activities are subject to control as a result, for instance, of the imposition of European Community or United Nations trade sanctions against particular countries or regions. Licences to export arms and other goods controlled for strategic reasons are issued by the UK Secretary of State for Trade and Industry (DTI) acting through the Export Control Organization (ECO). Licences are approved on the advice of the UK Foreign and Commonwealth office, the Ministry of Defence and, where sustainable development issues are involved, the Department for International Development.

In France, decisions relating to exports of conventional arms are taken at the Prime Minister level. He or she is assisted by the Commission Interministérielle pour l'Etude des Exportations de Matériels de Guerre (CIEEMG (Inter-ministerial Commission for the Study of Military Equipment Exports)), chaired by the Secretary General of National Defence. The procedure governing arms exports is published in the *Journal Officiel* (Official Gazette). It is accompanied, as a rule, by a clause prohibiting re-exports and, in the event of transfers of classified information, by a security agreement. The export controls for dual-use goods were introduced in France by a decree of 1944. Since 1995, export controls for dual-use goods are implemented in accordance with rules defined by the European regime. Export controls are assumed by the French authorities, which issue export licences for each export of dual-use goods to a country outside the European Union. A similar procedure is applied to the transmissions of software or technologies by electronic means, fax or telephone.

In the United States, the export control system is based on the Export Administration Act and the Munitions Control Act. These laws control all export of goods, services and ideas from the United States. The determinants for controls are national security, foreign policy, short supply and nuclear non-proliferation.

Export licences in the US are issued by the Department of Commerce, which administers the Export Administration Act.[8] In consultation with other government agencies – particularly the Departments of State, Defense and Energy – the Commerce Department has drawn up a list of commodities whose export is considered particularly sensitive. In addition, a list of countries differentiates nations according to their political relationship with the United States. Finally, there is a list for each country of individual firms that are considered to be unreliable trading partners because of past trade-diversion activities.

After an export licence application has been filed, specialists in the Department of Commerce match the commodity to be exported with the critical commodities list, a file containing information about products that are either particularly sensitive to national security or controlled for other purposes. The product is then matched with the country of destination and the recipient company. If no concerns regarding any of the three exist, an export licence is issued. This process may sound overly cumbersome, but it does not apply in equal measure to all exports. Most international business activities can be carried out under NLR conditions, which stands for 'no licence required'. NLR provides blanket permission to export to most trading partners, provided that neither the end-user nor the end-use is considered sensitive. However, the process becomes more complicated and cumbersome when products incorporating high-level technologies are involved. The exporter must then apply for an export licence, which consists of written authorization to send a product abroad. However, even in most of these cases, licence applications can be submitted via the Internet and licensing forms can be downloaded from it.

The international business repercussions of export controls are important. It is one thing to design an export control system that is effective and that restricts those international business activities subject to important national concerns. It is, however, quite another when controls lose their effectiveness and when one country's firms are placed at a competitive disadvantage with firms in other countries whose control systems are less extensive or even non-existent.

F**O**CUS ON

POLITICS

The EU Code of Conduct Fails to Prevent French Helicopters Being Produced Under Licence in India and Transferred to Nepal

Between June 2003 and September 2004, India supplied a number of Lancer attack helicopters to Nepal. Hindustan Aeronautics Ltd (HAL) produced the helicopters in co-operation with the French firm Eurocopter. Components and parts made in several other EU countries were also used. The sale of EU attack helicopters to Nepal created controversy and seriously threatened the credibility and effectiveness of the EU Code of Conduct in view of the political turmoil in Nepal and the likelihood that such helicopters would be used against civilian targets.

The Lancer is based upon the Cheetah attack helicopter that has been produced in India under licence from Eurocopter since 1970. Eurocopter has also been closely involved in the development of the Advanced Light Helicopter. Eurocopter has also assisted in development of India's Druv advanced light helicopter. The French Company, Turbomeca, has provided engines for the Cheetah, Lancer and Advanced Light Helicopters. Although France remains the principal EU member state involved with the production of these helicopters in India, a number of other European companies have also been reported as supplying components or sub-systems for helicopters manufactured by Hindustan Aeronautics. For example the ALH reportedly contains Italian components for the flight control and the hydraulic system, British hydraulic pack components and rocket pods manufactured by a Belgian company.

India seems to have weaker controls on the export of military helicopters than its EU counterparts. In 2002, in an effort to boost its arms sales, India removed the 'blacklist' of countries to which it would not export weapons. In February 2003, the Chairman of Hindustan Aeronautics stated that 'we have our own advanced light helicopter design and to export it we do not need any permission'.

The close involvement of France with the production of attack helicopters in India, via licensed production agreements and the incorporation of components or sub-systems from other EU member states into these helicopters raises serious concerns. Criterion 7 of the EU Code requires EU member states to consider the 'risk that . . . equipment will be diverted within the buyer country or re-exported under undesirable conditions', and to consider 'the capability of the recipient country to exert effective export controls'. The continued involvement of EU-based companies in the production of Indian attack helicopters seriously undermines the credibility of the EU Code and its effectiveness in stopping the proliferation of arms to conflict or human rights crisis zones.

Sources: www.hal-india.com; 'French aerospace company eyes India for manufacturing base', Businessline, Chennai: 27 November 2002; *International Defense Review*, 15 January 1999; 'India drops arms export blacklist', BBC News, 28 October 2002; 'We are open to outsourcing from private industry', Businessline, Chennai, 12 February 2003.

A New Environment for Export Controls

Terrorist attacks have again highlighted the importance of export controls. Restricting the flow of materials can be crucial in avoiding the development of weapons of mass destruction; restricting technology can limit the ability to target missiles; restricting the flow of funds can inhibit the subsidization of terrorist training.

Nowadays, the principal focus of export controls must rest on the developing world. Quite a number of countries from this region want chemical and nuclear weapons and the technology to make use of them. For example, a country such as Libya can do little with its poison gas shells without a suitable delivery system.[9] Iran and its nuclear programme have ignited political controversy and major concerns in the developed world but have been supported by countries such as China, Russia, Pakistan and North Korea. As a result, export controls have moved from a 'strategic balance' to a 'tactical balance' approach. Nevertheless, even though the political hot spots addressed may be less broad in terms of their geographic expanse, the peril emanating from regional disintegration and local conflict may be just as dangerous to the world community as earlier strategic concerns with the Soviet Union.[10]

Another major change consists of the loosening of mutual bonds among allied nations. For many years the United States, Western Europe and Japan, together with emerging industrialized nations, held a generally similar strategic outlook. This outlook was driven by the common desire to reduce or at least contain the influence of the Soviet Union. However, with the disintegration of the Soviet Union in 1991, individual national interests that had been subsumed by the overall strategic objective gained in importance. As a consequence, differences in perspectives, attitudes and outlooks can now lead to ever-growing conflicts among the major players in the trade field.

Major change has also resulted from the increased foreign availability of high-technology products. In the past decade, the number of participants in the international trade field has grown rapidly. High-technology products are available worldwide from many sources. The broad

F○CUS ON

Iran's Nuclear Aspirations

As the Cold War ended, the strategic environment around Iran changed. China and North Korea supplied conventional weapons and nuclear assistance to Iran. Pakistan and China signed long-term nuclear co-operation agreements with Iran in 1987 and 1990, respectively. Accords with both countries involved training personnel and in the case of China, the accord included an agreement to provide Iran with a 27 kW miniature neutron source reactor (MNSR) and two 300 MW Qinshan power reactors. Western intelligence suspected that Pakistan, which many estimated had succeeded in manufacturing a nuclear bomb in 1986, provided Iran with nuclear assistance. The Soviet Union, traditionally an ally of Iraq, had also indicated an interest in co-operating with Iran. In January 1995, the Russian Federation formally announced that it would complete the construction of the Bushehr reactors and signed an agreement with Iran to build three additional reactors at the site.

Since the signing of these agreements, the United States has continuously expressed its opposition to the Bushehr deal because of fears that the deal could provide Iran with knowledge and technology to support a nuclear weapons programme. Despite many technical delays (misfit of original Siemens equipment with Russian technology) and efforts by the United States to stall the project, frequently by lobbying the Russian government for the cancellation of the deal, Iran has made significant progress. Over the years, the United States has successfully blocked several of Iran's nuclear agreements, such as those with Argentina (uranium enrichment and heavy water production facilities), China (plutonium-producing research reactor, two power reactors and a uranium conversion plant) and Russia (heavy water production plant). In 1995, it became evident that Iran may be pursuing nuclear weapons by procuring dual-use items from Western firms. Iran and Russia concluded a secret protocol stipulating, among other things, construction of a gas centrifuge enrichment facility. The fear was that Iran might learn how to construct a similar clandestine facility and then produce weapons-grade uranium undetected. The United States then imposed extensive sanctions on Iran and successfully pressured Russia and other potential suppliers, mostly in Europe, to halt exports of sensitive dual-use nuclear technology to Iran, such as high-voltage switches that could trigger a nuclear weapon and specialized remote manipulators designed to handle heavy volumes of radioactive material and possibly intended for a uranium or plutonium reprocessing plant.

Sources: 'Sanctions against Iran "unacceptable", Russian minister', AFP, 17 November 2003, www.iranexpert.com/; de Borchgrave, A., 'Iran in bombsights?' *Washington Times*, 5 July 2004; www.nti.org accessed on 12 April 2007.

availability makes any denial of such products more difficult to enforce. If a nation does control the exports of widely available products, it imposes a major competitive burden on its firms.

The speed of change and the rapid dissemination of information and innovation around the world has also shifted. For example, the current life cycle of computer chips is only 18 months. More than 70% of the data processing industry's sales resulted from the sale of devices that did not exist two years earlier.[11] This enormous technical progress is accompanied by a radical change in computer architecture. Instead of having to replace a personal computer or a workstation with a new computer, it is possible now to simply exchange microprocessors or motherboards with new, more efficient ones. Furthermore, today's machines can be connected to more than one microprocessor and users can customize and update configurations almost at will. Export controls that used to be based largely on capacity criteria have become almost irrelevant because they can no longer fulfil the function assigned to them. A user simply acquires additional chips, from whomever, and uses expansion slots to enhance the capacity of his or her computer.

The question arises as to how much of the latest technology is required for a country to engage in 'dangerous' activity. For example, nuclear weapons and sophisticated delivery systems were developed by the United States and the Soviet Union long before supercomputers became available. Therefore, it is reasonable to assert that researchers in countries working with equipment that is less than state of the art, or even obsolete, may well be able to achieve a threat capability that can result in major destruction and affect world safety.

From a control perspective, there is also the issue of equipment size. Due to their size, supercomputers and high-technology items used to be fairly difficult to hide and any movement of such products was easily detectable. Nowadays, state-of-the-art technology has been miniaturized. Much leading-edge technological equipment is so small that it can fit into a briefcase and most equipment is no larger than the luggage compartment of a car. Given these circumstances, it has become difficult to supervise closely the transfer of such equipment.

There are several key export control problem areas for firms and policy makers. First is the continuing debate about what constitutes military-use products, civilian-use products and dual-use items. Increasingly, goods are of a dual-use nature, typically commercial products that have potential military applications. The classic example is a pesticide factory that, some years later, was revealed to be a poison gas factory.[12] It is difficult enough to clearly define weapons. It is even more problematic to achieve consensus among nations regarding dual-use goods. For example, what about quite harmless screws if they are to be installed in rockets or telecommunications equipment used by the military? The problem becomes even greater with attempts to classify and list subcomponents and regulate their exportation. Individual country lists will lead to a distortion of competition if they deviate markedly from each other. The very task of drawing up any list is itself fraught with difficulty when it comes to components that are assembled. For example, according to German law the Patriot missile consists of only simple parts whose individual export is permissible. The earlier Focus on Politics shows how slippery the slope can be.

Even if governments were to agree on lists and continuously updated them, the resulting control aspects would be difficult to implement. Controlling the transfer of components within and among companies across economic areas such as NAFTA or the EU would significantly slow down business. Even more importantly, subjecting only the export of physical goods to surveillance is insufficient. The transfer of knowledge and technology is of equal or greater importance. Weapons-relevant information can easily be exported via books, periodicals and disks, and therefore their content would also need to be controlled. Foreigners would need to be prevented from gaining access to such sources during visits or from making use of data networks across borders. Attendance at conferences and symposia would have to be regulated, the flow of data across national borders would have to be controlled and today's communication systems and highways such as the Internet would have to be scrutinized. All these concerns have led to the emergence of controls of deemed exports. These controls address people rather than products in those instances where knowledge transfer could lead to a breach of export restrictions. More information is available at www.bis.doc.gov/.

Conflicts can also result from the desire of nations to safeguard their own economic interests. Due to different industrial structures, these interests vary between nations. For example, Germany, with a strong world market position in machine tools, motors and chemical raw materials, will think differently about manufacturing equipment controls than a country such as the United States, which sees computers as an area of its competitive advantage.

The terrorist attacks on Washington DC and New York have led to a renewal of international collaboration in the export-control field. Policies are being scrutinized as to their sensibility in light of the dangers of proliferation and international terrorism. Closer collaboration among countries has resulted in an easing of export-control policies in the technology field.[13] Determined to bring US economic as well as military power to bear in the fight against terrorism, the Bush Administration has also used policy both as a stick and as a carrot by deploying preferential trade measures, removing existing controls coupled with loans to reward allies and imposing new sanctions to intimidate adversaries.[14] The role of export controls and their sophistication can therefore be expected to increase.

Regulating International Business Behaviour

Home countries may implement special laws and regulations to ensure that the international business behaviour of firms in their country is conducted within appropriate *moral* and *ethical boundaries*. The definition of appropriateness may vary from country to country and from government to government. Therefore, the content, enforcement and impact of such regulations on firms may vary substantially among nations. As a result, the international manager must walk a careful line, balancing the expectations held in different countries.

One major area in which nations attempt to govern international business activities involves boycotts. As an example, Arab nations have developed a blacklist of companies that deal with Israel. Furthermore, Arab customers frequently demand assurance that products they purchase are not manufactured in Israel and that the supplier company does not do any business with Israel. The goal of these actions clearly is to impose a boycott on business with Israel. US political ties to Israel caused the US government to adopt anti-boycott laws to prevent US firms from complying with the boycott. The laws include a provision to deny foreign income tax benefits to companies that comply with the boycott. They also require notifying the US government if boycott requests are received. US firms that comply with the boycott are subject to heavy fines and to denial of export privileges. For more information, see www.bis.doc.gov/AntiboycottCompliance.

Boycotts, however, may also spring from the reactions of disgruntled consumers or legislators. For example, the United States Congress, unhappy with the lack of French support in the campaign against Iraq, officially renamed foods with the word 'French' in them and placed French foreign direct investment under scrutiny. Another example, reported in the next Focus on Politics shows how Iran and Saudi Arabia vented their anger economically over the publication of offensive cartoons of Muhammad in a Danish newspaper.

F⦾CUS ON

POLITICS   Iran's Boycott of Danish Goods

Iranian government officials announced a suspension of all trade and economic ties with Denmark to protest against provocative caricatures of the Prophet Muhammad that first appeared in a Danish newspaper and have been republished in other newspaper and periodicals around Europe. The cartoons first appeared in Denmark's *Jyllands-Posten* portraying Prophet Muhammad with a bomb in his turban.

The argument over the publication of the controversial cartoons added to already tense ties amid growing concerns in the European Union and in the United States that Iran is aiming to develop nuclear weapons.

A European Union official declared that Brussels had not been able to confirm the Iranian boycott and confirmation was awaited from Danish authorities and companies, which would be notified first of Iran's government decision.

The European Union is Iran's main trade partner. In 2004, the 25 EU members had combined exports to Iran worth €11.8 billion, while their combined imports were valued at €9.2 billion. Danish share in that trade was 1.86%. Danish exports to Iran comprise mainly machinery as well as pharmaceutical and medical products (about 0.3% of the total Danish export). Iranian imports in Denmark consist mainly of oil, petrochemicals and agricultural products.

Saudi Arabian businesses began a boycott of Danish goods on 26 January 2006, when supermarkets put up signs urging shoppers to stop buying Danish goods and removed all Danish products from the shelves.

'There are Danish companies that are affected by the boycott but it is too early to say whether it will have consequences for [the Danish] economy, which is sound', said Danish Prime Minister Anders Fogh Rasmussen at a news conference. The EU spokesman Johannes Laitenberger warned that even though Iran is not a member of the World Trade Organization, the EU would take measures against Tehran if it sought to boycott European goods. The EU made similar threats of trade and political sanctions against Saudi Arabia and other Middle East governments at the WTO and elsewhere, if they are found to be behind boycotts of Danish goods over the cartoon controversy.

Iranian Commerce Minister Masoud Mirkazemi told state-run radio that all contracts and negotiations with Danish companies would be suspended. Iran's Health Ministry declared that it was cancelling all previously approved business deals for medical equipment and medication with Danish companies.

Meanwhile the EU and the US pushed through a resolution at the UN's nuclear monitoring agency in Vienna, Austria, forwarding concerns over Iran's nuclear programme to the UN Security Council. The council has the power to impose economic and political sanctions on Iran.

Sources: Adapted from 'EU warns Iran over boycott of Danish goods' *China Daily*, 8 February 2006, www.chinadaily.com.cn/english/doc/2006-02/08/content_518203.htm, (accessed 13 April 2007) www.ec.europa.eu/comm/external_relations/iran/intro/index.htm, (accessed 13 April 2007.)

Caught in a web of governmental activity, firms may be forced either to lose business or pay substantial fines. This is especially true if the firm's products are competitive but not unique, so that the supplier can opt to purchase them elsewhere. The heightening of such conflict can sometimes force companies to search for new and possibly risky ways to circumvent the law or to withdraw operations totally from a country.

Another area of regulatory activity affecting the international business efforts of firms is antitrust laws. These laws often apply to international operations as well as to domestic business. In many countries, antitrust agencies watch closely when a firm buys a company, engages in a joint venture with a foreign firm or makes an agreement abroad with a competing firm in order to ensure that the action does not result in restraint of competition.

An interesting example is the recent acquisition in Britain of the supermarket giant Safeway by the much smaller rival Morrisons. The bids announced were as follows. Morrisons offered £2.9 billion; Sainsbury outlined a £3.2 billion offer. The US hyper-giant Wal-Mart, owner of the UK's third largest supermarket chain ASDA, as well as the strongest British chain Tesco showed interest. Why was Safeway attracting so much interest? Retailers prefer to expand by taking over existing retail space. Thus, the opportunity to buy Safeway's 479 stores in one go represented a rare chance. Success would mean a huge competitive advantage for the rival winning the takeover battle.

At the time of the bidding, Sainsbury was ranked third in the UK supermarket league, after losing its top position to Tesco in the 1990s and its second position to ASDA in the early 2000s. A key factor in the British government's decision on whether to allow a takeover to proceed was the size of the combined group in the market. A share of over 25% is seen as anti-competitive. At the time of the bid, Sainsbury had 17% market share and Safeway 11%, and so their combined market share would be above 25%. Wal-Mart would face a similar problem, with a takeover of Safeway bringing its British market share well above 25%. Tesco had beyond 25% of the share of the market, but its managers believed they could persuade the competition watchdog that taking over 75% of all Safeway stores would not greatly distort the market. The world's biggest retailer Wal-Mart had the deepest pockets and if competition issues were resolved it would be in the strongest position from financial point of view.

In the end, however, competition issues proved to be an insurmountable obstacle. Morrisons had the upper hand in the takeover battle because of its small size, which did not raise serious competition issues. Morrisons operated in the north of England only and had just over 100 stores. The company's financial success had taken it into the FTSE 100 index of leading shares and given it the opportunity to launch a bid for Safeway, a firm with more than four times as many stores. After a five month investigation, the British competition watchdog blocked Morrisons' much larger rivals, Wal-Mart, Tesco and Sainsbury, from buying out the Safeway chain, saying any such deal would operate against the public interest. On 26 September 2003 Morrisons was given the go-ahead to buy Safeway. The next year, Morrisons sold 114 Safeway stores and a distribution centre to rival Somerfield for £260 million. Morrisons also sold its Safeway subsidiaries in Jersey and Guernsey to CI Traders, an AIM-listed Jersey-based company, for £51 million. Morrisons stated the sale confirmed its strategy of focusing its UK business.

Given the increase in worldwide co-operation among companies, however, the wisdom of extending antitrust legislation to international activities is being questioned. Some limitations to these tough antitrust provisions were already implemented decades ago. For example, in the United States the Webb-Pomerene Act of 1918 excludes from antitrust prosecution firms co-operating to develop foreign markets. This law was passed as part of an effort to aid export efforts in the face of strong foreign competition by oligopolies and monopolies. The exclusion of international activities from antitrust regulation was further enhanced by the Export Trading Company Act of 1982, which ensures that co-operating firms are not exposed to the threat of treble damages. Further steps to loosen the application of antitrust laws to international business are under consideration because of increased competition from strategic alliances and global mega corporations.

Firms operating abroad are also affected by laws against bribery and corruption. In many countries, payments or favours are a way of life and 'a greasing of the wheels' is expected in return for government services. As a result, many companies doing business internationally are routinely forced to pay bribes or do favours for foreign officials in order to gain contracts. Every year, businesses pay huge amounts of money in bribes to win friends, influence and contracts. These bribes are conservatively estimated to run to US$80 billion a year – roughly the amount that the UN believes is needed to eradicate global poverty. The US Commerce Department reports that, annually, bribery is believed to be a factor in commercial contracts worth US$145 billion.[15]

Corruption is particularly widespread in nations where the administrative apparatus enjoys excessive and discretionary power and where there is a lack of transparency of laws and processes. Poverty, insufficient salaries of government servants and income inequalities also tend to increase corruption.[16] Fighting corruption is therefore not only an issue of laws and ethics, but also of creating an environment that makes honesty possible and desirable.

Presently corruption is recognized to be one of the world's greatest problems. Its impact on business is considerable as corruption impedes economic growth, distorts competition and represents serious legal risks. Corruption is also very costly for business, with the extra financial burden estimated to add at least 10% to the costs of doing business in many parts of the world.

The international legal fight against corruption has gained momentum in more recent times through the Organization for Economic Co-operation and Development (OECD) Convention on Combating Bribery of Foreign Public Officials in International Business Transactions and through the entering into force of the first globally agreed instrument, the United Nations Convention against Corruption (UNCAC) in December 2005.

In the 1970s, a major national debate erupted in the United States about these business practices, led by arguments that US firms have an ethical and moral leadership obligation and that contracts won through bribes do not reflect competitive market activity. As a result, the Foreign Corrupt Practices Act was passed in 1977, making it a crime for US executives of publicly traded firms to bribe a foreign official in order to obtain business.

A number of US firms have complained about the act, arguing that it hinders their efforts to compete internationally against companies whose home countries have no such anti-bribery laws. The problem is one of ethics versus practical needs and, to some extent, of the amounts involved. For example, it may be hard to draw the line between providing a generous tip and paying a bribe in order to speed up a business transaction. Many business executives believe that the United States should not apply its moral principles to other societies and cultures in which bribery and corruption are endemic. To compete internationally, executives argue, they must be free to use the most common methods of competition in the host country.

On the other hand, applying different standards to executives and firms based on whether they do business abroad or domestically is difficult to do. Also, bribes may open the way for shoddy performance and loose moral standards among executives and employees and may result in a spreading of general unethical business practices. Unrestricted bribery could result in firms concentrating on how to bribe best rather than on how to best produce and market their products. Typically, international businesses that use bribery fall into three categories: those who bribe to counterbalance the poor quality of their products or their high price; those who bribe to create a market for their unneeded goods; and, in the bulk of cases, those who bribe to stay competitive with other firms that bribe.[17] In all three of these instances, the customer is served poorly, the prices increase and the transaction does not reflect economic competitiveness.

The international manager must carefully distinguish between reasonable ways of doing business internationally – that is, complying with foreign expectations – and outright bribery and corruption. To assist the American manager in this task, the 1988 US Trade Act (which applies only and exclusively to the US) clarifies the applicability of the Foreign Corrupt Practices legislation. The revisions outline when a manager is expected to know about violation of the act and they draw a distinction between the facilitation of routine governmental actions and governmental policy decisions. Routine actions concern issues such as the obtaining of permits and licenses, the processing of governmental papers (such as visas and work orders), the providing of mail and phone service and the loading and unloading of cargo. Policy decisions refer mainly to situations in which the obtaining or retaining of a contract is at stake. While the facilitation of routine actions is not prohibited, the illegal influencing of policy decisions can result in the imposition of severe fines and penalties. The risks inherent in bribery have grown since 1999, when the OECD adopted a treaty criminalizing the bribery of foreign public officials, moving well beyond its previous discussions, which only sought to outlaw the tax deductibility of improper payments. The Organization of American States (OAS) has also officially condemned bribery. Similarly, the World Trade Organization has decided to consider placing bribery rules on its agenda. In addition, non-governmental organizations such as Transparency International are conducting widely publicized efforts to highlight corruption and bribery and even to rank countries on a Corruption Perceptions Index (www.transparency.de).

These issues place managers in the position of having to choose between home-country regulations and foreign business practices. This choice is made even more difficult because diverging standards of behaviour are applied to businesses in different countries. However, the gradually emerging consensus among international organizations may eventually level the playing field.

A final, major issue that is critical for international business managers is that of general standards of behaviour and ethics. Increasingly, public concerns are raised about such issues as environmental protection, global warming, pollution and moral behaviour. However, these issues are not of the same importance in every country. What may be frowned upon or even illegal in one nation may be customary or at least acceptable in others. For example, the cutting down of the Brazilian rain forest may be acceptable to the government of Brazil, but scientists and concerned consumers may object vehemently because of the effect on global warming and other climatic changes. The export of US tobacco products may be legal but results in accusations of exporting death to developing nations. China may use prison labour in producing products for export, but US law prohibits the importation of such products. Mexico may permit the use of low safety standards for workers, but the buyers of Mexican products may object to the resulting dangers.

International firms must understand the conflicts in standards and should assert leadership in implementing change. Not everything that is legally possible should be exploited for profit. By acting on existing, leading-edge knowledge and standards, firms will be able to benefit in the long term through consumer goodwill and the avoidance of later recriminations.

International executives are 'selling' the world on two key issues: one is the benefit of market forces that result in the interplay of supply and demand. This interplay in turn uses price signals instead of government decree to adjust activities, thrives on competition and works within an environment of respect for profitability and private property. The second key proposition is that international marketers will do their best to identify market niches and bring their products and services to customers around the globe. Since these activities take up substantial financial resources, they provide individuals with the opportunity to invest their funds in the most productive and efficient manner.

Key underlying dimensions of both of these issues are managerial and corporate virtue, vision and veracity. Unless the world can believe in what executives say and do and trust their global activities, it will be hard, if not impossible, to forge a global commitment between those doing the marketing and the ones being marketed to. It is therefore of vital interest to executives to ensure that corruption, bribery, lack of transparency and the misleading of consumers, investors and employees are systematically relegated to the history books – where they belong. It will be the extent of openness, responsiveness, long-term thinking and truthfulness that will determine the degrees of freedom of international business.[18]

HOST COUNTRY POLITICAL AND LEGAL ENVIRONMENT

The politics and laws of a host country affect international business operations in a variety of ways. The good manager will understand these dimensions of the countries in which the firm operates so that he or she can work within existing parameters and can anticipate and plan for changes that may occur.

Political Action and Risk

Firms usually prefer to conduct business in a country with a stable and friendly government, but such governments are not always easy to find. Managers must therefore continually monitor the government, its policies and its stability to determine the potential for political change that could adversely affect corporate operations.

There is political risk in every nation, but the range of risks varies widely from country to country. In general, political risk is lowest in countries that have a history of stability and consistency. Political risk tends to be highest in nations that do not have this sort of history. In a number of countries, however, consistency and stability that were apparent on the surface have been quickly swept away by major popular movements that drew on the bottled-up frustrations of the population. Three major types of political risk can be encountered: ownership risk, which exposes property and life; operating risk, which refers to interference with the ongoing operations of a firm; and transfer risk,

	Loss May Be the Result of:	
Contingencies May Include:	The actions of legitimate government authorities	Events caused by factors outside the control of government
The involuntary loss of control over specific assets without adequate compensation	• Total or partial expropriation • Forced divestiture • Confiscation • Cancellation or unfair calling of performance bonds	• War • Revolution • Terrorism • Strikes • Extortion
A reduction in the value of a stream of benefits expected from the foreign-controlled affiliate	• Non-applicability of 'national treatment' • Restriction in access to financial, labour, or material markets • Control on prices, outputs, or activities • Currency and remittance restrictions • Value-added and export performance requirements	• Nationalistic buyers or suppliers • Threats and disruption to operations by hostile groups • Externally induced financial constraints • Externally imposed limits on imports or exports

Figure 4.1: Exposure to political risk.

Source: José de la Torre and David H. Neckar (1990) 'Forecasting Political Risks for International Operations', in H. Vernon-Wortzel and L. Wortzel (eds), *Global Strategic Management: The Essentials,* 2nd edition, John Wiley & Sons, Inc., 195. Reproduced with permission.

which is mainly encountered when attempts are made to shift funds between countries. Firms can be exposed to political risk due to government actions or even actions outside the control of governments. The type of actions and their effects are classified in Figure 4.1.

A major political risk in many countries is that of conflict and violent change. A manager will want to think twice before conducting business in a country in which the likelihood of such change is high. To begin with, if conflict breaks out, violence directed toward the firm's property and employees is a strong possibility. Guerrilla warfare, civil disturbances and terrorism often take an anti-industry bent, making companies and their employees potential targets. International corporations are often subject to major threats, even in countries that boast great political stability. Sometimes the sole fact that a firm is market oriented is sufficient to attract the wrath of terrorists. Following US military strikes in Afghanistan, in the spring of 2002 a group of suspected Muslim militants in Pakistan kidnapped and murdered journalist Daniel Pearl, a reporter with *The Wall Street Journal*, the flagship of US business journalism.

International terrorists frequently target US facilities, operations and personnel abroad. Since the September 11 attacks on the World Trade Centre and the Pentagon, such attacks have also taken place within the United States. US firms, by their nature, cannot have the elaborate security and restricted access of US diplomatic offices and military bases. As a result, United States businesses are the primary target of terrorists worldwide and remain the most vulnerable targets in the future.[19] Ironically enough, in many instances, the businesses attacked or burned are the franchisees of US business concepts. Therefore, the ones suffering most from such attacks are the local owners and local employees. The methods used by terrorists against business facilities include bombing, arson, hijacking and sabotage. To obtain funds, the terrorists resort to kidnapping executives, armed robbery and extortion.[20] To reduce international terrorism, recent experience has demonstrated that international collaboration is imperative to identify and track terrorist groups and to systematically reduce their safe havens and financial support. In spite of such efforts, terrorism is likely to continue. As former US senators Hart and Rudman have written:

> prudence requires we assume . . . adversaries . . . have learned from the attacks how vulnerable the US and other countries are. They will also have observed that relatively low-cost terrorist operations . . . can inflict extensive damage and profound disruption. . . . As long as catastrophic attacks are likely to yield tangible results in undermining our economy and way of life, undertaking these attacks will be attractive to those who regard the US and its allies as their enemy.[21]

As a consequence, governments are likely to continue imposing new regulations and restrictions intended to avert terrorist acts. For example, increasingly complex customs clearance and international logistical requirements or specific requirements imposed to enhance security systems all combine to increase the cost of doing business internationally. Moreover, these security measures will also tend to lessen the efficiency with which international business channels can function.[22]

In many countries, particularly in the developing world, coups d'état can result in drastic changes in government. The new government often will attack foreign firms as remnants of a Western-dominated colonial past, as has happened in Cuba, Nicaragua and Iran. Even if such changes do not represent an immediate physical threat, they can lead to policy changes that may have drastic effects. The past decades have seen coups in Ghana, Ethiopia, Pakistan and Ivory Coast, for example, that have seriously impeded the conduct of international business.

Less drastic, but still worrisome, are changes in government policies that are not caused by changes in the government itself. These occur when, for one reason or another, a government feels pressured to change its policies toward foreign businesses. The pressure may be the result of nationalist or religious factions or widespread anti-Western feeling.

A broad range of policy changes is possible as a result of political unrest. All of the changes can affect the company's international operations, but not all of them are equal in weight. Except for extreme cases, companies do not usually have to fear violence against their employees, although violence against company property is quite common. Also common are changes in policy that result from a new government or a strong new stance that is nationalist and opposed to foreign investment. The most drastic public steps resulting from such policy changes are usually expropriation and confiscation.

Expropriation is the transfer of ownership by the host government to a domestic entity with payment of compensation. Expropriation was an appealing action to many countries because it demonstrated their nationalism and transferred a certain amount of wealth and resources from foreign companies to the host country immediately. It did have costs to the host country, however, to the extent that it made other firms more hesitant to invest there. Expropriation does not relieve the host government of providing compensation to the former owners. However, these compensation negotiations are often protracted and frequently result in settlements that are unsatisfactory to the owners. For example, governments may offer compensation in the form of local, non-transferable currency or may base compensation on the book value of the firm. Even though firms that are expropriated may deplore the low levels of payment obtained, they frequently accept them in the absence of better alternatives.

The use of expropriation as a policy tool has sharply decreased over time. In the mid-1970s, more than 83 expropriations took place in a single year. By the turn of the century, the annual average had declined to fewer than three. Apparently, governments have come to recognize that the damage they inflict on themselves through expropriation exceeds the benefits they receive.[23]

Confiscation is similar to expropriation in that it results in a transfer of ownership from the firm to the host country. It differs in that it does not involve compensation for the firm. Some industries are more vulnerable than others to confiscation and expropriation because of their importance to the host

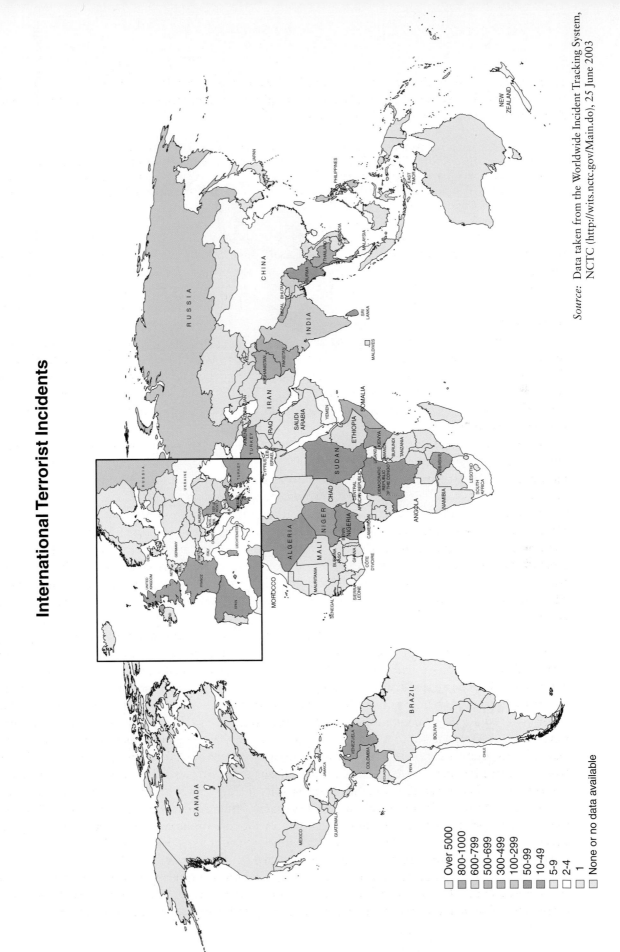

International Terrorist Incidents

Legend:
- Over 5000
- 800–1000
- 600–799
- 500–699
- 300–499
- 100–299
- 50–99
- 10–49
- 5–9
- 2–4
- 1
- None or no data available

Source: Data taken from the Worldwide Incident Tracking System, NCTC (http://wits.nctc.gov/Main.do), 25 June 2003

Top 10 Terrorist Incident Location

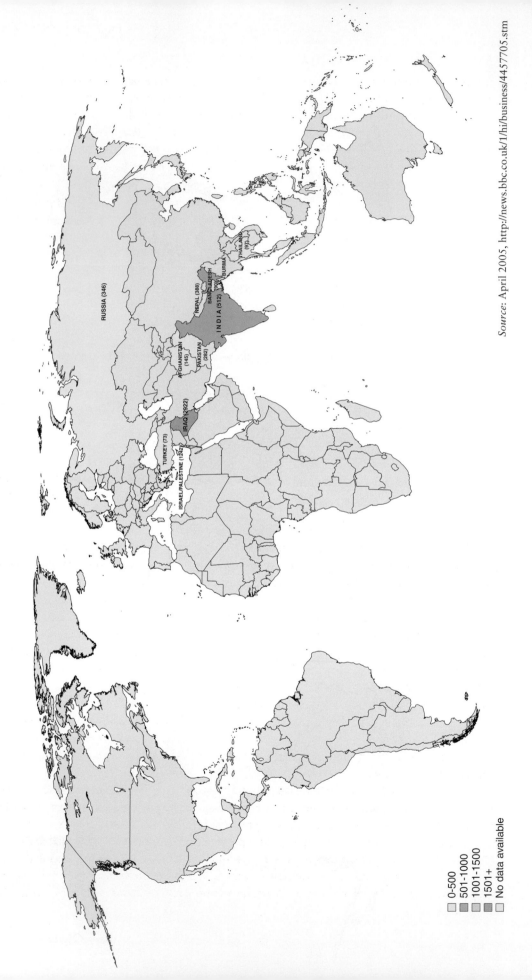

RUSSIA (346)

NEPAL (388)

BANGLADESH (300)

BURMA

THAILAND (97)

INDIA (512)

AFGHANISTAN (145)

PAKISTAN (282)

IRAQ (2922)

TURKEY (73)

ISRAEL/PALESTINE (1242)

0-500
501-1000
1001-1500
1501+
No data available

Source: April 2005, http://news.bbc.co.uk/1/hi/business/4457705.stm

country's economy and their lack of ability to shift operations. For this reason, such sectors as mining, energy, public utilities and banking have frequently been targets of such government actions.

Confiscation and expropriation constitute major political risks for foreign investors. Other government actions, however, are equally detrimental to foreign firms. Many countries are turning from confiscation and expropriation to more subtle forms of control, such as domestication. The goal of domestication is the same – that is, to gain control over foreign investment – but the method is different. Through domestication, the government demands transfer of ownership and management responsibility. It can impose local content regulations to ensure that a large share of the product is locally produced or demand that a larger share of the profit is retained in the country. Changes in labour laws, patent protection and tax regulations are also used for purposes of domestication.

Domestication can have profound effects on an international business operation for a number of reasons. If a firm is forced to hire nationals as managers, poor co-operation and communication can result. If domestication is imposed within a very short time span, corporate operations overseas may have to be headed by poorly trained and inexperienced local managers. Domestic content requirements may force a firm to purchase its supplies and parts locally. This can result in increased costs, less efficiency and lower-quality products. Export requirements imposed on companies may create havoc for their international distribution plans and force them to change or even shut down operations in third countries.

Finally, domestication usually shields an industry within one country from foreign competition. As a result, inefficiencies will be allowed to thrive due to a lack of market discipline. This will affect the long-run international competitiveness of an operation abroad and may turn into a major problem when, years later, domestication is discontinued by the government.

If government action consists of weakening or not enforcing intellectual property right (IPR) protection, companies run the risk of losing their core competitive edge. Such steps may temporarily permit domestic firms to become quick imitators. Yet, in the longer term, they will not only discourage the ongoing transfer of technology and knowledge by multinational firms, but also reduce the incentive for local firms to invest in innovation and progress.

Poor IPR legislation and enforcement in the otherwise lucrative markets of Asia illustrate a clash between international business interests and developing nations' political and legal environments. Businesses attempting to enter the markets of China, Indonesia, Malaysia, Singapore, Taiwan, Thailand and the Philippines face considerable risk in these countries, which have the world's worst records for copyright piracy and intellectual property infringements. But these newly industrialized countries argue that IPR laws discriminate against them because they impede the diffusion of technology and artificially inflate prices. They also point to the fact that industrialized nations such as the United States and Japan violated IPR laws during earlier stages of development. In fact, the United States became a signatory to the Berne Convention on copyrights only in 1989 – around one hundred years after its introduction – and Japan disregarded IPR laws in adapting Western technologies during the 1950s. Furthermore, although newly industrialized nations are becoming increasingly aware that strong IPR protection will encourage technology transfer and foreign investment, the weak nature of these countries' court structures and the slow pace of legislation often fail to satisfy the needs of their rapidly transforming economies.[24]

Due to successful international negotiations in the Uruguay Round, the World Trade Organization now has agreement on significant dimensions of the trade-related aspects of intellectual property rights (TRIPS) (www.wto.org). This agreement sets minimum standards of protection to be provided by each member country for copyrights, trademarks, geographical indications, industrial designs, patents, layout designs of integrated circuits and undisclosed information such as trade secrets and test data.[25] Although not all-encompassing, these standards provide substantial assurances of protection, which after an implementation delay for the poorest countries, will apply to virtually all parts of the world.

One might ask why companies would choose to do business in risky markets. However, as with anything international (or any business for that matter), the issue is not whether there is any risk but rather the degree of risk that exists. Key links to risk are the dimension of reward. With appropriate rewards, many risks become more tolerable. For example, between 1991 and 1997 the average return on foreign direct investment in Africa was higher than in any other region, according to the UN Conference on Trade and Development. This is partly because the perceived risk of doing business in very poor countries is so great that firms tend to invest only in projects that promise quick profits. But it is also because there are good opportunities. For brave businesspeople, there may be rich returns in unexpected places.[26]

Economic Risk

Most businesses operating abroad face a number of other risks that are less dangerous, but probably more common, than the drastic ones already described. A host government's political situation or desires may lead it to impose economic regulations or laws to restrict or control the international activities of firms.

Nations that face a shortage of foreign currency will sometimes impose controls on the movement of capital into and out of the country. Such controls may make it difficult for a firm to remove its profits or investments from the host country. Sometimes exchange controls are also levied selectively against certain products or companies in an effort to reduce the importation of goods that are considered to be luxuries or to be sufficiently available through domestic production. Such regulations often affect the importation of parts, components or supplies that are vital to production operations in the country. They may force a firm to alter its production programme or, worse yet, shut down its entire plant. Prolonged negotiations with government officials may be necessary to reach a compromise on what constitutes a 'valid' expenditure of foreign currency resources. Because the goals of government officials and corporate managers are often quite different, such compromises, even when they can be reached, may result in substantial damage to the international operations of the firm.

Countries may also use tax policy toward foreign investors in an effort to control multinational corporations and their capital. Tax increases may raise much-needed revenue for the host country, but they can severely damage the operations of foreign investors. This damage, in turn, will frequently result in decreased income for the host country in the long run. The raising of tax rates needs to be carefully differentiated from increased tax scrutiny of foreign investors. Many governments believe that multinational firms may be tempted to shift tax burdens to lower-tax countries by using artificial pricing schemes between subsidiaries. In such instances, governments are likely to take measures to obtain their fair contribution from multinational operations. In the United States, for example, increased focus on the taxation of multinational firms has resulted in various back-tax payments by foreign firms and the development of new corporate pricing policies developed in collaboration with the Internal Revenue Service.[27]

The international executive also has to worry about price controls. In many countries, domestic political pressures can force governments to control the prices of imported products or services, particularly in sectors considered highly sensitive from a political perspective, such as food or healthcare. A foreign firm involved in these areas is vulnerable to price controls because the government can play on citizens' nationalistic tendencies to enforce the controls. Particularly in countries that suffer from high inflation, frequent devaluations or sharply rising costs, the international executive may be forced to choose between shutting down the operation or continuing production at a loss in the hope of recouping profits when the government loosens or removes its price restrictions. Price controls can also be administered to prevent prices from being too low. Governments have enacted antidumping laws, which prevent foreign competitors from pricing their imports unfairly low in order to drive domestic competitors out of the market. Since dumping charges depend heavily on the definition of 'fair' price, a firm can sometimes become the target of such accusations quite unexpectedly. Proving that no dumping took place can become quite onerous in terms of time, money and information disclosure.

Managing the Risk

Managers face the risk of confiscation, expropriation, domestication or other government interference whenever they conduct business overseas, but ways exist to lessen the risk. Obviously, if a new government comes into power and is dedicated to the removal of all foreign influences, there is little a firm can do. In less extreme cases, however, managers can take actions that will reduce the risk, provided they understand the root causes of the host country's policies.

Adverse governmental actions are usually the result of nationalism, the deterioration of political relations between home and host country, the desire for independence or opposition to colonial remnants. If a host country's citizens feel exploited by foreign investors, government officials are more likely to take anti-foreign action. To reduce the risk of government intervention, the international firm needs to demonstrate that it is concerned with the host country's society and that it considers itself an integral part of the host country, rather than simply an exploitative foreign corporation. Ways of doing this include intensive local hiring and training practices, better pay, contributions to charity and societally useful investments. In addition, the company can form joint ventures with local partners to demonstrate that it is willing to share its gains with nationals. Although such actions will not guarantee freedom from political risk, they certainly lessen the exposure.

Another action that can be taken by corporations to protect against political risk is the close monitoring of political developments. Increasingly, private sector firms offer such monitoring assistance, permitting the overseas corporation to discover potential trouble spots as early as possible and to react quickly to prevent major losses.

Firms can also take out insurance to cover losses due to political and economic risk. Most industrialized countries offer insurance programmes for their firms doing business abroad.

© Ian Marriott, Wolf Production, Photographers by Design. Reproduced with permission.

In Germany, for example, Hermes Kreditanstalt (www.hermes.de) provides exporters with insurance. In the United States, the Overseas Private Investment Corporation (OPIC) (www.opic.gov) can cover three types of risk insurance: currency inconvertibility insurance, which covers the inability to convert profits, debt service and other remittances from local currency into US dollars; expropriation insurance, which covers the loss of an investment due to expropriation, nationalization or confiscation by a foreign government; and political violence insurance, which covers the loss of assets or income due to war, revolution, insurrection or politically motivated civil strife, terrorism and sabotage. The cost of coverage varies by country and type of activity, but for manufacturers it averages US$0.35 for US$100 of coverage per year to protect against inconvertibility, US$0.50 to protect against expropriation and US$0.45 to compensate for damage to business income and assets from political violence.[28] Usually the policies do not cover commercial risks and, in the event of a claim, cover only the actual loss – not lost profits. In the event of a major political upheaval, however, risk insurance can be critical to a firm's survival.

The discussion to this point has focused primarily on the political environment. Laws have been mentioned only as they appear to be the direct result of political change. However, the laws of host countries need to be considered on their own to some extent, for the basic system of law is important to the conduct of international business.

Legal Differences and Restraints

Countries differ in their laws as well as in their use of the law. For example, over the past decade the United States has become an increasingly litigious society in which institutions and individuals are quick to initiate lawsuits. Court battles are often protracted and costly and even the threat of a court case can reduce business opportunities. In contrast, Japan's tradition tends to minimize the role of the law and of lawyers. On a per capita basis, Japan has only about 5% of the number of lawyers in the United States.[29] Whether the number of lawyers is cause or effect, the Japanese tend not to litigate. Litigation in Japan means that the parties have failed to compromise, which is contrary to Japanese tradition and results in loss of face. A cultural predisposition therefore exists to settle conflicts outside the court system.

Over the millennia of civilization, many different laws and legal systems have emerged. King Hammurabi of Babylon codified a series of decisions by judges into a body of laws. Legal issues in many African tribes were settled through the verdicts of clansmen. A key legal perspective that survives today is that of theocracy, such as Hebrew law and Islamic law (the Shariah) that are the result of the dictates of God, scripture, prophetic utterances and practices and scholarly interpretations.[30] These legal systems have faith and belief as their key focus and are a mix of societal, legal and spiritual guidelines.

Although legal systems are important to society, from an international business perspective, the two major legal systems worldwide can be categorized into common law and code law. Common law is based on tradition and depends less on written statutes and codes than on precedent and custom. (Common law jurisdiction originated in England and is the system of law in the United States, Cyprus, Ireland and the UK. Malta's jurisdiction is based on both common and code law. All other 23 countries in the EU apply code law jurisdiction.) Code law, on the other hand, is based on a comprehensive set of written statutes. Countries with code law try to spell out all possible legal rules explicitly. Code law is based on Roman law and is found in the majority of the nations of the world.

In general, countries with the code law system have much more rigid laws than those with the common law system. In the latter, courts adopt precedents and customs to fit cases, allowing a better idea of basic judgement likely to be rendered in new situations. The differences between code law and common law and their impact on international business, although wide in theory, are not as broad in practice. One reason is that many common-law countries, including the United States, have adopted commercial codes to govern the conduct of business.

Host countries may adopt a number of laws that affect the firm's ability to do business. Tariffs and quotas, for example, can affect the entry of goods. Special licences for foreign goods may be required.

Other laws may restrict entrepreneurial activities. In Argentina, for example, pharmacies must be owned by the pharmacist. This legislation prevents an ambitious businessperson from hiring druggists and starting a pharmacy chain. Similarly, the law prevents the addition of a drug counter to an existing business such as a supermarket and thus the broadening of the product offering to consumers.

Specific legislation may also exist regulating what does and does not constitute deceptive advertising. Many countries prohibit specific claims that compare products to the competition or restrict the use of promotional devices. Even when no laws exist, regulations may hamper business operations. For example, in some countries, firms are required to join the local chamber of commerce or become a member of the national trade association. These institutions in turn may have internal sets of rules that specify standards for the conduct of business that may be quite confining.

Seemingly innocuous local regulations that may easily be overlooked can have a major impact on the international firm's success. For example, Japan had an intricate process regulating the building of new department stores or supermarkets. The government's desire to protect smaller merchants brought the opening of new, large stores to a virtual standstill. Since department stores and supermarkets serve as the major conduit for the sale of imported consumer products, the lack of new stores severely affected opportunities for market penetration of imported merchandise.[31] Only after intense pressure from the outside did the Japanese government decide to reconsider the regulations. Another example concerns the growing global controversy that surrounds the use of genetic technology. Governments increasingly devise new rules that affect trade in genetically modified products. Australia introduced a mandatory standard for foods produced using bio-technology, which prohibits the sale of such products unless the food has been assessed by the Australia New Zealand Food Authority.

Other laws may be designed to protect domestic industries and reduce imports. For example, although foodstuffs and domestic goods are taxed at a 10% rate, Russia charges a 20% value-added tax on most imported goods, assesses high excise taxes on goods such as cigarettes, automobiles and alcoholic beverages, and provides a burdensome import licensing regime for alcohol to depress Russian demand for imports.[32]

Finally, the interpretation and enforcement of laws and regulations may have a major effect on international business activities. For example, in deciding what product can be called a 'Swiss' Army knife or 'French' wine, the interpretation given by courts to the meaning of a name can affect consumer perceptions and sales of products.

The Influencing of Politics and Laws

To succeed in a market, the international manager needs much more than business know-how. He or she must also deal with the intricacies of national politics and laws. Although to understand fully another country's legal political system will rarely be possible, the good manager needs to be aware of its importance and to work with people who do understand how to operate within the system. To do so is particularly important for multinational corporations. These firms work in many countries and must manage relationships with a large number of governments. Often, these governments have a variety of ideologies, which may require different corporate responses. To be strategically successful, the firm must therefore be able to formulate and implement political activities on a global scale.[33]

Many areas of politics and law are not immutable. Viewpoints can be modified or even reversed and new laws can supersede old ones. Therefore, existing political and legal restraints do not always need to be accepted. To achieve change, however, some impetus for it – such as the clamours of a constituency – must occur. Otherwise, systemic inertia is likely to allow the status quo to prevail.

The international manager has various options. One is to simply ignore prevailing rules and expect to get away with it. Pursuing this option is a high-risk strategy because the possibility of objection and even prosecution exists. A second, traditional, option is to provide input to trade negotiators and expect any problem areas to be resolved in multilateral negotiations. The drawbacks to this option are, of course, the quite time-consuming process involved and the lack of control by the firm.

A third option involves the development of coalitions and constituencies that can motivate legislators and politicians to consider and ultimately implement change. This option can be pursued in various ways. One direction can be the recasting or redefinition of issues. Often, specific terminology leads to conditioned, though inappropriate, responses. For example, before China's accession to the World Trade Organization in 2001, the country's trade status with the United States had been highly controversial for many years. The US Congress had to decide annually whether or not to grant most favoured nation (MFN) status to China. The debate on this decision was always very contentious and acerbic and often framed around the question as to why China deserved to be treated the 'most favoured way'. Lost in the debate was often the fact that the term 'most favoured' was simply taken from WTO terminology and only indicated that trade with China would be treated like that with any other country. Only in late 1999 was the terminology changed from MFN to NTR (normal trade relations). Even though there was still considerable debate regarding China, at least the controversy about special treatment had been eliminated.[34]

Beyond terminology, firms can also highlight the direct links and their costs and benefits to legislators and politicians. For example, a manager can explain the employment and economic effects of certain laws and regulations and demonstrate the benefits of change. The picture can be enlarged by including indirect links. For instance, suppliers, customers and distributors can be asked to help explain to decision makers the benefit of change. In addition, the public at large can be involved through public statements or advertisements.

Developing such coalitions is not an easy task. Companies often seek assistance in effectively influencing the government decision-making process. Typical categories of firm-level political behaviour are lobbying, public/government relations, industry alliances and associations, and political incentives.[35] Lobbying usually works best when narrow economic objectives or single-issue campaigns are involved. Typically, lobbyists provide this assistance. Usually, there are well-connected individuals and firms that can provide access to policy makers and legislators in order to communicate new and pertinent information.

Many US firms have representatives in Washington, DC, as well as in state capitals and are quite successful at influencing domestic policies. Often, however, they are less adept at ensuring proper representation abroad even though, for example, the European Commission in Brussels wields far-reaching economic power. For example, a survey of US international marketing executives found that knowledge and information about foreign trade and government officials was ranked lowest among critical international business information needs. This low ranking appears to reflect the fact that many US firms are far less successful in their interactions with governments abroad and far less intensive in their lobbying efforts than are foreign entities in the United States.[36]

Many countries and companies have been effective in their lobbying in the United States. As an example, Brazil has retained nearly a dozen US firms to cover and influence trade issues. Brazilian citrus exporters and computer manufacturers have hired US legal and public relations firms to provide them with information on relevant US legislative activity. The Banco do Brasil also successfully lobbied for the restructuring of Brazilian debt and favourable US banking regulations.

The other forms of political behaviour are more useful when it comes to general issues applicable to a wide variety of firms or industries or when long-term policy directions are at stake. In such instances, the collaboration and power of many market actors can help sway the direction of policy.

Although representation of the firm's interests to government decision makers and legislators is entirely appropriate, the international manager must also consider any potential side effects. Major questions can be raised if such representation becomes very overt. Short-term gains may be far outweighed by long-term negative repercussions if the international firm is perceived as exerting too much political influence.

INTERNATIONAL RELATIONS AND LAWS

In addition to understanding the politics and laws of both home and host countries, the international manager must also consider the overall international political and legal environment. This is important because policies and events occurring among countries can have a profound impact on firms trying to do business internationally.

International Politics

The effect of politics on international business is determined by both the bilateral political relations between home and host countries and by multilateral agreements governing the relations among groups of countries.

The government-to-government relationship can have a profound influence in a number of ways, particularly if it becomes hostile. President Bush's characterization in February 2002 of Iran, Iraq and North Korea as an 'axis of evil' aggravated already unstable political relationships and threatened to set back negotiations by US companies to secure lucrative oil deals.[37] In another example, although the internal political changes in the aftermath of the Iranian revolution certainly would have affected any foreign firm doing business in Iran, the deterioration in US–Iranian political relations that resulted had a significant additional impact on US firms, which were injured not only by the physical damage caused by the violence, but also by the anti-American feelings of the Iranian people and their government. The resulting clashes between the two governments subsequently destroyed business relationships, regardless of corporate feelings or agreements on either side.

International political relations do not always have harmful effects. If bilateral political relations between countries improve, business can benefit. One example is the improvement in Western relations with Central Europe following the official end of the Cold War. The political warming opened the potentially lucrative former Eastern bloc markets to Western firms.

The overall international political environment has effects, whether good or bad, on international business. For this reason, the manager must strive to remain aware of political currents and relations worldwide and attempt to anticipate changes in the international political environment so that his or her firm can plan for them.

International Law

International law plays an important role in the conduct of international business. Although no enforceable body of international law exists, certain treaties and agreements are respected by a number of countries and profoundly influence international business operations. For example the WTO defines internationally acceptable economic practices for its member nations. Although it does not directly deal with individual firms, it does affect them indirectly by providing some predictability in the international environment.

The Patent Cooperation Treaty (PCT) provides procedures for filing just one international application for designating countries in which a patent is sought, which has the same effect as filing national applications in each of those countries. Similarly, the European Patent Office examines applications and issues national patents in any of its member countries. Other regional offices include the African Industrial Property Office (ARIPO), the French-speaking African Intellectual Property Organization (OAPI) and one in Saudi Arabia for six countries in the Gulf region.

International organizations such as the United Nations and the OECD have also undertaken efforts to develop codes and guidelines that affect international business. These include the Code on International Marketing of Breast-milk Substitutes, which was developed by the World Health Organization (WHO) (www.who.int/en) and the UN Code of Conduct for Transnational Corporations. Even though there are 34 such codes in existence, the lack of enforcement ability hampers their full implementation.

In addition to multilateral agreements, firms are affected by bilateral treaties and conventions between the countries in which they do business. For example, a number of countries have signed bilateral Treaties of Friendship, Commerce and Navigation (FCN). The agreements generally define the rights of firms doing business in the host country. They normally guarantee that firms will be treated by the host country in the same manner in which domestic firms are treated. Although these treaties provide for some sort of stability, they can also be cancelled when relations worsen.

The international legal environment also affects the manager to the extent that firms must concern themselves with jurisdictional disputes. Because no single body of international law exists, firms are usually restricted by both home and host country laws. If a conflict occurs between contracting parties in two different countries, a question arises concerning which country's laws are to be used and in which court the dispute is to be settled. Sometimes the contract will contain a jurisdictional clause, which settles the matter with little problem. If the contract does not contain such a clause, however, the parties to the dispute have a few options. They can settle the dispute by following the laws of the country in which the agreement was made or they can resolve it by obeying the laws of the country in which the contract will have to be fulfilled. Which laws to use and in which location to settle the dispute are two different decisions. As a result, a dispute between a US exporter and a French importer could be resolved in Paris but be based on New York State law. The importance of such provisions was highlighted by the lengthy jurisdictional disputes surrounding the Bhopal incident in India.

In cases of disagreement, the parties can choose either arbitration or litigation. Litigation is usually avoided for several reasons. It often involves extensive delays and is very costly. In addition, firms may fear discrimination in foreign countries. Therefore, companies tend to prefer conciliation and arbitration, because they result in much quicker decisions. Arbitration procedures are often spelled out in the original contract and usually provide for an intermediary who is judged to be impartial by both parties. Intermediaries can be representatives of chambers of commerce, trade associations or third-country institutions. One key non-governmental organization handling international commercial disputes is the International Court of Arbitration, founded in 1923 by the International Chamber of Commerce (ICC: www.iccwbo.org). Each year it handles arbitrations in some 48 different countries with arbitrators of some 57 different nationalities. Arbitration is usually faster and less expensive than litigation in the courts. In addition, the limited judicial recourse available against arbitral awards, as compared with court judgements, offers a clear advantage. Parties that use arbitration rather than litigation know that they will not have to face a prolonged and costly series of appeals. Finally, arbitration offers the parties the flexibility to set up a proceeding that can be conducted as quickly and economically as the circumstances allow. For example, a multimillion dollar ICC arbitration was completed in just over two months.[38]

SUMMARY

The political and legal environment in the home and host countries and the laws and agreements governing relationships among nations are important to the international business executive. Compliance is mandatory in order to do business successfully abroad. To avoid the problems that can result from changes in the political and legal environment, it is essential to anticipate changes and to develop strategies for coping with them. Whenever possible, the manager must avoid being taken by surprise and letting events control business decisions.

Governments affect international business through legislation and regulations, which can support or hinder business transactions. An example is when export sanctions or embargoes are imposed to enhance foreign policy objectives. Similarly, export controls are used to preserve national security. Nations also regulate the international business behaviour of firms by setting standards that relate to bribery and corruption, boycotts and restraint of competition.

Through political actions such as expropriation, confiscation or domestication, countries expose firms to international risk. Management therefore needs to be aware of the possibility of such risk and alert to new developments. Many private sector services are available to track international risk situations. In the event of a loss, firms may rely on insurance for political risk or seek redress in court. International legal action, however, may be quite slow and may compensate for only part of the loss.

Managers need to be aware that different countries have different laws. One clearly pronounced difference is between code law countries, where all possible legal rules are spelled out, and common law countries such as the United States, where the law is based on tradition, precedent and custom.

Managers must also pay attention to international political relations, agreements and treaties. Changes in relations or rules can mean major new opportunities and occasional threats to international business. Even though conflict in international business may sometimes lead to litigation, the manager needs to be aware of the alternative of arbitration, which may resolve the pending matter more quickly and at a lower cost.

QUESTIONS FOR DISCUSSION

1. Discuss this potential dilemma: 'High political risk requires companies to seek a quick payback on their investments. Striving for a quick payback, however, exposes firms to charges of exploitation and results in increased political risk'.
2. Discuss this statement: 'The national security that export control laws seek to protect may be threatened by the resulting lack of international competitiveness of US firms'.
3. Discuss the advantages and disadvantages of common law and code law.
4. The United States has been described as a litigious society. How does frequent litigation affect international business?
5. After you hand your passport to the immigration officer in country X, s/he misplaces it. A small 'donation' would certainly help to find it again. Should you give the officer the money? Is this a business expense to be charged to your company? Should it be tax deductible?

INTERNET EXERCISE

According to the anti-corruption monitoring organization Transparency International, which countries have the highest levels of corruption? Which have the lowest levels? (Use the Corruption Perception Index found at www.transparency.de.) What problems might an exporter have in doing business in a country with high levels of corruption?

TAKE A STAND

Peer to peer online sharing has become a lucrative business that allows online service providers such as Kazaa to enable its users to swap music and videos without paying for them and prevents artists from receiving royalties. Consequently, Kazaa and other file-sharing services have been the subject of blistering legal and public relations campaigns by the entertainment industry aimed at shutting down their businesses or at least undermining consumer confidence in them. Senator Orrin Hatch, a musician himself, said that if nothing else could stop people from stealing copyrighted works, he would support using programmes to damage the computers of those who do.

FOR DISCUSSION

Despite all of this, file sharing is thriving and although Kazaa says it does not support piracy, companies usually cannot control how consumers use its software. Should the government intervene?

Source: 'Beyond Kazaa, a grand plan: executive seeks partnership with showbiz'. *The Washington Post*, E01 6-19-03.

PART 2

INTERNATIONAL BUSINESS AND MARKETS

Operating internationally requires managers to be aware of a highly complex environment. Domestic and international environmental factors and their interaction have to be recognized and understood. In addition, ongoing changes in these environments have to be appreciated.

Part 2 delineates the macro factors and institutions affecting international business. It explains the workings of international business as well as the workings of the international monetary system and financial markets. This part includes a chapter on doing business in emerging markets.

CHAPTER 5

Financial Markets

- The Market for Currencies

- The Purpose of Exchange Rates

- Monetary Systems of the Twentieth Century

- The European Monetary System and the Euro

- International Money Markets

- International Capital Markets

- International Banking and Bank Lending

- International Security Markets

LEARNING OBJECTIVES

- To understand how currencies are traded and quoted on world financial markets.

- To examine the links between interest rates and exchange rates.

- To understand the similarities and differences between domestic sources of capital and international sources of capital.

- To examine how the needs of individual borrowers have changed the nature of the instruments traded on world financial markets in the past decade.

- To understand how the debt crises of the 1980s and 1990s are linked to the international financial markets and exchange rates.

CURRENCIES AND THE FEAR OF FLOATING

After 1945, the USA emerged from the Second World War with the world's gold reserves, the largest industrial base and a surplus of dollars backed by gold. During the 1950s and the 1960s Cold War, the US was generous to key allies such as Germany and Japan, to allow the economies of Asia and Western Europe to flourish as a counter to communism. Stability was reached by opening the US to imports from Japan and West Germany. The costly Vietnam War led to a drain of US gold reserves in the 1960s. By 1968 the drain had reached crisis levels. In August 1971, President Nixon finally broke the Bretton Woods Agreement and refused to redeem dollars for gold. He did not have enough gold to give. This situation opened a most remarkable phase of world economic history. After 1971, the dollar was fixed not to an ounce of gold, something measurable, but was fixed only to the printing presses of the US Treasury and Federal Reserve. The dollar became a political currency – do you have 'confidence' in the US as the defender of the Free World?

Currencies floated up and down against the dollar. Financial markets were slowly deregulated. Controls were lifted. Offshore banking was allowed, with unregulated hedge funds and financial derivatives.

What soon became clear to US Treasury and Federal Reserve circles after 1971 was that they could exert more global influence via debt – US Treasury debt – than they ever did by running trade surpluses. One man's debt is the other's credit. All key commodities, above all, oil, were traded globally in dollars thus demand for dollars continued, despite the fact that the US created more dollars than its own economy justified. Soon, its trade partners held so many dollars that they feared the creation of a dollar crisis. Instead, they systematically inflated and actually weakened their own economies to support the Dollar System, fearing a global collapse. The first shock came with the 1973 price increase in oil by 400%. Germany, Japan and the world was devastated, unemployment soared. The dollar gained.

This Dollar System is the real source of a global inflation that we have witnessed in Europe and worldwide since 1971. In the years between 1945 and 1965, total supply of dollars grew a total of only some 55%. Those were the golden years of low inflation and stable growth. After Nixon's break with gold, dollars expanded by more than 2000% between 1970 and 2001!

The dollar is still the only global reserve currency. This means other central banks must hold dollars as reserve to guarantee against currency crises, to back their export trade, to finance oil imports and so on. In 2008, some 67% of all central bank reserves are dollars. Gold is but a tiny share now and euros only about 15%. Until the creation of the euro, there was not even a theoretical rival to the dollar reserve currency role.

What is little understood is how the role of US trade deficits and the Dollar System are connected. The United States has followed a deliberate policy of trade deficits and budget deficits for most of the past two decades. In this way the US has locked the rest of the world into dependence on a US money system. So long as the world accepts US dollars as money value, the US enjoys unique advantage as the sole printer of those dollars. The trick is to get the world to accept it. The history of the past 30 years is about how this was done, using the WTO, the IMF and the World Bank.

What has evolved is a mechanism more effective than any the British Empire had with India and its colonies under the Gold Standard. So long as the US is the sole military superpower, the world will continue to accept inflated US dollars as payment for its goods. Countries such as Argentina, Congo or Zambia are forced to get dollars to get the IMF seal of approval. Industrial trading nations are forced to earn dollars to defend their own currencies. The total effect of the US financial, political and trade policy has been to maintain the unique role of the dollar in the world economy. It is no accident that the greatest financial centre in the world is New York. It is the core of the global Dollar System.

It works as follows: a German company, say BMW, gets dollars for its car sales in the USA. It turns the dollars over to the Bundesbank or ECB (European Central Bank) in exchange for euros it can use. The German central bank thus builds up its dollar currency reserves. Since the oil shocks of the 1970s, the need to have dollars to import oil became national security policy for most countries, Germany included. Boosting dollar exports was a national goal. But since the Bundesbank could no longer get gold for their dollars, the issue became what to do with the mountain of dollars their trade earned. They decided to at least earn an interest rate by buying safe, secure US Treasury bonds. So long as the US had a large budget deficit, there were plenty of bonds to buy.

Today, most foreign central banks hold US Treasury bonds or similar US government assets as their 'currency reserves'. They in fact hold an estimated US$1 trillion to US$1.5 trillion of US Government debt. The US economy is addicted to foreign borrowing. It is able to enjoy a far higher living standard than if it had to use its own savings to finance its consumption. America lives off the borrowed money of the rest of the world in the Dollar System. In effect, the German workers at BMW build the cars and give them away to Americans for free when the central bank uses the dollars to buy US bonds.

Today, the US trade deficit runs at an unbelievable US$500 billion and the dollar does not collapse. Why? In May and June alone, the Bank of China and Bank of Japan bought US$100 billion of US Treasury and other government debt even when the value of those bonds was falling. They did it to save their exports by manipulating the yen to dollar to prevent a rising yen.

Because the world payments system, and most importantly, the world capital markets – stocks, bonds, derivatives – are dollar markets, the dollar overwhelms all others. The European Central Bank could offer an alternative. We shall certainly wait and see if it is able to do so.

After sinking for the first half of 2003, the dollar came up for air, regaining some of its value against the euro in the second half of the year and now it is rather low again. It has plunged again, pulled under by America's huge current-account deficit. The US dollar has lost a lot of its value against the yen and many other Asian currencies although most of the Asian economies have large balance-of-payments surpluses.

The biggest dollar surplus country today is China. Globalization is in fact just a code word for dollar-ization. The Chinese Yuan is fixed to the dollar. The US is being flooded with cheap Chinese goods, often outsourced by US multinationals. China today has the largest trade surplus with the US, more than US$100 billion a year. Japan is second with US$70 billion. Canada with US$48 billion, Mexico with US$37 billion and Germany with US$36 billion make the rest of top 5 trade deficit countries, a total deficit of almost US$300 billion of the colossal US$480 deficit in 2002. This gives a clue to US foreign policy priorities.

In effect, the US has succeeded in getting foreign surplus countries to invest their own savings, to be a creditor to the US, by buying Treasury bonds. Asian countries such as Indonesia export capital to the US instead of the reverse!

Should debt be repaid? The central banks just keep buying new debt, rolling the old debts over. The debts of the USA are the assets of the rest of the world, the basis of their credit systems! The second key to the Dollar System deals with poorer debtor countries. Here the US influence is strategic in the key multilateral institutions of finance – the World Bank, the IMF and the WTO. Entire countries such as Argentina, Brazil or Indonesia are forced to devalue currencies relative to the dollar, privatize key state industries and cut subsidies, all to repay dollar debt, most often to private US banks.

If other currencies cling to the dollar, then others such as the euro will have to rise disproportionately if America's deficit is to be trimmed.

And cling they do. The Chinese yuan and the Malaysian ringgit are pegged to the dollar and protected by capital controls. The Hong Kong dollar is also tied to the US dollar through a currency board. Officially, other Asian currencies float but central banks have been intervening on a grand scale in the foreign-exchange market to hold down their currencies as the dollar has weakened.

In a free market, China's currency would surely rise. But demands from foreigners are likely to fall on deaf ears. The Chinese government is worried about rising unemployment as jobs are lost in unprofitable state companies and deflation remains an issue. And, so long as the yuan is pegged to the dollar, other Asian countries will have a big reason to resist appreciation too.

International financial markets serve as links between the financial markets of each individual country and as independent markets outside the jurisdiction of any one country. The market for currencies is the heart of this international financial market. International trade and investment are often denominated in a foreign currency, and so the purchase of the currency precedes the purchase of goods, services or assets.

This chapter provides a detailed explanation to the structure and functions of the foreign currency markets, the international money markets and the international securities markets.

Sources: Abstracted from 'Fear of Floating', *The Economist.com*, 10 July 2003; F.W. Engdahl (2006) 'Crisis of the US Dollar System', *Global Research*, 14, October.

THE MARKET FOR CURRENCIES

The market for currencies (Forex trading market) cannot actually be found physically. Instead, the market is a large network of central banks and individual investors all engaged in the process of currency exchange. Because the Forex market deals with countries all over the world, the market must remain open 24 hours a day. It follows the three markets: the United States of America, Europe and Asia. This presents a problem to even the more successful investors. It is simply not possible for any human being to stay up 24 hours a day so that they have up-to-date information on the market.

The price of any one country's currency in terms of another country's currency is called a foreign currency exchange rate. For example, the exchange rate between the US dollar ($, USD or US$) and the European euro (€ or EUR) may be '1.1478 dollars per euro', or simply abbreviated as US$1.1478/€. This is the same exchange rate as when stated 'EUR1.00 = US$ 1.1478'. Since most international business activities require at least one of the two parties to first purchase the country's currency before purchasing any good, service or asset, a proper understanding of exchange rates and exchange rate markets is very important to the conduct of international business.

A word about currency symbols: as already noted, the letters US$ and EUR or € are often used as the symbols for the US dollar and the European Union's euro. These are the computer symbols (ISO-4217 codes). The field of international finance suffers, however, from a lack of agreement when it comes to currency abbreviations. This chapter uses the more common symbols used in the financial press – US$ and € in this case. As a practitioner of international finance, however, stay on your toes. Every market, every country and every firm, may have its own set of symbols. For example, the symbol for the British pound sterling can be £ (the pound symbol), GBP (Great Britain pound), STG (British pound sterling) or ST£ (pound sterling).

Exchange Rate Quotations and Terminology

The order in which the foreign exchange rate is stated is sometimes confusing to the uninitiated. For example, when the rate between the US dollar and the European euro was stated above, US$1.1478/€, a direct quotation on the US dollar was used. This is simultaneously an indirect quotation on the European euro. The direct quote on any currency is when that currency is stated first; an indirect quotation refers to when the subject currency is stated second. Figure 5.1 illustrates both forms, direct and indirect quotations, for major world currencies for Wednesday, 23 July 2003.

Most of the quotations listed in Figure 5.1 are spot rates. A spot transaction is the exchange of currencies for immediate delivery. Although it is defined as immediate, in practice settlement actually occurs two business days following the agreed-upon exchange. The other time-related quotations listed in Figure 5.1 are the forward rates. Forward exchange rates are contracts that provide for two parties to exchange currencies on a future date at an agreed-upon exchange rate. Forwards are typically traded for the major volume currencies for maturities of 30, 90, 120, 180 and 360 days (from the present date). The forward, like the basic spot exchange, can be for any amount of currency. Forward contracts serve a variety of purposes but their primary purpose is to allow a firm to lock in a future rate of exchange. This is a valuable tool in a world of continually changing exchange rates.

The quotations listed will also occasionally indicate if the rate is applicable to business trade (the commercial rate) or for financial asset purchases or sales (the financial rate). Countries that have government regulations regarding the exchange of their currency may post official rates, while the markets operating outside their jurisdiction will list a floating rate. In this case, any exchange of currency that is not under the control of its government is interpreted as a better indication of the currency's true market value.

Direct and Indirect Quotations

The Wall Street Journal quotations (Figure 5.1) list rates of exchange between major currencies, both in direct and indirect forms. The exchange rate for the Japanese yen (¥) versus the US dollar in the third column is ¥118.89/US$. This is a direct quote on the Japanese yen and an indirect quote on the US dollar. The inverse of this spot exchange rate for the same day is listed in the first column, the direct quote on the US dollar, US$.008 411/¥. The two forms of the exchange rate are of course equal, one being the inverse of the other:[1]

$$\frac{1}{¥118.89/US\$} = US\$0.008411/¥$$

Luckily, world currency markets do follow some conventions to minimize confusion. With only a few exceptions, most currencies are quoted in direct quotes versus the US dollar (SF/US$, Baht/US$, Pesos/US$), also known as European terms. The major exceptions are currencies at one time or another associated with the British Commonwealth (including the Australian dollar) and now the

EXCHANGE RATES

The foreign exchange mid-range rates below apply to trading among banks in amounts of US$1 million and more, as quoted at 4 p.m. Eastern time by Reuters and other sources. Retail transactions provide fewer units of foreign currency per dollar.

Country	US$ Equiv.		Currency Per US$	
	Wed	Tue	Wed	Tue
Argentina (Peso)-y	0.3600	0.3594	2.7778	2.7824
Australia (Dollar)	0.6595	0.6515	1.5163	1.5349
Bahrain (Dinar)	2.6523	2.6522	0.3770	0.3770
Brazil (Real)	0.3454	0.3470	2.8952	2.8818
Canada (Dollar)	0.7153	0.7062	1.3980	1.4160
1-month forward	0.7140	0.7049	1.4006	1.4186
3-months forward	0.7120	0.7029	1.4045	1.4227
6-months forward	0.7091	0.7004	1.4102	1.4278
Chile (Peso)	0.001421	0.001420	703.73	704.23
China (Renminbi)	0.1208	0.1208	8.2781	8.2782
Colombia (Peso)	0.0003467	0.0003472	2884.34	2880.18
Czech. Rep. (Koruna)				
Commercial rate	0.03569	0.03509	28.019	28.498
Denmark (Krone)	0.1544	0.1524	6.4767	6.5617
Ecuador (US Dollar)	1.0000	1.0000	1.0000	1.0000
Egypt (Pound)-y	0.1637	0.1637	6.1099	6.1099
Hong Kong (Dollar)	0.1282	0.1282	7.8003	7.8003
Hungary (Forint)	0.004311	0.004244	231.96	235.63
India (Rupee)	0.02169	0.02169	46.104	46.104
Indonesia (Rupiah)	0.0001162	0.0001188	8606	8418
Israel (Shekel)	0.2282	0.2276	4.3821	4.3937
Japan (Yen)	0.008411	0.008394	118.89	119.13
1-month forward	0.008419	0.008403	118.78	119.01
3-months forward	0.008436	0.008418	118.54	118.79
6-months forward	0.008460	0.008443	118.20	118.44
Jordan (Dinar)	1.4104	1.4104	0.7090	0.7090
Kuwait (Dinar)	3.3371	3.3318	0.2997	0.3001
Lebanon (Pound)	0.0006634	0.0006634	1507.39	1507.39
Malaysia (Ringgit)-b	0.2632	0.2632	3.7994	3.7994
Mexico (Peso)				
Floating rate	0.0946	0.0958	10.5675	10.4341

Country	US$ Equiv.		Currency Per US$	
	Wed	Tue	Wed	Tue
New Zealand (Dollar)	0.5801	0.5755	1.7238	1.7376
Norway (Krone)	0.1377	0.1356	7.2622	7.3746
Pakistan (Rupee)	0.01732	0.01735	57.737	75.637
Peru (new Sol)	0.2880	0.2881	3.4722	3.4710
Phillippines (Peso)	0.01853	0.01860	53.967	53.763
Poland (Zloty)	0.2598	0.2560	3.8491	3.9063
Russia (Ruble)-a	0.03295	0.03296	30.349	30.340
Saudi Arabia (Riyal)	0.2667	0.2666	3.7495	3.7509
Singapore (Dollar)	0.5696	0.5692	1.7556	1.7569
Slovak Rep. (Koruna)	0.02709	0.02674	36.914	37.397
South Africa (Rand)	0.1334	0.1321	7.4963	7.5700
South Korea (Won)	0.0008468	0.0008454	1180.92	1182.87
Sweden (Krona)	0.1245	0.1222	8.0321	8.1833
Switzerland (Franc)	0.7424	0.7345	1.3470	1.3615
1-month forward	0.7430	0.7350	1.3459	1.3605
3-months forward	0.7440	0.7360	1.3441	1.3587
6-months forward	0.7454	0.7374	1.3416	1.3561
Taiwan (Dollar)	0.02911	0.02910	34.353	34.364
Thailand (Baht)	0.02379	0.02389	42.035	41.859
Turkey (Lira)	0.00000071	0.00000072	1408451	1388889
UK (Pound)	1.6083	1.5975	0.6218	0.6260
1-month forward	1.6052	1.5943	0.6230	0.6272
3-months forward	1.5990	1.5885	0.6254	0.6295
6-months forward	1.5903	1.5796	0.6288	0.6331
United Arab (Dirham)	0.2723	0.2722	3.6724	3.6738
Uruguay (Peso)				
Financial	0.03720	0.03720	26.882	26.882
Venezuela (Bolivar)	0.000626	0.000626	1597.44	1597.44
SDR	1.3951	1.3920	0.7168	0.7184
Euro	1.1478	1.1330	0.8712	0.8826

Special Drawing Rights (SDR) are based on exchange rates for the US, British and Japanese currencies.

Source: International Monetary Fund

KEY CURRENCY CROSS RATES

	Dollar	Euro	Pound	SFranc	Peso	Yen	CdnDir
Late New York Trading Wednesday, July 23, 2003							
Canada	1.3980	1.6046	2.2484	1.0379	0.13229	0.01176	••••
Japan	118.89	136.46	191.21	88.265	11.251	••••	85.043
Mexico	10.5675	12.1293	16.996	7.8453	••••	0.08888	7.5589
Switzerland	1.347	1.5461	2.1664	••••	0.12746	0.01133	0.9635
UK	0.62180	0.7137	••••	0.4616	0.05884	0.00523	0.44476
Euro	0.87120	••••	1.4012	0.64680	0.08244	0.00733	0.62319
US	••••	1.1478	1.6083	0.74240	0.09463	0.00841	0.71530

Source: Reuters

Figure 5.1: Exchange rate and cross rate tables.

Source: The Wall Street Journal, Thursday, 24 July 2003. Eastern Edition (staff produced copy only) by The Wall Street Journal. Copyright 2003 by Dow Jones & Co. Inc.

European euro. These currencies are customarily quoted as US dollars per pound sterling or US dollars per Australian dollar, known as **American terms**. Once again, it makes no real difference whether you quote US dollars per Japanese yen or Japanese yen per US dollar, as long as you know which is being used for the transaction.

Figure 5.2, the foreign currency quotations from the *Financial Times* of London, provides wider coverage of the world's currencies, including many of the lesser-known and traded. The quotes shown in the figure are for 19 July 2003.

Cross Rates

Although it is common among exchange traders worldwide to quote currency values against the US dollar, it is not necessary. Any currency's value can be stated in terms of any other currency. When the exchange rate of a currency is stated without using the US dollar as a reference, it is referred to as a **cross rate**. For example, if the Japanese yen and European euro are both quoted versus the US dollar, they would appear as ¥118.89/US$ and US$1.1478/€. But if the ¥/€ cross rate is needed, it is simply a matter of multiplication:

$$¥118.89/US\$ \times US\$1.1478/€ = ¥136.46/€$$

The yen per euro cross rate of 136.46 is the third leg of the triangle of currencies, which must be true if the first two exchange rates are known. If one of the exchange rates changes due to market forces, the others must adjust for the three exchange rates again to align. If they are out of alignment, it would be possible to make a profit simply by exchanging one currency for a second, the second for a third and the third back to the first. This is known as **triangular arbitrage**. Besides the potential profitability of arbitrage that may occasionally occur, cross rates have become increasingly common in a world of rapidly expanding trade and investment.

Percentage Change Calculations

The quotation form is important when calculating the percentage change in an exchange rate. For example, if the spot rate between the Japanese yen and the US dollar changed from ¥125/US$ to ¥150/US$, the percentage change in the value of the Japanese yen is:

$$\frac{¥125/US\$ - ¥150/US\$}{¥150/US\$} \times 100 = -16.67\%$$

The Japanese yen has declined in value versus the US dollar by 16.67%. This is consistent with the intuition that it now requires more yen (150) to buy a dollar than it used to (125).

The same percentage change result can be achieved by using the inverted forms of the same spot rates (indirect quotes on the Japanese yen), if care is taken to also 'invert' the basic percentage change calculation. Using the inverse of ¥125/US$ (US$0.0080/¥) and the inverse of ¥150/US$ (US$0.0067/¥), the percentage change is still −16.67%:

$$\frac{US\$0.0067/¥ - US\$0.0080/US\$}{US\$0.0080/¥} \times 100 = -16.67\%$$

If the percentage changes calculated are not identical, it is normally the result of rounding errors introduced when inverting the spot rates. Both methods are identical, however, when calculated properly.

CURRENCY RATES

Jul 18	Currency	Dollar Closing mid	Dollar Day's change	Euro Closing mid	Euro Day's change	Pound Closing mid	Pound Day's change
Argentina	(Peso)	2.8050	+0.0200	3.1451	+0.0305	4.4429	+0.0138
Australia	(A$)	1.5511	+0.0181	1.7392	+0.0247	2.4569	+0.0188
One Month		–	–	1.7431	+0.0248	2.4598	+0.0188
One Year		–	–	1.7837	+0.0253	2.4897	+0.0192
Bahrain	(Dinar)	0.3770	–	0.4228	+0.0011	0.5972	−0.0024
Bolivia	(Boliviano)	7.6792	–	8.6104	+0.0223	12.1636	−0.0491
Brazil	(R$)	2.8750	+0.0135	3.2236	+0.0234	4.5539	+0.0031
Canada	(C$)	1.4106	+0.0151	1.5817	+0.0211	2.2344	+0.0151
One Month		1.413	+0.0151	1.5829	+0.0211	2.2338	+0.0150
Three Month		1.4173	+0.0151	1.5848	+0.0209	2.232	+0.0147
One Year		1.4331	+0.0144	1.5922	+0.0201	2.2224	+0.0136
Chile	(Peso)	701.050	+2.8000	786.052	+5.1640	1110.43	−0.0300
Colombia	(Peso)	2883.60	−5.58	3233.12	+2.12	4567.32	−27.32
Costa Rica	(Colon)	400.920	+0.1700	449.552	+1.3930	635.037	−2.2960
Czech Rep.	(Koruna)	28.6064	+0.0755	32.0750	+0.1675	45.3113	−0.0628
One Month		28.6347	+0.0757	32.0777	+0.1679	45.2687	−0.0624
One Year		28.8974	+0.0770	32.1047	+0.1683	44.811	−0.6000
Denmark	(DKr)	6.8304	−0.0182	7.4343	−0.0012	10.5022	−0.0715
One Month		6.6364	−0.0180	7.4342	−0.0011	10.4914	−0.0711
Three Month		6.6473	−0.0181	7.4333	−0.0010	10.4688	−0.0713
One Year		6.6929	−0.0171	7.4357	+0.0001	10.3786	−0.0685
Egypt	(Egypt £)	6.1487	–	6.8943	+0.0178	9.7393	−0.0394
Estonia	(Kroon)	13.9534	−0.0377	15.6453	−0.0017	22.1015	−0.1493
Hong Kong	(HK$)	7.7992	−0.0001	8.7449	+0.0224	12.3536	−0.0501
One Month		7.7999	−0.0001	8.7378	+0.0226	12.3309	−0.0500
Three Month		7.8012	–	8.7238	+0.0227	12.2863	−0.0499
One Year		7.8154	−0.0004	8.6829	+0.0220	12.1193	−0.0494
Hungary	(Forint)	236.955	+0.1200	265.686	+0.8220	375.325	−1.3260
One Month		238.79	+0.2300	267.5016	+0.9519	377.503	−1.1590
One Year		253.55	−0.8200	281.6909	−0.1814	393.177	−2.8570
India	(Rs)	48.2400	−0.0200	51.8466	+0.1564	73.2418	−0.2641
One Month		46.3613	+0.0238	51.9356	+0.1614	73.2924	−0.2582
One Year		47.2825	+0.0325	52.5302	+0.1716	73.3203	−0.2441
Indonesia	(Rupiah)	8330.00	+71.50	9340.01	+104.12	13194.30	+60.40
One Month		–	–	9331.58	+104.13	13168.88	+60.33
One Year		–	–	9254.52	+103.12	12917.22	+59.40
Iran	(Rial)	8230.00	–	9228.30	+24.69	13035.90	−52.70
Israel	(Shk)	4.4350	+0.0050	4.9728	+0.0185	7.0248	0.0205
Japan	(Y)	118.905	+0.1500	133.322	+0.5120	188.340	−0.5220
One Month		188.78	+0.1450	133.0615	+0.5034	187.78	−0.5320
Three Month		118.56	+0.1450	132.5816	+0.5097	186.725	−0.5220
One Year		117.495	+0.1700	130.5354	+0.5276	182.2	0.4620
Kenya	(Shilling)	75.0500	+0.3000	84.1499	+0.5532	118.876	−0.0030
Kuwait	(Dinar)	0.3004	+0.0002	0.3368	+0.0010	0.4758	−0.0016
One Month		0.3008	+0.0002	0.3369	+0.0011	0.4754	−0.0016
One Year		0.3036	+0.0005	0.3373	+0.0014	0.4708	−0.0010
Malaysia	(M$)	3.8000	–	4.2608	+0.0110	6.0190	−0.0243
Mexico	(New Peso)	10.3605	+0.0115	11.6167	+0.0429	16.4105	−0.0480
One Month		10.3949	+0.0111	11.6448	+0.0427	16.4333	−0.0487
Three Month		10.479	+0.0113	11.7182	+0.0432	16.5033	−0.0492
One Year		10.9438	−0.0002	12.1584	+0.0312	16.9704	−0.0684
New Zealand	(NZ$)	1.7527	+0.0343	1.9652	+0.0435	2.7762	+0.0434
One Month		–	–	1.9703	+0.0437	2.7805	+0.0435
One Year		–	–	2.0231	+0.0459	2.8238	−0.0458
Nigeria	(Naira)	129.750	−0.1000	145.482	+0.2640	205.518	−0.9890
Norway	(NKr)	7.4198	−0.0580	8.3195	−0.0433	11.7526	−0.1397
One Month		7.4376	−0.0579	8.3318	−0.0431	11.758	−0.1395
Three Month		7.4635	−0.0577	8.3461	−0.0425	11.7542	−0.1390
One Year		7.5726	−0.0562	8.4131	−0.0405	11.7427	−0.1347
Pakistan	(Rupee)	57.6900	−0.0600	64.6850	+0.1002	91.3781	−0.4646
Peru	(New Sol)	3.4684	−0.0011	3.8890	+0.0088	5.4939	−0.0239
Phillipines	(Peso)	53.7250	+0.1500	60.2392	+0.3236	85.0978	−0.1053
One Month		53.9835	+0.1460	60.4744	+0.3203	85.3425	−0.1129
Three Month		54.5655	+0.1520	61.0180	+0.3282	85.9353	−0.1089

Jul 18	Currency	Dollar Closing mid	Dollar Day's change	Euro Closing mid	Euro Day's change	Pound Closing mid	Pound Day's change
One Year		57.353	+0.1865	63.7185	+0.3712	88.9367	−0.0671
Poland	(Zloty)	3.9824	−0.0226	4.4653	−0.0138	6.3080	−0.0615
One Month		3.9968	−0.0225	4.4773	−0.0136	6.3185	−0.0614
One Year		4.1321	−0.0229	4.5907	−0.0136	6.4076	−0.0615
Romania	(Leu)	32764.00	+21.50	36736.60	+119.00	51896.50	−175.50
Russia	(Rouble)	30.4252	−0.0198	34.1143	+0.0661	48.1920	−0.2262
Saudi Arabia	(SR)	3.7502	−0.0001	4.2050	+0.0108	5.9402	−0.0241
One Month		3.7518	−0.0002	4.2029	+0.0107	5.9313	−0.0242
One Year		3.7668	−0.0005	4.1849	+0.0103	5.8412	−0.0241
Singapore	(S$)	1.7632	+0.0019	1.9770	+0.0072	2.7929	−0.0081
One Month		1.7627	+0.0020	1.9746	+0.0073	2.7866	−0.0081
One Year		1.7566	+0.0021	1.9515	+0.0074	2.7239	−0.0076
Slovakia	(Koruna)	37.6187	+0.2154	42.1800	+0.3500	59.5862	+0.1018
One Month		37.7852	+0.2154	42.3285	+0.3507	59.7346	+0.1007
One Year		39.3812	+0.2739	43.7521	+0.4166	61.068	+0.1810
Slovenia	(Tolar)	109.160	−0.5050	234.521	+0.0420	331.299	−2.1420
South Africa	(R)	7.6825	−0.0437	8.6140	−0.0266	12.1686	−0.1188
One Month		7.7548	−0.0439	8.6871	−0.0266	12.2594	−0.1194
Three Month		7.881	−0.0452	8.8129	−0.0276	12.4116	−0.1221
One Year		8.3415	−0.0472	9.2672	−0.0285	12.9349	−0.1256
South Korea	(Won)	1182.55	+3.55	1325.93	+7.40	1873.10	−1.92
One Month		1185.70	+3.55	1328.27	+7.42	1874.47	−1.93
Three Month		1191.75	+3.50	1332.68	+7.37	1876.89	−2.09
One Year		1213.30	+2.55	1347.96	+6.30	1881.45	−3.59
Sweden	(SKr)	8.2541	−0.0077	9.2550	−0.0154	13.0742	−0.0650
One Month		8.2668	−0.0075	9.2608	+0.0157	13.069	−0.0647
Three Month		8.2896	−0.0077	9.2700	+0.0157	13.0555	−0.0649
One Year		8.3896	−0.0057	9.3208	+0.0178	13.0097	−0.0612
Switzerland	(SFr)	1.3707	−0.0041	1.5369	−0.0007	2.1711	−0.0154
One Month		1.3697	−0.0041	1.5344	−0.0006	2.1654	−0.0154
Three Month		1.3679	−0.0041	1.5296	−0.0007	2.1542	−0.154
One Year		1.3601	−0.0040	1.5111	−0.0005	2.1092	−0.148
Taiwan	(T$)	34.4700	+0.0400	38.6495	+0.1447	54.5988	−0.1569
One Month		34.425	+0.0275	38.5642	+0.1309	54.4224	−0.1760
One Year		34.085	+0.0250	37.8680	+0.1255	52.8552	−0.1734
Thailand	(Bt)	41.7500	+0.0700	46.8122	+0.1993	66.1299	−0.1559
One Month		41.752	+0.0700	46.7722	+0.1997	66.0057	−0.1554
One Year		41.825	+0.0700	46.4781	+0.1975	64.873	−0.1518
Tunisia	(Dinar)	1.2979	−0.0015	1.4553	+0.0021	2.0559	−0.0106
Turkey	(Lira)	1403500	+25500	1573675	+32588	2223074	+31572
UAE	(Dirham)	3.6730	−0.0001	4.1184	+0.0106	5.8178	−0.0237
One Month		3.6731	−0.0001	4.1147	+0.0105	5.8178	−0.0236
One Year		3.6755	−0.0001	4.0834	+0.0104	5.6995	−0.0231
UK (0.6313)*	(£)	1.5840	−0.0063	0.7079	+0.0047	–	–
One Month		1.581	−0.0062	0.7086	+0.0047	–	–
Three Month		1.575	−0.0063	0.7100	+0.0047	–	–
One Year		1.5508	−0.0061	0.7165	+0.0048	–	–
Uruguay	(Peso)	26.7650	+0.0500	30.0103	+0.1335	42.3944	−0.0918
USA	($)	–	–	1.1213	+0.0029	1.5840	−0.0063
One Month		–	–	1.1202	+0.0029	1.581	−0.0062
Three Month		–	–	1.1183	+0.0029	1.575	−0.0063
One Year		–	–	1.1110	+0.0029	1.5508	−0.0061
Venezuela	(Bolivar)	1598.00	–	1791.76	+4.64	2531.15	−10.23
Vietnam	(Dong)	15513.00	−2.00	17394.00	+42.80	24571.80	−102.50
Euro (0.8918)*	(Euro)	1.1213	+0.0030	–	–	1.4126	−0.0094
One Month		1.1203	+0.0030	–	–	1.4112	−0.0093
Three Month		1.1183	+0.0030	–	–	1.4083	−0.0094
One Year		1.111	+0.0030	–	–	1.3957	−0.0092
SDR		–	0.72090	–	0.80835	+0.0019	1.141900	–

*The closing mid-point rates for the Euro and £ against the US$ are shown in brackets. The other figures in the dollar column of both the Euro and Sterling rows are in the reciprocal form in line with market convention. †Floating rate now shown for Argentina. ‡Official rate set by Malaysian government. The WM/Reuters rate for the valuation of capital assets is 3.80 MYR/US$. Rates are derived from the WM/REUTERS 4pm (London time) CLOSINGSPOT and FORWARD RATE services. Some values are rounded by the F.T. The exchange rates printed in this table are also available on the Internet at http://www.FT.com.

Euro Locking Rates: Austrian Schilling 13.7603. Belgium/Luxembourg Franc 40.3399, Finnish Markha 5.94573, French Franc 6.55957, German Mark 1.95583, Greek Drachma 340.75, Irish Punt 0.787564, Italian Lira 1936.27, Netherlands Guilder 2.20371, Portuguese Escudo 200.482, Spanish Peseta 166.386.

Figure 5.2: Guide to world currencies.

Source: Financial Times, 19/20 July 2003, 16. Reproduced by permission of the Financial Times.

Foreign Currency Market Structure

The market for foreign currencies is a worldwide market that is informal in structure. This means that it has no central place, pit or floor, like the floor of the New York Stock Exchange, where the trading takes place. The 'market' is actually the thousands of telecommunications links among financial institutions around the globe and it is open nearly 24 hours a day. Someone, somewhere, is nearly always open for business. Figure 5.3 illustrates how the trading day moves with the sun for the four largest trading centres – Tokyo, Singapore, London and New York. As described in the Focus on e-Commerce on page 130, trading is also moving to the Internet.

For example, Table 5.1 reproduces a computer screen from one of the major international financial information news sources, Reuters. This is the spot exchange screen, called FXFX, which is

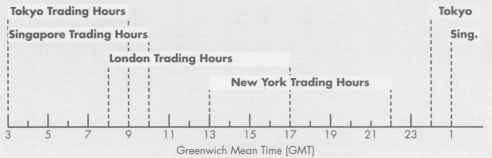

Currency trading takes place *nearly* 24 hours a day – around the globe. The trading day for the four largest city trading centres begins in Tokyo, with Singapore opening one hour later at 1:00 GMT. London, the centre of the international financial markets, opens at 8:00 GMT, followed by New York at 13:00 GMT.

Figure 5.3: Global currency trading: the trading day.

Source: Based on data found at http://www.currenex.com/efx/efx.shtml?efx&.

13:07	CCY	Page	Name	Reuters Spot Rates	CCY	HI euro	Lo FXFX
13.06	GBP	AIBN	AL IRISH	N.Y.	1.7653/63 * GBP	1.7710	1.7630
13.06	CHF	CITX	CITIBANK	ZUR	1.5749/56 * CHF	1.5750	1.5665
13.06	JPY	CHNY	CHEMICAL	N.Y.	128.53/58 * JPY	128.70	128.23
13.02	XEV	PRBX	PRIVAT	COP	1.1259/68 * XEV	1.1304	1.1255

Column 1: Time of entry of the latest quote to the nearest minute (British Standard time).
Column 2: Currency of quotation (bilateral with the US dollar); quotes are currency per US$, except for the British pound sterling (dollars per unit of pound) and the European Currency Unit (dollars per unit of XEV). The currency symbols are as follows: GBP – British pound sterling; CHF – Swiss franc; JPY – Japanese yen; XEV – European Currency Unit.
Column 3: Mnemonic of inputting bank. Allows the individual trader to dial up the correct page (by this mnemonic) where the trader can see the full set of spot and forward quotes for this and other currencies being offered by this bank.
Column 4: Name of the inputting bank.
Column 5: Branch location of that bank from which the quote has emanated (so that an inquiring trader can telephone the correct branch); N.Y. – New York; ZUR – Zurich; LDN – London.
Column 6: Spot exchange rate quotation, bid quote, then offer quote.
Column 7: Recent high price for this specific quote.
Column 8: Recent low price for this specific quote.

Source: Adapted from C. A. E. Goodhart and L. Figliuoli (1991) 'Every Minute Counts in Financial Markets', *Journal of International Money and Finance*, 10, 23–52, reproduced with permission from Elsevier

Table 5.1: Typical foreign currency quotations on a Reuters screen.

available to all subscribers to the Reuters news network. The screen serves as a bulletin board, where all financial institutions wanting to buy or sell foreign currencies can post representative prices. Although the rates quoted on these computer screens are indicative of current prices, the buyer is still referred to the individual bank for the latest quotation due to the rapid movement of rates worldwide. There are also hundreds of banks operating in the markets at any moment that are not listed on the brief sample of Reuters FXFX page.[2] The speed with which this market moves, the multitude of players playing on a field that is open 24 hours a day and the circumference of the earth with its time and day differences produce many different 'single prices'. The Focus on Culture on page 130 illustrates how trading occurs between traders themselves.

Market Size and Composition

Until recently there was little data on the actual volume of trading on world foreign currency markets. Starting in the spring of 1986, however, the Federal Reserve Bank of New York, along with other major industrial countries' central banks through the auspices of the Bank for International Settlements (BIS), started surveying the activity of currency trading every three years. Some of the principal results are shown in Figure 5.4.

Growth in foreign currency trading has been nothing less than astronomical. The survey results for the month of April 1998 indicate that daily foreign currency trading on world markets exceeded US$1 500 000 000 000 (a trillion with a *t*). In comparison, the annual (not daily) US government budget deficit has never exceeded US$300 billion and the US merchandise trade deficit has never topped US$200 billion.

The majority of the world's trading in foreign currencies is still taking place in the cities where international financial activity is centred: London, New York and Tokyo. A recent survey by the US

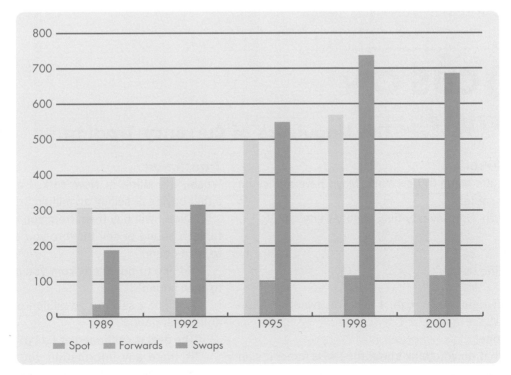

Figure 5.4: Global foreign exchange market turnover (daily averages in April, billions of US dollars).

Source: Bank for International Settlements, 'Central Bank Survey of Foreign Exchange and Derivatives Market Activity in April 2001', October 2001, www.bis.org.

Federal Reserve of currency trading by financial institutions and independent brokers in New York reveals additional information of interest. Approximately 66% of currency trading occurs between 1 p.m. and 5 p.m. (Greenwich Mean Time), with 29% between 5 p.m. and 9 p.m. and the remaining 5% between 9 p.m. and 8 a.m. the next day.

FOCUS ON

E-BUSINESS · Online Global Currency Exchange

Currenex, Inc. is the first independent and open online global currency exchange, linking institutional buyers and sellers worldwide. Operational today, Currenex's Internet-based service, Fxtrades, provides banks, corporate treasury departments, institutional funds/asset managers, government agencies, international organizations and central banks instant access to the US$1 trillion daily global foreign exchange market through multiple price discovery mechanisms on an open, impartial exchange.

Fxtrades is a real-time FX marketplace that provides secure and comprehensive FX trading from initiation and execution to settlement and reporting. As members in the Currenex exchange, CFOs, treasurers and fund managers can approach currency transactions knowing that they are able to secure the most competitive bid while improving operational efficiencies, increasing productivity and providing tight integration with back office operations.

Currenex, founded in 1999, has major multinational members including MasterCard International and Intel Corporation, as well as more than 25 global market-making banks, among them ABN Amro, Barclays Capital and Merrill Lynch.

Source: www.currenex.com.

FOCUS ON

CULTURE · The Linguistics of Currency Trading

Conversation

'Yoshi, it's Maria in New York. May I have a price on twenty cable?'

'Sure. One seventy-five, twenty-thirty'.

'Mine twenty'.

'All right. At 1.7530, I sell you twenty million pounds'.

'Done'.

'What do you think about the Swiss franc? It's up 100 pips'.

Translation

'Yoshi, it's Maria in New York. I am interested in either buying or selling 20 million British pounds'.

'Sure. I will buy them from you at 1.7520 dollars to each pound or sell them to you at 1.7530 dollars to each pound'.

'I'd like to buy them from you at 1.7530 dollars to each pound'.

'All right. I sell you 20 million pounds at 1.7530 dollars per pound'.

'The deal is confirmed at 1.7530'.

'Is there any information you can share with me about the fact that the Swiss franc has risen one one-hundredth of a franc against the US dollar in the past hour?'

'I saw that. A few German banks have been buying steadily all day. . .'.

'Yes, German banks have been buying Swiss francs all day, causing the price to rise a little. . .'.

Source: Adapted from Adam Gonelli (1993) *The Basics of Foreign Trade and Exchange*, The Federal Reserve Bank of New York, Public Information Department.

Three reasons typically given for the enormous growth in foreign currency trading are as follows:

- ***Deregulation of International Capital Flows:*** it is easier than ever to move currencies and capital around the world without major governmental restrictions. Much of the deregulation that has characterized government policy over the past 10 to 15 years in the United States, Japan and the European Union has focused on financial deregulation.
- ***Gains in Technology and Transaction Cost Efficiency:*** it is faster, easier and cheaper to move millions of dollars, yen or euros around the world than ever before. Technological advancements, not only in the dissemination of information but also in the conduct of exchange or trading, have added greatly to the ability of individuals working in these markets to conduct instantaneous arbitrage (some would say speculation).
- ***The World Is a Risky Place:*** many argue that the financial markets have become increasingly volatile over recent years, with larger and faster swings in financial variables such as stock values and interest rates adding to the motivations for moving more capital at faster rates.

THE PURPOSE OF EXCHANGE RATES

If countries are to trade, they must be able to exchange currencies. To buy wheat or corn or DVD recorders, the buyer must first have the currency in which the product is sold. A French firm purchasing consumer electronic products manufactured in Japan must first exchange its euros for Japanese yen, and then purchase the products. And each country has its own currency.[3] The exchange of one country's currency for another should be a relatively simple transaction, but it is not.

What Is a Currency Worth?

At what rate should one currency be exchanged for another currency? For example, what should the exchange rate be between the US dollar and the Japanese yen? The simplest answer is that the exchange rate should equalize purchasing power. For example, if the price of a movie ticket in the United States is US$6, the 'correct' exchange rate would be one that exchanges US$6 for the amount of Japanese yen it would take to purchase a movie ticket in Japan. If ticket prices are ¥540 in Japan, the exchange rate that would equalize purchasing power would be:

$$\frac{¥540}{US\$6} = ¥90/US\$$$

Therefore, if the exchange rate between the two currencies is ¥90/US$, the cinemagoer can purchase a ticket regardless of which country he or she is in. This is the theory of purchasing power parity (PPP), generally considered the definition of what exchange rates ideally should be. The purchasing power parity exchange rate is simply the rate that equalizes the price of the identical product or service in two different currencies:

Price in Japan = Exchange rate × Price in US

If the price of the same product in each currency is $P^{\yen}$ and $P^{\$}$ and the spot exchange rate between the Japanese yen and the US dollar is $S^{\yen/\$}$, the price in yen is simply the price in dollars multiplied by the spot exchange rate:

$$P^{\yen} = S^{\yen/\$} \times P^{\$}$$

If this is re-arranged (dividing both sides by $P^{\$}$), the spot exchange rate between the Japanese yen and the US dollar is the ratio of the two product prices:

$$\frac{P^{\yen}}{S^{\yen/\$}} = P^{\$}$$

These prices could be the price of just one good or service, such as the cinema ticket mentioned previously, or they could be price indices for each country that cover many different goods and services. Either form is an attempt to find comparable products in different countries (and currencies) in order to determine an exchange rate based on purchasing power parity. The question then is whether this logical approach to exchange rates actually works in practice.

The Law of One Price

The version of purchasing power parity that estimates the exchange rate between two currencies using just one good or service as a measure of the proper exchange for all goods and services is called the Law of One Price. To apply the theory to actual prices across countries, we need to select a product that is identical in quality and content in every country. To be truly theoretically correct, we would want such a product to be produced entirely domestically, so that there are no import factors in its construction.

Where would one find such a perfect product? McDonald's. Table 5.2 presents what *The Economist* magazine calls 'the golden-arches standard'. What it provides is a product that is essentially the same the world over and is produced and consumed entirely domestically.

The Big Mac Index compares the actual exchange rate with the exchange rate implied by the purchasing power parity measurement of comparing Big Mac prices across countries. For example, using the Big Mac prices quoted in Table 5.2, the average price of a Big Mac in the United States on a specific date was US$2.71. On that same date, the price of a Big Mac in Mexico, in pesos, was Peso23.00. These relative Big Mac prices are then used to calculate the implied purchasing power parity exchange rate between the two currencies:

$$\frac{\text{Peso23.00}}{\text{US\$2.71}} = \text{Peso8.4871/US\$}$$

The exchange rate between the Mexican peso and the US dollar should be – according to purchasing power parity theory – Peso8.4871/US$ (or Peso8.49/US$ rounded to two decimal places as in Table 5.2). The actual exchange rate in the marketplace on that date was Peso10.53/US$. This means that the *market* valued a dollar at 10.53 pesos, when the *theory* valued the dollar at 8.49 pesos. Therefore, if one is to believe the Big Mac Index, the Mexican peso was undervalued by 19%.

MONETARY SYSTEMS OF THE TWENTIETH CENTURY

The mixed fixed/floating exchange rate system operating today is only the latest stage of a continuing process of change. The systems that have preceded the present system varied between gold-based standards (*The Gold Standard*) and complex systems in which the US dollar

	Big Mac prices		Implied PPP[a] of the Dollar	Actual Dollar Exchange Rate 22 April 22nd	Under(−)/Over (+) Valuation Against the Dollar (%)
	In Local Currency	In Dollars			
United States[b]	US$2.71	2.71			
Argentina	Peso 4.10	1.43	1.51	2.88	−47
Australia	A$3.00	1.86	1.11	1.61	−31
Brazil	Real 4.55	1.48	1.68	3.07	−45
Britain	£1.99	3.14	1.36[c]	1.58[c]	+16
Canada	C$3.20	2.21	1.18	1.45	−18
Chile	Peso 1400	1.95	517	716	−28
China	Yuan 9.90	1.20	3.65	8.28	−56
Czech Rep	Koruna 56.57	1.96	20.9	28.9	−28
Denmark	DKr27.75	4.10	10.2	6.78	+51
Egypt	Pound 8.00	1.35	2.95	5.92	−50
Euro area	€2.71	2.97	1.00[d]	1.10[d]	+10
Hong Kong	HK$11.50	1.47	4.24	7.80	−46
Hungary	Forint 490	2.18	181	224	−19
Indonesia	Rupiah 16 100	1.84	5941	8740	−32
Japan	¥262	2.19	96.7	120	−19
Malaysia	M$5.04	1.33	1.86	3.80	−51
Mexico	Peso 23.00	2.18	8.49	10.53	−19
New Zealand	NZ$3.95	2.21	1.46	1.78	−18
Peru	New Sol 7.90	2.29	2.92	3.46	−16
Philippines	Peso 65.00	1.24	24.0	52.5	−54
Poland	Zloty 6.30	1.62	2.32	3.89	−40
Russia	Rouble 41.00	1.32	15.1	31.1	−51
Singapore	S$3.30	1.86	1.22	1.78	−31
South Africa	Rand 13.95	1.84	5.15	7.56	−32
South Korea	Won 3300	2.71	1218	1220	nil
Sweden	SKr30.00	3.60	11.1	8.34	+33
Switzerland	SFr6.30	4.59	2.32	1.37	+69
Taiwan	NT$70.00	2.01	25.8	34.8	−26
Thailand	Baht 59.00	1.38	21.8	42.7	−49
Turkey	Lira 3 750 000	2.34	1 383 764	1 600 500	−14
Venezuela	Bolivar 3700	2.32	1365	1598	−15

[a]Purchasing power parity: local price divided by price in United States.
[b]Average of New York, Chicago, San Francisco and Atlanta.
[c]Dollars per pound.
[d]Dollars per euro.

Table 5.2: The hamburger standard.

largely took the place of gold (*The Bretton Woods Agreement*). To understand why the dollar, the euro and the yen are floating today, it is necessary to return to the (pardon the pun) *golden oldies*.

The Gold Standard

Although there is no recognized starting date, the gold standard as we call it today began sometime in the 1880s and extended up through the outbreak of the First World War. **The gold standard** was premised on three basic ideas:

- a system of fixed rates of exchange existed between participating countries;
- 'money' issued by member countries had to be backed by reserves of gold;
- gold would act as an automatic adjustment, flowing in and out of countries and automatically altering the gold reserves of that country if imbalances in trade or investment did occur.

Under the gold standard, each country's currency would be set in value per ounce of gold. For example, the US dollar was defined as US$20.67 per ounce, while the British pound sterling was defined as £4.2474 per ounce. Once each currency was defined versus gold, the determination of the exchange rate between the two currencies (or any two currencies) was simple:

$$\frac{\text{US\$20.57/ounce of gold}}{\text{£4.2474/ounce of gold}} = \text{US\$4.8665/£}$$

The use of gold as the pillar of the system was a result of historical tradition and not anything inherently unique to the metal gold itself. It was shiny, soft, rare and generally acceptable for payment in all countries.

The Inter-war Years, 1919–1939

The 1920s and 1930s were a tumultuous period for the international monetary system. The British pound sterling, the dominant currency prior to the First World War, survived the war but was greatly weakened. The US dollar returned to the gold standard in 1919 but gold convertibility was largely untested across countries throughout the 1920s, as world trade took a long time to recover from the destruction of the war. With the economic collapse and bank runs of the 1930s, the US was forced to once again abandon gold convertibility.

The economic depression of the 1930s was worldwide. As all countries came under increasingly desperate economic conditions, many countries resorted to isolationist policies and protectionism. World trade slowed to a trickle and with it the general need for currency exchange. It was not until the latter stages of the Second World War that international trade and commerce once again demanded a system for currency convertibility and stability.

The Bretton Woods Agreement, 1944–1971

The governments of 44 of the Allied Powers gathered together in Bretton Woods, New Hampshire, USA, in 1944 to plan for the post-war international monetary system. The British delegation, headed by Lord John Maynard Keynes, the famous economist, and the US delegation, headed by Secretary of the Treasury Henry Morgenthau Jr. and director of the Treasury's monetary research department, Harry D. White, laboured long and hard to reach an agreement. In the end, all parties agreed that a post-war system would be stable and sustainable only if it was able to provide sufficient liquidity to countries during periods of crisis. Any new system had to have facilities for the extension of credit for countries to defend their currency values.

After weeks of debate, the Bretton Woods Agreement was reached. The plan called for the following:

- fixed exchange rates between member countries, termed an 'adjustable peg';
- establishment of a fund of gold and currencies available to members for stabilization of their respective currencies (the *International Monetary Fund*);
- establishment of a bank that would provide funding for long-term development projects (the *World Bank*).

Like the gold standard at the turn of the century, all participants were to establish par values of their currencies in terms of gold. Unlike the prior system, however, there was little if any convertibility of currencies for gold expected; convertibility was versus the US dollar ('good as gold'). In fact, the only currency officially convertible to gold was the US dollar (pegged at US$35/ounce). It was this reliance on the value of the dollar and the reliance on the economic stability of the US economy, in fact, which led to 25 years of relatively stable currency and to the system's eventual collapse.

Times of Crisis, 1971–1973

On 15 August, 1971, President Richard Nixon of the United States announced that 'I have instructed [Treasury] Secretary [John B.] Connally to suspend temporarily the convertibility of the dollar into gold or other assets'. With this simple statement, President Nixon effectively ended the fixed exchange rates established at Bretton Woods more than 25 years earlier.

In the weeks and months following the August announcement, world currency markets devalued the dollar, although the United States had only ended gold convertibility, not officially declared the dollar's value to be less. In late 1971, the Group of Ten finance ministers met at the Smithsonian Institution in Washington DC to try to piece together a system to keep world markets operational. First, the dollar was officially devalued to US$38/ounce of gold (as if anyone had access to gold convertibility). Second, all other major world currencies were revalued against the dollar (the dollar was relatively devalued) and all would now be allowed to vary from their fixed parity rates by plus/minus 2.25% from the previous 1.00%.

Without convertibility of at least one of the member currencies to gold, the system was doomed from the start. Within weeks, currencies were surpassing their allowed deviation limits; revaluations were occurring more frequently; and the international monetary system was not a 'system', it was chaos. Finally, world currency trading nearly ground to a halt in March 1973. The world's currency markets closed for two weeks. When they re-opened, major currencies (particularly the US dollar) were simply allowed to float in value. In January 1976, the Group of Ten once again met, this time in Jamaica and the Jamaica Agreement officially recognized what the markets had known for years – the world's currencies were no longer fixed in value.

Floating Exchange Rates, 1973–Present

Since March 1973, the world's major currencies have floated in value versus each other. This flotation poses many problems for the conduct of international trade and commerce, problems that are themselves the subject of entire courses of study (*currency risk management* for one). The inability of a country, a country's government to be specific, to control the value of its currency on world markets has been a harsh reality for most.

Throughout the 1970s, if a government wished to alter the current value of its currency or even slow or alter a trending change in the currency's value, the government would simply buy or sell its own currency in the market using its reserves of other major currencies. This process of direct intervention was effective as long as the depth of the government's reserve pockets kept up with the volume of trading on currency markets. For these countries – both then and today – the primary problem is maintaining adequate foreign exchange reserves.

By the 1980s, however, the world's currency markets were so large that the ability of a few governments (the United States, Japan and Germany to name three) to move a market simply through direct intervention was over. The major tool now left was for government (at least when operating alone) to alter economic variables such as interest rates to alter the *motivations* and *expectations* of market participants for capital movements and currency exchange. During periods of relative low inflation (a critical assumption), a country that wishes to strengthen its currency versus others might raise domestic interest rates to attract capital from abroad. Although relatively effective in many cases, the downside of this policy is that it raises interest rates for domestic consumers and investors alike, possibly slowing the domestic economy. The result is that governments today must often choose between an external economic policy action (raising interest rates to strengthen the currency) and a domestic economic policy action (lowering interest rates to stimulate economic activity).

There is, however, one other method of currency value management that has been selectively employed in the past 15 years, termed co-ordinated intervention. After the US dollar had risen in value dramatically over the 1980 to 1985 period, the Group of Five, or G5, nations (France, Japan, West Germany, United States and United Kingdom) met at the Plaza Hotel in New York in September 1985 and agreed to a set of goals and policies, the Plaza Agreement. These goals were to be accomplished through co-ordinated intervention among the central banks of the major nations. By the Bank of Japan (Japan), the Bundesbank (Germany) and the Federal Reserve (United States) all simultaneously intervening in the currency markets, they hoped to reach the combined strength level necessary to push the dollar's value down. Their actions met with some success in that instance, but there have been few occasions since then of co-ordinated intervention.

THE EUROPEAN MONETARY SYSTEM AND THE EURO

In the week following the suspension of dollar convertibility to gold in 1971, the finance ministers of a number of the major countries of Western Europe discussed how they might maintain the fixed parities of their currencies independent of the US dollar. By April 1972, they had concluded an agreement that was termed the 'snake within the tunnel'. The member countries agreed to fix parity rates between currencies with allowable trading bands of 2.25% variance. As a group they would allow themselves to vary by 4.5% versus the US dollar. Although the effort was well intentioned, the various pressures and crises that rocked international economic order in the 1970s, such as the OPEC price shock of 1974, resulted in a relatively short life for the 'snake'.

In 1979 a much more formalized structure was put in place among many of the major members of the European Community. The European Monetary System (EMS) officially began operation in March 1979 and once again established a grid of fixed parity rates among member currencies. The EMS was a much more elaborate system for the management of exchange rates than its predecessor 'snake'. The EMS consisted of three different components that would work in concert to preserve fixed parities (also termed central rates).

First, all countries that were committing their currencies and their efforts to the preservation of fixed exchange rates entered the Exchange-Rate Mechanism (ERM). Although all the currencies of the countries of the European Union would be used in the calculation of important indices for management purposes, several countries chose not to be ERM participants. Participation in the ERM technically required that countries accept bilateral responsibility of maintaining the fixed rates.

The second element of the EMS was the actual grid of bilateral exchange rates with their specified band limits. As under the Smithsonian Agreement and the former snake, member currencies were allowed to deviate 62.25% from their parity rate. Some currencies, however, such as the Italian lira, were originally allowed larger bands (610% variance) due to their more characteristic volatility.

The third and final element of the EMS was the creation of the European Currency Unit (ECU). The ECU was a weighted average index of the currencies that are part of the EMS. Each currency was weighted by a value reflecting the relative size of that country's trade and gross domestic product. This allowed each currency to be defined in units per ECU.

The need for fixed exchange rates within Europe was clear. The countries of Western Europe trade among themselves to a degree approaching interstate commerce in the United States. It was therefore critical to the economies and businesses of Europe that exchange rates be as stable as possible. Although it had its critics, the EMS was generally successful in providing exchange-rate stability.

The Maastricht Treaty and the Euro

In an attempt to maintain the momentum of European integration, the members of the European Union concluded the Maastricht Treaty in December 1991. The treaty, besides laying out long-term goals of harmonized social and welfare policies in the Union, specified a timetable for the adoption of a single currency to replace all individual currencies. This was a very ambitious move. The Maastricht Treaty called for the integration and co-ordination of economic and monetary policy so that few financial differences would exist by the time of currency unification in 1997.

On 31 December 1998, the final fixed rates between the 11 participating currencies and the euro were put into place. On 1 January 1999, the euro (with its official symbol '€') was officially launched as a single currency for the European Union. This new currency will eventually replace all the individual currencies of the participating member states, resulting in a single, simple, efficient medium of exchange for all trade and investment activities.

'Why' Monetary Unification?

According to the European Union, 'economic and monetary union (EMU) is a single currency area within the European Union single market in which people, goods, services and capital move without restrictions'. Beginning with the Treaty of Rome in 1957 and continuing with the Single European Act of 1987, the Maastricht Treaty of 1992 and the Treaty of Amsterdam of 1997, a core set of European countries has been working steadily toward integrating their individual countries into one larger, more efficient domestic market. Even after the launch of the 1992 Single Europe programme, however, a number of barriers to true openness remained. The use of different currencies was thought to still require both consumers and companies to treat the individual markets separately. And currency risk of cross-border commerce still persisted. The creation of a single currency is to move beyond these last vestiges of separated markets.

The growth of global markets and the increasing competitiveness of the Americas and Asia drove the members of the European Union in the 1980s and 1990s to take actions that would allow their people and their firms to compete globally. The reduction of barriers across all member countries to allow economies of scale (size and cost per unit) and scope (horizontal and vertical integration) was thought to be Europe's only hope to not be left behind in the new millennium. The economic potential of the EU is substantial. The successful implementation of a single, strong and dependable currency for the conduct of 'life' could well alter the traditional dominance of the US dollar as the world's currency.

Fiscal Policy and Monetary Policy

The monetary policy for the EMU is conducted by the newly formed European Central Bank (ECB), which according to its founding principles in the Maastricht Treaty has one singular responsibility: to safeguard the stability of the euro. Following the basic structures that were used in the establishment of the Federal Reserve System in the United States and the Bundesbank in Germany, the ECB is free of political pressures that historically have caused monetary authorities to yield to employment pressures by inflating economies. The ECB's independence allows it to focus simply on the stability of the currency without falling victim to history's trap.

The ECB is headquartered in Frankfurt and became operational in June 1998. It became responsible for the entire monetary policy of the 11 participating states on 1 January 1999. It consists of a president' whose term is eight years, assisted by a vice president and four executives from member states. The ECB's governing council sets interest rates in conjunction with the directors of the individual national central banks. These national central banks now – in conjunction with the ECB – form the European System of Central Banks (ESCB). The ECB establishes policy and the ESCB is responsible for implementation, regulation and enforcement. The ECB has the job of ensuring that payments move smoothly across all EU borders, not just within the euro area. It is at the heart of a real-time network for large payments transactions in euros, known as TARGET, which helps EU financial markets work more efficiently. TARGET2, which upgrades the technology, started in November 2007. TARGET2 Securities is also to be implemented. This has the potential to save financial markets more than €200 million a year from more efficient settlement across borders for securities transactions. The ECB and the European Commission are working jointly on a Single Euro Payments Area (SEPA). This will make virtually all forms of cross-border euro payment faster and no more expensive than domestic payments by 2010. At the moment, only credit transfers up to €50 000 are treated like domestic payments and it is virtually impossible to make some types of payment (e.g., direct debits) cross-border. SEPA will bring down costs for everyone from large companies to parents wanting to send money regularly to students at a foreign university.

Fixing the Value of the Euro

The 31 December 1998 fixing of the rates of exchange between national currencies and the euro resulted in the conversion rates shown in Table 5.3. These are permanent fixes for these currencies. As illustrated, there are 11 EU member states that initially adopted the euro. The British, as has been the case since the passage of the Maastricht Treaty, are sceptical of increasing EU infringement on their sovereignty, including the euro itself. Although it is one of the newest members, Sweden has failed to see significant benefits from EU membership and is also sceptical of EMU participation. Sweden rejected euro membership in September 2003, as noted in the accompanying Focus on Politics (below). Denmark, like Britain and Sweden, has a strong political element that is highly nationalistic and has opted for now not to participate. The Greeks, however, were very much in favour of participation but could not initially qualify because of the size of their fiscal deficits and national debt, as well as inflation. However, Greece joined the EMU on 1 January 2001. The euro notes and coins were introduced in January 2002. In January 2007 Slovenia joined the Euro Zone and on 1 January 2008 Cyprus and Malta became members of the EMU. Slovakia planned to adopt the euro on 1 January 2009. Bulgaria, the Czech Republic, Estonia, Hungary, Latvia, Lithuania, Poland, Romania and Sweden have no target date for joining.

The European Union has been very careful to differentiate the euro from its predecessor the ECU (European Currency Unit). The euro is actually money, whereas the ECU was an index of money. The ECU was never legal tender under European law, whereas the euro is legal tender. The ECU's value was based on the composition currencies of the European Union's participants in the European Monetary System, whereas the euro is a completely independent currency or money that is exchangeable into other currencies but not dependent on them for its value. The primary purpose for the ECU's existence was the construction of the exchange rate bands for the conduct of the ERM of the EMS. The euro replaced all individual currencies.

Previous Currency	Symbol	Per Euro	
Belgian or Luxembourg francs	BEF/LUF	40.3399	1 euro = 40.3399 BEF or LUF
Deutschemarks	DEM	1.95583	1 euro = 1.95583 DEM
Spanish peseta	ESP	166.386	1 euro = 166.386 ESP
French francs	FRF	6.55957	1 euro = 6.55957 FRF
Irish punts	IEP	0.787564	1 euro = 0.787564 IEP
Italian lira	ITL	1936.27	1 euro = 1936.27 ITL
Netherlands guilders	NLG	2.20371	1 euro = 2.20371 NLG
Austrian shillings	ATS	13.7603	1 euro = 13.7603 ATS
Portuguese escudo	PTE	200.482	1 euro = 200.482 PTE
Finnish marks	FIM	5.94573	1 euro = 5.94573 FIM

Table 5.3: The fixing of the exchange rates to the euro (€).

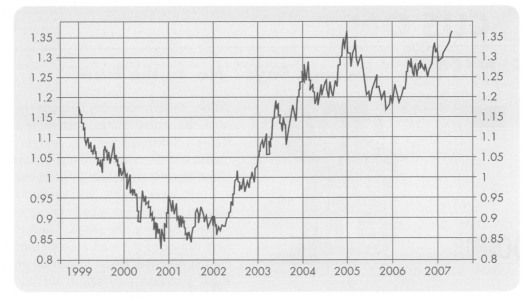

Figure 5.5: Monthly average exchange rates: US dollars per euro.
Source: © 2003 by Prof. Werner Antweiler, University of British Columbia, Vancouver, BC, Canada.

On 4 January 1999, the euro began trading on world currency markets. Its introduction was a smooth one, with trading heavy and relatively stable. The euro's value has first fallen substantially, and then risen substantially, against the dollar since its inception. In both 2000 and 2001 its value neared US$0.85/€, but in December 2005 surged to over US$1.35/€. Figure 5.5 illustrates the euro's value versus the US dollar after its inception. An example projection for the exchange rate between the two currencies is shown on Figure 5.6.

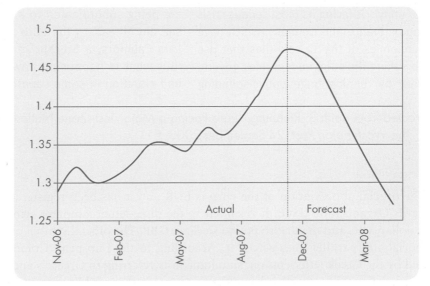

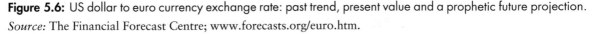

Figure 5.6: US dollar to euro currency exchange rate: past trend, present value and a prophetic future projection.
Source: The Financial Forecast Centre; www.forecasts.org/euro.htm.

F◯CUS ON

POLITICS Sweden Says ´No´ to the Euro

Europe's common currency, the euro – introduced four and one half years ago as a global competitor to the dollar and the most visible symbol of the continent's post-war unity – is facing its most serious crisis since its inception. France and Germany, which have the biggest economies of the 12 countries that use the euro, are breaking the strict budget rules governing the currency by running huge public-spending deficits. Growth continues to sputter in the euro zone, while the United States is showing initial signs of recovery. Unemployment has risen to 12.5 million in the EU. And the near-record-high value of the currency is hurting competitiveness by dampening exports.

Last week voters in Sweden overwhelmingly rejected adopting the euro in favour of keeping their national currency, the krona. Sweden's entry would have expanded the euro zone's economy just 3.6% but the rejection, based in part on voters' concerns about problems they see in the euro zone, could strengthen resistance in the other two holdouts in the 15-country European Union, Britain and Denmark.

'The outcome of the Swedish referendum was no surprise', said Dominique Barbet, senior economist for the French bank BNP Paribas. 'The euro zone is definitely not looking attractive right now'. He added, 'We knew from the beginning that the euro zone was not a perfect monetary zone'.

The euro's current troubles are highlighting the enormous difficulties of melding a dozen disparate economies into a single monetary union. It shows that despite statements of integration and European unity, many countries are willing to break ranks when they feel their national interests are being subordinated to a common goal. 'I don't see any threat' to the euro zone as a whole, said Lars Calmfors, a Stockholm University economist. 'But what is happening now is serious and it's a bad situation in some countries'.

Source: Abstracted from Keith B. Richburg, 'Euro Facing a Major Test: Zone Nations Show Willingness to Break Ranks', *The Washington Post*, 24 September 2003, E1.

The official abbreviation of the euro is EUR and it has been registered with the International Standards Organization (ISO). It is similar to the three-letter computer symbols used for the United States dollar, US$ and the British pound sterling, GBP. The official symbol of the euro is €, an E with two horizontal parallel lines across it. According to the European Commission, the symbol was inspired by the Greek letter epsilon, simultaneously referring to Greece's ancient role as the source of European civilization, as well as being the first letter in the word Europe.

Where the euro's value will go in the coming months and years is now a matter of markets. The fundamental factors that affect the supply and demand for any currency – inflation, monetary and fiscal policy, balance of payments – will now all drive the value of the euro. Many pundits believe the inherent strength and structure of the ECB will continue to provide a sound footing for the growth of EU business and therefore the continued health of the euro's value on world currency markets. It is important to note, however, that the long-term goal of most exchange rate policies is stability, not *strength* or *weakness*.

INTERNATIONAL MONEY MARKETS

A money market is traditionally defined as a market for deposits, accounts or securities that have maturities of one year or less. The international money markets, often termed the Eurocurrency markets, constitute an enormous financial market that is in many ways outside the jurisdiction and supervision of world financial and governmental authorities.

Eurocurrency Markets

A Eurocurrency is any foreign currency-denominated deposit or account at a financial institution outside the country of the currency's issuance. For example, US dollars that are held on account in a bank in London are termed Eurodollars. Similarly, Japanese yen held on account in a Parisian financial institution are classified as Euroyen. The 'Euro' prefix does not mean these currencies or accounts are only European.

Eurocurrency Interest Rates

What is the significance of these foreign currency-denominated accounts? Simply put, it is the purity of value that comes from no governmental interference or restrictions with their use. Eurocurrency accounts are not controlled or managed by governments (e.g., the Bank of England has no control over Eurodollar accounts); therefore, the financial institutions pay no deposit insurance, hold no reserve requirements and normally are not subject to any interest rate restrictions with respect to such accounts. Eurocurrencies are one of the purest indicators of what these currencies should yield in terms of interest. Sample Eurocurrency interest rates are shown in Table 5.4.

There are hundreds of different major interest rates around the globe but the international financial markets focus on a very few, the interbank interest rates. Interbank rates charged by banks to banks in the major international financial centres such as London, Frankfurt, Paris, New York, Tokyo, Singapore and Hong Kong are generally regarded as 'the interest rate' in the respective

Interest Rate/ Exchange Rate	Maturity	Eurodollar Interest Rates (%)	Europound Interest Rates (%)
	1 month	1.900	3.850
	3 months	1.920	4.040
	6 months	2.200	4.260
	12 months	2.500	4.650
Exchange rates: Spot rate		US$1.4178/£	
Forward rates	1 month	US$1.4155/£	
	3 months	US$1.4104/£	
	6 months	US$1.4035/£	
	12 months	US$1.3887/£	

Table 5.4: Exchange rates and Eurocurrency interest rates.

market. The interest rate that is used most often in international loan agreements is the Eurocurrency interest rate on US dollars (Eurodollars) in London between banks: the London Interbank Offer Rate (**LIBOR**). Because it is a Eurocurrency rate, it floats freely without regard to governmental restrictions on reserves, deposit insurance or any other regulation or restriction that would add expense to transactions using this capital. The interbank rates for other currencies in other markets are often named similarly, PIBOR (Paris Interbank Offer Rate), MIBOR (Madrid Interbank Offer Rate), HIBOR (either Hong Kong or Helsinki Interbank Offer Rate), SIBOR (Singapore Interbank Offer Rate). Whereas LIBOR is the offer rate – the cost of funds 'offered' to those acquiring a loan – the equivalent deposit rate in the Euromarkets is LIBID (the London Interbank Bid Rate), the rate of interest other banks can earn on Eurocurrency deposits.

How do these international Eurocurrency and interbank interest rates differ from domestic rates? Answer: not by much. They generally move up and down in unison by currency, but often differ by the percentage by which the restrictions alter the rates of interest in the domestic markets. For example, because the Euromarkets have no restrictions, the spread between the offer rate and the bid rate (the loan rate and the deposit rate) is substantially smaller than in domestic markets. This means the loan rates in international markets are a bit lower than domestic market loan rates and deposit rates are a bit higher in the international markets than in domestic markets. This is, however, only a big-player market. Only well-known international firms, financial or non-financial, have access to the quantities of capital necessary to operate in the Euromarkets. But as described in the following sections on international debt and equity markets, more and more firms are gaining access to the Euromarkets to take advantage of deregulated capital flows.

Linking Eurocurrency Interest Rates and Exchange Rates

Eurocurrency interest rates also play a large role in the foreign exchange markets themselves. They are, in fact, the interest rates used in the calculation of the forward rates we noted earlier. Recall that a forward rate is a contract for a specific amount of currency to be exchanged for another currency at a future date, usually 30, 60, 90, 180 or even 360 days in the future. Forward rates are calculated from the spot rate in effect on the day the contract is written along with the respective Eurocurrency interest rates for the two currencies.

For example, to calculate the 90-day forward rate for the US dollar–British pound cross rate, the spot exchange rate is multiplied by the ratio of the two Eurocurrency interest rates – the Eurodollar and the Europound rates. Note that it is important to adjust the interest rates for the actual period of time needed, 90 days (3 months) of a 360-day financial year:

$$\text{90-Day Forward Rate} = \text{Spot} \times \frac{1 + \left(i_{90}^{\$} \times \frac{90}{360} \right)}{1 + \left(i_{90}^{\pounds} \times \frac{90}{360} \right)}$$

Now, plugging in the spot exchange rate of US\$1.4178/£ and the two 90-day (3-month) Eurocurrency interest rates from Table 5.4 (1.92% for the dollar and 4.04% for the pound), the 90-day forward exchange rate is:

$$\text{90-Day Forward Rate} = \$1.4178/\pounds \times \frac{1 + \left(0.0192 \times \frac{90}{360} \right)}{1 + \left(0.0404 \times \frac{90}{360} \right)} = \$1.4104/\pounds$$

The forward rate of 1.4104/£ is a 'weaker rate' for the British pound than the current spot rate. This is because one British pound will yield US\$1.4178 in the spot market but only US\$1.4104 in the forward market (at 90 days). The British pound would be said to be 'selling forward at a discount', while the dollar would be described as 'selling forward at a premium' because its value is stronger at the 90-day forward rate.

Why is this the case? The reason is that the 90-day Eurocurrency interest rate on the US dollar is lower than the corresponding Eurocurrency interest rate on the British pound. If it were the other way around – if the US dollar interest rate were higher than the British pound interest rate – the British pound would be selling forward at a premium. The forward exchange rates quoted in the markets, and used so frequently in international business, simply reflect the difference in interest rates between currencies.

INTERNATIONAL CAPITAL MARKETS

Just as with the money markets, the international capital markets serve as links among the capital markets of individual countries, as well as constituting a separate market of their own – the capital that flows into the Euromarkets. Firms can now raise capital, debit or equity, fixed or floating interest rates, in any of a dozen currencies, for maturities ranging from 1 month to 30 years, in the international capital markets. Although the international capital markets have traditionally been dominated by debt instruments, international equity markets have shown considerable growth in recent years.

The international financial markets can be subdivided in a number of ways. The following sections describe the international debt and equity markets for securitized and non-securitized capital. This is capital that is separable and tradable, such as a bond or a stock. Non-securitized, a fancy term for bank loans, was really the original source of international capital (as well as the international debt crisis).

Defining International Financing

The definition of what constitutes an international financial transaction is dependent on two fundamental characteristics: (1) whether the borrower is domestic or foreign; and (2) whether the borrower is raising capital denominated in the domestic currency or a foreign currency. These two characteristics form four categories of financial transactions, as illustrated in Figure 5.7.

- *Category 1: Domestic Borrower/Domestic Currency.* This is a traditional domestic financial market activity. A borrower who is resident within the country raises capital from domestic financial institutions denominated in local currency. All countries with basic market economies have their own domestic financial markets, some large and some quite small. This is still by far the most common type of financial transaction.
- *Category 2: Foreign Borrower/Domestic Currency.* This is when a foreign borrower enters another country's financial market and raises capital denominated in the local currency. The international dimension of this transaction is based only on who the borrower is. Many borrowers, both public and private, increasingly go to the world's largest financial markets to raise capital for their enterprises. The ability of a foreign firm to raise capital in another country's financial market is sometimes limited by that government's restrictions on who can borrow, as well as the market's willingness to lend to foreign governments and companies that it may not know as well as domestic borrowers.
- *Category 3: Domestic Borrower/Foreign Currency.* Many borrowers in today's international markets need capital denominated in a foreign currency. A domestic firm may actually issue a bond to raise capital in its local market where it is known quite well, but raise the capital in the form of a foreign currency. This type of financial transaction occurs less often than the previous two types because it requires a local market in foreign currencies, a Eurocurrency market. A number of countries, such as the United States, highly restrict the amount and types of financial transactions in

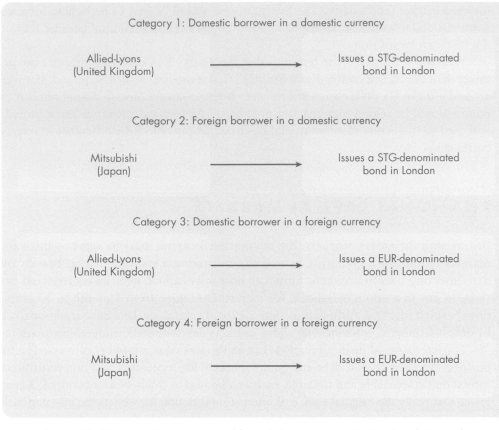

Figure 5.7: Categorizing international financial transactions: issuing bonds in London.

foreign currency. International financial centres such as London and Zurich have been the traditional centres of these types of transactions.

- **Category 4: Foreign Borrower/Foreign Currency.** This is the strictest form of the traditional Eurocurrency financial transaction, a foreign firm borrowing foreign currency. Once again, this type of activity may be restricted by which borrowers are allowed into a country's financial markets and which currencies are available. This type of financing dominates the activities of many banking institutions in the offshore banking market.

Using this classification system, it is possible to categorize any individual international financial transaction. For example, the distinction between an international bond and a Eurobond is simply that of a Category 2 transaction (foreign borrower in a domestic currency market) and a Category 3 or 4 transaction (foreign currency denominated in a single local market or many markets).

INTERNATIONAL BANKING AND BANK LENDING

Banks have existed in different forms and roles since the Middle Ages. Bank loans have provided nearly all of the debt capital needed by industry since the start of the Industrial Revolution. Even in this age in which securitized debt instruments (bonds, notes and other types of tradable paper) are growing as sources of capital for firms worldwide, banks still perform a critical role by providing capital for medium-sized and smaller firms, which dominate all economies.

The Locations of the World's International Finance Centres and International Offshore Financial Centres

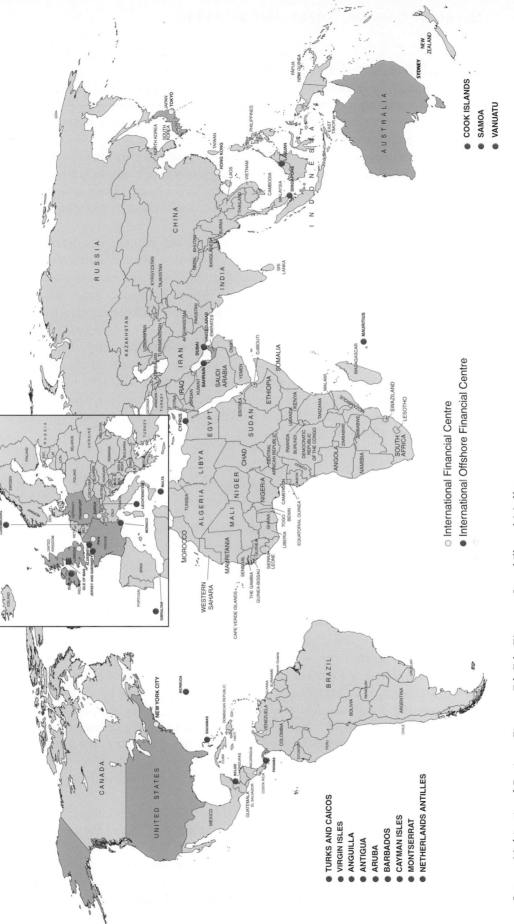

○ International Financial Centre

● International Offshore Financial Centre

● TURKS AND CAICOS
● VIRGIN ISLES
● ANGUILLA
● ANTIGUA
● ARUBA
● BARBADOS
● CAYMAN ISLES
● MONTSERRAT
● NETHERLANDS ANTILLES

● COOK ISLANDS
● SAMOA
● VANUATU

Source: Multinational Business Finance, 7th Ed., Eiteman, Stonehill, and Moffett.

Note: International Financial Centres (IFCs) are the traditional centres of international financial activity, and normally include the conduct of both domestic and international financial transactions. *International Offshore Financial Centres (IOFCs)* are centres of offshore financial activities only (no interaction is allowed with the domestic financial or business community), and normally exist because of specific tax laws and provisions which encourage their establishment and allow them special treatment.

Structure of International Banking

Similar to the foreign direct investment decision sequence, banks can expand their cross-border activities in a variety of ways. Like all decisions involving exports and direct investment, increasing the level of international activity and capability normally requires placing more capital and knowledge at risk to be able to reap the greater benefits of expanding markets.

A bank that wants to conduct business with clients in other countries but does not want to open a banking operation in that country can do so through correspondent banks or representative offices. A correspondent bank is an unrelated bank (by ownership) based in the foreign country. By the nature of its business, it has knowledge of the local market and access to clients, capital and information that a foreign bank does not.

A second way that banks may gain access to foreign markets without actually opening a banking operation there is through representative offices. A representative office is basically a sales office for a bank. It provides information regarding the financial services of the bank but cannot deliver the services itself. It cannot accept deposits or make loans. The foreign representative office of a bank will typically sell the bank's services to local firms that may need banking services for trade or other transactions.

If a bank wants to conduct banking business within the foreign country, it may open a branch banking office, a banking affiliate or even a wholly owned banking subsidiary. A branch banking office is an extension of the parent bank and is not independently financed from the parent. The branch office is not independently incorporated and therefore is commonly restricted in the types of banking activities that it may conduct. Branch banking is by far the most common form of international banking structure used by banks.

INTERNATIONAL SECURITY MARKETS

Although banks continue to provide a large portion of the international financial needs of government and business, it is the international debt securities markets that have experienced the greatest growth in the past decade. The international security markets include bonds, equities and private placements.

The International Bond Market

The international bond market provides the bulk of financing. The four categories of international debt financing discussed previously particularly apply to the international bond markets. Foreign borrowers have been using the large, well-developed capital markets of countries such as the United States and the United Kingdom for many years. These issues are classified generally as foreign bonds as opposed to Eurobonds. Each has gained its own pet name for foreign bonds issued in that market. For example, foreign bond issues in the United States are called Yankee bonds, in the United Kingdom Bulldogs, in the Netherlands Rembrandt bonds and in Japan they are called Samurai bonds. When bonds are issued by foreign borrowers in these markets, they are subject to the same restrictions that apply to all domestic borrowers. If a Japanese firm issues a bond in the United States, it must still comply with all rules of the US Securities and Exchange Commission, including the fact that they must be dollar-denominated.

Bonds that fall into Categories 3 and 4 are termed Eurobonds. The primary characteristic of these instruments is that they are denominated in a currency other than that of the country in which they are sold. For example, many US firms may issue Euroyen bonds on world markets. These bonds are sold in international financial centres such as London or Frankfurt but they are denominated in Japanese yen. Because these Eurobonds are scattered about the global markets, most are a type of bond known as a bearer bond. A bearer bond is owned officially by whoever is holding it, with no master registration list being held by government authorities who then track who is earning interest income from bond investments.[4] Bearer bonds have a series of small coupons that border the bond itself. On an annual basis, one of the coupons is cut or 'clipped' from the bond and taken to a banking institution that is one of the listed paying agents. The bank will pay the holder of the coupon the interest payment due and usually no official records of payment are kept.

International Equity Markets

Firms are financed with both debt and equity. Although the debt markets have been the centre of activity in the international financial markets over the past three decades, there are signs that international equity capital is becoming more popular. As more and more firms raise capital in the international equity markets, they may also find themselves more vulnerable to market reactions to war and terrorism, as described in the following Focus on Culture.

Again using the same categories of international financial activities, the Category 2 transaction of a foreign borrower in a domestic market in local currency is the predominant international equity activity. Foreign firms often issue new shares in foreign markets and list their stock on major stock exchanges such as those in New York, Tokyo or London. The purpose of foreign issues and listings is to expand the investor base in the hope of gaining access to capital markets in which the demand for shares of equity ownership is strong.

FOCUS ON

CULTURE   Equity Market Crises in the Twentieth Century

The largest equity market losses in the past century were primarily related to war and terrorism and their associated economic devastation.

Country	Event	Equity Market Losses (Real Returns) (%)
US	Terrorist attacks, 11 September, 2001	−14
US	October 1987 stock market crash	−23
US	Bear market, 2000–2001	−37
US	Wall Street crash of 1929	−60
UK	Bear market, 1973–1974	−71
Germany	Second World War, 1945–1948	−91
Japan	Second World War, 1944–1947	−97

Source: Adapted from Elroy Dimson, Paul Marsh and Mike Staunton (2002) *Triumph of the Optimists, 101 Years of Global Investment Returns*, Princeton University Press, 58.

A foreign firm that wants to list its shares on an exchange in the United States does so through American Depository Receipts. These are the receipts to bank accounts that hold shares of the foreign firm's stock in that firm's country. The equities are actually in a foreign currency, and so by holding them in a bank account and listing the receipt on the account on the American exchange, the shares can be revalued in dollars and re-divided so that the price per share is more typical of that of the US equity markets (US$20 to US$60 per share frequently being the desired range).

There was considerable growth in recent years in the Euro-equity markets. A Euro-equity issue is the simultaneous sale of a firm's shares in several different countries, with or without listing the shares on an exchange in that country. The sales take place through investment banks. Once issued, most Euro-equities are listed at least on the computer screen quoting system of the International Stock Exchange (ISE) in London, the SEAQ. As of late 1994, the Frankfurt stock exchange was the most globalized of major equity exchanges, with more than 45% of the firms listed on the exchange being foreign. At the same time, 18.8% of the firms on the London exchange were foreign, New York was a distant third with 7.6% foreign firms, and Tokyo fourth with less than 6%.

Private Placements

One of the largest and largely unpublicized capital markets is the private placement market. A private placement is the sale of debt or equity to a large investor. The sale is normally a one-time-only trans-action in which the buyer of the bond or stock purchases the investment and intends to hold it until maturity (if debt) or until repurchased by the firm (if equity). How does this differ from normal bond and stock sales? The answer is that the securities are not resold on a secondary market such as the domestic bond market or the New York or London stock exchanges. If the security was intended to be publicly traded, the issuing firm would have to meet a number of disclosure and registration requirements with the regulatory authorities.

Historically, much of the volume of private placements of securities occurred in Europe, with a large volume being placed with large Swiss financial institutions and large private investors. But in recent years the market has grown substantially across all countries as the world's financial markets have grown and as large institutional investors (particularly pension funds and insurance firms) have gained control over increasing shares of investment capital.

Gaining Access to International Financial Markets

Although the international markets are large and growing, this does not mean they are for everyone. For many years, only the largest of the world's multinational firms could enter another country's capital markets and find acceptance. The reasons are information and reputation.

Financial markets are by definition risk-averse. This means they are very reluctant to make loans to or buy debt issued by firms that they know little about. Therefore, the ability to gain access to the international markets is dependent on a firm's reputation, its ability to educate the markets about what it does, how successful it has been and its patience. The firm must in the end be willing to expend the resources and effort required to build a credit reputation in the international markets. If successful, the firm may enjoy the benefits of new, larger and more diversified sources of the capital it needs.

The individual firm, whether it is a burger stand serving the international tastes of office workers in London or a major multinational firm such as Honda of Japan, is affected by exchange rates and international financial markets. Although the owner of the burger stand probably has more important and immediate problems than exchange rates to deal with, it is clear that firms such as Honda see the movements in these markets as critically important to their long-term competitiveness.

SUMMARY

This chapter has spanned the breadth of the international financial markets from currencies to capital markets. The world's currency markets expanded threefold in only six years and there is no reason to believe this growth will end. It is estimated that more than US$1 trillion worth of currencies change hands daily and the majority of it is US dollars, euros or Japanese yen. These are the world's major floating currencies.

But the world's financial markets are much more than currency exchanges. The rapid growth in the international financial markets – both on their own and as links between domestic markets – has resulted in the creation of a large and legitimate source of finance for the world's multinational firms. The recent expansion of market economics to more and more of the world's countries and economies sets the stage for further growth for the world's currency and capital markets, but also poses the potential for new external debt crises.

QUESTIONS FOR DISCUSSION

1. What is the purpose of an exchange rate?
2. Who trades currencies? Why?
3. What is a forward exchange rate?
4. What is a currency worth?
5. Why is the Big Mac a good indicator of purchasing power parity?
6. Why would a gold standard probably not work today?
7. What is a 'Eurocurrency?'
8. Why was the euro created to replace the individual currencies of the European Union member states?
9. How are exchange rates and interest rates combined to form forward exchange rates?
10. What are the major sources of debt and equity for multinational firms trying to raise capital in the international markets?

INTERNET EXERCISES

1. The IMF, World Bank and United Nations are only a few of the major world organizations that track, report and aid international economic and financial development. Using the following web sites and others that may be linked to them, briefly summarize the economic outlook for the developed and emerging nations of the world. For example, the full text of Chapter 1 of the *World Economic Outlook*, published annually by the World Bank, is available through the IMF's web page.

   • International Monetary Fund, www.imf.org/
   • United Nations, www.unsystem.org/
   • The World Bank Group, www.worldbank.org/
   • Europa (EU) Homepage, www.europa.eu.int/
   • Bank for International Settlements, www.bis.org/

2. Current economic and financial statistics and commentaries are available via the IMF's web page under 'What's New', 'Fund Rates' and the 'IMF Committee on Balance of Payments Statistics'. For an in-depth examination of the IMF's ongoing initiative on the validity of these statistics, termed metadata, visit the IMF's Dissemination Standards Bulletin Board listed below:

   • International Monetary Fund, www.imf.org/
   • IMF's Dissemination Standards Bulletin Board, www.dsbb.imf.org/

3. American Depository Receipts (ADRs) now make up more than 10% of all equity trading on US stock exchanges. As more companies based outside of the United States list on US markets, the need to understand the principal forces that drive ADR values increases with each trading day. Beginning with JP Morgan's detailed description of the ADR process and current ADR trading activity, prepare a briefing for senior management in your firm encouraging them to consider internationally diversifying the firm's liquid assets portfolio with ADRs.

- JP Morgan, www.JPMorgan.com

TAKE A STAND

More and more companies from emerging markets are listing their shares on the world's largest equity markets – such as London, Paris, New York and Tokyo. By listing their shares they are opening the door to investors and their capital, from around the world, allowing the firms to gain access to larger quantities of capital at cheaper rates sooner. But they are also giving up their exclusive ownership. No longer are investors limited to the citizens of one country; after listing, the companies are owned by the 'citizens of the world'. Companies such as Nokia, once owned and operated by the citizens of Finland, or Cemex of Mexico, are now largely owned by large groups of institutional investors from New York and London.

FOR DISCUSSION

1. In order for companies to compete in the twenty-first century, they need global access to capital, which means the ability to raise large quantities at the lowest possible internationally available price. A company that wishes to remain largely domestic in ownership is doomed to slower growth versus global multinationals, and in the end may simply be doomed altogether.
2. The ability to restrict ownership of firms to the residents of their own home country is the prerogative of all companies and one that should not be given up lightly. What defines culture, society and the economic context of nationalism is at the heart of the globalization debate. Not only should the concept of shareholder value maximization be tempered, but also the very definition of who the shareholders ought to be.

CHAPTER
6

Economic Integration

- Levels of Economic Integration
- Arguments Surrounding Economic Integration
- European Integration
- North American Economic Integration
- Other Economic Alliances
- Economic Integration and the International Manager
- Cartels and Commodity Price Agreements

LEARNING OBJECTIVES

- To review types of economic integration among countries.
- To examine the costs and benefits of integrative arrangements.
- To understand the structure of the European Union and its implications for firms within and outside Europe.
- To explore the emergence of other integration agreements, especially in the Americas and Asia.
- To suggest corporate response to advancing economic integration.

BUILDING BLOCS TOWARD WORLDWIDE FREE TRADE

Regional groupings based on economics have become increasingly important over the last 10 years. Thirty-two such groupings are estimated to be in existence: three in Europe, four in the Middle East, five in Asia and 10 each in Africa and the Americas. Trade within the three major blocs – the American, European and Asian – has grown rapidly, while trading among the blocs or with outsiders is either declining or growing far more moderately.

Some of these groupings around the world have the superstructure of nation-states (such as the European Union); some (such as the ASEAN Free Trade Area (AFTA), are multinational agreements that may be more political arrangements than cohesive trading blocs at present. Increasingly, new blocs are made up of several independent blocs; for example, the European Economic Area is composed of the EU member nations and the nations belonging to the European Free Trade Area (EFTA). Some arrangements are not trading blocs *per se*, but work to further them. The Free Trade Area of the Americas (FTAA) is a foreign policy initiative designed to further democracy in the region through incentives to capitalistic development and trade liberalization. The Andean Common Market and MERCOSUR have both indicated an intention to negotiate with the parties of the North American Free Trade Agreement (NAFTA) to create a hemispheric market. Regional economic integration in Asia has been driven more by market forces than by treaties and by a need to maintain balance in negotiations with Europe and North America. Broader formal agreements are in formative stages; for example, the Asia-Pacific Economic Cooperation (APEC) initiated in 1989 would bring together partners from multiple continents and blocs. AFTA members are joined by such economic powerhouses as China, South Korea, Taiwan and the United States.

Regional groupings are constantly being developed in multiple ways either internally, by adding new dimensions to the existing ones, or by creating new blocs. In 1995, informal proposals were made to create a new bloc between NAFTA and EU members called TAFTA, the Transatlantic Free Trade Area. Since the elimination of the Soviet Union in 1991, 12 former republics have tried to forge common economic policies, but thus far only Belarus, Kazakhstan and Russia are signatories. In 2002, 12 EU countries adopted the euro as a common currency and eliminated their respective national currencies and in 2004, the EU expanded to 25 nations, accepting eight Central European and two Mediterranean countries to the European Union. On 1 January 2007, two Southeast European countries, Bulgaria and Romania, became members of the EU. On the same date, the first ex-Communist country to be accepted as an EU member state, Slovenia, became the 13th member state of the euro zone.

Companies are facing ever-intensifying competition within these blocs but, at the same time, can take advantage of emerging opportunities. As new countries join blocs, fears that these blocs are nothing but protectionism on a grander scale are allayed. As governments liberalize their industrial sectors and allow for competition, they give birth to companies that are not only competitive regionally but also globally.

Sources: 'A Nervous New Arrival on the European Union's Bloc', *The Economist*, 30 August 2003, 16–18; 'Mega Europe 25 states, 450 million citizens', *Business Week*, 25 November 2002, 62; *The World Factbook 2003*, available at www.cia.gov/; 'The Euro: What You Need to Know', *The Wall Street Journal*, 4 January 1999, A5, A6; 'World Trade Growth Slower in 1998 after Unusually Strong Growth in 1997', World Trade Organization press release, 16 April 1999, www.wto.org; 'American Politics, Global Trade', *The Economist*, 27 September 1997, 23–26; and Ilkka A. Ronkainen, 'Trading Blocs: Opportunity or Demise for International Trade?', *Multinational Business Review* 1 (Spring 1993): 1–9; 'Brussels says yes to Bulgaria, Romania', *Financial Times*, 26 September 2006; 'Ex-communist Slovenia joins euro' BBC News, 1 January 2007, http://news.bbc.co.uk/2/hi/europe/6222115.stm, accessed 13 April 2007.

INTRODUCTION

The benefits of free trade and stable exchange rates are available only if nation-states are willing to give up some measure of independence and autonomy. This has resulted in increased economic integration around the world with agreements among countries to establish links through movement of goods, services, capital and labour across borders. Some predict, however, that the regional trading blocs of the new economic world order will divide into a handful of protectionist super states that, although liberalizing trade among members, may raise barriers to external trade.

Economic integration is best viewed as a spectrum. At one extreme we might envision a truly global economy in which all countries share a common currency and agree to a free flow of goods, services and factors of production. At the other extreme would be a number of closed economies, each independent and self-sufficient. The various integrative agreements in effect today lie along the middle of this spectrum. The most striking example of successful integration is the historic economic unification that is taking place around the world today. These developments were discussed in this chapter's opening vignette. Some countries, however, give priority to maintaining economic self-sufficiency and independence, through their ranks have thinned considerably, with countries such as Vietnam becoming heavily involved in international trade and investment as well as regional economic integration through membership of two blocs. Even North Korea is now considered as a possible future market by companies such as Coca-Cola.

This chapter will begin with an explanation of the various levels of economic integration. The level of integration defines the nature and degree of economic links among countries. The major arguments both for and against economic integration will be reviewed. Next, the European Union, the North American Free Trade Agreement, Asia-Pacific Economic Co-operation and other economic alliances will be discussed. Finally, possible strategic moves by international managers in response to integration are outlined.

LEVELS OF ECONOMIC INTEGRATION

A trading bloc is a preferential economic arrangement among a group of countries. The forms it may take are shown in Table 6.1. From least to most integrative, they are the free trade area, the customs union, the common market and the economic union.[1] It should be noted that countries (or groups of countries) may give preferential treatment to other countries on the basis of historic ties or due to political motivations. Examples include the European Union's granting preferential access for selected products from their former colonies under the Lomé Convention or similar treatment by the United States of Caribbean nations

Stage of Integration	Abolition of Tariffs and Quotas Among Members	Common Tariff and Quota System	Abolition of Restrictions on Factor Movements	Harmonization and Unification of Economic Policies and Institutions
Free trade area	Yes	No	No	No
Customs union	Yes	Yes	No	No
Common market	Yes	Yes	Yes	No
Economic union	Yes	Yes	Yes	Yes

Source: Franklin R. Root, 1992, *International Trade and Investment*, South-Western Publishing Company, Cincinnati, OH, 254

Table 6.1: Forms of international economic integration.

(the Caribbean Basin Initiative). Since the benefits are unidirectional, these arrangements are not considered to be part of economic integration.

The Free Trade Area

The free trade area is the least restrictive and loosest form of economic integration among countries. In a free trade area, all barriers to trade among member countries are removed. Therefore, goods and services are freely traded among member countries. No discriminatory taxes, quotas, tariffs or other trade barriers are allowed. Sometimes a free trade area is formed only for certain classes of goods and services. An agricultural free trade area, for example, implies the absence of restrictions on the trade of agricultural products only. The most notable feature of a free trade area is that each country continues to set its own policies in relation to non-members. In other words, each member is free to set any tariffs, quotas or other restrictions that it chooses on trade with countries outside the free trade area. Among such free trade areas the most notable are the European Free Trade Area (EFTA) and the North American Free Trade Agreement (NAFTA).

As an example of the freedom members have in terms of their policies toward non-members, Mexico has signed a number of bilateral free trade agreements with other blocs (e.g., the European Union) and nations (e.g., Chile) to both improve trade and attract foreign direct investment. Similarly, the United States has free trade agreements with Israel, Jordan, Chile, Singapore and is in negotiations with the five Central American countries that formed the Central American Common Market. Future discussions on free trade may involve such diverse countries as Morocco, Australia and selected southern African nations.[2]

The Customs Union

The customs union is one step further along the spectrum of economic integration. Like the members of a free trade area, members of a customs union dismantle barriers to trade in goods and services among themselves. In addition, however, the customs union establishes a common trade policy with respect to non-members. Typically, this takes the form of a common external tariff, where imports from non-members are subject to the same tariff when sold to any member country. Tariff revenues are then shared among members according to a pre-specified formula. The Southern African Customs Union is the oldest and most successful example of economic integration in Africa.

The Common Market

Further still along the spectrum of economic integration is the common market. Like the customs union, a common market has no barriers to trade among members and has a common external trade policy. In addition, however, factors of production are also mobile among members. Factors of production include labour, capital and technology. Thus restrictions on immigration, emigration and cross-border investment are abolished. The importance of factor mobility for economic growth cannot be overstated. When factors of production are freely mobile, capital, labour and technology may be employed in their most productive uses.

Despite the obvious benefits, members of a common market must be prepared to co-operate closely in monetary, fiscal and employment policies. Furthermore, although a common market will enhance the productivity of members in the aggregate, it is by no means clear that individual member countries will always benefit. Because of these difficulties, the goals of common markets have proved to be elusive in many areas of the world, notably Central America and Asia. However, the objective of the Single European Act was to have a full common market in effect within the EU at the end of 1992. Although many of the directives aimed at opening borders and markets were implemented on schedule, some sectors, such as automobiles and telecommunications, took longer to be liberalized.

The Economic Union

The creation of a true economic union requires integration of economic policies in addition to the free movement of goods, services and factors of production across borders. Under an economic union, members would harmonize monetary policies, taxation and government spending. In addition, a common currency would be used by all members. This could be accomplished *de facto* or, in effect, by a system of fixed exchange rates. Clearly, the formation of an economic union requires nations to surrender a large measure of their national sovereignty to supranational authorities in community-wide institutions such as the European Parliament. The ratification of the Maastricht Treaty by all of the then 12 member countries created the European Union, effective from 1 January 1994. The treaty (jointly with the Treaty of Amsterdam, which took effect in 1999) set the foundation for economic and monetary union (EMU) with the establishment of the euro as a common currency by 1 January 1999. A total of 13 of the EU countries are currently part of 'Euroland' (Austria, Belgium, Finland, France, Germany, Greece, Holland, Ireland, Italy, Luxembourg, Portugal, Slovenia and Spain). In addition, moves may be made toward a political union with common foreign and security policy, as well as judicial co-operation.[3]

ARGUMENTS SURROUNDING ECONOMIC INTEGRATION

A number of arguments surround economic integration. They are centred on: (1) trade creation and diversion; (2) the effects of integration on import prices, competition, economies of scale and factor productivity; and (3) the benefits of regionalism versus nationalism.

Trade Creation and Trade Diversion

Economist Jacob Viner first formalized the economic costs and benefits of economic integration.[4] The question is whether similar benefits accrue when free trade is limited to one group of countries. The case examined by Viner was the customs union. The conclusion of Viner's analysis was that negative or positive effects may result when a group of countries trade freely among themselves but maintain common barriers to trade with non-members.

Viner's arguments can be highlighted with a simple illustration. In 1986, Spain formally entered the European Union (EU) as a member. Prior to membership, Spain – like all non-members such as the United States, Canada and Japan – traded with the EU and suffered the common external tariff. Imports of agricultural products from Spain or the United States had the same tariff applied to their products, for example, 20%. During this period, the United States was a lower-cost producer of wheat compared with Spain. US exports to EU members may have cost US$3.00 per bushel, plus a 20% tariff of US$0.60, for a total of US$3.60 per bushel. If Spain at the same time produced wheat at US$3.20 per bushel, plus a 20% tariff of US$0.64 for a total cost to EU customers of US$3.84 per bushel, its wheat was more expensive and therefore less competitive.

But when Spain joined the EU as a member, its products were no longer subject to the common external tariffs; Spain had become a member of the 'club' and therefore enjoyed its benefits. Spain was now the low-cost provider of wheat at US$3.20 per bushel, compared with the price of US$3.60 from the United States. Trade flows changed as a result. The increased export of wheat and other products by Spain to the EU as a result of its membership is termed trade creation. The elimination of the tariff literally created more trade between Spain and the EU. At the same time, because the United States was still outside of the EU, its products suffered the higher price as a result of tariff application. US exports to the EU fell. When the source of trading competitiveness is shifted in this manner from one country to another, it is termed trade diversion.

Whereas trade creation is distinctly positive in moving toward freer trade and therefore lower prices for consumers within the EU, the impact of trade diversion is negative. Trade diversion is inherently negative because the competitive advantage has shifted away from the lower-cost producer to the higher-cost producer. The benefits of Spain's membership are enjoyed by Spanish farmers (greater export sales) and EU consumers (lower prices). The two major costs are reduced tariff revenues collected and costs borne by the United States and its exports as a result of lost sales. In such cases, the injured party may seek compensation based on global trade rules. As a result of the European Union's expansion in 2004, the Japanese government argued that its exporters would lose sales of US$22 million in the new member countries in product categories such as autos and consumer electronics. The EU argued that the EU's expansion would benefit Japanese companies in the long term.[5]

From the perspective of non-members such as the United States, the formation or expansion of a customs union is obviously negative. Most damaged will naturally be countries that may need to have trade to build their economies, such as the developing countries. From the perspective of members of the customs union, the formation or expansion is only beneficial if the trade creation benefits exceed trade diversion costs. When Finland and Sweden joined the EU in 1995, the cost of an average food basket decreased by 10%. The only major item with a significant price increase was bananas due to the quota and tariff regime that the EU maintained in favour of its former colonies and against the major banana-producing nations in Latin America.

Reduced Import Prices

When a small country imposes a tariff on imports, the price of the goods will typically rise because sellers will increase prices to cover the cost of the tariff. This increase in price, in turn, will result in lower demand for the imported goods. If a bloc of countries imposes the tariff, however, the fall in demand for the imported goods will be substantial. The exporting country may then be forced to reduce the price of the goods. The possibility of lower prices for imports results from the greater market power of the bloc relative to that of a single country. The result may then be an improvement in the trade position of the bloc countries. Any gain in the trade position of bloc members, however, is offset by a deteriorating trade position for the exporting country. Again, unlike the win-win situation resulting from free trade, the scenario involving a trade bloc is instead win-lose.

Increased Competition and Economies of Scale

Integration increases market size and therefore may result in a lower degree of monopoly in the production of certain goods and services.[6] This is because a larger market will tend to increase the number of competing firms, resulting in greater efficiency and lower prices for consumers. Moreover, less energetic and productive economies may be spurred into action by competition from the more industrious bloc members.

Many industries, such as steel and automobiles, require large-scale production in order to obtain economies of scale in production. Therefore, certain industries may simply not be economically viable in smaller, trade-protected countries. However, the formation of a trading bloc enlarges the market so that large-scale production is justified. The lower per-unit costs resulting from scale economies may then be obtained. These lower production costs resulting from greater production for an enlarged market are called **internal economies of scale**. This is evident if the region adopts common standards, thus allowing not only for bigger markets for the companies but also enabling them to become global powerhouses. Ericsson and Nokia both benefited from the EU adopting the GSM standard for wireless communication to build scale beyond their small domestic markets.

In a common market, **external economies of scale** may also be present. Because a common market allows factors of production to flow freely across borders, the firm may now have access to cheaper capital, more highly skilled labour or superior technology. These factors will improve the quality of the firm's good or service, lower costs or both.

Higher Factor Productivity

When factors of production are freely mobile, the wealth of the common market countries, in aggregate, is likely to increase. The theory behind this contention is straightforward: factor mobility will lead to the movement of labour and capital from areas of low productivity to areas of high productivity. In addition to the economic gains from factor mobility, there are other benefits not so easily quantified. The free movement of labour fosters a higher level of communication across cultures. This, in turn, leads to a higher degree of cross-cultural understanding; as people move, their ideas, skills and ethnicity move with them.

Again, however, factor mobility will not necessarily benefit each country in the common market. A poorer country, for example, may lose badly needed investment capital to a richer country, where opportunities are perceived to be more profitable. Another disadvantage of factor mobility that is often cited is the brain-drain phenomenon. A poorer country may lose its most talented workers when they are free to search out better opportunities. More-developed member countries worry that companies may leave for other member countries where costs of operation, such as social costs, are lower. Many multinationals, such as Philips and Goodyear, have shifted their MERCOSUR production to Brazil from Argentina to take advantage of lower costs and incentives provided by the Brazilian government.[7]

Regionalism versus Nationalism

Economists have composed elegant and compelling arguments in favour of the various levels of economic integration. It is difficult, however, to turn these arguments into reality in the face of intense nationalism. The biggest impediment to economic integration remains the reluctance of nations to surrender a measure of their autonomy. Integration, by its very nature, requires the surrender of national power and self-determinism. An example of this can be seen in the following Focus on Integration Pains.

EUROPEAN INTEGRATION

Economic Integration in Europe from 1948 to the Mid-1980s

The period of the Great Depression from the late 1920s through the Second World War was characterized by isolationism, protectionism and fierce nationalism. The economic chaos and political difficulties of the period resulted in no serious attempts at economic integration until the end of the war. From the devastation of the war, however, a spirit of co-operation gradually emerged in Europe.

The first step in this regional co-operative effort was the establishment of the Organization for European Economic Co-operation (OEEC) in 1948 to administer Marshall Plan aid from the United States. Although the objective of the OEEC was limited to economic reconstruction following the war, its success set the stage for more ambitious integration progammes.

In 1952, six European countries (West Germany, France, Italy, Belgium, the Netherlands and Luxembourg) joined in establishing the European Coal and Steel Community (ECSC). The Treaty establishing the ECSC was signed in Paris on 18 April 1951 and entered into force on 24 July 1952, with a validity period of 50 years expiring on 23 July 2002. In the light of the establishment of the common market, the Treaty introduced the free movement of products without customs duties or taxes. It prohibited discriminatory measures or practices, subsidies, aids granted by States or special charges imposed by States and restrictive practices.

In 1957, the European Economic Community (EEC) was formally established by the *Treaty of Rome*. In 1967, ECSC and EEC as well as the European Atomic Energy Community (EURATOM) were merged to form the European Community (EC). The EEC created a common market that featured the elimination of most barriers to the movement of goods, services, capital and labour, the prohibition of most public policies or private agreements that inhibit market competition, a Common Agricultural

FOCUS ON

POLITICS   Integration Pains

© Getty Images. Reproduced with permission.

Trucks from Mexico cross the border into the United States. In defiance of veto threats from the White House and warnings from Mexico, the Senate approved a US$60.1 billion bill that subjects Mexican truckers to increased inspections, insurance and other requirements before entering the US.

Economic integration will not make everyone happy, despite promises of great benefits from the free flow of people, goods, services and money. More developed countries, such as the United States, France and Japan, fear a haemorrhage of jobs as companies shift their operations to less prosperous regions with lower wages or fewer governmental controls.

In NAFTA, more than 85% of the more than US$330 billion in US–Mexican trade in 2006 moved on trucks. More than 4.3 million commercial vehicles enter the United States from Mexico yearly through 25 border crossings in Arizona, California, New Mexico and Texas. Currently, all but a fraction are limited to a narrow strip along the border where freight is transferred to US-based truckers for delivery to final destinations. Under NAFTA, cross-border controls on trucking were to be eliminated by the end of 1995, allowing commercial vehicles to move freely in four US and six Mexican border states. But US truckers, backed by the Teamsters Union, would have none of this, arguing that Mexican trucks were dangerous and exceeded weight limits. The union also worried that opening of the border would depress wages, because it would allow US trucking companies to team up with lower-cost counterparts in Mexico. In early 2001, the NAFTA Arbitration Panel ruled that Mexican trucks must be allowed to cross US borders and in December the Senate finally approved a measure that permitted Mexican truckers to haul cargo on US roads as long as they are subject to strict safety and inspection rules. The Bush Administration, initially opposed to the bill on the grounds that it singled out Mexico for tougher inspections and therefore violated NAFTA, withdrew its opposition after the September 11th terrorist attacks, accepting that safety standards on truck traffic, especially hazardous cargo, are a top priority.

In the European Union, politicians blame other member countries for the loss of investment opportunities and the jobs they represent. France missed out to the United Kingdom when US vacuum-cleaner firm Hoover shifted European production to Scotland, where a flexible workforce agreed to limits on strike actions, lower wages and economies of scale, allowing the company to cut costs. France accused Britain of 'social dumping' – eroding workers' rights in a bid to attract foreign direct investment. In France, firm labour laws protect wages and pensions and make redundancy decisions costly for employers. In May 2002, in response to a bill that would make it even tougher to lay off employees, Italian-owned Moulinex-Brandt and British retailer Marks & Spencer decided to pull back operations in France. Moulinex-Brandt announced plans to close three factories, laying off over 2900 workers. Medef, a French employers' organization, insists that unless France reforms its legal and fiscal business environment, it will continue to lose jobs and wealth-creating enterprises to its competitors in Europe. France's law reducing the work week from 39 hours to 35 has not helped matters, either. PSA Peugeot Citroën has diverted jobs outside of its home base. Its workforce outside of France has doubled to 68 000 over the last decade, while the domestic workforce has dwindled to 4000. The expansion of the EU to cheaper-labour Central and Eastern European countries may erode that base further.

Sources: 'Mexican Trucks May Get Full Access', *The Washington Post*, 28 November 28, A4; 'Clocking Out', *The Wall Street Journal*, 8 August 2002, A1; 'Hogtied', *The Economist*, 17 January 2002; Lyzette Alvarez, 'Senate Votes to Let Mexican Trucks in US', *The New York Times*, 5 December 2001; 'Business Not As Usual', *The Economist*, 26 April 2001; 'US is Told to Let Mexican Trucks Enter', *The Wall Street Journal*, 7 February 2001, A2; Ben Fox, 'Border Nations Near Deal on Trucking', *The Associated Press*, 3 June 1999; 'The Trucks That Hold Back NAFTA', *The Economist*, 13 December 1997: 23–24; 'French Say United Europe Promotes "Job Poaching"', *The Washington Post*, 10 February 1993.

Policy (CAP) and a common external trade policy. Table 6.2 shows the founding members of the community in 1957, members who have joined since, as well as those invited to join early in the twenty-first century. The Treaty of Rome is a monumental document, composed of more than 200 articles. The main provisions of the treaty are summarized in Table 6.3. The document was (and is) quite ambitious. The co-operative spirit apparent throughout the treaty was based on the premise that the mobility of goods, services, labour and capital – the 'four freedoms' – was of paramount importance for the economic prosperity of the region. Founding members envisioned that the successful integration of the European economies would result in an economic power to rival that of the United States.

1957	1973–1986	1995	2004		2007
France	Great Britain (1973)	Austria	Czech Republic	Latvia	Bulgaria
West Germany	Ireland (1973)	Finland	Cyprus	Lithuania	Romania
Italy	Denmark (1973)	Sweden	Estonia	Malta	
Belgium	Greece (1981)		Hungary	Slovakia	
Netherlands	Spain (1986)		Poland		
Luxembourg	Portugal (1986)		Slovenia		

Table 6.2: Membership of the European Union.

1. Formation of a free trade area: the gradual elimination of tariffs and other barriers to trade among members.
2. Formation of a customs union: the creation of a uniform tariff schedule applicable to imports from the rest of the world.
3. Formation of a common market: the removal of barriers to the movement of labour, capital and business enterprises.
4. The adoption of common agricultural policies.
5. The creation of an investment fund to channel capital from the more advanced to the less developed regions of the community.

Table 6.3: Main provisions of the Treaty of Rome.

Some countries, however, were reluctant to embrace the ambitious integrative effort of the Treaty. In 1960, a looser, less integrated philosophy was endorsed with the formation of the European Free Trade Association (EFTA) by eight countries: Austria, Denmark, Finland, Norway, Portugal, Sweden, Switzerland and United Kingdom. Barriers to trade among member countries were dismantled, although each country maintained its own policies with non-member states. Since that time EFTA has lost much of its original significance due to its members joining the European Union (Denmark and the United Kingdom in 1973, Portugal in 1986 and Austria, Finland and Sweden in 1995). EFTA countries have co-operated with the EU through bilateral free trade agreements and, since 1994, through the European Economic Area (EEA) arrangement, which allows for free movement of people, goods, services and capital within the combined area of the EU and EFTA. Of the EFTA countries, Iceland and Liechtenstein (which joined the EEA in May 1995) have decided not to apply for membership in the EU. Norway was to have joined in 1995, but after a referendum declined membership, as it did in 1973. Switzerland's decision to stay out of the EEA (mainly to keep the heaviest EU truck traffic from its roads) has hampered its negotiations for membership in the EU. In 2000, however, it entered into a series of bilateral agreements to liberalize its trading relations with the EU.[8] In 2006, the Swiss Government declared the decision to base Swiss–EU relationships on bilateral agreements.

A conflict that intensified throughout the 1980s was between the richer and more industrialized countries and the poorer countries of the Mediterranean region. The power of the bloc of poorer countries was strengthened in the 1980s when Greece, Spain and Portugal became EU members. Many argue that the dismantling of barriers between the richer and poorer countries will benefit the poorer countries by spurring them to become competitive. However, it may also be argued that the richer countries have an unfair advantage and therefore should accord protection to the poorer members before all barriers are dismantled.

Another source of difficulty that intensified in the 1980s was the administration of the community's **common agricultural policy (CAP)**. Most industrialized countries, including the United States, Canada and Japan, have adopted wide-scale government intervention and subsidization schemes for the agriculture industry. In the case of the EU, however, these policies have been implemented on a community-wide, rather than national, level. The CAP includes: (1) a price-support system whereby EU agriculture officials intervene in the market to keep farm product prices within a specified range; (2) direct subsidies to farmers; and (3) rebates to farmers who export or agree to store farm products rather than sell them within the community. The implementation of these policies absorbs about two-thirds of the annual EU budget.

The CAP has caused problems both within the EU and in relationships with non-members. Within the EU, the richer, more industrialized countries resent the extensive subsidization of the more agrarian economies, including new member countries, such as Poland and Bulgaria. Outside trading partners, especially the United States, have repeatedly charged the EU with unfair trade practices in agriculture. Developing countries complain about the EUs average 20% tariffs against their agricultural exports to the bloc and their €73 billion subsidies to their own farmers.[9]

The European Union since the Mid-1980s

By the mid-1980s, a sense of 'Europessimism' permeated most discussions of European integration. Although the members remained committed in principle to the 'four freedoms', literally hundreds of obstacles to the free movement of goods, services, people and capital remained. For example, there were cumbersome border restrictions on trade in many goods and although labour was theoretically mobile, the professional certifications granted in one country were often not recognized in others.

Growing dissatisfaction with the progress of integration, as well as threats of global competition from Japan and the United States, prompted the EU to take action. A policy paper published in 1985 (now known as the 1992 White Paper) exhaustively identified the remaining barriers to the four freedoms and proposed means of dismantling them.[10] It listed 282 specific measures designed to make the four freedoms a reality.

The implementation of the White Paper proposals began formally in 1987 with the passage of the Single European Act, which stated that 'the community shall adopt measures with the aim of progressively establishing the internal market over a period expiring on 31 December 1992'. The Single European Act envisaged a true common market where goods, people and money could move as freely between Germany and France as they move between American states.

Progress toward the goal of free movement of goods has been achieved largely due to the move from a 'common standards approach' to a 'mutual recognition approach'. Under the common standards approach, EU members were forced to negotiate the specifications for literally thousands of products, often unsuccessfully. For example, because of differences in tastes, agreement was never reached on specifications for beer, sausage or mayonnaise. Under the mutual recognition approach, the laborious quest for common standards is in most cases no longer necessary. Instead, as long as a product meets legal and specification requirements in one member country, it may be freely exported to any other and customers serve as final arbiters of success.

Less progress toward free movement of people in Europe has been made than toward free movement of goods. The primary difficulty is that EU members have been unable to agree on a common immigration policy. As long as this disagreement persists, travellers between countries must pass through border checkpoints. Some countries – notably Germany – have relatively lax immigration policies, whereas others – especially those with higher unemployment rates – favour strict controls on immigration. A second issue concerning the free movement of people is the acceptability of professional certifications across countries. In 1993, the largest EU member countries passed all of the professional worker directives. This means that workers' professional qualifications will be recognized throughout the EU, guaranteeing them equal treatment in terms of employment, working conditions and social protection in the host country.

Attaining free movement of capital within the EU entails several measures. First, citizens will be free to trade in EU currencies without restrictions. Second, the regulations governing banks and other financial institutions will be harmonized. In addition, mergers and acquisitions will be regulated by the EU rather than by national governments. Finally, securities will be freely tradable across countries.

A key aspect of free trade in services is the right to compete fairly to obtain government contracts. Under the 1992 guidelines, a government should not give preference to its own citizens in awarding government contracts. However, little progress has been made in this regard. Open competition in public procurement has been calculated to save US$10 billion a year. Yet the non-national share of contracts has been 5% since 1992. Worse still, few unsuccessful bidders complain, for fear that they would be ignored in future bids.[11]

Project 1992 was always a part of a larger plan and more a process than a deadline.[12] Many in the EU bureaucracy argued that the 1992 campaign required a commitment to Economic and Monetary Union (EMU) and subsequently to political union. These sentiments were confirmed at the Maastricht summit in December 1991, which produced various recommendations to that effect. The ratification of the Maastricht Treaty in late 1993 by all of the 12 member countries of the EC created the *European Union* starting 1 January 1994. The treaty calls for a commitment to economic and monetary union and a move toward political union with common foreign and security policy.

Currently the EU has a population of more than 500 million, an area of 4.32 million square kilometres and comprises 27 countries: Austria, Belgium, Bulgaria, Cyprus, Czech Republic, Denmark, Estonia, Finland, France, Germany, Greece, Hungary, Ireland, Italy, Latvia, Lithuania, Luxembourg, Malta, Netherlands, Poland, Portugal, Romania, Slovakia, Slovenia, Spain, Sweden and the United Kingdom. Canary Islands (Spain), Azores and Madeira (Portugal), French Guyana, Guadeloupe, Martinique and Reunion (France) are sometimes listed separately even though they are legally a part of Spain, Portugal and France.

Despite the uncertainties about the future of the EU, new countries want to join. Most EFTA countries have joined or are EU applicants in spite of the fact that the EEA treaty gives them most of the benefits of a single market. They also want to have a say in the making of EU laws and regulations. Access to the EU is essential for the growth of the Baltic and Central European countries. At the same time, the EU hopes to underpin democracy and free markets in the once centrally planned dictatorships and create a zone of stability at the EU's eastern flank.[13] The enlargement will create investment opportunities for firms and ensure cheaper goods for consumers in the EU. Before investment occurs, however, productivity in the new member countries has to improve significantly. Turkey's application has been hindered by its poor human rights record, its unresolved dispute with Greece over Cyprus and internal problems with Kurdish separatists. After the EU enlargements in 2004 and 2007, the present EU overall enlargement strategy document was adopted by the European Commission on 8 November 2006. The progress of the candidate countries (Croatia, the former Yugoslav Republic of Macedonia and Turkey) and potential candidate countries (Albania, Bosnia and Herzegovina, Montenegro, Serbia and Kosovo under UN Security Council Resolution 1244) on their road towards the EU is assessed in the Commission progress reports published on 8 November 2006.

In the long term, countries such as Belarus, Moldova and the Ukraine may become membership candidates.

F●CUS ON

POLITICS

The historic development of the EU in dates is as follows:

- On 9 May 1950 the French Foreign Minister Robert Schuman presented his proposal of a united Europe, known as the Schuman declaration. It is considered to be the start of the creation of the European Union.
- On 23 July 1952 the Treaty of Paris entered into force marking the establishing of the European Coal and Steel Community (ECSC). Its founding members were the Benelux countries (Belgium, the Netherlands and Luxembourg), France, Italy and West Germany.
- In 1958 the ECSC member countries established the European Economic Community (EEC), which later became the European Community.
- On 1 January 1973 the First EU Enlargement took place – Denmark, Ireland and the United Kingdom acceded to the EC (Norway also signed the Treaty but failed the ratification due to a negative opinion in a national referendum on accession).
- On 1 January 1981 the Second EU Enlargement made Greece an EC member.
- In 1985 Greenland decided to leave the EC following a referendum after being granted home rule by Denmark six years earlier.
- On 1 January 1986 the Third EU Enlargement brought Portugal and Spain into the EC.

- On 3 October 1990 the ex-German Democratic Republic and West Germany reunified, making the former East Germany a part of the EC. The German reunification added to the EC's area and population, but not the number of member countries.
- On 1 November 1993 The Maastricht Treaty took effect, formally establishing the European Union.
- On 1 January 1995 the Fourth EU Enlargement made Austria, Finland and Sweden, members of the EU (Norway signed the Treaty for the second time but failed to ratify it due to a negative opinion in a national referendum on accession).
- On 1 May 2004 the First Wave of the Fifth Enlargement took place. Ten countries, Cyprus, the Czech Republic, Estonia, Hungary, Latvia, Lithuania, Malta, Poland, Slovakia and Slovenia acceded to the EU. The largest number of countries, territory and population were then admitted to the EU in the whole history of the Union.
- On 1 January 2007, in the Second Wave of the Fifth Enlargement, Bulgaria and Romania became members of the EU.
- On 15 December 2008 the Caribbean islands of Bonaire, Saba and Saint Eustatius became part of the Netherlands as special municipalities and will thereby also become part of the European Union.

Organization of the EU

The executive body of the EU is the European Commission (EC), headquartered in Brussels. It is composed of commissioners (two from each larger member country and one from each smaller member) and headed by a president. The European Commission embodies and upholds the general interest of the European Union and is the driving force in the Union's institutional system. Its four main roles are:

- To propose legislation to Parliament and the Council.
- To administer and implement Community policies.
- To enforce Community law (jointly with the Court of Justice).
- To negotiate international agreements, mainly those relating to trade and co-operation.

The Maastricht Treaty brought the terms of office of the European Parliament and the EC into close alignment: Colleges serve a five-year term and take up office six months after European Parliament elections, which are held on a fixed basis in the June of years ending in 4 and 9, e.g., 2009, 2014, etc.

Since the enlargement of the European Union on 1 January 2007, the College counts 27 Commissioners. They are each in charge of particular policy areas and meet collectively as the College of Commissioners. Before the last enlargement of the EU, the larger countries had two Commissioners and the remaining countries each had one. Presently each member country now has one Commissioner.

The Commissioners oversee directorates-general (or departments), such as agriculture, transportation and external relations. The Commissioners are appointed by the member states, but according to the Treaty of Rome, their allegiance is to the community, not to their home country. The European Commission's staff in Brussels numbers over 26 000 people. Presently the EU has 23 official languages: Bulgarian, Czech, Danish, Dutch, English, Estonian, Finnish, French, Gaelic, German, Greek, Hungarian, Italian, Latvian, Lithuanian, Maltese, Polish, Portuguese, Romanian, Slovak, Slovene, Spanish and Swedish. That is why more than 25% of those employed at the EC are interpreters and translators.

The Council of the European Union is the main legislative institution of the EU. Article 202 of the Maastricht Treaty the Council, in accordance:

- ensures co-ordination of the general economic policies of the member states;
- has power to take decisions;
- confers on the Commission, in the acts which the Council adopts, powers for the implementation of the rules that the Council lays down.

The Council may impose certain requirements in respect of the exercise of these powers. The Council may also reserve the right, in specific cases, to exercise directly implementing powers itself. The procedures referred to above must be consonant with principles and rules to be laid down in advance by the Council, acting unanimously on a proposal from the Commission and after obtaining the opinion of the European Parliament.

In effect, the Council performs the following functions:

- *Legislation:* The Council passes EU laws on the recommendations of the European Commission together with the European Parliament using the Co-decision procedure.
- *Approval of the EU budget:* The Council and the Parliament must agree on the EU budget.
- *Foreign and defence policy:* Although each member state is free to develop its own foreign and defence policy, the Council seeks to achieve a common foreign and defence policy for the member states.
- *Economic policy:* The Council also seeks to achieve a common economic policy for the member states.
- *Justice:* The Council seeks to co-ordinate the justice system of the member states, especially in areas such as terrorism.

The Court of Justice is composed of 27 Judges and eight Advocates General. The Judges and Advocates General are appointed by common accord by the governments of the member states for a renewable term of six years. They are chosen from among lawyers whose independence is beyond doubt and who possess the qualifications required for appointment, in their respective countries, to the highest judicial offices or who are of recognized competence. The Judges of the Court elect one of themselves as President of the Court for a renewable term of three years. The President directs the work and staff of the Court and presides at hearings and deliberations of the full Court or the Grand Chamber. The Advocates General assist the Court. They are responsible for presenting, with complete impartiality and independence, an 'opinion' in the cases assigned to them.

The European Parliament represents all citizens from the EU member countries. Its members are known as Members of the European Parliament (MEPs). MEPs are elected every five years by universal adult suffrage. Since 1 January 2007, there are 785 MEPs but their number will drop to 736 after the next election. The Maastricht and Amsterdam Treaties empowered the Parliament to veto legislation in certain policy areas and confer with the Council to settle differences in their respective drafts of legislation. Furthermore, the Parliament can question the Commission and Council, amend and reject the budget and dismiss the entire Commission.[14]

The entities and the process of decision making are summarized in Figure 6.1. Not shown are the Court of Auditors (who are to ensure the sound financial management of the EU) and the European

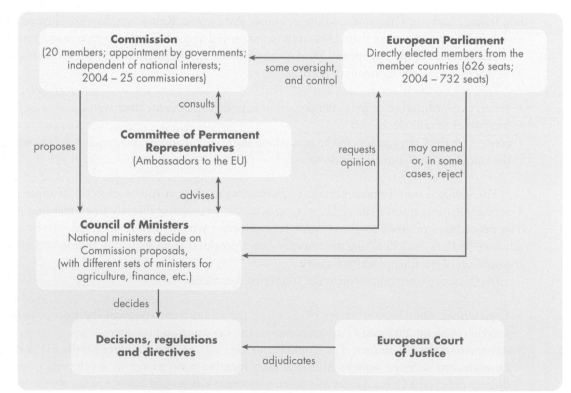

Figure 6.1: Organization and decision making of the EU.

Sources: 'EU Perustuslaki Voi Tuoda Suomeen Uuden Superministerin', *Helsingin Sanomat*, 1 August 2003, A6; schematic adapted from 'My, How You've Grown', *The Economist*, 25 January 1992, 31–32, © The Economist Newspaper Ltd, London.

Central Bank (ECB), which is responsible for monetary policy. The ECB is also responsible for the EU's single currency, the euro. The ECB's main task is to maintain the euro's purchasing power, thus providing price stability in the euro area. Since 1 January 1999 the ECB has been responsible for conducting monetary policy for the euro area – the world's second largest economy after that of the United States. The euro area came into being when responsibility for monetary policy was transferred from the national central banks of 11 EU member states, namely, Austria, Belgium, Finland, France, Germany, Ireland, Italy, Luxembourg, The Netherlands, Portugal and Spain to the ECB on 1 January 1999. Greece joined the euro area in 2001, followed by Slovenia, the 13th member of the euro area, in 2007. The creation of the euro area and a new supranational institution, the ECB, was a milestone in a long and complex process of European integration. To join the euro area, the 13 countries had to fulfil the convergence criteria, as will other EU member states prior to adopting the euro. The criteria set out the economic and legal preconditions for countries to participate successfully in Economic and Monetary Union.

Implications of the Integrated European Market

Perhaps the most important implication of the four freedoms for Europe is the economic growth that is expected to result.[15] Several specific sources of increased growth have been identified. First, there will be gains from eliminating the transaction costs associated with border patrols, customs procedures and so forth. Second, economic growth will be spurred by the economies of scale that will be achieved when production facilities become more concentrated, consolidated and integrated. Third, there will be gains from more intense competition among EU companies. Firms that were monopolists in one country will now be subject to competition from firms in other EU countries. The introduction of the euro has also added to the efficiencies, especially in terms of consolidation of firms across industries and across countries. Furthermore, countries in Euroland have been benefiting from cheaper transaction costs and reduced currency risks. Consumers and businesses have enjoyed greater price transparency and increased price-based competition.

The deepening EU integration has important implications for firms within and outside Europe. There are substantial benefits for those firms already operating in Europe. Those firms have advantages because their operations in one country can now be freely expanded into others and their products may be freely sold across borders. In a borderless Europe, firms have access to many more millions of consumers. In addition, the free movement of capital allows the firms to sell securities, raise capital and recruit labour throughout Europe. Firms have also gained substantial economies of scale in production and marketing. The extent of these economies of scale depends on the ability of the managers to find pan-regional segments or to homogenize tastes across borders through their promotional activity.

For firms from non-member countries, European integration presents various possibilities depending on the firm's position within the EU.[16] Table 6.4 provides four different scenarios with proposed courses of action. Well-established US-based multinational marketers such as H.J. Heinz and Colgate-Palmolive will be able to take advantage of the new economies of scale. For example, 3M plants used to turn out different versions of the company's products for various markets. Now, the 3M plant in Wales, for example, makes videotapes and videocassettes for all of Europe. Colgate-Palmolive has to watch out for competitors, such as Germany's Henkel, in the brutally competitive detergent market. At the same time, large-scale retailers, such as France's Carrefour and Germany's Aldi group, are undertaking their own efforts to exploit the situation with hypermarkets supplied by central warehouses with computerized inventories. Their procurement policies have to be met by companies such as Heinz. Many multinationals are developing pan-European strategies to exploit the emerging situation; that is, they are standardizing their products and processes to the greatest extent possible without compromising local input and implementation.

Company Status	Challenges	Response
Established multinational in one market/multiple markets	Exploit opportunities from improved productivity Meet challenge of competitors Cater to customers/intermediaries doing same	Pan-European strategy
Firm with one European subsidiary	Competition Loss of niche	Expansion Strategic alliances Rationalization Divestment
Exporter to Europe	Competition Access	European branch Selective acquisition Strategic alliance
No interest in Europe	Competition at home Lost opportunity	Entry

Source: Material drawn from John F. Magee, 1989, '1992 Moves Americans Must Make', *Harvard Business Review*, 67 (May–June), 78–84.

Table 6.4: Proposed company responses to European markets.

A company with a foothold in only one European market is faced with the danger of competitors who can use the strength of multiple markets. Furthermore, the elimination of barriers may do away with the company's competitive advantage. For example, more than half of the 45 major European food companies are in just one or two of the individual European markets and seriously lag behind broader-based US and Swiss firms. Similarly, automakers such as Fiat are nowhere close to the cross-manufacturing presence of Ford and GM. The courses of action include expansion through acquisitions or mergers, formation of strategic alliances (for example, AT&T's joint venture with Spain's Telfnica to produce state-of-the-art microchips), rationalization by concentrating only on business segments in which the company can be a pan-European leader and, finally, divestment.

Exporters from outside the EU need to worry about maintaining their competitive position and continued access to the market. Small and mid-sized US companies account for more than 60% of US exports to the EU. Their success is based on the relationships they have developed with their customers, especially in hi-tech.[17] Companies with a physical presence may be in a better position to assess and take advantage of the developments. Internet-systems provider WatchGuard Technologies has almost doubled its staff in Europe, from 12 to 20 in 2002 in the wake of the September 11th attacks, and despite increasing concern about viruses. In some industries, US marketers do not see a reason to be in Europe at all or to change from exporting to more involved modes of entry. Machinery and machine tools, for example, are in great demand in Europe and marketers in these companies say they have little reason to manufacture there.

The term Fortress Europe has been used to describe the fears of many US firms about a unified Europe. The concern is that while Europe dismantles internal barriers, it will raise external ones, making access to the European market difficult for US and other non-EU firms. In a move designed to protect European farmers, for example, the EU has occasionally banned the import of certain agricultural goods from the United States. The EU has also called on members to limit the number of US television programmes broadcast in Europe. Finally, many US firms are concerned about the relatively strict domestic content rules, such as geographic indications, recently passed by the EU. These rules require certain products sold in Europe to be manufactured with European inputs. One effect of the perceived threat of Fortress Europe has been an increased direct investment in Europe by US firms, due to fears that the EU will erect barriers to US exports and of the domestic content rules governing many goods.

NORTH AMERICAN ECONOMIC INTEGRATION

Although the EU is undoubtedly the most successful and well-known integrative effort, integration efforts in North America have gained momentum and attention. What started as a trading pact between two close and economically well-developed allies has already been expanded to include Mexico and long-term plans call for further additions. However, in North American integration the interest is purely economic; there are no constituencies for political integration.

US–Canada Free Trade Agreement

After three failed tries during the twentieth century, the United States and Canada signed a free trade agreement that came into effect on 1 January 1989. The agreement created a US$5 trillion continental economy. The two countries already had sectoral free trade arrangements; for example, one for automotive products had existed for over 20 years. Even before the agreement, however, the United States and Canada were already the world's largest trading partners and there were relatively few trade barriers. The new arrangement eliminated duties selectively in three stages over the 1989–1999 period.[18] For example, the first round eliminated a 3.9% tariff on US computers shipped to Canada as well as 4.9–22% duties on trade in whiskey, skates, furs and unprocessed fish. The sensitive sectors, such as textiles, steel and agricultural products, were not liberalized until the latter part of the transitionary period.

Both countries see the free trade agreement as an important path to world competitiveness. Although there have been some dislocations, due to production consolidation, for example, the pact has created 750 000 jobs in the United States and 150 000 in Canada. It has also added as much as 1% in growth to both countries' economies. Canada is the largest single nation trading partner of the United States. Trade between the United States and Canada exceeded US$499.3 billion in 2005 (a 12.6% increase over 2004). US trade with Canada represented nearly 19.4% of US total trade in 2005 and Canada purchased 23.4% of US exports. Although Canada is an important trading partner for the United States, the United States is the dominant trade partner for Canada. The United States supplied 56.6% of Canada's imports of goods in 2005 and purchased 84.0% of Canada's exports. Automobiles and auto parts are the top US exports to and imports from Canada. Computer equipment, electrical equipment, engines, turbo-engines, recorded media, optical equipment and precision instruments are other major US exports. Primary US imports from Canada, apart from those in the automotive industry, are energy (natural gas, petroleum products and electricity), engines, aircraft equipment, wood and paper products.

North American Free Trade Agreement (NAFTA)

Negotiations on a North American Free Trade Agreement (NAFTA) began in 1991 to create the world's largest free market with currently over 400 million consumers and a total output of nearly US$11 trillion.[19] The pact marked a bold departure: never before had industrialized countries created such a massive free trade area with a developing country neighbour.

Since Canada stands to gain very little from NAFTA (its trade with Mexico is 1% of its trade with the United States), much of the controversy has centred on the gains and losses for the United States and Mexico. Proponents have argued that the agreement gives US firms access to a huge pool of relatively low-cost Mexican labour at a time when demographic trends are indicating labour shortages in many parts of the United States. At the same time, many new jobs have been created in Mexico. The agreement gives firms in both countries access to millions of additional consumers and the liberalized trade flows will result in faster economic growth in both countries. The top 20 exports and imports between Mexico and the United States are in virtually the same industries, indicating intra-industry specialization and building of economies of scale for global competitiveness.[20] Overall, the corporate view toward NAFTA is overwhelmingly positive.

Opposition to NAFTA has been on issues relating to labour and the environment. US unions in particular worry about job loss to Mexico given lower wages and work standards, some estimating that six million US workers were vulnerable to job loss. A distinctive feature of NAFTA is the two side agreements that were worked out to correct perceived abuses in labour and in the environment in Mexico. The North American Agreement on Labour Cooperation (NAALC) was set up to hear complaints about worker abuse. Similarly, the Commission on Environmental Compliance was established to act as a public advocate on the environment. The side agreements have, however, had little impact, mainly because the mechanisms they created have almost no enforcement power.[21]

After a remarkable start in increased trade and investment, NAFTA suffered a serious setback due to significant devaluation of the Mexican peso in early 1995 and the subsequent impact on trade. Critics of NAFTA argued that too much was expected too fast of a country whose political system and economy were not ready for open markets. In response, advocates of NAFTA argued that there was nothing wrong with the Mexican real economy and that the peso crisis was a political one that would be overcome with time. As a matter of fact, with the help of the United States and the IMF, Mexico's economy started a strong recovery in 1996.

In the period of 1993–2004, total trade between the United States and its NAFTA partners increased 129.3%, yet total trade between the United States and non-NAFTA partners increased 123.8% in the same period. According to Hufbauer and Schott (2005)[22], overall, NAFTA has not caused *trade diversion*, aside from a few select industries such as textiles and apparel, in which rules of origin negotiated in the agreement were specifically designed to make US firms prefer Mexican manufacturers. The World Bank also showed that the aggregate NAFTA imports' percentage growth was accompanied by an almost similar increase of non-NAFTA imports, thus suggesting that increase in trade was not diversionary.

Reforms have turned Mexico into an attractive market in its own right. Mexico's gross domestic product has been expanding by about 3% every year since 1989 and exports to the United States have risen 21.6% a year to US$183 billion (86% of total) in 2005. By institutionalizing the nation's turn to open markets, the free trade agreement has attracted considerable new foreign investment.

The United States has benefited from Mexico's success. US exports to Mexico were more than double those to Japan at US$118 billion (53% of total) in 2005. The US major trading partners in 2005 were Canada 23.4%, Mexico 13.3%, Japan 6.1%, China 4.6%, UK 4.3% and Germany 3.1%. Although the surplus of US$1.3 billion in 1994 turned to a deficit of US$50.1 billion in 2005, these imports have helped in Mexico's growth and will, therefore, strengthen NAFTA in the long term. Furthermore, US imports from Mexico have been shown to have much higher US content than imports from other countries.[23] At present, co-operation between Mexico and the United States is taking new forms beyond trade and investment; for example, bi-national bodies have been established to tackle issues such as migration, border control and drug trafficking.[24]

Among the US industries to benefit are computers, autos, petrochemicals, financial services and aerospace. Aerospace companies such as Boeing, Honeywell and GE Aircraft Engines have recently made Mexico a centre for both parts manufacture and assembly. Aerospace is now one of Mexico's largest industries, second only to electronics, with 10 000 workers employed.[25] In Mexico's growth toward a more advanced society, manufacturers of consumer goods also stand to benefit. NAFTA has already had a major impact in the emergence of new retail chains, many established to handle new products from abroad.[26] Not only have US retailers, such as Wal-Mart, expanded to and in Mexico, but Mexican retailers, such as Grupo Gigante, have entered the US market.[27] Wal-Mart's use of lower tariffs, physical proximity and buying power is changing the Mexican retail landscape, as shown in the following Focus on Retail.

F◯CUS ON

RETAIL   Reshaping the World Retail Market

Wal-Mart saw the promise of the Mexican market in 1991 when it stepped outside of the United States for the first time by launching Sam's Clubs in 50–50 partnership with Cifra, Mexico's largest retailer. The local partner was needed to provide operational expertise in a market of significant culture and income differences from Wal-Mart's domestic one. Within months the first outlet – a bare-bones unit that sold bulk items at just above wholesale prices – was breaking all Wal-Mart records in sales. Although tariffs still made imported goods pricey, 'Made in the USA' merchandise also started appearing on the shelves.

After NAFTA took effect in 1994, tariffs tumbled, unleashing pent-up demand in Mexico for US-made goods. The trade treaty also helped eliminate some of the transportation headaches and government red tape that had kept Wal-Mart from fully realizing its competitive advantage. NAFTA resulted in many European and Asian manufacturers setting up plants in Mexico, giving the retailer cheaper access to more foreign brands.

Wal-Mart's enormous buying power has kept it ahead of its Mexican competitors who are making similar moves. Because Wal-Mart consolidates its orders for all goods it sells outside of the United States, it can wring deeper discounts from suppliers than its local competitors. Wal-Mart Mexico has repeatedly exploited NAFTA and other economic forces to trigger price wars. For example, rather than pocket the windfall that resulted when tariffs on Lasko brand floor fans fell from 20 to 2%, price cuts took place equal to the tariff reductions.

Behind Wal-Mart's success are increasingly price-conscious consumers. The greater economic security of NAFTA has helped tame Mexico's once fierce inflation. The resulting price stability has made it easier for Mexican consumers to spot bargains. In addition, Wal-Mart's clean, brightly lit interiors orderly and well-stocked aisles and consistent pricing policies are a relief from the chaotic atmosphere that still prevails in many local stores.

Wal-Mart's aggressive tactics have resulted in complaints as well. In 2002, Mexico's Competition Commission was asked to probe into reports that Wal-Mart exerts undue pressure on suppliers to lower their prices. Local retailers, such as Comerci, Gigante and Soriana, have seen their profits plummet but are forced to provide prices competitive to Wal-Mart's. In addition, they have engaged in aggressive rehauls of their operations. Soriana, for example, invested US$250 million in new stores in 2002. Soriana took out ads in local newspapers warning about 'foreign supermarkets' when regulators fined a Wal-Mart in Monterrey because a shelf price did not match the price on the checkout receipt.

Wal-Mart's success continues and it is now Mexico's top retailer. It already has 579 grocery stores, wholesale-club outlets and restaurants in Mexico.

Russia is expected to become Europe's biggest grocery market by 2020. Russia will overtake Germany as Europe's largest market in the next 10–12 years, with its estimated value rising 180% to €375 billion. In 2006 the Russian retail market was the fifth largest European market, after those of Germany, France, Britain and Italy, but constant increase in disposable income and developing trends of spending rather than saving means that the market is expected to grow rapidly.

Meanwhile the Russian retail market remains the most difficult market for Western retailers. One of the main reasons is that there is an established tradition of buying from small independent shops and local markets, especially among buyers in the Russian regions outside Moscow and St Petersburg, where only about 10% of grocery shopping is done in modern grocery stores. Moreover profit margins for the grocery sector are low. When Russians are shopping in modern grocery stores they are opting for discount outlets. Russia's five largest grocery retailers are all discounters. Pyaterochka, the largest of them, has a market share of just 1.8%.

Despite these barriers, the British retailer Marks & Spencer (M&S) has opened two stores in Moscow under a franchise agreement operated by the Turkish franchisee FIBA Group company, Marka Magazacilik AS, which operates 50 M&S outlets in Turkey. The German giant retailer, Metro, has also opened its first outlet in Moscow and plans to open a chain of stores in the near future. Since 2005 the Metro Group has become the highest-selling retailer in Russia. Presently the Group has more than 12 000 employees.

Reports in August 2006 suggested that Wal-Mart CEO Lee Scott met with Carrefour Chairman Luc Vandevelde in France for preliminary talks as a precursor to a Wal-Mart bid, Despite consistent denials from Carrefour, rumours had surfaced before about bids from both Tesco and Wal-Mart. Although Carrefour has been performing relatively under-par in recent years, its huge store network and global reach (it is the world's second largest retailer after Wal-Mart) make it an attractive target for rivals in the billion euro global retail sector. Meanwhile, as Carrefour announced lower-than-expected sales figures, its potential suitor – Wal-Mart – revealed in July 2006 that rising oil prices were beginning to affect profit levels. According to Lee Scott, not only do rising oil prices increase the cost of distribution, but they also reducing customer spending due to a significant reduction of disposable income. Scott said: 'The only real economic concern I have is that oil prices will erase improvements in employment and real income for an important segment of our customer base'.

Following meetings with Sainsbury's and Tesco in London, the Ulster Farmers' Union (UFU) has said that progress has been made in the ongoing saga over falling beef prices for the Northern Ireland province's farmers. Early in August 2006 the union's farmers picketed a Tesco store in Belfast over what they called 'disloyalty' to the region's meat sector in favour of cheaper South American meat imports. The protest at Tesco's Antrim Road outlet followed a collapse in farm gate beef prices in the province, which the farmers said was a result of the retailers stocking Brazilian beef imports instead of locally produced beef meat. At the time, Campbell Tweed (then Ulster Farmers' Union President) said that it was 'soul destroying' for farmers to see their produce being displaced by 'cheap imports from Brazil', while Tesco hit back at these allegations saying that any South American beef that was on sale in Tesco Northern Ireland stores was 'minimal' and part of a once off promotion. Tweed added that more than 95% of beef and lamb on sale on a regular basis in Tesco's Northern Ireland stores is sourced in the Antrim province. 'The meetings have been positive in the sense that it is clear that the supermarkets are committed to using large volumes of local beef', he also said. 'But volume is only one part of the equation and it is critical that farmers also receive a sustainable price for their produce. This is not the case at present in the beef industry and the supermarkets have a responsibility to address that'. According to the UFU, some beef producers are losing well over £100 on every animal sold and other farmers feel that their efforts to achieve Quality Assured Status have been 'undermined' by cheaper imports. 'The supermarkets are very powerful, but with that power comes responsibility', said Tweed after the meetings. 'If they are genuinely interested in maintaining a quality assured local supply base, they must send positive market signals to farmers. There is a commitment there to buy local, but we must see an urgent improvement in prices at the farm gate.'

Source: 'War of the Superstores', *Business Week*, 23 September 2002, 60; 'How Well Does Wal-Mart Travel?', *Business Week*, 3 September 2001, 82–84; 'How NAFTA Helped Wal-Mart Reshape the Mexican Market', *The Wall Street Journal*, 31 August 2001, A1–A2; Vijay Govindarajan and Anil K. Gupta, 'Taking Wal-Mart Global: Lessons from Retailing's Giant', *Strategy and Business*, Fourth Quarter, 1999, 45–56; www.checkout.ie/WorldReport.asp, accessed 17 April 2007.

Free trade does produce both winners and losers. Although opponents concede that the NAFTA agreement is likely to spur economic growth, they point out that segments of the US economy will be harmed by the agreement. Overall wages and employment for unskilled workers in the United States will fall because of Mexico's low-cost labour pool. US companies have been moving operations to Mexico since the early 1960s. The door was opened when Mexico liberalized export restrictions to allow for more so-called maquiladoras, over 3600 plants that make goods and parts or process food for export back to the United States. The supply of labour is plentiful, the pay and benefits are low and the work regulations are lax by US standards. In the last two decades, maquiladoras evolved from low-end garment or small-appliance assembly outfits to higher-end manufacturing of big-screen TVs, computers and auto parts. The factories shipped US$76.8 billion worth of goods (half of all Mexican exports), almost all of it to the United States.

But the arrangement is in trouble. The NAFTA treaty required Mexico to strip maquiladoras of their duty-free status by 2001. Tariff breaks formerly given to all imported parts, supplies, equipment and machinery used by foreign factories in Mexico now apply only to imports from Canada, Mexico and the United States. This effect is felt most by Asian factories since they still import a large amount of components from across the Pacific (for example, 97% of components for TVs assembled in Tijuana are imported, mostly from Asia). Europeans are less affected because of Mexico's free trade agreement with the EU, which eliminated tariffs gradually by 2007.[28] Wages have also been rising to US$3.52 an hour (up from US$2.29 in 1997) resulting in some low-end manufacturers of apparel and toys moving production to Asia.[29] While the Mexican government is eager to attract maquiladora investment, it is also keen to move away from using cheap labour as a central element of competitiveness.

Despite US fears of rapid job loss if companies send business south of the border, recent studies have put job gain or loss as almost a washout. The good news is that free trade has created higher-skilled and better-paying jobs in the United States as a result of growth in exports. As a matter of fact, jobs in exporting firms tend to pay 10–15% more than the jobs they replace. Losers have been US manufacturers of auto parts, furniture and household glass; sugar, peanut and citrus growers; and seafood and vegetable producers. The US Labour Department has certified 316 000 jobs as threatened or lost due to trade with Mexico and Canada. At the same time, the US economy has added some 20 million jobs in the years since NAFTA. The fact that job losses have been in more heavily unionized sectors has made these losses politically charged. In most cases, high Mexican shipping and inventory costs will continue to make it more efficient for many US industries to serve their home market from US plants. Outsourcing of lower-skilled jobs is an unstoppable trend for developed economies such as the United States. However, NAFTA has given US firms a way of taking advantage of cheaper labour while still keeping close links to US suppliers. Mexican assembly plants get 82% of their parts from US suppliers, whereas factories in Asia are using only a fraction of that.[30] Without NAFTA, entire industries might be lost to Asia rather than just the labour-intensive portions.

Countries dependent on trade with NAFTA countries are concerned that the agreement will divert trade and impose significant losses on their economies. Asia's continuing economic success depends largely on easy access to the North American markets, which account for more than 25% of annual export revenue for many Asian countries. Lower-cost producers in Asia are likely to lose some exports to the United States if they are subject to tariffs while Mexican firms are not and may, therefore, have to invest in NAFTA[31] Similarly, many in the Caribbean and Central America fear that the apparel industries of their regions will be threatened, as would much-needed investments.

NAFTA may be the first step toward a hemispheric bloc, but nobody expects it to happen any time soon. It took more than three years of tough bargaining to reach an agreement between the United States and Canada, two countries with parallel economic, industrial and social systems. The challenges of expanding free trade throughout Latin America will be significant. However, many of Latin America's groupings are making provisions to join NAFTA and create a hemispheric trade regime.[32] For this to happen, for example, many Latin nations will demand trade concessions in citrus, sugar, steel, apparel and other industries that the United States may, for political reasons, find extremely difficult to grant.[33] Overall, many US companies fear that Latin Americans will move closer to the European Union if free trade discussions do not progress. For example, both MERCOSUR and Mexico have signed free trade agreements with the EU.[34]

Latest Developments and Future Prospects for NAFTA

With the 10th anniversary of NAFTA in 2004, there has been renewed discussion of ways to enhance co-operation between the three NAFTA partners. The concept of deepening NAFTA – 'NAFTA plus' – has taken on added salience, in some quarters, since most of the gains resulting from tariff reduction of the agreement have been realized. Moreover, the Free Trade Agreements (FTAs) negotiated by the United States and Canada with other trading partners have diminished the relative advantage of NAFTA. In addition, since the September 11th, 2001, terrorist attacks there has been a perception in the business circles in both Canada and Mexico that continued economic access to the US market is strongly dependent on greater security co-operation with the United States. The Security and Prosperity Partnership (SPP), contains many initiatives that could lead to some measure of regulatory harmonization among the United States, Canada and Mexico. Moreover, in June 2006, the three nations launched a North American Competitiveness Council, which is made up of business leaders from each nation who examine proposals and provide recommendations to improve the competitiveness of North American business in the global marketplace.

An approach envisioned by US and Canadian business leaders and policy advocates is to create a North American security perimeter. This proposal responds to US fears of terrorism. Thus, a container landing at the Canadian port of Victoria headed for the United States would be inspected in Victoria, not at the Canadian–US border, thereby avoiding delays at border choke-points.

Another future avenue regarding the further integration of the North American economy is the creation of a customs union. Members of a customs union commonly eliminate tariffs among themselves and erect common barriers against the rest of the world. Both the US and Canada have already eliminated all tariffs between each other under NAFTA and have similar, though not identical, tariff schedules with third countries. Because all customs duties would be paid at port of entry at the perimeter of the customs union, the need for customs agents on the Canadian–US land border to collect revenue would be obviated.

The creation of a Common Market or Economic Union is also a future opportunity for NAFTA. A common market area would add free movement of labour and capital; thus, immigration and investment regulations would need to be harmonized or mutually recognized. An economic union similar to the European Union would also require harmonized or mutually recognized standards and regulations and perhaps some supranational institutions. Although the United States and Canada share many developed country level standards, this form of integration would need significant working out. For example, the United States would need to adopt the metric system to fulfil its obligations to harmonize standards. The North American members of an economic union will have to allow supranational entities to overrule laws passed by the US Congress or Canadian/Mexican Parliament. These issues simply illustrate the extent to which a North American economic integration would affect the governance of the United States, Canada and Mexico.

Many Canadian policy circles consider the opportunity of monetary union with the United States. This idea has been discussed in many forms. The Canadian dollar could be linked in value to the US dollar; Canada could adopt the US dollar; or a new North American currency (called the Amero by one proponent) could replace the US and Canadian dollars and later the Mexican peso. The supporters of the monetary union idea argue that it would force Canada to make the necessary structural adjustments that would make the Canadian economy more competitive, linking the macroeconomic policies of the United States and Canada. Canadian opponents of North American monetary union contend that it would lead to an unacceptable loss of political and economic sovereignty. However, in a monetary union in which macroeconomic convergence is achieved, this argument is not relevant. According to the opponents of monetary union, the US and Canadian economies respond differently to economic and political challenges, and hence need to utilize different adjustment mechanisms.

Further development and expansion of NAFTA has not yet occurred, and US plans to make Chile a member of the Agreement have not materialized.

OTHER ECONOMIC ALLIANCES

The world's developing countries have perhaps the most to gain from successful integrative efforts. Because many of these countries are also quite small, economic growth is difficult to generate internally. Many of these countries have adopted policies of *import substitution* to foster economic growth. With an import substitution policy, new domestic industries produce goods that were formerly imported. Many of these industries, however, can be efficient producers only with a higher level of production than can be consumed by the domestic economy. Their success, therefore, depends on accessible export markets made possible by integrative efforts.

Integration in Latin America

Before the signing of the US–Canada Free Trade Agreement, all of the major trading bloc activity in the Americas had taken place in Latin America. One of the longest-lived integrative efforts among developing countries was the Latin American Free Trade Association (LAFTA), formed in 1961. As the name suggests, the primary objective of LAFTA was the elimination of trade barriers. The 1961 agreement called for trade barriers to be gradually dismantled, leading to completely free trade by 1973. By 1969, however, it was clear that a pervasive protectionist ideology would keep LAFTA from meeting this objective and the target date was extended to 1980. In the meantime, however, the global debt crisis, the energy crisis and the collapse of the Bretton Woods system prevented the achievement of LAFTA objectives.

Two regional trading blocs were set up: the Andean Pact, later renamed the Andean Community and the Latin American Integration Association (ALADI). The Andean Pact was signed in 1968 by Bolivia, Colombia, Ecuador, Peru and Venezuela and was the first relatively successful Latin American regional grouping. The principal measures were a tariff reduction for international trade, the establishment of a common external tariff and the introduction of joint policies on the transportation of goods and economic co-operation in the functioning of selected industries. These measures facilitated government intervention in business activities in the member countries but somewhat restricted the implementation of free market mechanisms. The members intended to establish a common market by the mid-1990s, but market liberalization problems, a severe recession in the late 1990s and distrust between the member states impeded this objective. The organization continues to function as a customs union but the individual states are tending to seek bilateral agreements with non-member countries.

ALADI was formed in 1980 and was largely based on preferential tariff agreements between pairs of similarly developed member states. This led to more than 20 bilateral agreements and five sub-regional pacts, but economic co-operation and free trade between the member states failed to develop and consequently some of its members withdrew to form the Southern Common Market (MERCOSUR, see below).

The Central American Common Market (CACM) was formed by the Treaty of Managua in 1960. The CACM has often been cited as a model integrative effort for other developing countries. By the end of the 1960s, the CACM had succeeded in eliminating restrictions on 80% of trade among members. A continuing source of difficulty, however, is that the benefits of integration have fallen disproportionately to the richer and more developed members. Political difficulties in the area have also hampered progress. However, the member countries renewed their commitment to integration by negotiating free trade agreements with its trading partners. For example, a free trade agreement with the United States is considered desirable due to the complementary nature of trade flows, which exceed US$20 billion each year.

Integration efforts in the Caribbean have focused on the Caribbean Community and Common Market formed in 1968. Caribbean nations (as well as Central American nations) have benefited from the Caribbean Basin Initiative (CBI), which, since 1983, has extended trade preferences and granted access to the markets of the United States. Under NAFTA the preferences were lost, which meant that the Caribbean countries had to co-operate more closely with each other. They have argued that their small size entitles them to special concessions, especially in their fight against growing and trafficking in drugs.[35] Legislation by the United States to extend unilaterally NAFTA benefits to CBI countries to protect them from investment and trade diversion was passed in 2000.[36]

None of the activity in Latin America has so far been hemispheric; the Central Americans have their structures, the Caribbean nations theirs and the South Americans their own different forms. However, in a dramatic transformation, these nations are now looking for free trade as a salvation from stagnation, inflation and debt.

MERCOSUR or Mercosul (Mercado Comun del Sur or Mercado Comum do Sul)[37] was created by Argentina and Brazil in 1988 and expanded in 1991 to include Paraguay and Uruguay. Its foundation was preceded by 17 bilateral agreements between Argentina and Brazil in 1984–1988 to improve conditions for international trade. In 1996 Bolivia and Chile joined MERCOSUR as associate members. The largest economic bloc in Latin America, MERCOSUR still operates as a customs union but aspires to become a common market in the near future. The member states account for almost two thirds of the total Latin American economic output and the combined market consists of more than 230 million people. There is a high degree of economic unification among the member states. They have an open policy towards foreign direct investment but somewhat restrictive regulations on international trade. Brazil is the largest, richest in terms of natural resources and most influential economy in the bloc. Argentina has the largest middle class but has recently suffered from economic volatility. Within the bloc there are both integrative and divergent forces. For example, there are differing perspectives on the desired level and scope of economic integration as well as on protectionist measures that limit the degree of freedom to conduct international trade. This has had a negative impact on international competitiveness at the firm, industry, national and regional levels and limited the bargaining power of MERCOSUR *vis-à-vis* other powerful economic blocs. The ambition of the member states is to incorporate all the other Latin American countries (except Cuba) and turn MERCOSUR into a Free Trade Area of the Americas.

Despite their own economic challenges and disagreements over trade policy, the states in MERCOSUR have agreed to economic-convergence targets similar to those of the EU. These are in areas of inflation, public debt and fiscal deficits. Latin nations are realizing that if they do not unite, they will become increasingly marginal in the global market. In approaching the EU with a free trade agreement, for example, MERCOSUR members want to diversify their trade relationships and reduce their dependence on US trade.

The ultimate goal is a hemispheric free trade zone from Point Barrow, Alaska, to Patagonia. The first step to such a zone was taken in December 1994, when leaders of 34 countries in the Americas agreed to work toward the Free Trade Area of the Americas (FTAA) by 2005. Ministerials held since have established working groups to gather data and make recommendations in preparation for the FTAA negotiations. The larger countries have agreed to consider giving smaller and less-developed countries more time to reduce tariffs, to open their economies to foreign investment and to adopt effective laws in areas such as anti-trust, intellectual property rights, bank regulation and prohibitions on corrupt business practices. At the same time, the less-developed countries have agreed to include labour and environmental standards in the negotiations.[38]

Changes in corporate behaviour have been swift. Free market reforms and economic revival have had companies ready to export and to invest in Latin America. For example, Brazil's opening of its computer market resulted in Hewlett-Packard establishing a joint venture to produce PCs. Companies are also changing their approaches with respect to Latin America. In the past, Kodak dealt with Latin America through 11 separate country organizations. It has since streamlined its operations to five 'boundariless' companies organized along product lines and taking advantage of trade openings and centralized distribution, thereby making deliveries more efficient and decreasing inventory-carrying costs.[39]

Integration in Asia

The development in Asia has been quite different from that in Europe and in the Americas. Whereas arrangements in Europe and North America have been driven by political will, market forces may compel politicians in Asia to move toward formal integration. Although Japan is the dominant force in the area and might seem the choice to take leadership in such an endeavour, neither the Japanese themselves nor the other nations want Japan to do it. The concept of a 'Co-Prosperity Sphere' of 50 years ago has made nations wary of Japan's influence.[40] Also, in terms of economic and political distance, the potential member countries are far from each other, especially compared with the EU.

Asian interest in regional integration, however, is increasing for pragmatic reasons. First, European and American markets are significant for the Asian producers and some type of organization or bloc may be needed to maintain leverage and balance against the two other blocs. Second, given that much of the growth in trade for the nations in the region is from intra-Asian trade, having a common understanding and policies will become necessary.

A future arrangement is likely to use the frame of the most established arrangement in the region, the Association of Southeast Asian Nations (ASEAN). Before 1991, ASEAN had no real structures and consensus was reached through information consultations. In October 1991, the Heads of State and Government of ASEAN member countries (Brunei, Indonesia, Malaysia, Philippines, Singapore, Thailand, Vietnam and, since 1997, Cambodia, Myanmar and Laos) announced the formation of a customs union called ASEAN Free Trade Area (AFTA), which was made functional in 1992.

The objective of AFTA is to increase the ASEAN region's competitive advantage as a production base geared for the world market. A vital step in this direction is the liberalization of trade through the elimination of tariffs and non-tariff barriers among the ASEAN members. This activity has begun to serve as a catalyst for greater efficiency in production and long-term competitiveness. Moreover, the expansion of intra-regional trade is giving the ASEAN consumers wider choice and better quality consumer products. The 10 member countries agreed to reduce tariffs to a maximum level of 5% in 2003 and to create a customs union by 2010.

ASEAN now focuses on the development of product-specific mutual recognition arrangements in conformity assessment so that product-related standards and regulations do not become technical barriers to trade. ASEAN has also set the goal of harmonizing national standards with international ones, such as International Standards Organization (ISO), International Electrotechnical Commission (IEC) and International Telecommunications Union (ITU) standards, for 20 priority product groups. These 20 product groups are some of the most widely traded products in the region including important consumer durables, for example, radios, television sets, refrigerators, air conditioners and telephone sets. In 2005, ASEAN had a population of 570 million, a gross domestic product of US$1 064 351.3 million, total exports of US$765 544.8 million, imports of US$677 112.1 million and a trade surplus of US$88 432.7 million.

The Malaysians have pushed for the formation of the East Asia Economic Group (EAEG), which would add Hong Kong, Japan, South Korea and Taiwan to the list. This proposal makes sense because without Japan and the rapidly industrializing countries of the region such as South Korea and Taiwan, the effect of the arrangement would be small. Japan's reaction has been generally negative toward all types of regionalization efforts, mainly because it has the most to gain from free trade efforts. However, part of what has been driving regionalization has been Japan's reluctance to foster some of the elements that promote free trade, such as reciprocity.[41] Should the other trading blocs turn against Japan, its only resort may be to work toward a more formal trade arrangement in Pacific Asia.

Another formal proposal for co-operation would start building bridges between two emerging trade blocs. Some individuals have publicly called for a US–Japan common market. Given the differences on all fronts between the two, the proposal may be quite unrealistic at this time. Negotiated trade liberalization will not open Japanese markets due to major institutional differences, as seen in many rounds of successful negotiations but totally unsatisfactory results. The only solution for the US government is to forge better co-operation between the government and the private sector to improve competitiveness.[42]

In 1989, Australia proposed the Asia-Pacific Economic Co-operation (APEC) as an annual forum. The proposal called for ASEAN members to be joined by Australia, New Zealand, Japan, China, Hong Kong, Taiwan, South Korea, Canada and the United States. It was initially modelled after the Organization for Economic Co-operation and Development (OECD), which is a centre for research and high-level discussion. Since then, APECs goals have become more ambitious. At present, APEC has 20 members: Australia, Brunei Darussalam, Canada, Chile, China, Hong Kong as a part of China, Indonesia, Japan, Republic of Korea, Malaysia, Mexico, New Zealand, Papua New Guinea, Peru, the Philippines, Russia, Taiwan, Thailand, United States of America and Vietnam. The key objectives of APEC are to liberalize trade by 2020, to facilitate trade by harmonizing standards and to build human capacities for realizing the region's ambitions. The trade-driven economies of the region have the world's largest pool of savings, and the most advanced technologies and fastest growing markets. Therefore, companies with interests in the region are observing and supporting APEC-related developments closely, as shown in the Focus on Politics below.

However, the future actions of the other two blocs will determine how quickly and in what manner the Asian bloc, whatever it is, will respond. Also, the stakes are the highest for the Asian nations because their traditional export markets have been in Europe and North America and, in this sense, very dependent on free access.

FOCUS ON

POLITICS   In Support of Free Trade in Asia

General Motors (GM) – and all the major car makers – are driving into Asia. In the period of 2001–2010, vehicle sales in Asia are expected to grow by more than that of Europe and North America combined, making Asia the second largest automotive market with sales approaching 20 million vehicles per year. The world's largest industrial company has found the environmental challenges considerable despite the lure of substantial market potential made possible by the growing middle class. In addition to distribution challenges and aggressive competition from other manufacturers, both local and foreign, the most daunting challenges are barriers to free trade. For example, in Indonesia, GM faces competition from a local model, the Timor, which costs substantially less due to government supports (that is, lower duties on imported components). Before the resignation of President Suharto, the company was run by one of his sons.

To work around the trade barriers and get on solid footing in Asian markets, GM has invested heavily to build up local manufacturing and distribution. The company's build-up in Asia started in 1990 with the establishment of a regional office in Hong Kong and representative offices in Bangkok, Beijing, Jakarta and Kuala Lumpur. In 1994, GM's Asia headquarters were moved from Detroit to Singapore. Singapore not only provides co-ordination and support, but allows GM to tailor manufacturing, distribution and sales to local requirements. In Japan, GM now owns a 49% equity stake in Isuzu, while in China, the company established GM China as a separate entity. GM has two factories there and is planning further expansion. For example, through a US$100 million joint venture with Chinese state-owned car manufacturers, GM is making headway in the minivan sector, one of the fastest growing segments in the market. Another investment, a US$251 million stake in ailing automaker Daewoo Motor Company, gives GM a foothold in South Korea, Asia's second largest auto market. To highlight its presence in Asia, GM is investing US$450 million in a regional manufacturing facility in Thailand's Rayong Province to build the specially designed and engineered Opel 'Car for Asia'.

To combat protectionism and further the cause of free trade, GM has developed a three-pronged strategy. The first approach focuses on executives working with government representatives from the United States, the EU and Japan to dismantle what GM regards as the largest flaws. The company uses its clout as a major investor, but it can also call on support from industries that follow it into a new market, such as component manufacturers. On the second level, GM works within existing frameworks to balance the effects of nationalistic policies. In countries such as Indonesia and Malaysia, it develops company-specific plans to preserve avenues of sales even under challenging circumstances. Finally, GM is also pursuing its business strategy in Asia's free trade areas. Since it will be a long time before barriers are taken down in the Asia Pacific Economic Co-operation Forum (APEC), its immediate focus is on the ASEAN Free Trade Area (AFTA). GM is hopeful that the automotive sector will be a beneficiary of tariff reductions – provided that member governments can be persuaded that such cuts are in their best interests.

Sources: Robyn Meredith, 'Crazy Like a Fox', *Forbes*, 8 July 2002, 74; Peter Wonacott, 'GMs Chinese Unit, Two Partners, Join Up to Make Minivehicles', *The Wall Street Journal*, 4 June 2002; 'US Auto Makers Demonstrate Commitment to Thailand', US–ASEAN Business Council press release, 12 May 1999, www.us–asean.org; 'GM Delays Plans to Open Big Thai Plant', *The Wall Street Journal*, 6 January 1998, A2; 'GM Presses for Free Trade in Asia', *Crossborder Monitor*, 15 January 1997, 1, 9. See also: www.GMBuyPower.com and www.gmautoworld.com.tw.

Economic integration has also taken place on the Indian subcontinent. In 1985, seven nations of the region (India, Pakistan, Bangladesh, Sri Lanka, Nepal, Bhutan and the Maldives) launched the **South Asian Association for Regional Co-operation (SAARC)** to be later joined by Afghanistan. Co-operation is limited to relatively non-controversial areas, such as agriculture and regional development. Elements such as the formation of a common market have not been included. The EU has consistently affirmed an interest in strengthening relationships with SAARC. The EU takes the view that it can help consolidate the ongoing integration process through its economic influence in the region, its own historical experience of economic and trade integration and of dealing with diversity, and its interest in crisis prevention. In 1996, the European Commission and the SAARC Secretariat signed a Memorandum of Understanding on Co-operation. In 1999, the EU and SAARC agreed to co-operate on improving market access for SAARC products into the EU market. The European Commission is currently designing a new, broader programme of co-operation with SAARC, which should notably seek to promote the harmonization of standards; facilitate trade; raise awareness about the benefits of regional co-operation; and promote business networking in the SAARC area.

The **Gulf Co-operation Council (GCC)** for the Arab States of the Gulf was created on 25 May 1981, and comprised the oil rich states of Bahrain, Kuwait, Oman, Qatar, Saudi Arabia and the United Arab Emirates. The unified economic agreement between the countries of the GCC was signed on 11 November 1981 in Riyadh, Saudi Arabia. In 2006, Yemen started negotiations for GCC membership and is expected to join in 2016. EU relations with GCC are channelled through a Co-operation Agreement signed in 1989 between the European Community and the GCC. The objective of this Agreement is to contribute to strengthening stability in a region of strategic importance and to facilitate political and economic relations. The Co-operation Agreement lays out the establishment of an annual Joint Council/Ministerial Meeting between the EU and the GCC foreign ministers as well as between senior officials at a Joint Co-operation Committee. Such EU–GCC meetings have been held at alternating locations. With respect to the implementation of the Co-operation Agreement, the Joint Council stressed its shared political will to further relations and co-operation in all areas besides trade and economic issues.

On specific areas such as counter-terrorism, there was a strong reaffirmation by both parties on their commitment to fight terrorism in all its forms and manifestations. The aftermath of the Iraq war and EU efforts towards the establishment of an EU Strategic Partnership for the Mediterranean and the Middle East provoked a renewed interest in EU–GCC relations. The European Commission is therefore seeking to enhance co-operation activities with the GCC within the framework of the Strategic Partnership for the Mediterranean and the Middle East, approved by the European Council in June 2004. Such co-operation should encompass the political, economic and social fields. Such enhanced co-operation will also open up possibilities for the European Commission to support the region's domestic reform efforts including areas such as education or human rights.

Integration in Africa

Africa's economic groupings range from currency unions among European nations and their former colonies to customs unions among neighbouring states. In addition to wanting to liberalize trade among members, African countries want to gain better access to European and North American markets for farm and textile products. Given that most of the countries are too small to negotiate with the other blocs, alliances have been the solution. In 1975, 16 West African nations attempted to create a megamarket large enough to interest investors from the industrialized world and reduce hardship through economic integration. The objective of the Economic Community of West African States (ECOWAS) was to form a customs union and eventual common market. Although many of its objectives have not been reached, its combined population of 160 million represents the largest economic entity in sub-Saharan Africa.

Other entities in Africa include the Common Market for Eastern and Southern Africa (COMESA), the Economic Community of Central African States (CEEAC), the Southern African Customs Union (SACU), the Southern African Development Community (SADC) and some smaller, less globally oriented blocs such as the Economic Community of the Great Lakes Countries, the Mano River Union and the East African Community (EAC).

The Treaty establishing COMESA was signed on 5 November 1993 in Kampala, Uganda. Current COMESA member countries are: Angola, Burundi, Comoros, Congo, Eritrea, Ethiopia, Kenya, Libya, Madagascar, Malawi, Mauritius, Namibia, Rwanda, Seychelles, Sudan, Swaziland, Tanzania, Uganda, Zambia and Zimbabwe. Its main focus is on the formation of a large economic and trading unit that is capable of overcoming some of the barriers that are faced by individual states. COMESA is an all-embracing development organization involving co-operation in all economic and social sectors. Nine of the member states formed a free trade area in 2000, with Rwanda and Burundi joining the FTA in 2004 and the Comoros and Libya in 2006.

At a summit meeting in December 1981, the leaders of the Central African Customs and Economic Union (UDEAC) agreed in principle to form a wider economic community of Central African states. On 18 October 1983 a new integration, later known as CEEAC, was established by the UDEAC members and the members of the Economic Community of the Great Lakes States (CEPGL) (Burundi, Rwanda and the then Zaire) as well as São Tome and Principe, beginning operations in 1985.

The Southern African Customs Union was established on 11 December 1969 with the signature of the Customs Union Agreement between Botswana, Lesotho, Namibia, South Africa and Swaziland. It entered into force on the 1 March 1970, thereby replacing the Customs Union Agreement of 1910. The SACU is the oldest customs union in the world. It meets annually to discuss matters related to the Agreement. There are also technical liaison committees, namely the Customs Technical Liaison Committee, the Trade and Industry Liaison committee and the *Ad hoc* Sub-Committee on Agriculture, which meet three times a year.

The Southern African Development Co-ordination Conference (SADCC) was the forerunner of the socio-economic co-operation known today as SADC. The adoption by nine majority-ruled southern African countries of the Lusaka declaration on 1 April 1980 paved the way for the formal establishment of SADCC in July 1981. SADCC was transformed into SADC on 17 August 1992 with the adoption of the Windhoek Declaration by the founding members of SADCC and newly independent Namibia. On 14 August 2001, the 1992 SADC treaty was amended. The headquarters of SADC is in Gaborone, Botswana. The current SADC member countries are Angola, Botswana, Democratic Republic of Congo, Lesotho, Madagascar, Malawi, Mauritius, Mozambique, Namibia, South Africa, Swaziland, Tanzania, Zambia and Zimbabwe. Seychelles joined SADC, in 1997, but left in 2004.

Most member countries are part of more than one bloc (for example, Tanzania is a member in both the EAC and SADC). The blocs, for the most part, have not been successful due to the small size of the members and lack of economic infrastructure to produce goods to be traded inside the blocs. Moreover, some of the blocs have been relatively inactive for substantial periods of time while their members endure internal political turmoil or even warfare among each other.[43] In 2002, African nations established the African Union (AU) for regional co-operation. Eventually, plans call for a pan-African parliament, a court of justice, a central bank and a shared currency.[44]

ECONOMIC INTEGRATION AND THE INTERNATIONAL MANAGER

Regional economic integration creates opportunities and challenges for the international manager. Economic integration may have an impact on a company's entry mode by favouring direct investment, because one of the basic rationales for integration is to generate favourable conditions for local production and inter-regional trade. By design, larger markets are created with potentially more opportunity. Harmonization efforts may result in standardized regulations, which can positively affect production and marketing efforts.

Decisions regarding integrating markets must be assessed from four different perspectives, which are examined in the next sections: the range and impact of changes resulting from integration; development of strategies to relate to these changes; organizational changes needed to exploit these changes; and strategies to influence change in a more favourable direction.[45]

Effects of Change

The first task is to create a vision of the outcome of the change. Change in the competitive landscape can be dramatic if scale opportunities can be exploited in relatively homogeneous demand conditions. This could be the case, for example, for industrial goods and consumer durables, such as cameras and watches, as well as for professional services. The international manager will have to take into consideration varying degrees of change readiness within the markets themselves; that is, governments and other stakeholders, such as labour unions, may oppose the liberalization of competition, especially when national champions such as airlines, automobiles, energy and telecommunications are

The European Union

Member Countries
Candidate Countries

NAFTA and CACM Countries

North American Free Trade Agreement (NAFTA) Member Countries

Central American Common Market (CACM) Member Countries

CARICOM and MERCOSUR Countries

BAHAMAS

HAITI

SAINT KITTS & NEVIS
ANTIGUA & BARBUDA
BELIZE
JAMAICA
MONTSERRAT
DOMINICA
SAINT LUCIA
SAINT VINCENT &
THE GRENADINES
BARBADOS
GRENADA
TRINIDAD & TOBAGO

GUYANA
SURINAM

BRAZIL

PARAGUAY

ARGENTINA

URUGUAY

Carribean Community (CARICOM)
Member Countries

Southern Common Market (MERCOSUR)
Member Countries

SADC, COMESA, ECOWAS and GCC Countries

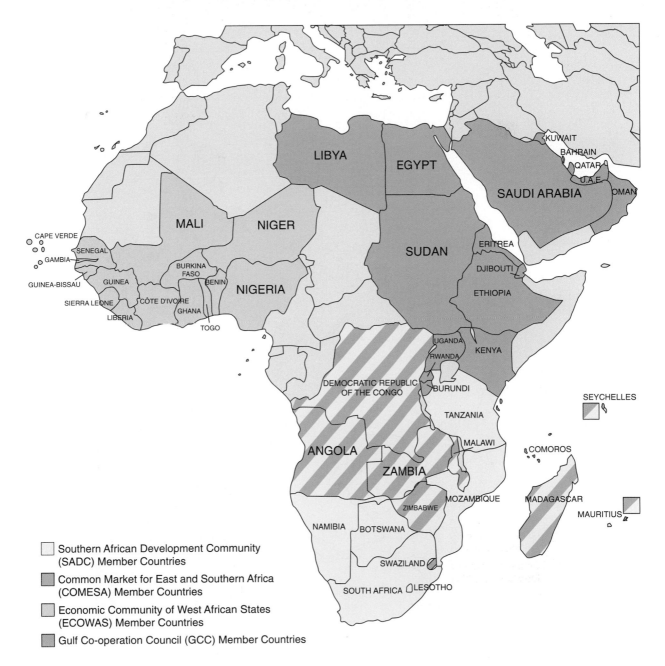

☐ Southern African Development Community (SADC) Member Countries

☐ Common Market for East and Southern Africa (COMESA) Member Countries

☐ Economic Community of West African States (ECOWAS) Member Countries

☐ Gulf Co-operation Council (GCC) Member Countries

ASEAN Countries

PHILIPPINES

INDONESIA

BRUNEI

MALAYSIA

VIETNAM

LAOS

THAILAND

CAMBODIA

MYANMAR

MALAYSIA

SINGAPORE

Association of Southeast Asian Nations
(ASEAN) Member Countries

OCED, Commonwealth and OPEC Countries

ST KITTS and NEVIS
ANTIGUA and BARBUDA
DOMINICA
ST LUCIA
BARBADOS
GRENADA
TRINIDAD and TOBAGO
ST VINCENT and THE GRENADINES

BRUNEI
FIJI
NAURU
SOLOMON ISLANDS
TUVALU
SAMOA
TONGA
VANUATU
KIRIBATI

☐ Organization for Economic Co-operation and Development (OECD) Member Countriesa

☐ Organization of Petroleum Exporting Countries (OPEC) Member Countries

☐ Commonwealth of Nations

☐ No current data available

concerned. However, with deregulation, monopolies have had to transform into competitive industries. In Germany, for example, the price of long-distance calls has fallen 40% forcing the former monopolist, Deutsche Telekom, to streamline its operations and seek new business abroad. By fostering a single market for capital, the euro is pushing Europe closer to a homogeneous market in goods and services, thereby exerting additional pressure on prices.[46]

Strategic Planning

The international manager will have to develop a strategic response to the new environment to maintain a sustainable long-term competitive advantage. Those companies already present in an integrating market should fill in gaps in goods and market portfolios through acquisitions or alliances to create a regional or global company.

It is increasingly evident that even a regional presence is not sufficient and sights need to be set on a presence beyond that. In industries such as automobiles, mobile telephony and retailing, blocs in the twenty-first century may be dominated by two or three giants leaving room only for niche players. Those with currently weak positions or no presence at all, will have to create alliances for market entry and development with established firms. For instance, the American firm General Mills created Cereal Partners Worldwide with Nestlé to establish itself in Europe and to jointly develop new market opportunities in Asia. An additional option for the international manager is leaving the market altogether in response to the new competitive conditions or the level of investment needed to remain competitive. For example, Bank of America sold its operations in Italy to Deutsche Bank once it determined the high cost of becoming a pan-European player.

Reorganization

Whatever the changes, they will call for company reorganization.[47] Structurally, authority will have to be more centralized so that regional programmes can be executed. In staffing, focus will have to be on individuals who understand the subtleties of consumer behaviour across markets and therefore can evaluate the similarities and differences among cultures and markets. In developing systems for the planning and implementation of regional programmes, adjustments will have to be made to incorporate views throughout the organization. If, for example, decisions on regional advertising campaigns are made at headquarters without consultation with country operations, resentment by the local staff will lead to less-than-optimal execution. The introduction of the euro means increased co-ordination in pricing as compared to the relative autonomy in price setting enjoyed by country organizations in the past. Companies may move corporate or divisional headquarters from the domestic market to be closer to the customer or centres of innovation. For example, after American company Procter & Gamble's reorganization, the fabric and home care business unit was headquartered in Brussels, Belgium.

Lobbying

International managers, as change agents, must constantly seek ways to influence the regulatory environment in which they must operate. Economic integration will involve various powers and procedures, such as the EU's Commission and its directives. The international manager is not powerless to influence such powers and procedures; a passive approach may result in competitors gaining an advantage or a disadvantageous situation emerging for the company. For example, it was very important for the US pharmaceutical industry to obtain tight patent protection as part of the NAFTA agreement and substantial time and money was spent on lobbying both the executive and legislative branches of the US government in the effort to meet its goal.

Often policy makers rely heavily on the knowledge and experience of the private sector in carrying out their own work. Influencing change will therefore mean providing policy makers with industry information such as test results. Lobbying will usually have to take place at multiple levels simultaneously; within the EU, this means the European Commission in Brussels, the European Parliament in Strasbourg or the national governments within the EU. US managers with substantial resources have established their own lobbying offices in Brussels, while smaller companies get their voices heard through joint offices or their industry associations. In terms of lobbying, US firms have been at an advantage given their experience in their home market; however, for many non-US firms, lobbying is a new, yet necessary, skill to be acquired. At the same time, managers in two or more blocs can work together to produce more efficient trade through, for example, Mutual Recognition Agreements (MRAs) on standards.[48]

CARTELS AND COMMODITY PRICE AGREEMENTS

An important characteristic that distinguishes developing countries from industrialized countries is the nature of their export earnings. While industrialized countries rely heavily on the export of manufactured goods, technology and services, the developing countries rely chiefly on the export of primary products and raw materials – for example, copper, iron ore and agricultural products. This distinction is important for several reasons. First, the level of price competition is higher among sellers of primary goods, because of the typically larger number of sellers and also because primary goods are homogeneous. This can be seen by comparing the sale of computers with, for example, copper. Only three of four countries are competitive forces in the computer market, whereas at least a dozen compete in the sale of copper. Furthermore, while goods differentiation and therefore brand loyalty are likely to exist in the market for computers, buyers of copper are likely to purchase on the basis of price alone. A second distinguishing factor is that supply variability will be greater in the market for primary goods because production often depends on uncontrollable factors such as weather. For these reasons, market prices of primary goods – and therefore developing country export earnings – are highly volatile.

Responses to this problem have included cartels and commodity price agreements. A cartel is an association of producers of a particular good. Although a cartel may consist of an association of private firms, our interest is in the cartels formed by nations. The objective of a cartel is to suppress the market forces affecting its good in order to gain greater control over sales revenues. A cartel may accomplish this objective in several ways. First, members may engage in price fixing. This entails an agreement by producers to sell at a certain price, eliminating price competition among sellers. Second, the cartel may allocate sales territories among its members, again suppressing competition. A third tactic calls for members to agree to restrict production and therefore supplies, resulting in artificially higher prices.

The most widely known cartel is the Organization of Petroleum Exporting Countries (OPEC), which consists of 11 oil-producing and exporting countries (Algeria, Indonesia, Iran, Iraq, Kuwait, Libya, Nigeria, Qatar, Saudi Arabia, United Arab Emirates and Venezuela). OPEC became a significant force in the world economy in the 1970s and its tactics include both price fixing and production quotas. Continued price increases brought the average price per barrel to nearly US$35 by 1981. In January 2008, oil prices hit a high of US$100.09 a barrel but have since fallen back as traders anticipate that slower economic growth will reduce energy demand. The Asian financial crisis resulted in a downturn for oil in the last years of the twentieth century.

OPECs market share has declined from its 55% peak in 1974 to 40% at present.[49] In addition, the cohesiveness among OPEC members has diminished. Sales often occurred at less than the agreed-upon price and production quotas were repeatedly violated. To keep the world economy running smoothly, co-operation from OPEC in terms of production amounts is necessary.[50] As a result of the oil embargo of 1974, the United States spearheaded the development of the International Energy Agency (IEA), the task of which was to gather stockpiles of oil to offset any supply shortage. Rather than acting as adversaries, the IEA and OPEC have agreed that the IEA will use its emergency stocks only as a last resort, and OPEC has promised to keep the world well-supplied with oil.[51]

International commodity price agreements involve both buyers and sellers in an agreement to manage the price of a certain commodity. Often, the free market is allowed to determine the price of the commodity over a certain range. However, if demand and supply pressures cause the commodity's price to move outside that range, an elected or appointed manager will enter the market to buy or sell the commodity to bring the price back into the range. The manager controls the buffer stock of the commodity. If prices float downward, the manager purchases the commodity and adds to the buffer stock. Under upward pressure, the manager sells the commodity from the buffer stock. This system is somewhat analogous to a managed exchange rate system, in which authorities buy and sell to influence exchange rates. International commodity agreements are currently in effect for sugar, tin, rubber, cocoa and coffee.

SUMMARY

Economic integration involves agreements among countries to establish links through the movement of goods, services and factors of production across borders. These links may be weak or strong depending on the level of integration. Levels of integration include the free trade area, customs union, common market and full economic union.

The benefits derived from economic integration include trade creation, economies of scale, improved terms of trade, the reduction of monopoly power and improved cross-cultural communication. However, a number of disadvantages may also exist. Most important, economic integration may work to the detriment of non-members by causing deteriorating terms of trade and trade diversion. In addition, no guarantee exists that all members will share the gains from integration. The biggest impediment to economic integration is nationalism; there is strong resistance to surrendering autonomy and self-determinism to co-operative agreements.

The most successful example of economic integration is the European Union. The EU has succeeded in eliminating most barriers to the free flow of goods, services and factors of production. In addition, the EU has made progress toward the evolution of a common currency and central bank, which are fundamental requirements of an economic union. In the Americas, NAFTA is paving the way for a hemispheric trade bloc.

A number of regional economic alliances exist in Africa, Latin America and Asia, but they have achieved only low levels of integration. Political difficulties, low levels of development and problems with cohesiveness have impeded integrative progress among many developing countries. However, many nations in these areas are seeing economic integration as the only way to prosperity in the future.

International commodity price agreements and cartels represent attempts by producers of primary products to control sales revenues and export earnings. The former involves an agreement to buy or sell a commodity to influence prices. The latter is an agreement by suppliers to fix prices, set production quotas or allocate sales territories. OPEC, for example, has had inestimable influence on the global economy during the past 40 years.

QUESTIONS FOR DISCUSSION

1. Explain the difference between a free trade area and a customs union. Speculate why negotiations were held for a North American Free Trade Agreement rather than for a North American Common Market.
2. What problems might a member country of a common market be concerned about?
3. Construct an example of a customs union arrangement resulting in both trade creation and trade diversion.
4. Distinguish between external and internal economies of scale resulting from economic integration.
5. Are economic blocs (such as the EU and NAFTA) building blocs or stumbling blocs as far as worldwide free trade is concerned?
6. Suppose that you work for a medium-sized manufacturing firm in the USA. Approximately 20% of your sales are to European customers. What threats and opportunities does your firm face as a result of an integrated European market?

INTERNET EXERCISES

1. Compare and contrast two different points of view on expanding free trade by accessing the web sites of The Business Roundtable, an industry coalition promoting increased access to world markets (www.brtable.org), and the AFL–CIO, American Federation of Labour–Congress of Industrial Organizations (www.aflcio.org).
2. The euro will be either a source of competitive advantage or disadvantage for managers. Using 'Euro case study: Siemens', available at http://news.bbc.co.uk/1/hi/events/the_launch_of_emu/euro_facts/224550.stm, assess the validity of the two points of view.

TAKE A STAND

The European Union is the most significant market in the world for bananas, consuming over 39% of the world's output. That is why a decision by the EU Farm Council attracted attention among both banana-growing nations and those consuming them. The decision was made to favour imports coming from EU countries, mainly British, French and Spanish former colonies in Africa, Caribbean and the Pacific, under a preferential trading agreement called the Lomé Convention. Other producing countries would be subject to a quota of 2.2 million tonnes with a 20% tariff. All imports beyond that amount would be subject to a 170% tariff.

The EU's stated reason for the decision was to protect the former colonies in what, for some of them, is their main source of revenue. For example, in the case of St. Lucia, more than 60% of its export revenue is from bananas. One of the other (hidden agenda) reasons was to attempt to curb American influence in the banana trade. The United States is home to three of the major companies in the business: Chiquita, Del Monte and Dole.

The Caribbean nations have favoured the decision as a consideration of smaller nations' right to exist with a decent standard of living, self-determination and independence. Their main concern is that free trade would soon put their growers out of business due to the inherent ineffi-ciencies of smaller farms. In Latin America, the view was quite the opposite. For countries such as Ecuador, Costa Rica, Colombia and Honduras, the restrictions resulted in losses of US$1 billion and 170 000 jobs. The unit-costs of production in Latin America are typically 2.5 times less than in the Caribbean.

Initially, the United States acted as an interested observer given that it is not a banana-growing nation (except for small amounts grown in Hawaii). However, at the request of Chiquita, the United States filed a complaint with the World Trade Organization. The main driver was the danger-ous precedent of inaction if the EU banana regime went unchallenged. Unless deterred, the EU could possibly enjoy similar measures in other sectors of agriculture.

FOR DISCUSSION

1. Is the involvement of the United States in the 'banana wars' justified?
2. Are there any other ways the EU countries could support their former colonies apart from erecting trade barriers?

CHAPTER

7

The Challenge of Emerging Markets

- Doing Business with Changing Economies
- Adjusting to Global Change
- State Enterprises and Privatization
- The Role of the Multinational Firm

LEARNING OBJECTIVES

- To understand the special concerns that must be considered by the international manager when dealing with emerging market economies.
- To survey the vast opportunities for trade offered by emerging market economies.
- To understand why economic change is difficult and requires much adjustment.
- To become aware that privatization offers new opportunities for international trade and investment.

HIGH-TECH TEACHING IN CHINA

Blackboard Inc. is a Washington, DC-based e-learning firm that was created in 1994. The Blackboard system gives students and faculty members an individualized Internet-based file space that is a part of a central system. This allows students and teachers to collect, share, discover and manage important materials from articles, research papers, presentations and multimedia files. Blackboard includes web applications to help instructors manage student submissions, maintain grade records and permit e-mail communication among class participants.

The technology is appealing to users because it is not particularly complex and allows professors and students alike to quickly incorporate it into coursework. Blackboard's software is currently being used in 60 countries by more than 3000 universities, 600 of which are located outside of the United States. Blackboard produces the software in twelve languages and the software is able to accommodate a large number of users – 95 000 at one Mexican university alone.

The company has entered into a joint venture with Cernet Corporation, a Chinese education company established by the Ministry of Education, to provide e-learning capabilities for Chinese universities. Blackboard will provide an online platform where professors can post class assignments and announcements, conduct tests or quizzes and initiate online discussions. Blackboard will also be used to provide preparation services for college entrance exams, the GRE and TOEFL. Blackboard's current expansion into China represents a huge opportunity for the company. In its first years the Blackboard system will be available to six universities in China and up to 100 000 students are expected to use it!

The potential for growth is high. Estimates are that within five years, 5–10 million Chinese students will be using Blackboard. In 10 years, more than 20 million users could be served. China has tremendous market potential with more than 230 million students and the Chinese government plans to wire all schools, elementary through university level, by 2010. Blackboard facilitates the Chinese educational reform initiatives, by offering more modern teaching methods that emphasize student involvement and creativity. First year revenue from the venture is expected to be between US$3 and US$5 million.

There are, however, some risks associated with expansion into China. Many education analysts point out that China's per capita education spending is low when compared with Western education systems. For Western systems, buying a product like Blackboard is a fairly minor outlay; for Chinese universities it is an expensive proposition. It may therefore be difficult for the company to convince universities to spend their limited resources on the Blackboard system.

Another issue of contention is intellectual property rights. By uploading articles and other content onto Blackboard, faculty and students could inadvertently be violating various copyright laws. Were such a violation to be prosecuted, the situation could be embarrassing and expensive for the university and instructor involved. The past poor record of China's payments for intellectual property is making Blackboard cautious.

Sources: www.washingtonpost.com/wp-dyn/articles/A17254-2003Sep2.html; www.iht.com/articles/108305.html; and www.blackboard.com/b3/guest/news/pressdetail.asp?tid=254.

INTRODUCTION

This chapter addresses major societal, economic and ideological shifts that take place in the global economy. The focus is on the changing economies of Asia, particularly China, India and Pakistan; Latin America, specifically, Brazil, Argentina and Chile; and Africa, notably Morocco, South Africa and Nigeria. These nations are called emerging economies because they are gradually becoming integrated into the global economy. The second type of changing economies are the transition economies – found in Eastern Europe, the former Soviet Union and other formerly socialist states. Transition economies have experienced a shift in economic thinking from central planning to a market-based model. Finally, we will look at the lesser-developed markets of Africa, Latin America and some of Asia, which lack economic freedom and transparency. The economic change in these markets is presented and the role of privatization is discussed.

The rise of new players in world trade has important implications for the international business manager both in terms of opportunities and risks, as this chapter's opening vignette has shown. Privatization is addressed because the increasing transition of economic activity from government ownership into private hands presents a substantial shift in market orientation and offers new opportunities for trade and investment. Developmental issues are presented to reflect the special needs of large regions of the world and the resulting special responsibilities of international business.

DOING BUSINESS WITH CHANGING ECONOMIES

The major emerging economies are those of China, India, Pakistan, Southeast Asia and other rapidly growing nations such as Brazil, Indonesia and Malaysia. Broadly defined, an emerging market is a country making an effort to change and improve its economy with the goal of raising its performance to that of the world's more economically advanced nations.[1] Improved economies can benefit emerging-economy countries through higher personal income levels and better standards of living, more exports, increased foreign direct investment and more stable political structures. Developed countries also benefit from their access to the human and natural resources of emerging nations by getting lower cost products and services.

The biggest emerging markets display factors that make them strategically important: favourable consumer demographics, rising household incomes and increasing availability of credit, as well as increasing productivity resulting in more attractive prices.[2] As computer-factory workers in China and software programmers in India increase their incomes, they become consumers. The number of people in the world with the equivalent of US$10 000 in annual income will double, to 2 billion,

FOCUS ON

COMPETITION

From Global Partners to Global Competitors

China's membership in the World Trade Organization in 2001 signalled a new era in global business ties. Its entry was perceived as local acceptance of globalization and capitalism and signalled to the world that China was a most relevant market. Investment flooded into China. As the infrastructure grew, popular franchises such as KFC and Subway emerged and Chinese exports flooded international markets. The country had adopted the notion that an unregulated market, a level playing field, allows the true economic victor to emerge.

China's acceptance of market norms created an era of unprecedented growth in the country. Nearly every economic indicator pointed to the exponential growth of the economy. The country has expanded from having regional hegemony to becoming a major global player that competes for global resources such as oil.

From the US's point of view, China's growth complicated relations between the two superpowers. Fearing that the country will use its expanding economy to challenge the American model of international relations, US foreign policy hawks tried to use economic tools as leverage against China. In 2003, the US passed a number of tariffs aimed at decreasing Chinese textile exports and lessening the US trade deficit.

As China grows, so do its businesses and their economic influence. But instead of using their newfound influence to spur global co-operation, many Chinese businesses have resorted to blocking market-oriented reforms at home. They have supported tariffs on foreign products and higher taxes on investors from abroad to consolidate their economic supremacy.

Some of the Chinese discontent with foreign business has been triggered by US and EU policies. When the China National Offshore Oil Corp (CNOOC) attempted to buy Unocal, a US oil company, in 2005, American legislators rallied against the deal by accusing China of attempting to monopolize the energy market. The American veto of the acquisition discredited the American notion that democracy and capitalism are the keys to success. With further degradation of the legitimacy of the American economic model, China will be more likely to block reforms of its controlled system and society, complicating future American business investment.

The EU has claimed to be the neutral arbiter in this dispute. It uses the institutional frameworks of the WTO to support Chinese growth and democratization. In 2004, the EU and China launched a €20 billion programme under the auspices of the WTO to assist Chinese industry, government and civil society. The programme's bolstering of democracy in all levels of society may create a business atmosphere that is most conducive to foreign businesses.

Sources: Chen, Wu. 'View From China: Less Admiration for US Business'. *CFO Magazine*, 1 November 2005, www.cfo.com/article.cfm/5077996; 'Bilateral Trade Issues: China' (2005) Bulletin of the EC on EU–China trade.

by 2015 – and 900 million of those newcomers to the consumer class will be in emerging markets. General Electric (GE), for example, expects to get as much as 60% of its revenue growth from emerging markets over the next decade.[3]

Transition economies are a second type of changing economy, and include the new market economies emerging out of once centrally planned economies of the former Soviet Union, East Germany (now unified with West Germany), and the Eastern and Central European nations (Albania, Bulgaria, the Czech and Slovak Republics, Hungary, Poland and Romania). Transition economies have experienced a shift in economic thinking from central planning to market orientation since the

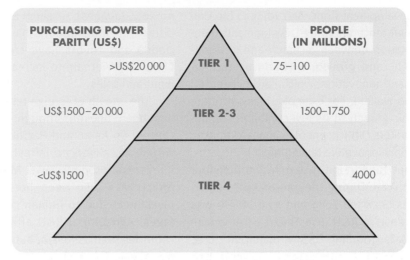

Figure 7.1: The world economic pyramid.

Source: United Nations Development Reports, 2002, www.un.org.

fall of the Soviet empire. Many believe that business ties between the Western world and transition economies are a recent phenomenon. That is not the case. In the 1920s, for example, GE and RCA helped develop the Soviet electrical and communications industries. However, due to the political divide between communism and capitalism and the colonial status of some transition economies in the late 1940s, Western corporations had limited international business contact with transition economies.[4] Socialist nations perceived international corporations as a front for Western and capitalist imperialism. Western managers, in turn, often saw socialism as a threat to the market system and the Western world in general.

The third type of changing economy is the lesser-developed economy. Lesser-developed markets are economies that lack market institutions and the thrust towards economic freedom and transparency. Four billion people in the world live in poverty, subsisting on less than US$1500 a year (see Figure 7.1). Less-developed markets comprise countries in Africa (e.g., Morocco, Zimbabwe and the Congo), Asia (e.g., Laos, Cambodia and Vietnam) and Latin America (e.g., Colombia, Ecuador and Haiti). Many of these countries are former colonies of the Western states and have experienced much civil unrest since decolonization. Civil war, corruption and human rights abuses deterred Western investment, leaving the economic infrastructure of these countries underdeveloped and stranding millions of people in poverty.

FOCUS ON

INVESTMENT   R&D Investment: Pathway to Growth

Globalization includes the expansion of businesses into emerging economies and less-developed nations. Much of the expansion is seen by the public as McDonald's in Brazil and Starbucks in China. However, a relatively new phenomenon is foreign direct investment for research and development (R&D) in these countries.

Firms are moving their business infrastructure, specifically the product development and customer support sectors, into these markets. Start-up barriers such as capital requirements and industrial experience are low. The expectation is that the move will lower costs and improve the skills of workers in these locations. The local presence also allows firms to adapt more easily to the needs of the local population.

The advantages are also numerous for emerging and lesser-developed economies that agree to host research and development firms. According to the United Nations Conference on Trade Development, there is a high correlation between research and development investment and growth. R&D drives technological change and innovation, which cause increased productivity and welfare. For example, many attribute India's economic growth to its investment in technology sector workers, which enables many domestic start-ups to supply innovative technology.

The hotspot for foreign research and development has been Asia. During the rise of Asia's emerging economies between 1989 and 1999, there was an 18-fold increase in R&D investment by American companies in Asia, totalling US$1.4 billion. In 2004, Intel employed 1500 IT professionals in India and Motorola had a 2000-person R&D institute in China. Other companies such as Ericsson, Intel, Nokia and SAP have also invested in research in Asia. Most notably, Japanese research and development expenditures in other nations have grown most rapidly. Honda and Toyota have created R&D affiliates in China and Vietnam to increase motorcycle development and sales.

The growth of foreign research and development has been uneven, though. Most investment has centred on Asian and Pacific markets with a robust workforce, advanced infrastructure and reasonable intellectual property laws. Mexico, Brazil and South Africa have also been hotspots for foreign R&D investment due to human capital and legal advantages. Agricultural R&D affiliates have emerged in countries such as Kenya, but are still in their embryonic stages. These successful countries have all maximized foreign investment by transferring technology and innovation to their society.

Sources: W. Kuemmerle (1999) 'The Drivers of Foreign Direct Investment into Research and Development: An Empirical Investigation'. *Journal of International Business Studies*, 30, 1–24; United Nations Conference on Trade and Development, 'Globalisation of R&D and Developing Countries', May 2006.

For information regarding the population and GDP of changing economies, consult Table 7.1. It is evident that insufficient economic opportunity results in migration pressure from developing nations into industrialized ones. Successful economic transition is a key tool to reduce such migration. If people have a reasonable chance for economic prosperity at home, they are less likely to leave. Some also say that the hope and property brought on by a successful economy will decrease the likelihood that a country will become a terrorist haven. Ownership gives people something to lose and deters them from risky ventures such as terrorism.

A Brief Overview of Transition Economies

Due to differing politics and ideology, the economic and international business history of transition economies is quite different from those of the Western world. The former Soviet system of foreign trade dates to a decree signed by Lenin on 22 April 1918. It established that the state would have a monopoly on foreign trade and that all foreign trade operations were to be concentrated in the hands of organizations specifically authorized by the state. Over time, this system of a state-controlled monopoly was also imposed on the East European satellites of the Soviet Union and adopted as models for the People's Republic of China and other emerging economies, such as India.

In the mid-1980s, the Soviet Union developed two new political and economic programmes: perestroika and glasnost. Perestroika fundamentally reformed the Soviet economy by improving the overall technological and industrial base as well as the quality of life for Soviet citizens through increased availability of food, housing and consumer goods. Glasnost complemented those efforts by encouraging the free exchange of ideas and discussion of problems, pluralistic participation in decision making and increased availability of information.[5] These measures were in turn complemented by

	Population (Millions)[a]	GDP (US$ Billions)[b]	GDP Per Capita (US$)[c]
Key emerging economies			
Brazil	188.0	1655.0	8800
China	1314.0	10021.0	7800
India	1095.3	4164.0	3800
Indonesia	245.5	948.3	3900
Iran	68.7	599.8	8700
Malaysia	24.4	313.2	12800
Mexico	107.4	1149.0	10700
Nigeria	131.9	191.4	1500
Pakistan	165.8	437.5	2600
Thailand	64.6	596.5	9200
Key transition economies			
Albania	3.6	20.46	5700
Belarus	10.3	83.00	8100
Bulgaria	7.4	79.0	10700
Czech Republic	10.2	225.5	22000
Hungary	10.0	175.0	17500
Kyrgyzstan	5.2	10.73	2100
Poland	38.5	554.5	14400
Russia	142.9	1746.0	12200
Ukraine	46.7	364.4	7800
Key lesser-developed economies			
Bolivia	9.0	27.87	3100
Cambodia	13.9	38.89	2800
Guatemala	12.3	61.38	5000
Kenya	34.7	41.48	1200
Mozambique	19.7	29.17	1500
Niger	12.5	12.36	1000
Paraguay	6.5	31.26	4800
Vietnam	84.4	262.5	3100

Source: The World Factbook 2007, CIA
[a]July 2006 estimates.
[b]2006 estimates measured in purchasing power parity.
[c]2006 estimates measured in purchasing power parity.

Table 7.1: Population of changing economies.

reform in the foreign trade sector. For the first time, national agencies, large enterprises and research institutes were authorized to handle their own foreign transactions directly. Other socialist countries rapidly copied the Soviet Union and began to invite foreign investors and to privatize state enterprises.

By late 1989, all the individual shifts resulted in the emergence of a new economic and geopolitical picture. The Iron Curtain disappeared and, within three years, the Communist empire ceased to exist. Market reforms and democracy emerged as key desires in former Soviet satellite states. Many looked to the West for investment and ended their economic dependence on the Soviet Union. The economic transition for former socialist states was tedious and harsh. Austerity programmes were introduced and the prices of subsidized products were adjusted upward to avoid distorted trade flows due to distorted prices. To avoid inflation, wages were kept in check. Governments aimed to stimulate productivity with pay-for-performance practices and entire industries were either privatized or shut down. This situation led to a significant decrease in the standard of living, political discord and a desire by some for a return to the old days.

Currently, many former socialist states work to become part of Western markets. The European Union has welcomed Poland, Slovakia, the Czech Republic and the Baltic states. In 2004, the EU expanded to 25 members accepting eight Central European and two Mediterranean countries to the Union. Bulgaria and Romania joined in 2007. Despite some of the uncertainties about the future cohesiveness of the EU, new nations are also eager to become EU members in the long run. Ukraine and Belarus have developed co-operation agreements with the EU but have made no official plans to join as yet.

A Brief Overview of Emerging Economies

Emerging economies are the new economic power-houses and are referred to by many as the success stories of the age of globalization. In the post-war period many emerging economies started out as weak markets hindered by oppressive regimes, corruption and a lack of transparency. However, many emerging economies, driven by a desire for freedom and integration with the world, addressed these problems with key reforms of social and economic policies. International institutions, such as the International Monetary Fund (IMF) and World Bank, fostered economic growth in these countries. International aid allowed emerging economies to begin to address the problems of poverty, famine and authoritarianism. Western business activity in emerging economies gave these nations an incentive to continue democracy, growth and the improvement of infrastructure.

The two largest emerging economies are India and China. These economies are significant due to their size and demographics. They have a high number of scientists and Internet users (see Table 7.2). India's population is over one billion and China's is about 1.3 billion.[6] Together, these countries account for over 30% of the world's population. Therefore, they represent a large consumer and employment base for international business. Technology and an increased standard of living have greatly transformed these societies. The number of international links through English speakers, Internet users and scientists continues to grow within China and India – encouraging international businesses and nurturing domestic firms. The number of white-collar jobs in China and India has even led to a reverse brain drain – where many of the scientists who left their country in the 1990s are returning home to find lucrative jobs.[7]

The reforms of the Chinese economy towards market-oriented structure serve as an example of the changes in emerging economies. After decades of political and economic isolation, in 1979, China opened its economy by unleashing a series of market-based reforms that hoped to increase productivity, living standards and technological quality. China pursued both agricultural and industrial reforms. The commune system, an agricultural structure in which an entire village was responsible for harvesting a plot of land, was disbanded and more self-management was encouraged within state enterprises. Under the new policies, economic output grew by 10%. Soon, an overheating economy

	Population (Millions)	Scientists	Literacy Rate	Internet Users
China	1,314[a]	282,000[c]	90.9%[a]	111.0[e]
India	1,095[b]	296,000[d]	59.5%[a]	50.6[f]

[a]2005 CIA World Factbook estimates.
[b]2006 CIA World Factbook estimates.
[c]2004 estimate, Ministry of Science and Technology of the People's Republic of China.
[d]2004 estimate, National Science and Technology Management Information System, Government of India.
[e]2006 estimate, etForecasts.com.
[f]2006 estimate, China Internet Network Information Centre.

Table 7.2: Human capital of India and China.

caused leaders to recast their reforms. In 1992, the Chinese government revealed a Ten Year Plan to continue China's transition into a 'socialist market economy'. Since then, China has turned into the world's third largest economy (in terms of purchasing power parity) and has experienced economic growth rates of 8–10% in the mid-2000s. China is now a major participant in world trade. It joined the World Trade Organization in 2001 and amended its constitution to provide for basic property rights. Chinese exports totalled US$762.3 billion in 2005, with the US importing US$243.5 billion and the EU importing US$218 billion.[8] At the same time, the US exported US$41.8 billion of goods into China, leaving a sizeable trade deficit of US$201.7 billion. The EU exported US$61.5 billion to China and generated a trade deficit of US$156.5 billion.

The changes in China's economy have also given rise to changes in China's culture. The number of Chinese English speakers is growing so rapidly that British Prime Minister Gordon Brown remarked that 'by 2025, the number of English-speaking Chinese is likely to exceed the number of native English speakers in the rest of the world'.[9] New cultural values are emerging that stress growth, scarcity and productivity. These values were formalized by the Chinese president Hu Jintao in eight rules, commonly referred to as 'China's Eight Commandments'.

India's economy also began the move to a market-oriented structure in the early 1990s. Industrial liberalization, de-control of foreign investment and exchange regimes and significantly reduced tariffs have now made India the 12th largest economy in the world, with a 2006 GDP growth of about 7.0%. India's main advantage is its large English-speaking population – a remnant of British colonialism. The English-speaking population attracts many service-based companies into India. For example, computer companies such as Dell have moved their customer support centres and communications operations to India. India's economy has been propelled by the boost in service exports and modernization provided by a large information technology sector. Software exports grossed US$17.2 billion in 2004. However, India's growth is constrained by bureaucracy and corruption. Also inhibiting are high fiscal deficits, which totalled US$123 billion in 2004.[10]

A Brief Overview of Lesser-Developed Economies

The political developments of the mid-twentieth century have impeded the economic growth of many nations, casting them as lesser-developed economies with little economic freedom, few legitimate institutions and very limited transparency. The decolonization movement liberated many countries from Western colonizers, but left them mired in conflict between factions competing for power in the newly formed vacuum. Civil war overtook the Congo, a network of countries in West Africa and Somalia. During the Cold War, the economic transformation of lesser-developed economies became a secondary concern for the major powers. Instead, the US and Soviet Union armed and supported governments in lesser-developed nations to achieve pre-eminence based on geopolitical calculations. These moves gave rise to many authoritarian regimes that escalated civil wars, rather than promoting peace and economic growth.

As colonies, many lesser-developed economies were extraction sites for valuable natural resources that were shipped to the West. The Congo is rich in cadmium (the material used to make cell phone batteries); Equatorial Guinea and the countries of the Niger Delta possess substantial oil reserves; Liberia and Sierra Leone contain profitable diamond mines; Cambodian timber is highly priced. However, these resources have often been more of a curse, rather than a blessing, for lesser-developed economies. Control of these resources by one faction often led to an asymmetric distribution of wealth. Resources flow into war chests, as in the case of Liberia's 'Blood Diamonds'. Massive corruption also inhibits the improvement of domestic economies. The oil companies of the Niger Delta are notorious for poor environmental records and have been accused of violently suppressing locals. The international community has taken some steps to reduce the exploitation of lesser-developed economies. For example, The Kimberly Process has outlined guidelines for the diamond trade that aims to stem the profitability of illegal diamonds. However, international agreements are nearly useless if nations do not enforce them.

Alleviating the problems of lesser-developed nations has become more of a humanitarian, rather than economic, concern. Because these countries lack the infrastructure, literacy and legitimate institutions of emerging economies, businesses are less interested in their progress. It remains often the responsibility of international organizations, humanitarian non-governmental organizations and individual governments to ensure prosperity and stability in lesser-developed economies.

The Realities of Economic Change

For Western firms, the political and economic shifts converted latent but closed markets into markets offering very real and vast opportunities. Yet the shifts are only the beginning of a process. The announcement of an intention to change does not automatically result in change itself. For example, the abolition of a centrally planned economy does not create a market economy. Laws permitting the emergence of private sector entrepreneurs do not create entrepreneurship. The reduction of price controls does not immediately make goods available or affordable. Deeply ingrained systemic differences between the transition economies and Western firms continue. Highly prized, fully accepted fundamentals of the market economy, such as the reliance on competition, support of the profit motive and the willingness to live with risk on a corporate and personal level, are not yet fully accepted. Major changes still need to take place. The evaluation of risk is therefore especially precarious because the established models of risk assessment do not seem to apply.[11] It is therefore useful to review the major economic and structural dimensions of the changes taking place in order to identify major shortcomings and opportunities for international business.

Many transition economies face major **infrastructure shortages**. Transportation systems, particularly those leading to the West, require vast improvement. Long-haul trucking is an extremely expensive and difficult mode of transportation. Warehousing facilities are either lacking or very poor outside the major cities. A lack of refrigeration facilities places severe handicaps on trans-shipments of perishable products.[12] The housing stock is in need of major overhaul. Market intermediaries often do not exist. Payments and funds-transfer systems are inadequate. These infrastructure shortcomings will inhibit economic growth for years to come.

Capital shortages are also a major constraint. Catching up with the West in virtually all industrial areas requires major capital infusions. Even though major programmes have been designed to attract hidden personal savings into the economy, transition economies must rely to a large degree on attracting capital from abroad. Continued domestic uncertainties and high demand for capital around the world make this difficult. In light of existing inefficiencies, corruption[13] and domestic uncertainties, it is also a major task to ensure that the capital remains in the country. Often, **capital flight** more than compensates for any incoming foreign investment, thus leaving the domestic capital markets in a precarious position.

Firms doing business with transition economies often encounter interesting demand conditions. Buyers' preferences are frequently vague and undefined. Available market information is inaccurate. For example, knowledge about pricing, advertising, research and trading is very limited and few institutions are able to research demand and channel supply accurately. As a result, even if they want to, it is quite difficult for corporations to respond to demand. In emerging markets, consumption patterns can change rapidly. Companies that can anticipate these discontinuities can exploit them. When the Chinese government decided to develop an affordable housing programme nationwide, supplemented by a new mortgage system, it meant that thousands of households would be moving to new dwellings in the next several years. Research among Chinese consumers showed that these families would then also be willing to spend money to keep their homes in good condition (as compared with their previous homes where kitchens and bathroom facilities were shared). A surge in the demand for household cleaning products was to be expected and companies such as Procter & Gamble readied themselves for it.[14]

Investors find that these countries have substantial knowledge resources to offer. For example, it is claimed that Russia and Central Europe possess about 35–40% of all researchers and engineers in the world.[15] At the same time, however, these nations suffer from the disadvantages imposed by a lack of management skills. In the past, management mainly consisted of skilful manoeuvring within the allocation process. Central planning, for example, required firms to request tools seven years in advance; material requirements needed to be submitted two years in advance. Ordering was done haphazardly, because requested quantities were always reduced and surplus allocations could always be traded with other firms. The driving mechanism for management was therefore not responsiveness to existing needs but rather to plan fulfilment through the development of a finely honed **allocation mentality**, which waited for instructions from above.

Commitment by managers and employees to their work is difficult to find. Many employees are still caught up in old work habits, which consisted of never having to work a full shift due to other commitments and obligations. The notion that 'they pretend to pay us and we pretend to work' is still strong. The dismantling of the past policy of the 'Iron Rice Bowl', which made layoffs virtually impossible, reduces rather than increases such commitment.

The new environment also complicates managerial decision making. Even simple changes often require an almost unimaginable array of adjustments of licences, taxes, definitions and government rules. The challenges to managers in emerging markets are not restricted to the governmental front. The success of operations frequently rests on managers' ability to compete effectively with unconventional competition such as product counterfeiters, product diverters and informal competitors who ignore local labour and tax laws.[16]

To cope with all these challenges, transition economies need trained managers. Since no large supply of such individuals exists, much of the training must be newly developed. Simply applying established Western guidelines to such training is inappropriate due to the differences in the people to be trained and the society in which they live. Business learning in transition economies must focus on key business issues such as marketing, strategic planning, international business and financial analysis. However, it must not just focus on the transmission of knowledge but also aim to achieve behavioural change. Given the lack of market orientation in the previous business environment, managers must adapt their behaviour in areas such as problem solving, decision making, the development of customer orientation and **team building**. In addition, the attitudes held by managers toward business and Western teaching approaches must be taken into consideration. One often finds substantial reluctance to accept new business knowledge and practice.

ADJUSTING TO GLOBAL CHANGE

Both institutions and individuals tend to display some resistance to change. The resistance grows as the speed of change increases. It does not necessarily indicate a preference for the earlier conditions but rather a concern about the effects of adjustment and a fear of the unknown. Major shifts have occurred both politically and economically in Central and Eastern Europe as well as the former Soviet Union, accompanied by substantial dislocations. Therefore, resistance should be expected. Deeply entrenched interests and traditions are not easily supplanted by the tender and shallow root of market-oriented thinking. The understanding of links and interactions cannot be expected to grow overnight. For example, greater financial latitude for firms also requires that inefficient firms be permitted to go into bankruptcy – a concept not cherished by many. The need for increased efficiency and productivity causes sharp reductions in employment – a painful step for the workers affected. The growing ranks of unemployed are swelled by the members of the military who have been brought home or demobilized. Concurrently, wage reforms threaten to relegate blue-collar workers, who were traditionally favoured by the socialist system, to second-class status, while permitting the emergence of a new entrepreneurial class of the rich, an undesirable result for those not participating in the upswing. Retail price reforms endanger the safety net of larger population segments and widespread price changes introduce inflation. It is difficult to accept a system where there are winners and losers, particularly for those on the losing side. As a result, an increase in ambivalence and uncertainty may well produce rapid shifts in economic and political thinking.

Presently, about a half of China's labour force is engaged in agricultural production and produces extremely high yields due to intensive cultivation and innovation in fertilizer technology. Despite the strong agricultural sector, many Chinese regions remain underdeveloped and lack running water, electricity and schools. In 2003, more than 152 million Chinese citizens, mostly from rural inland areas, lived on less than US$1 a day.[17] Chinese social spending and industrial investment centres on large coastal cities such as Shanghai. As a result, many people migrate from the rural areas to the cities – creating a new class of poor rural migrants. More recent Chinese policies have begun to focus on reducing rural poverty. The government has waived agricultural taxes and invests in the development of rural infrastructure such as sewers and basic farmland. As a result, the threat of displacement is high for traditional producers in industrialized nations.

Job shifts have led to decreasing employment in the manufacturing sector of industrialized nations. For example, US manufacturing employment in 2006, at 14.2% of the total, had decreased below the levels of when it was officially measured in 1867.[18] In the period 1970–2001, German manufacturing dropped by more than 13% points, and in Japan, manufacturing employment dropped by 6.5% points during the same time.[19] With less demand for manufacturing jobs in developed nations, hourly compensation rates dropped accordingly. As demonstrated in Figure 7.2, between 1994 and 2004, hourly compensation rates grew at a slower pace in established manufacturing powerhouses such as the US and Japan. To soften the blow against domestic manufacturers posed by emerging manufacturing economies, industrialized countries have taken protective measures such as tariffs and regulations. However, these measures will only delay the needed adjustments in economic structure. Therefore, it can be expected that wage distortions still occur in countries, which maintain a relative manufacturing employment overhang.[20]

All of these declines in employment reflected a transfer of manufacturing away from the industrialized nations toward the emerging economies. Figure 7.3 shows how the proportion of manufacturing has grown rapidly in nations such as Indonesia, Malaysia and South Korea.[21]

Due to domestic economic dislocations, the pressure is on post-industrial nations to restrict the inflow of trade from the transition and emerging economies. Giving in to such pressure, however, would be highly detrimental to the further development of these new market economies. The countries in transition need assistance in their journey. Providing them with open markets is the best form of assistance, much more valuable than the occasional transfer of aid funds. Rapid changes and substantial economic dislocation have caused many individuals and policy makers in the emerging economies to become suspicious and wary of market approaches. Unless wealthy nations convincingly

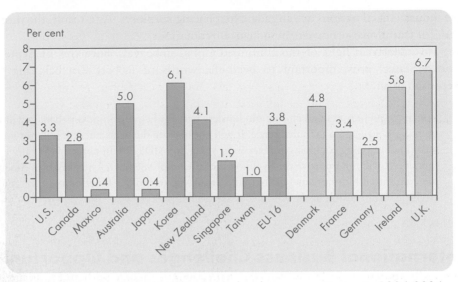

Figure 7.2: Average annual growth rates in hourly compensation costs, 1994–2004.

Source: Bureau of Labor Statistics www.dol.gov/asp/media/reports/chartbook/chart3_2.htm, accessed 20 April 2006.

demonstrate how competition, variety, trade and freedom of choice can improve the quality of life, the opportunity to transform post-socialist and less-developed societies may be jeopardized. The wealthy nations share the burden of global economic adjustment – a responsibility that has grown over the years.

But it is not just in the emerging economies that major changes have come about. The shifts experienced there also have major impact on the established market economies of the West. Take the reorientation of trade flows. With traditional and 'forced' trade relationships vanishing, many more countries exert major efforts to become new partners in global trade. They attempt to export much more of their domestic production. Many of the exports are in product categories such as agriculture, basic manufacturing, steel, aluminium and textiles, which are precisely the economic sectors in which

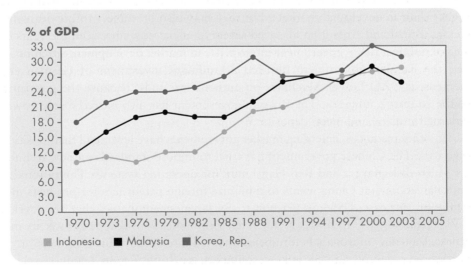

Figure 7.3: Manufacturing (value added) as a percentage of GDP.

Source: World Bank World Development Indicators Database.

the industrialized nations are already experiencing surpluses. As a result, the threat of displacement is high for traditional producers in industrialized nations.

Particularly in light of the continued global upheavals since the 11 September attacks on the United States, it is important to heed the words of Robert Zoellick, the United States Trade Representative:

> Erecting new barriers and closing old borders will not help the impoverished. It will not feed hundreds of millions struggling for subsistence. It will not liberate the persecuted. It will not improve the environment in developing countries or reverse the spread of AIDS. It will not help the railway orphans I visited in India. It will not improve the livelihoods of the union members I met in Latin America. It will not aid the committed Indonesians I visited who are trying to build a functioning, tolerant democracy in the largest Muslim nation in the world.[22]

International Business Challenges and Opportunities

Ironically, as economies grow, so does their economic linkage with and leverage over each other. This newfound power can instil hostility against foreign businesses. For example, the Chinese financial community's admiration for the US has lessened as the two countries have begun to compete for energy.[23]

Currently, most sourcing opportunities from China and India are for manufactured and industrial products such as garments and apparel, which reflect the past orientation of R&D expenditures towards traditional industrial sectors. Over time, however, services and technology may play a larger role. For example, both India and China are rapidly becoming major competitors in the production of cellular phones and mobile communications. This is correlated with a higher standard of living in the countries and the role of technology transfer through economic ties. In 2005, India was expected to have 70 million mobile phone users and 54 million cable TV subscribers. Due to increasing economic ties, China and the US signed *The US–China Science and Technology Agreement*, which creates a framework for bilateral co-operation in marine conservation, renewable energy, health and other topics. China also has high-profile scientific co-operation with Japan and the EU. Therefore, even if they are not interested in entertaining the emerging economies, the international business manager would be wise to maintain relationships with them in order not to lose a potentially valuable source of supply.[24]

Growth does not guarantee its overall appeal and potential. The growth rates may be consistently higher than in developed markets, but they may also be subject to greater volatility. For example, Russia, Brazil and Argentina all faced severe financial crises between the years 1999 and 2001. The role of political risk – government interference in market development situations – is high. For example, the Russian government blocked a landmark investment of German engineering company Siemens in OAO Power Machines on antitrust grounds, because the government deemed it vital to the country's interests. The Russian government has also barred foreign-owned companies from bidding for its oil and metal deposits.[25]

In other instances, emerging market governments have leveraged their position as hosts to foreign investors. The Chinese government has tried to impose standards on new technologies, such as EVD for video-disk players and Red Flag Linux for operating systems. The rational behind this 'techno-nationalism' is that China wants to minimize foreign patent fees for products made and sold domestically (in this case, US$4.50 per unit to six Japanese companies that are developing the underlying DVD technology).[26] In Brazil, a Dutch telecommunications company took six months and eight government agency approvals before being granted a temporary business licence.[27] For data analysing barriers to economic success in key economies, see Table 7.3. In a country such as Singapore, where one can start a business in six days, innovation and growth are high. By contrast, the fact that a new business takes 153 days to start up in Mozambique prevents business development and innovation.

	Average Time to Start a Business (Days)	Number of Necessary Procedures to Start a Business
Britain	18	6
China	48	13
Germany	24	9
India	71	11
Mali	42	13
Mozambique	153	14
Poland	31	10
Russia	33	8
Singapore	6	6
Sweden	16	3
United States	5	5

Source: 2005 estimates, World Bank World Development Indicators.

Table 7.3: Business climates in key economies.

Another concern is the current and future competition from emerging market companies. Chinese companies have been able to develop powerful global brands in a very short period of time. Some have been developed from the domestic base in a step-by-step manner (e.g., Haier in appliances and Geely in cars) or through acquisitions of existing global brands (such as TCL for TVs and Lenovo by IBM for computers).[28] Another concern is based on economic and national security. Companies, such as GE, Microsoft, Cisco and Intel, have all established R&D operations in China, thereby training foreign scientists and possibly giving the omnipresent Chinese government access to proprietary technologies.

The pressure of change, however, also presents vast opportunities for the expansion of international business activities. Large populations offer new potential consumer demand and production capability. Many opportunities arise out of the enthusiasm with which a market orientation is embraced in some nations. Companies that are able to tap into the desire for an improved standard of living can develop new demand on a large scale.

One major difficulty encountered is the frequent unavailability of convertible currency. Products, however necessary, often cannot be purchased by emerging market economies because no funds are available to pay for them. As a result, many countries resort to **barter** and countertrade. This places an additional burden on the international manager, who must not only market products to the clients but also market the products received in return to other consumers and institutions.

Problems also have arisen from the lack of protection some of the countries afford to intellectual property rights. Firms have complained about frequent illegal copying of films, books and software and about the counterfeiting of brand-name products. Unless importers can be assured that government safeguards will protect their property, trade and technology transfer will be severely inhibited.

Problems can be encountered when attempting to source products from emerging market economies. Many firms have found that selling is not part of the economic culture in some countries. The few available descriptive materials are often poorly written and devoid of useful information. Obtaining additional information about a product may be difficult and time-consuming.

The quality of the products obtained can be a major problem. In spite of their great desire to participate in the global marketplace, many producers still tend to place primary emphasis on product performance. They often neglect issues of style and product presentation. Therefore, the international manager must require manufacturers to improve quality and offer prompt delivery using advanced information technology.

Nevertheless, many international business opportunities exist. Some transition economies have products that are unique in performance. Although they could not be traded during a time of ideological conflict, they are becoming successful global products in an era of new trade relations. For example, research shows that Russian tractors can be sold successfully in the United States. A study found that many of the previously held negative attitudes about imports from transition economies have been modified by the changed political climate.[29] These nations can offer consumers in industrialized nations a variety of products at low costs once their labour force can perform at an international level.

Currently, most sourcing opportunities from Eastern Europe and the Commonwealth of Independent States are for industrial products that reflect the past orientation of R&D expenditures. Over time, however, consumer products may play a larger role, sometimes even a surprising one. For example, both Hungary and China are rapidly becoming major competitors in the production and export of *foie gras*, the famed delicacy made from goose or duck livers. Derided for decades as France's contribution to capitalist greed and decadence, this product is increasingly supplied at more competitive prices by emerging market economies.[30] There are also substantial opportunities for technology transfer. For example, the former Soviet training programme for cosmonauts, which prepared space travellers for long periods of weightlessness, actually provides quite useful information for US manufacturers of exercise equipment. Therefore, even if not interested in entering the transition economies, the international business manager should maintain relationships in order not to lose a potentially valuable source of supply.

STATE ENTERPRISES AND PRIVATIZATION

One other area where the international business manager must deal with a period of transition is that of the state-owned enterprise. These firms represent a formidable pool of international suppliers, customers and competitors. Many of them are located in emerging market economies and are currently being converted into privately owned enterprises. This transition also presents new opportunities.

Reasons for State-Owned Enterprises

A variety of economic and non-economic factors has contributed to the existence of state-owned enterprises. Two primary ones are national security and economic security. Many countries believe that, for national security purposes, certain industrial sectors must be under state control. Typically, these sectors include telecommunications, airlines, banking and energy.

Economic security reasons are primarily cited in countries that are heavily dependent on specific industries for their economic performance. This may be the case when countries are heavily commodity dependent. Governments frequently believe that, given such heavy national dependence on a particular sector, government control is necessary to ensure national economic health.

Other reasons also contributed to the development of state-owned enterprises. On occasion, the sizeable investment required for the development of an industry is too large to come from the private sector. Therefore, governments close the gap between national needs and private sector resources by developing these industries themselves. In addition, governments often decide to rescue failing private enterprises by placing them in government ownership. In doing so, they fulfil important policy objectives, such as the maintenance of employment, the development of depressed areas or the increase of exports.

Some governments also maintain that state-owned firms may be better for the country than privately held companies because they may be more societally oriented and therefore contribute more to the greater good. This was particularly the case in areas such as telecommunications and transportation, where profit maximization, at least from a governmental perspective, was not always seen as the appropriate primary objective. Rather, social goals such as employment may be valued much higher than profits or rates of return.[31]

The Effect of State-Owned Enterprises on International Business

There are three types of activities where the international manager is likely to encounter state-owned enterprises: market entry, the sourcing or marketing process and international competition. On occasion, the very existence of a state-owned enterprise may inhibit or prohibit foreign market entry. For reasons of development and growth, governments frequently make market entry from the outside quite difficult so that the state-owned enterprise can perform according to plan. Even if market entry is permitted, the conditions under which a foreign firm can conduct business are often substantially less favourable than the conditions under which state-owned enterprises operate. Therefore, the international firm may be placed at a competitive disadvantage and may not be able to perform successfully even though economic factors would indicate success.

The international manager also faces a unique situation when sourcing from or marketing to state-owned enterprises. Even though the state-owned firm may appear to be simply another business partner, it is ultimately an extension of the government and its activities. This may mean that the state-owned enterprise conducts its transactions according to the overall foreign policy of the country rather than according to economic rationale. For example, political considerations can play a decisive role in purchasing decisions. Contracts may be concluded for non-economic reasons rather than be based on product offering and performance. Contract conditions may depend on foreign policy outlook, prices may be altered to reflect government displeasure and delivery performance may change to 'send a signal'. Exports and imports may be delayed or encouraged depending on the current needs of government.

Finally, the international firm also may encounter international competition from state-owned enterprises. Very often, the concentration of such firms is not in areas of comparative advantage but rather in areas that are most beneficial for the government owning the firm. Policy objectives often are much more important than input costs. Sometimes, state-owned enterprises may not even know the value of the products they buy and sell because price levels have such a low priority. As a result, the international manager may be confronted with competition that is very tough to beat.

Privatization

Governments and citizens have increasingly recognized the drawbacks of government control of enterprises. Competition is restrained, which results in lower quality of goods and reduced innovation. Citizens are deprived of lower prices and of choice. The international competitiveness of state-controlled enterprises typically declines, often resulting in the need for growing government subsidies. In addition, rather than focusing on business, many government-controlled corporations have become grazing grounds for political appointees or vote winners through job allocations. As a result, many government-owned enterprises excel only at losing money.[32]

It is possible to reduce the cost of governing by changing government's role and involvement in the economy. Through privatization, budgets can be reduced and more efficient – not fewer – services can be provided. Privatized goods and services are often more competitive and more innovative. Two decades of experience with privatization indicate that private enterprises almost invariably outperform state-run companies.[33] The conversion of government monopolies into market-driven activities also tends to attract foreign investment capital, bringing additional know-how and financing to enterprises. Finally, governments can use proceeds from privatization to fund other pressing domestic needs.

The methods of privatization vary from country to country. Some nations come up with a master plan for privatization, whereas others deal with it on a case-by-case basis. The Treuhandanstalt of

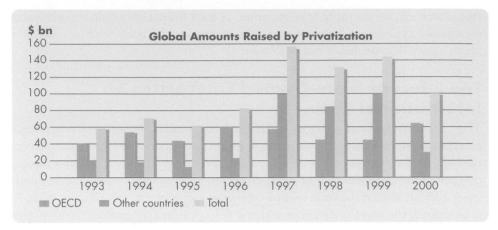

Figure 7.4: Trends in global privatization.

Source: Organization for Economic Co-operation and Development (2001) *Financial Market Trends*, **79**(June). Copyright OECD, 2001, www.oecd.org.

Germany, for example, which was charged with disposing of most East German state property, aimed to sell firms but also to maximize the number of jobs retained. In other countries, ownership shares are distributed to citizens and employees. Some nations simply sell to the highest bidder in order to maximize the proceeds. For example, Mexico has used most of its privatization proceeds to amortize its internal debt, resulting in savings of nearly US$1 billion a year in interest payments. As Figure 7.4 shows, governments have raised substantial amounts through privatization. The Focus on Politics below shows that, in spite of its many advantages, the support for privatization is not unanimous. Too often, the process itself and the distribution of the funds obtained appear to be corrupt or at least not very transparent.

The purpose of most privatization programmes is to improve productivity, profitability and product quality and to shrink the size of government. As companies are exposed to market forces and competition, they are expected to produce better goods and services at lower costs. Privatization also intends to attract new capital for these firms so that they can carry out necessary adjustments and improvements. Since local capital is often scarce, privatization efforts increasingly aim to attract foreign capital investment. Privatization, however, is no magic wand. Its key benefits come from corporate adjustments, which are often quite painful. Increased business activity can also have negative externalities such as pollution, thereby draining government resources. Pollution costs the Chinese economy 7–10% every year. To lessen waste and save the country's vanishing forests, China passed a 5% tax on disposable chopsticks in 2006.[34]

F⬤CUS ON

POLITICS   'For Sale' Signs Up in Russia

Nearly 10 years after the fall of communism, Russia has finally allowed the sale of real estate property. Advocates for the measure say that the move is needed to convert Russia into a market economy. Andrei Neschadin, executive director of the Expert Institute, an independent Moscow-based think-tank, explains that 'the expansion of commercial activity, the growth of towns and cities, has long hinged upon this question. A normal market in land will eventually make us a normal country at last.' He argues that with a stable set of laws supporting the ownership rights over land and property, wealthy Russians and foreign investors will begin to sink money into the Russian real estate markets. Anatoly Manillia, deputy director of the Centre for Political Research, adds, 'the lack of private property in land has been the major logjam in all our efforts to attract investment, fight corruption and build a dynamic market economy'.

As it stands now there is a black market to exchange property but because law does not govern these transactions, the process usually involves bribing government officials – which makes many international companies nervous. Bribery and corruption are illegal in most Western nations and the Organization for Economic Co-operation and Development in 1999 adopted a treaty criminalizing the bribery of foreign public officials. The Foreign Corrupt Practices Act also makes it a crime for companies publicly traded in the United States to bribe a foreign official in order to obtain business.

Opponents of private land ownership, the communist party among others, see it as another opportunity for the rich to rob the majority of the Russian people. The privatization efforts in Russia over the last decade have been disorderly and were tainted by allegations of corruption that nearly always proved to be true. Ordinary Russians are sceptical after such an ill-fated transition to capitalism and are willing to listen to communist claims that 'another mass robbery of their national heritage is afoot'. Yeygeny Kozlov is in charge of the municipal land department for the city of Kolomna. Even he concedes that people 'are suspicious now that changes will only work against them. People remember how a few people became rich through privatization and the rest were impoverished and they worry'. This is an issue of contention within Russia and shows one of the country's major dilemmas. How can Russia become a market economy and attract foreign capital without disenfranchising its people?

Sources: Peter Baker, 'Russia Allows 'For Sale' Signs on Urban Property', *Washington Post,* 27 October 2001, A24; Fred Weir, 'Russia: Tough Capitalist Frontier Opens Up', *Christian Science Monitor,* www.csmonitorarchive.com, accessed 3 September 2002.

The trend toward privatization offers unique opportunities for international managers. Existing firms, both large and small, can be acquired at low cost, often with governmental support through tax exemptions, investment grants, special depreciation allowances and low-interest-rate credits. The purchase of such firms enables the international firm to expand operations without having to start from scratch. In addition, since wages are often low in the countries where privatization takes place, there is a major opportunity to build low-cost manufacturing and sourcing bases. Furthermore, the international firm can also act as a catalyst by accelerating the pace of transferring business skills and technology and boosting trade prospects. In short, the very process of change offers new opportunities to the adept manager.

The Less-Developed Markets[35]

The time may have come to look at the four billion people in the world who live in poverty, subsisting on less than US$1500 a year (see Figure 7.1). Despite initial scepticism, companies are finding that they can make profits while at the same time having a positive effect on the sustainable livelihoods of people not normally considered potential customers.[36] However, it will require radical departures from the traditional business models: for example, new partnerships (ranging from local governments to not-for-profit organizations) and new pricing structures (allowing customers to rent or lease, rather than buy).

The first order of business is to learn about the needs, aspirations and habits of targeted populations for which traditional intelligence gathering may not be the most effective. Hewlett-Packard has an initiative called World e-Inclusion which, working with a range of global and local partners, aims to sell, lease or donate a billion dollars' worth of satellite-powered computer products and services to markets in Africa, Asia, Eastern Europe, Latin America and the Middle East. To engage with communities in Senegal, Hewlett-Packard partnered with Joko Incorporated, a company founded by revered Senegalese pop star Youssou n'Dour.

In the product area, companies must combine advanced technology with local insights. Hindustan Lever (part of Unilever) learned that low-income Indians, usually forced to settle for low-quality products, wanted to buy high-end detergents and personal care products but could not afford them in quantities available. In response, the company developed extremely low-cost packaging material and other innovations that allowed for a product priced in pennies instead of the US$4 to US$15 price of the regular containers. The same brand is on all of the product forms, regardless of packaging. Given that these consumers do not shop at supermarkets, Lever employs local residents with pushcarts who take small quantities of the sachets to kiosks.

Due to economic and physical isolation of poor communities, providing access can lead to a thriving business. In Bangladesh (with income levels of US$200 per year), GrameenPhone Ltd leases access to wireless phones to villagers. Every phone is used by an average of 100 people and generates US$900 in revenue a month – two to three times the revenue generated by wealthier users who own their phones in urban areas. Similarly, the Jhai Foundation, an American-Lao foundation, is helping villagers in Laos obtain Internet access. The first step, however, was to develop an inexpensive and robust computer. The computer has no moving, and very few delicate, parts. Instead of a hard disk, it relies on flash-memory chips and instead of an energy-guzzling glass cathode ray tube, its screen is a liquid-crystal display.

The emergence of these markets presents a great opportunity for companies. It also creates a chance for business, government and civil society to join together in a common cause to help the poor aspiring to join the world market economy. Lifting billions of people from poverty may help avert social decay, political chaos, terrorism and environmental deterioration, which is certain to continue if the gap between rich and poor countries continues to widen.

THE ROLE OF THE MULTINATIONAL FIRM

All problems aside, the market potential of transition and emerging economies is enormous. It is this promise that is paramount to understanding the developing role of multinational firms in transition economies. They enter because they see substantial profit potential. This potential, however, may not be attained quickly and firms must time their entry and activity to pace themselves for the long race.

The experience to date in many transition economies has been mixed in terms of business success. Many of the newly formed purely domestic businesses have experienced relatively short life spans often characterized by rapid growth and significant profitability, albeit short lived in duration. The causes of failure typically are problems in general business management, the institution of new government regulations or taxes, or regulatory failures.

Multinational firms, however, have experienced higher rates of success in transition economies for a variety of reasons. First, foreign firms have had a tendency to enter – at least initially – service sectors that allowed high profit potential with minimal capital investments. This permits a first-stage entry with little capital at risk. Many of these service-sector market niches, such as insurance, Internet-based telecommunication services, security sales and brokerage services and management consulting, to name a few, are 'markets' that simply did not exist under the prior economic system.

As multinational firms gain experience and knowledge of the local markets, they may then increase the size of their capital investments, for example in the form of acquisitions or greenfield investments. The local market is then used as an export base to neighbouring and other transition and emerging economies, taking advantage of long-standing links across countries for trade and commerce. At this point, the domestic market is not the focus of the firm's activity. With few exceptions, the profit potential is seen as cost-based access to other external markets.

This export orientation of the multinational firm is quite consistent with the economic policy goals of many economies. They are often sorely in need of export earnings. Having a multinational firm use their economic system as 'base camp' for export-led development adds employment and infrastructure support. This is also one of the factors contributing to the special privileges accorded to foreign multinationals by host governments, such as preferential import duties, corporate tax breaks and subsidized labour. In fact, many multinationals quickly find their access to local capital through the rapidly developing domestic financial sector to be easier than that of other domestic borrowers, because many domestic companies are effectively excluded from accessing necessary capital. This is in many ways an unfortunate result of the lower-risk profile of the multinational firm compared with recently established domestic enterprises. If not balanced by encouragement for domestic firms, this disadvantage may result in growing criticism of multinational firms and their impact on vulnerable economies. It can also lead to renewed nationalist pressures on governments and reduce the ability of multinational firms to expand their activities globally.

As multinational firms mature in transition or emerging economies, many find that the domestic market itself represents a legitimate market opportunity on a stand-alone basis. Although this is the commonly assumed goal of privatization, it is not always achieved. For example, as global firms expand their presence in an economy, thereby expanding their offerings in industrial and retail products and services, they may quickly become net importers of capital equipment and other necessary inputs for providing the high level of economic goods demanded by the populace. Due to simultaneous investments by many firms, they may also find many more competitors in this new market than they had expected.

Many economies now recognize that if they are to develop businesses that are world-class competitors and not just poor domestic copies of foreign firms, they must somehow tap the knowledge base already thriving within successful global firms. Frequently, multinational firms are invited to begin joint ventures only with domestic parties. This in itself is often difficult, given that these domestic businesses or entities rarely have significant capital to contribute but rather bring to the table non-quantifiable contributions such as market savvy and emerging business networks.

For example, in the global telecommunications industry, access to capital is only one of the many needs for industrial development. The technical know-how of the world's key global players is also needed for the development of a first-class industry. Countries such as Hungary, Indonesia and Brazil have invited foreign companies in conjunction with domestic parties to form international joint ventures to bid for the rights to develop large segments or geographic areas within their borders. This requirement is intended to serve as a way of tapping the enormous technical and market knowledge base and commitment of established multinational firms. Without their co-operation, the ability to close the gap with the leading global competitors may be impossible.

Often the multinational firm is invited into an economy to bring capital and technical and market know-how to help improve existing second-class companies. For example, in the early 1990s, General Motors negotiated extensively with the Polish government on the establishment of a joint venture with one of the government-owned automotive manufacturers. GM would provide capital and technology, while the Polish automotive manufacturer contributed its own existing asset base, workers already in place and access to a potentially large market. The problem confronted by GM and so many other multinational firms in similar circumstances is that they view the contributions of their domestic partner to be less significant than the potential loss of technical and intellectual property and the risks associated with maintaining the multinational firm's own reputation and quality

FOCUS ON

ENTREPRENEURSHIP

Meeting Need and Opportunity in Developing Markets

Micronutrient deficiencies or a lack of vitamins and minerals, such as vitamin A, iron and zinc, are believed to afflict about two billion children around the world. The impact on the learning capabilities of these children and their overall health and mortality is high. With vitamin pills costly to distribute and pill-taking hard to enforce, fortification of foods offers the most promising prospects for combating these deficiencies.

Developing a fortified drink that is cheap, effective and with no aftertaste is a challenge for any company. Attempts in the past failed either because technology was not advanced enough for the idea to work or because development efforts resulted in drinks that were priced too high for the customers most in need. For some companies the idea of dealing with the poorest markets in the world has not been appealing due to the lack of immediate growth prospects.

Coca-Cola has introduced 'Project Mission' in Botswana to launch a drink to combat anaemia, blindness and other afflictions common in poorer parts of the world. The drink, called Vitango, is like the company's Hi-C orange-flavoured drink but contains 12 vitamins and minerals chronically lacking in the diets of people in developing countries. Vitango will put the company in head-to-head competition with Procter & Gamble, which has a similar drink called Nutristar. The latter is sold in Venezuela in most food stores in flavours such as mango and passion fruit and promises 'taller, stronger and smarter kids'.

The project satisfies multiple objectives for the Coca-Cola Company. First, it could help boost sales at a time when global sales of carbonated drinks are slowing and, second, it will help in establishing relationships with governments and other local constituents that will serve as a positive platform for the Coca-Cola brand. The market for such nutritional drinks may be limited but entering the markets offers both Coca-Cola and Procter & Gamble the chance to play the role of good corporate citizen at a time when being perceived as such is increasingly important for multinational corporations. 'It is the right thing to do', says Steven Heyer, Coca-Cola's president and chief operating officer for noncarbonated beverages. 'The marginal cost is low and the return to society is high.'

Aiming their products at the developing world, the companies have to tread carefully (remembering Nestlé's debacle with infant formula). To succeed they will have to win the support of nutrition and health experts. No claims are being made that these drinks are a one-stop-shop for health but merely a supplement to a healthy diet.

Sources: C. K. Prahalad and Stuart L. Hart, 'The Fortune at the Bottom of the Pyramid', *Strategy and Business*, first quarter, 2002, 35–47; 'Drinks for Developing Countries', *Wall Street Journal*, 27 November 2001, B1, B6; and Dana James, 'B2–4B Spells Profits', *Marketing News*, 5 November 2001, 1, 11–12.

standards. In addition, it is frequently more expensive to retool an existing manufacturing facility than it is simply to start fresh with a greenfield facility. These are difficult partnerships and each and every one requires extended discussion, negotiation and special 'chemistry' for success.

Multinational corporations are very often the only ones that can realistically make a difference in solving some of the problems in developing markets, as shown in the above Focus on Entrepreneurship. Developing new technologies or products is a resource-intensive task and requires knowledge transfer from one market to another. Without multinationals as catalysts, non-governmental organizations, local governments and communities will continue to flounder in their attempts to bring development to the poorest nations in the world.[37]

SUMMARY

Special concerns must be considered by the international manager when dealing with former centrally planned economies in transition. Although the emerging market economies offer vast opportunities for trade, business practices may be significantly different from those to which the executive is accustomed.

In the emerging market economies, the key to international business success will be an understanding of the fact that societies in transition require special adaptation of business skills and time to complete the transformation. Due to their growing degree of industrialization, other economies are also becoming part of the world trade and investment picture. It must be recognized that these global changes will, in turn, precipitate adjustments in industrialized nations, particularly in the manufacturing and trade sectors. Adapting early to these changes can offer new opportunities to the international firm.

Often the international manager is also faced with state-owned enterprises that have been formed in non-communist nations for reasons of national or economic security. These firms may inhibit foreign market entry and they frequently reflect in their transactions the overall domestic and foreign policy of the country rather than any economic rationale. The current global trend toward privatization offers new opportunities to the international firm through investment or by offering business skills and knowledge to assist in the success of privatization.

QUESTIONS FOR DISCUSSION

1. Planning is necessary, and yet central planning is inefficient. Why?
2. Discuss the observation that 'Russian products do what they are supposed to do – but only that'.
3. How can and should the West help Central and Eastern European countries?
4. How can Central and Eastern European managers be trained to be market oriented?
5. Where do you see the greatest potential in future trade between emerging market economies and industrialized nations?
6. What are the benefits of privatization?
7. Why do most transition economy governments require foreign multinationals to enter business via joint ventures with existing domestic firms?
8. Why do foreign multinationals often have advantaged access to capital in emerging economies over purely domestic companies?

INTERNET EXERCISES

1. Identify the key programmes and information services offered to exporters operating in the former Soviet Union through the US Department of Commerce. (Refer to Commerce's Business Information Service for the Newly Independent States, BISNIS, www.ita.doc.gov.)

2. What role does the European Bank for Reconstruction and Development play in transforming the formerly communist economies of Eastern Europe and the Soviet Union? (Refer to the web site www.ebrd.com.)

TAKE A STAND

With the demise of the communist economies of Central and Eastern Europe and the former Soviet Union, as well as the advances in international communication and information technologies, globalization is an accomplished fact. Although many countries grow to unprecedented levels of wealth and economic security, others continue to experience permanent debt and instability. Activists are warning of the dangers of 'savage capitalism', where social safety nets are dismantled and the greedy are ensured a constant supply of exploitable cheap labour from the world's poorest countries.

FOR DISCUSSION

Pope John Paul II urged adapting to new needs, modifying the rules of the marketplace and developing new models of sharing between rich and poor countries. How do you evaluate the risk of the greediness of a few, which leaves many on the margin of survival?

PART 3

INTERNATIONAL BUSINESS STRATEGY

8 Entry and Expansion

9 Strategic Planning, Organization, Implementation and Control

In order to operate successfully abroad, firms must prepare for their market entry. Key in the preparation is the conduct of research to build a knowledge base of country-specific issues and market-specific opportunities and concerns.

Once such a base is established, the company can enter international markets, initially through exporting and international intermediaries. Over time, expansion can occur through foreign direct investment and lead to the formation of the multinational corporation.

Concurrent to the entry and expansion, the firm must engage in substantial strategic planning. The planning and the subsequent steps necessary for organization, implementation and control represent the content of this part.

CHAPTER
8

Entry and Expansion

- The Role of Management
- Motivations to Go Abroad
- Strategic Effects of Going International
- Entry and Development Strategies
- International Intermediaries
- Local Presence
- A Comprehensive View of International Expansion

LEARNING OBJECTIVES

- To learn how firms gradually progress through an internationalization process.
- To understand the strategic effects of internationalization on the firm.
- To study the various modes of entering international markets.
- To understand the role and functions of international intermediaries.
- To learn about the opportunities and challenges of co-operative market development.

EXPANDING A BUSINESS

Triumph TBS is a Welsh company and the leading manufacturer of steel storage products for the office environment in the UK. The company was established in 1946 as a family owned business. In 2007, its turnover was in the region of £60 million with the majority being generated in the UK and Ireland. The company recognized that in order to ensure sustainable growth, and also to prepare it for a potential sale, the business needed to be increased in volume and be geographically diversified. Given the practically unlimited number of potential export markets, a strategy needed to be developed to offer a sensible selection of target markets.

Following this strategy, a country specific tactic needed to be developed. Agreed tactics needed to be implemented within a timeframe. After a number of consultations it was decided to choose a mix of mature and emerging markets in order to achieve various stages of market penetration and profit generation. A shortlist of target countries was developed and agreed on, including Portugal, Austria, Belgium, Russia and China.

Portugal was chosen because the market accepts English literature and it is driven by similar dynamics to the UK market. It was suggested that the ideal strategy was to find an importing dealer to act as main distributor. A number of criteria were set, such as involvement with the community, reputation, market coverage and quality of showroom and service. Once a dealership was identified and approached, an introduction was made to Triumph and the export director was accompanied to Lisbon, where a consulting company facilitated the negotiations.

Austria was chosen because it is one of the healthiest economies in Europe, with good market potential and above-average growth rate. It was suggested that the ideal strategy for Austria was to appoint a self-employed sales agent who had to have a showroom. A suitable candidate was identified and invited to Wales. A local consulting company facilitated the meeting, moderated and assisted in negotiation and closing.

For China it was suggested that the ideal strategy was to find a key dealer who had the resources, the reputation, know-how and the attitude to represent and commit to a Western supplier. The dealership had to be in the high-end of the market, with established relationships to projects of Western corporations in China. After a market visit and an extensive search and selection process, an ideal dealership was identified and introduced to the client, with an agreement eventually entered.

The same strategy was recommended for Russia and executed in the same way: a market and dealership visit helped to screen potential candidates and eventually a suitable dealer was introduced to the client.

In Belgium, a competing manufacturer was identified as the ideal partner to team up with. Products proved to be mutually complementary and Triumph could benefit from an established distribution structure. After due diligence showed no areas of concern an agreement between both companies was facilitated.

Sources: Triumph Bureau Systems; www.scribd.com/doc/295936/Case-Study-Export-Development, accessed 1 March 2008.

INTRODUCTION

International business holds out the promise of large new market areas, and yet firms cannot simply jump into the international marketplace and expect to be successful. They must adjust to needs and opportunities abroad, have quality products, understand their customers and do their homework to understand the vagaries of international markets. The rapid globalization of markets, however, reduces the time available to adjust to new market realities.

This chapter is concerned with firms preparing to enter international markets and companies expanding their current international activities. Initial emphasis is placed on export activities with a focus on the role of management in starting up international operations and a description of the basic stimuli for international activities. Entry modes for the international arena are highlighted and the problems and benefits of each mode are discussed. The role of facilitators and intermediaries in international business is described. Finally, alternatives that involve a local presence by the firm are presented.

THE ROLE OF MANAGEMENT

Management dynamism and commitment are crucial to a firm's first steps toward international operations. Typically, managers of firms with a strong international performance are active, aggressive and display a high degree of international orientation.[1] Such an orientation is indicated by substantial global awareness and cultural sensitivity.[2] Conversely, the managers of firms that are unsuccessful or inactive internationally usually exhibit a lack of determination or devotion to international business.

The issue of managerial commitment is a critical one because foreign market penetration requires a vast amount of market development activity, sensitivity toward foreign environments, research and innovation. Regardless of what the firm produces or where it does business internationally, managerial commitment is crucial for enduring stagnation and sometimes even setbacks and failure. After all, it is top management that determines the willingness to take risk, to introduce new products, to seek new solutions to problems and to strive continuously to succeed abroad.[3] To achieve such a commitment, it is important to involve all levels of management early on in the international planning process and to impress on all players that the effort will only succeed with a commitment that is company-wide.[4]

Initiating international business activities takes the firm in an entirely new direction, quite different from adding a product line or hiring a few more people. For a firm, going international means that a fundamental strategic change is taking place. Companies that initiate international expansion efforts and succeed with them, typically begin to enjoy operational improvements – such as positioning strengths in competition – long before financial improvements appear.[5]

The decision to export usually comes from the highest levels of management, typically the owner, president, chairman or vice president of marketing.[6] The carrying out of the decision – that is, the implementation of international business transactions – is then the primary responsibility of marketing personnel. It is important to establish an organizational structure in which someone has the specific responsibility for international activities. Without such a responsibility centre, the focus necessary for success can easily be lost. Such a centre need not be large. For example, just one person assigned part time to international activities can begin exploring and entering international markets.

The first step in developing international commitment is to become aware of international business opportunities. Management must then determine the degree and timing of the firm's internationalization. For instance, a German corporation that expands its operation into Austria, Belgium, the Netherlands and Switzerland is less international than a German corporation that launches operations in Algeria, Brazil, India and Japan. Moreover, if a German-based corporation already has activities in the United States, setting up a business in Canada does not increase its degree of internationalization as much as if Canada was the first 'bridgehead' in North America.[7]

Management must decide the timing of when to start the internationalization process and how quickly it should progress. For example, market entry might be desirable as soon as possible because clients are waiting for the product or because competitors are expected to enter the market shortly. In addition, it may be desirable to either enter a market abroad selectively or to achieve full market coverage from the outset. Decisions on these timing issues will determine the speed with which management must mobilize and motivate the people involved in the process.[8] It must be kept in mind that a firm-wide international orientation does not develop overnight but rather needs time to grow. Internationalization is a matter of learning, of acquiring experiential knowledge. A firm must learn about foreign markets and institutions but also about its own internal resources in order to know what it is capable of when exposed to new and unfamiliar conditions.[9] Planning and execution of an export venture must be incorporated into the firm's strategic management process. A firm that sets no strategic goals for its export venture is less likely to make the venture a long-term success.[10] As markets around the world become more linked and more competitive, the importance of developing and following a strategy becomes increasingly key to making things better.[11]

Management is often much too preoccupied with short-term, immediate problems to engage in sophisticated long-run planning. As a result, many firms are simply not interested in international business. Yet certain situations may lead a manager to discover and understand the value of going international and decide to pursue international business activities. One trigger factor can be international travel, during which new business opportunities are discovered. Alternatively, the receipt of information can lead management to believe that international business opportunities exist. Unsolicited orders from abroad are an example. Research in Scotland has shown that two thirds of small exporting firms started to do so because of unsolicited approaches from buyers or third parties. Management's entrepreneurial spirit manifested itself by following through on the lead.[12] Nonetheless, although such management by serendipity may be useful in a start-up phase, it is no substitute for effective planning when it comes to setting the long-term strategic corporate direction.

Managers who have lived abroad and learned foreign languages or are particularly interested in foreign cultures are more likely to investigate whether international business opportunities would be appropriate for their firms. Countries or regions with high levels of immigration may, over time, benefit from greater export success due to more ties, better information and greater international business sensitivity through their new residents.

New management or new employees can also introduce an international orientation. For example, managers entering a firm may already have had some international business experience and may use this experience to further the business activities of their new employer.

MOTIVATIONS TO GO ABROAD

Normally, management will consider international activities only when stimulated to do so. A variety of motivations can push and pull individuals and firms along the international path. An overview of the major motivations that have been found to make firms go international is provided in Table 8.1.

Proactive Motivations	Reactive Motivations
Profit advantage	Competitive pressures
Unique products	Overproduction
Technological advantage	Declining domestic sales
Exclusive information	Excess capacity
Tax benefit	Saturated domestic markets
Economies of scale	Proximity to customers and ports

Table 8.1: Major motivations to firms.

Proactive motivations represent stimuli for firm-initiated strategic change. Reactive motivations describe stimuli that result in a firm's response and adaptation to changes imposed by the outside environment. In other words, firms with proactive motivations go international because they want to; those with reactive motivations go international because they have to.

Proactive Motivations

Profits are the major proactive motivation for international business. Management may perceive international sales as a potential source of higher profit margins or of more added-on profits. Of course, the profitability expected when planning to go international is often quite different from the profitability actually obtained. Profitability is often linked with international growth – yet many corporate international entry decisions are made based on expectations of market growth rather than on actual market growth.[13] Particularly in start-up operations, initial profitability may be quite low due to the cost of getting ready for going international and the losses resulting from early mistakes.[14] The gap between expectation and reality may be especially large when the firm has not previously engaged in international business. Even with thorough planning, unexpected influences can change the profit picture substantially. Shifts in exchange rates, for example, may drastically affect profit forecasts.

Unique products or a technological advantage can be another major stimulus. A firm may produce goods or services that are not widely available from international competitors. Again, real and perceived advantages must be differentiated. Many firms believe that they offer unique products or services, even though this may not be the case internationally. If products or technologies are unique, however, they certainly can provide a competitive edge. What needs to be considered is how long such an advantage will last. The length of time is a function of the product, its technology and the creativity of competitors. In the past, a firm with a competitive edge could often count on being the sole supplier to foreign markets for years to come. This type of advantage has shrunk dramatically because of competing technologies and the frequent lack of international patent protection.

Special knowledge about foreign customers or market situations may be another proactive stimulus. Such knowledge may result from particular insights by a firm, special contacts an individual may have, in-depth research or simply from being in the right place at the right time (for example, recognizing a good business situation during a vacation trip). Although such exclusivity can serve well as an initial stimulus for international business, it will rarely provide prolonged motivation because competitors can be expected to catch up with the information advantage. Only if firms build up international information advantage as an ongoing process, through, for example, broad market scanning or special analytical capabilities, can prolonged corporate strategy be based on this motivation.

Tax benefits can also play a major motivating role. Many governments use preferential tax treatment to encourage exports. As a result of such tax benefits, firms can offer their product at a lower cost in foreign markets or can accumulate a higher profit. However, international trade rules make it increasingly difficult for governments to use tax subsidies to encourage exports. For example, to counteract the value-added tax refund provided to exporters by the European Union, the United States has provided for tax deferment for its exporters. This deferment originally called the Domestic International Sales Corporation (DISC) and now known as the Extraterritorial Income Tax Exclusion (ETI) has repeatedly been found to be in violation of World Trade Organization (WTO) rules and subject to abolishment or retaliatory tariffs by trading partners.

A final major proactive motivation involves economies of scale. International activities may enable the firm to increase its output and therefore rise more rapidly on the learning curve. The Boston Consulting Group has shown that the doubling of output can reduce production costs by up to 30%. Increased production for international markets can therefore help to reduce the cost of production for domestic sales and make the firm more competitive domestically as well.[15]

Reactive Motivations

Reactive motivations influence firms to respond to environmental changes and pressures rather than blaze new trails. Competitive pressures are one example. A company may worry about losing domestic market share to competing firms that have benefited from the economies of scale gained through international business activities. Further, it may fear losing foreign markets permanently to competitors that have decided to focus on these markets. Since market share is usually most easily retained by firms that initially obtain it, some companies may enter the international market head over heels. Quick entry, however, may result in equally quick withdrawal once the firm recognizes that its preparation has been inadequate.

Similarly, overproduction may represent a reactive motivation. During downturns in the domestic business cycle, foreign markets can provide an ideal outlet for excess inventories. International business expansion motivated by overproduction does not usually represent full commitment by management but rather a temporary safety valve. As soon as domestic demand returns to previous levels, international business activities are curtailed or even terminated. Firms that have used such a strategy once may encounter difficulties when trying to employ it again because many international customers are not interested in temporary or sporadic business relationships.

Declining domestic sales, whether measured in sales volume or market share, have a similar motivating effect. Goods marketed domestically may be at the declining stage of their product life cycle. Instead of attempting to push back the life cycle process domestically or in addition to such an effort, firms may opt to prolong the product life cycle by expanding the market. Such efforts often meet with success, particularly with high-technology products that are outmoded by the latest innovation. Such 'just-dated' technology may enable vast progress in manufacturing or services industries and, most importantly, may make such progress affordable. For example, a hospital without any imaging equipment may be much better off acquiring a 'just-dated' MRI machine, rather than waiting for enough funding to purchase the latest state-of-the-art equipment.

Excess capacity can also be a powerful motivator. If equipment for production is not fully used, firms may see expansion abroad as an ideal way to achieve broader distribution of fixed costs. Alternatively, if all fixed costs are assigned to domestic production, the firm can penetrate foreign markets with a pricing scheme that focuses mainly on variable cost. Yet such a view is feasible only for market entry. A market-penetration strategy based on variable cost alone is unrealistic because, in the long run, fixed costs have to be recovered to replace production equipment.

The reactive motivation of a saturated domestic market has similar results to that of declining domestic sales. Again, firms in this situation can use the international market to prolong the life of their good and even of their organization.

A final major reactive motivation is that of proximity to customers and ports. Physical and psychological closeness to the international market can often play a major role in the international business activities of the firm. For example, a firm established near a border may not even perceive itself as going abroad if it does business in the neighbouring country. Except for some firms close to the Canadian or Mexican border, this factor is much less prevalent in the United States than in many other nations. Most European firms automatically go abroad simply because their neighbours are so close.

In this context, the concept of psychological distance needs to be understood. Geographic closeness to foreign markets may not necessarily translate into real or perceived closeness to the foreign customer. Sometimes cultural variables, legal factors and other societal norms make a foreign market that is geographically close seem psychologically distant. For example, research has shown that US firms perceive Canada to be much closer psychologically than Mexico. Even England, mainly because of the similarity in language, is perceived by many US firms to be much closer than Mexico or other Latin American countries, despite the geographic distances. However, in light of the reduction of trade barriers as a result of the North American Free Trade Agreement (NAFTA) and a growing proportion of the US population with Hispanic background, this long-standing perception may be changing rapidly.

It is important to remember two major issues in the context of psychological distance. First, some of the distance seen by firms is based on perception rather than reality. For example, many UK firms may see the United States as psychologically very close because the English language is spoken in both. However, the attitudes and values of managers and customers may vary substantially between markets. Too much of a focus on the similarities may let the firm lose sight of the differences. Many Canadian firms have incurred high costs in learning this lesson when entering the United States. Second, closer psychological proximity does make it easier for firms to enter markets. Therefore, for firms new to international business it may be advantageous to begin this new activity by entering the psychologically closer markets first in order to gather experience before venturing into markets that are farther away.

In general, firms that are most successful in international business are usually motivated by proactive – that is, firm internal – factors. Proactive firms are also frequently more service oriented than reactive firms. Further, proactive firms tend to be more marketing and strategy oriented than reactive firms, which have as their major concern operational issues. The following Focus on Entrepreneurship describes the proactive efforts of an exporter. The clearest differentiation between the two types of firms can probably be made after the fact by determining how they initially entered international

F CUS ON

ENTREPRENEURSHIP

An International Bug

How did a small Phoenix-based environmental cleanup company boost international sales from zero to 25% of annual revenues? By proactively going for the world!

First, Dan Kelley, CEO of Tierra Dynamic Company and his 30 employees had to discover a very special 'bug'. Tierra Dynamic patented a discovery called the *bio sparge*, a naturally occurring bacterium that Tierra cultivates and then induces to eat spilled hydrocarbons at an accelerated rate. According to Kelley, 'this technique remediates soil three times faster than other methods now on the market, a significant advantage when you're concerned about carcinogens that can cause cancers and other health problems'.

Second, Kelley discovered a gaping hole in the international market for his product – and leaped to fill that hole. Kelley comments, 'The environmental industry is new to many developing countries and we can compete better over there than we can in more developed countries....There's a big void in the market and we're happy to fill it.'

Third, Kelley identified locations that required environmental cleanup, focusing on Brazil and Argentina, as well as Indonesia, Malaysia and Singapore. His market analysis was based primarily on the environmental regulation enforcement priorities of a given country.

Next came the practical issue of setting up shop on foreign soil. Kelley prefers working with a local partner, one who has the necessary local contacts but who lacks the requisite technology.

After five years, Tierra found a match, then another and eventually secured an international reputation for environmental cleanup within emerging markets. Tierra created a joint venture company called Mileto-Innovative Remediation Technologies in its target country of Argentina. Kelley is optimistic as he has gone there for the long run.

Tierra Dynamic is currently negotiating the rights to another patented technology that can destroy not only hydrocarbons but also PCBs, a lethal source of carcinogens that can be found in soil and water. As for the future of environmental cleanup, Kelley hopes new technologies will continue to protect the health of families worldwide.

Source: Doug Barry (2002) 'Have Microbes, Will Travel: Small Sun Belt Company Finds Niche in Cleaning Up After Others', *Export America*, 3(2), February.

markets. Proactive firms are more likely to have solicited their first international order, whereas reactive firms frequently begin international activities after receiving an unsolicited order from abroad.

STRATEGIC EFFECTS OF GOING INTERNATIONAL

Going international presents the firm with new environments, entirely new ways of doing business and a host of wide-ranging new problems. The problems can consist of strategic considerations, such as service delivery and compliance with government regulations. In addition, the firm has to focus on start-up issues, such as how to find and effectively communicate with customers and operational matters, such as information flows and the mechanics of carrying out an international business transaction. This involves a variety of new documents, including commercial invoices, bills of lading, consular invoices, inspection certificates and shipper's export declarations. The paperwork is necessary to comply with various domestic, international or foreign regulations. The regulations may be designed to control international business activities, to streamline the individual transaction or, as in the case of the shipper's export declaration, to compile trade statistics.

The firm needs to determine its preparedness for internationalization by assessing its internal strengths and weaknesses. This preparedness has to be evaluated in the context of the globalization of the industry within which the firm operates, because this context will affect the competitive position and strategic options available to the firm.[16]

Unusual things can happen to both risk and profit. Management's perception of risk exposure grows in light of the gradual development of expertise, the many concerns about engaging in a new activity and uncertainty about the new environment it is about to enter. Domestically, the firm has gradually learned about the market and therefore managed to decrease its risk. In the course of international expansion, the firm now encounters new and unfamiliar factors, exposing it to increased risk. At the same time, because of the investment needs required by a serious international effort, immediate profit performance may slip. In the longer term, increasing familiarity with international markets and the diversification benefits of serving multiple markets will decrease the firm's risk below the previous 'domestic only' level and increase profitability as well. In the short term, however, managers may face an unusual and perhaps unacceptable, situation: rising risk accompanied by decreasing profitability. In light of this reality, which is depicted in Figure 8.1, many executives are tempted not to initiate international activities or to discontinue them.[17]

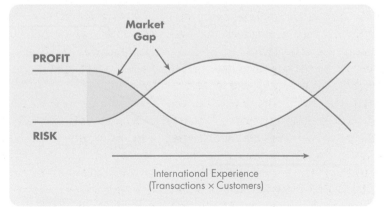

Figure 8.1: Profit and risk during early internationalization.

Source: Michael R. Czinkota (2001) 'A National Export Development Policy for New and Growing Businesses', in *Best Practices in International Business*, M. Czinkota and I. Ronkainen (eds), South-Western, Cincinnati, OH, 35–45. Reproduced by permission of Michael Czinkota.

Understanding the changes in risk and profitability can help management overcome the seemingly prohibitive cost of going international, because the negative developments may only be short term. Yet, success does require the firm to be a risk taker and firms must realize that satisfactory international performance will take time.[18] Satisfactory performance can be achieved in three ways: effectiveness, efficiency and competitive strength. Effectiveness is characterized by the acquisition of market share abroad and by increased sales. Efficiency is manifested later by rising profitability. Competitive strength refers to the firm's position compared to other firms in the industry and, due to the benefits of international experience, is likely to grow. The international executive must appreciate the time and performance dimensions associated with going abroad in order to overcome short-term setbacks for the sake of long-term success.

ENTRY AND DEVELOPMENT STRATEGIES

In the following sections we present the most typical international entry and expansion strategies. The evolution of a manufacturer's decision on entry mode is presented in Figure 8.2. The international entry and expansion strategies are exporting and importing, licensing and franchising. Another key way to expand is through a local presence, either via inter-firm co-operation or foreign direct investment. These can take on many forms such as contractual agreements, equity participation and joint ventures or direct investment conducted by the firms alone.

Exporting and Importing

Firms can be involved in exporting and importing in an indirect or direct way. Indirect involvement means that the firm participates in international business through an intermediary and does not deal with foreign customers or firms. Direct involvement means that the firm works with foreign customers or markets with the opportunity to develop a relationship. Firms typically opt for direct involvement based on cost decisions. Transaction cost theory postulates that firms will evaluate and compare the costs of integrating an operation internally, as compared to the cost of using an external party to

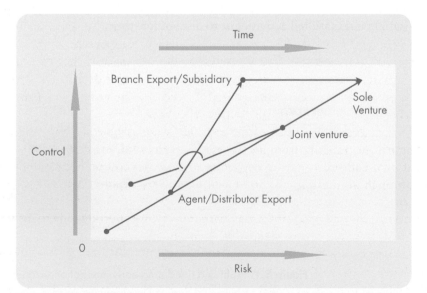

Figure 8.2: Evolution of a manufacturer's decision on entry mode.
Source: F. Root (1994) *Entry Strategies for International Markets*. Jossey-Bass Inc. Publishers.

act for the firm abroad.[19] Once it becomes easier and more efficient for a firm to conduct all the research, negotiations, shipping and monitoring itself, rather than paying someone else to do it, the firm is likely to become a direct exporter or importer.

The end result of exporting and importing is similar whether the activities are direct or indirect. In both cases, goods and services either go abroad or come to the domestic market from abroad, and goods may have to be adapted to suit the targeted market. However, the different approaches have varying degrees of impact on the knowledge and experience levels of firms. The less direct the involvement of the firm, the less likely is the internal development of a storehouse of information and expertise on how to do business abroad;, information that the firm can draw on later for further international expansion. Therefore, although indirect activities represent a form of international market entry, they may not result in growing management commitment to international markets or increased capabilities in serving them.

Many firms are indirect exporters and importers, often without their knowledge. As an example, merchandise can be sold to a domestic firm that in turn sells it abroad. This is most frequently the case when smaller suppliers deliver products to large multinational corporations, which use them as input to their foreign sales. Foreign buyers may also purchase products locally and then send them immediately to their home country. Although indirect exports may be the result of unwitting participation, some firms also choose this method of international entry as a strategic alternative that conserves effort and resources while still taking advantage of foreign opportunities.

At the same time, many firms that perceive themselves as buying domestically may in reality buy imported products. They may have long-standing relations with a domestic supplier who, because of cost and competitive pressures, has begun to source products from abroad rather than to produce them domestically. In this case, the buyer firm has become an indirect importer.

Firms that opt to export or import directly have more opportunities ahead of them. They learn more quickly the competitive advantages of their products and can therefore expand more rapidly. They also have the ability to control their international activities better and can forge relationships with their trading partners, which can lead to further international growth and success.

However, the firms are also faced with obstacles. These hurdles include identifying and targeting foreign suppliers and/or customers and finding retail space, all of which are processes that can be very costly and time-consuming. Some firms are overcoming such barriers through the use of mail-order catalogues or electronic commerce ('storeless' distribution) networks. In Japan, for example, 'high-cost rents, crowded shelves and an intricate distribution system have made launching new products via conventional methods an increasingly difficult and expensive proposition. Direct marketing via e-Commerce eliminates the need for high-priced shop space.'[20] In addition, particularly in industry sectors characterized by very thin profit margins, survival is determined by sales volume. Under such conditions, a large market size is essential for success – pointing many firms in the direction of international markets reached through electronic business.[21]

As a firm and its managers gather experience with exporting, they move through different levels of commitment, ranging from awareness, interest, trial, evaluation and, finally, adaptation of an international outlook as part of corporate strategy. Of course, not all firms will progress with equal speed through all these levels. Some will do so very rapidly, perhaps encouraged by success with an electronic commerce approach and move on to other forms of international involvement such as foreign direct investment. Others may withdraw from exporting, due to disappointing experiences or as part of a strategic resource allocation decision.[22]

Increasingly, there are many new firms that either start out with an international orientation or develop one shortly after their establishment. Such **mininationals** or **born global** firms (covered in more detail in Chapter 9) emerge particularly in industries that require large numbers of customers and in countries that only offer small internal markets. They tend to be small and young[23] and often make heavy use of electronic commerce in reaching out to the world. In some countries more than one third of new companies have been reported to export within two years.[24] Firms, managers and governments therefore need to be much quicker than they have been in the past when it comes to introducing firms to and preparing them for the international market.

INTERNATIONAL INTERMEDIARIES

Both direct and indirect importers and exporters frequently make use of trade intermediaries who can assist with troublesome yet important details such as documentation, financing and transportation. The intermediaries can also identify foreign suppliers and customers and help the firm with long- or short-term market penetration efforts. Major types of international intermediaries are export management companies and trading companies. Together with export facilitators, the intermediaries can bring the global market to the domestic firm's doorstep and help overcome financial and time constraints. The list below shows those areas in which a trade intermediary can be particularly helpful:[25]

- knows foreign market competitive conditions;
- has personal contacts with potential foreign buyers;
- evaluates credit risk associated with foreign buyers;
- has sales staff to call on current foreign customers in person;
- assumes responsibility for physical delivery of product to foreign buyer.

It is the responsibility of the firm's management to decide how to use intermediaries. Options range from using their help for initial market entry to developing a long-term strategic collaboration. It is the degree of corporate involvement in and control of the international effort that determines whether the firm operates as an indirect or direct internationalist.

Export Management Companies

Firms that specialize in performing international business services as commission representatives or as distributors are known as export management companies (EMCs). Most EMCs are quite small. Many were formed by one or two principals with experience in international business or in a particular geographic area. Their expertise enables them to offer specialized services to domestic corporations.

EMCs have two primary forms of operation: they take title to goods and distribute internationally on their own account; or they perform services as agents. They often serve a variety of clients, and thus their mode of operation may vary from client to client and from transaction to transaction. An EMC may act as an agent for one client and as a distributor for another. It may even act as both for the same client on different occasions.

When working as an agent, the EMC is primarily responsible for developing foreign business and sales strategies and establishing contacts abroad. Because the EMC does not share in the profits from a sale, it depends heavily on a high sales volume, on which it charges commission. The EMC may therefore be tempted to take on as many products and as many clients as possible to obtain a high sales volume. As a result, the EMC may spread itself too thin and may be unable adequately to represent all the clients and products it carries. The risk is particularly great with small EMCs.

EMCs that have specific expertise in selecting markets because of language capabilities, previous exposure or specialized contacts appear to be the ones most successful and useful in aiding client firms in their international business efforts. For example, they can co-operate with firms that are already successful in international business but have been unable to penetrate a specific region. By sticking to their area of expertise and representing only a limited number of clients, such agents can provide quite valuable services.

When operating as a distributor, the EMC purchases products from the domestic firm, takes title and assumes the trading risk. Selling in its own name, it has the opportunity to reap greater profits than when acting as an agent. The potential for greater profit is appropriate, because the EMC has drastically reduced the risk for the domestic firm while increasing its own risk. The burden of the merchandise acquired provides a major motivation to complete an international sale successfully. The domestic firm selling to the EMC is in the comfortable position of having sold its merchandise and received its money without having to deal with the complexities of the international market. On the other hand, it is less likely to gather much international business expertise.

Compensation of EMCs

The mechanism of an EMC may be very useful to the domestic firm if such activities produce additional sales abroad. However, certain activities must take place and must be paid for. As an example, a firm must incur market development expenses to enter foreign markets. At the very least, product availability must be communicated, goods must be shown abroad and visits must be arranged or contacts must be established. These activities must be funded.

One possibility is a fee charged to the manufacturer by the EMC for market development, sometimes in the form of a retainer and often on an annual basis. The retainers vary and are dependent on the number of products represented and the difficulty of foreign market penetration. Frequently, manufacturers are also expected to pay all or part of the direct expenses associated with foreign market penetration. These expenses may involve the production and translation of promotional product brochures, the cost of attending trade shows, the provision of product samples or trade advertising.

Alternatively, the EMC may demand a price break for international sales. In one way or another, the firm that uses an EMC must pay the EMC for the international business effort. Otherwise, despite promises, the EMC may simply add the firm and product in name only to its product offering and do nothing to achieve international success.

Power Conflicts between EMCs and Clients

The EMC faces the continuous problem of retaining a client once foreign market penetration is achieved. Many firms use an EMC's services mainly to test the international arena, with the clear desire to become a direct participant once successful operations have been established. Of course, this is particularly true if foreign demand turns out to be strong and profit levels are high. The conflict between the EMC and its clients, with one side wanting to retain market power by not sharing too much international business information and the other side wanting to obtain that power, often results in short-term relationships and a lack of co-operation. Since international business development is based on long-term efforts, this conflict frequently leads to a lack of success.

For the concept of an export management company to work, both parties must fully recognize the delegation of responsibilities, the costs associated with those activities and the need for information sharing, co-operation and mutual reliance. Use of an EMC should be viewed just like a domestic channel commitment, requiring a thorough investigation of the intermediary and the advisability of relying on its efforts, a willingness to co-operate on a relationship rather than on a transaction basis and a willingness to reward its efforts properly. The EMC in turn must adopt a flexible approach to managing the export relationship. As access to the Internet is making customers increasingly sophisticated and world-wise, export management companies must ensure that they continue to deliver true value added. They must acquire, develop and deploy resources such as new knowledge about foreign markets or about export processes in order to lower their client firms' export-related transaction costs and therefore remain a useful intermediary.[26] By doing so, the EMC lets the client know that the cost is worth the service and thereby reduces the desire for circumvention.

Trading Companies

Another major intermediary is the trading company. The concept was originated by the European trading houses such as the Fuggers of Augsburg, Germany. Later on, monarchs chartered traders to form corporate bodies that enjoyed exclusive trading rights and protection by the naval forces in exchange for tax payments. Examples of such early trading companies are the Oost-Indische Compagnie of the Netherlands, formed in 1602, followed shortly by the British East India Company and La Compagnie des Indes chartered by France.[27] Today, the most famous trading companies are the *sogo shosha* of Japan. For example, Mitsubishi, Mitsui and C. Itoh have become household names around the world. The nine trading company giants of Japan act as intermediaries for about one third of the country's exports and two fifths of its imports.[28] The general trading companies play a unique role in world commerce by importing, exporting, countertrading, investing and manufacturing. Their vast size allows them to benefit from economies of scale and perform their operations at high rates of return, even though their profit margins are less than 2%.

Four major reasons have been given for the success of the Japanese *sogo shosha*. First, by concentrating on obtaining and disseminating information about market opportunities and by investing huge funds in the development of information systems, the firms have the mechanisms and organizations in place to gather, evaluate and translate market information into business opportunities. Second, economies of scale permit the firms to take advantage of their vast transaction volume to obtain preferential treatment by, for example, negotiating transportation rates or even opening up new transportation routes and distribution systems. Third, the firms serve large internal markets, not only in Japan but also around the world and can benefit from opportunities for countertrade. Finally, *sogo shosha* have access to vast quantities of capital, both within Japan and in the international capital markets. They can therefore carry out transactions that are too large or risky to be palatable or feasible for other firms.[29] In spite of changing trading patterns, these giants continue to succeed by shifting their strategy to expand their domestic activities in Japan, entering more newly developing markets, increasing their trading activities among third countries and forming joint ventures with non-Japanese firms.

Expansion of Trading Companies

For many decades, the emergence of trading companies was commonly believed to be a Japan-specific phenomenon. Japanese cultural factors were cited as the reason why such intermediaries could operate successfully only from that country. In the last few decades, however, many other governments have established trading companies. In countries as diverse as Brazil, Republic of Korea and Turkey, trading companies handle large portions of national exports.[30] The reason these firms have become so large is due, in good measure, to special and preferential government incentives, rather than market forces alone. Therefore, they may be vulnerable to changes in government policies.

In the United States, trading companies in which firms could co-operate internationally were initially permitted through the Webb-Pomerene associations established in 1918. In the 1930s these collaborative ventures accounted for about 12% of US exports, but by 2002 their share had dropped to less than 1%. Another US governmental approach to export trade facilitation was export trading company (ETC) legislation designed to improve the export performance of small and medium-sized firms. Bank participation in trading companies was permitted and businesses were encouraged to join together to export or offer export services.

Permitting banks to participate in ETCs was intended to allow ETCs better access to capital and therefore permit more trading transactions and easier receipt of title to goods. The relaxation of anti-trust provisions in turn was meant to enable firms to form joint ventures more easily. The cost of developing and penetrating international markets would then be shared, with the proportional share being, for many small and medium-sized firms, much easier to bear. As an example, in case a warehouse is needed in order to secure foreign market penetration, one firm alone does not have to bear all the costs. A consortium of firms can jointly rent a foreign warehouse. Similarly, each firm need not station a service technician abroad at substantial cost. Joint funding of a service centre by several firms makes the cost less prohibitive for each one. The trading company concept also offers a one-stop shopping centre for both the firm and its foreign customers. The firm can be assured that all international functions will be performed efficiently by the trading company and at the same time, the foreign customer will have to deal with few individual firms.

Although ETCs seem to offer major benefits to US firms that want to go abroad, they have not been very extensively used. By 2003, only 190 individual ETC certificates had been issued by the US Department of Commerce. Since some of the certificates covered all the members of trade associations, more than 5000 companies were part of an ETC.[31]

Private Sector Facilitators

Facilitators are entities outside the firm that assist in the process of going international. They supply knowledge and information but do not participate in the transaction. Such facilitators can come both from the private and the public sector.

Major encouragement and assistance can result from the statements and actions of other firms in the same industry. Information that would be considered proprietary if it involved domestic operations is often freely shared by competing firms when it concerns international business. The information not only has source credibility but also is viewed with a certain amount of fear, because a too-successful competitor may eventually infringe on the firm's domestic business.

A second influential group of private sector facilitators is distributors. Often a firm's distributors are engaged, through some of their business activities, in international business. To increase their international distribution volume, they encourage purely domestic firms to participate in the international market. This is true not only for exports but also for imports. For example, a major customer of a manufacturing firm may find that materials available from abroad, if used in the domestic production process, would make the product available at lower cost. In such instances, the customer may approach the supplier and strongly encourage foreign sourcing.

Banks and other service firms, such as accounting and consulting firms, can serve as major facilitators by alerting their clients to international opportunities. Although historically these service providers follow their major multinational clients abroad, increasingly they are establishing a foreign presence on their own. Frequently, they work with domestic clients on expanding market reach in the hope that their service will be used for any international transactions that result. Given the extensive information network of many service providers – banks, for example, often have a wide variety of correspondence relationships – the role of these facilitators can be major. Like a mother hen, they can take firms under their wings and be pathfinders in foreign markets.

Chambers of commerce and other business associations that interact with firms can frequently heighten their interest in international business. Yet, in most instances, such organizations function mainly as secondary intermediaries, because true change is brought about by the presence and encouragement of other managers.

Public Sector Facilitators

Government efforts can also facilitate the international efforts of firms. In the United States, for example, the Department of Commerce provides major export assistance, as do other federal organizations such as the Small Business Administration and the Export-Import Bank. Most countries maintain similar export support organizations. Table 8.2 provides the names of selected export promotion agencies from around the globe, together with their web addresses. Employees of these organizations typically visit firms and attempt to analyse their international business opportunities. Through rapid access to government resources, these individuals can provide data, research reports, counselling and financing information to firms. Government organizations can also sponsor meetings that bring

Australia	Australian Trade Commission	www.austrade.gov.au
Canada	Export Development Corporation	www.edc.ca/
France	Centre Français du Commerce Extérieur	www.cfce.fr/
Germany	Federal Office of Foreign Trade Information (BfAI)	www.bfai.com
India	India Trade Promotion Organization (ITPO)	www.indiatradepromotion.org
Japan	Japan External Trade Organization (JETRO)	www.jetro.go.jp
Singapore	International Enterprise Singapore	www.iesingapore.gov.sg
South Korea	Trade-Investment Promotion Agency (KOTRA)	www.kotra.or.kr/
United Kingdom	Overseas Trade Services	www.dti.gov.uk
United Nations/World Trade Organization	International Trade Centre	www.intracen.org
United States	Export-Import Bank	www.exim.gov
	International Trade Administration	www.ita.doc.gov
	Foreign Agricultural Service	www.fas.usda.gov

Table 8.2: Selected export promotion agencies around the globe.

interested parties together and alert them to new business opportunities abroad. Key governmental support is also provided when firms are abroad. By receiving information and assistance from their embassies, many business ventures abroad can be made easier.

Increasingly, organizations at the state and local level are also active in encouraging firms to participate in international business. Many states and provinces have formed agencies for economic development that provide information, display products abroad, conduct trade missions and sometimes even offer financing. Similar services can also be offered by state and local port authorities and by some of the larger cities. State and local authorities can be a major factor in facilitating international activities because of their closeness to firms.

Educational institutions such as universities and community colleges can also be major international business facilitators. They can act as trade information clearinghouses, facilitate networking opportunities, provide client counselling and technical assistance, and develop trade education programmes.[32] They can also develop course projects that are useful to firms interested in international business. For example, students may visit a firm and examine its potential in the international market as a course requirement. With the skill and supervision of faculty members to help the students develop the final report, such projects can be useful to firms with scarce resources, while exposing students to real-world problems.

Licensing

Under a licensing agreement, one firm permits another to use its intellectual property for compensation designated as royalty. The recipient firm is the licensee. The property licensed might include patents, trademarks, copyrights, technology, technical know-how or specific business skills. For example, a firm that has developed a bag-in-the-box packaging process for milk can permit other firms abroad to use the same process. Therefore, licensing can also be called the export of intangibles.

Licensing has intuitive appeal to many would-be international managers. As an entry strategy, it requires neither capital investment nor detailed involvement with foreign customers. By generating royalty income, licensing provides an opportunity to exploit research and development already conducted. After initial costs, the licensor can reap benefits until the end of the licence contract period. Licensing also reduces the risk of expropriation because the licensee is a local company that can provide leverage against government action.

Licensing may help to avoid host-country regulations applicable to equity ventures. It also may provide a means by which foreign markets can be tested without major involvement of capital or management time. Similarly, licensing can be used as a strategy to pre-empt a market before the entry of competition, especially if the licensor's resources permit full-scale involvement only in selected markets. Licensing also relieves the originating company from having to come up with culturally responsive changes in every market. As the Focus on Culture below shows, the local licensees can worry about that part.

A special form of licensing is trademark licensing, which has become a substantial source of worldwide revenue for companies that can trade on well-known names and characters such as Burberry and Dolce and Gabbana (D&G). Trademark licensing permits the names or logos of designers, literary characters, sports teams or movie stars to appear on clothing, games, foods and beverages, gifts and novelties, toys and home furnishings. Licensors can make huge profits with little effort, whereas licensees can produce a brand or product that consumers will recognize immediately. Trademark licensing is possible, however, only if the trademark name conveys instant recognition.

Licensing is not without disadvantages. It is a very limited form of foreign market participation and does not in any way guarantee a basis for future expansion. As a matter of fact, quite the opposite may take place. In exchange for the royalty, the licensor may create its own competitor not only in the market for which the agreement was made but also for third-country markets.

Licensing has also come under criticism from many governments and supranational organizations. They have alleged that licensing provides a mechanism for corporations in industrialized countries to capitalize on older technology. These accusations have been made even though licensing offers a foreign entity the opportunity for immediate market entry with a proven concept. It therefore eliminates the risk of R&D failure, the cost of designing around the licensor's patents and the fear of patent-infringement litigation.

FOCUS ON

CULTURE   TV Programme Licences Are International

For most of the history of television, American programming has dominated the airwaves in the United States and abroad. The most popular shows in any given country were likely to be American concepts produced by American firms. The cop show, the sitcom and the western are all television concepts developed in the US.

The privatization of many state-run television enterprises during the 1980s created more competition and increased demand worldwide for American programming. The new commercial stations lacked the expertise needed to produce hit shows in a cost-effective way, and so they filled their many open hours of airtime by purchasing programming from the United States.

American companies took advantage of high demand and prices skyrocketed. The trend continued through the 1990s as prices increased fivefold. During a bidding war in Britain, for example, the price of each episode of *The Simpsons* went up to US$1.5 million. American companies also bundled their offerings and forced television stations to buy less popular programming along with popular shows.

Over time, the situation abroad has changed. Local stations have become more adept at developing and producing their own programming. Tastes also changed as consumers demanded television shows more reflective of their own cultural values and preferences. All this means that stations no longer rely on American programming to win prime-time ratings battles.

In addition to claiming a larger share of their domestic markets, European production companies have turned the tables with licensing agreements. Now they develop winning television shows and license the idea to other companies for production in their own country.

Today, some of the most successful reality TV series showing in the US were pioneered overseas. One example is the Dutch hit show 'Big Brother'. New concepts are being developed, tested in foreign markets and exported all the time. The British television hit 'Pop Idol' gave rise to licensed versions in Poland, South Africa and the United States. In the new international television market, winning ideas can come from any country.

Sources: www.endemol.com, accessed 14 May 2003; Bill Brioux, 'Excuse Me, Is that a Canadian Idol?' *Edmonton Sun*, 23 October 2002.

Franchising

Franchising is the granting of the right by a parent company (the franchisor) to another, independent entity (the franchisee) to do business in a prescribed manner. The right can take the form of selling the franchisor's products or using its name, production and marketing techniques or general business approach.[33] Usually franchising involves a combination of many of those elements. The major forms of franchising are manufacturer–retailer systems (such as car dealerships), manufacturer–wholesaler systems (such as soft drink companies) and service-firm–retailer systems (such as lodging services and

© Getty Images. Reproduced with permission.

Gulf Arab tourists eat at a KFC franchise in the Lebanese mountain resort town of Bhamdoun, Lebanon. Tourists visiting Lebanon are mainly Arabs who see the country as a safer haven from potential harassment or travel inconveniences than Europe or the US. Lebanon is seeking to regain its former position as a regional tourism hot spot.

fast-food outlets). In 2002, global franchise sales increased by almost 16 000 franchisors and more than 1 million franchisees were estimated to be worth close to US$1.5 trillion.[34]

Typically, to be successful in international franchising, the firm must be able to offer unique products or unique selling propositions. A franchise must also offer a high degree of standardization, which does not require 100% uniformity but international recognizability. Concurrent with this recognizability, the franchisor can and should adapt to local circumstances. Food franchisors, for example, will vary the products and product lines offered depending on local market conditions and tastes.

Key reasons for the international expansion of franchise systems are market potential, financial gain and saturated domestic markets. From a franchisee's perspective, the franchise is beneficial because it reduces risk by implementing a proven concept. There are also major benefits from a governmental perspective. The source country does not see a replacement of exports or an export of jobs. The recipient country sees franchising as requiring little outflow of foreign exchange, because the bulk of the profits generated remain within the country.[35]

Franchising has been growing rapidly but government intervention is a major problem. In the Philippines, for example, government restrictions on franchising and royalties hindered Computer-Land's Manila store from offering a broader range of services, leading to a separation between the company and its franchisee. Selection and training of franchisees represents another problem area. Many franchise systems have run into difficulty by expanding too quickly and granting franchises to unqualified entities. Although the local franchisee knows the market best, the franchisor still needs to understand the market for product adaptation and operational purposes. The franchisor, in order to remain viable in the long term, needs to co-ordinate the efforts of individual franchisees – for example, to share ideas and engage in joint undertakings, such as co-operative advertising.

LOCAL PRESENCE

Inter-firm Co-operation

The world is too large and the competition too strong for even the largest companies to do everything independently. Technologies are converging and markets are becoming integrated, making the costs and risks of both goods and market development ever greater. Partly as a reaction to and partly to exploit the developments, management in multinational corporations has become more pragmatic about what it takes to be successful in global markets. The result has been the formation of *strategic alliances* with suppliers, customers, competitors and companies in other industries to achieve multiple goals.

A strategic alliance (or partnership) is an informal or formal arrangement between two or more companies with a common business objective. It is something more than the traditional customer–vendor relationship but something less than an outright acquisition. The alliances can take forms ranging from informal co-operation to joint ownership of worldwide operations. For example, Texas Instruments has reported agreements with companies such as IBM, Hyundai, Fujitsu, Alcatel and L. M. Ericsson using such terms as 'joint development agreement', 'co-operative technical effort', 'joint program for development', 'alternative sourcing agreement' and 'design/exchange agreement for co-operative product development and exchange of technical data'.[36]

Reasons for Inter-firm Co-operation

Strategic alliances are used for many different purposes by the partners involved. Market development is one common focus. Penetrating foreign markets is a primary objective of many companies. In Japan, Motorola is sharing chip designs and manufacturing facilities with Toshiba to gain greater access to the Japanese market. Some alliances aim to defend home markets. With no orders coming in for nuclear power plants, Bechtel Group has teamed up with Germany's Siemens to service existing US plants. Another key focus is to either share the risk of engaging in a particular activity in a particular market or to share the resource requirements of an activity.[37] The costs of developing new jet engines are so vast that they force aerospace companies into collaboration. One such consortium was formed by United Technologies' Pratt & Whitney division, Britain's Rolls-Royce, Motoren-und-Turbinen Union from Germany, Fiat of Italy and Japanese Aero Engines (made up of Ishikawajima Heavy Industries and Kawasaki Heavy Industries).[38] Some

Partner *Strength...*	+ Partner *Strength...*	= Joint Objective
Pepsico *marketing clout for canned beverages*	**Lipton** *recognized tea brand and customer franchise*	*To sell canned iced tea beverages jointly*
Philips *consumer electronics innovation and leadership*	**Levi Strauss** *fashion design and distribution*	*Outdoor wear with integrated electronic equipment for fashion-conscious consumers*
KFC *established brand and store format, and operations skills*	**Mitsubishi** *real estate and site-selection skills in Japan*	*To establish a KFC chain in Japan*
Siemens *presence in range of telecommunications markets worldwide and cable-manufacturing technology*	**Corning** *technological strength in optical fibres and glass*	*To create a fibre-optic-cable business*
Ericsson *technological strength in public telecommunications networks*	**Hewlett-Packard** *computers, software, and access to electronics-channels*	*To create and market network management systems*

Figure 8.3: Complementary strengths create value.

Sources: 'Portable Technology Takes the Next Step: Electronics You Can Wear', *Wall Street Journal*, 22 August 2000, B1, B4; Joel Bleeke and David Ernst, 'Is Your Strategic Alliance Really a Sale?' (1995) *Harvard Business Review*, 73(January–February), 97–105; Melanie Wells, 'Coca-Cola Proclaims Nestea Time for CAA', *Advertising Age*, 30 January 1995, 2. See also www.pepsico.com; www.lipton.com; www.kfc.com; www.siecor.com; www.ericsson.com; and www.hp.com.

alliances are formed to block and co-opt competitors.[39] For example, Caterpillar formed a heavy equipment joint venture with Mitsubishi in Japan to strike back at its main global rival, Komatsu, in its home market.

The most successful alliances are those that match the complementary strengths of partners to satisfy a joint objective. Often the partners have different product, geographic or functional strengths that the partners build on, rather than use to fill gaps.[40] Some of the major alliances created on this basis are provided in Figure 8.3.

Types of Inter-firm Co-operation

Each form of alliance is distinct in terms of the amount of commitment required and the degree of control each partner has. The equity alliances – minority ownership, joint ventures and consortia – feature the most extensive commitment and shared control. The different types of strategic alliances are summarized in Figure 8.4, using the extent of equity involved and the number of partners in the endeavour as defining characteristics.

In informal co-operation, partners work together without a binding agreement. This arrangement often takes the form of visits to exchange information about new products, processes and technologies, or may take the more formal form of the exchange of personnel for limited amounts of time. Often such partners are of no real threat in each other's markets and are of modest size in comparison to the competition, making collaboration necessary.[41] The relationships are based on mutual trust and friendship and may lead to more formal arrangements, such as contractual agreements or joint projects.

For contractual agreements, strategic alliance partners may join forces for joint R&D, joint marketing or joint production. Similarly, their joint efforts might include licensing, cross-licensing or cross-marketing activities. Nestlé and General Mills had an agreement whereby Honey Nut Cheerios and Golden Grahams were made in General Mills's US plants and shipped in bulk to Europe for

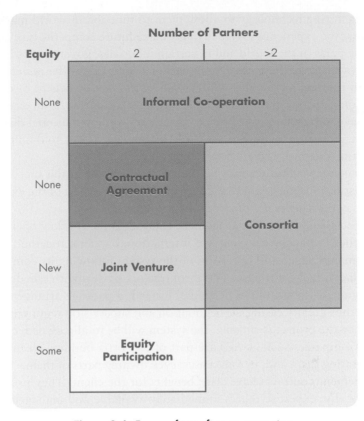

Figure 8.4: Forms of inter-firm co-operation.

Source: Adapted with permission from Bernard L. Simonin (1991) *Transfer of Knowledge of International Strategic Alliances: A Structural Approach*, unpublished dissertation, the University of Michigan, Ann Arbor. Reproduced with permission.

packaging by Nestlé. Such an arrangement – complementary marketing (also known as piggybacking) – allows firms to reach objectives that they cannot reach efficiently by themselves.[42] The alliance between General Mills and Nestlé evolved into a joint venture, Cereal Partners Worldwide, which markets both companies' products in Europe and Asia. Firms can also have a reciprocal arrangement whereby each partner provides the other access to its market. The New York Yankees and Manchester United sell each others' licensed products and develop joint sponsorship programmes. International airlines share hubs, co-ordinate schedules and simplify ticketing. Alliances such as Star (joining United and Lufthansa), Oneworld (British Airways and American Airlines) and Sky Team (Delta and Air France) provide worldwide coverage for their customers both in the travel and shipping communities.

Contractual agreements also exist for outsourcing. For example, General Motors buys cars and components from South Korea's Daewoo and Siemens buys computers from Fujitsu. As corporations look for ways simultaneously to grow and maintain their competitive advantage, outsourcing has become a powerful new tool for achieving those goals. Contract manufacturing allows the corporation to separate the physical production of goods from the research and development and marketing stages, especially if the latter are the core competencies of the firm. Benefits of such contracting are to improve company focus on higher value-added activities, to gain access to world-class capabilities and to reduce operating costs. Contract manufacturing has been criticized because of the pressure it puts on the contractors to cut prices and, thereby, labour costs. However, such work does provide many companies, especially in developing countries, the opportunity to gain the necessary experience in product design and manufacturing technology to allow them to function in world markets. Some have even voiced concerns that the experience eventually may make future competitors of current partners.

In some parts of the world and in certain industries, governments insist on complete or majority ownership of firms. In these cases, multinational companies offer *management contracts*, selling their expertise in running a company while avoiding the risk or benefit of ownership. Depending on the contract, doing so may even permit some measure of control. As an example, the manufacturing process may have to be relinquished to local firms, and yet international distribution may be required for the product. A management contract could maintain a strong hold on the operation by ensuring that all distribution channels remain firmly controlled.

A management contract may be the critical element in the success of a project. For example, financial institutions may gain confidence in a project because of the existence of a management contract and may even make it a precondition for funding.[43]

One specialized form of management contract is the turnkey operation. Here, the arrangement permits a client to acquire a complete international system, together with skills sufficient to allow unassisted maintenance and operation of the system following its completion.[44] The client need not search for individual contractors or subcontractors or deal with scheduling conflicts or with difficulties in assigning responsibilities or blame. Instead, a package arrangement focuses responsibility on one entity, thus greatly easing the negotiation and supervision requirements and subsequent accountability. When the project is running, the system will be totally owned, controlled and operated by the customer. Companies such as AES are part of consortia building electric power facilities around the world, operating them and, in some cases, even owning parts of them.

Management contracts have clear benefits for the client. They provide organizational skills not available locally, expertise that is immediately available and management assistance in the form of support services that would be difficult and costly to replicate locally. For example, hotels managed by the Sheraton Corporation have access to Sheraton's worldwide reservation system. Management contracts today typically involve the training of locals to take over the operation after a given period.

Similar advantages exist for the supplier. The risk of participating in an international venture is substantially lowered, while significant amounts of control are still exercised. Existing know-how that has been built up through substantial investment can be commercialized and frequently the impact of fluctuations in business volume can be reduced by making use of experienced personnel who otherwise would have to be laid off. Accumulated service knowledge should be used internationally and management contracts permit firms to do just that.

Equity Participation

Many multinational corporations have acquired minority ownerships in companies that have strategic importance for them, in order to ensure supplier ability and build formal and informal working relationships. One example is Ford Motor Company's 33.4% share of Mazda. The partners continue operating as distinctly separate entities but each enjoys the strengths the other partner provides. For example, thanks to Mazda, Ford has excellent support in the design and manufacture of subcompact cars, while Mazda has improved access to the global marketplace. Equity ownership in an innovator may also give the investing company first access to any new technology developed.

Another significant reason for equity ownership is market entry and support of global operations. For example, Telefónica de Espana has acquired varying stakes in Latin American telecommunications systems – a market that is the fastest-growing region of the world after Asia.

Joint Ventures

A joint venture can be defined as the participation of two or more companies in an enterprise in which each party contributes assets, has some equity and shares risk.[45] The venture is also considered long term. The reasons for establishing a joint venture can be divided into three groups: (1) government policy or legislation; (2) one partner's needs for other partners' skills; and (3) one partner's needs for other partners' attributes or assets.[46] Equality of the partners or of their contribution is not necessary. In some joint ventures, each partners' contributions – typically consisting of funds, technology, plant or labour – also vary.

The key to a joint venture is the sharing of a common business objective, which makes the arrangement more than a customer–vendor relationship but less than an outright acquisition. The partners' rationales for entering into the arrangement may vary. An example is New United Motor Manufacturing Inc. (NUMMI), the joint venture between Toyota and GM. Toyota needed direct access to the US market, and GM benefited from the technology and management approaches provided by its Japanese partner.

Joint ventures may be the only way in which a firm can profitably participate in a particular market, because many governments restrict equity participation in local operations by foreigners. Other entry modes may be limited; for example, exports may be restricted because of tariff barriers. Joint ventures are valuable when the pooling of resources results in a better outcome for each partner than if each were to conduct its activities individually. This is particularly true when each partner has a specialized advantage in areas that benefit the venture. For example, a firm may have new technology and yet lack sufficient capital to carry out foreign direct investment on its own. Through a joint venture, the technology can be used more quickly and market penetration achieved more easily. Similarly, one of the partners may have a distribution system already established or have better access to local suppliers, either of which permits a greater volume of sales in a shorter period of time.

Joint ventures also permit better relationships with local government and other organizations such as labour unions. Government-related reasons are the main rationale for joint ventures to take place in less-developed countries. If the local partner is politically influential, the new venture may be eligible for tax incentives, grants and government support. Negotiations for certifications or licences may be easier because authorities may not perceive themselves as dealing with a foreign firm. Relationships between the local partner and the local financial establishment may enable the joint venture to tap local capital markets. The greater experience (and therefore greater familiarity) with the local culture and environment of the local partner may enable the joint venture to benefit from greater insights into changing market conditions and needs.

Many joint ventures fall short of expectations and/or are disbanded. An unsuccessful joint venture can be dissolved, usually without significant penalty to the participants, whereas an unsuccessful merger, acquisition, or even the quest for an acquisition may leave a company so weakened that it becomes a takeover target. Centrus is an example of an unsuccessful joint venture. Formed by Cinergy, Florida Progress and New Century Energies to develop long-distance telephone service, it was cancelled when the participants determined that market conditions did not favour the venture.

The most common reasons for failure of a joint venture typically relate to conflicts of interest, problems with disclosure of sensitive information and disagreements over how profits are to be shared. There is also often a lack of communication before, during and after formation of the venture. In some cases, managers have been more interested in the launching of the venture than the actual running of the enterprise. Many of the problems stem from a lack of careful consideration in advance of how to manage the new endeavour. A partnership works on the basis of trust and commitment or not at all.

Typical disagreements cover the whole range of business decisions, including strategy, management style, accounting and control, marketing policies and strategies, R&D and personnel. The joint venture may, for example, identify a particular market as a target only to find that one of the partners already has individual plans for it. US partners have frequently complained that their Japanese counterparts do not send their most competent personnel to the joint venture; instead, because of their lifetime employment practice, they get rid of less competent managers by sending them to the new entities.

Similarly, the issue of profit accumulation and distribution may cause discontent. If one partner supplies the joint venture with a good, the partner will prefer that any profits accumulate at headquarters and accrue 100% to one firm rather than at the joint venture, where profits are divided according to equity participation. Such a decision may not be greeted with enthusiasm by the other partner. Once profits are accumulated, their distribution may lead to dispute. For example, one partner may insist on a high payout of dividends because of financial needs, whereas the other may prefer the reinvestment of profits into a growing operation.

Consortia

A new drug can cost US$500 million to develop and bring to market; a mainframe computer or a telecommunications switch can require US$1 billion. Some US$7 billion goes into creating a new generation of computer chips. To combat the high costs and risks of research and development, research consortia have emerged in the United States, Japan and Europe. For example, Ericsson, Panasonic, Samsung, Siemens, Sony, Motorola, Nokia and Psion have formed Symbian to develop technologies for wireless communication. Headquartered in the UK, the firm also has offices in Japan, Sweden and the United States.

Since the passage of the Joint Research and Development Act of 1984 (which allows both domestic and foreign firms to participate in joint basic research efforts in the US without the fear of antitrust action), well over 100 consortia have been registered in the United States. The consortia pool their resources for research into technologies ranging from artificial intelligence to semiconductor manufacturing. (The major consortia in those fields are MCC and Sematech.) The European Union has five mega projects to develop new technologies registered under the names EUREKA, ESPRIT, BRITE, RACE and COMET. Japanese consortia have worked on producing the world's highest-capacity memory chip and advanced computer technologies. On the manufacturing side, the formation of Airbus Industries secured European production of commercial jets. The consortium, now backed by the European Aeronautic Defence and Space Company (EADS), which emerged from the link-up of the German DaimlerChrysler Aerospace AG, the French Aerospatiale Matra and CASA of Spain,[47] has become a prime global competitor especially in the development of mega-liners.

Managerial Considerations

The first requirement of inter-firm co-operation is to find the right partner. Partners should have an orientation and goals in common and should bring complementary and relevant benefits to the endeavour. The venture makes little sense if the expertise of both partners is in the same area; for example, if both have production expertise but neither has distribution know-how. Patience should be exercised; a deal should not be rushed into, nor should the partners expect immediate results. Learning should be paramount in the endeavour while at the same time partners must try not to give away core secrets to each other.[48]

Second, the more formal the arrangement is, the greater the care that needs to be taken in negotiating the agreement. In joint venture negotiations, for example, extensive provisions must be made for contingencies. The points to be explored should include the following:

- clear definition of the venture and its duration;
- ownership, control and management;
- financial structure and policies;
- taxation and fiscal obligation;
- employment and training;
- production;
- government assistance;
- transfer of technology;

- marketing arrangements;
- environmental protection;
- record keeping and inspection;
- settlement of disputes.[49]

These issues have to be addressed before the formation of the venture; otherwise, they eventually surface as points of contention. A joint venture agreement, although comparable to a marriage agreement, should contain the elements of a divorce contract. In case the joint venture cannot be maintained to the satisfaction of partners, plans must exist for the dissolution of the agreement and for the allocation of profits and costs. Typically, however, one of the partners buys out the other partner(s) when partners decide to part ways.

A strategic alliance, by definition, also means a joining of two corporate cultures, which can often be quite different. To meet this challenge, partners must have frequent communication and interaction at three levels of the organization: top management, operational leaders and workforce levels. Trust and relinquishing control are difficult not only at the top but also at levels where the future of the venture is determined. A dominant partner may determine the corporate culture but even then the other partners should be consulted. The development of specific alliance managers may be advised to forge the net of relationships both within and between alliance partners and, therefore, to support the formal alliance structure.[50]

Strategic alliances operate in a dynamic business environment and must therefore adjust to changing market conditions. The agreement between partners should provide for changes in the original concept so that the venture can flourish and grow. The trick is to have a prior understanding as to which party will take care of which pains and problems so that a common goal is reached.

Government attitudes and policies have to be part of the environmental considerations of corporate decision makers. Although some alliances may be seen as a threat to the long-term economic security of a nation, in general, links with foreign operators should be encouraged. For example, the US government urged major US airlines to form alliances with foreign carriers to gain access to emerging world markets, partly in response to the failure to achieve free access to all markets through the negotiation of so-called 'open-skies' agreements.[51]

Full Ownership

For some firms, foreign direct investment requires, initially at least, 100% ownership. The reason may have an ethnocentric basis; that is, management may believe that no outside entity should have an impact on corporate decision making. Alternatively, it may be based on financial concerns. For example, the management of IBM held the belief in the early 1990s that by relinquishing a portion of its ownership abroad, it would be setting a precedent for shared control with local partners that would cost more than any possible gains.[52] In some cases, IBM withdrew operations from countries rather than agree to government demands for local ownership.

In order to make a rational decision about the extent of ownership, management must evaluate the extent to which total control is important to the success of its international marketing activities. Often full ownership may be a desirable, but not a necessary, prerequisite for international success. At other times it may be essential, particularly when strong links exist within the corporation. Interdependencies between and among local operations and headquarters may be so strong that nothing short of total co-ordination will result in an acceptable benefit to the firm as a whole.[53]

Increasingly, however, the international environment is hostile to full ownership by multinational firms. Government action through outright legal restrictions or discriminatory actions is making the option less attractive. There seems to be a distinct 'liability of foreignness' to which multinational firms are exposed. Such disadvantages can result from government resentment of greater opportunities by multinational firms. But they can also be the consequence of corporate actions such as the decision to have many expatriates rotate in top management positions, which may weaken the standing of a subsidiary and its local employees.[54]

To overcome market barriers abroad, firms can either build competitive capabilities from scratch or acquire them from local owners.[55] The choice is often to accept a reduction in control or lose the opportunity to operate efficiently in a country. In addition to formal action by the government, the general conditions in the market may make it advisable for the firm to join forces with local entities. Table 8.3 compares the conditions of application, advantages and disadvantages of the major entry modes.

Entry Mode	Conditions for Implementation	Advantages	Disadvantages
Exporting	• Limited sales potential of the target market • High target country production costs • Liberal import policies • High level of risk	• Lowest possible investment • Gradual exposure to international markets • Lowest possible risk • Allows speedy market entry • Maximizes economies of scale of existing facilities	• High transportation costs • Prices increase due to price escalation • Tariff barriers can make exporting non-applicable • Need to use intermediaries • Limits opportunities to learn
Licensing	• Significant import and investment barriers • Availability of legal protection of intellectual property rights • Substantial psychological distance • Licensee unlikely to become competitor	• Easy mode of entry • Entering markets with huge barriers to investment • Quick entry • Allows high return on investment	• Control over the operations of licensee difficult • Impedes co-ordination of international operations • Cross-licensing may mitigate risk • Unfavourable spill-over effects
Joint ventures	• High import barriers • High sales potential • Some risk – needs to share • Government restriction on foreign ownership • Availability of suitable partner	• Opportunities to benefit from knowledge exchange • Sharing risk • Present high learning potential	• Risk of conflict due to information asymmetry • Control proportionate to ownership participation • Difficult strategic co-ordination • Managerial issues a challenge
Foreign direct investment	• Significant import barriers • Small psychological distance • High sales potential • Low level of risk	• Increases control • Allows high flexibility in serving international markets • Quick and direct feedback from the market	• Most expensive mode of market entry • Riskiest mode of market entry • May be challenging in terms of managing local resources

Table 8.3: Comparison of conditions of implementation, advantages and disadvantages of various entry modes.

A COMPREHENSIVE VIEW OF INTERNATIONAL EXPANSION

The central driver of internationalization is the level of managerial commitment. This commitment will grow gradually from an awareness of international potential to the adaptation of international business as a strategic business direction. It will be influenced by the information, experience and perception of management, which in turn is shaped by motivations, concerns and the activities of change agents.

Management's commitment and its view of the capabilities of the firm will then trigger various international business activities, which can range from indirect exporting and importing to more direct involvement in the global market. Eventually, the firm may then expand further through measures such as joint ventures, strategic alliances or foreign direct investment.

All of the developments, processes and factors involved in the overall process of going international are linked to each other. A comprehensive view of these links is presented schematically in Figure 8.5.

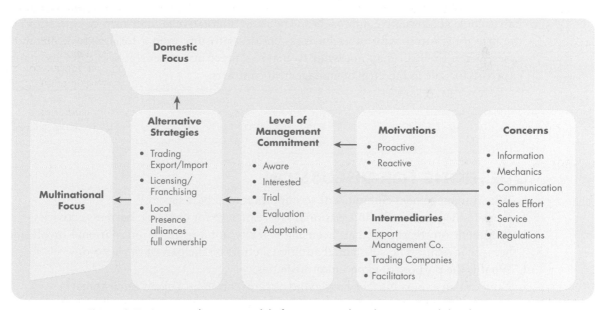

Figure 8.5: A comprehensive model of international market entry and development.

SUMMARY

Firms do not become experienced in international business overnight but rather progress gradually through an internationalization process. The process is triggered by different motivations to go abroad. The motivations can be proactive or reactive. Proactive motivations are initiated by aggressive management, whereas reactive motivations are the defensive response of management to environmental changes and pressures. Firms that are primarily stimulated by proactive motivations are more likely to enter international business and succeed.

In going abroad, firms encounter multiple problems and challenges, which range from a lack of information to mechanics and documentation. In order to gain assistance in its initial international experience, the firm can make use of either intermediaries or facilitators. Intermediaries are outside companies that actively participate in an international transaction. They are export management companies or trading companies. In order for these intermediaries to perform international business functions properly, however, they must be compensated, which results in a reduction of profits.

International facilitators do not participate in international business transactions but do contribute knowledge and information. Increasingly, facilitating roles are played by private sector groups, such as industry associations, banks, accountants or consultants, and by universities and federal, state and local government authorities.

Apart from exporting and importing, alternatives for international business entry are licensing, franchising and local presence. The basic advantage of licensing is that it does not involve capital investment or knowledge of foreign markets. Its major disadvantage is that licensing agreements typically have time limits, are often proscribed by foreign governments and may result in creating a competitor. The use of franchising as a means of expansion into foreign markets has increased dramatically. Franchisors must learn to strike a balance between adapting to local environments and standardizing to the degree necessary to maintain international recognizability.

Full ownership is becoming more unlikely in many markets as well as industries and the firm has to look at alternative approaches. The main alternative is inter-firm co-operation, in which the firm joins forces with other business entities, possibly even a foreign government. In some cases, when the firm may not want to make a direct investment, it will offer its management expertise for sale in the form of management contracts.

QUESTIONS FOR DISCUSSION

1. Why is management commitment so important to export success?
2. Explain the benefits that international sales can have for domestic business activities.
3. Comment on the stance that 'licensing is really not a form of international involvement because it requires no substantial additional effort on the part of the licensor'.
4. What is the purpose of export intermediaries?
5. How can an export intermediary avoid circumvention by a client or customer?
6. The rate of expropriation has been 10 times greater for a joint venture with the host government than for a 100% owned subsidiary, according to a study on expropriation since 1960. Is this not contrary to logic?
7. Comment on the observation that 'a joint venture may be a combination of Leonardo da Vinci's brain and Carl Lewis's legs; one wants to fly, the other insists on running'.
8. Why would an internationalizing company opt for a management contract over other modes of operation? Relate your answer especially to the case of hospitality companies such as Hyatt, Marriott and Novotel.

INTERNET EXERCISES

1. What forms of export assistance are offered by the Small Business Administration and the Export-Import Bank (consult their web sites at www.sba.gov and www.exim.gov.)?
2. Prepare a one-page memo to a foreign company introducing your product or service. Include a contact listing of 10 businesses in foreign countries looking to import your

particular product. Include the company name, address and other contact information along with special requirements of the company that you note from their posting of an offer to buy. Cite the sources from which you prepared your list.

Sample sources of trade leads:

- www.business-europa.co.uk
- www.tradenet.gov
- www.mnileads.com

3. Working conditions in subcontract factories have come under criticism for wages and working conditions. Using Nike's response (see http://www.nike.com/nikebiz/nikebiz.shtml?page=25), assess the type of criticisms heard and the ability of a company to address them.

TAKE A STAND

China's trade and investment activities have grown substantially since the 1980s. Yet there are many who question the ethics of supporting a regime that has systematically ignored important rights. Many organizations have called for global customers to boycott goods made in China. These groups cite basic human rights violations including China's lack of employment standards and rights, its oppressive policy toward Tibet and its forced abortion and sterilization programmes as reasons why Chinese goods should be boycotted.

FOR DISCUSSION

Conversely, others believe the best way to improve human rights in China and bring about democracy is through trade and investment. Foreign direct investment and multinational corporations operating in China are portrayed as important engines for change that will generate reformation of the government and improve the lives of the Chinese people. Nevertheless, does this stance ultimately send the message that economic priorities trump ethical concerns, or can they coexist?

CHAPTER 9

- Globalization
- The Strategic Planning Process
- Organizational Structure
- Implementation
- Controls

Strategic Planning, Organization, Implementation and Control

LEARNING OBJECTIVES

- To outline the process of strategic planning and to examine the external and internal factors determining the conditions for development of strategy and resource allocation.

- To illustrate how best to use the environmental conditions within the competitive challenges and resources of the firm to develop effective programmes.

- To suggest how to achieve a balance between local and regional/global priorities and concerns in the implementation of strategy.

- To describe alternative organizational structures for international operations and to highlight factors affecting those decisions.

- To indicate roles for country organizations in the development of strategy and implementation of programmes.

- To outline the need for and challenges of controls in international operations.

THE CHANGING LANDSCAPE OF GLOBAL MARKETS

Global markets for everything from cars to telecommunications have witnessed major consolidations in the last five years. Not only are companies playing the global game by being in all major and even minor markets of the world but also they are doing so by acquiring local players.

The beer industry has become the latest global battleground. The business has been more fragmented than most: the top four brewing companies have had less than one third of the global market (whereas the top four spirits makers easily control more than half of their markets). That is changing rapidly and dramatically as companies are pushing to acquire strong local brands and their distribution networks to push their already established global brands.

A major change occurred in 2002, when Anheuser-Busch lost its position as the number one company in the world for the first time in 50 years. South African Breweries (SAB) became the new leader after the acquisition of Miller Brewing Company and a 21% market share in the US beer market. Anheuser-Busch remained in control of nearly half of US sales but it has identified the need to expand globally as well. For example, in China (which boasts the second largest beer market in the world), by 2003 Anheuser-Busch had increased its share to 9.9% in Tsingtao, China's largest brewery. Thus in 2003 Anheuser-Busch regained its world market leadership. In Mexico, Anheuser-Busch owns 50% of Grupo Modelo and in Argentina and Chile, it has a share of the CCU brewery. Increasingly, however, its expansion has been challenged by its competitors. In Italy, SABMiller beat Anheuser-Busch by acquiring its former licensee Birra Peron to make its first major Western European move.

After years of standing on the sidelines, Dutch Heineken has been active in acquiring companies around the world. In Egypt, it bought a majority stake in Al Ahram Beverages to use the company's fruit-flavoured, non-alcoholic beverages as an entry to other Muslim markets. The next major battleground for Heineken and its competitors is Central and Eastern Europe, where Heineken acquired Karlovacka Pivovar in Croatia and Austrian BBAG, which has breweries in the Czech Republic, Hungary, Poland and Romania.

In 2004, the merger of Brazilian group Companhia de Bebidas das Américas (AmBev) with Belgium-based Interbrew created the largest brewing company in the world called Inbev. The significance of the deal is clear from the fact that Inbev now has a 15% share of the global beer market, taking it ahead of Anheuser-Busch and SABMiller. In 2006, Inbev had sales of €13.5 billion and a presence in 156 countries worldwide focusing primarily on three core brands: Stella Artois, Beck's and Brahma. Inbev's brand portfolio also includes a wide range of local and speciality beers.

With the recent changes, the 10 largest brewing companies now control more than 50% of the world beer markets, with the top 40 in charge of 83%. With the five largest companies increasing their production at a much faster rate than those following them, further consolidation of power is to be expected.

Heineken's World

Heineken operates in 170 countries and below is a sampling of that presence:

- *The Netherlands:* Heineken, Amstel, Kylian, Lingen's Blond, Murphy's Irish Red;
- *United States:* Heineken, Amstel, Paulaner, Moretti;

- **China:** Tiger, Reeb;
- **Singapore:** Heineken, Tiger;
- **France:** Heineken, Amstel, Buckler, Desperados;
- **Italy:** Heineken, Amstel, Birra Moretti;
- **Bulgaria:** Zagorka, Amstel, Heineken;
- **Poland:** Heineken, Zywiec;
- **Kazakhstan:** Tian Shan, Amstel;
- **Panama:** Soberana, Panama;
- **Egypt:** Fayrouz;
- **Israel:** Maccabee, Gold Star;
- **Nigeria:** Amstel Malta, Maltina.

Sources: 'Waking Up Heineken', *Business Week*, 8 September 2003, 68–72; 'In Search of Froth: Beer in Europe', *The Economist*, 28 June 2003, 89; 'Anheuser-Busch Raises Its Stake in Chinese Brewer', *Wall Street Journal*, 30 June 2003, A24; 'Panimoiden Keskittyminen on Kiivaassa Vauhdissa', *Kauppalehti*, 10 June 2003, 14–15; 'Heineken Brews Comeback Plans for US Market', *Wall Street Journal*, 27 May 2003, B1; 'The Interbrew-Ambev Merger Story' at www.icmr.icfai.org/casestudies/catalogue/Business%20Strategy2/BSTR137, accessed 9 May 2007.

GLOBALIZATION

The transformations in the world marketplace have been extensive and, in many cases, rapid. Local industries operating in protected national economies are challenged in integrated global markets contested by global players. National borders are becoming increasingly irrelevant as liberalization and privatization take place. This has then led to such phenomena as the growing scale and mobility of the world's capital markets and many companies' ability to leverage knowledge and talent across borders.[1] Even the biggest companies in the biggest home markets cannot survive by taking their situation as a given if they are in global industries such as automotive, banking, consumer electronics, entertainment, pharmaceuticals, publishing, travel services, home appliances or beer brewing, as shown in the opening vignette. Rather than seeking to maximize their share of the pie in home markets, they have to seek to maximize the size of the pie by having a presence in all the major markets of the world. Companies from emerging markets, such as China, have entered the megamarkets of North America and Europe not only to gain necessary size but also to gain experience in competing against global players in their home markets.[2]

Globalization reflects a business orientation based on the belief that the world is becoming more homogeneous and that distinctions between national markets are not only fading but, for some products, will eventually disappear. As a result, companies need to globalize their international strategy by formulating it across markets to take advantage of underlying market, cost, environmental and competitive factors.

As shown in Figure 9.1, globalization can be seen as the culmination of a process of international market entry and expansion. Before globalization, companies used to a great extent a country-by-country multidomestic strategy with each country organization operated as a profit centre. Each national entity marketed a range of different products and services targeted to different customer segments, using different strategies with little or no co-ordination of operations between countries.

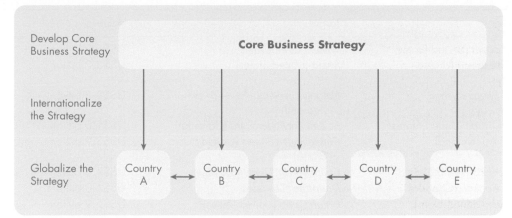

Figure 9.1: Evolution of global strategy.

Source: George S. Yip (2002) *Total Global Strategy II*, Prentice Hall, Upper Saddle River, NJ, 4.

However, as national markets become increasingly similar and economies of scale become increasingly important, the inefficiencies of duplicating product and programme development and manufacture in each country become more apparent and the pressure to leverage resources and co-ordinate activities across borders gains urgency. Similarly, the number of customers operating globally, as well as the same or similar competitors faced throughout the major markets, add to the need for strategy co-ordination and integration.

Globalization Drivers[3]

Both external and internal factors will create the favourable conditions for development of strategy and resource allocation on a global basis. These factors can be divided into market, cost, environmental and competitive factors.

Market Factors

The world customer identified by Ernst Dichter has gained new meaning today.[4] For example, Kenichi Ohmae has identified a new group of consumers, emerging in the triad of Europe, the Far East and North America, whom marketers can treat as a single market exhibiting the same spending habits.[5] More than 700 million in number, these consumers have similar educational backgrounds, income levels, lifestyles, use of leisure time and aspirations. One reason given for the similarities in their demand is a level of purchasing power (at least 10 times greater than that of less-developed countries or emerging markets) that translates into higher diffusion rates for certain products. Another reason is that developed infrastructures – diffusion of telecommunications and advanced transportation infrastructure – lead to attractive markets for other products. Similarities in demand conditions throughout the triad facilitate product design and the transferability of other programme elements.

At the same time, channels of distribution are becoming more global; that is, a growing number of retailers are now showing great flexibility in their strategies for entering new geographic markets.[6] Some are already world powers (e.g., Benetton and McDonald's), whereas others are pursuing aggressive growth (e.g., Aldi and IKEA). Also noteworthy are cross-border retail alliances, which expand the presence of retailers to new markets quite rapidly.

Cost Factors

Avoiding cost inefficiencies and duplication of effort are two of the most powerful globalization drivers. A single-country approach may not be large enough for the local business to achieve all

Acquirer	Target	Value	Date Announced
Weyerhauser (United States)	*Willamette Industries*	US$6.2 billion	28/1/02
Mead Westvaco (United States)	*Mead* (United States)	US$3.2 billion	29/8/01
Norske Skogindustrier (Norway)	*Fletcher Challenge Paper* (New Zealand)	US$2.5 billion	3/4/00
Smurfit-Stone (United States)	*St. Laurent Paperboard* (Canada)	US$1.0 billion	23/2/00
Stora Enso (Finland)	*Consolidated Papers* (United States)	US$3.9 billion	22/2/00
Int'l Paper (United States)	*Champion Int'l* (United States)	US$7.3 billion	12/5/00
Abitibi-Consol. (Canada)	*Donohue* (Canada)	US$4.0 billion	11/2/00
Int'l Paper (United States)	*Union Camp* (United States)	US$5.9 billion	24/11/98
Stora (Sweden)*ᵃ*	*Enso* (Finland)*ᵃ*	Undisclosed	2/6/98

Sources: 'Weyerhauser Company and Willamette Industries Sign Definitive Merger Agreement', Willamette Industries, Inc., press release, 28 January 2002, www.wii.com; 'Paper Merger Attains Size Without Adding Huge Debt', *Wall Street Journal*, 30 August 2001, B4; 'International Paper Has Its Work Cut Out For It', *Wall Street Journal*, 15 May 2000, A4; 'Stora Enso to Buy Consolidated Papers', *Wall Street Journal*, 23 February 2000, A3, A8. See also, www.storaenso.com; www.internationalpaper.com; www.upm-kymmene.com; www.abicon.com and www.weyerhaeuser.com.
ᵃMerger of equals.

Table 9.1: Consolidation in the paper industry 1998–2002.

possible economies of scale and scope as well as synergies, especially given the dramatic changes in the marketplace. Take, for example, pharmaceuticals. In the 1970s, developing a new drug cost about US$16 million and took four years to go to the market. The drug could be produced in Britain or the United States and eventually exported. Now, developing a new drug costs from US$500 million to US$1 billion and takes as long as 12 years, with competitive efforts close behind. For the leading companies, annual R&D budgets can run to US$5–8 billion. Only a global product for a global market can support that much risk.[7] Size has become a major asset, which partly explains the many mergers and acquisitions in industries such as aerospace, pharmaceuticals and telecommunications. The paper industry underwent major regional consolidation between 1998 and 2000, as shown in Table 9.1. The US International Paper Company won Champion International in a tense bidding contest with Finland's UPM-Kymmene to protect its home market position. As a result, UPM-Kymmene immediately targeted Sappi Ltd, a South African magazine-paper maker with significant North American operations and two US-based paper makers, Mead and Bowater.[8] In the heavily contested consumer goods sectors, launching a new brand may cost as much as US$100 million, meaning that companies such as Unilever and Procter & Gamble are not necessarily going to spend precious resources on one-country projects.

In many cases, expanded market participation and activity concentration can accelerate the accumulation of learning and experience. General Electric's philosophy is to be first or second in the world in a business or to get out. This can be seen, for example, in its global effort to develop premium computed tomography (CT), a diagnostic scanning system. GE swapped its consumer electronics business with the French Thomson for Thomson's diagnostic imaging business. At the same time, GE established GE Medical Systems Asia in Tokyo, anchored on Yokogawa Medical Systems, which is 75% owned by GE.

Environmental Factors

As shown earlier in this book, government barriers have fallen dramatically in recent years to further facilitate the globalization of markets and the activities of companies within them. For example, the forces pushing toward a pan-European market are very powerful: the increasing wealth and mobility of European consumers (favoured by the relaxed immigration controls), the accelerating flow of information across borders, the introduction of new products where local preferences are not well established and the publicity surrounding the integration process itself all promote globalization.[9] Also, the resulting removal of physical, fiscal and technical barriers is indicative of the changes that are taking place around the world on a greater scale.

At the same time, rapid technological evolution is contributing to the process. For example, Ford Motor Company is able to accomplish its globalization efforts by using new communications methods, such as teleconferencing, intranet and CAD/CAM links, as well as travel, to manage the complex task of meshing car companies on different continents.[10] Newly emerging markets will benefit from advanced communications by being able to leapfrog stages of economic development. Places that until recently were incommunicado in Brazil, China, Egypt, Hungary or Saudi Arabia are rapidly acquiring state-of-the-art telecommunications that will let them foster both internal and external development.[11]

A new group of global players is taking advantage of today's more open trading regions and newer technologies. **Mininationals** or **born globals** (newer companies with sales between US$200 million and US$1 billion) are able to serve the world from a small number of manufacturing bases, compared with having to build a plant in a number of countries as established multinational corporations once had to do. Their smaller administrative apparatus has allowed these mininationals to move swiftly to seize new markets and develop new products – a key to global success.[12] This phenomenon is highlighted in the following Focus on Entrepreneurship.

Competitive Factors

Many industries are already dominated by global competitors that are trying to take advantage of the three sets of factors mentioned earlier. To remain competitive, a company may have to be the first to do something or to be able to match or pre-empt competitors' moves. Products are now introduced, upgraded and distributed at rates unimaginable a decade ago. Without a global network, carefully researched ideas may be picked off by other global players. This is what Procter & Gamble and Unilever did to Kao's Attack concentrated detergent, which they mimicked and introduced into Europe and the United States before Kao could react.

With the triad markets often flat in terms of growth rate and fiercely competitive, many global marketers are looking for new markets and for new product categories for growth. Nestlé, for example, is setting its sights on consumer markets in fast-growing Asia, especially China, and has diversified into pharmaceuticals by acquiring Alcon and becoming a major shareholder in the world's number one cosmetics company, France's L'Oreal.[13] Between 1985 and 2000, Nestlé spent US$26 billion on acquisitions and another US$18 billion from 2001 to 2002.

Market presence may be necessary to execute global strategies and to prevent others from having undue advantage in unchallenged markets. Caterpillar faced mounting global competition from Komatsu but found out that strengthening its products and operations was not enough to meet the challenge. Although Japan was a small part of the world market, as a secure home base (no serious competitors), it generated 80% of Komatsu's cash flow. To put a check on its major global competitor's market share and cash flow, Caterpillar formed a heavy-equipment joint venture with Matsushita to serve the Japanese market.[14] Similarly, when Unilever tried to acquire Richardson-Vicks in the United States, Procter & Gamble saw this as a threat to its home market position and outbid its archrival for the company.

The Outcome

The four globalization drivers have affected countries and sectors differently. Although some industries are truly globally contested, such as paper and pulp and soft drinks, some sectors, such as

FOCUS ON

Mininationals Leap into Global Markets

'We were nobody – too small for people to pay attention to us', recalls Hong Lu of his first attempts to take his fledgling California-based company, Unitech Telecom, into Beijing in 1993. China, with its population of 1.3 billion and extremely low teledensity, seemed the optimal market for Unitech's telecommunications-access equipment. Locked out by towering multinationals Motorola, Lucent and Siemens, Lu quickly shifted his attention to Hangzhou, a mid-coastal university city. With its population of 1 million, Hangzhou offered a solid customer base, an educated workforce and easier access to government-owned phone companies. Within a year, Unitech posted sales of almost US$4 million into China. Following a merger with Starcom, a telecommunications software company with manufacturing facilities in China, revenues skyrocketed. Today, UTStarcom generates sales in excess of $165 million a year and has expanded into Taiwan, the Philippines, South Korea and Japan.

UTStarcom is a prime example of the small- to medium-sized firms that are reinventing the global corporation. The success of these mininationals proves that sheer size is no longer a buffer against competition, especially in markets that demand specialized or customized products. Electronic process technology allows mininationals to compete on price and quality – often with greater flexibility than larger rivals. In today's open trading regions, they are able to serve the world from a handful of manufacturing bases. Less red tape means that they are able to move swiftly in seizing new markets and developing new products, typically in focused markets. In many cases, these new markets were developed by the mininationals themselves. For example, Symbol Technologies, Inc., of Holtsville, New York, invented handheld laser scanners and now dominates this field. In a sector that did not exist in 1988, Cisco Systems Inc, of San Jose, California, grew from a mininational into a multinational corporation with 36 786 employees in more than 430 offices in 60 countries. Through its partnerships, Cisco sells its computer networking systems into a total of 115 countries. Other mininationals continue to focus on their core products and services, growing and excelling at what they do best. An empirical study of exporting firms established in the last 10 years found that more than half could be classified as born globals.

The lessons from these new generation global players are to: (1) keep focused and concentrate on being number one or number two in a technology niche; (2) stay lean by having small headquarters to save on costs and accelerate decision making; (3) take ideas and technologies to and from wherever they can be found; (4) take advantage of employees regardless of nationality to globalize thinking; and (5) solve customers' problems by involving them rather than pushing standardized solutions on them.

As a result of being flexible, mininationals are better able to weather storms, such as the Asian crisis, by changing emphases in the geographical operations.

Sources: China Success Story at www.utstar.com, accessed 25 September 2003; Øystein Moen and Per Servais (2002) 'Born Global or Gradual Global? Examining the Export Behaviour of Small and Medium-Sized Enterprises', *Journal of International Marketing*, 10(3), 49–72; Øystein Moen (2002) 'The Born

Globals: A New Generation of Small European Exporters', *International Marketing Review*, 19(2), 156–175; Gary Knight (2000) 'Entrepreneurship and Marketing Strategy: The SME Under Globalization', *Journal of International Marketing* 8(2), 12–32; 'Corporate Profile', *Cisco Systems 2000 Annual Report* at www.cisco.com; Grossman, 'Great Leap into China', *Inc. Magazine*, 15 October 1999; 'Turning Small into an Advantage', *Business Week*, 13 July 1998, 42–44; Michael W. Rennie, 'Born Global' (1993) *The McKinsey Quarterly*, 4, 45–52; 'Mininationals Are Making Maximum Impact', *Business Week*, 6 September 1993, 66–69.

government services, are still quite closed and will open up as a decades-long evolution. Commodities and manufactured goods are already in a globalized state, and many consumer goods are accelerating toward more globalization. Similarly, the leading trading nations of the world display far more openness than low-income countries, thus advancing the state of globalization in general. The expansion of the global trade arena is summarized in Figure 9.2. The size of markets estimated to be global in the year 2000 was well over US$21 billion, boosted by new sectors and markets becoming available. For example, although financially unattractive in the short- to medium term, low-income markets may be attractive for learning the business climate, developing relationships and building brands for the future. Hewlett-Packard, through its e-Inclusion initiative, is looking at speech interfaces for the Internet, solar applications and cheap devices that connect with the web.[15]

Leading companies by their very actions drive the globalization process. There is no structural reason why soft drinks should be at a more advanced stage of globalization while beer and spirits remain more local except for the opportunistic behaviour of Coca-Cola. Similarly, Nike and Reebok have driven their business in a global direction by creating global brands, a global customer segment and a global supply chain. By creating a single online trading exchange for all their parts and suppliers, General Motors, Ford and DaimlerChrysler created a worldwide market of US$240 billion in automotive components.[16]

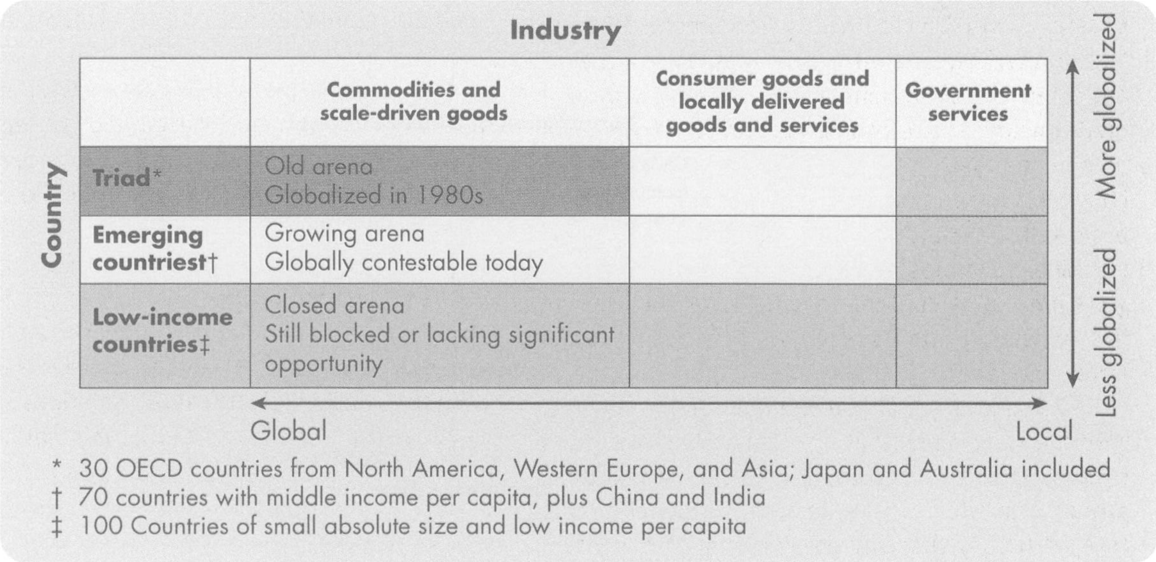

Industry				
Country		**Commodities and scale-driven goods**	**Consumer goods and locally delivered goods and services**	**Government services**
Triad*		Old arena Globalized in 1980s		
Emerging countries†		Growing arena Globally contestable today		
Low-income countries‡		Closed arena Still blocked or lacking significant opportunity		

Global ← → Local

More globalized ↑ / Less globalized ↓

* 30 OECD countries from North America, Western Europe, and Asia; Japan and Australia included
† 70 countries with middle income per capita, plus China and India
‡ 100 Countries of small absolute size and low income per capita

Figure 9.2: The global landscape by industry and market.

Source: Adapted and updated from Jagdish N. Sheth and Atul Parkatiyar (2001) 'The Antecedents and Consequences of Integrated Global Marketing', *International Marketing Review*, 19(1), 16–29; Jane Fraser and Jeremy Oppenheim (1997) 'What's New About Globalization?' *The McKinsey Quarterly*, 2, 173.

THE STRATEGIC PLANNING PROCESS

Given the opportunities and challenges provided by the new realities of the marketplace, decision makers have to engage in strategic planning to match markets with products and other corporate resources more effectively and efficiently to strengthen the company's long-term competitive advantage. Although the process has been summarized as a sequence of steps in Figure 9.3, many of the stages can occur in parallel. Furthermore, feedback as a result of evaluation and control may restart the process at any stage.

It has been shown that for globally committed marketers, formal strategic planning contributes to both financial performance and non-financial objectives.[17] These benefits include raising the efficacy of new-product launches, cost-reduction efforts and improving product quality and market-share performance. Internally, these efforts increase cohesion and improve understanding of different units' points of view.

Understanding and Adjusting the Core Strategy

The planning process has to start with a clear definition of the business for which strategy is to be developed. Generally, the strategic business unit (SBU) is the unit around which decisions are based. In practice, SBUs represent groupings with product-market similarities based on: (1) needs or wants to be met; (2) end-user customers to be targeted; or (3) the good or service used to meet the needs of specific customers. For a global company such as Black & Decker, the options may be to define the business to be analysed as the home improvement business, the do-it-yourself business or the power tool business. Ideally, each of these SBUs should have primary responsibility and authority in managing its basic business functions.

Figure 9.3: Global strategy formulation.
(The authors appreciate the contributions of Robert M. Grant in the preparation of this figure.)

This phase of the planning process requires the participation of executives from different functions, especially marketing, production, finance, logistics and procurement. Geographic representation should be from the major markets or regions as well as from the smaller, yet emerging, markets. With appropriate members, the committee can focus on products and markets as well as competitors whom they face in different markets, whether they are global, regional or purely local. Heading this effort should be an executive with the highest-level experience in regional or global markets. For example, one global firm called on the president of its European operations to come back to headquarters to head the global planning effort. This effort calls for commitment by the company itself both in calling on the best talent to participate in the planning effort and later in implementing their proposals.

It should be noted that this assessment against environmental realities may mean a dramatic change in direction and approach. For example, the once-separate sectors of computing and mobile telephony will be colliding and the direction of future products is still uncertain. The computer industry believes in miniaturizing the general-purpose computer, whereas the mobile-phone industry believes in adding new features (such as photo-messaging, gaming and location-based information) to its existing products.[18] The joint venture between Ericsson and Sony aims at taking advantage of this trend, something that neither party can do on its own.

Market and Competitive Analysis

Planning on a country-by-country basis can result in spotty worldwide market performance. The starting point for global strategic planning is to understand the underlying forces that determine business success that are common to the different countries in which the firm competes. Planning processes that focus simultaneously across a broad range of markets provide global marketers with tools to help balance risks, resource requirements, competitive economies of scale and profitability, to gain stronger long-term positions.[19] On the demand side this requires an understanding of the common features of customer requirements and choice factors. In terms of competition, the key is to understand the structure of the global industry in order to identify the forces that will drive competition and determine profitability.[20]

For the Ford Motor Company, strategy begins not with individual national markets but with understanding trends and sources of profit in the global vehicle market. What are the trends in world demand? What are the underlying trends in lifestyles and transportation patterns that will shape customer expectations and preferences with respect to safety, economy, design and performance? What is the emerging structure of the industry, especially with regard to consolidation among both vehicle manufacturers and their suppliers? What will determine the intensity of competition among the different vehicle manufacturers? The level of excess capacity (currently about 40% in the worldwide auto industry) is likely to be a key influence.[21] If competition is likely to intensify, which companies will emerge the winners? An understanding of scale economies, state of technology and the other factors that determine cost efficiency is likely to be critically important.

Internal Analysis

Organizational resources have to be used as a reality check for any strategic choice because they determine a company's capacity for establishing and sustaining competitive advantage within global markets. Industrial giants with deep pockets may be able to establish a presence in any market they wish, whereas more thinly capitalized companies may have to move cautiously. Human resources may also present a challenge for market expansion. A survey of multinational corporations revealed that good marketing managers, skilled technicians and production managers were especially difficult to find. This difficulty is further compounded when the search is for people with cross-cultural experience to run future regional operations.[22]

At this stage it is imperative that the company assess its own readiness for the necessary moves. This means a rigorous assessment of organizational commitment to global or regional expansion, as well as an assessment of the good's readiness to face the competitive environment. In many cases this has meant painful decisions to focus on certain industries and to leave others. For example, Finnish Nokia, one of the world's largest manufacturer of cellular phones, started its rise in the industry when a decision was made at the company in 1992 to focus on digital cellular phones and to sell off dozens of other product lines (as diverse as PCs, tyres and toilet tissue). By focusing its efforts on this line, the company was able to bring new products to market quickly, build economies of scale into its manufacturing and concentrate on its customers, thereby communicating a commitment to their needs. Nokia's current 40% share allows it the best global visibility of and by the market.[23]

Formulating Global Marketing Strategy

The first step in the formulation of global strategy is the choice of competitive strategy to be employed followed by the choice of country markets to be entered or to be penetrated further.

Choice of Competitive Strategy

In dealing with the global markets, the manager has three general strategic options, as shown in Figure 9.4: (1) cost leadership; (2) differentiation and (3) focus.[24] A focus strategy is defined by its emphasis on a single industry segment within which the orientation may be either toward low cost or differentiation. Any one of these strategies can be pursued on a global or regional basis or the manager may decide to mix and match strategies as a function of market or product dimensions.

In pursuing cost leadership, the company offers an identical product or service at a lower cost than competition. This often means investment in economies of scale and strict control of costs, such as overheads, research and development and logistics. Differentiation, whether it is industry wide or focused on a single segment, takes advantage of the manager's real or perceived uniqueness on elements such as design or after-sales service. It should be noted, however, that a low-price, low-cost strategy does not imply a commodity situation.[25] Although European and US technical standards differ, mobile phone manufacturers such as Nokia and Motorola design their phones to be as similar as possible to hold down manufacturing costs. As a result, they can all be made on the same production line, allowing the manufacturers to shift rapidly from one model to another to meet changes in demand and customer requirements. In the case of IKEA, the low-price approach is associated with clear positioning and a unique brand image focused on a clearly defined target audience of 'young people of all ages'. Similarly, companies that opt for high differentiation cannot forget the monitoring of costs. One common denominator of consumers around the world is their quest for value for their

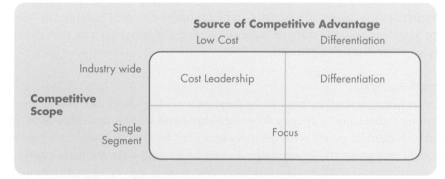

Figure 9.4: Competitive strategies.

Source: Michael Porter (1987) *Competitive Advantage*, The Free Press, New York, ch. 1. Reproduced by permission of Simon & Schuster.

money. With the availability of information increasing and levels of education improving, customers are poised to demand even more of their suppliers.

Most global companies combine high differentiation with cost containment to enter markets and to expand their market shares. Flexible manufacturing systems using mostly standard components and total quality management, reducing the occurrence of defects, are allowing companies to customize an increasing amount of their production, while at the same time saving on costs. Global activities will in themselves permit the exploitation of economies of scale not only in production but also in marketing activities, such as promotion.

Country-Market Choice

A global strategy does not imply that a company should serve the entire globe. Critical choices relate to the allocation of a company's resources among different countries and segments. The usual approach is first to start with regions and further split the analysis by country. Many managers use multiple levels of regional groupings to follow the organizational structure of the company, for example splitting Europe into northern, central and southern regions, which display similarities in demographic and behavioural traits. An important consideration is that data may be more readily available if existing structures and frameworks are used.[26]

Various **portfolio models** have been proposed as tools for this analysis. They typically involve two measures – internal strength and external attractiveness.[27] As indicators of internal strength, the following variables have been used: relative market share, product fit, contribution margin and market presence, which would incorporate the level of support by constituents as well as resources allocated by the company itself. Country attractiveness has been measured using market size, market growth rate, number and type of competitors, governmental regulation, as well as economic and political stability. An example of such a matrix is provided in Figure 9.5.

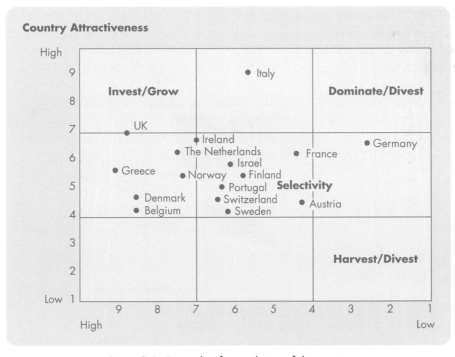

Figure 9.5: Example of a market-portfolio matrix.

Source: Adapted from Gilbert D. Harrell and Richard O. Kiefer (1993), 'Multinational Market Portfolios in Global Strategy Development', *International Marketing Review*, 10, 60–72. Reproduced with permission of Emerald Group Publishing Limited in the format Textbook via Copyright Clearance Center.

The matrix on country attractiveness and company strength is applied here to the European markets. Markets in the invest/grow position will require continued commitment by management in research and development, investment in facilities and the training of personnel at the country level. In cases of relative weakness in growing markets, the company's position may have to be strengthened (through acquisitions or strategic alliances) or a decision to divest may be necessary.[28] For example, Procter & Gamble decided to pull out of the disposable nappy markets in Australia and New Zealand due to well-entrenched competition, international currency fluctuations and importation of products from distant production facilities into the markets.[29]

It is critical that those involved in the planning endeavour to consider potential competitors and their impact on the markets should they enter. For example, rather than license software for their next-generation mobile phones from Microsoft, the largest makers (with a combined market share of 80% of the mobile handset market) established a software consortium called Symbian to produce software of their own. This will allow the participants to try out many different designs without having to start from scratch every time or be dependent on a potential competitor.[30]

Portfolios should also be used to assess market, product and business inter-linkages. This effort should use increasing market similarities through corporate adjustments by setting up appropriate strategic business units and the co-ordination of programmes. The presentation in Figure 9.6 shows a market-product-business portfolio for a global food company, such as Nestlé. The interconnections are formed by common target markets served, sharing of research and development objectives, use of similar technologies and the benefits that can be drawn from sharing common marketing experience. The example suggests possibilities within regions and between regions: frozen food both in Europe and the United States and ice cream throughout the three mega-markets.

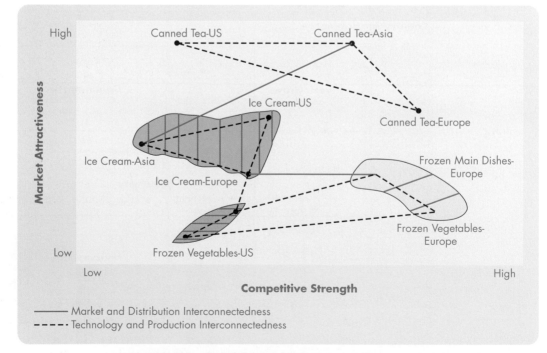

Figure 9.6: Example of strategic interconnectedness matrix.

Source: Adapted from Susan P. Douglas and C. Samuel Craig (1996) 'Global Portfolio Planning and Market Interconnectedness', *Journal of International Marketing*, 4(1), 93–110. Reproduced with permission of Emerald Group Publishing Limited in the format Textbook via Copyright Clearance Center.

Finally, the portfolio assessment also needs to be put into a larger context. The Korean market and the Korean vehicle manufacturers may not independently warrant urgent action on the part of the leading companies. However, as a part of the global strategic setting in the automotive industry, both the market and its companies become critically important. The Republic of Korea, along with China and Japan, is one of the three most important vehicle markets in Asia and can be considered an ideal platform for exporting to other parts of the continent and beyond. Although Korean vehicle manufacturers, such as Daewoo Motor Company and Samsung Motors, were heavily in debt, acquiring them would bring about the aforementioned benefits. Both Ford and GM wanted to acquire Daewoo to attain the top-producer position in the world. Renault, which wanted to acquire Samsung, saw synergistic benefits in that Samsung relies heavily on technology from Nissan, acquired by Renault earlier. There were also other indirect benefits; whoever acquired Daewoo would gain the number one spot in both Poland and Romania, long deemed crucial for tapping growth in Eastern European markets.[31]

In 2001, GM bought a stake of most of Daewoo Motor's productive assets and formed the GM Daewoo company, which started operations on 17 October 2002. Investing US$400 million, GM and its partners Suzuki and SAIC held a stake of 66.7% of GM Daewoo. The remaining equity stake of 33.3% was held by Korea Development Bank and several Korean investors. By August 2005, GM's share in GM Daewoo was 50.9%. GM Daewoo has manufacturing plants in Korea and an assembly plant in Vietnam. Its cars are marketed in over 150 countries worldwide with annual sales of more than 1 million vehicles.

In choosing country markets, a company must make decisions beyond those relating to market attractiveness and company position. A market expansion policy will determine the allocation of resources among various markets. The basic alternatives are concentration on a small number of markets and diversification, which is characterized by growth in a relatively large number of markets.

The conventional wisdom of globalization requires a presence in all of the major triad markets of the world. In some cases, markets may not be attractive in their own right but may have some other significance, such as being the home market of the most demanding customers, thereby aiding in product development or being the home market of a significant competitor (a pre-emptive rationale). For example, Procter & Gamble 'rolled' its Charmin bath tissue into European markets in 2000 to counter an upsurge in European paper products sales by its global rival Kimberly-Clark.[32] Also, the German PC maker Maxdata is taking aim at the US market based on the premise that if it can compete with the big multinationals (Dell, Compaq, Hewlett-Packard and Gateway) at home, there is no reason why it cannot be competitive in North America as well.[33]

Therefore, for global companies, three factors should determine country selection: (1) the stand-alone attractiveness of a market (e.g., China in consumer products due to its size); (2) global strategic importance (e.g., Finland in shipbuilding due to its lead in technological development in vessel design); and (3) possible synergies (e.g., entry into Latvia and Lithuania after successful operations in the Estonian market, given significant market similarities).

Segmentation

Effective use of segmentation, that is, the recognition that groups within markets differ sufficiently to warrant individual approaches, allows global companies to take advantage of the benefits of standardization (such as economies of scale) while addressing the unique needs and expectations of a specific target group. This approach means looking at markets on a global or regional basis, thereby ignoring the political boundaries that define markets in many cases. The identification and cultivation of such inter-market segments is necessary for any standardization of programmes to work.[34]

The emergence of segments that span across markets is already evident in the world marketplace. Global companies have successfully targeted the teenage segment, which is converging as a result of common tastes in sports and music fuelled by their computer literacy, travels abroad and, in many countries, financial independence.[35] Furthermore, a media revolution is creating a common fabric of attitudes and tastes among teenagers. Today satellite TV and global network concepts such as MTV are both helping create this segment and providing global companies an access to the teen audience around the world. For example, Reebok used a global ad campaign to launch its Instapump line of trainers in the United States, Germany, Japan and 137 other countries. Given that teenagers around the world are concerned with social issues, particularly environmentalism, Reebok has introduced a new ecological climbing shoe made from recycled and environmentally sensitive materials. Similarly, two other distinct segments have been detected to be ready for a pan-regional approach, especially in Europe. One includes trendsetters who are wealthier and better educated and tend to value independence, refuse consumer stereotypes and appreciate exclusive products. The second one includes Europe's businesspeople who are well-to-do, regularly travel abroad and have a taste for luxury goods.

The greatest challenge for the global company is the choice of an appropriate base for the segmentation effort. The objective is to arrive at a grouping or groupings that are substantial enough to merit the segmentation effort (for example, there are nearly 230 million teenagers in the Americas, Europe and the Asia-Pacific, with the teenagers of the Americas spending nearly US$60 billion of their own money yearly) and are reachable as well by the marketing effort (for example, the majority of MTVs audience consists of teenagers).

The possible bases for segmentation are summarized in Figure 9.7. Managers have traditionally used environmental bases for segmentation. However, using geographical proximity, political system characteristics, economic standing or cultural traits as stand-alone bases may not provide relevant data for decision making. Using a combination of them, however, may produce more meaningful

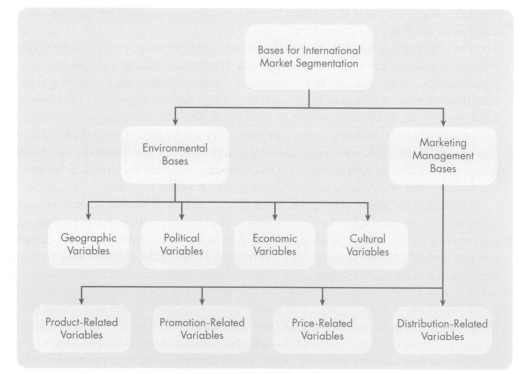

Figure 9.7: Bases for global market segmentation.

Source: Imad B. Baalbaki and Naresh K. Malhotra (1993) 'Marketing Management Bases for International Market Segmentation: An Alternate Look at the Standardization/Customization Debate', *International Marketing Review*, 10(1), 19–44. Reproduced with permission of Emerald Group Publishing Limited in the format Textbook via Copyright Clearance Center.

Segment	Characteristics	Geographics
Strivers	More likely to be men; place more emphasis on material and professional goals	One third of people in developing Asia; one quarter in Russia and developed Asia
Devouts	22% of adults; women more than men; tradition and duty are paramount	Africa, Asia, Middle East; least common in Europe
Altruists	18% of adults; larger portion of females; interested in social issues and welfare of society; older	Latin America and Russia
Intimates	15% of population; personal relationships and family	Europeans and North Americans
Fun Seekers	12% of population; youngest group	Developed Asia
Creatives	10% worldwide; strong interest in education, knowledge and technology	Europe and Latin America

Source: Tom Miller, 'Global Segments from 'Strivers' to 'Creatives',' *Marketing News*, 20 July 1998, 11. Reproduced with permission of American Marketing Association in the format Textbook via Copyright Clearance Center. See also www.ropercenter.uconn.edu.

Table 9.2: Global segments based on cultural values.

results. One of the segments pursued by global companies around the world is the middle-class family. Defining the composition of this global middle class is tricky, given the varying levels of development among nations in Latin America and Asia. However, some experts estimate that 23% of the world population enjoy middle-class lives, some 250 million in India alone.[36] Using household income alone may be quite a poor gauge of class. Income figures ignore vast differences in international purchasing power. Chinese consumers, for example, spend less than 5% of their total outlays on rent, transportation and health, while a typical US household spends 45 to 50%. Additionally, income distinctions do not reflect education or values – two increasingly important barometers of middle-class status. A global segmentation effort using cultural values is presented in Table 9.2.

It has also been proposed that markets that reflect a high degree of homogeneity with respect to marketing mix variables could be grouped into segments and thereby targeted with a largely standardized strategy.[37] Whether bases related to product, promotion, pricing or distribution are used, their influence should be related to environmentally based variables. Product-related bases include the degree to which products are culture-based, which stage of the life cycle they occupy, consumption patterns, attitudes toward product attributes (such as country of origin), as well as consumption infrastructure (for example, telephone lines for modems). The growth of microwave sales, for example, has been surprising in low-income countries; however, microwaves have become status symbols and buying them more of an emotional issue. Many consumers in these markets also want to make sure they get the same product as available in developed markets, thereby eliminating the need in many cases to develop market-specific products. Adjustments will have to be made, however. Noticing that for reasons of status and space, many Asian consumers put their refrigerators in their living rooms, Whirlpool makes refrigerators available in striking colours such as red and blue.

With promotional variables, the consumers' values and norms may necessitate local solutions rather than opting for a regional approach. Similar influences may be exerted by the availability or lack of media vehicles or government regulations affecting promotional campaigns. On the pricing side, dimensions such as customers' price sensitivity may lead the manager to go after segments that insist on high quality despite high price in markets where overall purchasing power may be low to ensure global or regional uniformity in the marketing approach. Affordability is a major issue for customers, whose buying power may fall short for at least the time being. Offering only one option may exclude potential customers of the future who are not yet part of a targeted segment. Companies like Procter & Gamble and Gillette offer an array of products at different price points to attract customers and to keep them as they move up the income scale.[38] As distribution systems converge, for example, with the increase of global chains, markets can also be segmented by outlet types that reach environmentally defined groups.

Global Programme Development

Decisions need to be made regarding how best to use the conditions set by globalization drivers within the framework of competitive challenges and the resources of the firm. Decisions will have to be made in four areas: (1) the degree of standardization in the product offering; (2) the marketing programme beyond the product variable; (3) location and extent of value-adding activities; and (4) competitive moves to be made.

Product Offering

Globalization is not equal to standardization except in the case of the core product or the technology used to produce the product. The components used in a personal computer may to a large extent be standard, with the localization needed only in terms of the peripherals; for example, IBM produces 20 different keyboards for Europe alone. Product standardization may result in significant cost savings upstream. For example, Stanley Works' compromise between French preferences for hand-saws with plastic handles and 'soft teeth' and British preferences for wooden handles and 'hard teeth' – to produce a plastic-handled saw with 'hard teeth' – allowed consolidation for production and resulted in substantial economies of scale. At Whirlpool, the use of common platforms allow European and American appliances to share technology and suppliers to lower cost and to streamline production. Many of the same components are used for products that eventually are marketed to segments looking for top-of-the-line or no-frills versions.[39]

Similar differences in customer expectations have Bestfoods selling 15 versions of minestrone soup in Europe. Shania Twain's double CD *Up!* is an example of catering to multiple segments at the same time: both discs contain the same 19 tracks but one with the effects pop fans appreciate, the other with country and western dimensions. A third disc with 'an Asian Indian vibe' replaces the 'country disc' in Europe.[40]

Marketing Approach

Nowhere is the need for the local touch as critical as in the execution of the marketing programme. Uniformity is sought especially in elements that are strategic (e.g., positioning) in nature, whereas care is taken to localize necessary tactical elements (e.g., distribution). This approach has been called glocalization. For example, Unilever achieved great success with a fabric softener that used a common positioning, advertising theme and symbol (a teddy bear) but differing brand names (e.g., Snuggle, Cajoline, Kuschel-weich, Mimosin and Yumos) and bottle sizes. Gillette scored a huge success with its Sensor shaver when it was rolled out in the United States, Europe and Japan with a common approach based on the premise that men everywhere want the same thing in a shave. Although the language of its TV commercials varied, the theme ('the best a man can get') and most of the footage were the same. A comparison of the marketing mix elements of two global marketers is given in Table 9.3. Notice that adaptation is present even at Coca-Cola, which is acknowledged to be one of the world's most global companies.

Location of Value-Added Activities

Globalization strives for cost reductions by pooling production or other activities or exploiting factor costs or capabilities within a system. Rather than duplicating activities in multiple or even all country organizations, a firm concentrates its activities. For example, Texas Instruments has designated a single design centre and manufacturing organization for each type of memory chip. To reduce high

Marketing Mix Elements	Adaptation		Standardization	
	Full	Partial	Partial	Full
Product			N	C
Brand name			N	C
Product positioning		N		C
Packaging			C/N	
Advertising theme		N		C
Pricing		N	C	
Advertising copy	N			C
Distribution	N	C		
Sales promotion	N	C		
Customer service	N	C		

Key: C: Coca-Cola; N: Nestlé.
Source: John A. Quelch and Edward J. Hoff (1986) 'Customizing Global Marketing', *Harvard Business Review*, (Boston: Harvard Business School Publishing Division), May–June, 61. Reprinted by permission of Harvard Business School.

Table 9.3: Globalization of the marketing mix.

costs and to be close to markets, it placed two of its four new US$250-million memory chip plants in Taiwan and Japan. To reduce high R&D costs, it entered into a strategic alliance with Hitachi. Many global companies have established R&D centres next to key production facilities so that concurrent engineering can take place every day on the factory floor. To enhance the global exchange of ideas, the centres have joint projects and are in real-time contact with each other.

The quest for cost savings and improved transportation methods has allowed some companies to concentrate customer service activities rather than having them present in all country markets. For example, Sony used to have repair centres in all of the Scandinavian countries and Finland; today, all service and maintenance activities are actually performed in a regional centre in Stockholm, Sweden. Similarly, MasterCard has teamed up with Mascon Global in Chennai, India, where MasterCard's core processing functions – authorization, clearing and settlement – for worldwide operations are handled.[41]

To show commitment to a given market, both economically and politically, centres may be established in these markets. Philips Electronics has chosen China as their Asian centre for global product research and development.[42]

Competitive Moves

A company with regional or global presence will not have to respond to competitive moves only in the market where it is being attacked. A competitor may be attacked in its profit sanctuary to drain its resources, or its position in its home market may be challenged.[43] When Fuji began cutting into Kodak's market share in the United States, Kodak responded by drastically increasing its penetration in Japan and created a new subsidiary to deal strictly with that market. In addition, Kodak solicited the support of the US government to gain more access to Japanese distribution systems that Kodak felt were unfairly blocked from them.

Cross-subsidization, the use of resources accumulated in one part of the world to fight a competitive battle in another, may be the competitive advantage needed for the long term.[44] One major market lost may mean losses in others, resulting in a domino effect. Jockeying for overall global leadership may result in competitive action in any part of the world. This has manifested itself in the form of 'wars' between major global players in industries such as soft drinks, automotive tyres, computers and wireless phones. The opening of new markets often signals a new battle, as happened in the 1990s in Russia, in Mexico after the signing of the North American Free Trade Agreement and in Vietnam after the normalization of relations with the United States. Given their multiple bases of operation, global companies may defend against a competitive attack in one country by countering in another country or, if the competitors operate in multiple businesses, countering in a different product category altogether. In the wireless phone category, the winners in the future will be those who can better attack less-mature markets with cheaper phones, while providing Internet-based devices elsewhere.[45]

In a study of how vehicle manufacturers develop strategies that balance the conflicting pressures of local responsiveness and regional integration in Europe, Japanese marketers were found to practise standardization in model offerings but to respond selectively to differences in market conditions by manipulating prices and advertising levels.[46]

Implementing Global Programmes

The successful global companies of the future will be those that can achieve a balance between the local and the regional/global concerns. Companies that have tried the global concept have often run into problems with local differences. Especially early on, global programmes were seen as standardized efforts dictated to the country organizations by headquarters. For example, when Coca-Cola re-entered the Indian market in 1993, it invested most heavily in its Coke brand, using its typical global positioning, and had its market leadership slip to Pepsi. Recognizing the mistake, Coke re-emphasized a popular local cola brand (Thums Up) and refocused the Coke brand advertising to be more relevant to the local Indian consumer.[47] In the past 10 years, Coca-Cola has been acquiring local soft-drink brands (such as Inca Cola in Peru), which now account for 10% of company sales.[48]

Challenges

Pitfalls that handicap global programmes and contribute to their suboptimal performance include market-related reasons, such as insufficient research and a tendency to over-standardize, as well as internal reasons, such as inflexibility in planning and implementation.

If a product is to be launched on a broader scale without formal research as to regional or local differences, the result may be failure. An example of this is Lego A/S, the Danish toy manufacturer, which decided to transfer sales promotional tactics successful in the US market unaltered to other markets, such as Japan. This promotion included approaches such as 'bonus packs' and gift promotions. However, Japanese consumers considered these promotions wasteful, expensive and not very appealing.[49] Going too local has its drawbacks as well. With too much customization or with local production, the marketer may lose its import positioning. For example, when Miller Brewing Company started brewing Löwenbräu under licence, the brand lost its prestigious import image. Often, the necessary research is conducted only after a programme has failed to meet set objectives.

Globalization by design requires a balance between sensitivity to local needs and deployment of technologies and concepts globally. This means that neither headquarters nor independent country managers can alone call the shots. If country organizations are not part of the planning process, or if adoption is forced on them by headquarters, local resistance in the form of the not-invented-here syndrome (NIH) may lead to the demise of the global programme or, worse still, to an overall decline in morale. Subsidiary resistance may stem from resistance to any idea originating from the outside or from valid concerns about the applicability of a concept to that particular market. Without local commitment, no global programme will survive.

Localizing Global Moves

The successful global companies of the twenty-first century will be those that can achieve a balance between country managers and global product managers at headquarters. This balance may be achieved by a series of actions to improve a company's ability to develop and implement global strategy. These actions relate to management processes organization structures and overall corporate culture, all of which should ensure cross-fertilization within the firm.[50]

Management Processes

In the multidomestic approach, country organizations had very little need to exchange ideas. Globalization, however, requires transfer of information not only between headquarters and country organizations but also between the country organizations themselves. By facilitating the flow of information, ideas are exchanged and organizational values strengthened. Information exchange can be achieved through periodic meetings of marketing managers or through worldwide conferences to allow employees to discuss their issues and local approaches to solving them. IBM, for example, has a Worldwide Opportunity Council that sponsors fellowships for employees to listen to business cases from around the world and develop global platforms or solutions. IBM has found that some country organizations find it easier to accept input of other country organizations than that coming directly from headquarters.

Part of the preparation for becoming global has to be personnel interchange. Many companies encourage (or even require) mid-level managers to gain experience abroad during the early or middle stages of their careers. The more experience people have in working with others from different nationalities – getting to know other markets and surroundings – the better a company's global philosophy, strategy and actions will be integrated locally.

The role of headquarters staff should be that of co-ordination and leveraging the resources of the corporation. For example, this may mean activities focused on combining good ideas that come from different parts of the company to be fed into global planning. Many global companies also employ world-class staffs whose role should be to consult subsidiaries by upgrading their technical skills and to focus their attention not only on local issues but also on those with global impact.

Globalization calls for the centralization of decision-making authority far beyond that of the multidomestic approach. Once a strategy has been jointly developed, headquarters may want to permit local managers to develop their own programmes, within specified parameters and subject to approval, rather than forcing them to adhere strictly to the formulated strategy. For example, Colgate-Palmolive allows local units to use their own approaches but only if they can prove they can beat the global 'benchmark' version. With a properly managed approval process, effective control can be exerted without unduly dampening a country manager's creativity.

Overall, the best approach against the emergence of the NIH syndrome is using various motivational policies such as: (1) ensuring that local managers participate in the development of strategies and programmes; (2) encouraging local managers to generate ideas for possible regional or global use; (3) maintaining a product portfolio that includes local as well as regional and global brands; and (4) allowing local managers control over their budgets so that they can respond to local customer needs and counter global competition (rather than depleting budgets by forcing them to participate only in uniform campaigns). By acknowledging this local potential, global companies can pick up successful brands in one country and make them cross-border stars. Since Nestlé acquired British confectionary maker Rowntree Mackintosh, it has increased its exports by 60% and made formerly local brands, such as After Eight Dinner mints, pan-European hits. When an innovation or a product is deemed to have global potential, rolling it out in other regions or worldwide becomes an important consideration.

Organization Structures

Various organization structures have emerged to support the globalization effort. Some companies have established global or regional product managers and their support groups at headquarters. Their task is to develop long-term strategies for product categories on a worldwide basis and to act as the support system for the country organizations. This matrix structure focused on customers, which has replaced the traditional country-by-country approach, is considered more effective in today's global marketplace according to companies that have adopted it.

Whenever a product group has global potential, firms such as Procter & Gamble, 3M and Henkel create strategic-planning units to work on the programmes. These units, such as 3M's EMATs (European Marketing Action Teams) consist of members from the country organizations that market the products, managers from both global and regional headquarters, as well as technical specialists.

To deal with the globalization of customers, companies such as Hewlett-Packard and DHL are extending national account management programmes across countries, typically for the most important customers.[51] In a study of 165 multinational companies, 13% of their revenue came from global customers (revenue from all international customers was 46%). Although relatively small, these 13% come from the most important customers, who cannot be ignored.[52] AT&T, for example, distinguishes between international and global customers and provides the global customers with special services including a single point of contact for domestic and international operations and consistent worldwide service. Executing global account management programmes builds relationships with important customers and also allows for the development of internal systems and interaction.

Technology has allowed companies to take unique advantage of strengths that are present in different parts of the world. A powerful new business model for organizations may be emerging, as shown in the following Focus on e-Business.

F CUS ON

E-BUSINESS   Taking Globalism to the Extremes

A new breed of high-tech companies is defying conventional wisdom about how corporations ought to operate. While most large companies have extensive worldwide operations, these new players aim to transcend nationality altogether. Some leading examples are included below.

Trend Micro
Having a computer-virus response centre in low-cost Manila and six smaller centres scattered around the globe allows this American/Japanese/Taiwanese company to guarantee delivery of inoculations against major viruses in less than two hours. No rival has comparable reach.

Logitech International
With dual headquarters in Switzerland and Silicon Valley, Logitech competes effectively with Microsoft

in computer peripherals. Its advantage is that the main manufacturing decisions are made in Taiwan, enabling the company to make quick decisions about whether to manufacture products in Chinese facilities or to farm them out.

Wipro
The company's vice-chairman is in the United States so he can work the client base in the largest market for technology services, but 17 000 out of 20 000 engineers and consultants are in India, where annual cost per employee is less than one fifth that of Silicon Valley.

Cognos
The Canadian/American company's international orientation has changed the way it makes software. In the past, it released different versions for each

country. Currently, it ships business software, designed for multinational customers, that includes all the major languages, plus data on local currencies and tax regulations.

What is unique about these entities is that many operations are virtual. Top executives and core corporate functions are placed in different countries to gain a competitive edge through the availability of talent and capital, low cost or proximity to their most important customers. To deal with the gaps between time zones and cultures, these companies operate like virtual computer networks. Thanks to the Internet, they can communicate in real time via e-mail, instant messaging or videoconferencing.

However, the model is not without its challenges. Executives are separated by oceans and time zones, making it difficult to maintain basic communications and routines that traditional companies take for granted.

Sources: 'Borders Are So Twentieth Century', *Business Week*, 22 September 2003, 68–73; Julian Birkinshaw and Tony Sheehan, 'Managing the Knowledge Lifecycle', *Sloan Management Review*, 2002, 44(Fall), 75–83; 'The Stateless Corporation', *Business Week*, 14 May 1990, 98–106.

Corporate Culture

Whirlpool's corporate profile states the following:

> Beyond selling products around the world, being a global home-appliance company means identifying and respecting genuine national and regional differences in customer expectations but also recognising and responding to similarities in product development, engineering, purchasing, manufacturing, marketing and sales, distribution and other areas. Companies which exploit the efficiencies from these similarities will outperform others in terms of market share, cost, quality, productivity, innovation and return to shareholders.[53]

In truly global companies, very little decision making occurs that does not support the goal of treating the world as a single market: planning for and execution of programmes take place on a worldwide basis.

An example of a manifestation of the global commitment is a global identity that favours no specific country (especially not the 'home country' of the company). The management features several nationalities and whenever teams are assembled, people from various country organizations get represented. The management development system has to be transparent, allowing non-national executives an equal chance for the fast track to top management.[54]

In determining the optimal combination of products and product lines to be marketed, a firm should consider options for individual markets as well as transfer of products and brands from one region or market to another. This will often result in a particular country organization marketing product lines and goods that are a combination of global, regional and national brands.

Decisions on specific targeting may result in the choice of a narrowly defined segment in the countries chosen. This is a likely strategy of specialized products to clearly definable markets, for example, ocean-capable sailing boats. Catering to multiple segments in various markets is typical of consumer-oriented companies that have sufficient resources for broad coverage.

Globalization has become one of the most important strategy issues for managers in the past 15 years. Many forces, both external and internal, are driving companies to globalize by expanding and co-ordinating their participation in foreign markets. The approach is not standardization, however. Managers may indeed occasionally be able to take identical concepts and approaches around the world, but most often they must be customized to local tastes. Internally, companies must make sure that country organizations around the world are ready to launch global products and programmes as if they had been developed only for their markets. The firms that are able to exploit commonalities across borders, and to do so with competent marketing managers in country organizations, will see the benefits in their overall performance.[55]

ORGANIZATIONAL STRUCTURE

The basic functions of an organization are to provide: (1) a route and locus of decision making and co-ordination and (2) a system for reporting and communications. Increasingly, the co-ordination and communication dimensions have to include learning from the global marketplace through the company's different units.[56] These networks are typically depicted in the organizational chart.

Organizational Designs

The basic configurations of international organizations correspond to those of purely domestic ones; the greater the degree of internalization, the more complex the structures can become. The types of structures that companies use to manage foreign activities can be divided into three categories, based on the degree of internationalization:

- Little or no formal organizational recognition of international activities of the firm. This category ranges from domestic operations handling an occasional international transaction on an ad hoc basis to firms with separate export departments.
- International division. Firms in this category recognize the ever-growing importance of the international involvement.
- Global organizations. These can be structured by product, area, function, process or customer, but ignore the traditional domestic–international split.

Hybrid structures may exist as well, in which one market may be structured by product, another by areas. Matrix organizations have merged in large multinational corporations to combine product-specific, regional and functional expertise. As worldwide competition has increased dramatically in many industries, the latest organizational response is networked global organizations in which heavy flows of hardware, software and personnel take place between strategically interdependent units to establish greater global integration. The ability to identify and disseminate best practices throughout the organization is an important competitive advantage for global companies. For example, a US vehicle manufacturer found that in the face of distinctive challenges presented by the local environment, Brazilian engineers developed superior seals, which the company then incorporated in all its models worldwide.[57]

Little or No Formal Organization

In the very early stages of international involvement, domestic operations assume responsibility for international activities. The role of international activities in the sales and profits of the corporation is initially so minor that no organizational adjustment takes place. No consolidation of information or authority over international sales is undertaken or is necessary. Transactions are conducted on a case-by-case basis, either by the resident expert or quite often with the help of facilitating agents, such as freight forwarders.

As demand from the international marketplace grows and interest within the firm expands, the organizational structure will reflect it. As shown in Figure 9.8, an export department appears as a separate entity. This may be an outside export management company – that is, an independent company that becomes the de facto export department of the firm. This is an indirect approach to international involvement in that very little experience is accumulated within the firm itself.

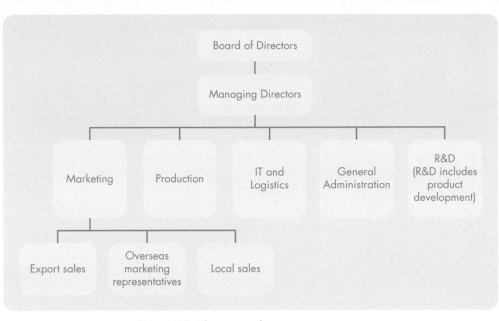

Figure 9.8: The export department structure.

Alternatively, a firm may establish its own export department, hiring a few seasoned individuals to take responsibility for international activities. Organizationally, the department may be a sub-department of marketing (as shown in Figure 9.8) or may have equal ranking with the various functional departments. The choice will depend on the importance assigned to overseas activities by the firm. The export department is the first real step toward internationalizing the organizational structures. It should be a fully fledged marketing organization and not merely a sales organization; that is, it should have the resources for market research and market-development activities (such as trade show participation).

Licensing as an international entry mode of market entry may be assigned to the R&D function despite its importance to the overall international strategy of the firm. A formal liaison among the export, marketing, production and R&D functions has to be formed for the maximum utilization of licensing.[58] If licensing indeed becomes a major activity for the firm, a separate manager should be appointed.

The more the firm becomes involved in foreign markets, the more quickly the export department structure will become obsolete. For example, the firm may undertake joint ventures or direct foreign investments, which require those involved to have functional experience. The firm therefore typically establishes an international division.

Some firms that acquire foreign production facilities pass through an additional stage in which foreign subsidiaries report directly to the president or to a manager specifically assigned the duty. However, the amount of co-ordination and control that are required quickly establish the need for a more formal international organization in the firm.

The International Division

The international division centralizes in one entity, with or without separate incorporation, all the responsibility for international activities (Figure 9.9 illustrates the international division of an American company). The approach aims to eliminate a possible bias against international operations that may exist if domestic divisions are allowed to serve international customers independently. In some cases, international markets have been treated as secondary to domestic markets. The international division concentrates international expertise, information flows concerning

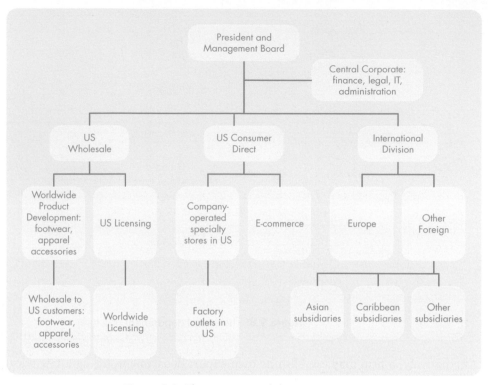

Figure 9.9: The international division structure.

foreign market opportunities and authority over international activities. However, manufacturing and other related functions remain with the domestic divisions to take advantage of economies of scale.

To avoid putting the international division at a disadvantage in competing for products, personnel and corporate services, co-ordination between domestic and international operations is necessary. Co-ordination can be achieved through a joint staff or by requiring domestic and international divisions to interact in strategic planning and to submit the plans to headquarters. Further, many corporations require and encourage frequent interaction between domestic and international personnel to discuss common problems in areas such as product planning. Co-ordination is also important because domestic operations are typically organized along product or functional lines, whereas international divisions are geographically oriented.

International divisions best serve firms with few products that do not vary significantly in terms of their environmental sensitivity and with international sales and profits that are still quite insignificant compared with those of the domestic divisions.[59] Companies may outgrow their international divisions as their sales outside of the domestic market grow in significance, diversity and complexity. European companies have traditionally used international divisions far less than their US counterparts due to the relatively small size of their domestic markets. Nestlé, Nokia or Philips, for example, would have never grown to their current prominence by relying on their home markets alone. Although international divisions were popular among US companies in the 1980s and 1990s, globalization of markets and the increased share of overseas sales have seen international divisions being replaced with global structures.[60] For example, Loctite, a leading marketer of sealants, adhesives and coatings, moved from an international division to a global structure by which the company is managed by market channel (e.g., industrial automotive and electronics industry); this enabled Loctite employees to synergize efforts and expertise worldwide.[61]

Global Organizational Structures

Global structures have grown out of competitive necessity. In many industries, competition is on a global basis, with the result that companies must have a high degree of reactive capability.

Six basic types of global structures are available:

- Global product structure, in which product divisions are responsible for all manufacture and marketing worldwide.
- Global area structure, in which geographic divisions are responsible for all manufacture and marketing in their respective areas.
- Global functional structures, in which functional areas (such as production, marketing, finance and personnel) are responsible for the worldwide operations of their own functional area.
- Global customer structures, in which operations are structured based on distinct worldwide customer groups.
- Mixed – or hybrid – structures, which may combine the other alternatives.
- Matrix structures, in which operations have reporting responsibility to more than one group (typically, product, functions or area).

Product Structure

The **product structure** is the form most often used by multinational corporations.[62] The approach gives worldwide responsibility to strategic business units for the marketing of their product lines, as shown in Figure 9.10. Most consumer-product firms use some form of this approach, mainly because

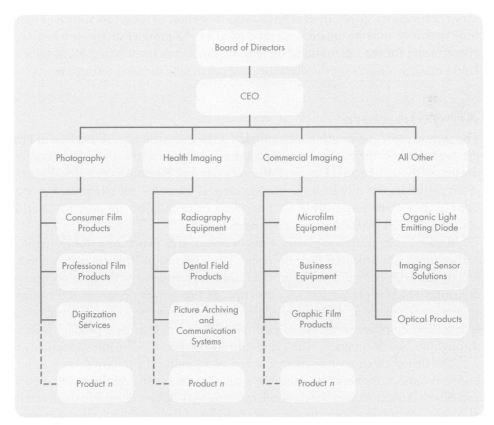

Figure 9.10: The global product structure (Kodak).

Source: www.kodak.com/US/en/corp/aboutKodak/bu.shtml. © Eastman Kodak Company.

of the diversity of their products. One of the major benefits of the approach is improved cost efficiency through centralization of manufacturing facilities. This is crucial in industries in which competitive position is determined by world market share, which in turn is often determined by the degree to which manufacturing is rationalized.[63]

Adaptation to this approach may cause problems, because it is usually accompanied by consolidation of operations and plant closings. A good example is Black & Decker, which rationalized many of its operations in its worldwide competitive effort against Makita, the Japanese power-tool manufacturer. Similarly, Goodyear reorganized itself into a single global organization with a complete business-team approach for tyres and general products. The move was largely prompted by tightening worldwide competition.[64] In a similar move, Ford merged its large and culturally distinct European and North American automotive operations by vehicle platform type to make more efficient use of its engineering and product development resources against rapidly globalizing rivals.[65] The Ford Focus, Ford's compact car introduced in 1999, was designed by one team of engineers for worldwide markets.

Other benefits of the product structure are the ability to balance the functional inputs needed for a product and the ability to react quickly to product-specific problems in the marketplace. Even smaller brands receive individual attention. Product-specific attention is important because products vary in terms of the adaptation they need for different foreign markets. All in all, the product approach is ideally suited to the development of a global strategic focus in response to global competition.

At the same time, the product structure fragments international expertise within the firm because a central pool of international experience no longer exists. The structure assumes that managers will have adequate regional experience or advice to allow them to make balanced decisions. Co-ordination of activities among the various product groups operating in the same markets is crucial to avoid unnecessary duplication of basic tasks. For some of these tasks, such as market research, special staff functions may be created and then filled by the product divisions when needed. If they lack an appreciation for the international dimension, product managers may focus their attention only on the larger markets or only on the domestic, and fail to take the long-term view.

Area Structure

The second most commonly used approach is the area structure, illustrated in Figure 9.11. Such firms are organized on the basis of geographical areas; for example, operations may be divided into those dealing with Asia-Pacific, Europe, Latin America and North America. Ideally, no special preference is given to the region in which the headquarters is located – for example, Europe or North America. Central staffs are responsible for providing co-ordination support for worldwide planning and control activities performed at headquarters.

Regional integration is playing a major role in area structuring; for example, many multinational corporations have located their European headquarters in Brussels, where the EU has its headquarters. In some US companies, North American integration led to the development of a North American division, which replaced the US operation as the power centre of the company. Organizational changes were made at 3M as a result of NAFTA, with the focus on three concepts: simplification, linkage and empowerment. As an example, this means that new-product launches are co-ordinated throughout North America, with standardizing of as many elements as feasible and prudent.[66]

The driver of structural choices may also be cultural similarity, such as in the case of Asia, or historic connections between countries, such as in the case of combining Europe with the Middle East and North Africa. As new markets emerge, they may be first delegated to an established country organization for guidance with the ultimate objective of having them be equal partners with others in the organization. When Estonia regained its independence and started its transformation to a market economy, many companies assigned the responsibility of the Estonian unit's development to their

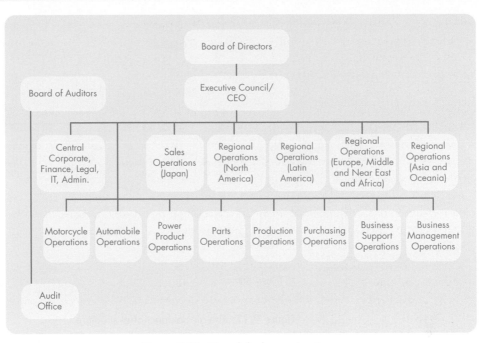

Figure 9.11: The global area structure.

country organization in Finland. In Latvia's case, the Swedish country organization got the job, whereas in Lithuania it is the Norwegian country organization.

The area approach follows the marketing concept most closely because individual areas and markets are given concentrated attention. If market conditions with respect to product acceptance and operating conditions vary dramatically, the area approach is the one to choose. Companies opting for this alternative typically have relatively narrow product lines with similar end-uses and end-users. However, expertise is needed in adapting the product and its marketing to local market conditions. Once again, to avoid duplication of effort in product management and in functional areas, staff specialists – for product categories, for example – may be used.

Without appropriate co-ordination from the staff, essential information and experience may not be transferred from one regional entity to another. Also, if the company expands its product lines and if end markets begin to diversify, the area structure may become inappropriate.

Some managers may feel that going into a global product structure may be too much, too quickly and opt, therefore, to have a regional organization for planning and reporting purposes. The objective may also be to keep profit or sales centres of similar size at similar levels in the corporate hierarchy. If a group of countries has small sales as compared with other country operations, they may be consolidated into a region. The benefit of a regional operation and regional headquarters would be the more efficient co-ordination of programmes across the region (as opposed to globally), a more sensitized management to country-market operations in the region and the ability to have the region's voice heard more clearly at global headquarters (as compared to what an individual, especially smaller, country operation could achieve).[67]

Functional Structure

Of all the approaches, the functional structure is the simplest from the administrative viewpoint because it emphasizes the basic tasks of the firm – for example, manufacturing, sales and

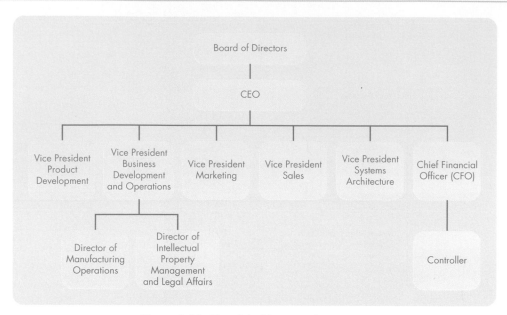

Figure 9.12: The global functional structure.

research and development. The approach, illustrated in Figure 9.12, works best when both products and customers are relatively few and similar in nature. Co-ordination is typically the key problem; therefore, staff functions are created to interact between the functional areas. Otherwise, the company's operational and regional expertise may not be exploited to the fullest extent possible.

A variation of the functional approach is one that uses processes as a basis for structure. The process structure is common in the energy and mining industries, where one corporate entity may be in charge of exploration worldwide and another may be responsible for the actual mining operations.

Customer Structure

Firms may also organize their operations using the customer structure, especially if the customer groups they serve are dramatically different – for example, consumers and businesses and governments. Catering to such diverse groups may require concentrating specialists in particular divisions. The product may be the same but the buying processes of the various customer groups may differ. Governmental buying is characterized by bidding, in which price plays a larger role than when businesses are the buyers.

Mixed Structure

In some cases, mixed or hybrid organizations exist. A mixed structure combines two or more organizational dimensions simultaneously. It permits adequate attention to product, area or functional needs as needed by the company. The approach may only be a result of a transitional period after a merger or an acquisition or it may come about due to unique market characteristics or product line. It may also provide a useful structure before the implementation of a worldwide matrix structure.[68]

Naturally, organizational structures are never as clear-cut and simple as presented here. Whatever the basic format, product, functional and area inputs are needed. Alternatives could include an initial product structure that would subsequently have regional groupings or an initial regional

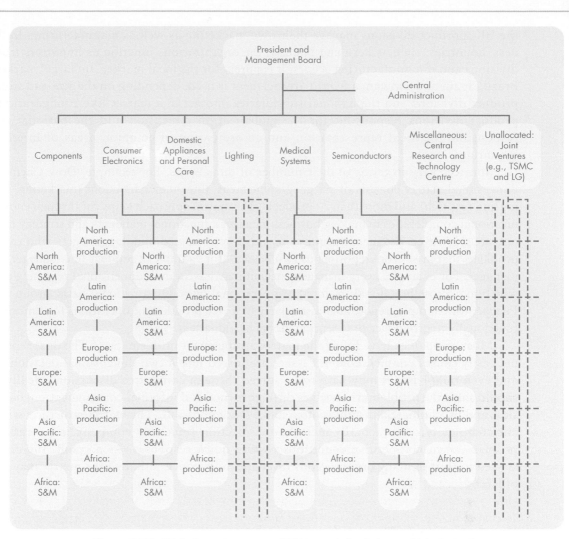

Figure 9.13: Global matrix structure (S&M stands for Sales and Marketing).

structure with subsequent product groupings. However, in the long term, co-ordination and control across such structures become tedious.

Matrix Structure

In an attempt to facilitate the planning for, and organizing and controlling of, interdependent businesses, critical resources, strategies and geographic regions, many multinational corporations have adopted the **matrix structure**.[69] Business is driven by a worldwide business unit (for example, photographic products or commercial and information systems) and implemented by a geographic unit (for example, Europe or Latin America). The geographical units, as well as their country subsidiaries, serve as the 'glue' between autonomous product operations.

Organizational matrices integrate the various approaches already discussed, as the example in Figure 9.13 illustrates. The seven product divisions (which are then divided into 60 product groups) have rationalized manufacturing to provide products for continent-wide markets rather than lines of products for individual markets.[70] These product groups adjust to changing market conditions; for example, the Components division has been slated to be merged into the other divisions due to lack of stand-alone profitability.[71] In 'key' markets, such as, France, Japan and the UK, product divisions manage their own marketing as well as manufacturing. In 'local business' countries, such as Peru and Nigeria, the organizations function as importers from product divisions and if manufacturing occurs, it is purely for the local market. In 'large' markets, such as Brazil, Spain and Taiwan, a hybrid arrangement is used, depending on the size and situation. The product divisions and the national subsidiaries interact in a matrix-like configuration, with the product divisions responsible for the globalization dimension and the national subsidiaries responsible for local representation and co-ordination of common areas of interest, such as recruiting.

Matrices vary in terms of their number of dimensions. For example, Dow Chemical's three-dimensional matrix consists of five geographic areas, three major functions (marketing, manufacturing and research) and more than 70 products. The matrix approach helps cut through enormous organizational complexities in making business managers, functional managers and strategy managers cooperate. However, the matrix requires sensitive, well-trained middle managers who can cope with problems that arise from reporting to two bosses – for example, a product-line manager and an area manager. For example, every management unit may have a multidimensional reporting relationship, which may cross functional, regional or operational lines. On a regional basis, group managers in Europe, for example, report administratively to a vice president of operations for Europe but report functionally to group vice presidents at global headquarters.

Most companies have found the matrix arrangement problematic.[72] The dual reporting channel easily causes conflict, complex issues are forced into a two-dimensional decision framework and even minor issues may have to be solved through committee discussion. Ideally, managers should solve the problems themselves through formal and informal communication; however, physical and psychological distances often make that impossible. The matrix structure, with its inherent complexity, may actually increase the reaction time of a company, a potentially serious problem when competitive conditions require quick responses. As a result, the authority has started to shift in many organizations from area to product, although the matrix may still be used officially.

Evolution of Organizational Structures

Companies have been shown to develop new structures in a pattern of stages as their products diversify and share of foreign sales increases.[73] At the first stage of autonomous subsidiaries reporting directly to top management, the establishment of an international division follows. As product diversity and the importance of the foreign marketplace increase, companies develop global structures to co-ordinate subsidiary operations and to rationalize worldwide production. As multinational corporations have been faced with simultaneous pressures to adapt to local market conditions and to rationalize production and globalize competitive reactions, many have opted for the matrix structure. The matrix structure probably allows a corporation to best meet the challenges of global markets (to be global and local, big and small, decentralized with centralized reporting) by allowing the optimizing of businesses globally and maximizing performance in every country of operation.[74] The evolutionary process is summarized in Figure 9.14.

Whatever the organizational arrangement may be, the challenge of employees working in 'silos' remains. Employee knowledge tends to be fragmented, with one unit's experience and know-how inaccessible to other units. Therefore, the wheel gets reinvented each time – at considerable cost to the company and to the frustration to those charged with tasks. Information technology can be used to synchronize knowledge across even the most complicated and diverse organizations.[75] At Procter & Gamble, for example, brand managers use a standardized, worldwide ad-testing system that allows them to access every ad the company has ever run, providing examples of how to meet particular needs.

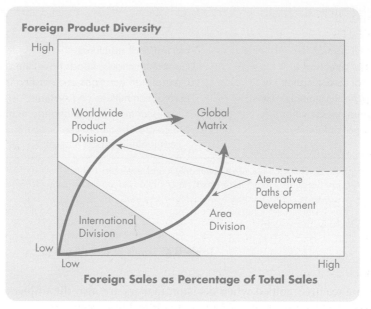

Figure 9.14: Evolution of international structures.

Source: From Christopher A. Bartlett (1986) 'Building and Managing the Transnational: The New Organizational Challenge', in *Competition in Global Industries*, Michael E. Porter (ed.), Harvard Business School Press, Boston, MA, 368. Reproduced by permission of Harvard Business School Publishing.

IMPLEMENTATION

Organizational structures provide the frameworks for carrying out decision-making processes. However, for that decision making to be effective, a series of organizational initiatives are needed to develop strategy to its full potential; that is, to secure implementation both at the national level and across markets.[76]

Locus of Decision Making

Organizational structures themselves do not indicate where the authority for decision making and control rests within the organization nor do they reveal the level of co-ordination between the units. The different levels of co-ordination between country units are summarized in Table 9.4. Once a suitable structure is found, it has to be made to work by finding a balance between the centre and country organizations.

If subsidiaries are granted a high degree of autonomy, the system is called decentralization. In decentralized systems, controls are relatively loose and simple and the flows between headquarters and subsidiaries are mainly financial; that is, each subsidiary operates as a profit centre. On the other hand, if controls are tight and the strategic decision making is concentrated at headquarters, the system is described as centralization. Firms are typically neither completely centralized nor decentralized; for example, some functions of the firm – such as finance – lend themselves to more centralized decision making; others – such as promotional decisions – do so far less. Research and development in organizations is typically centralized, especially in cases of basic research work. Some companies have, partly due to governmental pressures, added R&D functions on a regional or local basis. In many cases, however, variations are product and market based; for example, Corning Incorporated's TV tube strategy requires global decision making for pricing and local decision making for service and delivery.

The basic advantage of allowing maximum flexibility at the country-market level is that subsidiary management knows its market and can react to changes more quickly. Problems of motivation

Level	Description
5. Central control	No national structures
4. Central direction	Central functional heads have line authority over national functions
3. Central co-ordination	Central staff functions in co-ordinating role
2. Co-ordinating mechanisms	Formal committees and systems
1. Informal co-operation	Functional meetings: exchange of information
0. National autonomy	No co-ordination between decentralized units, which may even compete in export markets

Level 5 = highest; Level 0 = lowest. Most commonly found levels are 1–4.
Source: Norman Blackwell, Jean-Pierre Bizet, Peter Child and David Hensley (1995) 'Creating European Organisations That Work', Michael R. Czinkota and Ilkka A. Ronkainen (eds), *Readings in Global Marketing*, The Dryden Press, London, 376–385. From Czinkota, Readings in Global Marketing-HSIE, 1E. © 1995 South-Western, a part of Cengage Learning, Inc. Reproduced by permission.

Table 9.4: Levels of co-ordination.

and acceptance are avoided when decision makers are also the implementers of the strategy. On the other hand, many multinationals faced with global competitive threats and opportunities have adopted a global strategy formulation, which by definition requires a higher degree of centralization. What has emerged as a result can be called co-ordinated decentralization. This means that overall corporate strategy is provided from headquarters, while subsidiaries are free to implement it within the range agreed on in consultation between headquarters and the subsidiaries.

However, companies moving into this new mode may face significant challenges. Among these systemic difficulties is the lack of widespread commitment to dismantling traditional national structures, driven by an inadequate understanding of the larger, global forces at work. Power barriers from perceived threats to the personal roles of national managers, especially if their tasks are under the threat of being consolidated into regional organizations, can lead to proposals being challenged without valid reason. Finally, some organizational initiatives (such as multicultural teams or corporate chat rooms) may be jeopardized by the fact the people do not have the necessary skills (e.g., language ability) or that an infrastructure (e.g., intranet) may not exist in an appropriate format.[77]

One particular case is of special interest. Organizationally, the forces of globalization are changing the country manager's role significantly. When country operations were largely stand-alone, country managers enjoyed considerable decision-making autonomy as well as entrepreneurial initiative, with profit-and-loss responsibility, oversight of multiple functions and the benefit of distance from headquarters. Today, however, many companies have to emphasize global and regional priorities, which means that the power has to shift at least to some extent from the country manager to worldwide strategic business unit and product-line managers. Many of the local decisions are now subordinated to global strategic moves. However, regional and local programmes still require an effective local management component. Therefore, the future country manager will have to wear many hats in balancing the needs of the operation for which he or she is directly responsible with those of the entire region or strategic business unit.[78] To emphasize the importance of the global/regional dimension in the country manager's portfolio, many companies have tied the country manager's compensation to how the company performs globally or regionally, not just in the market for which the manager is responsible.

Factors Affecting Structure and Decision Making

The organizational structure and locus of decision making in a multinational corporation are determined by a number of factors, such as: (1) its degree of involvement in international operations; (2)

the products the firm markets; (3) the size and importance of the firm's markets; and (4) the human resource capability of the firm.[79]

The effect of the degree of involvement on structure and decision making was discussed earlier in the chapter. With low degrees of involvement, subsidiaries can enjoy high degrees of autonomy as long as they meet their profit targets. The same situation can occur even with the most globally oriented companies but within a different framework. Consider, for example, Philips USA, which generates 20% of the company's worldwide sales. Even more important, it serves as a market that is on the leading edge of digital media development. Therefore, it enjoys independent status in terms of local policy setting and managerial practices but is still, nevertheless, within the parent company's planning and control system.

The firm's country of origin and the political history of the area can also affect organizational structure and decision making. For example, Swiss-based Nestlé, with only 3 to 4% of its sales from its small domestic market, has traditionally had a highly decentralized organization. Moreover, European history for the past century – particularly the two world wars – has often forced subsidiaries of European-based companies to act independently to survive.

The type and variety of products marketed will affect organizational decisions. Companies that market consumer products typically have product organizations with high degrees of decentralization, allowing for maximum local flexibility. On the other hand, companies that market technologically sophisticated products – such as General Electric, which markets turbines – display centralized organizations with worldwide product responsibilities.

Going global has recently meant transferring world headquarters of important business units abroad. For example, Philips has moved headquarters of several of its global business units to the United States, including its Digital Video Group, Optimal Storage and Flat Panel Display activities, to Silicon Valley.

Apart from situations that require the development of an area structure, the unique characteristics of particular markets or regions may require separate and specific considerations for the firm. For example, when it was set up, AT&T's China division was the only one of 20 divisions in the world based on geography rather than on product or service line. Furthermore, it was the only one to report directly to the CEO.[80]

The human factor in any organization is critical. Managers at both headquarters and the country organizations must bridge the physical and cultural distances separating them. If country organizations have competent managers who rarely need to consult headquarters about their challenges, they may be granted high degrees of autonomy. In the case of global organizations, local management must understand overall corporate goals in that decisions that meet the long-term objectives may not be optimal for the individual local market.

The Networked Global Organization

No international structure is ideal and some have challenged the wisdom of even looking for one. They have recommended attention to new processes that would, in a given structure, help to develop new perspectives and attitudes that reflect and respond to the complex, opposing demands of global integration and local responsiveness. The question thus changes from which structural alternative is best to how the different perspectives of various corporate entities can better be taken into account when making decisions. In structural terms, nothing may change. As a matter of fact, Philips has not changed its basic matrix structure, and yet major changes have occurred in internal relations. The basic change was from a decentralized federation model to a networked global organization, the effects of which are depicted in Figure 9.15. The term glocal has been coined to describe this approach.[81]

Companies that have adopted the approach have incorporated the following three dimensions into their organizations: (1) the development and communication of a clear corporate vision; (2) the

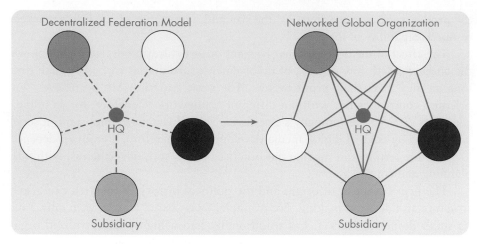

Figure 9.15: The networked global organization.

Source: Thomas Gross, Ernie Turner and Lars Cederholm (1997) 'Building Teams for Global Operations', *Management Review*, June, 34. Reproduced with permission of American Management Association in the format Textbook via Copyright Clearance Center.

effective management of human resource tools to broaden individual perspectives and develop identification with corporate goals; and (3) the integration of individual thinking and activities into the broad corporate agenda.[82] The first dimension relates to a clear and consistent long-term corporate mission that guides individuals wherever they work in the organization. Examples of this are Johnson & Johnson's corporate credo of customer focus and NEC's C&C (computers and communications). The second dimension relates both to the development of global managers who can find opportunities in spite of environmental challenges as well as creating a global perspective among country managers. The last dimension relates to the development of a co-operative mind-set among country organizations to ensure effective implementation of global strategies. Managers may believe that global strategies are intrusions on their operations if they do not have an understanding of the corporate vision, if they have not contributed to the global corporate agenda or if they are not given direct responsibility for its implementation. Defensive, territorial attitudes can lead to the emergence of the 'not-invented-here' syndrome; that is, country organizations objecting to or rejecting an otherwise sound strategy.

For example, in an area structure, units (such as Europe and North America) may operate quite independently, sharing little expertise and information with the other units. Although they are supposed to build links to headquarters and other units, they may actually be building walls. To tackle this problem, Nissan established four management committees that meet once a month to supervise regional operations. Each committee includes representatives of the major functions (e.g., manufacturing, marketing and finance) and the committees (for Japan, Europe, the United States and general overseas markets) are chaired by Nissan executive vice presidents based in Japan. The CEO attends the committee meetings periodically but regularly.[83]

This network avoids the problems of effort duplication, inefficiency and resistance to ideas developed elsewhere by giving subsidiaries the latitude, encouragement and tools to pursue local business development within the framework of the global strategy. Headquarters considers each unit a source of ideas, skills, capabilities and knowledge that can be used for the benefit of the entire organization. This means that subsidiaries must be upgraded from mere implementers and adaptors to contributors and partners in the development and execution of worldwide strategies. Efficient plants may be converted into international production centres, innovative R&D units converted into centres of excellence (and thus role models) and leading subsidiary groups given the leadership role in developing new strategies for the entire corporation. These centres of excellence are discussed in the following Focus on Entrepreneurship.

F◯CUS ON

ENTREPRENEURSHIP   Centres of Excellence

Country-market operations are gaining more significant roles as companies scan the world for ideas that can cross borders. The consensus among managers is that many more countries can be the birthplaces and incubators for solutions that can be applied on a worldwide basis. This realization has given rise to centres of excellence both in global manufacturing and service firms.

Centres of excellence have common themes. First, they are established in areas that top management considers to be of strategic importance to the firm. Given the increasing importance of emerging and developing markets, many companies are convinced that an intimate understanding of these new markets can only be achieved through proximity. Consequently, Unilever has installed innovation centres in 19 countries to develop unique solutions for these markets. Second, the heart of each centre of excellence is the leading-edge knowledge of a small number of individuals responsible for the continual maintenance and upgrading of the knowledge in question. Within ABB, for example, ABB Strömberg in Finland has worldwide responsibility for the electric drives, a category for which it is the recognized world leader. Third, centres of excellence typically have a dual role: to leverage and/or transfer the current leading-edge capabilities and continually to fine-tune and enhance those capabilities so that they remain state of the art. For example, Corning has

established a Centre for Marketing Excellence where sales and marketing staff from all of Corning's businesses – from glass to television components – will be able to find help with marketing intelligence, strategies, new product lines and e-Business.

Centres of excellence can emerge in three formats: charismatic, focused or virtual. Charismatic centres of excellence are individuals who are internationally recognized for their expertise in a function or an area. These individuals are called upon to build, through mentoring relationships, a capability in the firm that has been lacking. The most common type are focused centres of excellence, which are based on a single area of expertise, be it technological or product-based. The centre has an identifiable location from which the members provide advice and leadership. In virtual centres of excellence, the core individuals live and work around the world and keep in touch through electronic means and meetings. The knowledge of dispersed individuals is brought together, integrated into a coherent whole and disseminated throughout the firm.

An increasingly important determinant of competitive advantage is the ability to make proprietary knowledge available and usable on a global scale. Centres of excellence are a way for companies to exploit their geographically dispersed expertise more effectively.

Sources: Julian Birkinshaw and Tony Sheehan (2002) 'Managing the Knowledge Life Cycle', *Sloan Management Review,* 44(Fall), 75–83; Erin Strout (2000) 'Reinventing a Company', *Sales and Marketing Management,* 152(February), 86–92; Karl Moore and Julian Birkinshaw (1998) 'Managing Knowledge in Global Service Firms', *Academy of Management Executive,* 12(4), 81–92.

Promoting Internal Co-operation

The global business entity in today's environment can only be successful if it is able to move intellectual capital within the organization; that is, take ideas and move them around, faster and faster.[84]

One of the tools is teaching. For example, at Ford Motor Company, teaching takes three distinct forms as shown in Table 9.5. Ford's approach is similarly undertaken at many leading global companies. The focus is on teachable points of view; that is, an explanation of what a person knows and believes about what it takes to succeed in his or her business.[85] For example, GE's Jack Welch coined the term

Programme	Participants	Teachers	Components
Capstone	24 senior executives at a time	The leadership team	• About 20 days' training annually • Six-month team projects • 360-degree feedback • Community service
Business Leadership	All Ford salaried employees – 100 000	The participants' managers	• Three days' training annually • 100-day team projects • 360-degree feedback • Community service • Exercises contrasting old and new Ford
Executive Partnering	Promising young managers	The leadership team	• Eight weeks shadowing senior executives
Let's Chat about the Business	Everyone who receives e-mail at Ford – about 100 000	CEO	• Weekly e-mails describing Ford's new approach to employees' business
Customer-Driven Six Sigma	1900 full-time employees awarded 'Black Belt' in 2001	The leadership team	• Five days of intensive instruction • 'Learn-by-doing' learning model • Teams assigned multiple problem-solving projects

Sources: Ford Motor Company Annual Report 2000 and 2001 Corporate Citizenship Report, www.ford.com, accessed 14 March 2002; Suzy Wetlaufer (1999) 'Driving Change: An Interview with Ford Motor Company's Jacques Nasser', *Harvard Business Review*, 77(March–April), 76–88.

Table 9.5: Teaching programmes at Ford Motor Co.

'boundarylessness' to describe the means by which people can act without regard to status or functional loyalty and can look for better ideas from anywhere. Top leadership of GE spends considerable time at GE training centres interacting with up-and-comers from all over the company. Each training class is given a real, current company problem to solve and the reports can be career makers (or breakers).

A number of benefits arise from this approach. First, a powerful teachable point of view can reach the entire company within a reasonable period by having students become teachers themselves. At PepsiCo, the CEO passed his teachable point to 110 executives who then passed it to 20 000 people within 18 months. Second, participants in teaching situations are encouraged to maintain the international networks they develop during the sessions. It should be noted that teachers do not necessarily need to be only top managers. When GE launched a massive effort to embrace e-Commerce, many managers found that they knew little about the Internet. Following a London-based manager's idea to have an Internet mentor, GE encourages all managers to have one for a period of time for training each week.[86]

Another method to promote internal co-operation for global strategy implementation is the use of international teams or councils. In the case of a new product or programme an international team of managers may be assembled to develop strategy. Although final direction may come from headquarters, it has been informed of local conditions, and implementation of the strategy is enhanced because local-country managers were involved in its development. The approach has worked even in cases involving seemingly impossible market differences. Both Procter & Gamble and Henkel have successfully introduced pan-European brands, the strategy for which was developed by various European teams. These teams consisted of country managers and staff personnel to make easier eventual problems in strategy implementation and to avoid unnecessarily long and disruptive discussions about the fit of a new product to individual markets.

On a broader and longer-term basis, companies use councils to share **best practice**; for example, an idea that may have saved money or time or a process that is more efficient than existing ones. Most professionals at the leading global companies are members of multiple councils. In some cases, it is important to bring in members of other constituencies (e.g., suppliers, intermediaries and service providers) to such meetings to share their views and experiences and make available their own best practice for benchmarking.

Although technology has made such teamwork possible wherever the individual participants may be, relying only on technology may not bring about the desired results; 'high-tech' approaches inherently mean 'low touch', at the expense of results. Human relationships are still paramount.[87] A common purpose binds team members to a particular task, which can only be achieved through trust through face-to-face meetings. At the start of its 777 project, Boeing brought members of the design team from a dozen different countries to Everett, Washington, USA, and gave them the opportunity to work together for up to 18 months. Beyond learning to function effectively within the company's project management system, they also shared experiences which, in turn, engendered a level of trust between individuals that later enabled them to overcome obstacles raised by physical separation. The result was a design and launch in 40% faster time than with comparable projects.

The term *network* also implies two-way communications between headquarters and subsidiaries and between subsidiaries themselves. This translates into intercultural communication efforts focused on developing relationships.[88] This communication can take the form of newsletters or regular and periodic meetings of appropriate personnel, but new technologies are allowing businesses to link far-flung entities and eliminate the traditional barriers of time and distance.

Intranets integrate a company's information assets into a single accessible system using Internet-based technologies such as e-mail, news groups and the web. In effect, the formation of **virtual teams** becomes a reality. For example, employees at Levi Strauss & Co. can join an electronic discussion group with colleagues around the world, watch the latest Levi's commercials or comment on latest business programmes or plans.[89] 'Let's Chat About the Business' e-mails go out at Ford every Friday at 5 p.m. to about 100 000 employees to share information throughout the company and encourage dialogue. In many companies, the annual videotaped greeting from management has been replaced by regular and frequent e-mails (called e-briefs at GE). The benefits of intranet are: (1) increased productivity in that there is no longer a time lag between an idea and the information needed to assess and implement it; (2) enhanced knowledge capital, which is constantly updated and upgraded; (3) facilitated teamwork enabling online communication at insignificant expense; and (4) incorporation of best practice at a moment's notice by allowing managers and functional-area personnel to make up-to-the-minute decisions anywhere in the world.

As can be seen from the discussion, the networked approach is not a structural adaptation but a procedural one, calling for a change in management mentality. It requires adjustment mainly in the co-ordination and control functions of the firm. And although there is still considerable disagreement as to which of the approaches work, some measures have been shown to correlate with success. Of the many initiatives developed to enhance the workings of a networked global organization, such as cross-border task forces and establishment of centres of excellence, the most significant was the use of electronic networking capabilities.[90]

Further adjustment in organizational approaches is required as businesses face new challenges such as emerging markets, global accounts and the digitization of business.[91] Emerging markets present the company with unique challenges such as product counterfeiters and informal competitors who ignore local labour and tax laws. How these issues are addressed may require organizational rethinking. Colgate-Palmolive, for example, grouped its geographies under two different organizations: one responsible for mature, developed economies and the other for high-growth, emerging markets.[92] Global account managers need to have skills and the empowerment to work across functional areas and borders to deliver quality service to the company's largest clients. Finally, digital business, such as business-to-business and business-to-consumer Internet-based activities, needs to be brought into the mainstay of the businesses' activities and structures, and not seen as a separate activity.

The Role of Country Organizations

Country organizations should be treated as a source of supply as much as a source of demand. Quite often, however, headquarters managers see their role as the co-ordinators of key decisions and controllers of resources, and perceive subsidiaries as implementers and adaptors of global strategy in their respective local markets. Furthermore, they may see all country organizations as the same. This view severely limits use of the firm's resources and deprives country managers of the opportunity to exercise their creativity.[93]

The role that a particular country organization can play naturally depends on that market's overall strategic importance as well as its organizational competence. Using these criteria, four different roles emerge, as shown in Figure 9.16.

The role of a strategic leader can be played by a highly competent national subsidiary located in a strategically critical market. Such a country organization serves as a partner of headquarters in developing and implementing strategy. Procter & Gamble's Eurobrand teams, which analyse opportunities for greater product and marketing programme standardization, are chaired by a brand manager from a 'lead country'. For example, a strategic leader market may have products designed specifically with it in mind. Nissan's Z-cars have always been designated primarily for the US market, starting with the 240Z in the 1970s to the 350Z introduced in 2002.[94] The new model was designed by the company's La Jolla studio, in California.

A contributor is a country organization with a distinctive competence, such as product development. Increasingly, country organizations are the source of new products. For US firms, these range from IBM's recent breakthrough in superconductivity research, generated in its Zurich lab, to

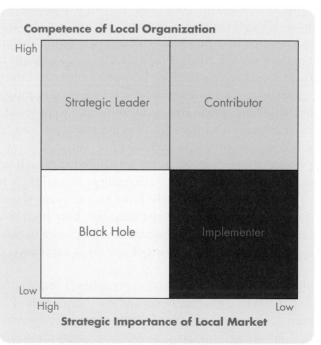

Figure 9.16: Roles for country organizations.

Source: Christopher Bartlett and Sumantra Ghoshal (1986) 'Tap Your Subsidiaries for Global Reach', *Harvard Business Review*, (Boston: Harvard Business School Publishing Division), 64(November–December), 87–94. Reproduced with permission of Harvard Business School Publishing.

low-end innovations such as Procter & Gamble's liquid Tide, made with a fabric-softening compound developed in Europe.[95] A contributor designation may be a function of geography as well. American companies such as Carrier, IBM and Hewlett-Packard use their units in Finland to penetrate the Russian market.[96] For products or technologies with multiple applications, leadership may be divided among different country operations. For example, DuPont delegates responsibility for each different application of Lycra to managers in a country where the application is strongest; that is, Brazil for swimwear and France for fashion. The global brand manager for Lycra ensures that those applications come together in an overall strategy.[97]

Implementers provide the critical mass for the global effort. These country organizations may exist in smaller, less-developed countries in which there is less corporate commitment for market development, and they exist mostly for sales purposes. Although most entities are given this role, it should not be slighted because the implementers provide the opportunity to capture economies of scale and scope that are the basis of a global strategy.

The **black hole** situation is one in which the international company has a low-competence country organization – or no organization at all – in a highly strategic market. A company may be in a black hole situation because it has read the market incorrectly (for example, penetration of the beverage market in Japan may require a local partner) or because government may restrict its activities (for example, foreign banks are restricted in terms of activities and geography in China). If possible, the marketer can use strategic alliances or acquisitions to change its competitive position. Whirlpool established itself in the European Union by acquiring Philips' white goods operation and has used joint ventures to penetrate the Chinese market. If governmental regulations hinder the scale of operations, the firm may use its presence in a major market as an observation post to keep up with developments before a major thrust for entry is executed (for example, with China's WTO membership, the banking sector should start opening up).

Depending on the role of the country organization, its relationship with headquarters will vary from loose control, based mostly on support, to tighter control to ensure that strategies get implemented appropriately. Yet, in each of these cases, it is imperative that country organizations have enough operating independence to cater to local needs and provide motivation to country managers. For example, an implementer's ideas concerning the development of a regional or global strategy or programme should be heard.

Country organization initiative is the principal means by which global companies can tap into new opportunities in markets around the world.[98] For instance, customers' unmet demands in a given market may result not only in the launch of a local product but also subsequently in its roll-out regionally or even globally. This may mean that subsidiaries are allowed to experiment with projects that would not be seen as feasible by headquarters. For example, developing products for small-scale power generation using renewable resources may not generate interest in Honeywell's major markets and subsidiaries but may well be something that one of its developing-country subsidiaries should investigate. In executing global strategies, country-specific buy-in is best secured through involvement of these organizations at the critical points in strategy development. Strategy formulaters should make sure that appropriate implementation can be achieved at the country level.

CONTROLS

The function of the organizational structure is to provide a framework in which objectives can be met. A set of instruments and processes is needed, however, to influence the performance of organizational members so as to meet the goals. Controls focus on the means to verify and correct actions that differ from established plans. Compliance needs to be secured from subordinates through different means of co-ordinating specialized and interdependent parts of the organization.[99] Within an organization, control serves as an integrating mechanism. Controls are designed to reduce uncertainty, increase predictability and ensure that behaviours originating in separate parts of the organization are compatible and in support of common organizational goals despite physical, psychological and temporal distances.

The critical issue here is the same as with organizational structure: What is the ideal amount of control? On the one hand, headquarters needs controls to ensure that international activities contribute the greatest benefit to the overall organization. On the other hand, these controls should not be construed as a code of laws and subsequently allowed to stifle local initiative.

This section will focus on the design and functions of control instruments available for international business operations, along with an assessment of their appropriateness. Emphasis will be placed on the degree of formality of controls used by firms.

Types of Controls

Most organizations display some administrative flexibility, as demonstrated by variations in how they apply management directives, corporate objectives or measurement systems. A distinction should be made, however, between variations that have emerged by design and those that are the result of autonomy. The first are the result of a management decision, whereas typically the second have grown without central direction and are based on emerging practices. In both instances, some type of control will be exercised. Controls that result from headquarters initiative rather than those that are the consequences of tolerated practices will be discussed here. Firms that wait for self-emerging controls often experience rapid international growth but subsequent problems in product-line performance, programme co-ordination and strategic planning.[100]

Whatever the system, it is important in today's competitive environment to have internal benchmarking. This relates to organizational learning and sharing of best practices throughout the corporate system to avoid the costs of reinventing solutions that have already been discovered. A description of the knowledge transfer is provided in the following Focus on e-Business. Three critical features are necessary in sharing best practice. First, there needs to be a device for organizational memory. For example, at Xerox, contributors to solutions can send their ideas to an electronic library where they are indexed and provided to potential adopters in the corporate family. Second, best practice must be updated and adjusted to new situations. For example, best practice adopted by a company's China office will be modified and customized and this learning should then become part of the database. Finally, best practice must be legitimized. This calls for a shared understanding that exchanging knowledge across units is organizationally valued and that these systems are important mechanisms for knowledge exchange. Use can be encouraged by including an assessment in employee performance evaluations of how effectively employees share information with colleagues and use the databases.

FOCUS ON

E-BUSINESS   Knowledge across Boundaries

Spurred by competitive pressures, global knowledge networks allow multinationals to share information and best practices across geographically dispersed units and time zones. Corporations save millions of dollars each year as a result of the up-to-the-minute knowledge transfer and feedback that such networks allow. In addition, the bonds that develop between employees in locations scattered around the globe are instrumental in achieving global objectives. Whether the goal is customer loyalty, increased production efficiency or retention of skilled employees, a knowledge-sharing network focused on improvement of operational practices worldwide helps multinationals meet the challenge of building a cohesive, global, corporate culture.

Ford Motor Company has established 25 'communities of practice' organized around functions. For example, painters in every assembly plant around the world belong to the same community. If local employees find a better way of conducting any of the 60-plus steps involved in painting, a template for that improvement is disseminated to all plants where the process can be replicated. From 1995 to 2000, Ford has discovered a total of 8000 better ways of doing business through its Best Practices Replication Plan, saving more than US$886 million in operating efficiencies.

Eureka, a knowledge-sharing system at Xerox Corp., saves the company between US$25 million and US$125 million a year, depending on how the numbers are tallied. The system connects service technicians around the world who provide information and, more importantly, feedback intended to improve Xerox's electronic product documentation. Eureka has evolved into an easy-access problem-solving database, with more than 30 000 tips submitted by technicians in every country in which Xerox operates. The success of Eureka inspired Xerox to create knowledge-sharing systems to benefit other operational functions. Focus 500 allows the company's top 500 executives to share information on their interactions with customers and industry partners. Project Library details costs, resources and cycle times of more than 2000 projects. It is a vital resource in improving Six Sigma quality in project management. PROFIT allows salespeople to submit hot selling tips – with cash incentives for doing so.

The 2001 merger of energy giants Texaco and Chevron represented an opportunity to integrate global knowledge networks. Active in nearly 180 countries, ChevronTexaco expects to leverage its knowledge systems into millions of dollars in cost savings. The company's information technology-enabled infrastructure allows scientists across the globe to work in virtual teams. More than 50 000 employees share platforms for every business process and communication, allowing real-time interactions among global workforces.

Sources: Louise Lee, 'The Other Instant Powerhouse in Energy Trading', *Business Week*, 26 November 2001; Kristine Ellis (2001), 'Sharing Best Practices Globally', *Training*, July; www.chevrontexaco.com.

In the design of the control systems, a major decision concerns the object of control. Two major objects are typically identified: output and behaviour.[101] Output controls include balance sheets, sales data, production data, product-line growth and performance reviews of personnel. Measures of output are accumulated at regular intervals and forwarded from the foreign locale to headquarters, where they are evaluated and critiqued based on comparisons to the plan or budget. Behavioural controls require the exertion of influence over behaviour after – or, ideally, before – it leads to action. Behavioural controls can be achieved through the preparation of manuals on such topics as sales techniques to be made available to subsidiary personnel or through efforts to fit new employees into the corporate culture.

To institute either of these measures, instruments of control have to be decided upon. The general alternatives are either bureaucratic/formalized control or cultural control. Bureaucratic controls consist of a limited and explicit set of regulations and rules that outline the desired levels of performance. Cultural controls, on the other hand, are much less formal and are the result of shared beliefs and expectations among the members of an organization. Table 9.6 provides a schematic explanation of the types of controls and their objectives.

Bureaucratic/Formalized Control

The elements of a bureaucratic/formalized control system are: (1) an international budget and planning system; (2) the functional reporting system; and (3) policy manuals used to direct functional performance.

The term *budgets* refers to shorter-term guidelines regarding investment, cash and personnel policies, and *plans* refers to formalized plans with more than a one-year horizon. The budget and

| Object of Control | Type of Control | | Characteristics of Control |
	Pure Bureaucratic/ Formalized Control	Pure Cultural Control	
Output	Formal performance reports	Shared norms of performance	HQ sets short-term performance target and requires frequent reports from subsidiaries
Behaviour	Company policies, manuals	Shared philosophy of management	Active participation of HQ in strategy formulation of subsidiaries

Sources: Peter J. Kidger (2001) 'Management Structure in Multinational Enterprises: Responding to Globalisation', *Employee Relations*, August, 69–85; B.R. Baliga and Alfred M. Jaeger (1984) 'Multinational Corporations: Control Systems and Delegation Issues', *Journal of International Business Studies*, 15(Fall), 25–40.

Table 9.6: Comparison of bureaucratic and cultural control mechanisms.

planning process is the major control instrument in headquarters–subsidiary relationships. Although systems and their execution vary, the objective is to achieve as good a fit as possible with the objectives and characteristics of the firm and its environment.

The budgetary period is typically one year, because it is tied to the accounting systems of the multinational. The budget system is used for four main purposes: (1) allocation of funds among subsidiaries; (2) planning and co-ordination of global production capacity and supplies; (3) evaluation of subsidiary performance; and (4) communication and information exchange among subsidiaries, product organizations and corporate headquarters.[102] Long-range plans vary dramatically, ranging from two years to ten years in length and are more qualitative and judgemental in nature. However, shorter periods such as two years are the norm, considering the added uncertainty of diverse foreign environments.

Although firms strive for uniformity, achieving it may be as difficult as trying to design a suit to fit the average person. The processes themselves are much formalized in terms of the schedules to be followed.

Control can also be seen as a mechanism to secure co-operation of local units. For example, although a company may grant substantial autonomy to a country organization in terms of strategies, headquarters may use allocation of production volume as a powerful tool to ensure compliance. Some of the ways for headquarters to gain co-operation of country organizations are summarized in Figure 9.17. Some of the methods used are formal, such as approval of strategic plans and personnel selection, whereas others are more informal, including personal contact and relationships, as well as international networking.[103]

Since the frequency of reports required from subsidiaries is likely to increase due to globalization, it is essential that subsidiaries see the rationale for the often time-consuming exercise. Two approaches, used in tandem, can facilitate the process: participation and feedback. The first refers to avoiding the perception at subsidiary levels that reports are 'art for art's sake' by involving the preparers in the actual use of the reports. When this is not possible, feedback about their consequences is warranted. Through this process, communication is enhanced as well.

On the behavioural front, headquarters may want to guide the way in which subsidiaries make decisions and implement agreed-upon strategies. US-based multinationals tend to be far more formalized than their Japanese and European counterparts, with a heavy reliance on manuals for all major functions.[104] The manuals discuss such items as recruitment, training, motivation and dismissal policies. The use of manuals is in direct correlation with the required level of reports from subsidiaries, discussed in the previous section.

Cultural Control

As seen from the country comparisons, most countries (outside the US) place less emphasis on formal controls, because they are viewed as too rigid and too quantitatively oriented. Instead, multinational

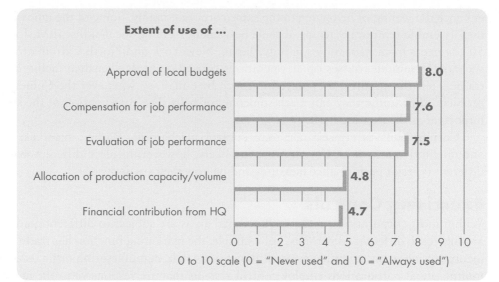

Extent of use of ...

Approval of local budgets	8.0
Compensation for job performance	7.6
Evaluation of job performance	7.5
Allocation of production capacity/volume	4.8
Financial contribution from HQ	4.7

0 1 2 3 4 5 6 7 8 9 10

0 to 10 scale (0 = "Never used" and 10 = "Always used")

Figure 9.17: Securing country–organization co-operation.

Source: Henry P. Conn and George S. Yip (2001) 'Global Transfer of Critical Capabilities', in Michael R. Czinkota and Ilkka A. Ronkainen (eds), *Best Practices in International Business*, South-Western, Mason, OH, 256–274.

corporations emphasize corporate values, and culture and evaluations are based on the extent to which an individual or entity fits in with the norms. Cultural controls require an extensive socialization process to which informal, personal interaction is central. Substantial resources have to be spent to train the individual to share the corporate cultures or 'the way things are done at the company'.[105] To build common vision and values, managers spend a substantial share of their first months at Matsushita in what the company calls 'cultural and spiritual training'. They study the company credo, the 'Seven Spirits of Matsushita', and the philosophy of the founder, Konosuke Matsushita, and learn how to translate the internalized lessons into daily behaviour and operational decisions. Although more prevalent in Japanese organizations, many Western entities have similar programmes, such as Philips's 'organization cohesion training' and Unilever's 'indoctrination'. This corporate acculturation is critical to achieving the acceptance of possible transfers of best practice within the organization.[106]

The primary instruments of cultural control are the careful selection and training of corporate personnel and the institution of self-control. The choice of cultural controls can be justified if the company enjoys a low turnover rate; the controls are thus applied when companies can offer and expect lifetime or long-term employment, as many firms do in Japan.

In selecting home-country nationals and, to some extent, third-country nationals, multinational corporations are exercising cultural control. The assumption is that the managers have already internalized the norms and values of the company and they tend to run a country organization with a more global view. In some cases, the use of headquarters personnel to ensure uniformity in decision making may be advisable; for example, Volvo uses a home-country national for the position of chief financial officer. Expatriates are used in subsidiaries not only for control purposes but also to effect change processes. Companies control the efforts of management specifically through compensation and promotion policies, as well as through policies concerning replacement.

When the expatriate corps is small, headquarters can still exercise its control through other means. Management training programmes for overseas managers as well as time at headquarters will indoctrinate individuals to the company's ways of doing things. Similarly, formal visits by headquarters teams (for example, for a strategy audit) or informal visits (perhaps to launch a new product) will enhance the feeling of belonging to the same corporate family. Some of the innovative global companies assemble temporary teams of their best talent to build local skills. IBM, for example, drafted 50 engineers from its facilities in Italy, Japan, New York and North Carolina to run three-week to six-month training courses on all operations carried on at its Shenzhen facility in China. After the trainers left the country, they stayed in touch by e-mail, so whenever the Chinese managers have a problem, they know they can reach someone for help. The continuation of the support has been as important as the training itself.[107]

Corporations rarely use one pure control mechanism. Rather, most use both quantitative and qualitative measures. Corporations are likely, however, to place different levels of emphasis on different types of performance measures and on how they are derived.

Exercising Controls

Within most corporations, different functional areas are subject to different guidelines because they are subject to different constraints. For example, the marketing function has traditionally been seen as incorporating many more behavioural dimensions than manufacturing or finance. As a result, many multinational corporations employ control systems that are responsive to the needs of the function. Yet such differentiation is sometimes based less on appropriateness than on personalities. It has been hypothesized that manufacturing subsidiaries are controlled more intensively than sales subsidiaries, because production more readily lends itself to centralized direction and technicians and engineers adhere more firmly to standards and regulations than salespeople.[108]

Similarly, the degree of control imposed will vary by subsidiary characteristics, including location. For example, since Malaysia is an emerging economy in which managerial talent is in short supply, headquarters may want to participate more in all facets of decision making. If a country-market witnesses economic or political turmoil, controls may also be tightened to ensure the management of risk.[109]

In their international operations, US-based multinationals place major emphasis on obtaining quantitative data. Although this allows for good centralized comparisons against standards and benchmarks, or cross-comparisons among different corporate units, it entails several drawbacks. In the international environment, new dimensions – such as inflation, differing rates of taxation and exchange rate fluctuations – may distort the performance evaluation of any given individual or organizational unit. For the global corporation, measurement of whether a business unit in a particular country is earning a superior return on investment relative to risk may be irrelevant to the contribution an investment may make worldwide or to the long-term results of the firm. In the short term, the return may even be negative.[110] Therefore, the control mechanism may quite inappropriately indicate reward or punishment.

Standardizing the information received may be difficult if the various environments involved fluctuate and require frequent and major adaptations. Further complicating the issue is the fact that although quantitative information may be collected monthly or at least quarterly, environmental data may be acquired annually or 'now and then', especially when a crisis seems to loom on the horizon. To design a control system that is acceptable not only to headquarters but also to the organization and individuals abroad, great care must be taken to use only relevant data. Major concerns, therefore, are the data collection process and the analysis and use of data. Evaluators need management information systems that provide for greater comparability and equity in administering controls. The more behaviourally based and culture-oriented controls are, the more care needs to be taken.

In designing a control system, management must consider the costs of establishing and maintaining it versus the benefits to be gained. Any control system will require investment in a management structure and in systems design. Consider, for example, costs associated with cultural controls: personal interaction, use of expatriates and training programmes are all quite expensive. Yet these expenses may be justified by cost savings through lower employee turnover, an extensive worldwide information system and an improved control system.[111] Moreover, the impact goes beyond the administrative component. If controls are misguided or too time-consuming, they can slow or undermine the strategy implementation process and thus the overall capability of the firm. The result will be lost opportunities or, worse yet, increased threats. In addition, time spent on reporting takes time from everything else and if the exercise is seen as mundane, it results in lowered motivation. A parsimonious design is therefore imperative. The control system should collect all the information required and trigger all the intervention necessary; however, it should not lead to the pulling of strings by a puppeteer.

The impact of the environment has to be taken into account, as well, in two ways. First, the control system must measure only those dimensions over which the organization has actual control. Rewards or sanctions make little sense if they are based on dimensions that may be relevant to overall corporate performance but over which no influence can be exerted, such as price controls. Neglecting the factor of individual performance capability would send the wrong signals and severely harm motivation. Second, control systems have to be in harmony with local regulations and customs. In some cases, however, corporate behavioural controls have to be exercised against local customs even though overall operations may be affected negatively. This type of situation occurs, for example, when a subsidiary operates in markets in which unauthorized facilitating payments are a common business practice.

Corporations are faced with major challenges in appropriate and adequate control systems in today's business environment. Given increased local government demands for a share in companies established, controls can become tedious, especially if the multinational corporation is a minority partner. Even if the new entity is a result of two companies joining forces through a merger – such as the one between Ciba and Sandoz to create Novartis – or two companies joining forces to form a new entity – such as Siecor established by Siemens AG and Corning Incorporated – the backgrounds of the partners may be different enough to cause problems in devising the required controls.

SUMMARY

Managers need to engage in strategic planning to better adjust to the realities of the new marketplace. Understanding the firm's core strategy (i.e., what business they are really in) starts the process and this assessment may lead to adjustments in what business the company may want to be in. In formulating global strategy for the chosen business, the decision makers have to assess options and make choices about markets and competitive strategy to be used in penetrating them. This may result in the choice of one particular segment across markets or the exploitation of multiple segments in which the company has a competitive advantage. In manipulating and implementing programmes for maximum effect in the chosen markets, the old adage, 'think globally, act locally', becomes a critical guiding principle both as far as customers are concerned and in terms of country organization motivation.

The structures and control mechanisms needed to operate in the international business field are discussed. The elements define relationships between the entities of the firm and provide the channels through which the relationships develop. The fundamental tests of organizational design are whether there is a fit with the company's overall marketing strategy and whether it reflects the strengths of the entities within the organization.[112]

International firms can choose from a variety of organizational structures, ranging from a domestic organization that handles ad hoc export orders to a fully fledged global organization. The choice will depend heavily on the degree of internationalization of the firm, the diversity of international activities and the relative importance of product, area, function and customer variables in the process. A determining factor is also the degree to which headquarters wants to decide important issues concerning the whole corporation and the individual subsidiaries. Organizations that function effectively still need to be revisited periodically to ensure that they remain responsive to a changing environment. Some of the responsiveness is showing up not as structural changes but rather in how the entities conduct their internal business.

In addition to organization, the control function takes on major importance for multinationals, due to the high variability in performance resulting from divergent local environments and the need to reconcile local objectives with the corporate goal of synergism. Although it is important to grant autonomy to country organizations so that they can be responsive to local market needs, it is of equal importance to ensure close co-operation among units to optimize corporate effectiveness.

Control can be exercised through bureaucratic means, which emphasize formal reporting and evaluation of benchmark data, or through cultural means, in which norms and values are understood by the individuals and entities that make up the corporation. US firms typically rely more on bureaucratic controls, whereas multinational corporations from other countries frequently run operations abroad through informal means and rely less on stringent measures.

The implementation of controls requires great sensitivity to behavioural dimensions and the environment. The measurements used must be appropriate and reflective of actual performance rather than marketplace vagaries. Similarly, entities should be judged only on factors over which they have some degree of control.

QUESTIONS FOR DISCUSSION

1. What is the danger in oversimplifying the globalization approach? Would you agree with the statement that 'if something is working in a big way in one market, you better assume it will work in all markets?'
2. What are the critical ways in which globalization and standardization differ?
3. In addition to teenagers as a global segment, are there possibly other groups with similar traits and behaviours that have emerged worldwide?
4. Why is the assessment of internal resources critical as early as possible in developing a global strategic plan?
5. Outline the basic reasons why a company does not necessarily have to be large and have years of experience to succeed in the global marketplace.
6. What are the basic reasons why country operations would not embrace a new regional or global plan (i.e., why the not-invented-here syndrome might emerge)?
7. Firms differ, often substantially, in their organizational structures even within the same industry. What accounts for the differences in their approaches?
8. Discuss the benefits gained by adopting a matrix form of organizational structure.
9. What changes in the firm and/or in the environment might cause a firm to abandon the functional approach?
10. Is there more to the not-invented-here syndrome than simply hurt feelings on the part of those who believe they are being dictated to by headquarters?
11. 'Implementers are the most important country organizations in terms of buy-in for a global strategy'. Comment.
12. How can systems that are built for global knowledge transfer be used as control tools?

INTERNET EXERCISES

1. Using the material available at their web site (www.unilever.com), suggest ways in which Unilever's business groups can take advantage of global and regional strategies due to interconnections in production and marketing.

2. Bestfoods is one of the largest food companies in the world, with operations in more than 60 countries and products sold in 110 countries in the world. Based on the brand information given (http://www.bestfoods.com/about.asp), what benefits does a company derive from having a global presence?

3. Improving internal communications is an objective for networked global organizations. Using the web site of the Lotus Development Corporation (www.lotus.com) and their section on solutions and success stories, outline how companies have used Lotus Notes to help them interactively share information.

4. Using company and product information available on their web sites, determine why Dow (www.dow.com) and Siemens (www.siemens.com) have opted for global product/business structures for their organizations.

TAKE A STAND – STRATEGY

Asian cars, once scorned by European consumers, are now in high demand in Western Europe. Sales of Japanese brands rose 7.4% in 2003, while the overall market shrank by 2.2%. Recent steady gains have helped boost Japanese market share to 12.4%. Korean makers, such as Hyundai, have been able to gain a foothold and have a 1.7% share. By contrast, every European maker (except for Citroën) lost ground in 2003.

During the 1990s, Japanese carmakers' top priority was winning in the US market. In Europe, they maintained low-key operations and invested little. Market share hovered around 10% for a decade. Now, boosted by their success in the United States (where they have a 29.1% market share), they are ready to repeat their success in Europe, the world's most competitive market. All restrictions on Japanese auto imports were removed in 2000, giving them free access throughout the countries members of the EEA. (Japan had 'voluntarily restricted' its exports to Europe to 993 000 cars before that.)

The Japanese success is not just based on price. Asian makers are mastering the art of European car allure as well. They are building local design centres and tapping into the best talent pools on the continent: that is, cars with Japanese DNA in line with tastes of European consumers. In addition, they are using technological finesse. Knowing the European preference for diesel engines, Honda's and Nissan's new models all feature diesel engines. In the past five years, Toyota has redesigned its European models' interiors, added manual transmissions, tailored engines and handling to more rigorous driving habits, and boosted sales by 48%.

FOR DISCUSSION

1. Are the Japanese likely to conquer the European market to the same degree as they did in the United States?

2. Should the European Union have continued its restrictions on Japanese car imports to protect its own companies?

TAKE A STAND – ORGANIZATION

A new executive team at Parker Pen were impressed with the overall success many companies had with globalization. Up to that point, Parker Pen's subsidiaries had enjoyed a high degree of autonomy, which, in turn, had resulted in diverse product lines and there were 40 different advertising agencies handling the Parker Pen account worldwide. The new team wanted to streamline and rid the company of replicated efforts. The goal was to have 'one look, one voice', with the entire planning taking place at headquarters.

The idea of selling pens the same way around the world did not sit well with many Parker Pen units. Pens were indeed the same but markets, they believed, were different. France and Italy fancied expensive fountain pens, while northern Europe was a ballpoint market. In some markets, Parker could assume an above-the-fray stance; in others it would have to get into the trenches and compete on price.

Headquarters initially stated that directives were to be used only as starting points and that they allowed for ample local flexibility. The subsidiaries saw it differently and some fought the scheme all the way. Conflict arose, with one of the new executive team members shouting at one of the meetings, 'Yours is not to reason why; yours is to implement'.

FOR DISCUSSION

1. Could this situation have been avoided altogether?
2. What should companies do if headquarters–subsidiary conflicts emerge?

PART 4

INTERNATIONAL BUSINESS OPERATIONS

When a firm enters and establishes itself in international markets, it is important to devise and implement strategies that will help provide a competitively advantageous position. Part 4 focuses on important overarching dimensions such as supply-chain management, as well as on the traditional functional areas of marketing, finance, accounting, taxation and human resource management.

CHAPTER
10

Marketing, Logistics and Supply-Chain Management

- Marketing in International Business Operations
- Target Market Selection
- Marketing Management
- International Logistics Defined
- Supply-Chain Management
- Dimensions of International Logistics
- International Packaging Issues
- International Storage Issues
- Management of International Logistics

LEARNING OBJECTIVES

- To describe how environmental differences generate new challenges for the international marketing manager.
- To compare and contrast the merits of standardization versus localization strategies for country markets.
- To discuss market-specific and global challenges facing the marketing functions: product, price, distribution and promotion.
- To understand the importance of logistics and supply-chain management as crucial tools for competitiveness.
- To learn about materials management and physical distribution.
- To learn why international logistics is more complex than domestic logistics.
- To see how the transportation infrastructure in host countries often dictates the options open to the manager.

BEING A GOOD SPORT GLOBALLY

In any given country, the majority of corporate sponsorship goes to sports. Of the nearly US$25 billion spent worldwide in 2002, two thirds was allocated to sports. Within sports, the two flagship events are the football World Cup and the Olympic Games (both summer and winter). Sponsors want to align themselves with – and create – meaningful sport-related moments for consumers. At the same time, consumers associate sponsors of sporting events with leadership, teamwork, pursuit of excellence, as well as friendship.

Sponsorships have been a cornerstone of the Coca-Cola Company's marketing

© Getty Images. Reproduced with permission.

efforts for 100 years, starting with their use of sports stars such as world champion cyclist Bobby Walthour in ads in 1903. Presently, the company is the world's biggest sports sponsor with total sponsorship-related expenses at $1 billion annually. These activities span different types of sports and various geographies (as shown below).

Coca-Cola spent US$26 million for its sponsorship of the World Cup in 2002, which gave it the right to use the World Cup logo/trademarks, exclusive positioning and branding around the event, as well as premium perimeter advertising positions at every game. Sponsorships include a guarantee that no rival brands can be officially linked to the tournament or use the logo or trademarks. To assure exclusivity, FIFA (football's governing body) bought all key advertising hoarding space around the main stadia for the tournament and this space was offered to the sponsors first. In addition, every main sponsor got 250 tickets for each game of the tournament for promotional purposes or corporate entertainment (of key constituents, such as intermediaries or customers).

Each country organization within Coca-Cola decided which programmes it wanted to use during sponsorship depending on its goals, which are jointly set by local managers and headquarters. For example, in Rio de Janeiro, the company erected huge TV screens on which people could watch the games. Given that Ecuador qualified for the tournament for the first time in its history, this fact was played up in local advertising. In Japan, the company used I-mode phones, in addition to traditional media, to create meaningful and relevant connections with the World Cup.

Naturally, there is always substantial overlap in programmes between markets, with headquarters' 20-person team in charge of the co-ordination effort. One example of this was an online World Cup game that headquarters created in conjunction with Yahoo! and then helped each interested country to localize. Another global programme was Coca-Cola Go! Stadium Art, which allowed consumers and artists to compete to create ads that ran in the various stadia throughout the tournament. The company also joined forces with other sponsors for cross-promotional efforts; for example, with Adidas to give away the Official Match Ball, with McDonald's for consumer promotions and with Toshiba on a cyber-cup tournament.

Although marketers have become far more demanding in terms of their sponsorships, the World Cup is one of the few global events available. Pulling out would mean allowing a competitor to step in (e.g., when Vauxhall left in 1998, Hyundai took its place.)

Although measuring the return on such investment is challenging, Coca-Cola evaluates dimensions such as the number of new corporate customers that sell Coke in their stores, the incremental amount of promotional/display activity and new vending placement. The influence on the brand is the most difficult to establish; World Cup sponsorship has been suggested to have boosted its presence especially in the emerging and developing markets.

Coca-Cola's Sports Sponsorships

- Olympics (since 1928):
  - supports athletes and teams in nearly 200 countries in exchange for exclusive rights in non-alcoholic beverage category through 2008;
  - official soft/sports drink (Coca-Cola, PowerAde);
  - runs marketing programmes in over 130 countries.
- Football:
  - FIFA partner since 1974 – signed landmark eight-year agreement through 2006 to be official soft/ sports drink at Men's World Cup 2002/2006, Women's World Cup 1999/2003, Confederation Cup competitions, under 20/under 17 World Youth Championships;
  - also sponsors Copa America, Asian Football Confederation, over 40 national teams.
- Basketball:
  - signed 100-year agreement in 1998 for Sprite to be official soft drink of NBA/WNBA;
  - advertising in over 200 countries.
- Others:
  - Coca-Cola Classic: official soft drink of National Football League;
  - Surge/PowerAde: official soft drink of National Hockey League;
  - Coca-Cola Classic/PowerAde: official soft drink/sports drink of Rugby World Cup;
  - sponsor of International Paralympics/Special Olympics.

Sources: 'Still Waiting for that Winning Kick, *Business Week*, 21 October 2002, 116–118; 'The Best Global Brands', *Business Week*, 5 August 2002, 92–94; 'World Cup: Sponsors Need to Get in the Game', *Business Week*, 17 June 2002, 52; 'World Cup Marketing', *Advertising Age Global*, March 2002, 17–30; 'Too Many Players on the Field', *Advertising Age*, 10 December 2001, 3.

MARKETING IN INTERNATIONAL BUSINESS OPERATIONS

Marketing is the process of planning and executing the conception, pricing, promotion and distribution of ideas, goods and services to create exchanges that satisfy individual and organizational objectives.[1] The concepts of satisfaction and exchange are at the core of marketing. For an exchange to take place two or more parties have to come together physically or electronically and they must communicate and deliver things of perceived value. Customers should be perceived as information seekers who evaluate marketers' offerings in terms of their own drives and needs. When the offering is consistent with their needs, they tend to choose the good or service; if it is not, another alternative is chosen. A key task of the marketer is to recognize the ever-changing nature of needs and wants. Marketing techniques apply not only to goods but also to ideas and services. Additionally, well over 50% of all marketing activities are business marketing – directed at other businesses, governmental entities and various types of institutions.

The task of the international marketer is to seek new opportunities in the world marketplace and satisfy emerging needs through creative management of the firm's goods, pricing, distribution and promotional policies that have been called the technical universals of marketing.[2] By its very nature, marketing is the most sensitive of business functions to environmental effects and influences.

The analysis of target markets is the first of the international marketer's challenges. Potential and existing markets need to be evaluated and priorities established for each, ranging from rejection to a temporary holding position to entry. Decisions at the level of the overall marketing effort must be made with respect to the selected markets and a plan for future expansion must be formulated. The closer that potential target markets are in terms of their geographical, cultural and economic distance, the more attractive they typically become to the international marketer.

A critical decision in international marketing concerns the degree to which the overall marketing programme should be standardized or localized. The ideal is to standardize as much as possible without compromising the basic task of marketing: satisfying the needs and wants of the target market. Many multinational marketers are adopting globalization strategies that involve the standardization of good ideas, while leaving the implementation to local entities.

The technical side of marketing management is universal but environments require adaptation within all the mix elements. The degree of adaptation will vary by market, good or service marketed and overall company objectives.

TARGET MARKET SELECTION

The process of target market selection involves narrowing down potential country markets to a feasible number of countries and market segments within them. Rather than try to appeal to everyone, firms best use their resources by: (1) identifying potential markets for entry; and (2) expanding selectively over time to those deemed attractive.

Identification and Screening

A four-stage process for screening and analysing foreign markets is presented in Figure 10.1. It begins with very general criteria and ends with product-specific market analyses. The data and the methods needed for decision making change from secondary to primary as the steps are taken in sequence. Although presented here as a screening process for choosing target markets, the process is also applicable to change of entry mode or even divestment.

If markets were similar in their characteristics, the international marketer could enter any one of the potential markets. However, differences among markets exist in three dimensions: physical, psychic and economic.[3] Physical distance is the geographic distance between home and target countries. Psychic or cultural distance refers to differences in language, tradition and customs between two countries. Economic distance translates into the target market's ability to pay. Generally, the greater the overall distance between two countries, the less knowledge the marketer has about the target market.

The four stages in the screening process are: preliminary screening, estimation of market potential, estimation of sales potential and identification of segments.

Preliminary Screening

The preliminary screening process must rely chiefly on secondary data for country-specific factors as well as product- and industry-specific factors. Country-specific factors typically include those that would indicate the market's overall buying power; for example, population, gross national product in total and per capita, total exports and imports and production of cement, electricity and steel.[4] Product-specific factors narrow the analysis to the firm's specific areas of operation. A company such

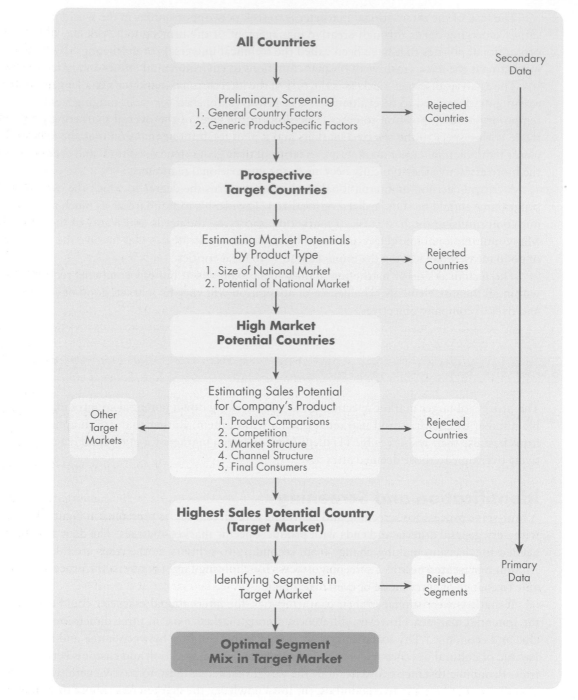

Figure 10.1: The screening process in target market choice.

Source: Adapted from Franklin R. Root (1994) *Entry Strategies from International Markets*, Lexington Books, D.C. Heath and Co., 56. Reproduced with permission of John Wiley & Sons, Inc.

as Motorola, manufacturing for the automotive aftermarket, is interested in the number of passenger cars, trucks and buses in use. The statistical analyses must be accompanied by qualitative assessments of the impact of cultural elements and the overall climate for foreign firms and products. A market that satisfies the levels set becomes a prospective target country.

Estimating Market Potential

Total market potential is the sales, in physical or monetary units, that might be available to all firms in an industry during a given period under a given level of industry marketing effort and given environmental conditions.[5] The international marketer needs to assess the size of existing markets and forecast the size of future markets. A number of techniques, both quantitative and qualitative, are available for this task.

Income elasticity of demand is the relationship between demand and economic progress. The share of income spent on necessities reflects the level of development of the market as well as the money left for other purchases. When consumption per capita of a product category is mapped against GDP/GNP per capita, it reflects a diminishing rate in consumption as income rise.

If the data are available for product-specific analysis, the simplest way to establish a market-size estimate is to conduct a market audit, which adds together local production and imports with exports deducted from the total. However, in many cases, data may not exist, be current or be appropriate. In such cases, market potentials may have to be estimated by methods such as analogy. This approach is based on the use of proxy variables that have been shown to correlate with the demand for the product in question. The market size for a product (such as video games) in country A is estimated by comparing a ratio for an available indicator (e.g., PC ownership) for country A and country B and using this ratio in conjunction with market data available on videogames for country B.

In similar fashion, a country or a group of countries may be used as a proxy for an entire region. For example, Coca-Cola Company launched Georgia, a ready-to-drink coffee brand developed in Japan, in Northern Europe as a test for wider international rollout.[6] The choice was based on the fact that Northern Europe leads the world in per capita consumption of coffee in general.

Despite the valuable insight generated through these techniques, caution should be used in interpreting the results. All the quantitative techniques are based on historical data that may be obsolete or inapplicable because of differences in cultural and geographic traits of the market. Further, with today's technological developments, lags between markets are no longer at a level that would make all the measurements valid. Moreover, the measurements look at a market as an aggregate; that is, no regional differences are taken into account.

In addition to these quantitative techniques that rely on secondary data, international marketers can use various survey techniques. They are especially useful when marketing new technologies. A survey of end-user interest and responses may provide a relatively clear picture of the possibilities in a new market. Surveys can also be administered through a web site or through e-mail.[7]

Comparing figures for market potential with actual sales will provide the international marketer with further understanding of his or her firm's chances in the market. If the difference between potential and reality is substantial, the reasons can be evaluated using gap analysis. The differences can be the result of usage, distribution or product line gaps.[8]

Estimating Sales Potential

Even when the international marketer has gained an understanding of markets with the greatest overall promise, the firm's own possibilities in those markets are still not known. Sales potential is the share of the market potential that the firm can reasonably expect to get over the longer term. To arrive at an estimate, the marketer needs to collect product- and market-specific data. The data will have to do with the following:

- competition – strength, likely reaction to entry;
- market – strength of barriers;
- consumers – ability and willingness to buy;
- product – degree of relative advantage, compatibility and complexity;
- channel structure – access to retailers.

Identifying Segments

Within the markets selected, individuals and organizations will vary in their wants, resources, geographical locations, buying attitudes and buying practices. Initially, the firm may cater to one or only a few segments and later expand to others, especially if the product is innovative. Segmentation is indicated when segments are indeed different enough to warrant individualized attention, are large enough for profit potential and can be reached through the methods that the international marketer wants to use.

Once the process is complete for a market or group of markets, the international marketer may begin it again for another one. When growth potential is no longer in market development, the firm may opt for market penetration.

Concentration versus Diversification

Choosing a market expansion policy involves the allocation of effort among various markets. The major alternatives are concentration on a small number of markets or diversification, which is characterized by growth in a relatively large number of markets in the early stages of international market expansion.[9]

Expansion Alternatives

Either concentration or diversification is applicable to market segments or to total markets, depending on the resource commitment the international marketer is willing and able to make. One option is a dual-concentration strategy, in which efforts are focused on a few segments in a limited number of countries. Another is a dual-diversification strategy, in which entry is to most segments in most available markets. The first is a likely strategy for small firms or firms that market specialized products to clearly definable markets, for example, ocean-capable sailing boats. The second is typical for large consumer-oriented companies that have sufficient resources for broad coverage. Market concentration/segment diversification opts for a limited number of markets but for wide coverage within them, putting emphasis on company acceptance. Market diversification/segment concentration usually involves the identification of a segment, possibly worldwide, to which the company can market without major changes in its marketing mix.

Factors Affecting Expansion Strategy

Expansion strategy is determined by the factors relating to market, mix and company that are listed in Table 10.1. In most cases, the factors are interrelated.

Market-Related Factors

These factors are the ones that were influential in determining the attractiveness of the market in the first place. In the choice of expansion strategy, demand for the firm's products is a critical factor. With high and stable growth rates in certain markets, the firm will most likely opt for a concentration strategy. If the demand is strong worldwide, diversification may be attractive. The uniqueness of the firm's offering with respect to competition is also a factor in the expansion strategy. If lead time over competition is considerable, the decision to diversify may not seem urgent.

In many product categories marketers, knowingly or unknowingly, will be affected by spill over effects. Consider, for example, the impact that satellite channels have had on advertising in Europe or Asia, where ads for a product now reach most of the markets. Where geographic (and psychic) distances are short, spill-over is likely and marketers are most likely to diversify.

Government constraints can be a powerful motivator in a firm's expansion. Although government barriers may naturally prevent new market entry, marketers may seek access through using new entry modes, adjusting marketing programmes or getting into a market before entry barriers are erected.

Factor	Diversification	Concentration
Market growth rate	Low	High
Sales stability	Low	High
Sales response function	Concave	S curve
Competitive lead time/response	Short	Long
Spillover effects	High	Low
Need for product adaptation	Low	High
Need for communication adaptation	Low	High
Economies of scale in distribution	Low	High
Extent of constraints	Low	High
Programme control requirements	Low	High

Source: Adapted from Igal Ayal and Jehiel Zif (1979) 'Marketing Expansion Strategies in Multinational Marketing', *Journal of Marketing*, 43(Spring), 89. Reproduced with permission of American Marketing Association in the format Textbook via Copyright Clearance Center

Table 10.1: Factors affecting the choice between concentration and diversification strategies.

Mix-Related Factors

These factors relate to the degree to which marketing mix elements – primarily product, promotion and distribution – can be standardized. The more that standardization is possible, the more diversification is indicated.

Depending on the product, each market will have its own challenges. Whether constraints are apparent (such as tariffs) or hidden (such as tests or standards), they will complicate all the other factors. Nevertheless, regional integration has allowed many marketers to diversify their efforts.

Company-Related Factors

These include the objectives set by the company for its international operations and the policies it adopts in those markets.

The opportunity to take advantage of diversification is available for all types of companies, not only the large ones. For example, Symbol Technologies invented the handheld laser scanner and now dominates the field worldwide. Cisco Systems claims 50% of the world market for gear that connects networks of computers, a field not in existence 10 years ago.[10]

MARKETING MANAGEMENT

After target markets are selected, the next step is the determination of marketing efforts at appropriate levels. A key question in international marketing concerns the extent to which the elements of the marketing mix – product, price, place and distribution – should be standardized. The marketer also faces the specific challenges of adjusting each of the mix elements in the international marketplace.

Standardization versus Adaptation

The international marketer must first decide what modifications in the mix policy are needed or warranted. Three basic alternatives in approaching international markets are available:

- Make no special provisions for the international marketplace but, instead, identify potential target markets and then choose products that can easily be marketed with little or no modification.

Factors encouraging standardization	Factors encouraging adaptation
• Economies in product R&D • Economies of scale in production • Economies in marketing • Control of marketing programmes • 'Shrinking' of the world marketplace	• Differing use conditions • Government and regulatory influences • Differing buyer behaviour patterns • Local initiative and motivation in implementation • Adherence to the marketing concept

Table 10.2: Standardization versus adaptation.

• Adapt to local conditions in each and every target market (the multi-domestic approach).
• Incorporate differences into a regional or global strategy that will allow for local differences in implementation (globalization approach).

In today's environment, standardization usually means cross-national strategies rather than a policy of viewing foreign markets as secondary and therefore not important enough to have products adapted for them. Ideally, the international marketer should think globally and act locally, focusing on neither extreme (full standardization nor full localization). Global thinking requires flexibility in exploiting good ideas and products on a worldwide basis regardless of their origin. Factors that encourage standardization or adaptation are summarized in Table 10.2.

The adaptation decision will also have to be assessed as a function of time and market involvement. The more companies learn about local market characteristics in individual markets, the more they are able to establish similarities and as a result, standardize their approach. This market insight gives them legitimacy with local constituents in developing a common understanding of the extent of standardization versus adaptation.[11]

Factors Affecting Adaptation

Even when marketing programmes are based on highly standardized ideas and strategies, they depend on three sets of variables: (1) the market(s) targeted; (2) the product and its characteristics; and (3) company characteristics, including factors such as resources and policy.

Questions of adaptation have no easy answers. Marketers in many firms rely on decision-support systems to aid in programme adaptation, whereas others consider every situation independently. All goods must, of course, conform to environmental conditions over which the marketer has no control. Further, the international marketer may use adaptation to enhance its competitiveness in the marketplace.

Marketing Mix Policy

Goods or services form the core of the firm's international operations. The factors affecting product adaptation to foreign market conditions are summarized in Figure 10.2. The changes vary from minor ones, such as translation of a user's manual, to major ones, such as a more economical version of the product.

Product Policy

Studies of product adaptation show that the majority of products have to be modified for the international marketplace one way or another. Changes typically affect packaging, measurement units, labelling, product constituents and features, usage instructions and, to a lesser extent, logos and brand names.[12] Product adaptation is often a company's response to government regulations. Some of the requirements may serve no purpose other than a political one (such as protection of domestic industry or response to political pressures). Because of the sovereignty of nations, individual firms must comply but they can influence the situation either by lobbying directly or through industry associations to have the issue raised during trade negotiations.

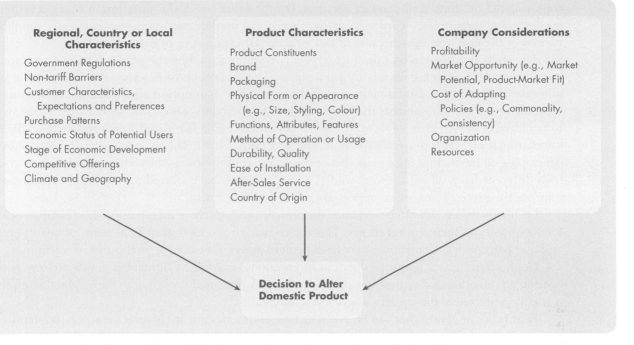

Regional, Country or Local Characteristics

Government Regulations
Non-tariff Barriers
Customer Characteristics,
    Expectations and Preferences
Purchase Patterns
Economic Status of Potential Users
Stage of Economic Development
Competitive Offerings
Climate and Geography

Product Characteristics

Product Constituents
Brand
Packaging
Physical Form or Appearance
    (e.g., Size, Styling, Colour)
Functions, Attributes, Features
Method of Operation or Usage
Durability, Quality
Ease of Installation
After-Sales Service
Country of Origin

Company Considerations

Profitability
Market Opportunity (e.g., Market
    Potential, Product-Market Fit)
Cost of Adapting
    Policies (e.g., Commonality,
    Consistency)
Organization
Resources

Decision to Alter Domestic Product

Figure 10.2: Factors affecting product adaptation decisions.

Source: Adapted from V. Yorio (1983) *Adapting Products for Export*, The Conference Board, New York, 7. Used with permission of The Conference Board.

The member countries of the European Economic Area (EEA) are imposing standards in more than 10 000 product categories ranging from toys to tractor seats. Although US companies such as Murray Manufacturing have had to change their products to comply with the standards (in Murray's case, making its lawnmowers quieter), they will be able to produce one European product in the future. Overall, most producers are forced to improve quality of all their products because some product rules require adoption of an overall system approved by the International Standards Organization (ISO).[13]

Product decisions made by marketers of consumer products are especially affected by local behaviour, tastes, attitudes and traditions – all reflecting the marketer's need to gain the customer's approval. A piece of knowledge of cultural and psychic differences may be the key to success. For example, Brazilians rarely eat breakfast or they eat it at home; therefore, Dunkin' Donuts markets doughnuts as snacks, as dessert and for parties. To further appeal to Brazilians, doughnuts are made with local fruit fillings such as papaya and guava.[14]

Often no concrete product changes are needed, only a change in the product's **positioning**, which is the perception by consumers of the firm's brand in relation to competitors' brands.

Non-tariff barriers include product standards, testing or approval procedures, subsidies for local products and bureaucratic red tape. The non-tariff barriers affecting product adjustments usually concern elements outside the core product. Because non-tariff barriers are usually in place to keep foreign products out or to protect domestic producers, getting around them may be the single toughest problem for the international marketer.

The monitoring of competitors' product features, as well as determining what has to be done to meet and beat them, is critical to product-adaptation decisions. Competitive offerings may provide a baseline against which resources can be measured.

Management must take into account the stage of economic development of the overseas market. As a country's economy advances, buyers are in a better position to buy and to demand more sophisticated products and product versions. On the other hand, the situation in some developing markets may require backward innovation; that is, the market may require a drastically simplified version of the firm's product because of lack of purchasing power or of usage conditions.

The country of origin of a product, typically communicated by the phrase 'made in (country)', has considerable influence on quality perceptions. The perception of products manufactured in certain countries is affected by a built-in positive or negative assumption about quality. One study of machine tool buyers found that the United States and Germany were rated higher than Japan, with Brazil rated below all three of them.[15] These types of findings indicate that steps must be taken by the international marketer to overcome or at least neutralize biases. The issue is especially important to developing countries that need to increase exports and for importers who source products from countries different from where they are sold.[16] Some countries have started promotional campaigns to improve their overall images in support of exports and investment.[17]

Company policy will often determine the presence and degree of adaptation. Most companies aim for consistency in their market efforts. This means that all products must fit in terms of quality, price and user perceptions. Consistency may be difficult to attain, for example, in the area of warranties.

Counterfeiting is a major problem in international markets. Counterfeit goods are any goods bearing an unauthorized representation of a trademark, patented invention or copyrighted work that is legally protected in the country where it is marketed.

Four types of action that can be taken against counterfeiting are legislative action, bilateral and multilateral negotiations, joint private sector action and measures taken by individual firms. Governments have enacted special legislation and set country-specific negotiation objectives for reciprocity and retaliatory options for intellectual property protection.

Pricing Policy

This is the only element in the marketing mix that is revenue generating; all the others are costs. It should therefore be used as an active instrument of strategy in the major areas of marketing decision making. Pricing in the international environment is more complicated than in the domestic market, however, because of such factors as government influence, different currencies and additional costs. International pricing situations can be divided into four general categories: export pricing, foreign market pricing, price co-ordination and intra-company, or transfer, pricing. Three general price-setting strategies in international marketing are a standard worldwide price, dual pricing, which differentiates between domestic and export prices, and market-differentiated pricing.[18]

Standard worldwide pricing is based on average unit costs of fixed, variable and export-related costs. In dual pricing, domestic and export prices are differentiated and two approaches are available: the cost-plus method and the marginal cost method. The cost-plus strategy involves the actual costs; that is, a full allocation of domestic and foreign costs to the product. Although this type of pricing ensures margins, the final price may put the product beyond the reach of the customer. As a result, some exporters resort to flexible cost-plus strategy, wherein discounts are provided when necessary as a result of customer type, intensity of competition or size of order. The marginal cost method considers the direct costs of producing and selling for export as the floor beneath which prices cannot be set. Fixed costs for plants, R&D, domestic overhead and domestic marketing costs are disregarded. An exporter can thus lower export prices to be competitive in markets that otherwise might have been considered beyond access.

On the other hand, market-differentiated pricing is based on a demand-oriented strategy and is thus more consistent with the marketing concept. This method also allows consideration of competitive forces in setting export price. The major problem is the exporter's perennial dilemma: lack of information. Therefore, in most cases, marginal costs provide a basis for competitive comparisons, on which the export price is set.

Price escalation is due to costs incurred in modifying goods for foreign markets, operational costs relating to exporting and costs incurred in entering foreign markets. The combined effect of both clear-cut and hidden costs results in export prices far in excess of domestic prices.

Inexpensive imports often trigger accusations of dumping – that is, selling goods overseas for less than in the exporter's home market, at a price below the cost of production, or both. Dumping ranges from predatory to unintentional. Predatory dumping is the tactic of a foreign firm that intentionally sells at a loss in another country to increase its market share at the expense of domestic producers. This amounts to an international price war. Unintentional dumping is the result of time lags between the date of sales transactions, shipment and arrival. Prices, including exchange rates, can change in such a way that the final sales price is below the cost of production or below the price prevailing in the exporter's home market.

F CUS ON

LOGISTICS   Export Documentation

A firm must deal with numerous forms and documents when exporting to ensure that all goods meet local and foreign laws and regulations.

A **bill of lading** is a contract between the exporter and the carrier indicating that the carrier has accepted responsibility for the goods and will provide transportation in return for payment. The bill of lading can also be used as a receipt and to prove ownership of the merchandise. There are two types of bills: negotiable and non-negotiable. **Straight bills of lading** are non-negotiable and are typically used in prepaid transactions. The goods are delivered to a specific individual or company. **Shipper's order** bills of lading are negotiable; they can be bought, sold or traded while the goods are still in transit and are used for letter of credit transactions. The customer usually needs the original or a copy of the bill of lading as proof of ownership to take possession of the goods.

A *commercial invoice* is a bill for the goods stating basic information about the transaction, including a description of the merchandise, total cost of the goods sold, addresses of the shipper and seller, and delivery and payment terms. The buyer needs the invoice to prove ownership and to arrange payment. Some governments use the commercial invoice to assess customs duties.

Other export documents that may be required include export licences, consular invoices (used to control and identify goods, they are obtained from the country to which the goods are being shipped), certificates of origin, inspection certification, dock and/or warehouse receipts, destination control statements (which serve to notify the carrier and all foreign parties that the item may only be exported to certain destinations), insurance certificates, shipper's export declarations (used to control exports and compile trade statistics) and export packaging lists.

The documentation required depends on the merchandise in the shipment and its destination. The number of documents required can be quite cumbersome and costly, creating a deterrent to trade. For example, before the introduction of document simplification, it was estimated that the border-related red tape and controls within the then-European Community cost European companies €7.3 billion in extra administrative costs and delays annually. To eliminate the barriers posed by all this required documentation, Europe introduced the Single Administrative Document (SAD), which led to the elimination of nearly 200 customs forms required of truck drivers when travelling from one member country to another.

To ensure that all documentation required is accurately completed and to minimize potential problems, firms just entering the international market should consider using freight forwarders, who specialize in handling export documentation. Freight forwarders increasingly choose to differentiate themselves through the development of sophisticated information management systems, particularly with electronic data interchange (EDI).

FOCUS ON

Terms of Shipment and Sale

The responsibilities of the buyer and the seller should be spelled out as they relate to what is and is not included in the price quotation and when ownership of goods passes from seller to buyer. **Incoterms** are the internationally accepted standard definitions for terms of sale set by the International Chamber of Commerce (ICC) since 1936. The Incoterms 2000 went into effect on 1 January 2000, with significant revisions to better reflect changing transportation technologies and the increased use of electronic communications. Although the same terms may be used in domestic transactions, they gain new meaning in the international arena. The terms are grouped into four categories, starting with the term whereby the seller makes the goods available to the buyer only at the seller's own premises (the 'E'-terms), followed by the group whereby the seller is called upon to deliver the goods to a carrier appointed by the buyer (the 'F'-terms). Next are the 'C'-terms, whereby the seller has to contract for carriage but without assuming the risk of loss or damage to the goods or additional costs after the dispatch and finally the 'D'-terms, whereby the seller has to bear all costs and risks to bring the goods to the destination determined by the buyer.

Prices quoted *ex-works* **(EXW)** apply only at the point of origin and the seller agrees to place the goods at the disposal of the buyer at the specified place on the date or within the fixed period. All other charges are for the account of the buyer.

One of the new Incoterms is **free carrier (FCA)**, which replaced a variety of **free on board (FOB)** terms (see below) for all modes of transportation except vessel. FCA (named inland point) applies only at a designated inland shipping point. The seller is responsible for loading goods into the means of transportation; the buyer is responsible for all subsequent expenses. If a port of exportation is named, the costs of transporting the goods to the named port are included in the price.

Free alongside ship (FAS) at a named US port of export means that the exporter quotes a price for the goods, including charges for delivery of the goods alongside a vessel at the port. The seller handles the cost of unloading and wharfage; loading, ocean transportation and insurance are left to the buyer.

Free on board **(FOB)** applies only to vessel shipments. The seller quotes a price covering all expenses up to and including delivery of goods on an overseas vessel provided by or for the buyer.

Under **cost and freight (CFR)** to a named overseas port of import, the seller quotes a price for the goods, including the cost of transportation to the named port of debarkation. The cost of insurance and the choice of insurer are left to the buyer.

With **cost, insurance and freight (CIF)** to a named overseas port of import, the seller quotes a price including insurance, all transportation and miscellaneous charges to the point of debarkation from the vessel. If other than waterway transport is used, the terms are **CPT (carriage paid to)** or **CIP (carriage and insurance paid to)**.

With **delivered duty paid (DDP)**, the seller delivers the goods, with import duties paid, including inland transportation from import point to the buyer's premises. With **delivered duty unpaid (DDU)**, only the destination customs duty and taxes are paid by the consignee. Ex-works signifies the maximum obligation for the buyer; delivered duty paid puts the maximum burden on the seller.

Careful determination and clear understanding of terms used and their acceptance by the parties involved are vital to avoid misunderstandings and disputes. These terms are also powerful competitive tools. The exporter should therefore learn what importers usually prefer in the particular market and what the specific transaction may require. An inexperienced importer may be discouraged by a quote such as 'ex-plant Jessup, Maryland', whereas 'CIF Helsinki' will assure the Finnish importer that many additional costs will only be in the familiar home environment.

When taking control of transportation costs, however, the exporter must know well in advance what impact the additional costs will have on the bottom line. If the approach is implemented incorrectly, exporters can be faced with volatile shipping rates, unexpected import duties and restive customers. Most exporters do not want to go beyond the CIF quotation because of uncontrollables and unknowns in the destination country. Whatever terms are chosen, the programme should be agreed to by the exporter and the buyer(s) rather than imposed solely by the exporter.

Foreign market pricing is the pricing in the individual markets in which the firm operates. It is determined by corporate objectives, costs, customer behaviour and market conditions, market structure and environmental constraints. All of these factors vary from country to country and pricing policies of the multinational corporation must vary as well.

Significant price gaps in various country markets in which a company operates lead to the emergence of grey markets/parallel importation. The term refers to brand-name imports that enter a country legally but outside regular, authorized distribution channels. The proponents of grey marketing argue for their right to 'free trade' by pointing to manufacturers who are both overproducing and overpricing in some markets. The main beneficiaries are consumers, who benefit from lower prices, and discount distributors, who now have access to the good.

Transfer or intra-company pricing is the pricing of sales to members of the corporate family. Four main transfer pricing possibilities have emerged over time: (1) transfer at direct cost; (2) transfer at direct cost plus additional expenses; (3) transfer at a price derived from end-market prices; and (4) transfer at an arm's length price (the price that unrelated parties would have reached on the same transaction). The OECD has issued transfer pricing guidelines including methodology and documentation scenarios to assist in the compliance process.

Distribution Policy

Channels of distribution provide the essential links that connect producers and customers. The channel decision is the longest term of the marketing mix decisions in that it cannot be readily changed. In addition, it involves relinquishing some of the control the firm has over the marketing of its products. The term channel design refers to the length and width of the channel employed. Channel design is determined by factors that can be summarized as *the 11 Cs:* customer, culture, competition, company, character, capital, cost, coverage, control, continuity and communication. Although there are no standard answers to channel design, the international marketer can use the 11 Cs as a checklist to determine the proper approach to reach target audiences before selecting channel members to fill the roles. The first three factors are given, in that the company must adjust its approach to the existing structures. The other eight are controllable to a certain extent by the marketer.

Promotional Policy

The international marketer must choose a proper combination of the various promotional tools – advertising, personal selling, sales promotion and publicity – to create images among the intended target audience. The choice will depend on the target audience, company objectives, the product or service marketed, the resources available for the endeavour and the availability of promotional tools in a particular market. The focus may not only be on a product or service but the company's overall image.

International logistics is concerned with the flow of materials into, through and out of the international corporation and therefore includes materials management as well as physical distribution. The logistician must recognize the total systems demands on the firm, its suppliers and customers in order to develop trade-offs between various logistics components. By taking a supply-chain perspective, the manager can develop logistics systems that are supplier- and customer-focused and highly efficient. Implementation of such a system requires close collaboration between all members of the supply chain.

F⊙CUS ON

Distribution and Supply-Chain Management – Logistics in China

On a midsummer day in Shanghai, a dozen workers load cases of brand-name imported wine onto a small, uncovered and unrefrigerated truck, which will spend hours on poor roads to the central city. Martin Tong, a manager for a computer-peripherals maker, waits impatiently for seven days for computer parts to come from Shanghai to Sichuan, China's most populous province. Stacks of DVD players and cases of Hennessy XO cognac stand idle at Shanghai's loading docks, quickly losing value while waiting for truckers to return from previous deliveries.

To compete globally, China tries to adopt international best practices: firms in the technology, telecommunications, insurance and petroleum industries have rapidly closed the performance gap with their global competitors. Yet, best practices in logistics have yet to proliferate in China. The cost for its inadequate logistical infrastructure is enormous: US$230 billion, or 20% of GDP, is dedicated to logistics each year.

China's transportation-bottleneck costs can easily outweigh its gains from trade, a McKinsey and Co. study asserts. Poor infrastructure, continued restrictions for foreign entrance in logistics and transportation, inefficient freight operators and corruption are only some of the barriers separating multinational companies from the 1.3 billion potential Chinese consumers. Total shipping costs in China are 40–50% more expensive than in the United States. Of 673 Shanghai trucking firms surveyed, 400 are cottage operators with less than two vehicles and only four have fleets of more than 100. In addition, only 20% of China's freight trucks are containerized, leaving most transported merchandise bouncing about in open-back vehicles.

Although 70% of Fortune 500s global firms leverage their competitive advantage by outsourcing to third-party logistics (3PL) providers, China has yet to catch on, with only 2% of its companies employing 3PLs. Outsourcing to 3PLs allows manufacturers to minimize costs and focus on the core competency of creating better products. Since 3PL providers represent many firms, they have greater leverage with freight carriers and can demand lower transportation prices and better service. Moreover, 3PL companies are better equipped and experienced at integrating logistics functions into a firm's existing supply chain.

A major block for foreign 3PL firms planning to enter the Chinese market is the Ministry of Foreign Trade and Economic Co-operation. This government office heavily regulates the logistics industry with complicated approval processes for logistics joint ventures, limitations on required licences and cumbersome and inefficient customs clearance procedures.

With the expected increase in the volume of cargo shipped between China and the rest of the world due to WTO accession, Chinese authorities plan to improve their logistics operations. Spending billions of US dollars to modernize its rail and road systems, China is also updating its Shanghai port, the fifth largest in the world, to perform on the same level as the Hong Kong and Singapore ports. Although enormous potential exists in the Chinese consumer market, logistical challenges sharply limit that potential.

Sources: Ben Dolven, 'The Perils of Delivering the Goods', *Far Eastern Economic Review*, 25 September 2002; Diana Huang and Mark Kadar, 'Third-Party Logistics in China: Still a Tough Market', *Mercer Report on Travel and Transport,* Winter 2003, www.mercermc.com, accessed February 2003; 'Moving Goods in China', McKinsey & Co., February 2002, www.mckinsey.de, accessed February 2003.

International logistics differs from domestic activities in that it deals with greater distances, new variables and greater complexity because of national differences. One major factor to consider is transportation. The international manager needs to understand transportation infrastructures in other countries and modes of transportation such as ocean shipping and air shipping. The choice among these modes will depend on the customer's demands and the firm's transit time, predictability and cost requirements. In addition, non-economic factors such as government regulations weigh heavily in this decision.

Inventory management is another major consideration. Inventories abroad are expensive to maintain yet often crucial for international success. The logistician must evaluate requirements for order cycle times and customer service levels to develop an international inventory policy that can also serve as a strategic management tool.

F CUS ON

LOGISTICS   Ocean Shipping

Ocean shipping is a key mode for international freight movement. Three types of vessels operating in ocean shipping can be distinguished by their service: **liner service, bulk service** and tramp or charter service. Liner service offers regularly scheduled passage on established routes. Bulk service mainly provides contractual services for individual voyages or for prolonged periods of time. **Tramp service** is available for irregular routes and scheduled only on demand.

In addition to the services offered by ocean carriers, the type of cargo a vessel can carry is also important. Most common are conventional (break bulk) cargo vessels, container ships and roll-on/roll-off vessels. Conventional cargo vessels are useful for oversized and unusual cargoes but may be less efficient in their port operations. **Container ships** carry standardized containers that greatly facilitate the loading and unloading of cargo and intermodal transfers. As a result, the time the ship has to spend in port is reduced as are the port charges. **Roll-on/roll-off** (RO-RO) vessels are essentially oceangoing ferries.

Trucks can drive onto built-in ramps and roll off at the destination. Another vessel similar to the RO-RO vessel is the LASH (lighter aboard ship). LASH vessels consist of barges stored on the ship and lowered at the point of destination. The individual barges can then operate on inland waterways, a feature that is particularly useful in shallow water.

The availability of a certain type of vessel, however, does not automatically mean that it can be used. The greatest constraint in international ocean shipping is the lack of ports and port services. For example, modern container ships cannot serve some ports because the local equipment cannot handle the resulting traffic. The problem is often found in developing countries, where local authorities lack the funds to develop facilities. In some instances, governments may purposely limit the development of ports to impede the inflow of imports. Increasingly, however, governments have begun to recognize the importance of an appropriate port facility structure and are developing such facilities in spite of the large investments necessary.

F🔵CUS ON

LOGISTICS Air Shipping

Air shipping is available to and from most countries. This includes the developing world, where it is often a matter of national prestige to operate a national airline. The total volume of **airfreight** in relation to total shipping volume in international business remains quite small. However, 40% of the world's manufactured exports (by value) travel by air. Clearly, high-value items are more likely to be shipped by air, particularly if they have a high **density**, that is, a high weight-to-volume ratio.

Over the years, airlines have made major efforts to increase the volume of airfreight. Many of these activities have concentrated on developing better, more efficient ground facilities, automating air way-bills, introducing airfreight containers, and providing and marketing a wide variety of special services to shippers. In addition, some airfreight companies and ports have specialized and become partners in the international logistics effort.

Changes have also taken place within the aircraft. As an example, 40 years ago, the holds of large propeller aircraft could take only about 10 tonnes of cargo. Today's jumbo jets can load up to 120 metric tonnes of cargo with an available space of 636 cubic meters, and can therefore transport bulky products, such as locomotives. In addition, aircraft manufacturers have responded to industry demands by developing both jumbo cargo planes and combination passenger and cargo aircraft. The latter carry passengers in one section of the main deck and freight in another. These hybrids can be used by carriers on routes that would be uneconomical for passengers or freight alone.

From the shipper's perspective, the products involved must be appropriate for air shipment in terms of their size. In addition, the market situation for any given product must be evaluated. Airfreight may be needed if a product is perishable or if, for other reasons, it requires a short transit time. The level of customer service needs and expectations can also play a decisive role. For example, the shipment of an industrial product that is vital to the ongoing operations of a customer may be much more urgent than the shipment of packaged consumer products.

International packaging is important because it ensures arrival of the merchandise at the ultimate destination in safe condition. In developing packaging, environmental conditions such as climate and handling conditions must be considered.

The logistics manager must also deal with international storage issues and determine where to locate inventories. International warehouse space will have to be leased or purchased and decisions will have to be made about using foreign trade zones.

Implementing the logistics function with an overall supply-chain perspective that is responsive to environmental demands will increasingly be a requirement for successful global competitiveness.

INTERNATIONAL LOGISTICS DEFINED

International logistics is the design and management of a system that controls the forward and reverse flow of materials, services and information into, through and out of the international corporation. It encompasses the total movement concept by covering the entire range of operations concerned with movement, including therefore both exports and imports. By taking a systems approach, the firm explicitly recognizes the links among the traditionally separate logistics components within and outside of a corporation. As a result, the firm can develop just-in-time (JIT) delivery for lower inventory cost, electronic data interchange (EDI) for more efficient order processing and early supplier involvement (ESI) for better planning of goods development and movement. In addition, the use of such a systems approach allows a firm to concentrate on its core competencies and to form outsourcing alliances with other companies. For example, a firm can choose to focus on manufacturing and leave all aspects of order filling and delivery to an outside provider.

Two major phases in the movement of materials are of logistical importance. The first phase is materials management or the timely movement of raw materials, parts and supplies into and through the firm. The second phase is physical distribution, which involves the movement of the firm's finished product to its customers. In both phases, movement is seen within the context of the entire process. Stationary periods (storage and inventory) are therefore included. The basic goal of logistics management is the effective co-ordination of both phases and their various components to result in maximum cost effectiveness while maintaining service goals and requirements.

Key to business logistics are three major concepts, namely, the systems concept, the total cost concept and the trade-off concept. The systems concept is based on the notion that materials-flow activities within and outside of the firm are so extensive and complex that they can be considered only in the context of their interaction. Instead of each corporate function, supplier and customer operating with the goal of individual optimization, the systems concept stipulates that some components may have to work sub-optimally to maximize the benefits of the system as a whole. The systems concept intends to provide the firm, its suppliers and its customers, both domestic and foreign, with the benefits of synergies expected from the co-ordinated application of size. In order for the systems concept to work, information flows and partnership trust are instrumental.

A logical outgrowth of the systems concept is the development of the total cost concept. To evaluate and optimize logistical activities, cost is used as a basis for measurement. The purpose of the total cost concept is to minimize the firm's overall logistics cost by implementing the systems concept appropriately. In the international arena, the total cost concept must also incorporate the consideration of total after-tax profit, by taking the impact of national tax policies on the logistics function into account. The objective is to maximize after-tax profits rather than minimize total cost.

The trade-off concept recognizes the links within logistics systems that result from the interaction of their components. For example, locating a warehouse near the customer may reduce the cost of transportation. However, additional costs are associated with new warehouses. Managers can maximize performance of logistics systems only by formulating decisions based on the recognition and analysis of such trade-offs.

Logistics costs comprise between 10 and 30% of the total landed cost of an international order. Already, international firms have achieved many of the cost reductions that are possible in financing and production and are now using international logistics as a competitive tool. Technological advances and progress in communication systems and information-processing capabilities are particularly significant in the design and management of logistics systems.

SUPPLY-CHAIN MANAGEMENT

The integration of these three concepts has resulted in the new paradigm of supply-chain management, where a series of value-adding activities connects a company's supply side with its demand side. It has been defined by the Ohio State University Global SMC forum as 'the integration of business processes from end user through original suppliers that provide products, services and information that add value for customers'.[19] This approach views the supply chain of the entire extended enterprise, beginning with the supplier's suppliers and ending with consumers or end-users. The perspective

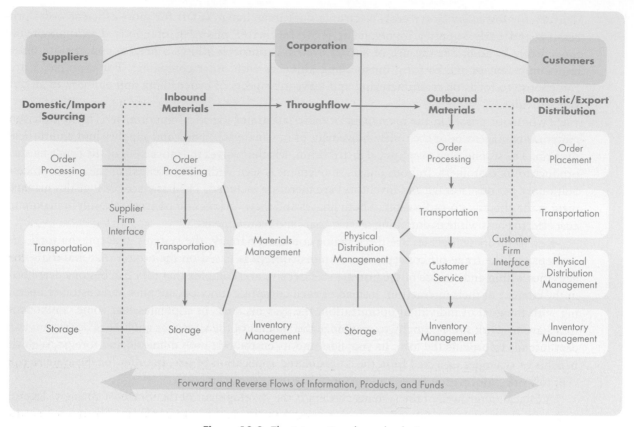

Figure 10.3: The international supply chain.

encompasses the entire flow of funds, products and information that form one cohesive link to acquire, purchase, convert/manufacture, assemble and distribute goods and services to the ultimate consumers.

Export supply-chain management skills facilitate the identification of attractive sources of supply and help firms develop a low-cost competitive supply position in export markets. They also help develop good relationships with suppliers and ensure quality inputs at reasonable prices delivered on a timely basis.[20] For example, Wal-Mart, the largest US retailer, has reduced inventories by 90%. This has saved the company hundreds of millions of dollars in inventory holding costs thus allowing it to offer low prices to its customers.[21] Technological developments have opened up supplier relationships for companies outside of the buyer's domestic market; however, the supplier's capability of providing satisfying goods and services will play the most critical role in securing long-term contracts. An overview of the international supply chain is shown in Figure 10.3.

DIMENSIONS OF INTERNATIONAL LOGISTICS

In domestic operations, logistics decisions are guided by the experience of the manager, possible industry comparisons, an intimate knowledge of trends and discovered heuristics – or general rules. In international business operations the long-term survival of businesses depends on an understanding of the differences inherent in the international logistics field.

International Transportation Issues

Transportation determines how and when goods will be received. The transportation issue can be divided into three components: infrastructure, the availability of modes and the choice of modes among the given alternatives.

In industrialized countries, firms can count on an established infrastructure or transportation network. Around the globe, however, major infrastructural variations will be encountered. Some countries may have excellent inbound and outbound transportation systems but weak internal transportation links. In such instances, shipping to the market may be easy but distribution within the market may represent a very difficult and time-consuming task.

The firm's logistics platform, which is determined by a location's ease and convenience of market reach under favourable cost circumstances, is a key component of a firm's competitive position. Since different countries and regions may offer alternative logistics platforms, the firm must recognize that such alternatives can be the difference between success and failure. The logistics manager must be informed about infrastructure projects abroad and at home and factor them into the firm's strategy. In some countries, for example, railroads may be an excellent transportation mode, far surpassing the performance of trucking, whereas in others the use of railroads for freight distribution may be a gamble at best.

International transportation frequently requires ocean or airfreight modes, which many corporations only rarely use domestically. In addition, combinations such as land bridges or sea bridges may permit the transfer of freight among various modes of transportation, resulting in intermodal movements. The international logistics manager must understand the specific properties of the different modes to be able to use them intelligently.

The international logistics manager must make the appropriate selection from the available modes of transportation. The decision will be heavily influenced by the needs of the firm and its customers. The manager must consider the performance of each mode on four dimensions: transit time, predictability, cost and non-economic factors.

Transit time is the period between departure and arrival of the carrier. It varies significantly between ocean freight and airfreight. For example, the 45-day transit time of an ocean shipment can be reduced to 24 hours if the firm chooses airfreight. A short transit time may reduce or even eliminate the need for an overseas depot. Overall, it has been estimated that each day that goods are in transit adds about 0.8% to the cost of the goods.

Perishable products require shorter transit times. Transporting them rapidly prolongs the shelf life in the foreign market. Air delivery may be the only way to enter foreign markets successfully with products that have a short life span. International sales of cut flowers have reached their current volume only as a result of airfreight.

Predictability is another important factor. As reliability is considered essential but relative, the delay of one day for airfreight tends to be seen as much more severe and 'unreliable' than the same delay for ocean freight. However, delays tend to be shorter in absolute time for air shipments. As a result, arrival time via air is more predictable. This attribute has a major influence on corporate strategy.

An important aspect of predictability is also the capability of a shipper to track goods at any point during the shipment. Tracking becomes particularly important as corporations increasingly obtain products from and send them to multiple locations around the world. Due to rapid advances in information technology, the ability to know where a shipment is has increased dramatically, while the cost of this critical knowledge has declined.

International transportation services are usually priced on the basis of both cost of the service provided and value of the service to the shipper. A logistics manager must decide whether the clearly higher cost of airfreight can be justified. In part, this will depend on the cargo's properties. The physical density and the value of the cargo will affect the decision. As a result, sending diamonds by

Characteristics of Mode	Mode of Transportation				
	Air	Pipeline	Highway	Rail	Water
Speed (1 = fastest)	1	4	2	3	5
Cost (1 = highest)	1	4	2	3	5
Loss and damage (1 = least)	3	1	4	5	2
Frequency[a] (1 = most)	3	1	2	4	5
Dependability (1 = best)	5	1	2	3	4
Capacity[b] (1 = best)	4	5	3	2	1
Availability (1 = best)	3	5	1	2	4

Source: Ronald H. Ballou (1998) *Business Logistics Management*, 4th edn, Prentice Hall, Upper Saddle River, NJ, 146
[a]Frequency: number of times mode is available during a given time period.
[b]Capacity: ability of mode to handle large or heavy goods.

Table 10.3: Evaluating transportation options.

airfreight is easier to justify than sending coal. Alternatively, a shipper can decide to mix modes of transportation in order to reduce overall cost and time delays.

Most important, however, are the supply-chain considerations of the firm. The manager must determine how important it is for merchandise to arrive on time, which, for example, will be different for standard garments versus high fashion dresses. The effect of transportation cost on price and the need for product availability abroad must also be considered. Simply comparing transportation modes on the basis of price alone is insufficient. The manager must factor in all corporate, supplier and customer activities that are affected by the modal choice and explore the full implications of each alternative. A useful overall comparison of different modes of transportation is provided in Table 10.3.

The transportation sector, nationally and internationally, both benefits and suffers from non-economic factors such as government involvement. For example, governmental pressure is exerted on shippers to use national carriers, even if more economical alternatives exist. Such preferential policies are most often enforced when government cargo is being transported. Restrictions are not limited to developing countries. For example, in the United States, the federal government requires that all travellers on government business use national flag carriers when available.

For balance of payments reasons, international quota systems of transportation have been proposed. The United Nations Conference on Trade and Development (UNCTAD) has recommended that 40% of the traffic between two nations be allocated to vessels of the exporting country, 40% to vessels of the importing country and 20% to third-country vessels. However, stiff international competition among carriers and the price sensitivity of customers frequently render such proposals ineffective, particularly for trade between industrialized countries.

International Inventory Issues

Inventories tie up a major portion of corporate funds. Annual inventory carrying costs (the expense of maintaining inventories) are heavily influenced by the cost of capital and industry-specific conditions. Just-in-time (JIT) inventory policies, which minimize the volume of inventory by making it available only when it is needed, are increasingly required by multinational manufacturers and distributors engaging in supply-chain management.

The purpose of establishing inventory systems – to maintain product movement in the delivery pipeline and to have a cushion to absorb demand fluctuations – is the same for domestic and international operations. The international environment, however, includes unique factors such as currency exchange rates, greater distances and duties.

In deciding the level of inventory to be maintained, the international manager must consider three factors: the order cycle time, desired customer service levels and use of inventories as a strategic tool.

Order cycle time is the total time that passes between the placement of an order and the receipt of the merchandise. Two dimensions are of major importance to inventory management: the length of the total order cycle and its consistency. In international business, the order cycle is frequently longer than in domestic business. It comprises the time involved in order transmission, order filling, packing and preparation for shipment and transportation. Supply-chain driven firms use electronic data interchange (EDI) rather than facsimile, telex, telephone or mail. EDI is the direct transfer of information technology between computers of trading partners.[22] The usual paperwork the partners send each other, such as purchase orders and confirmations, invoices and shipment notices are formatted into standard messages and transmitted via a direct link network or a third-party network. EDI can streamline processing and administration and reduce the costs of exchanging information.

The order-filling time may also increase because lack of familiarity with a foreign market makes the anticipation of new orders more difficult. Packing and shipment preparation require more detailed attention. Finally, of course, transportation time increases with the distances involved. Larger inventories may have to be maintained both domestically and internationally to bridge the time gaps.

Consistency, the second dimension of order cycle time, is also more difficult to maintain in international business. Depending on the choice of transportation mode, delivery times may vary considerably from shipment to shipment. The variation may require the maintenance of larger safety stocks to be able to fill demand in periods when delays occur.

Inventories can be used by the international corporation as a strategic tool in dealing with currency valuation changes or to hedge against inflation. By increasing inventories before an imminent devaluation of a currency instead of holding cash, the corporation may reduce its exposure to devaluation losses. Similarly, in the case of high inflation, large inventories can provide an important inflation hedge. In such circumstances, the international inventory manager must balance the cost of maintaining high levels of inventories with the benefits accruing from hedging against inflation or devaluation. Many countries, for example, charge a property tax on stored goods. If the increase in tax payments outweighs the hedging benefits to the corporation, it would be unwise to increase inventories before devaluation.

INTERNATIONAL PACKAGING ISSUES

Packaging is instrumental in getting the merchandise to the ultimate destination in a safe, maintainable and presentable condition. Packaging that is adequate for domestic shipping may be inadequate for international transportation because the shipment will be subject to the motions of the vessel on which it is carried. Added stress in international shipping also arises from the transfer of goods among different modes of transportation. Figure 10.4 provides examples of some sources of stress in intermodal movement that are most frequently found in international transportation.

The responsibility for appropriate packaging rests with the shipper of goods. The weight of packaging must be considered, particularly when airfreight is used, because the cost of shipping is often based on weight. At the same time, packaging material must be sufficiently strong to permit stacking in international transportation. Another consideration is that, in some countries, duties are assessed according to the gross weight of shipments, which includes the weight of packaging.

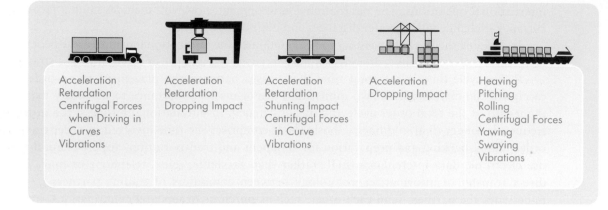

Figure 10.4: Stresses in intermodal movement.

Source: David Greenfield (1980), 'Perfect Packing for Export', *Handling and Shipping Management*, September issue.

One solution to the packaging problem in international logistics has been the development of intermodal containers – large metal boxes that fit on trucks, ships, railroad cars and planes and ease the frequent transfer of goods in international shipments. Developed in different forms for both sea and air transportation, containers also offer better use of carrier space because of standardization of size. The shipper therefore may benefit from lower transportation rates. In addition, containers can offer greater safety from pilferage and damage. Of course, at the same time, the use of containers allows thieves to abscond with an entire shipment rather than just parts of it. On some routes in Russia, for example, theft and pilferage of cargo are so common that liability insurers will not insure container haulers in the region.[23]

Overall, cost attention must be paid to international packaging. The customer who ordered and paid for the merchandise expects it to arrive on time and in good condition. Even with replacements and insurance, the customer will not be satisfied if there are delays. Dissatisfaction will usually translate directly into lost sales.

INTERNATIONAL STORAGE ISSUES

Although international logistics is discussed as a movement or flow of goods, a stationary period is involved when merchandise becomes inventory stored in warehouses. Heated arguments can arise within a firm over the need for and utility of warehousing internationally. On the one hand, customers expect quick responses to orders and rapid delivery. Accommodating the customer's expectations would require locating many distribution centres around the world. On the other hand, warehouse space is expensive. In addition, the larger volume of inventory increases the inventory carrying cost. Fewer warehouses allow for consolidation of transportation and therefore lower transportation rates to the warehouse. However, if the warehouses are located far from customers, the cost of outgoing transportation increases. The international logistician must consider the trade-offs between service and cost to the supply chain in order to determine the appropriate levels of warehousing.

The location decision addresses how many distribution centres to have and where to locate them. The availability of facilities abroad will differ from the domestic situation. Despite the high cost, international storage facilities should be established if they support the overall logistics effort. In many markets, adequate storage facilities are imperative to satisfy customer demands and to compete successfully. For example, since the establishment of a warehouse connotes a visible presence, in doing so a firm can convince local distributors and customers of its commitment to remain in the market for the long term.

Once the decision is made to use storage facilities abroad, the warehouse conditions must be carefully analysed. Proper bar coding of products and the use of package dimensions acceptable to the warehousing system are basic requirements. In contrast, in warehouses still stocked manually, weight limitations will be of major concern.

To optimize the logistics system, the logistician should analyse international product sales and then rank order products according to warehousing needs. Products that are most sensitive to delivery time might be classified as 'A' products. 'A' products would be stocked in all distribution centres and safety stock levels would be kept high. Products for which immediate delivery is not urgent could be classified as 'B' products. They would be stored only at selected distribution centres around the world. Finally, products for which there is little demand would be stocked only at headquarters. Should an urgent need for delivery arise, airfreight could again assure rapid shipment. Classifying products enables the international logistician to substantially reduce total international warehousing requirements and still maintain acceptable service levels.

Special Trade Zones

Areas where foreign goods may be held or processed and then re-exported without incurring duties are called foreign trade zones. The zones can be found at major ports of entry and also at inland locations near major production facilities.

The existence of trade zones can be quite useful to the international firm. For example, in some countries, the benefits derived from lower labour costs may be offset by high duties and tariffs. As a result, location of manufacturing and storage facilities in these countries may prove uneconomical. Foreign trade zones are designed to exclude the impact of duties from the location decision. This is done by exempting merchandise in the foreign trade zone from duty payment. The international firm can therefore import merchandise; store it in the foreign trade zone; and process, alter, test or demonstrate it – all without paying duties. If the merchandise is subsequently shipped abroad (that is, re-exported), no duty payments are ever due. Duty payments become due only if the merchandise is shipped into the country from the foreign trade zone.

All parties to the arrangement benefit from foreign trade zones. The government maintaining the trade zone achieves increased employment and investment. The firm using the trade zone obtains a spearhead in the foreign market without incurring all the costs customarily associated with such an activity. As a result, goods can be reassembled and large shipments can be broken down into smaller units. Also, goods can be repackaged when packaging weight becomes part of the duty assessment. Finally, goods can be given domestic 'made-in' status if assembled in the foreign trade zone. Thus, duties may be payable only on the imported materials and component parts rather than on the labour that is used to finish the product.

Export processing zones usually provide tax- and duty-free treatment for production facilities whose output is destined abroad. The maquiladoras of Mexico are one example of a programme that permits firms to take advantage of sharp differentials in labour costs. Firms can carry out the labour-intensive part of their operations in Mexico, while sourcing raw materials or component parts from other nations.

One country that has used trade zones very successfully for its own economic development is China. Through the creation of special economic zones, in which there are no tariffs, substantial tax incentives and low prices for land and labour, the government has attracted many foreign investors bringing in billions of dollars. The investors have brought new equipment, technology and managerial know-how and have increased local economic prosperity substantially.

For the logistician, the decision whether to use such zones mainly is framed by the overall benefit for the supply-chain system. Clearly, additional transport is required, warehousing facilities need to be constructed and materials handling frequency will increase. However, the costs may well be balanced by the preferential government treatment or by lower labour costs.

MANAGEMENT OF INTERNATIONAL LOGISTICS

The very purpose of a multinational firm is to benefit from system synergism and a persuasive argument can be made for the co-ordination of international logistics at corporate headquarters. Without co-ordination, subsidiaries will tend to optimize their individual efficiency but jeopardize the efficiency of the overall performance of the supply chain.

Centralized Logistics Management

A significant characteristic of the centralized approach to international logistics is the existence of headquarters staff who retain decision-making power over logistics activities affecting international subsidiaries. If headquarters exerts control, it must also take the primary responsibility for its decisions. Clearly, ill will may arise if local managers are appraised and rewarded on the basis of a performance they do not control. This may be particularly problematic if headquarters staff suffer from a lack of information or expertise.

To avoid internal problems, both headquarters staff and local management should report to one person. This person, whether the vice president for international logistics or the president of the firm, can then become the final arbiter to decide the firm's priorities.

Decentralized Logistics Management

When a firm serves many international markets that are diverse in nature, total centralization might leave the firm unresponsive to local adaptation needs. If each subsidiary is made a profit centre in itself, each one carries the full responsibility for its performance, which can lead to greater local management satisfaction and to better adaptation to local market conditions. Yet often such decentralization deprives the logistics function of the benefits of co-ordination. For example, although headquarters, referring to its large volume of overall international shipments, may be able to extract bottom rates from transportation firms, individual subsidiaries by themselves may not have similar bargaining power. The same argument applies also to the sourcing situation, where the co-ordination of shipments by the purchasing firm may be much more cost-effective than individual shipments from many small suppliers around the world.

Once products are within a specific market, however, increased input from local logistics operations should be expected and encouraged. At the very least, local managers should be able to provide input into the logistics decisions generated by headquarters.

Outsourcing Logistics Services

A third option, used by some corporations, is the systematic outsourcing of logistics capabilities. By collaborating with transportation firms, private warehouses or other specialists, corporate resources can be concentrated on the firm's core product.

Many firms whose core competency does not include logistics find it more efficient to use the services of companies specializing in international shipping. This is usually true for smaller shipping volumes, for example in cases when smaller import-export firms or smaller shipments are involved. Such firms prefer to outsource at least some of the international logistics functions, rather than detracting from staff resources and time. Some logistical services providers carve specific niches in the transnational shipping market, specializing for example in consumer goods forwarding. The resulting lower costs and better service make such third parties the preferred choice for many firms.

Going even further, one-stop logistics allows shippers to buy all the transportation modes and functional services from a single carrier, instead of going through the pain of choosing different third parties for each service. One-stop logistics ensures a more efficient global movement of goods via different transportation modes. Specialized companies provide EDI tracking services and take care of customs procedures; they also offer distribution services, such as warehousing and inventory management. Although the cost savings and specialization benefits of such a strategy seem clear, one must also consider the loss of control for the firm, its suppliers and its customers that may result from such outsourcing. Yet, contract logistics does not and should not require the handing over of control. Rather, it offers concentration on one's specialization – a division of labour. The control and responsibility toward the supply chain remain with the firm, even though operations may move to a highly trained outside organization.

SUMMARY

International marketer should look for opportunities in the world marketplace and satisfy new customers needs by applying creative marketing management approaches for the prosperity and competitiveness of the firm. As marketing is the most sensitive of all business functions to environmental effects and influences the challenges for the international marketer are huge. The most significant is the challenge of the analysis of the target market. Decisions at the level of the overall marketing effort must be made with respect to the selected markets and the for future international market expansion

The key decision an international marketer must make is the degree to which the marketing programme should be standardized or localized. The strive for standardization must not compromise the satisfaction of the specific customers needs. The degree of localization will vary across markets and will depend upon a variety of other factors among which environmental specifics and product categories.

As competitiveness becomes increasingly dependent on efficiency, international logistics and supply-chain management increase their importance.

International logistics deals with the materials management as well as physical distribution and is performed in and out of the international corporation. The implementation of such a complex system requires close collaboration among all members of the supply-chain management.

QUESTIONS FOR DISCUSSION

1. If, indeed, the three dimensions of distance are valid, to which countries would UK companies initially expand? Consider the interrelationships of the distance concepts.
2. Is globalization ever a serious possibility or is the regional approach the closest the international marketer can ever hope to get to standardization?
3. What are the possible exporter reactions to extreme foreign exchange rate fluctuations?
4. Argue for and against grey marketing.
5. Explain the key aspects of supply-chain management.
6. Explain the meaning and impact of transit time in international logistics.
7. How can an international firm reduce its order cycle time?
8. What role can the international logistician play in improving the environmental friendliness of the firm?

TAKE A STAND (1)

Ferrari is among the best-known names in high-performance automobiles. Many factors contribute to this, including the fact that only a select number of Ferraris are made annually and the amount sold in the United States, for example, is limited to about 1000. Usually, anyone placing an order would have to wait over two years for delivery of a car that costs between US$200 000 and US$300 000, depending on the model.

As a result of this shortage in supply, some importers and buyers have started importing these cars outside of the authorized channels (known as parallel importation or grey marketing). Due to the differences in government regulations in car features between, for example, the European Union and the United States, the US government requires that these nonconforming cars are reported to the Office of Vehicle Safety Compliance. The importer will have to explain how they will replace foreign parts with US parts and adjust the engineering to conform with US regulations. The bumpers, for example, are thicker in US versions; seat belt warning systems have to be added and speedometers must be adjusted from kilometres to miles. This practice had been going on for years with car manufacturers mostly looking the other way. However, when the high value of the dollar started making vehicle purchases directly from Europe 30–40% cheaper and the volume of these imports shot up, Ferrari felt it had to do something.

In late June 2001, Ferrari asked the US government to halt the importation of Ferrari Modenas and 550 Maranellos until the company had time to prepare its objections to grey-market imports. Ferrari's formal brief released later that summer stated that grey-market imports differed from their authorized (and specially manufactured) US counterparts in 'hundreds' of ways and could not be readily modified to meet US requirements. Ferrari countered criticism of its actions by stating that they were not doing so for business but for safety reasons.

FOR DISCUSSION

1. Should distribution be reserved only for intermediaries authorized by the originator?
2. Why is it that in most cases governments allow grey-market flows to exist? When should they take exception to this practice?

TAKE A STAND (2)

All customers like to choose from a wide variety of products and follow-up service for improvements or when things go wrong. Companies in turn are willing to provide the selection and service, as long as they are making money, directly or indirectly, by growing markets or retaining customers. In most instances, managers who desire to improve specific service levels in any region have to justify the ensuing benefits to the firm. Since the population of developing nations is mostly poor, it is difficult to justify high service levels. Therefore, even if people in these countries can afford to purchase a good, they may not receive the follow-up service that is available in industrialized nations. In other words, they pay more and get less.

FOR DISCUSSION

1. Should logistics cost differentials be determined on a market-by-market basis?
2. Should service delivery be cost-blind in order to delight customers?

CHAPTER

11

Financial Management

- What Is the Goal of Management?
- Import/Export Trade Financing
- Multinational Investing
- International Cash Flow Management
- Foreign Exchange Exposure
- Economic Exposure
- Countertrade

LEARNING OBJECTIVES

- To understand how value is measured and managed across the multiple units of the multinational firm.
- To understand how international business and investment activity alters and adds to the traditional financial management activities of the firm.
- To understand the three primary currency exposures that confront the multinational firm.
- To examine how exchange rate changes alter the value of the firm and how management can manage or hedge these exposures.

THE FINANCIAL CHALLENGES OF SCHERING-PLOUGH

Fred Hassan had something of a reputation for turning troubled companies around. But when he committed to move from Pharmacia to Schering-Plough, taking over as chairman and CEO in April 2003, he most likely was not really ready for what awaited him. Hassan had engineered a solution to Pharmacia's woes by arranging a merger with Monsanto to gain possession of the painkiller Celebrex. But given the problems of Schering-Plough, it may be some time before the company is in any condition to be the object of anyone's eye.

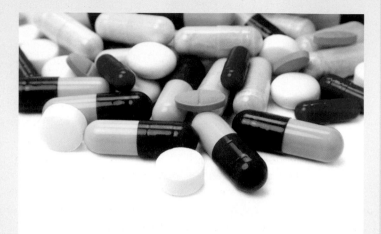

Schering-Plough's major allergy drug, Claritin, lost patent protection in November 2002 and Schering had moved it to the over-the-counter market quickly. Claritin's declines, combined with declining sales of nearly every major product in Schering's portfolio, sent sales and profits reeling in the first quarter of 2003. And it did not stop there. In the second quarter of 2003 Schering agreed to pay US$500 million in fines to the Food and Drug Administration related to what was termed 'sloppy manufacturing' and related problems in 2001 and 2002. And to add insult to injury, in September 2003 the Securities and Exchange Commission fined the company's previous chief executive, Richard Kogan, along with another senior executive, for passing on information about disappointing earnings to some investors privately before making the information public.

In August 2003 Schering-Plough acknowledged that it may not have enough cash in the United States to fund operations for the rest of the year if it maintained both its current spending levels and its dividends to stockholders. Although the company noted that it had significant cash reserves, a large portion of the company's US$3.6 billion in cash resides in overseas accounts. The company noted that it was not anxious to repatriate the cash from overseas, being unwilling to take on the heavy taxes associated with repatriating the money. After an extensive review of the company's failing financial health, in September 2003 Schering-Plough slashed its dividend by 68% (from 17 cents per share per quarter to 5.5 cents) and slated at least 1000 employees to leave under an early retirement programme.

Many of the firm's critics, however, did not see how the firm's actions were in the best interests of anyone. Avoiding tax ordinarily may ultimately benefit stockholders but not if the firm simultaneously slashes their returns in dividends. And the higher costs of early retirement are not a bargain for anyone involved either, except perhaps the retirees themselves.

Sources: Based on 'Schering-Plough Reiterates Warnings About Cash Shortage', *Wall Street Journal*, 13 August 2003; 'Schering-Plough Corp. Cuts Its Dividends 68%', *Wall Street Journal*, 22 August 2003, B5.

INTRODUCTION

What exactly is the leadership of the multinational firm attempting to achieve? Profit maximization – the first words that leap from the lips – is the simplest answer. But as is the case with much of global business, it is not quite that simple. Should leadership be maximizing the profits in the short run, the long run, for stockholders alone, or for all the stakeholders of the multinational organization?

WHAT IS THE GOAL OF MANAGEMENT?

Publicly traded companies seek to maximize shareholder wealth, which is also called *stockholder wealth maximization*. Stockholder wealth maximization dictates that the management of the company should actively seek to maximize the returns to stockholders by working to push share prices up and continually grow the dividends paid out to those same shareholders. This implies in the extreme, however, that management is not seeking to build value or wealth for the other stakeholders in the multinational enterprise: the creditors, management itself, employees, suppliers, communities in which these firms reside and even the government itself. Clearly the modern concept of free market capitalism is a near sole focus on building wealth for stockholders alone and has been frequently interpreted as extremely short-run in focus.

But this is not an accepted universal truth in global business. Continental European and Japanese firms have long pursued a wider definition of wealth maximization – *corporate wealth maximization* – which directs management to consider the financial and social health of all stakeholders, not focused exclusively on the financial returns of the multinational firm alone. This is not to say that the firm is not driven to maximize its profitability but it does direct the firm to consider and balance short-term financial goals against long-term societal goals of continued employment, community citizenship and public welfare needs – an extremely difficult task, at best.

These two different philosophies are not necessarily exclusive. Many firms attempt to find some balance between the two. The stockholder wealth maximization is in many ways much simpler and easier to pursue, having a single objective and in many ways a single client. Although simplistic and sometimes leading to the abuses that have been so widely reported in recent years (Enron, Worldcom and Tyco to name but a few), it has led to the development of the relatively more competitive global business. The Focus on Ethics that follows, highlighting the story of Enron, is but one example of how a lack of ethical balance may lead to ruin.

Although in many ways a kinder and gentler philosophy, corporate wealth maximization has the unenviable charge of attempting to meet the desires of multiple stakeholders. Decision making becomes slower, less decisive and frequently results in organizations that cannot meet the constantly growing pressures of a global marketplace that rewards innovation, speed and lower costs. The concerns of social impacts, environmental responsibility and sustainable development – although sounding good on the public relations releases – impose heavy burdens on organizations trying to compete in a wireless, Internet-based marketplace. The financial objectives of the multinational enterprise should be those that find the unique balance that works for them and their own corporate culture.

Global Financial Goals

The multinational firm, being a conglomeration of many firms operating in a multitude of economic environments, must determine for itself the proper balance between three primary financial objectives:

* maximization of consolidated, after-tax, income;
* minimization of the firm's effective global tax burden;
* correct positioning of the firm's income, cash flows and available funds.

F CUS ON

Stockholder Wealth Maximization and Corporate Culture: The Enron Debacle

Enron may be the classic tale of how the singular pursuit of one philosophy, in the absence of consideration of other interests or beliefs, can lead to ruin.

The company's origins were humble: a simple natural gas pipeline operator that saw considerable growth in the 1980s. As the 1980s drew to a close, however, the company's new management team saw new opportunities to build additional shareholder value in making markets in natural gas using the information that flowed naturally to the firm from its existing operations. The Enron story was the subject of countless business school case studies, news stories and Wall Street admiration.

Although now a global player, building and operating pipelines and power plants all over the world, the firm now found itself creating enormous profits through market-making, primarily in North America.

As the firm hired more and more of the young best and brightest – paying premium salaries and signing bonuses to the new graduates of the best MBA programmes – it built a corporate culture that was singularly focused on profits and greed. Without the healthy balance of wisdom and experience from a time-tested corporate culture, in many ways it became a naive and blind pursuer of stockholder wealth maximization.

By the late 1990s it became increasingly clear to many at the top of Enron that the story itself was losing steam and profits could not be sustained. Many believe that it was the company's own corporate culture, one based on nothing other than earnings-per-share growth, that led to many of the questionable ethical decisions and ultimately to its demise.

These goals are frequently inconsistent. The pursuit of one goal may result in a less desirable outcome in regard to another goal. Management must make decisions about the proper trade-offs between goals about the future (which is why people, and not computers, are employed as managers).

Genus Corporation

A sample firm aids in illustrating how the various components of the multinational firm fit together and how financial management must take decisions regarding trade-offs. Genus Corporation is a US-based manufacturer and distributor of extremity-stimulus medical supplies.[1] The firm's corporate headquarters and original manufacturing plant are in New Orleans, Louisiana.

Genus currently has three wholly owned foreign subsidiaries located in Brazil, Germany and China. In addition to the parent company selling goods in the domestic (US) market and exporting goods to Mexico and Canada, each of the foreign subsidiaries purchases sub-assemblies (transfers) from the parent company. The subsidiaries then add value in the form of specific attributes and requirements for the local-country market and distribute and sell the goods in the local market (Brazil, Germany and China).

The three countries where Genus has incorporated subsidiaries pose very different challenges for the financial management of the firm. These challenges are outlined in Figure 11.1.

Tax Management

Genus, like all firms in all countries, would prefer to pay less tax rather than more. Whereas profits are taxed at relatively low to moderate rates in China and Brazil, Germany's income tax

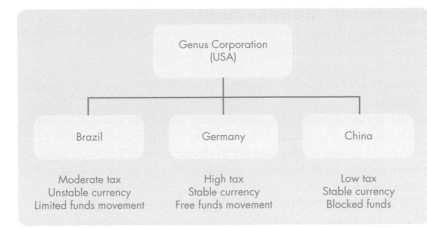

Figure 11.1: Genus corporation and foreign subsidiaries.

rate is relatively high. If Genus could 're-arrange' its profits among its units, it would prefer to make more of its profits in China and Brazil, given the lower tax burden placed on profits in those countries.

Currency Management

Ultimately, for valuation purposes, the most important attribute of any of the three country currencies is its ability to maintain its value versus the US dollar, the reporting currency of the parent company. In 2001, the euro was introduced in most of the EU countries. Although the value of the euro has fluctuated, it is one of the world's primary currencies, a major competitor to the US dollar, and is expected to maintain its value well over time. The Chinese renminbi (or yuan as it is sometimes called) is not freely convertible into other currencies without governmental approval and its value is therefore highly controlled and maintained. The Brazilian real, however, is of particular worry. In previous years the value of the Brazilian currency has been known to fall dramatically, wiping out the value of profits generated in Brazil when converted to any other currency, such as the dollar. As opposed to what tax management would recommend, Genus would prefer to 're-arrange' its profits into Germany and into euros for currency management purposes.

Funds Flow Management

The ability to move funds with relative ease and timeliness in a multinational firm is extremely important. For Genus, the German subsidiary experiences no problems with funds movements, because the German financial system is highly developed and open. Although Brazil possesses a number of bureaucratic requirements for justifying the movement of funds in and out of the country, it is still relatively open for moving funds cross-border. Genus's problems lie in China. The Chinese government makes it nearly impossible for foreign corporations to move funds out of China with any frequency, although bringing capital into China is not a problem. For funds management purposes, Genus would like to 're-arrange' its profits and cash flows to minimize having funds blocked up in China.

The challenge to financial management of the global firm is management's ability to find the right trade-off between these often conflicting goals and risks.

Multinational Management

A number of helpful reminders about multinational companies aid in describing the financial management issues confronting Genus:

- The primary goal of the firm, domestic or multinational, is the maximization of consolidated profits, after tax.
- *Consolidated profits* are the profits of all the individual units of the firm originating in many different currencies as expressed in the currency of the parent company, in this case, the US dollar. Consolidated profits are *not* limited to those earnings that have been brought back to the parent company (repatriated) and in fact these profits may never be removed from the country in which they were earned.
- Each of the incorporated units of the firm (the parent company and the three foreign subsidiaries) has its own set of traditional financial statements: statement of income, balance sheet and statement of cash flows. These financial statements are expressed in the local currency of the unit for tax and reporting purposes to the local government.

Table 11.1 provides an overview of one year's profits before and after tax on both the individual unit level and on the consolidated level, in both local currency and US dollar value.

The owners of Genus, its shareholders, track the firm's financial performance on the basis of its earnings per share (EPS). EPS is simply the consolidated profits of the firm, in the parent currency,

Unit (Currency)	Profit (Local Currency)	Income Tax Rate (%)	Taxes Payable (Local Currency)	Profit After Tax (Local Currency)	Exchange Rate (Currency/US)	Profit (US$)
US parent company (dollar)	4500	35	1575	2925	1.0000	US$2925.00
Brazilian subsidiary (real)	6250	25	1563	4688	2.5000	US$1875.00
German subsidiary (euro)	3000	35	1050	1950	1.1600	US$2262.00
Chinese subsidiary (Rmb)	2500	30	750	1750	8.500	US$205.88
Consolidated						
Profits after tax (000s of US$)						US$7267.88
Shares outstanding (000s)						10 000
Earnings per share (US$)						US$0.73

Notes:
1. Each individual unit of the company maintains its books in local currency as required by host governments.
2. The Brazilian real and Chinese renminbi are expressed as local currency per US dollar. The euro, however, as is common practice, is quoted in US dollars per euro.
3. Each individual unit's profits are translated into US dollars using the average exchange rate for the period (year).
4. US parent company's sales are derived from both sales to unrelated parties in the United States, Mexico (exporting) and Canada (exporting), as well as intra-firm sales (transfers) to the three individual foreign subsidiaries.
5. Tax calculations assume all profits are derived from the active conduct of merchandise trade and all profits are retained in the individual foreign subsidiaries (no dividend distribution from the foreign subsidiary back to the US parent company).

Table 11.1: Genus corporation's consolidated gross profits (in 000s).

divided by the total number of shares outstanding:

$$EPS = \frac{\text{Consolidated profits after tax}}{\text{Shares outstanding}} = \frac{\text{US\$}7,267,880}{10,000,000} = \text{US\$}0.73/\text{share}$$

Each affiliate is located within a country's borders and is therefore subject to all laws and regulations applying to business activities within that country. These laws and regulations include specific practices as they apply to corporate income and tax rates, currency of denomination of operating and financial cash flows, and conditions under which capital and cash flows may move into and out of the country.

Multinational financial management is not a separate set of issues from domestic or traditional financial management but reflects the additional levels of risk and complexity introduced by the conduct of business across borders. Business across borders introduces different laws, different methods, different markets, different interest rates and, most of all, different currencies.

The many dimensions of multinational financial management are most easily explained in the context of a firm's financial decision-making process in evaluating a potential foreign investment. Such an evaluation includes:

- capital budgeting, which is the process of evaluating the financial feasibility of an individual investment, whether it be the purchase of a stock, real estate or a firm;
- capital structure, which is the determination of the relative quantities of debt capital and equity capital that will constitute the funding of the investment;
- working capital and cash flow management, which is the management of operating and financial cash flows passing in and out of a specific investment project.

Multinational financial management means that all the above financial activities will be complicated by the differences in markets, laws and currencies. This is the field of financial risk management. Firms may intentionally borrow foreign currencies, buy forward contracts or price their products in different currencies to manage their cash flows that are denominated in foreign currencies.

Changes in interest and exchange rates will affect each of the above steps in the international investment process. All firms, no matter how 'domestic' they may seem in structure, are influenced by exchange rate changes. The financial managers of a firm that has any dimension of international activity, imports or exports, foreign subsidiaries or affiliates, must pay special attention to these issues if the firm is to succeed in its international endeavours. The discussion begins with the difficulties of simply getting paid for international sales: import/export financing.

IMPORT/EXPORT TRADE FINANCING

Unlike most domestic business, international business often occurs between two parties that do not know each other very well. Yet, in order to conduct business, a large degree of financial trust must exist. This financial trust is basically the trust that the buyer of a product will actually pay for it on or after delivery. For example, if a furniture manufacturer in Gdansk receives an order from a distributor located in Warsaw, the furniture maker will ordinarily fill the order, ship the furniture and await payment. Payment terms are usually 30 to 60 days. This is trade on an 'open account basis'. The furniture manufacturer has placed a considerable amount of financial trust in the buyer but normally is paid with little problem.

Internationally, however, financial trust is pushed to its limit. An order from a foreign buyer may constitute a degree of credit risk (the risk of not being repaid) that the producer (the exporter) cannot

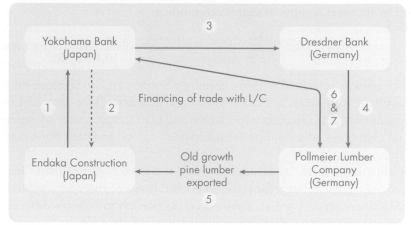

Figure 11.2: Trade financing with a letter of credit.

afford to take. The exporter needs some guarantee that the importer will pay for the goods. Other factors that tend to intensify this problem include the increased lag times necessary for international shipments and the potential risks of payments in different currencies. For this reason, arrangements that provide guarantees for exports are important to countries and companies wanting to expand international sales. This can be accomplished through a sequence of documents surrounding the letter of credit.

Trade Financing Using a Letter of Credit (L/C)

A lumber manufacturer in Germany, Pollmeier, receives a large order from a Japanese construction company, Endaka, for a shipment of beech hardwood lumber. Pollmeier has not worked with Endaka before and therefore seeks some assurance that payment for the lumber will actually be made. Pollmeier ordinarily does not require any assurance of the buyer's ability to pay (sometimes a small down payment or deposit is made as a sign of good faith) but an international sale of this size is too large a risk. If Endaka could not or would not pay, the cost of returning the lumber products to Germany would be prohibitive. Hence, the following sequence of events will complete the transaction (see Figure 11.2);

1. Endaka Construction (JAP) requests a letter of credit (L/C) to be issued by its bank, Yokohama Bank.
2. Yokohama Bank will determine whether Endaka is financially sound and capable of making the payments as required. This is a very important step because Yokohama Bank simply wants to guarantee the payment, not make the payment.
3. Yokohama Bank, once satisfied with Endaka's application, issues the L/C to a representative in Germany or to the exporter's bank, Dresdner Bank. The L/C guarantees payment for the merchandise if the goods are shipped as stipulated in accompanying documents. Customary documents include the commercial invoice, customs clearance and invoice, the packing list, certification of insurance and a bill of lading.
4. The exporter's bank assures Pollmeier that payment will be made after evaluating the letter of credit. At this point the credit standing of Yokohama Bank has been substituted for the credit standing of the importer itself, Endaka Construction.
5. When the lumber order is ready, it is loaded on board the shipper (called a common carrier). When the exporter signs a contract with a shipper, the signed contract serves as the receipt that the common carrier has received the goods and it is termed the bill of lading.

6. Pollmeier draws a *draft* against Yokohama Bank for payment. The draft is the document used in international trade to effect payment and explicitly requests payment for the merchandise, which is now shown to be shipped and insured consistent with all requirements of the previously issued L/C. (If the draft is issued to the bank issuing the L/C, Yokohama Bank, it is termed a bank draft. If the draft is issued against the importer, Endaka Construction, it is a trade draft.) The draft, L/C and other appropriate documents are presented to Dresdner Bank for payment.

7. If Dresdner Bank had *confirmed* the letter of credit from Yokohama Bank, it would immediately pay Pollmeier for the lumber and then collect from the issuing bank, Yokohama. If Dresdner Bank had not confirmed the letter of credit, it only passes the documents to Yokohama Bank for payment (to Pollmeier). The confirmed, as opposed to unconfirmed, letter of credit obviously speeds up payment to the exporter.

Regardless, with the letter of credit as the financial assurance, the exporter or the exporter's bank is collecting payment from the importer's bank, not from the importer itself. It is up to the specific arrangements between the importer (Endaka) and the importer's bank (Yokohama) to arrange the final settlement at that end of the purchase.

If the trade relationship continues over time, both parties will gain faith and confidence in the other. With this strengthening of financial trust, the trade financing relationship will loosen. Sustained buyer–seller relations across borders eventually end up operating on an open account basis similar to domestic commerce.

MULTINATIONAL INVESTING

Any investment, whether it be the purchase of stock, the acquisition of real estate or the construction of a manufacturing facility in another country, is financially justified if the present value of expected cash inflows is greater than the present value of expected cash outflows; in other words, if it has a positive net present value (NPV). The construction of a capital budget is the process of projecting the net operating cash flows of the potential investment to determine if it is indeed a good investment.

Capital Budget Components and Decision Criteria

All capital budgets are only as good as the accuracy of the cost and revenue assumptions. Adequately anticipating all the incremental expenses that the individual project imposes on the firm is critical to a proper analysis.

A capital budget is composed of three primary cash flow components:

* *Initial Expenses and Capital Outlays.* The initial capital outlays are normally the largest net cash outflow occurring over the life of a proposed investment. Because the cash flows occur up front, they have a substantial impact on the net present value of the project.
* *Operating Cash Flows.* The operating cash flows are the net cash flows the project is expected to yield once production is underway. The primary positive net cash flows of the project are realized in this stage; net operating cash flows will determine the success or failure of the proposed investment.
* *Terminal Cash Flows.* The final component of the capital budget is composed of the salvage value or resale value of the project at its end. The terminal value will include whatever working capital balances can be recaptured once the project is no longer in operation (at least by this owner).

The financial decision criterion for an individual investment is whether the net present value of the project is positive or negative.[2] The net cash flows in the future are discounted by the average cost of capital for the firm (the average of debt and equity costs). The purpose of discounting is to capture the fact that the firm has acquired investment capital at a cost (interest). The same capital could have been used for other projects of other investments. It is therefore necessary to discount the future cash flows to account for this foregone income of the capital; its opportunity cost. If NPV is positive, the project is an acceptable investment. If the project's NPV is negative, the cash flows expected to result from the investment are insufficient to provide an acceptable rate of return and the project should be rejected.

A Proposed Project Evaluation

The capital budget for a manufacturing plant in Singapore serves as a basic example. ACME, a US manufacturer of household consumer products, is considering the construction of a plant in Singapore in 2003. It will cost S$1 660 000 to build and will be ready for operation on 1 January 2004. ACME will operate the plant for three years and then sell it to the Singapore government.

To analyse the proposed investment, ACME must estimate what the sales revenues would be per year, the costs of production, the overhead expenses of operating the plant per year, the depreciation allowances for the new plant and equipment, and the Singapore tax rate on corporate income. The estimation of all net operating cash flows is very important to the analysis of the project. Often the entire acceptability of a foreign investment may depend on the sales forecast for the foreign project.

ACME needs US dollars, not Singapore dollars. The only way the stockholders of ACME will be willing to undertake the investment is if it will be profitable in terms of their own currency, the US dollar. This is the primary theoretical distinction between a domestic capital budget and a multinational capital budget. The evaluation of the project in the viewpoint of the parent will focus on whatever cash flows, either operational or financial, will find their way back to the parent firm in US dollars.

ACME must therefore forecast the movement of the Singapore dollar (S$) over the four-year period. The spot rate on 1 January 2003 is S$1.6600/US$. ACME concludes that the rate of inflation will be roughly 5% higher per year in Singapore than in the United States. If the theory of purchasing power parity holds, it should take roughly 5% more Singapore dollars to buy a US dollar per year. Using this assumption, ACME forecasts the exchange rate in the period 2003–2006.

After considerable study and analysis, ACME estimates that the net cash flows of the Singapore project, in Singapore dollars, would be those on line 1 in Table 11.2. Line 2 lists the expected exchange rate between Singapore dollars and US dollars over the four-year period, assuming it takes 5% more Singapore dollars per US dollar each year (thus the Singapore dollar is therefore expected to depreciate versus the US dollar). Combining the net cash flow forecast in Singapore dollars with the

Line #	Description	2003	2004	2005	2006
1	Net cash flow in S$	(1 660 000)	300 000	600 000	1 500 000
2	Exchange rate, S$/US$	1.6600	1.7430	1.8302	1.9217
3	Net cash flow in US$	(1 000 000)	172 117	327 833	780 559
4	Present value factor	1.0000	0.8621	0.7432	0.6407
5	Present value in US$	(1 000 000)	148 377	243 633	500 071
6	Net present value in US$	(107 919)			
7	Net present value in S$	5505			

Notes:
a. The spot exchange rate of S$1.6600/US$ is assumed to change by 5% per year, $1.6600 \times 1.05 = 1.7430$.
b. The present value factor assumes a weighted average cost of capital, the discount rate, of 16%. The present value factor then is found using the standard formula of $1/(1 + 0.16)^t$, where t is the number of years in the future (1, 2 or 3).

Table 11.2: Multinational capital budget: Singapore manufacturing facility.

expected exchange rates, ACME can now calculate the net cash flow per year in US dollars. ACME notes that although the initial expense is sizable, S$1 660 000 or US$1 000 000, the project produces positive net cash flows in its very first year of operations (2004) of US$172 117 and remains positive every year after.

ACME estimates that its cost of capital, both debt and equity combined (the weighted average cost of capital), is about 16% per year. Using this as the rate of discount, the discount factor for each of the future years is found. Finally, the net cash flow in US dollars multiplied by the present value factor yields the present values of each net cash flow. The net present value of the Singapore project is a negative US$107 919; hence, ACME may decide at this stage not to proceed with the project since its evaluation appears to be financially unacceptable.

Risks in International Investments

How is an international investment different from a domestic one? It is riskier, at least from the standpoint of cross-border risk. The higher risk of an international investment arises from the different countries, their laws, regulations, potential for interference with the normal operations of the investment project and obviously currencies, all of which are unique to international investment.

The risk of international investment is considered greater because an international investment will be within the jurisdiction of a different government. Governments have the ability to pass new laws, including the potential nationalization of the entire project. The typical problems that may arise from operating in a different country are changes in foreign tax laws, restrictions placed on when or how much in profits may be repatriated to the parent company and other types of restrictions that hinder the free movement of merchandise and capital among the proposed project, the parent and any other country relevant to its material inputs or sales.

The other major distinction between a domestic investment and a foreign investment is that the viewpoint or perspective of the parent and the project are no longer the same. The two perspectives differ because the parent only values cash flows it derives from the project. So, for example, in Table 11.2 the project generates sufficient net cash flows in Singapore dollars so that the project is acceptable from the project's viewpoint but not from the parent's viewpoint. Assuming the same 16% discount rate, the NPV in Singapore dollars is S$5505, while the NPV to the US parent was a negative US$107 919, as noted previously.

But what if the exchange rate were not to change at all – but remain *fixed* for the 2003–2006 period? The NPV would then be positive from both viewpoints (project NPV remains S$5505, parent's NPV is now US$3316). Or what if the Singapore government were to restrict the payment of dividends back to the parent firm or somehow prohibit the Singapore subsidiary from exchanging Singapore dollars for US dollars (capital controls)? Without cash flows in US dollars, the parent would have no way of justifying the investment. And all of this could occur while the project itself is sufficiently profitable when measured in local currency (Singapore dollars). This split between project and parent viewpoint is a critical difference in international investment analysis.

INTERNATIONAL CASH FLOW MANAGEMENT

Cash management is the financing of short-term or current assets but the term is used here to describe all short-term financing and financial management of the firm. Even a small multinational firm will have a number of different cash flows moving throughout its system at one time. The maintenance of proper liquidity, the monitoring of payments and the acquisition of additional capital when needed all require a great degree of organization and planning in international operations.

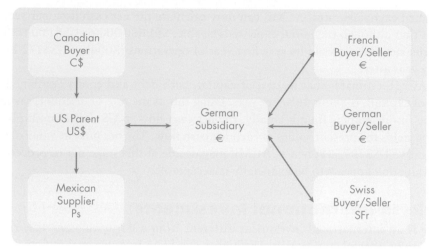

Figure 11.3: Operating and financing cash flows of a multinational firm.

Operating Cash Flows and Financing Cash Flows

Firms possess both operating cash flows and financing cash flows. Operating cash flows arise from the everyday business activities of the firm such as paying for materials or resources (accounts payable) or receiving payments for items sold (accounts receivable). In addition to the direct cost and revenue cash flows from operations, there are a number of indirect cash flows. The indirect cash flows are primarily licence fees paid to the owners of particular technological processes and royalties to the holders of patents of copyrights.

Financing cash flows arise from the funding activities of the firm. The servicing of existing funding sources, interest on existing debt and dividend payments to shareholders constitute potentially large and frequent cash flows. Periodic additions to debt or equity through new bank loans, new bond issuances or supplemental stock sales may also add to the volume of financing cash flows in the multinational firm.

Figure 11.3 provides an overview of how operating and financial cash flows may appear for a US-based multinational firm. In addition to having some export sales in Canada, it may import some materials from Mexico. The firm has gained access to several different European markets by first selling its product to its German subsidiary, which then provides the final touches necessary for sales in Germany, France and Switzerland. Sales and purchases by the parent with Canada and Mexico give rise to a continuing series of accounts receivable and accounts payable, which may be denominated in Canadian dollars, Mexican pesos or US dollars.

Intra-firm Cash Flows and Transfer Prices

Cash flows between the US parent and the German subsidiary will be both operational and financial in nature. The sale of the major product line to the German subsidiary creates intra-firm account receivables and payables. The payments may be denominated in either US dollars or euros. The intra-firm sales may, in fact, be two-way if the German subsidiary is actually producing a form of the product not made in the United States but needed there.

One of the most difficult pricing decisions many multinational firms must make concerns the price at which they sell their products to their own subsidiaries and affiliates. These prices, called transfer prices, theoretically are equivalent to what the same product would cost if purchased on the open market. However, it is often impossible to find such a product on the open market; it may be unique to the firm and its product line. The result is a price that is set internally and may result in the subsidiary being more or less profitable. This, in turn, has impacts on taxes paid in host countries. The following Focus on Politics illustrates what happens when governments and firms do not agree on transfer prices.

FOCUS ON

POLITICS   Swiss Unit Pays Penalty for Transfer Pricing Abuse

Tax authorities believe that Nippon Roche K.K. failed to declare taxable income totalling ¥14 billion between 1992 and 1995, according to sources familiar with the case. The income in question was allegedly transferred to the company's Swiss parent firm, Roche Holding Ltd., through a practice known as transfer pricing, in which a subsidiary pays artificially inflated prices for goods purchased from its overseas parent to cut taxable income in the host country.

The sources said Nippon Roche allegedly manipulated prices of raw materials for cancer drugs and other medicine purchased from F. Hoffman-La Roche Ltd, a drug company under Roche Holding. Nippon Roche could be ordered to pay an additional ¥3.8. billion in taxes for failing to declare ¥4.5 billion in taxable income between 1989 and 1991. Under an agreement with Swiss tax authorities earlier this year, Japanese tax authorities settled on a figure of some ¥5.5 billion 'for the amount of undeclared income transferred to the parent firm to avoid double taxation.

Source: 'Swiss Unit Faces Hefty Penalty for Tax Evasion', *Japan Times*, 10 November 1996.

The foreign subsidiary may also be using techniques, machinery or processes that are owned or patented by the parent firm and so must pay royalties and licence fees. The cash flows are usually calculated as a percentage of the sales price in Germany. Many multinational firms also spread the overhead and management expenses incurred at the parent over their foreign affiliates and subsidiaries that are using the parent's administrative services.

There are also a number of financing cash flows between the US parent and the German subsidiary. If the subsidiary is partially financed by loans extended by the parent, the subsidiary needs to make regular payments to the parent. If the German subsidiary is successful in its operations and generates a profit, dividends will be paid back to the parent. If, at some point, the German subsidiary needs more capital than it can retain from its own profits, it may need additional debt or equity capital. These obviously would add to the potential financial cash flow volume.

The subsidiary, in turn, is dependent on its sales in Germany (euro revenues), France (euro revenues) and Switzerland (Swiss franc revenues) to generate the needed cash flows for paying everyone else. This 'map' of operating and financing cash flows does not even attempt to describe the frequency of the various foreign currency cash flows or to assign the responsibility for managing the currency risks. The management of cash flows in a larger multinational firm, one with possibly 10 or 20 subsidiaries, is obviously complex. The proper management of the cash flows is, however, critical to the success of the multinational business.

Cash Management

The structure of the firm dictates how cash flows and financial resources can be managed. The trend in the past decade has been for the increasing centralization of most financial and treasury operations.

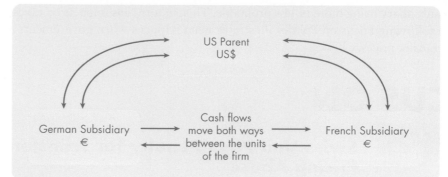

Figure 11.4: Netting and cash pooling of cash flows in the multinational firm.

The centralized treasury is often responsible for both funding operations and cash flow management. The centralized treasury may often enjoy significant economies of scale, offering more services and expertise to the various units of the firm worldwide than the individual units themselves could support. However, regardless of whether the firm follows a centralized or decentralized approach, there are a number of operating structures that help the multinational firm manage its cash flows.

Netting

Figure 11.4 expands our firm to two European subsidiaries, one in Germany and one in France. The figure illustrates how many of the cash flows between units of a multinational firm are two-way and may result in unneeded transfer costs and transaction expenses. Co-ordination between units simply requires planning and budgeting of intra-firm cash flows so that two-way flows are 'netted' against one another, with only one smaller cash flow as opposed to two having to be undertaken.

Netting can occur between each subsidiary and the parent and between the subsidiaries themselves (it is often forgotten that many of the activities in a multinational firm occur between subsidiaries and not just between individual subsidiaries and the parent). Netting is particularly helpful if the two-way flow is in two different currencies, because each would be suffering currency exchange charges for intrafirm transfers.

Cash Pooling

A large firm with a number of units operating both within an individual country and across countries may be able to economize on the amount of firm assets needed in cash if one central pool is used for cash pooling. With one pool of capital and up-to-date information on the cash flows in and out of the various units, the firm spends much less in terms of forgone interest on cash balances, which are held in safekeeping against unforeseen cash flow shortfalls.

For example, for the firm described in Figure 11.4, the parent and German and French subsidiaries may be able to consolidate all cash management and resources in one place – for example, New York (associated with the US parent). One cash manager for all units would be in a better position for planning inter-company payments, including controlling the currency exposures of the individual units. A single large pool also may allow the firm to negotiate better financial service rates with banking institutions for cash-clearing purposes. In the event that the cash manager would need to be closer to the individual units (both proximity and time zone), the two European units could combine to run cash from one or the other for both.

Leads and Lags

The timing of payments between units of a multinational is somewhat flexible. Again, this allows the management of payments between the French and German subsidiaries and between the parent and

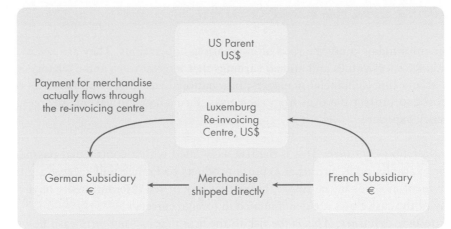

Figure 11.5: Establishing a re-invoicing centre in the multinational firm.

the subsidiaries to be much more flexible, allowing the firm not only to position cash flows where they are needed most but also to help manage currency risk. A foreign subsidiary that is expecting its local currency to fall in value relative to the US dollar may try to speed up or lead its payments to the parent. Similarly, if the local currency is expected to rise versus the dollar, the subsidiary may want to wait or lag payments until exchange rates are more favourable.

Re-Invoicing

Multinational firms with a variety of manufacturing and distribution subsidiaries scattered over a number of countries within a region may often find it more economical to have one office or subsidiary taking ownership of all invoices and payments between units.

For example, Figure 11.5 illustrates how our sample firm could be restructured to incorporate a re-invoicing centre. The site for the re-invoicing centre in this case is Luxembourg, a country that is known to have low taxes and few restrictions on income earned from international business operations. The Luxembourg subsidiary buys from one unit and sells to a second unit, therefore taking ownership of the goods and re-invoicing the sale to the next unit. Once ownership is taken, the sale/purchase can be re-denominated in a different currency, netted against other payments, hedged against specific currency exposures or re-priced in accordance with potential tax benefits of the re-invoicing centre's host country.

Internal Banks

Some multinational firms have found that their financial resources and needs are becoming too large or too sophisticated for the financial services that are available in many of their local subsidiary markets. One solution to this problem has been the establishment of an internal bank within the firm. The internal bank actually buys and sells payables and receivables from the various units, which frees the units of the firm from struggling for continual working capital financing and lets them focus on their primary business activities.

All these structures and management techniques are often combined in different ways to fit the needs of the individual multinational firm. Some techniques are encouraged or prohibited by laws and regulations (for example, many countries limit the ability to lead and lag payments), depending on the host country's government and stage of capital market liberalization. Multinational cash flow management requires flexibility in thinking – artistry in some cases – as much as technique on the part of managers.

FOREIGN EXCHANGE EXPOSURE

Companies today know the risks of international operations. They are aware of the substantial risks to balance sheet values and annual earnings that interest rates and exchange rates may inflict on any firm at any time. Financial managers, international treasurers and financial officers of all kinds are expected to protect the firm from such risks. Firms have, in varying degrees, three types of foreign currency exposure:

* *Transaction exposure.* This is the risk associated with a contractual payment of foreign currency. For example, a UK firm that exports products to France will receive a guaranteed (by contract) payment in euros in the future. Firms that buy or sell internationally have transaction exposure if any of the cash flows are denominated in foreign currency.
* *Economic exposure.* This is the risk to the firm that its long-term cash flows will be affected, positively or negatively, by unexpected future exchange rate changes. Although many firms that consider themselves to be purely domestic may not realize it, all firms have some degree of economic exposure.
* *Translation exposure.* This risk arises from the legal requirement that all firms consolidate their financial statements (balance sheets and income statements) of all worldwide operations annually. Therefore, any firm with operations outside its home country – operations that will be either earning foreign currency or valued in foreign currency – has translation exposure.

Transaction exposure and economic exposure are 'true exposures' in the financial sense. This means that they both present potential threats to the value of a firm's cash flows over time. The third exposure, translation, is a problem that arises from accounting. As illustrated by the following Focus on Culture, hedging the currency risks of a multinational company is a controversial issue for management today.

Transaction Exposure

Transaction exposure is the most commonly observed type of exchange rate risk. Only two conditions are necessary for a transaction exposure to exist: (1) a cash flow that is denominated in a foreign currency; and (2) the cash flow will occur at a future date. Any contract, agreement, purchase or sale that is denominated in a foreign currency that will be settled in the future constitutes a transaction exposure.

The risk of a transaction exposure is that the exchange rate might change between the present date and the settlement date. The change may be for the better or for the worse. For example, suppose that a UK firm signs a contract to purchase heavy rolled-steel pipe from a South Korean steel producer for 21 000 000 Korean won (KRW). The payment is due in 30 days upon delivery. The 30-day account payable, so typical of international trade and commerce, is a transaction exposure for the UK firm. The spot exchange rate on the date the contract is signed is KRW1862.09/GB£1. The UK firm would expect to pay

$$21\,000\,000/1\,862.09 = £11\,278$$

But the firm is not assured of what the exchange rate will be in 30 days. If the spot rate at the end of 30 days is KRW1900.02/GB£1, the UK firm would actually pay less. If, however, the exchange rate changed in the opposite direction, for example to KRW1780/GB£1, the payment could just as easily increase. This type of price risk – transaction exposure – is a major problem for international commerce.

F○CUS ON

To Hedge or Not to Hedge?

If Coca-Cola (nyse: KO-news-people) wanted international business, it sure got it. But now that 75% of its operating profit is generated outside the United States, the company may want to rethink its wish – especially since the strength of the dollar is expected to come back to bite the company's profits. It's concerning indeed: J.P. Morgan analyst John Faucher downgraded the company to market perform and predicted the firm will likely lower fiscal guidance when it announces fourth-quarter earnings at the end of the month. Caroline Levy, an analyst at UBS, also recently lowered earnings-per-share expectations for 2002 and 2003, from US$1.85 and US$2.06 to US$1.80 and US$2.00, respectively.

'I see the stock languishing', Levy says. 'There's not much downside but I don't see any catalysts for upside until there are signs of a global economic recovery'.

The timing couldn't be worse. Almost two years into his reign as Coca-Cola chief executive, Douglas Daft has, by most accounts, made decent progress improving the business. Now some Wall Street analysts accuse Daft of moving too slowly and some wonder how long he'll last in the position. Under Daft's direction, the company entered into an agreement with its bottling company, which had been a troubled relationship that hung over the stock. The company rolled out some new product lines including 'Diet Coke with Lemon'.

If it weren't for the little matter of currency, that might be true. Like most multinationals, Coca-Cola protects itself against foreign currency fluctuations by hedging but the results lately have been mixed. For 1999, the company gained US$87 million on its dealings but for 2000 it lost US$12 million. For 2002, Levy expects exposure to foreign currencies to shave off 5% of annual earnings (cutting earnings-per-share estimates by 5 cents), largely due to the Argentine peso and the South African rand. Further, Levy is concerned that if the Japanese yen remains depressed it could take a further bite out of 2003 earnings.

Source: Betsy Schiffman, 'Still Want to Teach the World to Sing?' 16 January 2002. Reprinted by permission of *Forbes Magazine* © 2004 Forbes, Inc., www.forbes.com

Transaction Exposure Management

Management of transaction exposures is usually accomplished by either natural hedging or contractual hedging. Natural hedging is the term used to describe how a firm might arrange to have foreign currency cash flows coming in and going out at roughly the same times and same amounts. This is referred to as natural hedging because the management or hedging of the exposure is accomplished by matching offsetting foreign currency cash flows and therefore, does not require the firm to undertake unusual financial contracts or activities to manage the exposure. For example, a Canadian firm that generates a significant portion of its total sales in euros may acquire euro debt. The euro earnings from sales could then be used to service the euro debt as needed. In this way, regardless of whether the exchange rate between the euro and the Canadian dollar goes up or down, the firm would be naturally hedged against the movement. If the euro went up in value against the Canadian dollar, the euros needed for debt service would be generated automatically by the export sales to the EU member states that have adopted the euro. Euro inflows would match euro cash outflows.

Contractual hedging is when the firm uses financial contracts to hedge the transaction exposure. The most common foreign currency contractual hedge is the forward contract, although other financial instruments and derivatives, such as currency futures and options are also used. The forward contract would allow the firm to be assured a fixed rate of exchange between the desired two currencies at the precise future date. The forward contract would also be for the exact amount of the exposure.

A hedge is an asset or a position whose value moves in the equal but opposite direction of the exposure. This means that if an exposure experienced a loss in value of €50, the hedge asset would offset the loss with a gain in value of €50. The total value of the position would not change. This would be termed a perfect hedge.

But perfect hedges are hard to find and many people would not use them if they were readily available. Why? The presence of a perfect hedge eliminates all downside risk but also eliminates all upside potential. Many businesses accept this two-sided risk as part of doing business. However, it is generally best to accept risk in the line of business, not in the cash-payment process of settling the business. As illustrated by the Focus on Ethics of Amazon.com, it is indeed possible to reap dramatic foreign currency gains.

F CUS ON

ETHICS The Role of Currency Gains in Amazon.com's Quest for Profits

Jeff Bezos, the CEO of Amazon.com, had promised that Amazon would turn a profit sometime in 2001. Although most analysts and investors did not believe him, he proved them wrong as Amazon .com reported a positive operating profit of US$59 million and a net income of US$5 million for the fourth quarter of 2001. He had indeed delivered on his promise.

One issue primary to all investors, however, is the quality of earnings. Although there are a number of technical components to earnings quality, one of the fundamental questions about reported earnings is whether they are sustainable. Did the earnings arise from operations or from one-time asset sales, investment gains or other nonsustainable transactions? In the case of Amazon.com, there was just one dimension to its quarterly profit return: the US$5 million in net income was, at least in part, the result of a one-time foreign currency gain in the quarter of US$16 million!

Risk Management versus Speculation

The distinction between managing currency cash flows and speculating with currency cash flows is sometimes lost among those responsible for the safekeeping of the firm's treasury. If the previous description of currency hedging is followed closely (the selection of assets or positions only to counteract potential losses on existing exposures), few problems should arise. Problems arise when currency positions or financial instruments are purchased (or sold) with the expectation that a specific currency movement will result in a profit, termed speculation.

There are a number of major multinational firms that treat their international treasury centres as 'service centres' but rarely do they consider financial management a 'profit centre'. One of the most visible examples of what can go wrong when currency speculation is undertaken for corporate profit occurred in Great Britain in 1991. A large UK food conglomerate, Allied-Lyons, suffered losses of £158 million on currency speculation after members of its international treasury staff suffered losses on currency positions at the start of the Persian Gulf War and then doubled-up on their positions in the following weeks in an attempt to recover previous losses. They lost even more.[3]

Currency Risk Sharing

Firms that import and export on a continuing basis have constant transaction exposures. If a firm is interested in maintaining a good business relationship with one of its suppliers, it must work with that supplier to assure it that it will not force all currency risk or exposure off on the other party on a continual basis. Exchange rate movements are inherently random; therefore some type of risk-sharing arrangement may prove useful.

If Ford (US) imports automotive parts from Honda (Japan) every month, year after year, major swings in exchange rates can benefit one party at the expense of the other. One solution would be for Ford and Honda to agree that all purchases by Ford will be made in Japanese yen as long as the spot rate on the payment date is between ¥120/US$ and ¥130/US$. If the exchange rate is between these values on the payment dates, Ford agrees to accept whatever transaction exposure exists (because it is paying in a foreign currency). If, however, the exchange rate falls outside of this range on the payment date, Ford and Honda will 'share' the difference. If the spot rate on settlement date is ¥110/US$, the Japanese yen would have appreciated versus the dollar, causing Ford's costs of purchasing automotive parts to rise. Since this rate falls outside the contractual range, Honda would agree to accept a total payment in Japanese yen that would result from a 'shared' difference of ¥10. Thus, Ford's total payment in Japanese yen would be calculated using an exchange rate of ¥115/US$.

Risk-sharing agreements like these have been in use for nearly 50 years on world markets. They became something of a rarity during the 1950s and 1960s, when exchange rates were relatively stable (under the Bretton Woods Agreement). But with the return to floating exchange rates in the 1970s, firms with long-term customer–supplier relationships across borders returned to some old ways of keeping old friends. And sometimes old ways work very well.

ECONOMIC EXPOSURE

Economic exposure, also called operating exposure, is the change in the value of a firm arising from unexpected changes in exchange rates. Economic exposure emphasizes that there is a limit to a firm's ability to predict cash flows or exchange rate changes in the medium to long term. All firms, either directly or indirectly, have economic exposure.

It is customary to think of only firms that actively trade internationally as having any type of currency exposure. But actually all firms that operate in economies affected by international financial events, such as exchange rate changes, are affected. A barber in Umeå, Sweden, seemingly isolated from exchange rate chaos, is still affected when the Swedish cronor (SEK) rises. If Swedish products become increasingly expensive to foreign buyers, Swedish manufacturers are forced to cut back production and lay off workers and businesses of all types decline – even the business of barbers. The impacts are real and they affect all firms, domestic and international alike.

How exposed is an individual firm in terms of economic exposure? It is impossible to say. Measuring economic exposure is subjective and for the most part it is dependent on the degree of internationalization present in the firm's cost and revenue structure, as well as potential changes over the long run. But simply because it is difficult to measure does not mean that management cannot take some steps to prepare the firm for the unexpected.

Impact of Economic Exposure

The impacts of economic exposure are as diverse as are firms in their international structure. Take the case of a US corporation with a successful UK subsidiary. The subsidiary manufactured and then distributed the firm's products in Great Britain, Germany and France. The profits of the UK subsidiary are paid out annually to the American parent corporation. What would be the impact on the profitability of the UK subsidiary and the entire US firm if the British pound suddenly fell in value against all other major currencies (as it did in September and October 1992)?

If the UK firm had been facing competition in Germany, France and its own home market from firms from those other two continental countries, it would now be more competitive. If the British pound is cheaper, so are the products sold internationally by UK-based firms. The UK subsidiary of the American firm would, in all likelihood, see rising profits from increased sales.

But what of the value of the UK subsidiary to the US parent corporations? The same fall in the British pound that allowed the UK subsidiary to gain profits would also result in substantially fewer US dollars when the British pound earnings are converted to US dollars at the end of the year. It seems that it is nearly impossible to win in this situation. Actually, from the perspective of economic exposure management, the fact that the firm's total value, subsidiary and parent together, is roughly similar as a result of the exchange rate change is desirable. Sound financial management assumes that a firm will profit and bear risk in its line of business, not in the process of settling payments on business already completed.

Economic Exposure Management

Management of economic exposure is being prepared for the unexpected. A firm such as Hewlett-Packard (HP), which is highly dependent on its ability to remain cost competitive in markets both at home (the US) and abroad, may choose to take actions now that would allow it passively to withstand any sudden unexpected rise of the dollar. This could be accomplished through diversification: diversification of operations and diversification of financing.

Diversification of operations would allow the firm to be desensitized to the impacts of any one pair of exchange rate changes. For example, a multinational firm such as Hewlett-Packard may produce the same product in manufacturing facilities in Singapore, the United States, Puerto Rico and Europe. If a sudden and prolonged rise in the dollar made production in the United States prohibitively expensive and uncompetitive, HP is already positioned to shift production to a relatively cheaper currency environment. Although firms rarely diversify production location for the sole purpose of currency diversification, it is a substantial additional benefit from such global expansion.

Diversification of financing serves to hedge economic exposure much in the same way as it did with transaction exposures. A firm with debt denominated in many different currencies is sensitive to many different interest rates. If one country or currency experiences rapidly rising inflation rates and interest rates, a firm with diversified debt will not be subject to the full impact of such movements. Purely domestic firms, however, are actually somewhat captive to the local conditions and are unable to ride out such interest rate storms as easily.

It should be noted that, in both cases, diversification is a passive solution to the exposure problem. This means that without knowing when or where or what the problem may be, the firm that simply spreads its operations and financial structure out over a variety of countries and currencies is prepared.

COUNTERTRADE

General Motors exchanged cars for a trainload of strawberries. Control Data swapped a computer for a package of Polish furniture, Hungarian carpet backing and Russian greeting cards. Uzbekistan, one of the new countries of the former Soviet Union, is offering the crude venom of vipers, toads, scorpions, black widows and tarantulas, as well as growth-controlling substances from snakes and lizards, in countertrade.[4] These are all examples of countertrade activities carried out around the world. As noted in the following Focus on Politics, countertrade is growing in volume as well as in complexity.

F◯CUS ON

The Booming Business of Countertrade

As the global economy continues its downward spiral, many Fortune 500 companies are turning to barter or countertrade arrangements to clear their warehouses of unsold stock, whether it be roller blades, sauerkraut, boxer shorts or corporate jets.

Barter allows companies to become more flexible and quicker in the face of international competition. Rather than selling old inventory for only 20 cents on the dollar in cash, firms can gain 80 cents or more by bartering. Big deals are increasingly found in corporate barter. In fact, in 2001, barter companies traded US$7.9 billion in goods and services worldwide. According to the International Reciprocal Trade Association (IRTA), the global recession will boost that figure by more than 20% in 2002, as companies dump stock surpluses and close-outs.

Barter companies deal in combination of cash and trade credits, which companies can exchange for business services, such as air travel and advertising. The deals have become increasingly complex and geographically dispersed, as the following examples illustrate:

- IBM's Mexico subsidiary exchanged 2600 outmoded computers worth US$1.7 million for US$1 million worth of Volkswagen vehicles, plus US$250 000 in trucking services and a quarter million worth of express-mail shipments.
- A cruise line used a barter company to trade US$1 million worth of empty cabins for US$1 million in trade credits. The cruise company used the credits, along with US$3 million in cash, for a US$4 million advertising campaign.
- A dental-care manufacturer exchanged 200 000 extra toothbrushes packaged in bulk for advertising worth twice the amount of the toothbrushes. A barter company repackaged the toothbrushes to be sold as a travel kit through a regional chain store.
- Volvo Cars of North America sold autos to the Siberian police force when it had no currency for the deal. A barter company accepted oil as payment for the vehicles and used the gains from its sale to provide Volvo with advertising credits equal to the value of the cars.

Sources: 'Juicy Stuff', *The Economist*, 7 February 2002; Paula L. Green, 'The Booming Barter Business', *Journal of Commerce*, 1 April 1997, 1A, 5A.

A Definition of Countertrade

Countertrade is a sale that encompasses more than an exchange of goods, services or ideas for money. In the international market, countertrade transactions 'are those transactions that have as a basic characteristic a linkage, legal or otherwise, between exports and imports of goods or services in addition to or in place of financial settlements'.[5] Historically, countertrade was mainly conducted in the form of *barter*, which is a direct exchange of goods of approximately equal value between parties, with no money involved. Such transactions were the very essence of business at times during which no money – that is, no common medium of exchange – existed or was available. Over time, money emerged as a convenient medium that unlinked transactions from individual parties and their joint timing and therefore permitted greater flexibility in trading activities.

Repeatedly, however, we can see returns to the barter system as a result of environmental circumstances. For example, because of the tight financial constraints of both students and the institution, Georgetown University during its initial years of operation after 1789 charged part of its tuition in foodstuffs and required students to participate in the construction of university buildings. During periods of high inflation in Europe in the 1920s, goods such as bread, meat and gold were seen as much more useful and secure than paper money, which decreased in real value by the minute. In the late 1940s, American cigarettes were an acceptable medium of exchange in most European countries, much more so than any particular currency except for the dollar.

Countertrade transactions have therefore always arisen when economic circumstances made it more acceptable to exchange goods directly rather than to use money as an intermediary. Conditions that encourage such business activities are lack of money, lack of value or faith in money, lack of acceptability of money as an exchange medium or greater ease of transaction by using goods.

Increasingly, countries and companies are deciding that, sometimes, countertrade transactions are more beneficial to them than transactions based on financial exchange alone. One reason is that the world debt crisis has made ordinary trade financing very risky. Many countries, particularly in the developing world, simply cannot obtain the trade credit or financial assistance necessary to pay for desired imports. Heavily indebted countries, faced with the possibility of not being able to afford imports at all, hasten to use countertrade to maintain at least some product inflow. However, it should be recognized that countertrade does not reduce commercial risk. Countertrade transactions will therefore be encouraged by stability and economic progress. Research has shown that countertrade appears to increase with a country's creditworthiness, because good credit encourages traders to participate in unconventional trading practices.[6]

The use of countertrade permits the covert reduction of prices and therefore allows the circumvention of price and exchange controls.[7] Particularly in commodity markets with cartel arrangements, such as oil or agriculture, this benefit may be very useful to a producer. For example, by using oil as a countertraded product for industrial equipment, a surreptitious discount (by using a higher price for the acquired products) may expand market share.

Another reason for the increase in countertrade is that many countries are again responding favourably to the notion of bilateralism. Thinking along the lines of 'you scratch my back and I'll scratch yours', they prefer to exchange goods with countries that are their major business partners.

Countertrade is also often viewed by firms and nations alike as an excellent mechanism to gain entry into new markets. When a producer believes that marketing is not its strong suit, the producer often hopes that the party receiving the goods will serve as a new distributor, opening up new international marketing channels and ultimately expanding the original market. For example, countertrade transactions agreed to between the Japanese firm NEC and the government of Egypt have resulted in a major increase of Japanese tourism to Egypt.[8]

Because countertrade is highly sought after in many large markets such as China, the former Eastern bloc countries, as well as South America, engaging in such transactions can provide major growth opportunities for firms. In increasingly competitive world markets, countertrade can be a good way to attract new buyers. By providing countertrade services, the seller is in effect differentiating its product from those of its competitors.[9]

Countertrade also can provide stability for long-term sales. For example, if a firm is tied to a countertrade agreement, it will need to source the product from a particular supplier, whether or not it wants to do so. This stability is often valued very highly because it eliminates, or at least reduces, vast swings in demand and thus allows for better planning. Countertrade, therefore, can serve as a major mechanism to shift risk from the producer to another party. In that sense, one can argue that countertrade offers a substitute for missing forward markets.[10] Finally, under certain conditions, countertrade can ensure the quality of an international transaction. In instances where the seller of technology is paid in output produced by the technology delivered, the seller's revenue depends on the success of the technology transfer and maintenance services in production. Therefore, the seller is more likely to be concerned about providing services, maintenance and general technology transfer.[11]

In spite of all the apparent benefits of countertrade, there are strong economic arguments against the activity. The arguments are based mainly on efficiency grounds. As Samuelson stated, 'Instead of there being a double coincidence of wants, there is likely to be a want of coincidence; so that, unless a hungry tailor happens to find an undraped farmer, who has both food and a desire for a pair of pants, neither can make a trade'.[12] Clearly, countertrade ensures that instead of balances being settled on a multilateral basis, with surpluses from one country being balanced by deficits with another, accounts must now be settled on a country-by-country or even transaction-by-transaction basis. Trade then results only from the ability of two parties or countries to purchase specified goods from one another rather than from competition. As a result, uncompetitive goods may be traded. In consequence, the ability of countries and their industries to adjust structurally to more efficient production may be restricted. Countertrade can therefore be seen as eroding the quality and efficiency of production and as lowering world consumption.

These economic arguments notwithstanding, however, countries and companies increasingly see countertrade as an alternative that may be flawed but worthwhile to undertake, because some trade is preferable to no trade. Both industrialized and developing countries exchange a wide variety of goods via countertrade; and as Table 11.3 shows, that countertrade knows few limits across goods.

Country		Exported Commodity	
A	B	A	B
Hungary	Ukraine	Foodstuffs Canned foods pharmaceuticals	Timber
Austria	Ukraine	Power station emissions control equipment	800 million kilowatts/year for 15 years
US (Chrysler)	Jamaica	200 pickup trucks	Equivalent value in iron ore
Ukraine	Czech Republic	Iron ore	Mining equipment
US (Pierre Cardin)	China	Technical advice	Silks and cashmeres
UK (Raleigh Bicycle)	CIS	Training CIS scientists in mountain bike production	Titanium for 30 000 bike frames per year
Indonesia	Uzbekistan	Indian tea	50 000 tonnes of cotton/year for three years
		Vietnamese rice Miscellaneous Indonesian products	
Zaire	Italy	Scrap iron	12 locomotives
China	Russia	212 railway trucks of mango juice	Passenger jet
Morocco	Romania	Citrus products	Several large ports/small harbours

Sources: American Countertrade Association, December 1996; Aspy P. Palia and Oded Shenkar (1991) 'Countertrade Practices in China', *Industrial Marketing Management*, 20, 58. www.i-trade.com

Table 11.3: A sample of barter agreements.

SUMMARY

Multinational financial management is both complex and critical to the multinational firm. Beginning with the very objective of management – stockholder wealth maximization or corporate wealth maximization – all traditional functional areas of financial management are affected by the internationalization of the firm. Capital budgeting, firm financing, capital structure, and working capital and cash flow management, all traditional functions, are made more difficult by business activities that cross borders and oceans, not to mention currencies and markets.

In addition to the traditional areas of financial management, international financial management must deal with the three types of currency exposure: (1) transaction exposure; (2) economic exposure; and (3) translation exposure. Each type of currency risk confronts a firm with serious choices regarding its exposure analysis and its degree of willingness to manage the inherent risks.

This chapter described not only the basic types of risk but also outlined a number of the basic strategies employed in the management of the exposures. Some of the solutions available today have only arisen with the development of new types of international financial markets and instruments, such as the currency swap. Others, such as currency risk-sharing agreements, are as old as exchange rates themselves.

QUESTIONS FOR DISCUSSION

1. What are the pros and cons of the two different theories of wealth maximization?
2. Why is it important to identify the cash flows of a foreign investment from the perspective of the parent rather than from just the project?
3. Is currency risk unique to international firms? Is currency risk good or bad for the potential profitability of the multinational?
4. Which type of currency risk is the least important to the multinational firm? Should resources be spent to manage this risk?
5. Are firms with no direct international business (imports and exports) subject to economic exposure?
6. Which type of firm do you believe is more 'naturally hedged' against exchange rate exposure, the purely domestic firm (the barber) or the multinational firm (subsidiaries all over the world)?
7. What are some of the causes for the resurgence of countertrade?
8. What forms of countertrade exist and how do they differ? What are their relative advantages and drawbacks?
9. How consistent is countertrade with the international trade framework?

INTERNET EXERCISES

1. Although major currencies such as the US dollar, the euro and the Japanese yen dominate the headlines, there are also many other currencies. Many of these currencies are traded in extremely thin and highly regulated markets, making their convertibility suspect. Finding quotations for these currencies is sometimes very difficult. Using some of the web pages listed below, see how many African currency quotes you can find. See Emerging Markets at www.emgmkts.com/.

2. Use the *Economist*'s web site to find the latest version of the Big Max Index of Currency over- and under-valuation. See www.economist.com.

3. The single unobservable variable in currency option pricing is the volatility, because volatility inputs are expected standard deviation of the daily spot rate for the coming period of the option's maturity. Using the London Stock Exchange and Philadelphia Stock Exchange web sites, pick one currency's volatility and research how its value has changed in recent periods and over historical periods.

4. Using the following major periodicals as starting points, find a current example of a firm with a substantial operating exposure problem. To help in your search, you might focus on businesses having major operations in countries with recent currency crises, either through devaluation or major home currency appreciation. Sources are *Financial Times* at www.ft.com/; *The Economist* at www.economist.com/; *Wall Street Journal* at www.wsj.com/.

5. In the World Trade Organization's Agreement on Government Procurement, how are *offsets* defined and what stance is taken toward them (refer to the government procurement page on the web site www.wto.org)?

TAKE A STAND

Many multinational companies believe that *hedging* is really nothing other than formalized *speculation*. Since many firms use the same complex financial instruments and derivatives that arbitragers and speculators use, they argue that companies are endangering their own future by allowing individuals within the organization to gamble with the company's own funds – for profit. And the profit only arises from the ability of the individual to 'beat the market'.

FOR DISCUSSION

1. Multinationals should accept foreign currency risks as part of doing business internationally and therefore should not spend precious resources and take unnecessary risks related to the use of financial derivatives for hedging. The cure is more harmful than the disease.

2. Multinationals must protect all their stakeholders – stockholders, creditors, employees and community – from the risks associated with conducting business in a global marketplace using currencies that bounce up and down in value. Although some hedging techniques may introduce new types of risks for the firm, it is in the entire firm's interest that it hedge significant cash flow risks and add certainty to the conduct of the firm's total business.

CHAPTER
12

- Managing Managers
- Managing Labour Personnel

Human Resource Management[1]

LEARNING OBJECTIVES

- To describe the challenges of managing managers and labour personnel in individual international markets and in worldwide operations.
- To examine the sources, qualifications and compensation of international managers.
- To assess the effects of culture on managers and management policies.
- To illustrate the different roles of labour in international markets, especially that of labour participation in management.

SEARCHING FOR GLOBAL EXECS

Many corporate decision makers have realized that human resources play at least as significant a role as advanced technology and economies of scale when it comes to competing successfully in the new global world order. A full 29% of Fortune 500 firms surveyed had nowhere near enough global leaders; 56% said they had fewer than needed; and two thirds said that the global leaders in their companies had less capability than was needed. The lacking global leaders are in three specific roles: running global business units or global functions and as country managers.

According to a survey of 1200 mid-sized US multinationals with annual sales of US$1 billion or less conducted by *International Business* magazine, senior executives seek managers who are culturally diverse but responsive to the direction of headquarters. Most US-based companies try to fill senior positions abroad with locals, using expatriates only for such specific projects as technology transfer. However, the same companies send their US middle managers the clear message that overseas operations are so important to corporate welfare that solid international experience is needed for advancement.

Although major markets in Europe and Asia possess deeper pools of managerial talent than ever before, many of these nationals prefer to work for domestic rather than foreign firms. In particularly short supply are marketing managers – 49% of the surveyed companies say that marketing is the hardest slot to fill. It is especially hard to find people who have the cross-cultural experience to make good regional managers.

Very few global leaders are born that way; that is, with an international childhood, a command of several languages and an education from an institution with an international focus. In most cases, they have to be trained and nurtured carefully. To make a business global, its leaders have to be able to: (1) see the world's challenges and opportunities; (2) think with an international mindset; (3) act with fresh, global-centric behaviours; and (4) mobilize a world-class team and company. A strong focus on Finland for a Nokia employee makes no sense. Three out of every five Nokia employees work outside of the company's home country and one out of three outside of Europe.

To achieve this, companies are using various approaches. For example, Molex, a manufacturer based in Illinois, USA, with 54 manufacturing plants in 19 countries worldwide, concentrates on filling its human resource management positions with host-country nationals. Malou Roth, vice president of human resources, training and development, explains that the company follows this practice not only so the managers can speak to employees in their own language and understand local legal requirements, but also so the managers will know which current US human resource practices will – and won't – work in their cultures.

Colgate-Palmolive promotes global leadership by hiring entry-level marketing candidates who have lived or worked abroad, speak more than one language or can demonstrate an existing aptitude for global business. Black & Decker has a team-based performance appraisal and feedback system, with members from around the world. South Korea's Sunkyong uses both classroom and action-learning projects that emphasize exposure to people throughout the company. NetFRAME Systems Inc., a maker of networking computers, gathers its expatriate and non-US managers at its California headquarters every quarter to encourage joint planning and problem solving on a global basis. Nortel manages each phase of its international transfers through candidate pools, informed self-selection, pre-departure training, support mechanisms, repatriation debriefing for employees and families and disseminating repatriates' international skills and knowledge throughout the company.

Companies that spend time and money creating and training global talent naturally want to retain it as long as possible. Loctite Corporation, maker of industrial adhesives, offers global opportunity, professional challenge and a competitive compensation package to keep its rising stars. Of the three approaches, claims the company, compensation is the least important to the managers.

Sources: Christopher Bartlett and Sumantra Ghoshal (2003) 'What is a Global Manager?' *Harvard Business Review*, 81(August), 99–107; Karl Moore (2003) 'Great Global Managers', *Across the Board*, 40(May/June), 38–42; 'Distractions Make Global Manager a Difficult Role', *Wall Street Journal*, 21 November 2000, B1, B18; 'Whither Global Leaders?' *HR Magazine*, May 2000, 83–88; Hal B. Gregersen, Allen J. Morrison and J. Stewart Black (1998) 'Developing Global Leaders for the Global Frontier', *Sloan Management Review*, 40(fall), 31–40; Shari Caudron, 'World-Class Execs', *Industry Week*, 1 December 1997, www.Industryweek.com; 'Globe Trotter: If It's 5:30, This Must Be Tel-Aviv', *Business Week*, 17 October 1994; Lori Ioannou, 'It's a Small World After All', *International Business*, February 1994, 82–88; Shawn Tully, 'The Hunt for the Global Manager', *Fortune*, 21 May 1990, 140–144; www.netframe.com; www.loctite.com; www.molex.com; www.blackanddecker.com; www.colgate.com; www.nortelnetworks.com; www.sk.co.kr

INTRODUCTION

Organizations have two general human resource objectives. The first is the recruitment and retention of a workforce made up of the best people available for the jobs to be done. The recruiter in international operations will need to keep in mind both cross-cultural and cross-national differences in productivity and expectations when selecting employees. Once they are hired, the firm's best interest lies in maintaining a stable and experienced workforce.

The second objective is to increase the effectiveness of the workforce. This depends to a great extent on achieving the first objective. Competent managers or workers are likely to perform at a more effective level if proper attention is given to factors that motivate them.

To attain the two major objectives, the activities and skills needed include:

- personnel planning and staffing, the assessment of personnel needs and recruitment;
- personnel training to achieve a perfect fit between the employee and the assignment;
- compensation of employees according to their effectiveness;
- an understanding of labour–management relations in terms of how the two groups view each other and how their respective power positions are established.

All of this means that human resource management must become a basic element of a company's expansion strategy. In a study of 76 European and US firms, a full 98% of the respondents had developed or were in the process of developing global human resource strategy. However, the majority reported that they had only moderate involvement in their company's overall business strategy. The task is, therefore, to establish human resources as not only a tactical element to fill needed positions but also one whose programmes affect overall business results.[2]

This chapter will examine the management of human resources in international business from two points of view, first that of managers and then that of labour.

MANAGING MANAGERS

The importance of the quality of the workforce in international business cannot be overemphasized, regardless of the stage of internationalization of the firm. Those in the early stages of internationalization focus on understanding cultural differences, whereas the more advanced are determined to manage and balance cultural diversity and eventually to integrate differences within the overall corporate culture. As seen in the chapter's opening vignette, international business systems are complex and dynamic and require competent people to develop and direct them.

Early Stages of Internationalization

The marketing or sales manager of the firm typically is responsible for beginning export activities. As foreign sales increase, an export manager will be appointed and given the responsibility for developing and maintaining customers, interacting with the firm's intermediaries and planning for overall market expansion. The export manager must also champion the international effort within the company because the general attitude among employees may be to view the domestic market as more important. Another critical function is the supervision of export transactions, particularly documentation. The requirements are quite different for international transactions than for domestic ones and sales or profits may be lost if documentation is not properly handled. The first task of the new export manager, in fact, is often to hire staff to handle paperwork that typically had previously been done by a facilitating agent, such as a freight forwarder.

The firm starting international operations will usually hire an export manager from outside rather than promote from within. The reason is that knowledge of the product or industry is less important than international experience. The cost of learning through experience to manage an export department is simply too great from the firm's standpoint. Further, the inexperienced manager would be put in the position of having to demonstrate his or her effectiveness almost at once.

The manager who is hired will have obtained experience through Foreign Service duty or with another corporation. In the early stages, a highly entrepreneurial spirit with a heavy dose of trader mentality is required. Even then, management should not expect the new export department to earn a profit for the first few years.

Advanced Stages of Internationalization

As the firm progresses from exporting to an international division to foreign direct involvement, human resources-planning activities will initially focus on need *vis-à-vis* various markets and functions. Existing personnel can be assessed and plans made to recruit, select and train employees for positions that cannot be filled internally. The four major categories of overseas assignments are: (1) CEO, to oversee and direct the entire operation; (2) functional head, to establish and maintain departments and ensure their proper performance; (3) trouble-shooters, who are used for their special expertise in analysing, and thereby preventing or solving, particular problems; and (4) white- or blue-collar workers.[3] Many technology companies have had to respond to shortages in skilled employees by globalized recruitment using web sites or by hiring head-hunters in countries such as China and India. For example, presently about a third of Nokia's worldwide workforce is comprised of non-Finns, whereas that share was about half in the late 1990s.[4]

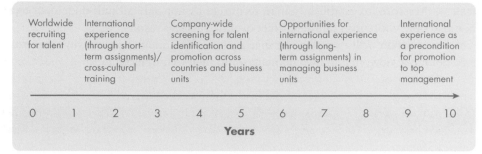

Figure 12.1: International management development.

Source: Adapted from Ingo Theuerkauf (1991) 'Reshaping the Global Organization', *McKinsey Quarterly*, 3, 104; Paul Evans, Vladimir Pucik and Jean-Louis Barsoux (2002) *The Global Challenge: Frameworks for International Human Resource Management*, McGraw-Hill/Irwin, New York, chs 2–4.

One of the major sources of competitive advantage of global corporations is their ability to attract talent around the world. The corporations need systematic management-development systems, with the objective of creating and carefully allocating management personnel. An example of this is provided in Figure 12.1. Increasingly, plans call for international experience as a prerequisite for advancement; for example, at Ford Motor Company, the goal is to have 100% of the top managers with international work experience with the company.[5]

In global corporations, there is no such thing as a universal global manager; instead a network of global specialists in four general groups of managers has to work together:[6]

- *Global business (product) managers* have the task to further the company's global-scale efficiency and competitiveness.
- *Country managers* have to be sensitive and responsive to local market needs and demands but, at the same time, be aware of global implications.
- *Functional managers* have to make sure that the corporation's capabilities in technical, manufacturing, marketing, human resource and financial expertise are linked and can benefit from each other.
- *Corporate executives* at headquarters have to manage interactions among the three groups of managers as well as identify and develop the talent to fill the positions.

As an example of this planning, in the Heineken company, a management review of human resources is conducted twice a year with each general manager of the operating companies, which are located in such countries as Canada, France, Ireland and Spain. The meeting is attended by the general manager, the personnel manager, the regional co-ordinating director in whose region the operating company is located and the corporate director of management development. Special attention is given to managers 'in the fast lane', the extent to which they are mobile, what might be done to foster their development and where they fit into succession planning.[7] Of course, any gaps must be filled by recruitment efforts.

Companies should show clear career paths for managers assigned overseas and develop the systems and the organization for promotion.[8] This approach serves to eliminate many of the perceived problems and thus motivates managers to seek out foreign assignments. Furthermore, when jobs open up, the company can quickly determine who is able and willing to take them. Foreign assignments can occur at various stages of the manager's tenure. In the early stages, assignments may be short-term, such as a membership in an international task force or 6–12 months at headquarters in a staff function. Later, an individual may serve as a business-unit manager overseas. Many companies use cross-postings to other countries or across product lines to further an individual's acculturation to the corporation.[9] A period in a head office department or a subsidiary will not only provide an understanding of different national cultures and attitudes but also improve an individual's 'know-who', and therefore establish the unity and common sense of purpose necessary for the proper implementation of global programmes.

At the most advanced stages of globalization, companies need to co-ordinate and leverage resources across borders. One of the most effective tools in achieving this aim are cross-border teams consisting of members of multiple nationalities.[10] For these teams to work, members need to have had the necessary experience to appreciate both global synergies and national/regional differences. Without assignments abroad, this is impossible.

Inter-firm Co-operative Ventures

Global competition is forging new co-operative ties between firms from different countries, thereby adding a new management challenge for the firms involved. Although many of the reasons for these alliances formation are competitive and strategic, the human resource function is critical to their implementation. As a matter of fact, some of the basic reasons so many of these ventures fail relate to human resource management; for example, managers from disparate venture partners cannot work together, or managers within the venture cannot work with the owners' managers.[11] As more ventures are created in newly emerging markets, the challenge of finding skilled local managers is paramount. If such talent is not secured, developing loyalty to the company may be difficult.[12]

Although the ingredients for success of the human resource function will differ with the type of co-operative venture, two basic types of tasks are needed.[13] The first task is to assign and motivate people in appropriate ways so that the venture will fulfil its set strategic tasks. This requires particular attention to such issues as job skills and compatibility of communication and other work styles. For example, some co-operative ventures have failed due to one of the partners' assigning relatively weak management resources to the venture or due to managers' finding themselves with conflicting loyalties to the parent organization and the co-operative venture organization. The second task is the strategic management of the human resources, that is, the appropriate use of managerial capabilities not only in the co-operative venture but also in other later contexts possibly back in the parent organization. An individual manager needs to see that an assignment in a co-operative venture is part of his or her overall career development.

Sources for Management Recruitment

The location and the nationality of candidates for a particular job are the key issues in recruitment. A decision will have to be made to recruit from within the company or, in the case of larger corporations, within other product or regional groups, or to rely on external talent. Similarly, decisions will have to be made whether to hire or promote locally or use expatriates; that is, home-country nationals or third-country nationals (citizens of countries other than the home or host country). Typically, 65% of expatriates are posted in subsidiaries, while the remaining 35% have assignments in their company's headquarters' country (i.e., they are 'inpatriates').[14] The major advantages and disadvantages of expatriates are summarized in Table 12.1.

In general, the choice process between expatriates and locals is driven by: (1) the availability and quality of the talent pool; (2) corporate policies and their cost; and (3) environmental constraints on the legal, cultural or economic front. Many countries still resist letting jobs go to foreigners but under pressure from employers in areas such as engineering and programming, the resistance is fading.[15] In the new economy, in which the physical location of work may not matter, the choice of becoming an expatriate may be the employee's. A new breed of telecommuters live countries or even continents apart from their companies' home offices.[16]

The advantages of appointing a national of the headquarters country in an overseas post are that the expat:

1. Knows the company's products and culture.
2. Relates easily and efficiently to corporate headquarters; speaks the verbal and cultural language.
3. Has technical or business skills not available locally.
4. May have special transferable capabilities (for example, opening operations in emerging markets).
5. Will protect and promote the interests of headquarters in international joint ventures and acquisitions and other situations requiring tight financial control.
6. Is unlikely to steal proprietary knowledge and set up competing businesses.
7. Does not put the country ahead of the company (unless he or she 'goes native').
8. Fits the company's need to develop future leaders and general managers with international experience.

The disadvantages of appointing an expat include:

1. High costs – covering relocation, housing, education, hardship allowance – often exceeding 200% of the home-country base.
2. Black-outs; 25% of expats have to be called home early.
3. Brown-outs: another 30–50% stay but underperform, leading to lost sales, low staff morale and a decline in local goodwill.
4. Prolonged start-up and wind-down time: in a typical three-year assignment the first year is spent unpacking and the third year is spent packing and positioning for the next move.
5. A short-sighted focus: expats with a three-year assignment tend to focus on the next career step rather than on building the local company.
6. Difficulty in finding experienced managers willing to move because of spouse's career, child's schooling or life-style and security concerns (e.g., in Middle Eastern countries).
7. Expats' concern about negative out-of-sight, out-of-mind impact on career development.
8. Re-entry problems: a high percentage of expats leave their companies after overseas assignments because jobs with similar breadth of responsibility are either not available or not offered.
9. Division of senior managers to overseas markets is difficult especially for smaller companies that do not yet have a lock on their domestic markets.

Source: John A. Quelch and Helen Bloom (1999) 'Ten Steps to a Global Human Resources Strategy', *Strategy and Business,* first quarter, 18–29. Reprinted with permission from strategy+business. Booz Allen Hamilton, Copyright 1999. www.state.gov

Table 12.1: The major advantages and disadvantages of expatriates.

The recruitment approach changes over the internationalization process of the firm. During the export stage, outside expertise is sought at first but the firm then begins to develop its own personnel for international operations. With expanded and more involved foreign operations, the firm's reliance on home-country personnel will be reduced as host-country nationals are prepared for management positions. The use of home-country and third-country nationals may be directed at special assignments, such as transfer of technology or expertise. The use of expatriates will continue as a matter of corporate policy to internationalize management and to foster the infusion of a particular corporate culture into operations around the world.

When international operations are expanded, a management development dilemma may result. Through internal recruitment, young managers will be offered interesting new opportunities. However, some senior managers may object to the constant drain of young talent from their units. Selective recruitment from the outside will help to maintain a desirable combination of inside talent and fresh blood. Furthermore, with dynamic market changes or new markets and new business development, outside recruitment may be the only available approach. Even in Japan, the taboo against hiring executives from other companies is breaking down. The practice of hiring from the top universities can no longer be dependent on the provision of the right people in all circumstances.[17]

Currently, most managers in subsidiaries are host-country nationals. The reasons include an increase in availability of local talent, corporate relations in the particular market and the economies realized by not having to maintain a corps of managers overseas. Local managers are generally more familiar with environmental conditions and how they should be interpreted. By employing local management, the multinational is responding to host-country demands for increased localization and providing advancement as an incentive to local managers. In this respect, however, localization can be carried too far. If the firm does not subscribe to a global philosophy, the manager's development is tied to the local operation or to a particular level of management in that operation. This has been an issue of contention, especially with Japanese employers in the United States. As a result, managers who outgrow the local operation may have nowhere to go except to another company.[18] Although the Japanese continue to express frustration in what they perceive to be disloyalty and opportunism on the part of US employees, they are starting to change their practices so that they can retain talented US nationals.[19]

Local managers, if not properly trained and indoctrinated, may see things differently from the way they are viewed at headquarters. As a result, both control and the overall co-ordination of programmes may be jeopardized. For the corporation to work effectively, of course, employees must first of all understand each other. Most corporations have adopted a common corporate language, with English as the *lingua franca*; that is, the language habitually used among people of diverse speech to facilitate communication. At most global companies, all top-level meetings are conducted in English. In some companies, two languages are officially in use; for example, at Nestlé both English and French are corporate languages. However, corporate training should focus on a broad spectrum of international communication skills rather than just a systematic knowledge of any one or two languages and should include such areas as cultural appreciation.[20]

A second goal is to avoid overemphasis on localization, which would prevent the development of an internationalized group of managers with a proper understanding of the impact of the environment on operations. To develop language skills and promote an international outlook in their management pools, multinational corporations are increasingly recruiting among foreign students at business schools in the United States, Western Europe and the Far East. When these young managers return home, following an initial assignment at corporate headquarters, they will have a command of the basic philosophies of multinational operations.

Cultural differences that shape managerial attitudes must be considered when developing multinational management programmes. For example, British managers place more emphasis than most other nationals on individual achievement and autonomy whereas French managers value competent supervision, sound company policies, fringe benefits, security and comfortable working conditions.[21]

The decision as to whether to use home-country nationals in a particular operation depends on such factors as the type of industry, the life-cycle stage of the product, the availability of managers from other sources and the functional areas involved. The number of home-country managers is typically higher in the service sector than in the industrial sector and overseas assignments may be quite short term. For example, many international hotel chains have established management contracts in China with the understanding that home-country managers will train local successors within three to five years. In the start-up phase of an endeavour, headquarters involvement is generally substantial. This applies to all functions, including personnel. Especially if no significant pool of local managers is available or their competence levels are not satisfactory, home-country nationals may be used. For control and communication reasons, some companies always maintain a home-country national as manager in certain functional areas, such as accounting or finance. On occasion, the need to control may be more specific. For example, expatriates may be used in joint ventures to ensure the proper use of funds or technologies by the local partner.[22]

The number of home-country nationals in an overseas operation rarely rises above 10% of the workforce and is typically about 1%. The reasons are both internal and external. In addition to the substantial cost of transfer, a manager may not fully adjust to foreign working and living conditions. Good corporate citizenship today requires multinational companies to develop the host country's workforce at the management level. Legal impediments to manager transfers may exist or other difficulties may be encountered. Many US-based hotel corporations, for example, have complained about delays in obtaining visas to the United States not only for managers but also for management trainees.

The use of third-country nationals is most often seen in large multinational companies that have adopted a global philosophy. The practice of some companies, such as Philips, is to employ third-country nationals as managing directors in subsidiaries. An advantage is that third-country nationals may contribute to the firm's overall international expertise. However, many third-country nationals are career international managers and they may become targets for raids by competitors looking for high levels of talent. They may be a considerable asset in regional expansion; for example, established subsidiary managers in Singapore might be used to start up a subsidiary in Malaysia. On the other hand, some transfers may be inadvisable for cultural or historical reasons, for example, transfers between Turkey and Greece.

The ability to recruit for international assignments is determined by the value an individual company places on international operations and the experience gained in working in them. Based on a survey of 1500 senior executives around the world, US executives still place less emphasis on international dimensions than their Japanese, Western European and Latin American counterparts. Although most executives agree that an international outlook is essential for future executives, 70% of foreign executives think that experience outside one's home country is important, compared with only 35% of US executives, and foreign language capability was seen as important by only 19% of US respondents, compared with 64% of non-US executives.[23]

In an era of regional integration, many companies are facing a severe shortage of managers who can think and operate regionally or even globally. Very few companies – even those characterizing themselves as global – have systematically developed international managers by rotating young executives through a series of assignments in different parts of the world.[24]

Selection Criteria for Overseas Assignments

The traits that have been suggested as necessary for the international manager range from the ideal to the real. One characterization describes 'a flexible personality, with broad intellectual horizons, attitudinal values of cultural empathy, general friendliness, patience and prudence, impeccable educational and professional (or technical) credentials – all topped off with immaculate health, creative resourcefulness and respect of peers. If the family is equally well endowed, all the better'.[25] In addition to flexibility and adaptability, they have to be able to take action where there is no precedent. Traits typically mentioned in the choosing of managers for overseas assignments are listed in Table 12.2. Their relative importance may vary dramatically, of course, depending on the firm situation, as well as where the choice is being made. The United States is particularly good at business literacy, whereas Latin Americans have developed the ability to cope with complex social relations.[26]

Competence	Adaptability	Personal Characteristics
Technical knowledge	Interest in overseas work	Age
Leadership ability	Relational abilities	Education
Experience, past performance	Cultural empathy	Sex
Area expertise	Appreciation of new management styles	Health
Language	Appreciation of environmental constraints	Marital relations
	Adaptability of family	Social acceptability

Table 12.2: Criteria for selecting managers for overseas assignment.

Competence Factors

An expatriate manager usually has far more responsibility than a manager in a comparable domestic position and must be far more self-sufficient in making decisions and conducting daily business. To be selected in the first place, the manager's technical competence level has to be superior to that of local candidates; otherwise, the firm would in most cases have chosen a local person. The manager's ability to do the job in the technical sense is one of the main determinants of ultimate success or failure in an overseas assignment.[27] However, management skills will not transfer from one culture to another without some degree of adaptation. This means that, regardless of the level of technical skills, the new environment still requires the ability to adapt the skills to local conditions. Technical competence must also be accompanied by the ability to lead subordinates in any situation or under any conditions.

Especially in global-minded enterprises, managers are selected for overseas assignments on the basis of solid experience and past performance. Many firms use the foreign tour as a step toward top management. By sending abroad internally recruited, experienced managers, the firm also ensures the continuation of corporate culture – a set of shared values, norms and beliefs and an emphasis on a particular facet of performance. Two examples are IBM's concern with customer service and 3M's concentration on innovation.

The role of factual cultural knowledge in the selection process has been widely debated. Area expertise includes knowledge of the basic systems in the region or market for which the manager will be responsible – such as the roles of various ministries in international business, the significance of holidays and the general way of doing business. None of these variables is as important as language, although language skill is not always highly ranked by firms.[28] A manager who does not know the language of the country may get by with the help of associates and interpreters but is not in a position to assess the situation fully. For instance, almost all Japanese representing their companies worldwide, speak English. As a matter of fact, some Japanese companies, such as Honda, have deployed some of their most talented executives to US operations.[29] Of the Americans representing US companies in China, Japan and South Korea only few know the local language well enough to use it in their work. The same holds true about British representatives in Southeast European countries. Some companies place language skills or aptitude in a larger context; they see a strong correlation between language skill and adaptability. Another reason to look for language competence in managers considered for assignments overseas is that all managers spend most of their time communicating.

Adaptability Factors

The manager's own motivation to a great extent determines the viability of an overseas assignment and consequently its success. The manager's interest in the foreign culture must go well beyond that of the average tourist if he or she is to understand what an assignment abroad involves. In most cases, the manager will need counselling and training to comprehend the true nature of the undertaking.

Adaptability means a positive and flexible attitude toward change. The manager assigned overseas must progress from factual cultural knowledge to interpretive cultural knowledge, trying as much as possible to become part of the new scene, which may be quite different from the one at home. The work habits of middle-level managers may be more lax, productivity and attention to detail less and overall environmental restrictions far greater. The manager on a foreign assignment is part of a multicultural team, in which both internal and external interactions determine the future of the firm's operations. For example, a manager from the United States may be used to an informal, democratic type of leadership that may not be applicable in countries such as Mexico or Japan, where employees expect more authoritarian leadership.[30]

Adaptability does not depend solely on the manager. Firms look carefully at the family situation because a foreign assignment often puts more strain on other family members than on the manager. As an example, a US engineering firm had serious problems in Italy that were traced to the inability of one executive's wife to adapt. She complained to other wives, who began to feel that they too suffered hardships and then complained to their husbands. Morale became so low that the company, after missing important deadlines, replaced most of the Americans on the job.[31] As a response, networks intended for expatriate spouses have been developed on corporate intranets to allow for exchange of advice and ideas.[32]

The characteristics of the family as a whole are important. Screeners look for family cohesiveness and check for marital instability or for behavioural difficulties in children. Abroad, the need to work together as a family often makes strong marriages stronger and causes the downfall of weak ones. Further, commitments or interests beyond the nuclear family affect the adjustment of family members to a new environment. Some firms use earlier transfers within the home country as an indicator of how a family will handle transfer abroad. With the dramatic increase in two-career households, foreign assignments may call for one of the spouses to sacrifice a career or, at best, to put it on hold. Increasingly transferees are requesting for spouse re-employment assistance.[33] As a result, corporations are forming consortia to try to tackle such problems. Members of the group interview accompanying spouses and try to find them positions with other member companies.[34] Increasingly, this also means male expatriate spouses who accompany their partners abroad.[35]

Personal Characteristics

Despite all of the efforts made by multinational companies to recruit the best person available, demographics still play a role in the selection process. Due to either a minimum age requirement or the level of experience needed, many foreign assignments go to managers in their mid-30s or older. Normally, companies do not recruit candidates from graduating classes for immediate assignment overseas. They want their international people first to become experienced and familiar with the corporate culture and this can best be done at headquarters' location.

Although the number of women in overseas assignments is only 18% according to one count, women are as interested as men in the assignments.[36] Corporate hiring practices may be based on the myth that women will not be accepted in the host countries. Many of the relatively few women managers report being treated as foreign business people and not singled out as women. These issues are highlighted in the Focus on Culture (below).

In the selection process, firms are concerned about the health of the people they may send abroad. Some assignments are in host countries with dramatically different environmental conditions from the home country and they may aggravate existing health problems. Moreover, if the candidate selected is not properly prepared, foreign assignments may increase stress levels and contribute to the development of peptic ulcers, colitis or other problems.

When candidates are screened, being married is usually considered a plus. Marriage brings stability and an inherent support system, provided family relations are in order. It may also facilitate adaptation to the local culture by increasing the number of social functions to which the manager is invited.

Social acceptability varies from one culture to another and can be a function of any of the other personal characteristics. Background, religion, race and gender usually become critical only in extreme cases in which a host environment would clearly reject a candidate based on one or more of these variables. The Arab boycott of the state of Israel, for example, puts constraints on the use of managers of Jewish origin in Arab countries. Women cannot negotiate contracts in many Middle Eastern countries. This still holds true even if the woman is president of the company.

F○CUS ON

CULTURE Women and the Global Corporate Ladder

There is growing evidence to suggest that women are making greater strides on the international front than ever before. The 2002 Global Relocation Survey, conducted by Windham International and the National Foreign Trade Council, provides various measures of this trend. A full 18% of American corporate expatriates are women, up from 10% in 1993.

Some argue that the numbers are relatively small due to commonly held myths about women in international business. The first is that women do not want to be international managers and the second is that foreigners' prejudice against them renders them ineffective, whether they are nationals or not.

In a study of more than 1000 graduating MBAs from schools in North America and Europe, females and males displayed equal interest in pursuing international careers. They also agreed that firms offer fewer opportunities to women pursuing international careers than to those pursuing domestic ones. Women expatriate managers agree that convincing superiors to let them go called for patience and persistence.

Expatriate women have generally reported numerous professional advantages to being female. Being highly visible (both internally and externally) has often been quoted as an advantage given that many women expatriates are 'firsts' for their companies. Foreign clients are curious about them, want to meet them and remember them after the first encounter. Emanuel Monogenis, a managing partner at the international search firm of Heidrick & Struggles, observed, 'My clients now see women as equals in top global searches. In fact, more and more executives are saying they prefer women because they feel they are willing to work harder and take less for granted than male counterparts. Many also believe women have more of a sensibility and insight into human behaviour and relationships than their male counterparts and this is highly valued in culturally diverse workforces.'

Sources: 2002 Global Relocation Trends Survey Report, Warren, NJ, USA: GMAC Relocation Services, 2003, available at www.gmacglobalrelocation.com; Virginia E. Schein (2001) 'A Global Look at Psychological Barriers to Women's Progress in Management', *Journal of Social Issues*, 57(winter), 675–689; 'Stay-at-Home Careers?' *Global Business*, January 2001, 62; Lori Ioannou (1994) 'Women's Global Career Ladder', *International Business*, December, 57–60; Nancy J. Adler and Dafna N. Izraeli (eds) (1994) *Competitive Frontiers: Women Managers in a Global Economy*, Blackwell Business, Cambridge, MA, Chapters 1 and 2; Diana Kunde, 'Management Opportunities for Women Brighten', *Washington Post*, 19 December 1993, H2; Anne B. Fisher, 'When Will Women Get to the Top?' *Fortune*, 21 September 1992, 44–56; www.heidrick.com

The Selection and Orientation Challenge

Due to the cost of transferring a manager overseas, many firms go beyond standard selection procedures and use adaptability screening as an integral part of the process. During the screening phase, the method most often used involves interviewing the candidate and the family. The interviews are conducted by senior executives, human relations specialists within the firm or outside firms. Interviewers ask the candidate and the family to consider the personal issues involved in the transfer; for example, what each will miss the most. In some cases, candidates themselves will refuse an assignment. In others, the firm will withhold the assignment on the basis of interviews that clearly show a degree of risk.

The candidate selected will participate in an orientation programme on internal and external aspects of the assignment. Internal aspects include issues such as compensation and reporting. External aspects are concerned with what to expect at the destination in terms of customs and

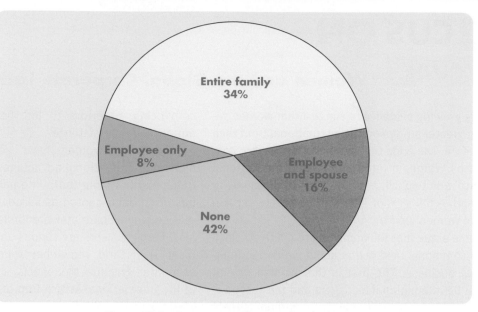

Figure 12.2: Companies offering cultural training.

Source: Lori Ioannou (1994) 'Cultivating the New Expatriate Executive', *International Business*, July, 46.

culture. The extent and level of the programmes will vary; for example, in a survey of 120 US companies, 42% reported having no cultural preparation training for their executives. A similar survey carried out of 145 companies revealed that 17% of the company executives had no cultural training. As shown in Figure 12.2, most programmes offered extend the orientation to the spouse or the entire family. If the company is still in the export stage, the emphasis in this training will be on interpersonal skills and local culture. With expatriates, the focus will be on both training and interacting with host-country nationals. Actual methods vary from area studies to sensitivity training.

The attrition rate in overseas assignments averages 40% among companies with neither adaptability screening nor orientation programmes, 25% among companies with cultural orientation programmes and 5–10% among companies that use both kinds of programmes. Considering the cost of a transfer, catching even one potentially disastrous situation pays for the programme for a full year. Most companies have no programme at all, however, and others provide them for higher level management positions only. Companies that have the lowest failure rates typically employ a four-tiered approach to expatriate use: (1) clearly stated criteria; (2) rigorous procedures to determine the suitability of an individual across the criteria; (3) appropriate orientation; and (4) constant evaluation of the effectiveness of the procedures.[37]

In this context, it is also important to make the length of the overseas appointment make sense for the individual, the family and the company. Three-year assignments are typical; however, in some cases when culture gaps are significant (as is in the case of Western and Eastern countries), it may be prudent to have longer tours.

It is important that the expatriate and his or her family feel the support continuing during their tour. A significant share of the dissatisfaction expressed pertains to perceived lack of support during the international experience, especially in cases of dual-career households.[38]

Culture Shock

The effectiveness of orientation procedures can be measured only after managers are overseas and exposed to security and socio-political tensions, health, housing, education, social network and

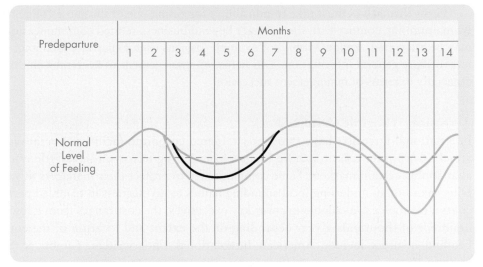

Figure 12.3: Culture shock cycle for an overseas assignment.
Note: Lines indicate the extreme severity with which culture shock may attack.
Source: L. Robert Kohls (1984) *Survival Kits for Overseas Living*, Intercultural Press, Yarmouth, ME, 68.

leisure activities, language, availability of products and services, and climate. Culture shock is the term used for the pronounced reactions to the psychological disorientation that is experienced in varying degrees when spending an extended period of time in a new environment.[39]

Of the locations around the world, those perceived to be the most pleasant have included Hong Kong, Rome, Buenos Aires, Dubai and Prague. The most difficult to live in include Karachi, Tiranë, Lagos, Saigon and Moscow.[40]

Causes and Remedies

The culture shock cycle for an overseas assignment may last about 14 months. Often goals set for a subsidiary or a project may be unrealistic or the means by which they are to be reached may be totally inadequate. All of these lead to external manifestations of culture shock, such as bitterness and even physical illness. In extreme cases, they can lead to hostility toward anything in the host environment.

The culture-shock cycle for an overseas assignment is presented in Figure 12.3. Four distinct stages of adjustment exist during a foreign assignment. The length of the stages is highly individual. The four stages are:

1. *Initial Euphoria.* Enjoying the novelty, largely from the perspective of a spectator.
2. *Irritation and Hostility.* Experiencing cultural differences, such as the concept of time, through increased participation.
3. *Adjustment.* Adapting to the situation; this in some cases leads to biculturalism and even accusations from corporate headquarters of 'going native'.
4. *Reentry.* Returning home to face a possibly changed home environment.

The manager may fare better at the second stage than other members of the family, especially if their opportunities for work and other activities are severely restricted. The fourth stage may actually cause a reverse culture shock when the adjustment phase has been highly successful and the return home is not desired. The home environment that has been idealized during the tour abroad may not be perfect after all and the loss of status and benefits enjoyed abroad may generate feelings of frustration.[41]

Firms themselves must take responsibility for easing one of the causes of culture shock: isolation. By maintaining contact with the manager beyond business-related communication, some of the shock may be alleviated. Exxon/Mobil, for example, assigns each expatriate a contact person at headquarters to share general information. This helps top management to keep tabs on the manager's progress especially in terms of management succession.

Terrorism: Tangible Culture Shock

International terrorists have frequently targeted corporate facilities, operations and personnel for attack. Corporate reactions have ranged from letting terrorism have little effect on operations to abandoning certain markets. Some companies try to protect their managers in various ways by fortifying their homes and using local-sounding names to do business in troubled parts of the world.[42] Of course, insurance is available to cover key executives; the cost ranges from a few thousand dollars to hundreds of thousands a year depending on the extent and location of the company's operations. Leading insurers include American International Underwriters, Chubb & Son and Lloyd's of London.[43]

The threat of terrorist activity may have an effect on the company's operations beyond the immediate geographic area of concern. Travel may be banned or restricted in times or areas threatened. An array of organizations has emerged to service companies with employees in the world's hot spots. For example, Rapid Air Support provides in-depth, up-to-the-minute information on government, security and military situations in various countries and is ready to pull out clients' employees when emergencies arise.[44]

Repatriation

Returning home may evoke mixed feelings on the part of the expatriate and the family. Their concerns are both professional and personal. Even in two years, dramatic changes may have occurred not only at home but also in the way the individual and the family perceive the foreign environment. At worst, reverse culture shock may emerge.

The most important professional issue is finding a proper place in the corporate hierarchy. If no provisions have been made, a returning manager may be caught in a holding pattern for an intolerable length of time. For this reason, Dow Chemical, for example, provides each manager embarking on an overseas assignment with a letter that promises a job at least equal in responsibility upon return. Furthermore, because of their isolation, assignments abroad mean greater autonomy and authority than similar domestic positions. Both financially and psychologically, many expatriates find the overseas position difficult to give up. Many executive perks, such as club memberships, will not be funded at home.

The family, too, may be reluctant to give up their special status. In India, for example, expatriate families have servants for most of the tasks they perform themselves at home. Many longer-term expatriates are shocked by increases in the prices of housing and education at home. For the many managers who want to stay abroad, this may mean a change of company or even career – from employee to independent business person. According to one survey, as many as 25% of returnees may leave their companies within two years of coming home (many of them taking expatriate assignments with new employers).[45]

This alternative is not an attractive one for the company, which stands to lose valuable individuals who could become members of an international corps of managers. Therefore, planning for repatriation is necessary.[46] A four-step process can be used for this purpose. The first step involves an assessment of foreign assignments in terms of environmental constraints and corporate objectives, making sure that the latter are realistically defined. The second stage is preparation of the individual for an overseas assignment, which should include a clear understanding of when and how repatriation takes place. Third, during the actual tour, the manager should be kept abreast of developments at headquarters, especially in terms of career paths. Finally, during the actual re-entry, the manager should receive intensive organizational re-orientation, reasonable professional adjustment time and counselling for the entire family on matters of, for example, finance. A programme of this type allows the expatriate to feel a close bond with headquarters regardless of geographical distance.

Compensation

A Japanese executive's salary in cash is quite modest by US and West European standards but he or she is comfortable in the knowledge that the company will take care of him or her. Compensation is paternalistic; for example, a manager with two children in college and a sizable mortgage would be paid more than a childless manager in a comparable job. As this example suggests, Japanese compensation issues go beyond salary comparisons. They include exchange rates, local taxes and what the money will buy in different countries. Many compensation packages include elements other than cash.

A firm's expatriate compensation programme has to be effective in: (1) providing an incentive to leave the home country on a foreign assignment; (2) maintaining a given standard of living; (3) taking into consideration career and family needs; and (4) facilitating re-entry into the home country.[47] To achieve these objectives, firms pay a high premium beyond base salaries to induce managers to accept overseas assignments. The costs to the firm are 2 to 2.5 times the cost of maintaining a manager in a comparable position at home. For example, the average compensation package of a US manager in Hong Kong is 32% higher than for a British manager. US firms traditionally offer their employees more high-value perks, such as bigger apartments.[48]

The compensation of the manager overseas can be divided into two general categories: (1) base salary and salary-related allowances; and (2) non-salary-related allowances. Although incentives to leave home are justifiable in both categories, they create administrative complications for the personnel department in tying them to packages at home and elsewhere. As the number of transfers increases, firms develop general policies for compensating the manager rather than negotiating individually on every aspect of the arrangement.

Base Salary and Salary-Related Allowances

A manager's base salary depends on qualifications, responsibilities and duties, just as it would for a domestic position. Furthermore, criteria applying to merit increases, promotions and other increases are administered as they are domestically. Equity and comparability with domestic positions are important, especially in ensuring that repatriation will not cause cuts in base pay. For administrative and control purposes, the compensation and benefits function in multinational corporations is most often centralized.

The cost of living varies considerably around the world, as can be seen in Table 12.3. The purpose of the cost of living allowance (COLA) is to enable the manager to maintain as closely as possible the same standard of living that he or she would have at home. COLA is calculated by determining a percentage of base salary that would be spent on goods and services at the foreign location. (Figures around 50% are typical.) The ratios will naturally vary as a function of income and family size. Fluctuating exchange rates will of course have an effect on the COLA as well and changes will call for reviews of the allowance.

Living cost comparisons for Americans residing in foreign areas are developed four times a year by the US Department of State Allowances Staff. For each post, two measures are computed: (1) a government index to establish post allowances for US government employees; and (2) a local index for use by private organizations. The government index takes into consideration prices of goods imported to posts and price advantages available only to US government employees.

| Location | Survey Date | Cost of living index[a] (Washington, DC = 100) | | | |
		Index	Effective Date	Family of 4[b]	Single
Melbourne, Australia	Mar. 2006	105	Aug. 2007	$26 500	$25 300
Brussels, Belgium	Oct. 2006	120	Aug. 2007	$50 200	$46 600
Paris, France	Dec. 2005	125	Aug. 2007	$87 200	$66 200
Frankfurt, Germany	Dec. 2005	117	Aug. 2007	$44 600	$43 000
Tokyo, Japan	Feb. 2006	168	Aug. 2007	$80 700	$75 700
Mexico City	Mar. 2007	124	Aug. 2007	$42 400	$40 400
The Hague, Netherlands	May. 2006	114	Aug. 2007	$59 600	$56 600
Geneva, Switzerland	Jun. 2007	163	Sep. 2007	$70 900	$64 100
London, UK	May. 2006	165	Aug. 2007	$77 800	$74 300

Source: www.state.gov
[a]Excluding housing and education.
[b]For a family of four members with an annual income of $77 793 and over.

Table 12.3: International cost comparisons.

The local index is used by many business firms and private organizations to determine the cost of living allowance for their American employees assigned abroad. Local index measures for 12 key areas around the world are shown in the index's accompanying table. Maximum housing allowances, calculated separately, are also given.

The index reports are issued four times annually under the title US Department of State Indexes of Living Costs Abroad, Quarters Allowances and Hardship Differentials by the US Department of Labor.

The foreign service premium is actually a bribe to encourage a manager to leave familiar conditions and adapt to new surroundings. Although the methods of paying the premium vary, as do its percentages, most firms pay it as a percentage of the base salary. The percentages range from 10 to 25% of base salary. One variation of the straightforward percentage is a sliding scale by amount – 15% of the first US$20 000, then 10% and sometimes a ceiling beyond which a premium is not paid. Another variation is by duration, with the percentages decreasing with every year the manager spends abroad. Despite the controversial nature of foreign service premiums paid at some locations, they are a generally accepted competitive practice.

The environments in which a manager will work and the family will live vary dramatically. For example, consider an American manager being assigned to London or Brisbane versus Dar es Salaam or Port Moresby, or Bogota or Buenos Aires. Some locations may require little, if any, adjustment. Other locations call for major adaptation because of climatic differences, political instability, inadequacies in housing, differences in education or recreation, or overall isolation. For example, a family assigned to Beijing may find that schooling is difficult to arrange, with the result that younger children go to school in Tokyo and the older ones in the United States. To compensate for this type of expense and adjustment, firms pay hardship allowances. For American managers, allowances are based on US State Department Foreign Post Differentials. The percentages vary from zero (e.g., the American manager in Helsinki) to 50% (as in Monrovia). The higher allowances typically include a danger pay extra added to any hardship allowance.[49]

Housing costs and related expenses are typically the largest expenditure in the expatriate manager's budget. Firms usually provide a housing allowance commensurate with the manager's salary level and position. When the expatriate is the country manager for the firm, the housing allowance will provide for suitable quarters in which to receive business associates. In most cases, firms set a range within which the manager must find housing. For common utilities, firms provide an allowance or pay the costs outright.

One of the major determinants of the manager's lifestyle abroad is taxes. A manager earning US$100 000 in Canada would pay nearly US$40 000 in taxes. For this reason, 90% of US multinational corporations have tax-equalization plans. When a manager's overseas taxes are higher than at home, the firm will make up the difference. However, in countries with a lower rate of taxation, the company simply keeps the difference. Starting in 2008, the exclusion is indexed for inflation.

Nonsalary-Related Allowances

Other types of allowances are made available to ease the transition into the period of service abroad. Typical allowances during the transition stage include: (1) a relocation allowance to compensate for the additional expense of a move, such as purchase of electric converters; (2) a mobility allowance as an incentive to managers to go overseas, usually paid in a lump sum and as a substitute for the foreign service premium (some companies pay 50% at transfer, 50% at repatriation); (3) allowances related to housing, such as home sale or rental protection, shipment and storage of household goods or provision of household furnishings in overseas locations; (4) automobile protection in terms of covering possible losses on the sale of a car or cars at transfer and having to buy others overseas, usually at a higher cost; (5) travel expenses, using economy-class transportation except for long flights (e.g., from Washington to Taipei); and (6) temporary living expenses, which may become substantial if housing is not immediately available – as for the expatriate family who had to spend a year at a hotel in Beijing, for example. Companies are also increasingly providing support to make up for income lost by the accompanying spouse.

Education for children is one of the major concerns of expatriate families. Free public schooling may not be available and the private alternatives expensive. In many cases, children may have to go to school in a different country. Firms will typically reimburse for such expenses in the form of an education allowance. In the case of college education, firms reimburse for one round-trip airfare every year, leaving tuition expenses to the family.

Finally, firms provide support for medical expenses, especially to provide medical services at a level comparable to the expatriate's home country. In some cases, this means travelling to another country for care; for example, from Malaysia to Singapore, where the medical system is the most advanced in Southeast Asia. Other health-related allowances are in place to allow the expatriate to leave the challenging location periodically for rest and relaxation. Leaves from hardship posts such as Port Moresby are routine.

Other issues should be covered by a clearly stated policy. Home leave is provided every year, typically after 11 months overseas, although some companies require a longer period. Home leaves are usually accompanied by consultation and training sessions at headquarters. At some posts, club memberships are necessary because: (1) the status of the manager requires them; and (2) they provide family members with access to the type of recreation they are used to in the home environment. Because they are extremely expensive – for example, a 'mandatory' golf club membership in Tokyo might cost thousands of dollars – the firm's assistance is needed.

Method of Payment

The method of payment, especially in terms of currency, is determined by a number of factors. The most common method is to pay part of the salary in the local currency and part in the currency of the manager's home country. Host-country regulations, ranging from taxation to the availability of foreign currency, will influence the decision. Firms themselves look at the situation from the accounting and administrative point of view and would like, in most cases, to pay in local currencies to avoid burdening the subsidiary. The expatriate naturally will want to have some of the compensation in his or her own currency for various reasons; for example, if exchange controls are in effect, to get savings out of the country upon repatriation may be very difficult.

Compensation of Host-Country Nationals

The compensation packages paid to local managers – cash, benefits and privileges – are largely determined as a function of internal equity and external competitiveness. Internal equity may be complicated because of cultural differences in compensation; for example, in Japan a year-end bonus of an additional month's salary is common. On the other hand, some incentive programmes to increase productivity may be unknown to some nationals. Furthermore, in many countries, the state provides benefits that may be provided by the firm elsewhere. Since the firm and its employees contribute to the programmes by law, the services need not be duplicated.

External competitiveness depends on the market price of trained individuals and their attraction to the firm. External competitiveness is best assessed through surveys of compensation and benefits levels for a particular market. The firm must keep its local managers informed of the survey results to help them realize the value of their compensation packages.

MANAGING LABOUR PERSONNEL

None of the firm's objectives can be realized without a labour force, which can become one of the firm's major assets or one of its major problems depending on the relationship that is established. Because of local patterns and legislation, headquarters' role in shaping the relations is mainly advisory, limited to setting the overall tone for the interaction. However, many of the practices adopted in one market or region may easily come under discussion in another, making it necessary for multinational corporations to set general policies concerning labour relations. Often multinational corporations have been instrumental in bringing about changes in the overall work environment in a country. And as decisions are made where to locate and how to streamline operations, education and training become important criteria for both countries and companies.

At many companies, educational programmes are a means of leveraging valuable company resources. Eastman Kodak has established eight training centres of excellence with functional specializations (e.g., technical training and general business education). In China, AT&T has provided customized technical training to the government workers who will run the AT&T-supplied telecommunications networks.[50]

Labour strategy can be viewed from three perspectives: (1) the participation of labour in the affairs of the firm, especially as it affects performance and well-being; (2) the role and impact of unions in the relationship; and (3) specific human resource policies in terms of recruitment, training and compensation.

Labour Participation in Management

Over the past 25 years, many changes have occurred in the traditional labour–management relationship as a result of dramatic changes in the economic environment and the actions of both firms and the labour force. The role of the worker is changing both at the level of the job performed and in terms of participation in the decision-making process. To enhance workers' roles in decision making, various techniques have emerged: self-management, co-determination, minority board membership and works councils. In striving for improvements in quality of work life, programmes that have been initiated include flex time, quality circles and work-flow re-organization. Furthermore, employee ownership has moved into the mainstream.

Labour Participation in Decision Making

The degree to which workers around the world can participate in corporate decision making varies considerably. Rights of information, consultation and co-determination develop on three levels:

	Direct Involvement of Workers[a]	Involvement of Representative Bodies[a]	Board Representation Standing[b]	Overall Standing[c]
Germany	3	1	1	A
Sweden	4	2	1	A
Norway	1	10	1	B
Netherlands	9	4	2	C
France	7	3	2	C
Belgium	5	6	3	D
Finland	2	9	3	D
Denmark	8	7	1	D
Israel	11	5	3	D
Italy	6	8	3	E
Great Britain	10	11	3	E

Sources: Adapted from Industrial Democracy in Europe International Research Group (1981) *Industrial Democracy in Europe*, Clarendon Press, Oxford, UK, 291; Industrial Democracy in Europe International Research Group (1993) *Industrial Democracy in Europe Revisited*, Oxford University Press, Oxford, UK, ch. 3
[a]Involvement is rated on an 11-point scale, where 1 stands for the greatest degree of involvement and 11 for almost no involvement.
[b]All cases without any kind of board participation are coded 3; the right to appoint two or more members, 1; the in-between category, 2.
[c]Rankings are from high (A) to low (E).

Table 12.4: Degree of worker involvement in decision making of firms.

- The shop-floor level or direct involvement; for example, the right to be consulted in advance concerning transfers.
- The management level or through representative bodies; for example, works council participation in setting of new policies or changing of existing ones.
- The board level: for example, labour membership on the board of directors.[51]

The extent of worker participation in decision making in 11 countries is summarized in Table 12.4. Yugoslavia, before its breakup, had the highest amount of worker participation in any country; self-management was standard through workers' councils, which decided all major issues including the choice of managing director and supervisory board. Currently, the greatest amount of co-operation between labour and capital in participative leadership exists in the Germanic group of European countries (namely, Austria, Germany, the Netherlands and Switzerland).[52]

In some countries, employees are represented on the supervisory boards to facilitate communication between management and labour by giving labour a clearer picture of the financial limits of management and by providing management with a new awareness of labour's point of view. The process is called co-determination. In Germany, companies have a two-tiered management system with a supervisory board and the board of managers, which actually runs the firm. In a firm with 20 000 employees, for example, labour would have 10 of the 20 supervisory board slots divided in the following way: three places for union officials and the balance to be elected from the workforce. At least one member must be a white-collar employee and one a managerial employee.[53] The supervisory board is legally responsible for the managing board.

In some countries, labour has minority participation. In the Netherlands, for example, works councils can nominate (not appoint) board members and can veto the appointment of new members appointed by others. In other countries, such as the United States, co-determination has been opposed by unions as an undesirable means of co-operation, especially when management–labour relations are confrontational.

A tradition in labour relations, especially in Britain, is works councils. They provide labour a say in corporate decision making through a representative body, which may consist entirely of workers or of a combination of managers and workers. The councils participate in decisions on overall working conditions, training, transfers, work allocation and compensation. In some countries, such as Finland and Belgium, workers' rights to direct involvement, especially as it involves their positions, are quite strong. The European Union's works council directive will ultimately require over 1000 multinational companies, both European and non-European, to negotiate works council agreements. The agreements will provide for at least one meeting per year to improving dialogue between workers and management.[54]

The countries described above are unusual across the world. In many countries and regions, workers have few, if any, of these rights. The result is long-term potential for labour strife in those countries and possible negative publicity elsewhere. Over a 10-year period from 1989 to 1998, the most working days lost occurred in Iceland, followed by Spain, Greece, Canada, Turkey and Italy. In 1998, the most strike-prone country was Denmark, where workers sought a sixth week of paid holiday through strikes.[55]

In addition to labour groups and the media, investors and shareholders are also scrutinizing multinationals' track records on labour practices. As a result, a company investing in foreign countries should hold to international standards of safety and health, not simply local standards. This can be achieved, for example, through the use of modern equipment and training. Local labour also should be paid adequately. This increases the price of labour, and yet ensures the best available talent and helps avoid charges of exploitation.[56] Companies subcontracting work to local or joint-venture factories need to evaluate industrial relations throughout the system not only to avoid lost production due to disruptions such as strikes but also to ensure that no exploitation exists at the facilities. Several large firms, such as Nike and Reebok, require subcontractors to sign agreements saying that they will abide by minimum wage standards.[57] Although companies have long been opposed to linking free trade to labour standards, the business community is rethinking its strategy mainly to get trade negotiations moving.[58]

Improvement of Quality of Work Life

The term quality of work life has come to encompass various efforts in the areas of personal and professional development. Its two clear objectives are to increase productivity and to increase the satisfaction of employees. Of course, programmes leading to increased participation in corporate decision making are part of the programmes; however, this section concentrates on individual job-related programmes: work redesign, team building and work scheduling.[59]

By adding both horizontal and vertical dimensions to the work, work redesign programmes attack undesirable features of jobs. Horizontally, task complexity is added by incorporating work stages normally done before and after the stage being redesigned. Vertically, each employee is given more responsibility for making the decisions that affect how the work is done. Japanese car manufacturers have changed some of the work routines in their plants in the United States. For example, at Honda's unit in Marysville, Ohio, workers reacted favourably to the responsibilities they had been given, such as inspecting their own work and instructing others. On the other hand, work redesign may have significant costs attached, including wage increases, facility change costs and training costs.

Closely related to work redesign are efforts aimed at team building. For example, in car plants, work is organized so that groups are responsible for a particular, identifiable portion of the car, such as interiors. Each group has its own areas in which to pace itself and to organize the work. The group must take responsibility for the work, including inspections, whether it is performed individually or in groups. The group is informed about its performance through a computer system. The team-building effort includes job rotation to enable workers to understand all facets of their jobs. Another approach to team building makes use of quality circles, in which groups of workers regularly meet to discuss issues relating to their productivity. Team-building efforts have to be adapted to cultural differences. In cultures that are more individualistic, incentive structures may have to be kept at the individual level and discussions on quality issues should be broad-based rather than precise.[60]

Flexibility in work scheduling has led to changes in when and how long workers are at the workplace. Flex time allows workers to determine their starting and ending hours in a given workday; for example, they might arrive between 7:00 and 9:30 a.m. and leave between 3:00 and 5:30 p.m. The idea spread from Germany to the European Union, and to other countries such as Switzerland, Japan, New Zealand and the United States. Some 40% of the Dutch working population holds flex- or part-time positions.[61] Despite its advantages in reducing absenteeism, flex time is not applicable to industries using assembly lines. Flexible work scheduling has also led to compressed workweeks – for example, the four-day week – and job sharing, which allows a position to be filled by more than one person.

Firms around the world also have other programmes for personal and professional development, such as career counselling and health counselling. All of them are dependent on various factors external and internal to the firm. Of the external factors, the most important are the overall characteristics of the economy and the labour force. Internally, the programmes must fit into existing organizational structures or management must be inclined toward change. In many cases, labour unions have been one of the major resisting forces. Their view is that firms are trying to prevent workers from organizing by allowing them to participate in decision making and management.

The Role of Labour Unions

When two of the world's largest producers of electro-technology, Swedish Asea and Switzerland's Brown Boveri, merged to remain internationally competitive in a market dominated by a few companies such as General Electric, Siemens, Hitachi and Toshiba, not everyone reacted positively to the alliance. For tax reasons, headquarters would not be located in Sweden and this caused the four main Swedish labour unions to oppose the merger. They demanded that the Swedish government exercise its right to veto the undertaking because Swedish workers would no longer have a say in their company's affairs if it were headquartered elsewhere.

The incident is an example of the role labour unions play in the operation of a multinational corporation. It also points up the concerns of local labour unions when they must deal with organizations directed from outside their national borders.

The role of labour unions varies from country to country, often because of local traditions in management–labour relations. The variations include the extent of union power in negotiations and the activities of unions in general. In Europe, especially in the Northern European countries, collective bargaining takes place between an employers' association and an umbrella organization of unions, on a national or a regional basis, establishing the conditions for an entire industry. At the other end of the spectrum, negotiations in Japan are on the company level and the role of larger-scale unions is usually consultative. Another striking difference emerges in terms of the objectives of unions and the means by which they attempt to attain them. In the United Kingdom, for example, union activity tends to be politically motivated and identified with political ideology. In the United States, the emphasis has always been on improving workers' overall quality of life.

Internationalization of business has created a number of challenges for labour unions. The main concerns that have been voiced are: (1) the power of the firm to move production from one country to another if attractive terms are not reached in a particular market; (2) the unavailability of data, especially financial information, to support unions' bargaining positions; (3) insufficient attention to local issues and problems while focusing on global optimization; and (4) difficulty in being heard by those who eventually make the decisions.[62] This has been countered by new activism to secure core labour standards as fundamental human rights, including freedom of association and the right to organize and bargain collectively.[63]

Although the concerns are valid, all the problems anticipated may not develop. For example, transferring production from one country to another in the short term may be impossible and labour strife in the long term may well influence such moves. To maintain participation in corporate decision making, unions are taking action individually and across national boundaries as seen in the Focus on Ethics below. Individual unions refer to contracts signed elsewhere when setting the agenda for their own negotiations. Supranational organizations such as the International Trade Secretariats and industry-specific organizations such as the International Metal Workers' Federation exchange information and discuss bargaining tactics. The goal is also to co-ordinate bargaining with multinational corporations across national boundaries. The International Labour Organization, a specialized agency of the United Nations, has an information bank on multinational corporations' policies concerning wage structures, benefits packages and overall working conditions.

The relations between companies and unions can be co-operative as well. Alliances between labour and management have emerged to continue providing well-paying factory jobs in the United

F○CUS ON

ETHICS   Global Unions versus Global Companies

From the labour point of view, the United States is perceived by European companies as more flexible and less costly. However, when these companies attempt to challenge US unions by downsizing the workforce to increase profitability, they meet resistance not only from the US unions but also from the international federations of trade unions. Conflict arises when there are different understandings of the role of labour unions.

Trelleborg, a Swedish metal and mining conglomerate with operations in eight European countries, expanded into the United States with the purchase of a plant in Copperhill, Tennessee, in 1991 after the owner went bankrupt. The plant was managed under Trelleborg's subsidiary, Boliden Intertrade Inc. The unions at Copperhill deferred over $5 million in wages to help keep the plant alive in the early 1990s. But labour–management relations deteriorated during contract negotiations in 1996, when Trelleborg insisted on sweeping changes in work rules. Boliden executives recognized that there would be a considerable loss of jobs but saw no other way to regain competitiveness.

The workers saw the changes as a direct assault on their seniority system and a threat to worker safety, and went on strike after their contract

expired. The company responded by hiring replacement workers and a squad of security guards. Two weeks later, the company said it had received a petition from its new employees indicating they did not want a union. Unions, on their part, demanded that Boliden withdraw its letter of de-recognition and remove the replacement workers.

US unions represent 16% of the public- and private-sector workforce but in Sweden the unionization rate is over 80%. Although strikes are relatively rare in Sweden, replacing workers during a walkout is virtually unheard of. Swedish workers also have the right to shut down a company during a strike by stopping delivery trucks and other services, all actions that are banned in the United States.

Union activity was not limited to local moves in Tennessee. Metal, the powerful Swedish labour union representing Swedish workers in the industry, was recruited to pressure the parent company in Sweden. The International Federation of Chemical, Energy, Mine and General Workers' Unions launched a campaign to pressure Trelleborg to rehire the Copperhill strikers. US and Canadian unions warned institutional investors and pension fund managers that an investment in Boliden could be risky. They made their warnings as Trelleborg executives were visiting North

America to raise $900 million in an initial public offering on the Toronto Stock Exchange.

Two months into the crisis, Trelleborg announced it would sell its US subsidiary.

Source: Jay Mazur (2000) 'Labor's New Internationalism', *Foreign Affairs*, 79(January/February), 79–93; Tim Schorrock (1997) 'Firm to Sell US Unit at Center of Labor Flap', *The Journal of Commerce*, 3 June, 3A: Joan Campbell (1994) *The European Labor Unions*, Greenwood Press, Greenwood, CT, 429; Tom DeVos (1981) *US Multinationals and Worker Participation in Management*, Quorum Books, Westport, CT, 195; www.trellgroup.se.

States in face of global competition. For example, the Amalgamated Clothing and Textile Workers Union of America and Xerox worked jointly to boost quality and cut costs to keep their jobs from going to Mexico, where wage rates were a fraction of US costs.[64]

Human Resource Policies

The objectives of a human resource policy pertaining to workers are the same as for management: to anticipate the demand for various skills and to have in place programmes that will ensure the availability of employees when needed. For workers, however, the firm faces the problem on a larger scale and does not have, in most cases, an expatriate alternative. This means that, among other things, when technology is transferred for a plant, it has to be adapted to the local workforce.

Although most countries have legislation and restrictions concerning the hiring of expatriates, many of them – for example some of the EU countries and certain oil-rich Middle Eastern countries – have offset labour shortages by importing large numbers of workers from countries such as Turkey and Jordan. The EU by design allows free movement of labour. A mixture of backgrounds in the available labour pool can put a strain on personnel development. As an example, the firm may incur considerable expense to provide language training to employees. In Sweden, a certain minimum amount of language training must be provided for all 'guest workers' at the firm's expense.

Bringing a local labour force to the level of competency desired by the firm may also call for changes. As an example, managers at Honda's plant in Ohio encountered a number of problems: labour costs were originally 50% higher and productivity 10% lower than in Japan. Cars produced there cost US$500 more than the same models made in Japan and then delivered to the United States. Before Honda began to produce the Accord in the United States, it flew 200 workers representing all areas of the factory to Japan to learn to build Hondas the Sayama way and then to teach their co-workers the skills.

Compensation of the workforce is a controversial issue. Payroll expenses must be controlled for the firm to remain competitive; on the other hand, the firm must attract in appropriate numbers the type of workers it needs. The compensation packages of US-based multinational companies have come under criticism, especially when their level of compensation is lower in developing countries than in the United States. Criticism has occurred even when the salaries or wages paid were substantially higher than the local average.

Comparisons of compensation packages are difficult because of differences in the packages that are shaped by culture, legislation, collective bargaining, taxation and individual characteristics of the job. In northern Europe, for example, new fathers can accompany their wives on a two-week paternity leave at the employer's expense.

These differences in compensation and benefits may come to a head in merger and acquisition situations. When Ford Motor acquired Volvo, planned changes included moving to a three-shift, round-the-clock production schedule just as in the United States, rather than the two shifts in Sweden.

Some of the differences are not changeable, however. Night-shift workers get paid the same as day-shift workers although they work only 30 hours a week because of a government-mandated allocation. Some benefits, such as a fitness centre that costs the company annually over US$600 000 to maintain, may come under scrutiny by the new owners.[65]

SUMMARY

A business organization is the sum of its human resources. To recruit and retain a pool of effective people for each of its operations requires: (1) personnel planning and staffing; (2) training activities; (3) compensation decisions; and (4) attention to labour–management relations.

Firms attract international managers from a number of sources, both internal and external. In the earlier stages of internationalization, recruitment must be external. Later, an internal pool often provides candidates for transfer. The decision then becomes whether to use home-country, host-country or third-country nationals. If expatriate managers are used, selection policies should focus on competence, adaptability and personal traits. Policies should also be set for the compensation and career progression of candidates selected for out-of-country assignments. At the same time, the firm must be attentive to the needs of local managers for training and development.

Labour can no longer be considered as simply services to be bought. Increasingly, workers are taking an active role in the decision making of the firm and in issues related to their own welfare. Various programmes are causing dramatic organizational change, not only by enhancing the position of workers but by increasing the productivity of the workforce as well. Workers employed by the firm are usually local, as are the unions that represent them. Their primary concerns in working for a multinational firm are job security and benefits. Therefore unions are co-operating across national boundaries to equalize benefits for workers employed by the same firm in different countries.

QUESTIONS FOR DISCUSSION

1. Is a 'supranational executive corps', consisting of cosmopolitan individuals of multiple nationalities who would be an asset wherever used, a possibility for any corporation?

2. Comment on this statement by Lee Iacocca: 'If a guy wants to be a chief executive 25 or 50 years from now, he will have to be well rounded. There will be no more of "Is he a good lawyer, is he a good marketing guy, is he a good finance guy?" His education and his experience will make him a total entrepreneur in a world that has really turned into one huge market. He better speak Japanese or German, he better understand the history of both of those countries and how they got to where they are and he better know their economics pretty cold.'

3. What additional benefit is brought into the expatriate selection and training process by adaptability screening?

4. A manager with a current base salary of US$100 000 is being assigned to Lagos, Nigeria. Assuming that you are that manager, develop a compensation and benefits package for yourself in terms of both salary-related and nonsalary-related items.

5. What accounts for the success of Japanese companies with both American unions and the more ferocious British unions? In terms of the changes that have come about, are there winners or losers among management and workers? Could both have gained?

6. Develop general policies that the multinational corporation should follow in dealing (or choosing not to deal) with a local labour union.

INTERNET EXERCISES

1. Paguro.net (available at www.paguro.net) is a network that puts expatriates, and especially their family members, in touch with each other. What benefits can be gained from individual or corporate membership of such a service?

2. Using a web site such as monster.com (http://workabroad.monster.com/articles/cost/) compare the cost of living in your home city versus Vienna, Austria; Brussels, Belgium; Shanghai, China; Bogota, Colombia; New York, USA; and New Delhi, India. What accounts for the differences present?

TAKE A STAND

US-based multinational corporations are increasingly debating whether they should establish grievance procedures for their non-union, non-managerial professional and technical employees. Firms such as IBM, Marriott, Bechtel and GE Power Systems have already installed procedures in an attempt to ensure organizational due process under such titles as 'Employee Dispute Resolution Programme' and 'Dispute Resolution Process: Employee Handbook'.

The rise of organizational due process in the private sector, both domestically and internationally, may be attributed to the void left by the declining institutional and economic power of unions in recent years. With industrial and trade unions retreating from the stage, multinational corporations are feeling more, not less, pressure to do what union leaders might have been pushing for in terms of employee rights. This results partly from a changing sense of employee relations and partly from a push to prevent unionization. For example, non-US car manufacturers have been able to keep unions out in their US facilities by offering attractive packages and working environments to their employees.

The biggest challenge may be that a non-union grievance procedure in which employees have complete confidence may be very difficult to create. The key tactical issues that need to be addressed for alternative dispute resolution and employee voice include the composition and nature of open-door policies and procedures and peer-review systems, as well as the operation of non-union grievance arbitration systems.

FOR DISCUSSION

1. Is providing a formal non-union grievance procedure merely an incidental feature in the operation of a multinational corporation or is it an ethical obligation for top management to fulfil?

2. Although there is no legal requirement that a corporation implement a system of due process in the workplace, how can such a procedure be viewed as a sound business decision?

CHAPTER 13

- Corporate Governance
- Accounting Diversity
- Principal Accounting Differences Across Countries
- International Taxation

Corporate Governance, Accounting and Taxation

LEARNING OBJECTIVES

- To explore the purpose and structure of corporate governance as it is practised globally.

- To examine the failures in corporate governance in recent years and how authorities are responding to these changes.

- To understand the differences between the European, the US and the Japanese approach to corporate governance.

- To understand how accounting practices differ across countries and how these differences may alter the competitiveness of firms in international markets.

- To isolate which accounting practices are likely to constitute much of the competitiveness debate in the coming decade.

- To examine the primary differences in international taxation across countries and in turn how governments deal with both domestic and foreign firms operating in their markets.

PARMALAT WENT BITTER

Following the financial scandals at Enron and WorldCom, European managers thought they had nothing to do with fraudulent behaviour. European chief executives boisterously argued that no such fraud was possible in Europe. Little did they know that the Italian company Parmalat would become a symbol of one of the largest financial frauds in history. The accounting calamity at Italian dairy-foods giant Parmalat had prosecutors scrambling to find out what happened to US$8.5–12 billion in vanished assets. Parmalat has turned out

to be the largest bankruptcy in European history, representing 1.5% of Italian GNP, which is proportionally larger than the combined ratio of the Enron and WorldCom bankruptcies to the US GNP.

Parmalat was headquartered in the central Italian city of Parma. It was launched as a family business and the *capofamiglia*, Calisto Tanzi, began expanding the business shortly after his father's death in 1961. He managed to develop it from a small sausage and cheese shop into an international food and beverage concern. Along the way, he formed close relationships with the Christian Democrats, who governed Italy throughout the post-war period.

The roots of the problem are traced back to 1997, when Parmalat decided to become a 'global player' using international acquisitions financed through debt. Soon, Parmalat became the third largest biscuit-maker in the United States. But such acquisitions, instead of bringing in profits, started, no later than 2001, to bring in red figures. Losing money on its productive activities, the company shifted more and more to the high-flying world of derivatives and other speculative enterprises.

Parmalat's founder and now former CEO Calisto Tanzi engaged the firm in several exotic enterprises, such as a tourist agency called Parmatour, and the purchase of the local soccer club Parma. Huge sums were poured into these two enterprises, which have been loss-makers from the very beginning. It has been reported that Parmatour, now closed, had a loss of at least €2 billion. While accumulating losses, and with debts to the banks, Parmalat started to built a network of offshore mail-box companies that were used to conceal losses, through a mirror-game that made them appear as assets, and the company started to issue bonds in order to collect money.

The security for such bonds was provided by the alleged assets represented by the offshore schemes. Bank of America, Citicorp and J.P. Morgan rated Parmalat bonds as sound financial paper, when they knew, or should have known, that they were worth nothing. Bank of America participated as a partner in some of Parmalat's acquisitions, and Citicorp is alleged to have built up the fraudulent accounting system. 'The Parmalat fraud has been mainly implemented in New York, with the active role of the Zini legal firm and of Citibank,' said San Diego lawyer Darren Robbins, a partner in the firm Milberg Weiss Bershad Hynes & Lerach, which is leading the class-action suit. 'We believe that Citigroup, by creating instruments like the sadly famous 'Buconero', has played a fundamental role in helping Parmalat to fake their balance sheets and hide their real financial situation.'

The New York-based Zini law firm named by Robbins played a role that seems to have come out of the movie *The Godfather*. Through Zini, firms owned by Parmalat were sold to certain American citizens with Italian surnames, only to be purchased again by Parmalat later. The whole operation was fake: the money for the sale in the first place came from other entities owned by Parmalat, and it served only to create 'liquidity' in the books. Thanks to that liquidity, Parmalat could keep issuing bonds. Mafia? Former CEO Tanzi declared to prosecutors in Parma that the fraudulent bonds system 'was fully the banks' idea'. Parmalat's former financial manager, Fausto Tonna, counterfeited Parmalat's balance sheets in order to provide security for the bonds, but 'it was the banks which proposed it to Tonna', Tanzi declared.

Tanzi's version was confirmed by Luciano Spilingardi, member of the Parmalat board. Bond issues were ordered by the banks, Spilingardi said to prosecutors, according to leaks published in the daily *La Repubblica*. 'I remember that one of the last issues of €150 million was presented to the board meeting as an explicit request by a foreign bank, which was ready to subscribe the entire bond. If I remember correctly, it was Deutsche Bank.' The request was accepted and the last Parmalat bond, issued in Summer 2003, made its way to the Cayman Islands offshore black hole. Meanwhile, the financial manager of Parmalat became Alberto Ferraris who came from . . . Citibank. In June 2003, before the last bond issue 'ordered' by Deutsche Bank, Parmalat's board had a new member: He was Luca Sala, a top manager coming from . . . Bank of America.

The Parmalat crisis finally broke out on 8 December 2003, when the company defaulted on a €150 million bond. The management claimed that this was because a customer, a speculative fund named Epicurum, did not pay its bills. Allegedly, Parmalat had won a derivatives contract with Epicurum, betting against the dollar. But it was soon discovered that Epicurum was owned by firms whose address was the same as some of Parmalat's own offshore entities. In other words, Epicurum was owned by Parmalat.

On 9 December, as rumours spread that Parmalat's claimed liquidity was not there, Standard & Poor's finally downgraded Parmalat bonds to junk status and in the next few days, Parmalat stocks fell 40%. On 12 December, Parmalat's management somehow found the money to pay the bond, but on 19 December came the end: Bank of America announced that an account with allegedly US$4.9 billion in liquidity claimed by Parmalat did not exist. When the bankruptcy was revealed Parmalat stocks fell an additional 66%.

In the subsequent investigation, Italian prosecutors said they had discovered that managers simply invented assets to offset as much as US$16.2 billion in liabilities and falsified accounts over a 15-year period, forcing the US$9.2 billion company into bankruptcy on 27 December 2003. Trading in Parmalat shares was suspended the same day.

Parmalat had 36 000 employees in 30 countries and it did US$3.3 billion in business in North America, where it not only sold its trademark milk-in-a-box but also owned Black Diamond Cheese, Archway Cookies LLC and Sunnydale Farms dairy. The US Securities and Exchange Commission has since sued Parmalat for misleading investors in a 'brazen fraud'. The scandal is also a fresh blow to the international accounting industry. Parmalat's auditor from 1990 to 1999 was the Italian branch of Grant Thornton International, one of the largest of the so-called second-tier US accounting firms. In 1999, Parmalat was forced to change its auditor under Italian law and it replaced Grant Thornton with the Italian unit of Deloitte Touche Tohmatsu. However, Grant Thornton continued to audit Parmalat's offshore entities. Neither firm uncovered what investigators say was years of blatant accounting fraud. Grant Thornton has issued a statement calling itself a 'victim' of the deceit. Deloitte points out that it first raised questions about Parmalat's accounts on 31 October 2003.

No one knows for certain whether missing funds were used to plug operating losses, pay creditors or illegally enrich management. Tanzi admitted to prosecutors on that he knew the company's accounts were being falsified to hide losses of as much as US$10 billion, mainly in Parmalat's Latin American subsidiaries. The fake balance sheet figures allowed Parmalat to continue borrowing. Tanzi also confessed to misappropriating some US$620 million to cover losses in other family owned companies.

The Italian Government speeded up the bankruptcy procedure in order to protect its industrial activity, payrolls and vendors from creditors' claims. The government appointed Enrico Bondi to present a reorganization plan by 20 January 2004. He was a man trusted by the banks. The same day, Paolo Raimondi, head of the Italian LaRouche movement, issued a statement in which he said that the Parmalat bankruptcy, like the Cirio, Enron and LTCM cases, 'are not isolated cases in an otherwise functioning system. Instead, they are the most evident manifestation of the bankruptcy of the entire financial system.' After pointing to the role of derivative speculation in the Parmalat case, Raimondi stressed that Citigroup and Bank of America, Parmalat's main financial partners, are 'the number two and three among banks involved in derivatives operations.' Because it is not just a firm at stake but the whole system, 'the solution must be a global one,' Raimondi said, pointing to LaRouche's proposal for a world financial reorganization called a New Bretton Woods. The Italian central banking system is not dissimilar to the US Federal Reserve or other central banking systems. Under the Bretton Woods system of regulations, however, it was partially under government control. This changed first in 1979, when deregulation freed the central bank from the obligation to buy government debt, and finally after 1992, when the largest shareholders of the Bank of Italy were privatized.

The bitterness is not only for those who created and implemented or simply preferred not to see or speak about the fraudulent financial operations but also for more than 100 000 Italians who owned Parmalat bonds. They were mostly families who had been advised by their banks to buy paper which is now worth nothing.

Sources: C. Celani, The Story Behind Parmalat's Bankruptcy, *Executive Intelligence Review*, 16 January 2004, www.larouchepub.com/other/2004/3102parmalat_invest.html; C. Sverige, The Parmalat scandal: Europe's ten-billion euro black hole, 6 January 2004, www.wsws.org/articles/2004/jan2004/parm-j06.shtml; How Parmalat Went Sour, *Business Week*, 12 January 2004, www.businessweek.com/magazine/content/04_02/b3865053_ mz054.htm.

INTRODUCTION

The structure and conduct of corporate governance and the methods used in the measurement of company operations, accounting, principles and practices, vary dramatically across countries. Corporate governance, as a result of the recent failures of Enron, Tyco, WorldCom, Parmalat and Health South to name but a few, has raised what was once an obscure topic of interest to regulators only to the front page of the daily papers. Key elements of corporate governance, the transparency of the firm's operations and financial results has stoked significant debate about both the accounting and tax practices of global companies. This chapter provides an overview of these issues and also presents current trends in both corporate practices and international regulatory approaches.

Taxation and accounting are fundamentally related. The principles by which a firm measures its sales and expenses, its assets and liabilities, all go into the formulation of profits, which are subject to taxation. The tax policies of more and more governments, in conjunction with accounting principles, are also becoming increasingly similar. Many of the tax issues of specific interest to officials, such as the avoidance of taxes in high-tax countries or the shielding of income from taxation by holding profits in so-called *tax havens*, are slowly being eliminated by increasing co-operation between governments. Like the old expression says, 'only death and taxes' are today, more than ever, inevitable. Although the average business manager cannot be expected to have a detailed understanding (or recall) of the multitudes of tax laws and accounting principles across countries, a basic understanding of many of these issues aids in the understanding of how firms may structure and operate their businesses globally with the perpetual commitment to create value. We begin with the debate raging over corporate governance of the modern corporation.

CORPORATE GOVERNANCE

The relationship among stakeholders used to determine and control the strategic direction and performance of an organization is termed corporate governance. The corporate governance of the organization is therefore the way in which order and process is established to ensure that decisions are made and interests are represented properly – for all stakeholders.

Although the governance structure of any company – domestic, international or multinational – is fundamental to its very existence, this subject has become the lightning rod of political and business debate in the past few years, because failures in governance in a variety of forms have led to corporate fraud and failure. Abuses and failures in corporate governance have dominated global business news in recent years. Beginning with the accounting fraud and questionable ethics of business conduct at Enron, culminating in its bankruptcy in the autumn of 2001, to the retirement pay package of Richard Grasso, the chairman of the New York Stock Exchange, in September 2003, failures in corporate governance have raised issues about the ethics and culture of the conduct of business.

The Goal of Corporate Governance

The single overriding objective of corporate governance is the optimization over time of the returns to shareholders. In order to achieve this, good governance practices should focus the attention of the board of directors of the corporation on this objective by developing and implementing a strategy for the corporation that ensures corporate growth and improvement in the value of the corporation's equity. At the same time, it should ensure an effective relationship with stakeholders.[1]

The most widely accepted statement of good corporate governance practices are those established by the Organization for Economic Co-operation and Development (OECD) in 1999:[2]

- *The Rights of Shareholders.* The corporate governance framework should protect shareholders' rights.
- *The Equitable Treatment of Shareholders.* The corporate governance framework should ensure the equitable treatment of all shareholders, including minority and foreign shareholders. All shareholders should have the opportunity to obtain effective redress for violation of their rights.
- *The Role of Stakeholders in Corporate Governance.* The corporate governance framework should recognize the rights of stakeholders as established by law and encourage active co-operation between corporations and stakeholders in creating wealth, jobs and the sustainability of financially sound enterprises.
- *Disclosure and Transparency.* The corporate governance framework should ensure that timely and accurate disclosure is made on all material matters regarding the corporation, including the financial situation, performance, ownership and governance of the company.
- *The Responsibilities of the Board.* The corporate governance framework should ensure the strategic guidance of the company, the effective monitoring of management by the board and the board's accountability to the company and the shareholders.

These principles obviously focus on several key areas – shareholder rights and roles, disclosure and transparency and the responsibilities of boards, which we will discuss in more detail below.

The Structure of Corporate Governance

Our first challenge is to try to capture what people mean when they use the expression 'corporate governance'. Figure 13.1 provides an overview of the various parties and their responsibilities associated with the governance of the modern corporation. The modern corporation is a complex organism living in a complex environment. Its actions and behaviours are directed and controlled by both internal forces and external forces.

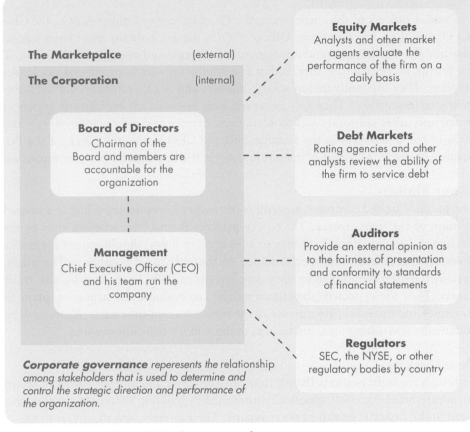

Figure 13.1: The structure of corporate governance.

The internal forces, the officers of the corporation (such as the Chief Executive Officer and the Board of Directors of the corporation (including the Chair of the Board), are those directly responsible for determining both the strategic direction and the execution of the company's future. But they are not acting within a vacuum; they are subject to the constant prying eyes of the external forces in the marketplace that question the validity and soundness of their decisions and performance. These include the equity markets in which the shares are traded, the analysts who critique their investment prospects, the creditors and credit agencies who lend them money, the auditors who testify to the fairness of their reporting and the multitude of regulators who oversee their actions in order to protect the public's investment.

The Board of Directors

The legal body that is accountable for the governance of the corporation is its Board of Directors. The board is composed of both employees of the organization (inside members) and senior and influential non-employees (outside members). Areas of debate surrounding boards include the following: (1) the proper balance between inside and outside members; (2) the means by which board members are compensated for their service; and (3) the actual ability of a board adequately to monitor and manage a corporation when board members are spending sometimes fewer than five days a year in board activities. Outside members, very often the current or retired chief executives of other major companies, may bring with them a healthy sense of distance and impartiality, which, although refreshing, may also result in limited understanding of the true issues and events within the company.

Officers and Management

The senior officers of the corporation, the Chief Executive Officer (CEO), the Chief Financial Officer (CFO) and the Chief Operating Officer (COO), are not only the most knowledgeable about the business but also the creators and directors of its strategic and operational direction. The management of the firm is, according to theory, acting as a contractor – as an *agent* – of stockholders to pursue value creation. They are motivated by salary, bonuses and stock options (positively) or by the risk of losing their jobs (negatively). They may, however, have biases of self-enrichment or personal agendas that the board and other corporate stakeholders must oversee and police. Interestingly enough, in more than 80% of the companies in the Fortune 500, the CEO is also the Chair of the Board. This is, in the opinion of many, a conflict of interest and not in the best interest of the company and its shareholders.

Equity Markets

The publicly traded company, regardless of country of residence, is highly susceptible to the changing opinion of the marketplace. The equity markets themselves, whether they be the New York Stock Exchange, London Stock Exchange or Mexico City Bolsa, should mirror the market's constant reflections on the promise and performance of the individual company. The analysts are those self-described experts employed by the many investment banking firms who also trade in these company shares. They are expected (sometimes naively) to evaluate the strategies, plans for execution of the strategies and financial performance of the firms on a real-time basis. Analysts depend on the financial statements and other public disclosures of the firm for their information.

Debt Markets

Although the debt markets (banks that provide loans and various forms of securitized debt such as corporate bonds) are not specifically interested in building shareholder value, they are indeed interested in the financial health of the company. Their interest, specifically, is in the company's ability to repay its debt in a timely and efficient manner. These markets, like the equity markets, must rely on the financial statements and other disclosures (public and private in this case) of the companies with which they work.

Auditors

Auditors are responsible for providing an external professional opinion as to the fairness and accuracy of corporate financial statements. In this process, they attempt to determine whether the firm's financial records and practices follow what in the United States is termed generally accepted accounting principles in regard to accounting procedures. But auditors are hired by the firms they are auditing, leading to a rather unique practice of policing their employers. The additional difficulty that has arisen in recent years is that the major accounting firms pursued the development of large consulting practices, often leading to a conflict of interest. An auditor not giving a clean bill of health to a client could not expect to gain many lucrative consulting contracts from that same firm in the near future.

Regulators

Publicly traded firms are subject to the regulatory oversight of both governmental organizations and non-governmental organizations. The Securities and Exchange Commission (SEC) in the US, for example, is a careful watchdog of the publicly traded equity markets, both in the behaviour of the companies themselves and of the various investors participating in those markets. The SEC and other authorities like it outside of the United States require a regular and orderly disclosure process of corporate performance in order that all investors may evaluate the company's investment value with adequate, accurate and fairly distributed information. This regulatory oversight is often focused on when and what information is released by the company, and to whom.

Publicly traded firms in the United States are also subject to the rules and regulations of the exchange in which they are traded (New York Stock Exchange, American Stock Exchange and NAS-DAQ are the largest). These organizations, typically categorized as 'self-regulatory' in nature, construct and enforce standards of conduct for both their member companies and themselves in the practice of share trading.

Comparative Corporate Governance

The origins of the need for a corporate governance process arise from the separation of ownership from management and from the views (which vary by culture) of who the stakeholders are and of what significance they hold. As a result, corporate governance practices differ across countries, economies and cultures. As described in Table 13.1, though, the various corporate governance structures may be classified by regime, and the regimes in turn reflect the evolution of business ownership and direction within the countries over time.

Market-based regimes, such as those of the United States and the United Kingdom, are characterized by relatively efficient capital markets in which the ownership of publicly traded companies is widely dispersed. *Family based systems*, such as those in many of the emerging markets, Asian markets and Latin American markets, not only started with strong concentrations of family ownership (as opposed to partnerships or small investment groups, which are not family based) but also have continued to be largely controlled by families even after going public. Bank-based and government-based regimes are those in which government ownership of property and industry has been the constant force over time, resulting in only marginal 'public ownership' of enterprise and, even then, subject to significant restrictions on business practices.

These regimes are therefore a function of at least three major factors in the evolution of global corporate governance principles and practices: financial market development, the degree of separation between management and ownership, and the concept of disclosure and transparency.

Financial Market Development

The depth and breadth of capital markets is critical to the evolution of corporate governance practices. Country markets that have had relatively slow growth, as in the emerging markets, or have industrialized rapidly using neighbouring capital markets (as in the case of Western Europe), may not form large public equity market systems. Without significant public trading of ownership shares, high

Regime basis	Characteristics	Examples
Market-based	Efficient equity markets; dispersed ownership	US, UK, Canada, Australia
Family based	Management and ownership is combined; family/majority and minority shareholders	Hong Kong, Indonesia, Malaysia, Singapore, Taiwan, France
Bank based	Government influence in bank lending; lack of transparency; family control	Korea, Germany
Government affiliated	State ownership of enterprise; lack of transparency; no minority influence	China, Russia

Source: Based on J. Tsui and T. Shieh (2004) 'Corporate Governance in Emerging Markets: An Asian Perspective', in *International Finance and Accounting Handbook*, 3rd edition, Frederick D.S. Choi (ed.), John Wiley & Sons, Inc., Hoboken, NJ, 24.4–24.6

Table 13.1: Comparative corporate governance regimes.

concentrations of ownership are preserved and few disciplined processes of governance are developed.

Separation of Management and Ownership

In countries and cultures in which the ownership of the firm has continued to be an integral part of management, agency issues and failures have been less of a problem. In countries such as the United States, in which ownership has become largely separated from management (and widely dispersed), aligning the goals of management and ownership is much more difficult.

Disclosure and Transparency

The extent of disclosure regarding the operations and financial results of a company vary dramatically across countries. Disclosure practices reflect a wide range of cultural and social forces, including the degree of ownership that is public, the degree to which government feels the need to protect investors' rights versus ownership rights and the extent to which family based and government-based business remains central to the culture. Transparency, a parallel concept to disclosure, reflects the visibility of decision-making processes within the business organization.

Note that the word 'ethics' has not been used. All of the principles and practices described so far have assumed that the individuals in roles of responsibility and leadership pursue them truly and fairly. That, however, has not always been the case.

The Case of Enron

Many of the issues related to corporate governance – and its failures – are best described by the case of Enron. Enron Corporation declared bankruptcy in November 2001 as a result of a complex combination of business and governance failures. As noted in its own board report as excerpted in the Focus on Ethics below, the failures involved organizations and individuals both inside and outside of Enron.

As it turns out, much of what Enron reported as 'earnings' were not. Much of the debt raised by the company via a number of partnerships was not disclosed in corporate financial statements as it should have been. Simultaneous to the over-reporting of profits and the under-reporting of debt was the massive compensation packages and bonuses earned by corporate officers. How did this happen?

- It appears that the executive officers of the firm were successful in managing the board of directors toward their own goals. Management had moved the company into a number of new markets in which the firm suffered substantial losses, resulting in re-doubled attempts on their part to somehow generate the earnings needed to meet Wall Street's unquenchable thirst for profitable growth.
- The board failed in its duties to protect shareholder interests by lack of due diligence and most likely by putting faith in the officers that proved undeserved. It is also important to note that Enron's legal advisers, some of whom reported to the board, also failed to provide leadership on a number of glaring instances of malfeasance.
- Enron's auditors, Arthur Andersen, committed serious errors in judgement regarding accounting treatment for many Enron activities, including the above partnerships. Andersen was reported to have had serious conflicts of interest, earning US$5 million in auditing fees from Enron in 2001 and more than US$50 million in consulting fees in the same year.
- Enron's analysts were, in a few cases, blinded by the sheer euphoria over Enron's latent successes in the mid- to late-1990s or else were working within investment banks that were earning substantial investment banking fees related to the complex partnerships. Although a few analysts continued to note that the company's earnings seemed strangely large relative to the falling cash flows reported, Enron's management was generally successful in arguing their point.

F⬤CUS ON

ETHICS Enron's Board on What Happened at Enron

'The tragic consequences of the related-party transactions and accounting errors were the result of failures at many levels and by many people: a flawed idea, self-enrichment by employees, inadequately designed controls, poor implementation, inattentive oversight, simple (and not so simple) accounting mistakes and overreaching in a culture that appears to have encouraged pushing the limits. Our review indicates that many of these consequences could and should have been avoided.'

Source: 'Report of Investigation: Special Investigative Committee of the Board of Directors of Enron Corporation', Board of Directors, Enron, 1 February 2002, 27–28.

The rise and fall of Enron is a story that is far from complete. It may be that in the end, however, the true moral of the story is not in the failure of any specific process in place within the American system of corporate governance, nor in the mistaken focus on fair-value accounting, nor in the lack of diligence of the board's own audit committee, but simply the failure of people in a wide variety of positions of leadership.

Good Governance and Reputation

Does good governance matter? This is actually a difficult question and the realistic answer has been, historically, largely dependent on outcomes. For example, as long as Enron's share price continued to rise dramatically throughout the 1990s, questions over transparency, accounting propriety and even financial facts were largely overlooked by all the stakeholders of the corporation. Yet, eventually, the fraud and deceit and failure of the multitude of corporate governance practices resulted in the bankruptcy of the firm, destroying not only the wealth of investors but also the careers, incomes and savings of so many of its basic stakeholders – its own employees. Ultimately, yes, good governance does matter. A lot.

A second way of valuing good governance is by measuring the attitudes and tendencies of the large global institutional investors who make the biggest decisions about where capital may go. A recent McKinsey study surveyed more than 200 institutional investors as to the value they placed on good governance. The survey results presented in Figure 13.2 quantify good governance in the premium that institutional investors would be willing to pay for companies with good governance within specific country markets. Although this is not exactly equivalent to saying who has 'good' and 'bad' corporate governance globally, it does provide some insight as to which countries' institutional investors see good governance as being scarce. It is again important to note that most of the emerging market nations have relatively few publicly traded companies, even today.

This is not a surprise to the 'sell-side', the companies themselves. Corporate leadership globally is increasingly concerned with the nature of its reputation and corporate governance failures are high on the list of issues that affect corporate reputation. Figure 13.3 presents survey results from 2003 in which CEOs were asked what external forces threatened their corporate reputation. Unethical behaviour and product or service problems tied for the most frequently cited causes for destruction of corporate reputation.

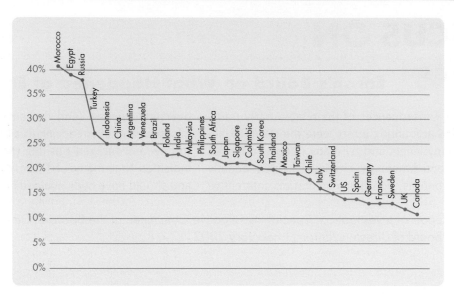

Figure 13.2: The value of good governance.

Source: Data complied from "McKinsey Global Investor Opinion Survey on Corporate Governance, 2002," McKinsey & Company, July 2002.

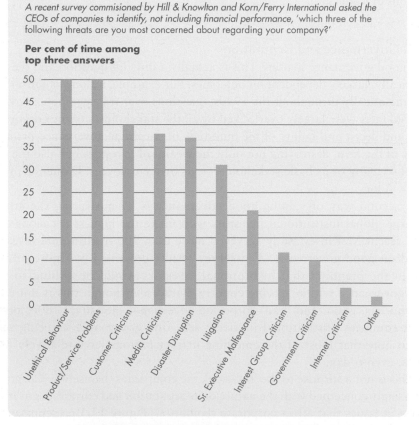

Figure 13.3: What threatens corporate reputation?

Source: '2003 Corporate Reputation Watch Survey', Hill & Knowlton and Korn/Ferry International. Korn Ferry Hill & Knowlton Corporate Reputation Watch, 2003. Used with permission.

Corporate Governance Reform

The debate regarding what needs to be done about corporate governance reform depends on which systems and regimes are deemed superior. To date, reform in the United States has been largely regulatory.

The US Response: Sarbanes–Oxley

The US Congress passed the Sarbanes–Oxley Act in July 2002. It had three major requirements: (1) CEOs of publicly traded firms must vouch for the veracity of the firm's published financial statements; (2) corporate boards must have audit committees drawn from independent (outside) directors; and (3) companies are prohibited from making loans to corporate officers and directors. The first provision – the so-called signature clause – has already had significant impact on the way in which companies prepare their financial statements. Although the provision was intended to instil a sense of responsibility and accountability in senior management (and therefore fewer explanations of 'the auditors signed-off on it'), the companies themselves have pushed the same procedure downward in their organizations, often requiring business unit managers and directors at lower levels to sign their financial statements.

Sarbanes–Oxley has been quite controversial internationally, as it is in conflict with a number of the existing corporate governance practices already in place in markets that view themselves as having better governance records than the United States. A foreign firm wishing to list or continue listing their shares on a US exchange must comply with the law. Some companies, such as Porsche, withdrew plans for a US listing specifically in opposition to Sarbanes–Oxley. Other companies, however – including many of the largest foreign companies traded on US exchanges, such as Unilever, Siemens and ST Microelectronics – have stated their willingness to comply, if they can find acceptable compromises between US law and the governance requirements and principles in their own countries.[3]

According to the 2007 Public Company Governance Survey of the US National Association of Corporate Directors (NACD), directors named strategic planning as their top concern followed by corporate performance, CEO succession and integration of strategy and compensation. The survey shows that the first three issues are perennially top concerns for directors but are also areas where directors indicate low levels of effectiveness. The area of CEO succession has been considered as least effective. There is also some disconnect between the areas of importance and effectiveness as shown in Figure 13.4.

The UK Approach

The UK government has commissioned several investigations of the corporate governance system. In 1992, the *Cadbury Report* presented an analysis of corporate governance best practice. In 1995, the *Greenbury Report* discussed renumeration; the *Hampel Report* in 1998 integrated suggestions on best practice and renumeration in the so called *Combined Code on Corporate Governance*. In 1999, the *Turnbull Report* produced Internal Control-Guidance for Directors on Combined Code. Following the Enron and WorldCom scandals in the US, the Combined Code was updated in 2003 to incorporate recommendations from reports on the role of non-executive directors (the *Higgs Report*) and the role of the audit committee (the *Smith Report*). At this time, the UK government confirmed that the Financial Reporting Council (FRC) was to have the responsibility for publishing and maintaining the Code. The FRC made further, limited, changes to the Code in 2006. Throughout all of these changes, the 'comply or explain' approach, first set out in the Cadbury Report, has been retained.

The FRC is the UK's independent regulator responsible for promoting confidence in corporate reporting and governance. The approach of the UK combines high standards of corporate governance

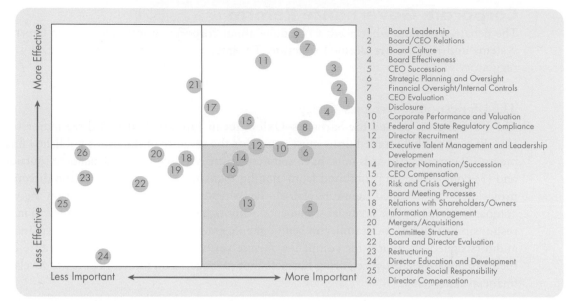

Figure 13.4: Public Company Governance Survey of the US National Association of Corporate Directors, 2007.

with relatively low associated costs. There is a relative lack of prescription as to how the company's board organizes itself and exercises its responsibilities. The Combined Code on Corporate Governance identifies good governance practices but companies can choose to adopt a different approach if that is more appropriate to their circumstances.

The UK approach starts from the position that good governance is a tool that can improve the board's ability to manage the company effectively as well as provide accountability to shareholders. To quote from the Cadbury Report: 'The effectiveness with which boards discharge their responsibilities determines Britain's competitive position. They must be free to drive their companies forward, but exercise that freedom within a framework of effective accountability. This is the essence of any system of good corporate governance.'

The key relationship is between the company and its shareholders, not between the company and the regulator. Boards and shareholders are encouraged to engage in dialogue on corporate governance matters. For the system to work effectively shareholders need to have appropriate and relevant information to enable them to make a judgement on the governance practices of the companies in which they invest. They also need the rights to enable them to influence the behaviour of the board when they are not content.

Under UK company law, shareholders have comparatively extensive voting rights, including the rights to appoint and dismiss individual directors and, in certain circumstances, to call an Extraordinary General Meeting of the company. Certain requirements relating to the AGM, including the provision of information to shareholders and arrangements for voting on resolutions, are also set out in company law, as are some requirements for information to be disclosed in the annual report and accounts. These include requirements for a Business Review (in which the board sets out, *inter alia*, a description of the principal risks and uncertainties facing the company) and a report on directors' remuneration, on which shareholders have an advisory vote. This framework is reinforced by the Listing Rules that must be followed by companies listed on the Main Market of the London Stock Exchange. The Listing Rules provide further rights to shareholders (e.g., by requiring that major transactions are put to a vote) and require certain information to be disclosed to the market. This includes the requirement to provide a 'comply or explain'

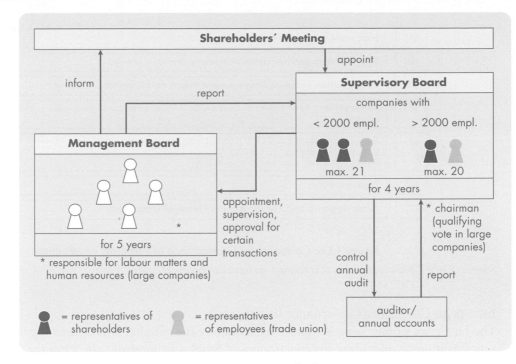

Figure 13.5: Governance structure of a German corporation.

Source: K. Macharzina, Centre for Research in Export and Technology Management, University of Hohenheim, Germany.

statement in the annual report explaining how the company has applied the Combined Code (or, in the case of companies incorporated outside the UK, to describe how the companies' governance practices differ from those set out in the Code).

German Corporate Governance System

A German stock corporation has been characterized by a two-tier board structure as shown in Figure 13.5. In 1998, Germany passed the *Control and Transparency Law* that increased the responsibility of the Management Board in German corporations in areas such as implementation of a risk-management system. Following this legal measure, in 2000, a panel of academics and business leaders, the Frankfurt Panel on Corporate Governance, was created. This panel was a private initiative, which had to explore the best practice in corporate governance, capital market issues and the needs of investors. At the same time, another private initiative, the Berlin Initiative, was launched. It drew together the experience and knowledge of German corporate board members, academics and an attorney. Those involved had to provide advice on modern internal corporate governance practice with an emphasis on the role, functions, composition and accountability of the Management Board.

Meanwhile, the government formed the Baums Commission, which brought together businesspeople, academics, politicians, representatives of trade unions and shareholders, and which worked out important recommendations and proposals for *the Code and the Transparency and Disclosure Law*. In 2002, the Cromme Commission developed the German Corporate Governance Code, which included mandatory disclosure, declaration of conformity, on a comply or explain basis. The Code addresses all major criticisms – especially from the international financial community, with reference to a stronger focus on stockholder interests, the peculiarity of the two-tier system, a greater transparency of the German corporate governance system (e.g., compensation system) and the independence of supervisory board members and auditors (see Figure 13.6).

(1)	**Foreword** (introduction to the two-tier system)
(2)	**Shareholders and the General Meeting** (invitation, proxies)
(3)	**Co-operation between Management Board and Supervisory Board**
(4)	**Management Board** (tasks and responsibilities, composition and compensation, conflicts of interest)
(5)	**Supervisory Board** (tasks and responsibilities, tasks and authorities of the Chairman, formation of committees, composition & compensation, conflicts of interest, examination of efficiency)
(6)	**Transparency**
(7)	**Reporting and Audit of the Annual Financial Statements**

Figure 13.6: Content of the German code of corporate governance.

Source: Code Commission, www.corporate-governance-code.de/.

European Corporate Governance Initiatives

The European Commission has aimed to harmonize the national laws addressing the issues of corporate governance, including the functioning of Stock Corporations. In 1968 the First EU directive spelled out the regulations on companies with liability. Between 1976 and 1984 the European Accountancy Code was developed. Its objective was to ensure co-ordination of the member states' legislation on the structure of public limited companies and the powers and obligations of their organs. This was followed by several drafts that attempted to unify all national systems but the final proposal had to be withdrawn by the Commission in 2001 due to political deadlock and the fundamental differences between member states' traditions in the company law field. This has led the Community legislature to leave national legislatures more room for manoeuvre and to allow companies more scope for exercising freedom of contract.

The European Commission wished to modernize company law and enhance the EU corporate governance systems. However, in 2002 a specially appointed group of experts concluded that a European Corporate Governance Code would not offer significant added value but would simply add an additional layer between international principles and national codes. Hence, the general recommendation was to adopt a common approach with a few essential rules and an adequate co-ordination of national corporate governance codes. In 2003, the EU accepted an Action Plan on Corporate Governance that included initiatives on the introduction of an Annual Corporate Governance Statement; the promotion of the role of (independent) non-executive or supervisory directors; the provision of a detailed disclosure of individual remuneration; and the creation of an European Corporate Governance Forum (including issuers, investors, regulators and academics).

The EU *Council Regulation on the Statute for a European Company* was adopted on 8 October 2001. It defined the rules for European Public Companies known as a Societas Europaea (SE), which is Latin for 'European Company'). There is also a statute allowing European Co-operative Societies. Since 2004, an SE can be registered in any member state of the European Union and the registration can be easily transferred to another member state. There is no EU-wide register of SEs (an SE is registered on the national register of the member state in which it has its head office), but each registration is to be published in the Official Journal of the European Union. Data show that by September 2007, at least 64 registrations have been reported. SEs can be created in the following ways: (1) by merger of national companies from different member states; (2) by the creation of a joint venture between companies (or other entities) in different member states; (3) by the creation of a SE subsidiary of a national company; and (4) by the conversion of a national company into an SE.

The objective of the Statute for a European company is

> to create a European company with its own legislative framework. This will allow companies incorporated in different Member States to merge or form a holding company or joint subsidiary, while avoiding the legal and practical constraints arising from the existence of fifteen different legal systems. To arrange for the involvement of employees in the European company and recognise their place and role in the company.
>
> (www.ec.europa.eu)

The minimum capital of an SE should be €120 000 and it can be easily transfered within the EU-Community without any need for dissolving the company in order to form a new one in another member state. The first examples of an SE are Strabag Bauholding (Austria), formed in October 2004, and Allianz AG (Germany), formed in September 2005.

The Japanese Approach to Corporate Governance

The Japanese corporate governance has been in transition due to the drastic change of its background economic market. The typical Japanese model of publicly held corporations had been developed in the economic growth era after the Second World War and reached its peak in the 1970s and 1980s. In the recession of the 1990s, the Japanese model was forced to change.

F⬤CUS ON

GOVERNANCE

Japan – The Corporate Governance Debate in Japan

Over the past decade, corporate governance has come to replace industrial policy and Japanese-style management as the key factor to explain Japanese business performance.

From the 1960s to the early 1990s, many observers focused on the close and co-operative relationship between Japan's economic ministries, especially Ministry of Finance and Ministry of International Trade and Industry and the companies under their jurisdiction, to explain Japan's economic success.

Those who felt uncomfortable giving government so much credit for Japan's economic success focused their attention on what they viewed to be the strengths of Japanese-style management, which included long-term employment, promotion and wages based on seniority, enterprise unions, low labour mobility, patient capital and keiretsu ties centred on main banks.

The bursting of the bubble economy in Japan in the early 1990s and the ensuing lost decade of economic stagnation have forced all but the staunchest advocates of the Japanese system to concede that changes are necessary to revive the economy. In recognition of the rise of market forces and the power of globalization, most now look to the government primarily to provide the macroeconomic environment for growth and see the enhancement of Japanese corporate competitiveness to be up to the private sector. This has led to the debate over corporate governance as a key to Japanese economic revival.

On one side of the debate are those who contend that Japanese corporate performance will improve only if Japanese companies adopt Western (primarily US) forms of corporate governance. This includes greater emphasis than at present on shareholder rights, information disclosure, transparency, profitability and management accountability.

Sony Corporation has been a frontrunner among Japanese companies in adopting certain aspects of US corporate governance. In 1997, the company reduced the number of board members from 38 to 10 and reinforced the role of outside board members. Sony's board now consists of three outside members and nine inside members. In 1998, Sony also established a nominating committee (consisting of one outside and five inside board members) responsible for selecting executives, and a compensation committee (consisting of two outside board members and a Sony counsellor) to determine executive compensation.

Although Sony is often cited as an example of change in Japanese corporate governance practices, it is atypical.

The arguments offered by those on the other side of the debate provide interesting insights into the Japanese *zeitgeist*. First, they argue that the purpose of a corporation in Japan differs from that in the West. Whereas the latter is aimed primarily to provide profits for shareholders, Japanese corporations exist fundamentally to produce economic value to Japan as a nation, which means that providing employment to the Japanese people is the highest priority. Second, the argument goes, given this difference in corporate purpose, Western notions of corporate governance have limited applicability in Japan. Whereas the West emphasizes the relationship between shareholders, management and the Board of Directors, Japanese corporations are beholden to their stakeholders, which include most importantly the employees, customers, suppliers, creditors and community.

Third, the opponents of change question whether conformity to Western corporate governance practices will lead to better economic performance. Here they cite the case of Toyota Motor Corporation, one of Japan's strongest and most successful companies and the first Japanese company to record annual group pre-tax profits exceeding one trillion yen. Toyota's Board of Directors consists of nearly 60 members, every single one a Toyota executive, who have consistently refuted the need to adopt Western modes of corporate governance.

Fourth, even if adopting Western practices were to improve profitability in the short term, the sceptics believe that such practices could have the corrosive effect of encouraging short-term profit-seeking at the expense of long-term investment, creating massive inequalities of income and wealth among employees and weakening commitment to the company as an institution, because the market might dictate that greater short-term value can accrue to shareholders if a company is sold off to the highest bidder. And such mergers and acquisitions may result in corporate restructuring that would almost certainly lead to unemployment.

Finally, the critics like to cite Enron's case, as a showcase of Western corporate governance at work.

Based on G. Fukushima, 'The Corporate Governance Debate', *Japan Times*, 8 April 2002; Global Communications Platform from Japan at www.glocom.org.

Japanese corporate governance by definition rests with the board of directors who are entitled to govern the company, supervise and monitor the company's management in order to promote effective management, and ensure accountability to shareholders. In practice, however, the role of management and the board of directors has been specifically defined.

The old option, *Kansayaku-Secchi-Gaisha* (System of Auditors), and the new option, *Iinkaitou-Secchi-Gaisha* (System of Committees), can be compared, as shown in Figures 13.7 and 13.8.

A comparison between the Japanese, EU, German and US corporate governance systems is shown in Table 13.2.

Board Structure and Compensation

Many critics have argued that the United States should move toward structural reforms more consistent with European standards. First, for example, prohibiting CEOs from also becoming Chair. Although this is increasingly common, there is no regulatory or other legal requirement to force the issue. Second, and more radically, would be to move toward the two-tiered structure of countries such as Germany, in which there is a supervisory board (largely outsiders and typically large – Siemens has 18 members) and a management board (predominantly insiders and smaller – Siemens has 8 members).

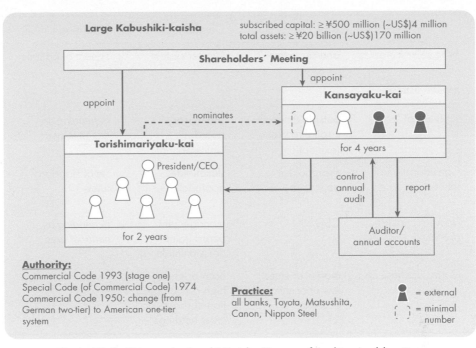

Figure 13.7: *Kansayaku-Secchi-Gaisha* (System of Auditors): old option.

Source: K. Macharzina, Centre for Research in Export and Technology Management, University of Hohenheim, Germany.

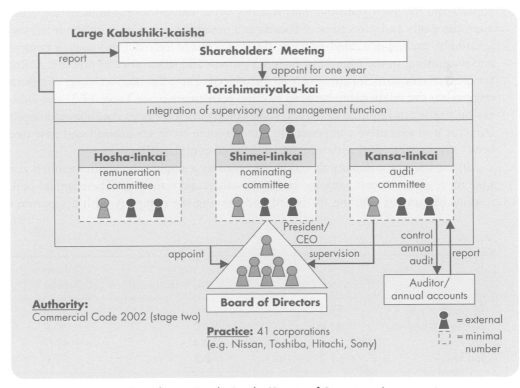

Figure 13.8: *Iinkaitou-Secchi-Gaisha* (System of Committees): new option.

Source: K. Macharzina, Centre for Research in Export and Technology Management, University of Hohenheim, Germany.

	USA	Germany	European Union	Japan
Type of structure	one-tier system	two-tier system	system of options	one-tier system (extended)
Mechanism of control –Internal –External	outside directors capital market (exit-option)	supervisory board (voice-option)	*depending on national laws*	informal rules and self-regulation
Consideration of interest	shareholder approach	stakeholder approach	set of standard rules	stakeholder approach (*Keiretsu*)
Decision-making process	CEO	management board (joint decision-making)	*depending on national laws*	*Torishimariyaku-kai* (principle of *Ringi*)
Corporate finance	market-oriented; low concentration of shares	bank-oriented; high concentration of shares and cross holdings		bank-oriented; high concentration of shares and cross holdings

Table 13.2: Comparison of the corporate governance systems.

The amount and form of board compensation are also under considerable debate. In the past, the United States was characterized by boards in which compensation was a combination of an annual stipend and the award of significant stock options. The stock option incentive, although intended to align the goals and objectives of boards and executive directors with the interests of stockholders, seemingly resulted in a mind-set more akin to the gift of lotto tickets – encouraging aggressive growth and accounting in the interest of earnings growth and share price appreciation. Recently, new rules for compensation disclosure have been introduced. There has been a change of control provisions that emphasizes the relationship between pay and performance (see Table 13.3) and although shareholder say on pay is not required in the US, some companies have been considering adopting this principle. Director and executive compensation have become more scrutinized and new taxation rules have been introduced to deal with the issue of deferred compensation.

In the UK, the company should be governed by a single board with members collectively responsible for leading the company and setting its values and standards. There should be a clear division of responsibilities for running the board and running the company with a separate Chair and Chief

	Overall (%)	CEO/President or Other Inside Director (%)	Outside Director (%)	Other (%)
Too high	35.7	30.4	40.4	30
Somewhat high	41.6	37.0	40.7	44.1
Just right	21.4	30.4	17.9	24.7
Too low	1.3	2.2	1.0	1.2

Source: NACD Public Company Governance Survey (2007). Reproduced by permission of the National Association of Corporate Directors, Washington, DC, www.nacdonline.org

Table 13.3: The level of CEO compensation, relative to their performance.

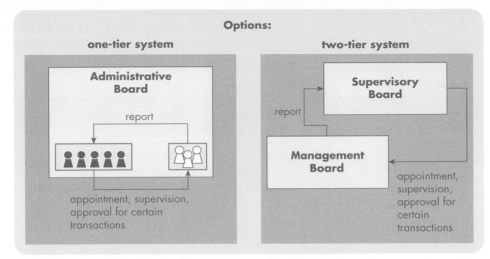

Figure 13.9: Governance structure of a Societas Europaes.

Executive. A balance of executive and independent non-executive directors is required – for larger companies at least 50% of the board members should be independent non-executive directors; smaller companies should have at least two independent directors. There should be formal and transparent procedures for appointing directors, with all appointments and re-appointments to be ratified by shareholders. The effectiveness of the board and its committees is evaluated on a regular basis and these evaluations are accompanied by formal and transparent procedures for setting executive remuneration. The remuneration committee is made up of independent directors and there is an advisory vote for shareholders. A strict requirement of the British corporate governance system is that a significant proportion of remuneration should be linked to performance.

The options recommended for the structure of Societas Europaes are shown in Figure 13.9. Within the governance mechanism of a company, it is inadvisable to set up a single European model of employee involvement. Nevertheless, there is a strict rule of protection of the employees' acquired rights. The establishment of a SE does not entail the disappearance or reduction of practices of employee involvement existing within the companies participating in the establishment of an SE. Moreover, a set of standard rules are set by the national legislation of the member states on the models of participation. According to these rules, employees are part of the supervisory board or the administrative board or are represented by a separate body; the general meeting may not approve the formation of an SE unless one of the models of participation defined in the Directive has been chosen and if management and employees do not reach a satisfactory arrangement, a set of standard rules becomes applicable. Overall, there are 25 different varieties of the SE in the EU Community due to the distinctness of legal systems, institutional arrangements and traditions. Although codes of best practice have been converging and the one- and two-tier systems have been in competition, there is no European company law and there are locational disadvantages for countries with extensive rights of co-determination/employee participation. Some of the differences in selected EU countries are shown in Table 13.4.

Transparency, Accounting and Auditing

The concept of transparency is also one that has been raised in a variety of different markets and contexts. Transparency is a rather common term used to describe the degree to which an investor – either existing or potential – can discern the true activities and value drivers of a company from the disclosures and financial results reported. For example, Enron was often considered a 'black box' when it came to what the actual operational and financial results and risks were for its multitude of

Country	Corporate Governance Structure	Co-determination (Participation of Labour)		
		No Seats	Up to $\frac{1}{3}$ of the Seats	$\frac{1}{3}$ up to $\frac{1}{2}$ of the Seats
Austria	two-tier			X
Belgium	one-tier	X		
Denmark	one-tier			X
Finland	choice		as a rule $\frac{1}{4}$	
France	choice		X	
Germany	two-tier			X
Italy	one-tier	X		
Luxemburg	one-tier		X	
Netherlands	two-tier	X		
Norway	choice			X
Poland	two-tier	X		
Portugal	one-tier	X		
Sweden	one-tier		X	
Spain	one-tier	X		
United Kingdom	one-tier	X		

Table 13.4: Corporate governance structure and co-determinination in Europe.

business lines. The consensus of corporate governance experts is that all firms, globally, should work toward increasing the transparency of the firm's risk–return proposition.

The accounting process itself, the way in which financial results and status of all firms are recorded, has now come under debate. The US system is characterized as strictly rule-based, rather than conceptually based, as is common in Western Europe. Many critics of US corporate governance practices point to this as a fundamental flaw, in which ever more clever accountants find ways to follow the rules, and yet not meet the underlying purpose for which the rules were intended. An extension of the accounting process debate is that of the role and remuneration associated with auditing – the process of using third parties, paid by the firm, to vet their reporting practices as being consistent with accepted accounting principles and practices. As the collapse of auditors Arthur Andersen illustrated following the Enron debacle, there are serious questions as to the faith investors can place in the results of this current practice.

In the UK, the board is responsible for presenting a balanced assessment of the company's position (including through the accounts) and maintaining a sound system of internal control. There are formal and transparent procedures for carrying out these responsibilities, including an audit committee made up of independent directors with the necessary experience.

In Germany, the audit committee is a particular sub-committee of the Supervisory Board's almost mandatory recommendation for companies with more than six Supervisory Board members. Until 1980, there was no tradition of audit committees in Germany. By 2005, 29 out of 30 DAX and 39 out of 50 MDAX listed companies had already established audit committees. The task of an audit committee is to improve Supervisory Board monitoring efficiency and effectiveness and ensure the necessary level of monitoring provided by the Supervisory Board as a whole. German audit committees do not show a unitary pattern. Although the composition of audit committees varies, it is quite common for more than 50% of their members to have accounting and/or industry experience. There is an indication that labour representatives have relatively little qualifications in tax issues and statutory audits.

Minority Shareholder Rights

Finally, the issue of minority shareholder rights continues to rage in many of the world's largest markets. Many of the emerging markets are still characterized by the family based corporate governance regime, where the family remains in control even after the firm has gone public. But what of the interests and voices of the other stockholders? How are their interests preserved in organizations in which families or private investors control all true decisions, including those made by the boards?

ACCOUNTING DIVERSITY

The fact that accounting principles differ across countries is not, by itself, a problem. The primary problem is that real economic decisions by lenders, investors or government policy makers may be distorted by the differences. Table 13.5 provides a simple example of the potential problems that may arise if two identical firms are operating in similar or dissimilar economic and accounting environments.

First, if two identical firms (in terms of structure, products and strategies) are operating in similar economic situations and are subject to similar accounting treatment (cell A), a comparison of their performance will be logical in practice and easily interpreted. The results of a competitive comparison or even an accounting audit (measurement and monitoring of their accounting practices) will lead to results that make sense. The two same firms operating in dissimilar economic situations will, when subject to the same accounting treatment, potentially look very different. And it may be that they should appear different if they are operating in totally different environments.

For example, one airline may depreciate its aircraft over five years, whereas another airline may depreciate over ten years. Is this justified? It is if the two identical air carriers are in fundamentally different economic situations. If the first airline flies predominantly short commuter routes, which require thousands of takeoffs and landings, and the second airline flies only long intercontinental flights, which require far fewer takeoffs and landings, the first may be justified in depreciating its fixed assets much faster. The airline with more frequent takeoffs and landings will wear out its aircraft more quickly, which is what the accounting principle of depreciation is attempting to capture.[4] The economic situations are different.

The most blatantly obvious mismatch of economic environments and accounting treatments in Table 13.5 is probably that of cell C. Two identical firms operating within the same economic environment that receive different accounting treatment are not comparable. The same firms, if placed in

Accounting Treatment	Economic Situation of Two Identical Firms	
	Similar	Dissimilar
Similar	[A] Logical practice Results are comparable	[B] May/may not be logical Results may/may not be comparable
Dissimilar	[C] Illogical practice Results are not comparable	[D] Logical practice Results may not be comparable

Source: Frederick D.S. Choi and Richard Levich (1992) 'International Accounting Diversity and Capital Market Decisions', in *Handbook of International Accounting*, John Wiley & Sons, Inc., Hoboken, NJ. Reproduced with permission of John Wiley & Sons, Inc.

Table 13.5: Accounting diversity and economic environments.

the same environment, would appear differently, with one potentially gaining competitive advantage over the other simply because of accounting treatment.

Finally, cell D offers the mismatch of different environments and different accounting treatments. Although logical in premise, the results are most likely incomparable in outcome. Identical firms in differing economic environments require differing approaches to financial measurement. But the fact that the results of financial comparison may not be usable is not an error; it is simply a fact of the differing markets in which the firms operate. As firms expand internationally, as markets expand across borders, as businesses diversify across currencies, cultures and economies, the movement toward cell A continues from market forces rather than from government intention.

PRINCIPAL ACCOUNTING DIFFERENCES ACROSS COUNTRIES

International accounting diversity can lead to any of the following problems in international business conducted with the use of financial statements: (1) poor or improper business decision making; (2) hindering the ability of a firm or enterprise to raise capital in different or foreign markets; and (3) hindering or preventing a firm from monitoring competitive factors across firms, industries and countries.

F⬤CUS ON

CULTURE   The Father of Accounting: Luca Pacioli Who?

Doctors have Hippocrates and philosophers have Plato. But who is the father of accounting? Knowing that accountants have long had inferiority complexes, two Seattle University professors have decided that the profession should have a father and that he should be Luca Pacioli.

But their anointing of the Renaissance scholar occasions an identity crisis. Hardly anyone – accountants included – has ever heard of Pacioli (pronounced pot-CHEE-oh-lee).

Five centuries ago, Pacioli published *Summa de Arithmetica, Geometria, Proportioni et Proportionalita*. It contained a slender tract for merchants on double-entry bookkeeping, which had been in wide use in Venice for years. Due to that, some accounting historians, including Professors Weis and Tinius, credit Pacioli with codifying accounting principles for the first time. That would seem to establish paternity.

Professor Vangermeersch, of the University of Rhode Island, says the origins of double-entry bookkeeping are open to question. 'If you're crediting people of past centuries for contributions to accounting, you should include Leonardo of Pisa, who brought Arabic numerals to the West; James Pelle, who initiated journal-entry systems; and Emile Garcke and J.M. Fells, who applied accounting to factory use', he said. All the men have another thing in common, he added: they are just as obscure as Luca Pacioli.

Even in literature, says Vangermeersch, the only famous accountant was Daniel Defoe, who wrote *Robinson Crusoe*. Unfortunately, Defoe was a terrible businessman and failed in a series of ventures. The professor observed, 'Even as a dissenter and pamphleteer, he was tarred and feathered by the public.'

Source: Abstracted from 'Father of Accounting Is a Bit of a Stranger to His Own Progeny', *Wall Street Journal*, 29 January 1993, A1, A6. Reprinted by permission of *The Wall Street Journal*, © 1993 Dow Jones & Company, Inc. All Rights Reserved Worldwide.

Origins of Differences

Accounting standards and practices are in many ways no different from any other legislative or regulatory statutes in their origins. Laws reflect the people, places and events of their time (see the Focus on Culture on page 400). Most accounting practices and laws are linked to the objectives of the parties who will use the financial information, including investors, lenders and governments.

Classification Systems

There are several ways to classify and group national accounting systems and practices. Figure 13.10 illustrates one such classification based on a statistically based clustering of practices across countries by C.W. Nobes. The systems are first subdivided into micro-based (characteristics of the firms and industries) and macro-uniform (following fundamental government or economic factors per country). The micro-based national accounting systems are then broken down into those that follow a theoretical principle or pragmatic concerns. The latter category includes the national accounting systems of countries as diverse as the United States, Canada, Japan, the United Kingdom and Mexico.

The macro-uniform systems, according to Nobes, are primarily used in European countries. The continental Europeans are typified by accounting systems that are formulated in secondary importance to legal organizational forms (Germany), for the apportionment and application of national tax laws (France, Spain, Italy) or the more pure forms of government and economic models (Sweden). An alternative approach to those in the European classification would be those used in Sweden and Germany, which have pushed their firms to adopt more widespread uniform standards. However, as with all classification systems, the subtle differences across countries can quickly make such classifications useless in practice. As the following sections will illustrate, slight differences can also yield significant competitive advantages or disadvantages to companies organized and measured under different financial reporting systems.

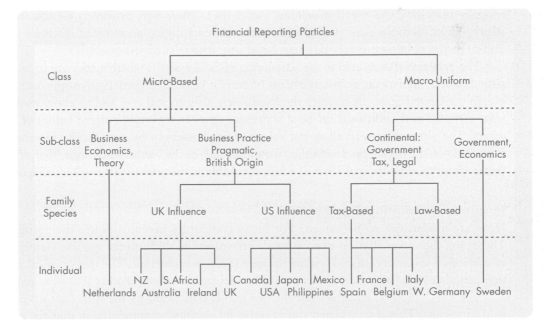

Figure 13.10: Nobes classification of national accounting systems.

Source: C.W. Nobes, 'International Classification of Accounting Systems', unpublished paper: April 1980, Table C, as cited in Frederick D.S. Choi and Gerhard G. Mueller (1992) *International Accounting*, 2nd edition, Prentice Hall, Englewood Cliffs, NJ, 34.

Principal Differences: The Issues

The resulting impact of accounting differences is to separate or segment international markets for investors and firms alike. Communicating the financial results of a foreign company operating in a foreign country and foreign currency is often a task that must be undertaken completely separately from the accounting duties of the firm. As long as significant accounting practices differ across countries, markets will continue to be segmented (and accountants may be required to be interpreters and marketers as much as bookkeepers).

Table 13.6 provides an overview of nine major areas of significant differences in accounting practices across countries.[5] There are, of course, many more hundreds of differences but the nine serve to highlight some of the fundamental philosophical differences across countries. Accounting differences are real and persistent and there is still the substantial question of competitive advantages and informational deficiencies that may result from these continuing differences across countries.

Accounting for Research and Development Expenses

Are research and development expenses capitalized or expensed as costs are incurred? Those who argue that there is no certainty that the R&D expenditures will lead to benefits in future periods would require immediate recognition of all expenses as in typical conservative practice. Alternatively, if R&D expenditures do lead to future benefits and revenues, the matching of expenses and revenues would be better served if the R&D expenditures were capitalized and expenses therefore spread out over the future benefit periods.

Accounting for Fixed Assets

How are fixed assets (land, buildings, machinery, equipment) to be expensed and carried? The assets constitute large outlays of capital, result in assets that are held by the firm for many years and yield benefits for many future years. All countries require companies to capitalize these fixed assets, so that they are depreciated over their future economic lives (once again spreading the costs out over periods roughly matching the revenue-earning useful life). There are, however, significant differences in depreciation methods used (straight-line, sum-of-years-digits, accelerated methods of cost recovery and so forth), resulting in very different expensing schedules across countries.

The primary issue related to the accounting of fixed assets is whether they are to be carried on company financial statements at historical cost or current value. The conservative approach, used for example, in the United States, is to carry the fixed assets at historical cost and to allow analysts to use their own methods and additional financial statement notes to ascertain current values of individual fixed assets. The alternative is to allow the values of fixed assets to be periodically re-valued up or down, depending on the latest appraised value. Countries such as the Netherlands argue that this is more appropriate, given that the balance sheet of a firm should show the present fair market value of all assets.

Inventory Accounting Treatment

How are inventories to be valued? For many companies inventories are their single largest asset. Therefore, the reconciliation of how goods are valued as sold (on the income statement) and valued as carried in inventory unsold (on the balance sheet) is important. The three typical inventory-valuation principles are LIFO (*last-in/first-out*), the average cost method and FIFO (*first-in/first-out*).

The LIFO method assumes that the last goods purchased by the firm (last-in) are the first ones sold (first-out). This is considered conservative by accounting standards in that the remaining inventory goods were the first ones purchased. The resulting expenses of cost of goods sold is therefore higher. The use of FIFO is thought to be more consistent theoretically with the matching of costs and revenues of actual inventory flows. FIFO is generally regarded as creating a more accurately measured balance sheet, as inventory is stated at the most recent prices.

	United States	Japan	United Kingdom	France	Germany	The Netherlands	Switzerland	Canada	Italy	Brazil	International Benchmark	International Allowed Alternative
Capitalization of research and development	Not allowed	Allowed in certain circumstances	Allowed in certain circumstances	Allowed in certain circumstances	Not allowed	Allowed in certain circumstances	Allowed in certain circumstances	Allowed in certain circumstances	Allowed in certain circumstances	Allowed	Required in certain circumstances	None
Fixed asset revaluation in excess of cost	Not allowed	Not allowed	Allowed	Allowed	Not allowed	Allowed in certain circumstances	Allowed in certain circumstances	Not allowed	Required in certain circumstances	Allowed	Not allowed	Allowed
Inventory valuation using LIFO	Allowed	Allowed	Allowed but rarely done	Allowed	Allowed in certain circumstances	Allowed	Allowed	Allowed	Allowed	Allowed but rarely done	Not allowed	Allowed
Finance leases capitalized	Required	Allowed in certain circumstances	Required	Allowed	Allowed in certain circumstances	Required	Allowed	Required	Not allowed	Allowed in certain circumstances	Required	None
Pension expense accrued during period of service	Required	Allowed	Required	Allowed	Required	Required	Allowed	Required	Allowed	Allowed	Required	None
Book and tax timing differences presented on the balance sheet as deferred tax	Required	Allowed in certain circumstances	Required in certain circumstances	Required	Allowed in certain circumstances	Required	Allowed	Required	Generally required	Required	Allowed	None
Current rate method used by foreign currency translation	Required for foreign operations whose functional currency is other than the reporting currency	Generally required	Required	Required for self-sustaining foreign operations	Allowed	Required for self-sustaining foreign operations	Allowed	Required for self-sustaining foreign operations	Required	Required	Required for self-sustaining foreign operations	None
Pooling method used for mergers	Required in certain circumstances	Allowed	Required in certain circumstances	Not allowed	Allowed in certain circumstances	Allowed but rarely done	Allowed but rarely done	Allowed in rare circumstances	Allowed in rare circumstances	Allowed but rarely done	Required in certain circumstances	None
Equity method used for 20–50% ownership	Required	Required	Required	Required	Required	Required	Allowed in certain circumstances	Required	Allowed	Required	Required	None

Source: William E. Decker, Jr. and Paul Brunner (2003) 'Summary of Accounting Principle Differences Around the World', in *International Finance and Accounting Handbook*, 3rd edition, Frederick D. S. Choi (ed.), John Wiley & Sons, Inc., Hoboken, NJ, 12.6. Reproduced with permission of John Wiley & Sons, Inc.

Table 13.6: Summary of principal accounting differences around the world.

Capitalizing or Expensing Leases

Are financing leases to be capitalized? The recent growth in popularity of leasing for its financial and tax flexibility has created a substantial amount of accounting discussion across countries. The primary question is whether a leased item should actually be carried on the balance sheet of the firm at all, because a lease is essentially the purchase of an asset only for a specified period of time. If not carried on the books, should the lease payments be expenses paid as if they were a rent payment?

Some argue that the lease results in the transfer of all risks and benefits of ownership to the firm (from the lessor to the lessee) and the lease contract should be accounted for as the purchase of an asset. This would be a capital lease and if the lessee borrowed money in order to acquire the asset, the lease payments of principal and interest should be accounted for in the same manner as the purchase of any other capital asset.

The alternative is that the lessee has simply acquired the rental use of the services of the asset for a specified period of time and payments on this operating lease should be treated only as rent. In this case the asset would remain on the books of the lessor.

Pension Plan Accounting

A private pension plan is the promise by an employer to provide a continuing income stream to employees after their retirement from the firm. The critical accounting question is whether the pension promise should be expensed and carried at the time the employee is working for the firm (providing a service to the firm that will not be fully paid for by the firm until all pension payments are completed) or expensed only as pension payments are made after retirement.

The primary problem with expensing the pension as the services are provided is that the firm does not know the exact amount or timing of the eventual pension payments. If it is assumed that these eventual pension payments can be reasonably approximated, the conservative approach is to account for the expenses as employee services are provided and to carry the pension liabilities on the books of the firm. In some countries, if it is believed that these pension liabilities cannot be accurately estimated, they will be expensed only as they are incurred on payment.

Accounting for Income Taxes

All countries require the payment of income taxes on earnings. However, the definition and timing of earnings can constitute a problem. In many countries, the definition of earnings for financial accounting purposes differs from earnings for tax purposes. The question then focuses on whether the tax effect should be recognized during the period in which the item appears on the income statement or during the period in which the item appears on the tax return.

If the expense is recognized during the period in which the item appears on the income statement, the tax gives rise to an associated asset or liability referred to as deferred tax. Some countries do not suffer the debate of whether the deferred tax should actually appear on the balance sheet of the firm by having all financial reporting follow tax rules.

Foreign Currency Translation

Corporations that operate in more than one country and one currency must periodically *translate* and *consolidate* all financial statements for home-country reporting purposes. The primary issues in foreign currency translation are which exchange rates should be used in the translation of currencies (historical or current rates) and how gains or losses resulting from the translation should be handled in the consolidation. The critical handling issue is whether the gains or losses are recognized in current income or carried on the consolidated balance sheet as an item under equity capital.

Figure 13.11 provides a simple decision-tree approach to translation of foreign affiliates for US corporations.

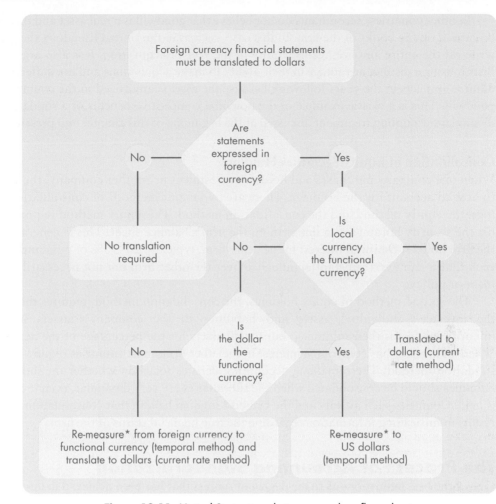

Figure 13.11: United States translation procedure flow chart.

*The term *re-measure* means to translate so as to change the unit of measure from a foreign currency to the functional currency.
Source: Frederick D.S. Choi and Gerhard G. Mueller (1992) *International Accounting*, 2nd edition, Prentice Hall, Englewood Cliffs, NJ, 169. Reproduced by permission of Pearson Education, Inc., Upper Saddle River, NJ.

Accounting for Mergers and Acquisitions

This is a relatively new issue in international accounting, given the sudden and rapid growth of merger and acquisition activity beginning in the United States and the United Kingdom in the 1980s. The primary accounting question is whether the assets and liabilities acquired should be carried at their original historic value or at the value at acquisition. In certain cases, however, it is believed that the shareholders of the acquired company end up owning shares of the acquirer and accountants argue that their assets and liabilities should not be re-valued but simply merged or pooled.

A second accounting issue of some concern is that often in the case of acquisitions, the price paid exceeds the fair value of the assets acquired. This is termed 'goodwill' and constitutes a significant accounting problem. Many accountants argue that this is a true value that is purchased and would not have been paid for if it did not exist. Even if goodwill is accepted as a legitimate economic value, the question remains as to how it is to be carried on the firm's balance sheet.

In other countries, accountants do not believe that goodwill is a real asset and therefore should not be carried on the books of the firm. In this case, such as in the United Kingdom, the firm is allowed to write off the entire amount against equity in the year of acquisition. It is also argued that this gives British firms a distinct advantage in their ability to make acquisitions and not suffer income statement dilution impacts in the years following because the asset is amortized in the countries that capitalize goodwill. This is a classic example of the potential competitive benefits of a similar activity receiving dissimilar accounting treatment discussed at the beginning of this chapter and presented in Table 13.5.

Consolidation of Equity Securities Holdings

When one company purchases and holds an investment in another company, the question arises as to how to account for the holdings. There are two major methods of consolidation of equity holdings: the equity method and the consolidation method. The equity method requires that the holder list the security holdings as a line item on the firm's balance sheet. This is generally required when the firm holds substantial interest in the other firm, typically 20–50% of outstanding voting shares, such that it can exert substantial influence over the other firm but not necessarily dictate management or policy.

The second method of equity holdings, the consolidation method, requires the addition of all of the investee's individual assets and liabilities to the company's assets and liabilities. A minority interest is then subtracted out for all assets for the percentage of the net asset not owned. When an investor has controlling interest in the other firm, most countries require the use of the consolidation method. The remaining accounting debates focus on whether the individual assets and liabilities should be consolidated when the subsidiaries are very dissimilar, even if controlling interest is held. Countries such as Italy and the United Kingdom believe that consolidation of dissimilar firms results in misleading information regarding the true financial status of the firms.

The Process of Accounting Standardization

One of the best indications as to the degree of success that has been achieved in international accounting standards is that there is still some conflict over the terminology of harmonization, standardization or promulgation of uniform standards. For example, the Focus on Culture and Russia's accounting rules on page 402 highlights the differing purposes for accounting in different countries. At the same time, the following Focus on Ethics that discusses corporate social responsibility at Starbucks provides insight into how companies are altering their performance reporting beyond traditional financial accounting.

As early as 1966, an Accountants International Study Group was formed by professional institutes in Canada, the United States and the United Kingdom to begin the study of significant accounting differences across countries. They were primarily only to aid in the understanding of foreign practices, not to form guidelines for more consistent or harmonious policies.

The establishment of the International Accounting Standards Committee (IASC) in 1973 was the first strong movement toward the establishment of international accounting standards. In the latter half of the 1970s, other international institutions such as the United Nations, the Organization for Economic Co-operation and Development (OECD) and the European Union also began forming study groups and analysing specific issues of confusion, such as corporate organization and varying degrees of disclosure required across countries.[6] The efforts of the European Union to harmonize standards between countries, not to standardize, is particularly important in understanding how accounting principles and practices may be reformed to allow individual country differences but at the same time minimize the economic distortions. Finally, in September 2003, the European Commission approved legislation requiring publicly traded companies to comply with IAS (International Accounting Standards) by 2005.

F⬤CUS ON

ETHICS   Corporate Social Responsibility and Starbucks

'Starbucks defines corporate social responsibility as conducting our business in ways that produce social, environmental and economic benefits to the communities in which we operate. In the end, it means being responsible to our stakeholders.

'There is growing recognition of the need for corporate accountability. Consumers are demanding more than 'product' from their favorite brands. Employees are choosing to work for companies with strong values. Shareholders are more inclined to invest in businesses with outstanding corporate reputations. Quite simply, being socially responsible is not only the right thing to do; it can distinguish a company from its industry peers.'

Corporate Social Responsibility Annual Report
Starbucks Coffee, Fiscal 2001, p. 3.

Starbucks found itself, somewhat to its surprise, an early target of the antiglobalist movement. Like

McDonald's before it, it appeared to be yet another American cultural imperialist, bringing a chain-store sameness to all countries everywhere. Like McDonald's, Starbucks found that its uniquely defined brand and experience did not have to conform to local cultural norms but could exist alongside traditional practices, creating its own market and successfully altering some consumer behaviours.

Unlike McDonald's, however, Starbucks was the purveyor of a commodity, coffee, which was priced and sold on global markets. Coffee was sourced from hundreds of thousands of small growers in Central and South America, many of which were severely impoverished by all global income and purchasing power standards. As coffee prices plummeted in the late 1990s, companies such as Starbucks were criticized for both benefiting from lower cost sourcing and for their unwillingness to help improve the economic conditions of the coffee growers themselves.

Starbucks has implemented a multitude of programmes to pursue its programme for corporate social responsibility (CSR) and pursue sustainable economic development for the people in its supply chain. Although not wishing to own the supply chain, Starbucks' strategy was a complex combination of altered business practices in procurement, direct support to the coffee growers and the formation of brands that would provide conduits for consumers wishing to support CSR initiatives. Starbucks has also been very clear as to why it is doing these things – because they are the right things to do.

Two other recent developments concerning international standardization merit special note. In 1985, the General Electric Company became the first major US corporation to acknowledge that the accounting principles underlying its 1984 financial statements 'are generally accepted in the United States and are consistent with standards issued by the International Accounting Standards Committee'.[7] Second, the Financial Accounting Standards Board (FASB), the organization in the United States charged with setting most standards for corporate accounting practices, committed itself to the full consideration of 'an international perspective' to all its work in the future.

F⬤CUS ON

CULTURE   Russia's Taxing Accounting Rules

CEOs don't like uncertainty. Moreover, boards of directors don't have much patience with financial statements that don't clearly present the financial health of an enterprise. All of which makes doing business in Russia a unique challenge, where the traditional focus has not been on profit but on control.

This focus is well stated in Pulitzer Prize winner Thomas L. Friedman's book, *The Lexus and the Olive Tree*. He writes:

'The purpose of the Soviet economy was not to meet the demand of consumers but to reinforce the control of the central government.... At a Soviet company that made bed frames, the managers were paid by the central government not according to how many bed frames they sold but on the basis of how much steel they consumed. The number of bed frames sold is a measure of consumer satisfaction.

The amount of steel produced and used is a measure of state power. In the Cold War, the Soviet Union was only interested in the latter.'[8]

As a result, reports BISNIS, the section at the US Department of Commerce that is the primary resource centre for US companies exploring business opportunities in Russia, Russian accounting regulations (RARs) were drafted and used for tax calculation and bookkeeping purposes and not designed for use by potential investors as measurement of a company's financial performance. With the increased interest of Western investment, however, the need for understandable, comparable, transparent, detailed and reliable financial statements has become apparent and the government of the Russian Federation has taken steps to promote accounting reforms.

Source: Adapted from 'Russia's Taxing Accounting Rules', *World Trade*, October 2000, by Scott T. Robertson.

INTERNATIONAL TAXATION

Governments alone have the power to tax. Each government wants to tax all companies within its jurisdiction without placing burdens on domestic or foreign companies that would restrain trade. Each country states its jurisdictional approach formally in the tax treaties that it signs with other countries. One of the primary purposes of tax treaties is to establish the bounds of each country's jurisdiction to prevent double taxation of international income.

Tax Jurisdictions

Nations usually follow one of two basic approaches to international taxation: a residential approach or a territorial or source approach. The residential approach to international taxation taxes the international income of its residents without regard to where the income is earned. The territorial approach to transnational income taxes all parties, regardless of country of residency, within its territorial jurisdiction.

Most countries in practice must combine the two approaches to tax foreign and domestic firms equally. For example, the United States and Japan both apply the residential approach to their own resident corporations and the territorial approach to income earned by non-residents within their territorial jurisdictions. Other countries, such as Germany, apply the territorial approach to dividends paid to domestic firms from their foreign subsidiaries; such dividends are assumed to be taxed abroad and are exempt from further taxation.

Within the territorial jurisdiction of tax authorities, a foreign corporation is typically defined as any business that earns income within the host country's borders but is incorporated under the laws of another country. The foreign corporation must usually surpass some minimum level of activity (gross income) before the host country assumes primary tax jurisdiction. However, if the foreign corporation owns income-producing assets or a permanent establishment, the threshold is automatically surpassed. Even so, it is not always easy to capture income.

Tax Types

Taxes are generally classified as direct and indirect. Direct taxes are calculated on actual income, either individual or firm income. Indirect taxes, such as sales taxes, severance taxes, tariffs and value-added taxes, are applied to purchase prices, material costs, quantities of natural resources mined and so forth. Although most countries still rely on income taxes as the primary method of raising revenue, tax structures vary widely across countries.

The value-added tax (VAT) is the primary revenue source for the European Union. A value-added tax is applied to the amount of product value added by the production process. The tax is calculated as a percentage of the product price less the cost of materials and inputs used in its manufacture, which have been taxed previously. Through this process, tax revenues are collected literally on the value added by that specific stage of the production process. Under the existing General Agreement on Tariffs and Trade (GATT), the legal framework under which international trade operates, value-added taxes may be levied on imports into a country or group of countries (such as the European Union) in order to treat foreign producers entering the domestic markets equally with firms within the country paying the VAT. Similarly, the VAT may be refunded on export sales or sales to tourists who purchase products for consumption outside the country or community. For example, an American tourist leaving London may collect a refund on all value-added taxes paid on goods purchased within the United Kingdom. The refunding usually requires documentation of the actual purchase price and the amount of tax paid.

F O CUS ON

ETHICS   Offshore Centres under Fire

The European Commission has long criticized so-called 'tax havens', such as the Channel Islands and the Isle of Man, as having lax regulations, even by offshore standards. Illegal entry of goods into the EU costs member countries' treasuries from €5 billion to €6 billion per year in lost revenues. For example, a smuggler's potential profit per truck- or container-load of merchandise ranges from €100 000 for agricultural produce to €1 million for cigarettes. The Commission also suspects high levels of fraud in the public sector.

Illegal money-sheltering is not exclusive to the European Community. From the Cook Islands, a protectorate of New Zealand, to Switzerland, famed for the secrecy of its bank accounts, money acquired through criminal or fraudulent means is hidden in phantom entities in offshore centres around the globe. A campaign by the Organization for Economic Co-operation and Development (OECD) seeks to crack down on tax havens in the Caribbean, as part of a wider effort to fight money laundering and financial crimes worldwide. US government officials claim that offshore money centres, long suspected of protecting the financial interests of the global drug-trafficking industry and of international mafia organizations, are also providing shelter for the assets of illegal terrorist groups and their supporters. Such charges can have a disastrous effect on the fragile economies that fall prey to them. Blacklisted by OECD, tiny island states such as Barbados fear that undue scrutiny of their financial institutions will irreparably damage their fledgling financial services industries, leading to economic collapse.

Offshore centres frequently come under attack as harbours for organizations that seek to evade corporate taxes. An increasing number of US companies, encouraged by their financial advisers, have incorporated in Bermuda as a means of lowering taxes without giving up the benefits of doing business in the United States. Tyco International, under investigation for corrupt accounting practices, saved US$400 million in taxes during 2001 by incorporating in Bermuda via a paper transaction. The company continued to operate in the United States.

Sources: 'Bermuda Havens to Be Reviewed', 1 March 2002, David Cay Johnston; 'US Corporations Are Using Bermuda to Slash Tax Bills', 18 February 2002; and 'Caribbean Tax Havens in Spotlight', 14 January 2001, *New York Times*; 'Offshore Centres' Regulations under Fire', *Financial Times*, 4 December 1996.

Income Categories and Taxation

There are three primary methods used for the transfer of funds across tax jurisdictions: royalties, interest and dividends. Royalties are under licence for the use of intangible assets such as patents, designs, trademarks, techniques or copyrights. Interest is the payment for the use of capital lent for the financing of normal business activity. Dividends are income paid or deemed paid to the shareholders of the corporation from the residual earnings of operations. When a corporation declares the percentage of residual earnings that is to go to shareholders, the dividend is declared and distributed.

Taxation of corporate income differs substantially across countries. Table 13.7 provides a summary comparison for Japan, Germany and the United States. In some countries, for example the United States and Japan, there is one corporate income tax rate applied to all residual earnings, regardless of what is retained versus what is distributed as dividends. In other countries, for example Germany, separate tax rates apply to distributed and undistributed earnings. (Note that Germany lists a specific corporate income tax rate for the branches of foreign corporations operating within Germany.)

Royalty and interest payments to non-residents are normally subject to withholding taxes. Corporate profits are typically double taxed in most countries, through corporate and personal taxes. Corporate income is first taxed at the business level with corporate taxes, and then a second time when the income of distributed earnings is taxed through personal income taxes. Withholding tax rates also differ by the degree of ownership that the corporation possesses in the foreign corporation. Minor ownership is termed portfolio, while major or controlling influence is categorized as substantial holdings. In the case of dividends, interest or royalties paid to non-residents, governments routinely apply withholding taxes to their payment in the reasonable expectation that the non-residents will not report and declare such income with the host-country tax authorities. Withholding taxes are specified by income category in all bilateral tax treaties. Notice in Table 13.7 the differentials in withholding taxes across countries by bilateral tax treaties. The US tax treaty with Germany results in a 0% withholding of interest or royalty payments earned by German corporations operating in the United States.

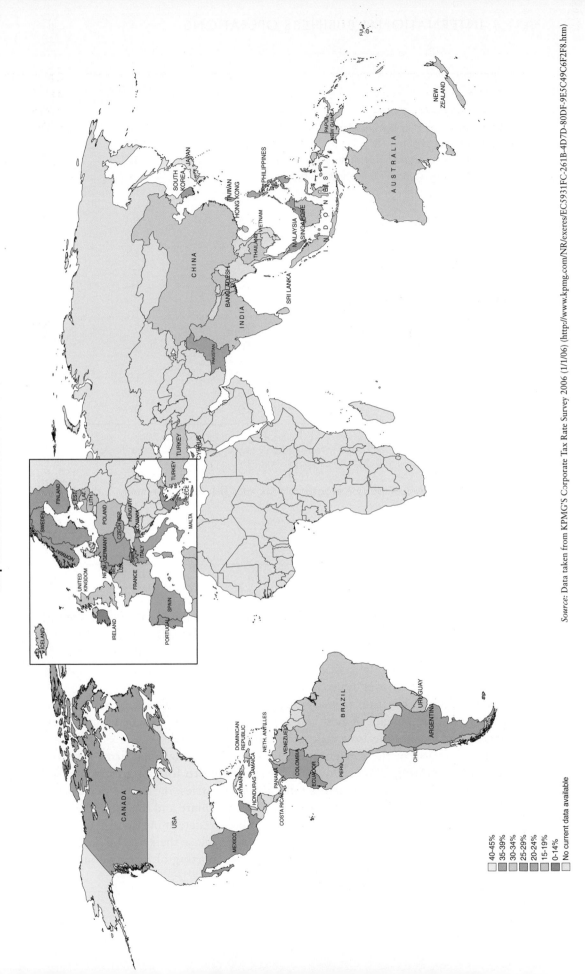

Corporate Tax Rates Around the World

Source: Data taken from KPMG'S Corporate Tax Rate Survey 2006 (1/1/06) (http://www.kpmg.com/NR/exeres/EC5931FC-261B-4D7D-80DF-9E5C49C6F2F8.htm)

40-45%
35-39%
30-34%
25-29%
20-24%
15-19%
0-14%
No current data available

Taxable Income Category	Japan	Germany	United States
Corporate income tax rates:			
Profits distributed to stockholders	37.5	30	35
Undistributed profits	37.5	45	35
Branches of foreign corporations	37.5	42	35
Withholding taxes on dividends (portfolio):			
With Japan	–	15	15
With Germany	15	–	15
With United States	15	5	–
Withholding taxes on dividends (substantial holdings):[a]			
With Japan	–	25	10
With Germany	10	–	5
With United States	10	10	–
Withholding taxes on interest:			
With Japan	–	10	10
With Germany	10	–	0
With United States	10	0	–
Withholding taxes on royalties:			
With Japan	–	10	10
With Germany	10	–	0
With United States	10	0	–

Source: *Corporate Taxes: A Worldwide Summary*, Price Waterhouse Coopers, 2003.
[a] 'Substantial holdings' for the United States apply only to intercorporate dividends. In Germany and Japan, 'substantial holdings' apply to corporate shareholders of greater than 25%.

Table 13.7: Comparison of corporate tax rates (%): Japan, Germany and the United States.

SUMMARY

Corporate government and accounting practices differ substantially across countries. The efforts of a number of international associates and agencies in the past two decades have, however, led to increasing co-operation and agreement among national accounting authorities. Real accounting differences remain and many of these differences still contribute to the advantaged competitive position of some countries' firms over international competitors.

International taxation is a subject close to the pocketbook of every multinational firm. Although the tax policies of most countries are theoretically designed not to change or influence financial and business decision making by firms, they often do.

The taxation of the foreign operations of US multinational firms involves the elaborate process of crediting US corporations for taxes paid to foreign governments. The combined influence of different corporate tax rates across countries, the degree of ownership and control a multinational may have or exercise in a foreign affiliate and the proportion of profits distributed to stockholders at home and abroad combine to determine the size of the parent's tax bill. As governments worldwide search for new ways to close their fiscal deficits and tax shortfalls, the pressures on international taxation and the reporting of foreign-source income will only increase.

QUESTIONS FOR DISCUSSION

1. What entities have what roles in corporate governance?
2. What are the major corporate governance regimes in the world today?
3. Why is there so much focus on boards in corporate governance reform?
4. Do you think all firms, in all economic environments, should operate under the same set of accounting principles?
5. What is the nature of the purported benefit that accounting principles provide UK firms over American firms in the competition for mergers and acquisitions?
6. Name two major indications that progress is being made toward standardizing accounting principles across countries.
7. What is the distinction between harmonizing accounting rules and standardizing accounting procedures and practices across countries?

INTERNET EXERCISES

1. In order to analyse an individual firm's operating exposure more carefully, it is necessary to have more detailed information available than is in the normal annual report. Choose a specific firm with substantial international operations, for example Coca-Cola or PepsiCo, and search the Security and Exchange Commission's Edgar Files for more detailed financial reports of their international operations. Search SEC EDGAR Archives at www.edgar-online.com.
2. The Financial Accounting Standards Board (FASB) promulgates standard practices for the reporting of financial results by companies in the United States. It also, however, often leads the way in the development of new practices and emerging issues around the world. One such major issue today is the valuation and reporting of financial derivatives and derivative agreements by firms. Use the FASB's home page and the web pages of several of the major accounting firms and other interest groups around the world to see current proposed accounting standards and the current state of reaction to the proposed standards. Use the FASB home page at www.fasb.org.
3. Using Nestlé's web page, check Current Press Releases for more recent financial results, including what the company reports as the primary currencies and average exchange rates used for translation of international financial results during the most recent period. See Nestlé: The World Food Company at www.ir.nestle.com.

TAKE A STAND

In August 2002, Connecticut-based Stanley Works, manufacturer of tools and hardware, was pressurized into dropping its initiative to undergo *corporate inversion* – reincorporate in Bermuda instead of the United States in order to reduce its overall tax burden. The Chief Executive Officer of Stanley, John Trani, only initiated such a controversial plan in order to try and reduce what he considered to be a globally uncompetitive tax burden suffered by US-based companies compared to their foreign competitors. (Ingersoll-Rand, US-based competitor to Stanley, successfully completed a corporate inversion offshore during the public debate about Stanley!)

The change in incorporation would not have altered anything about the company's operations, including jobs, wages, technology transfer, etc. It would, however, have reduced the taxes the company paid to the various units of the United States and individual state governments. In the end, Stanley withdrew the proposal after coming under extreme public attack by unions, federal, state and local government officials and even the business press. Most of the criticism was based on the assertion that a corporate inversion was un-American and unpatriotic, not that it was in any way illegal.

FOR DISCUSSION

1. Multinational companies should undertake any and all actions needed to maintain and grow their global competitiveness, including the reduction of tax burdens in whatever legal ways possible. Anything less than this results in an uncompetitive firm that is not acting in the best interest of stockholders.

2. Multinational companies have an obligation to all their stakeholders, employees, creditors, communities and governments, in addition to their stockholders. They have responsibilities to support the social and political ideals that have afforded them the comfort and convenience of growing and profiting from their national origins.

PART 5

FUTURE

14 New Horizons

The book concludes with a chapter focusing on new horizons of international business. Based on global research conducted by the authors, the section covers the newest developments, knowledge and speculations about international business, as well as information about professional and employment options in the international business field.

CHAPTER

14

New Horizons

- The International Business Environment
- Globalization and Trade Negotiations
- Government Policy
- The Future of International Business Management
- Knowledge and International Business
- Careers in International Business

LEARNING OBJECTIVES

- To understand the many changing dimensions that shape international business.
- To learn about and evaluate the international business forecasts made by a panel of experts.
- To understand the role and importance of knowledge in international business.
- To be informed about different career opportunities in international business.

IMPORTING ON THE INTERNET

Can't find a US-made snowboard at your local department store in Japan? Try the Internet. A US firm is creating what could be described as a Japanese cybermall, an online shopping service that enables US manufacturers and retailers to advertise and sell their products directly to consumers – in Japanese. The Japanese Internet service also teaches customers in Japan how to order products and services directly from the United States.

By setting up shop in local language cybermalls, firms couldtarget potential customers around the globe without the costly headaches that often scare them away from the international marketplace. Ion Global Portland has provided Japan-specific e-Business web site development, online marketing, strategic consulting and research services since 1995 to more than one hundred clients, including Amazon.com, British Telecom, Outpost.com, JC Penney, Nokia and PeopleSoft. The firm created a worldwide business consulting network spanning 10 countries.

Ion Global's electronic service averages 1000 unique users per day. More than 5000 people subscribe to its e-newsletter, according to owner Tim Clark. 'We're helping companies enter the Japanese market, companies that want to take a crack without paying for major magazine ads or huge marketing campaigns,' he said. The service is for companies 'interested in dealing directly with customers in Japan', through catalogue sales, for example, he said.

Here's how it works: a US manufacturer or retailer pays a fee for a display on the Import Centre site. The fee varies according to the size and complexity of the display, but runs from US$350 and up. Ion Global, whose staff includes fluent Japanese speakers, translates the copy into Japanese. For the Japanese consumer, the web site is an information resource for customers who want to buy products or services 'without going through middlemen or trading companies,' said Mr. Clark. Access is free of charge in Japan.

The site provides information about products featured on overseas e-Commerce sites that have received positive feedback from Japanese consumers. Japanese consumers visit the site both to learn about featured products and for help with composing English e-mail, interpreting sizes and units of measurement, and understanding different shipping methods.

Mickey Kerbel, president of Xtreme Inc., which makes snowboards, said he paid US$345 for a one-year listing and has sold about US$2000 worth of merchandise in only a couple of months since going online. 'The site provides a low-cost way to gain access to some of the world's most affluent customers,' said Tim Clark. Internet use in the Asia Pacific region is catching up to that of the United States. As of September 2002, Japan had close to 56 million Internet users. Some even claim that the Asia-Pacific region will become the world's largest Internet market by 2006. 'We're happy with the service and the list-building it has helped us with in the Japan market,' said Mike Delph, management information systems manager at US Cavalry, a Kentucky retailer of outdoor equipment and survival gear. He said he's amassed a large list of names through e-mail. 'We've had more responses from the [Import Centre] than we have on our own English language site,' said a system administrator for Blue Tech, a computer products retailer based in La Jolla, California.

Sources: www.nua.ie/surveys, accessed 2 October 2003; 'Corporate Fact Sheet', Ion Global web site, accessed 2 October 2003, www.ion-global.com; telephone interview with Tim Clark, 25 June 1999; William DiBenedetto, 'Home Shopping Internetwork: Buyers Find US Goods at Japanese Cybermall', *The Journal of Commerce*, 8 January 1996, 1A; Gartner's Dataquest, as cited by cyberatlas.internet.com, accessed 2 October 2003.

INTRODUCTION

All international businesses face constantly changing world economic conditions. This is not a new situation or one to be feared, because change provides the opportunity for new market positions to emerge and for managerial talent to improve the competitive position of the firm. Recognizing change and adapting creatively to new situations are the most important tasks of the international business executive, as this chapter's opening vignette shows.

Recently, changes are occurring more frequently, more rapidly and have a more severe impact. Due to growing real-time access to knowledge about and for customers, suppliers and competitors, the international business environment is increasingly characterized by high speed bordering on instantaneity.[1] In consequence, the past has lost much of its value as a predictor of the future. What occurs today may not only be altered in short order but be completely overturned or reversed. For example, political stability in a country can be completely disrupted over the course of a few months. A major, sudden decline in world stock markets leaves corporations, investors and consumers with strong feelings of uncertainty. Overnight currency declines result in an entirely new business climate for international suppliers and their customers. In all, international business managers today face complex and rapidly changing economic and political conditions.

This chapter discusses possible future developments in the international business environment, highlights the implications of the changes for international business management and offers suggestions for a creative response to the changes. The chapter will also explore the meaning of strategic changes as they relate to career choice and career path alternatives in international business.

THE INTERNATIONAL BUSINESS ENVIRONMENT

This section analyses the international business environment by looking at political, financial, societal and technological conditions of change and by providing a glimpse of possible future developments as envisioned by an international panel of experts.[2] The impact of these factors on doing business abroad, on international trade relations and on government policy is of particular interest to the international manager.

The Political Environment

The international political environment is undergoing a substantial transformation characterized by the reshaping of existing political blocs, the formation of new groupings and the break-up of old coalitions.

Planned versus Market Economies

The second half of the last century was shaped by the political, economic and military competition between the United States and the Soviet Union, which resulted in the creation of two virtually separate economic systems. This key adversarial posture has now largely disappeared, with market-based economic thinking emerging as the front-runner. Virtually all the former centrally planned economies are working on becoming market-oriented.

International business has made important contributions to this transition process. Trade and investment have offered the populace in these nations a new perspective, new options, new jobs and new alternatives for marketing their products and services. At the same time, the bringing together of two separate economic and business systems has resulted in new and sometimes devastating competition, a loss of government-ordained trade relationships and substantial dislocations and pain during the adjustment process.

Over the next years the countries of Central and Eastern Europe will continue to be attractive for international investment due to relatively low labour cost, low-priced input factors and large unused production capacities. This attractiveness will translate mainly into growing investment from Western Europe, for reasons of geographic proximity and attractive outsourcing opportunities. With the expansion of the European Union in 2004 and 2007, multinational corporations will recognize the limits to growth and cost containment in their traditional countries. They are likely to move aggressively further east in search of new customers and cheaper resources – a search that will result in a substantial inflow of direct investment into Central and Eastern Europe.

The North – South Relationship

The distinction between developed and lesser-developed countries (LDCs) is unlikely to change. The ongoing disparity between developed and developing nations is likely to be based, in part, on continuing debt burdens and problems with satisfying basic needs. As a result, political uncertainty may well result in increased polarization between the haves and have-nots, with growing potential for political and economic conflict. Demands for political solutions for economic problems are likely to increase. The World Trade Organization states that 2.6 billion people live on less than US$2 per day.[3] Some countries may consider migration as a key solution to population-growth problems, and yet many emigrants may encounter government barriers to their plans.

The developing countries of Africa continue to be a very cool region for international business purposes. Given the continent's size and diversity, it is unreasonable to expect similar economic conditions across all the nations of Africa. At any one time, some countries, their governments, their firms and the well-being of their citizens will differ sharply from others on the same continent. Nonetheless, there is an overwhelming forecast of the growing plight of Africa. There will continue to be a lack of any realistic debate on regime change and although virtually all African governments want enhanced trade opportunities to earn their own way, they do not have the technical wherewithal to carry out such plans. Ongoing crises triggered by the HIV/AIDS pandemic and by weak infrastructure continue to inhibit the capability of many governments to run their economies. They require not just investment programmes but also technical assistance on implementation procedures. International organizations need to go beyond the role of think tanks and become policy initiators. Non-governmental organizations and private firms attend to some of the most desperate needs caused by poor world gaps, but can offer only a temporary bridging rather than a permanent filling in of such an abyss.

State-owned companies are seen mostly as inefficient, high-cost enterprises that are hotbeds of patronage and corruption. Typically they are slow to adapt new technologies and, due to monopoly conditions and a lack of reward for excellence, provide a very low level of service. Similar shortcomings are likely to continue in the financial sector. Foreign investments continue to be largely in the extractive industries such as oil and gold, even though there are substantial new opportunities in other industries. There is likely to be little change until there is a sharp reduction in corruption, steep increases in transparency and major strengthening of the judiciary so that investors and business partners can develop confidence, commitment and trust. There must also be an emphasis on education and training because that triggers where the investments and jobs go.[4] It is not enough to expect a rising tide to raise all boats. There must also be significant effort expended to ensure the seaworthiness of the boat, the functioning of its sails and the capability of its crew. Market-oriented performance will be critical to success in the longer run.

In addition to internal reforms, African countries must also make choices and decide on whether and how to take advantage of innovations. Since there are very different, yet important arguments on each side, decisions are often difficult. The following Focus on Politics provides an example of such conflicting choices.

The issue of environmental protection will also be a major force shaping the relationship between the developed and the developing world. In light of the need and desire to grow their economies, however, there may be much disagreement on the part of the industrializing nations as to what approaches to take. Of key concern will be the answer to the question: Who pays? For example, placing large areas of land out of bounds for development will be difficult for nations that intend to pursue all options for further economic progress. Corporations in turn are likely to be more involved in protective measures if they are aware of their constituents' expectations and the repercussions of not meeting those expectations. Corporations recognize that by being environmentally responsible, a company can build trust and improve its image – therefore becoming more competitive. For example, in the early 1990s the first annual corporate environmental report was published; now over 2000 companies a year publish such reports.[5]

In light of divergent trends by different groups, three possible scenarios emerge. One scenario is that of continued international co-operation. The developed countries could relinquish part of their economic power to less-developed ones, thus contributing actively to their economic growth through a sharing of resources and technology. Although such cross-subsidization will be useful and necessary for the development of LDCs, it may reduce the rate of growth of the standard of living in the more developed countries. It would, however, increase trade flows between developed and less-developed countries and precipitate the emergence of new international business opportunities.

A second scenario is that of confrontation. Due to an unwillingness to share resources and technology sufficiently (or excessively, depending on the point of view), the developing and the developed areas of the world may become increasingly hostile toward one another. As a result, the volume of international business, both by mandate of governments and by choice of the private sector, could be severely reduced.

A third scenario is that of isolation. Although there may be some co-operation between them, both groups, in order to achieve their domestic and international goals, may choose to remain economically isolated. This alternative may be particularly attractive if each region believes that it faces unique problems and must therefore seek its own solutions.

Emerging Markets

Much of the growth of the global economy will be fuelled by the emerging markets of the Asia-Pacific region. There is also the increasing likelihood of a Free Trade Arrangement of the Americas, which will align the common economic interests of countries in South, Central and North America. Due to substantial natural resources and relatively low cost of production, such an agreement is likely to result in an increased flow of foreign direct investment and trade activity, emanating not only from the United States, but also from Europe and Japan.

The Asia-Pacific region is likely to be the hot spot in the next decade. For the industrialized nations, this development will offer a significant opportunity for exports and investment, but it will also diminish, in the longer term, the basis for their status and influence in the world economy. Although the nations in the region are likely to collaborate, they are not expected to form a bloc of the same type as the European Union or NAFTA. Rather, their relationship is likely to be defined in terms of trade and investment flows (e.g., Japan) and social contacts (e.g., the Chinese business community). A cohesive bloc may only emerge as a reaction to a perceived threat by other major blocs.

China is the leading hot prospect in international business for the coming decade. Its growth and capabilities are likely to provide for a forthcoming realignment of the world economy similar to that caused by Japan in the twentieth century. Even though there are likely to be significant conflicts between China and her major trading partners due to stiff competition, pressures for protection and product differentiation, China will be an assertive yet collaborative actor in international business and politics.

Indigenous developments combined with persistent, heavy foreign direct investment in China from industrialized nations will continue the growth of China as a low-cost manufacturing base for the world. These investments will increase in spite of ongoing unresolved political and legal issues,

F○CUS ON

Food Fight in Africa

Africa is the latest battleground in the ongoing war over genetically modified (GM) crops. GM crops grow from seeds that have had their DNA artificially changed by scientists, usually to make the plants more nutritious and resistant to disease and harsh weather conditions. Although farmers in the United States and China have greeted the new crops enthusiastically, there has been no such fanfare in Europe where the European Union (EU) has placed a five-year moratorium on new biotech products.

Now four of the world's largest agricultural companies – Monsanto, Dupont and Dow AgroSciences LLC from the United States and Syngenta AG of Switzerland – have announced plans to donate patent rights, seed varieties, laboratory know-how and other forms of agricultural aid to African scientists working to create plants resistant to disease, drought and insect damage. Proponents of GM crops argue that these donations will help bring food to the 190 million sub-Saharan Africans who are malnourished and regularly go to bed hungry. They consider the development of drought-resistant GM crops to be vital to feeding the African population. The agricultural companies support this initiative on humanitarian grounds but also acknowledge that they hope to create a market for their products in Africa. The companies are also aware of the bad publicity caused for pharmaceutical companies who appeared unwilling to help Africa battle its AIDS epidemic by supplying low-cost drugs.

Opponents of GM crops are outraged by the offer of patent rights and point out that the technology is unproven, innately dangerous and could do untold long-term damage to people, animals and the environment. They point to the 'Green Revolution' in Asia in the 1970s that greatly increased farm yields and fed an ever increasing percentage of the population in the face of rapid population growth. At the time the programmes were thought to be a major success. However, their dependence on pesticides and other poisons to lessen the effect of insects were later determined to have caused increased rates of birth defects and major environmental damage. Insects also began to become resistant to the pesticides. Now new and harsher poisons have to be used.

Opponents of GM crops argue that these seeds have not been adequately tested and pose unknown risks to the environment. They also question the motives of the agricultural companies. Although the companies are giving away the patents today, what happens as older varieties of GM crops are no longer as resistant to disease? Will the companies be as willing to give away technology in the future or will poor farmers have nothing to fall back on? Adding to the pressure on Africa is the threat that the EU will not import any genetically modified agricultural products. As a result, during a famine in southern Africa in the summer of 2002, the nation of Zambia refused to accept food aid in the form of genetically engineered corn from the United States, in order to protect its future exports.

Sources: www.washingtonpost.com/ac2/wp-dyn/A7970-2003Mar10, accessed 24 September 2003; Elizabeth Weise, 'Bio-Food Fight Centers on Africa Critics, Backers See Continent as Battleground', *USA Today*, 9 July 2002, D6.

which will increase risk and constrain the profitability of those investments. Nonetheless, it bears remembering that China is still a communist country and that her policies and thinking are not the same as those of highly industrialized nations. Firms in leading-edge-technology industries are likely to limit their production of sensitive materials in China.

During the coming years Chinese government officials as well as managers will discover how difficult it is to comply with agreed-upon WTO rules. Partner nations will insist, however, that adherence to such rules be relatively swift – particularly in light of large trade surpluses on the part of China. More stringent enforcement measures for intellectual property protection will be expected from the government, because the preservation of and payment for such rights will be crucial for the economic future of 'innovating' nations. At the same time, investors will work on forming strong local alliances to make piracy a key issue for local companies as well. If they have a stake to protect, they will stand up for their own and their partner's rights.

The investment inflow will also provide for an increased Chinese presence in branded goods around the world. China is likely to achieve a substantial takeaway of market share from the Asian tigers, such as Taiwan, Singapore and South Korea, but also from Western brands and manufacturers. As part of this effort Chinese firms will aim to raise their own profile. For example, rather than be the supplier of goods that are then marketed internationally under a Japanese or US label, Chinese firms will increasingly develop their own brand names and fight for their own name recognition, customer loyalty and market share.[6]

India may well be the country with the second highest opportunity for global economic growth and expansion. There will continue to be major opportunities for India due to its concentration on back-office operations and service industries. The quality of India's reputation will be of ongoing concern when compared with that of chief rival China. However, competitive advantages are present in English-language use as well as engineering-based education. Unlike China, India is also more likely to concentrate on services industries, with increasing capability to add value. For example, instead of remaining confined to supporting global medical transcription services, Indian physicians can increasingly read radiology scans and furnish expert opinions.

The reputation of India's workforce continues to be enhanced through its large and successful educational system even though it remains focused on implementation rather than creativity. Limits to economic growth and influence are likely to result from political developments from the continued opaqueness of government rules, as well as ongoing enmity with Pakistan. Although many experts believe that political conflict, both domestic and regional, nationalism and class structure may temper the ability of Indian companies to emerge as a worldwide competitive force, there is strong agreement that India's disproportionately large and specialized workforce in engineering and computer sciences makes the nation a power to be reckoned with.

Recently, several large emerging economies have been referred to as BRICS (Brazil, Russia, India, China and South Africa), with GDP of US$3.1876 trillion (measured in 2002). In 2006 their GDP accounted for more than 12% of the world's GDP. The territory of these big emerging markets covers almost 30% of the world's land. Their population comprises more than 45% of all people living on the earth. BRICS countries have been increasing their presence in the global economy. Not only have they enormous territory and human capital, but they control abundant and diverse natural factor endowments. The rate and level of their economic growth differs but any one of these countries has been developing at a much greater rate compared with the developed economies in the world. Although markets such as the US or the UK have become more saturated, the BRICS markets have been expanding and offering great new market potential. Apart from the five countries that fall into BRICS, there are certainly other emerging markets that have been developing at a great pace. Markets such as Malaysia, Indonesia, Argentina, Chile, Nigeria, Pakistan and the Ukraine, to mention a few, are also upcoming and warranting attention.

Brazil made a policy shift in the 1990s to open up to the global economy. The governments applied structural reforms and trade liberalization leading to effective long-term economic recovery and export-led growth. Lately, the Brazilian government has focused efforts into some specific economic sectors such as agribusiness and eco-business.

The Russian economy has accelerated its growth recently and domestic import substitution industries have been recovering. Although an enormous wealth of energy resources counts for the strength of the Russian economy, the country needs to move away from a resource-dependent economic structure, which is vulnerable to the instability of the commodity markets and exchange rate fluctuations, to a greater diversity of value-added activities in manufacturing and services.

From the economic point of view, India has grown mainly its service sector, benefiting from outsourcing. There are also expectations that India will develop into a labour market that will supply highly educated and skilled human resources to the rest of the world. Moreover, India is a big and promising consumption market with a growing disposable income and a rapidly expanding middle-class stratum of the society. The middle class has real purchasing power that drives consumption forward. To cope with the uncontrolled population growth, the development of the manufacturing sector is essential in order to generate jobs effectively. The government is committed to fostering the development of the pharmaceutical and biotech industries among others.

China is one of the most important emerging economies in the world. It is expected to be the new leader of the global economy by 2040 if not earlier. The speed of Chinese economic development and its success has called for re-thinking of the sources of competitive advantage of well-established multinational companies and all companies from the developed economies. Economic forecasts of major international agencies predict that emerging markets will continue to enjoy higher growth rates compared to developed countries in the long run. Thus, they will continue to present new opportunities for international business as well as challenges to incumbent competitors.

South Africa, since the abolishment of apartheid and democratization of its economy, has been following a strategy of economic growth through liberalization of the conditions for conducting business. Because of its relatively well-developed business infrastructure and the significant presence of South African firms throughout Africa, the country has potential to become a business gateway to southern Africa through tie-ups among South African firms and foreign business.

Some general economic indicators about Brazil, China, India and Russia are given in Figures 14.1–14.3.

The growth potential of the emerging economies may be threatened by uncertainty in terms of international relations and domestic policies, as well as social and political dimensions, particularly those pertaining to income distribution. Concerns also exist about infrastructural inadequacies, both physical – such as transportation – and societal – such as legal systems. The consensus of experts is, however, that growth in these countries will be significant.

A Divergence of Values

It might well be that different nations or cultures become increasingly disparate in terms of values and priorities. In some countries, the aim of financial progress and an improved quantitative standard of living may well give way to priorities based on religion or the environment. Even if nations share similar values, their priorities among these values may differ strongly. Within a market-oriented system, some countries may prioritize profits and efficiency, whereas others may place social harmony first, even at the cost of maintaining inefficient industries.

Such a divergence of values will require a major readjustment of the activities of the international corporation. A continuous scanning of newly emerging national values thus becomes imperative for the international executive.

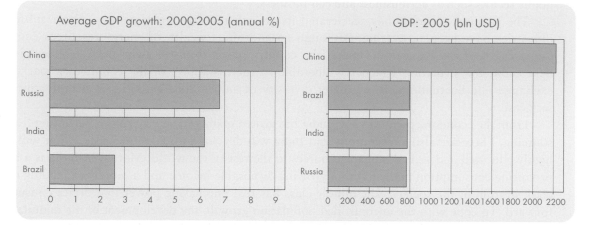

Figure 14.1: General economic indicators: GDP volume and GDP growth.

Source: World Bank (2006).

The International Financial Environment

Debt constraints and low commodity prices impose slow growth prospects for many developing countries. They will be forced to reduce their levels of imports and to exert more pressure on industrialized nations to open up their markets. Even if the markets are opened, however, demand for most primary products will be far lower than supply. Ensuing competition for market share will therefore continue to depress prices.

Developed nations have a strong incentive to help the debtor nations. The incentive consists of the market opportunities that economically healthy developing countries can offer and of national

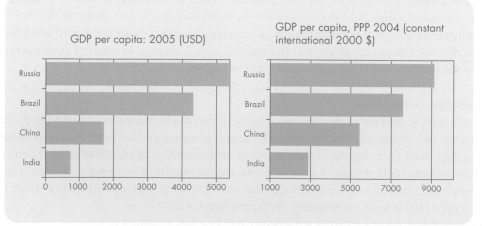

Figure 14.2: General economic indicators: GDP per capita.

Source: World Bank (2006).

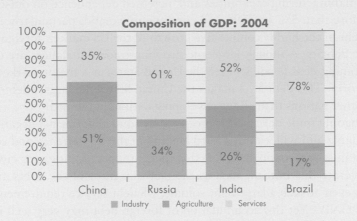

China has a relatively small service sector, and a relatively large share of industry in GDP. In reality, Russia may be a bit closer to China than appears in the graph due to transfer pricing schemes that shift a good share of oil profits to services (trade).

Composition of GDP: 2004

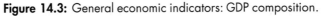

Figure 14.3: General economic indicators: GDP composition.

Source: World Development Indicators (2005).

security concerns. As a result, industrialized nations may very well find that funds transfers to debtor nations, accompanied by debt-relief measures such as debt forgiveness, are necessary to achieve economic stimulation at home.

The dollar will remain one of the major international currencies with little probability of gold returning to its former status in the near future. However, some international transaction volume in both trade and finance is increasingly likely to be denominated in non-dollar terms, using particularly the euro. The system of floating currencies is likely to continue, with occasional attempts by nations to manage exchange rate relationships or at least reduce the volatility of swings in currency values. However, given the vast flows of financial resources across borders, it would appear that market forces rather than government action will be the key determinant of a currency's value. Factors such as investor trust, economic conditions, earnings perceptions and political stability are therefore likely to have a much greater effect on the international value of currencies than domestic monetary and fiscal experimentation.

Given the close links among financial markets, shocks in one market will quickly translate into rapid shifts in others and easily overpower the financial resources of individual governments. Even if there should be a decision by governments to pursue closely co-ordinated fiscal and monetary policies, they are unlikely to be able to negate long-term market effects in response to changes in economic fundamentals.

A looming concern in the international financial environment will be the international debt load of the United States. Both domestically and internationally, the United States is incurring debt that would have been inconceivable only a few decades ago. For example, in the 1970s the accumulation of financial resources by the Arab nations was of major concern in the United States. Congressional hearings focused on whether Arab money was 'buying out America'. At that time, however, Arab holdings in the United States were US$10 billion to US$20 billion. Today the accumulation of foreign dollar holdings has reached much higher levels.

In 1985, the United States became a net negative investor internationally. A temporary weakening of the dollar is not to be confused with a long-term downward trend, particularly with a hands-off government policy. As a result, there are only short-term currency value advantages for new market opportunities abroad for US exporters. Unless there are strong productivity gains, there will be continued losses of manufacturing capabilities and increased dependence on outsourcing. Trade deficits, soon reaching more than 5% of GDP, will continue to expand, particularly in the consumer goods sector. Yet, in light of the highly competitive growth of the US market, foreign funds will continue to finance US trade deficits. Although large and growing trade imbalances are unsustainable over the long term, the coming decade will still see the United States as a major market and therefore growth engine for the world. This debt level makes the United States the largest debtor nation in the world, owing more to other nations than all the developing nations combined.

In light of ongoing trade deficits, it is projected by some that this net negative investment position will be unsustainable and will lead to a hard landing of the US currency and economy. Others argue against an unsustainable scenario, believing that there are special mitigating circumstances that let the United States tolerate this burden, such as the fact that most of the debts are denominated in US dollars and that, even at such a large debt volume, US debt-service requirements are only a relatively small portion of GNP.[7] Yet this accumulation of foreign debt may very well introduce entirely new dimensions into the international business relationships of individuals and nations. Once debt has reached a certain level, the creditor as well as the debtor is hostage to the loans.

Since foreign creditors expect a return on their investment, a substantial portion of future US international trade activity will have to be devoted to generating sufficient funds for such repayment. For example, at an assumed interest rate or rate of return of 10%, the international US debt level – without any growth – would require the annual payment of US$260 billion, which amounts to almost 27% of current US exports.[8] Therefore, it seems highly likely that international business will become a greater priority than it is today and will serve as a source of major economic growth for firms in the United States.

To some degree, foreign holders of dollars may also choose to convert their financial holdings into real property and investments in the United States. This will result in an entirely new pluralism in US society. It will become increasingly difficult and, perhaps, even unnecessary, to distinguish between domestic and foreign products – as is already the case with Hondas made in Ohio. Senators and members of Congress, governors, municipalities and unions will gradually be faced with conflicting concerns in trying to develop a national consensus on international trade and investment. National security issues may also be raised as major industries become majority owned by foreign firms.

Industrialized countries are likely to attempt to narrow the domestic gap between savings and investments through fiscal policies. Without concurrent restrictions on international capital flows, such policies are likely to meet with only limited success. Lending institutions have become more conservative in their financing, a situation that has hit not only small firms and developing countries, but also all financial institutions in developed countries. The current situation will have a far reaching impact on firms in the manufacturing and services sectors and even on the viability of nation states (the case of Iceland). It is a massive collapse that will redefine global trade and finance rules and probably change world balance of powers. The entire financial sector is likely to face continuous integration, ongoing bank acquisitions and a reduction in financial intermediaries. Customers will be able to assert their independence by increasingly being able to present their financial needs globally and directly to financial markets, thus obtaining better access to financial products and providers.

The Effects of Population Shifts

The population discrepancy between less-developed nations and the industrialized countries will continue to increase. In the industrialized world, a *population increase* will become a national priority, given the fact that in many countries, particularly in Western Europe, the population is shrinking. The shrinkage may lead to labour shortages and to major societal difficulties when a shrinking number of workers has to provide for a growing elderly population.

In the developing world, population stabilization will continue to be one of the major challenges of governmental policy. In spite of well-intentioned economic planning, continued rapid increases in population will make it more difficult to ensure that the pace of economic development exceeds population growth. If the standard of living of a nation is determined by dividing the GNP by its population, any increase in the denominator will require equal increases in the numerator to maintain the standard of living. With an annual increase in the world population of 100 million people, the task is daunting. It becomes even more complex when one considers that within countries with high population increases, large migration flows take place from rural to urban areas.

Urbanization is taking place at different speeds on various continents. In North America, the number of city dwellers overtook the rural population before 1940. In Europe, this happened after 1950 and in Latin America at the beginning of the 1960s. Today, these three continents are almost equally urbanized; 75% of Europeans and Latin Americans and 77% of North Americans are city dwellers, according to UN estimates. A similar process is occurring in Africa and Asia, which are still mainly rural. Their proportion of city dwellers rose from 25% in 1975 to a little more than 37% in 2001.[9] The turning point, when the figures will top 50%, is predicted to occur around 2025. Such movements and concentrations of people are likely to place significant stress on economic activity and the provision of services, but will also make it easier for marketers to direct their activities toward customers.

Of key concern in some countries is population balance. Technology has made it possible to predict with high accuracy the gender of a child. In many countries where family growth has been restricted, parents have developed a preference for male heirs. Over time, the result has been a skewed population in which males substantially outnumber females. Particularly for younger generations, this development has led to much greater difficulties in finding a partner for marriage. In consequence, some key cultural dimensions have changed. For example, it has been reported that in the state of Haryana, India, there are just 820 girls born for every 1000 boys. Girls of marriageable age are in such short supply that some parents are not only dropping their demands for wedding dowries (which have a centuries-old cultural tradition) but also offering a 'bride price' to families of prospective mates for their sons.[10] One can also argue that over time such imbalances can drive a society to develop family models such as polyandry – in which one woman may have more than one husband. It might also be possible that societies with a large surplus of young men are more prone to engage in wars.

The Technological Environment

The concept of the global village is commonly accepted today and indicates the importance of communication. Worldwide, the estimated number of people online in midyear 2008 was over 1.4 billion.[11] Asia has the largest number of Internet users, at more than 578 million people. Europe follows with over 384 million users, and the United States has over 284 million. Nonetheless, there is a wide digital gap around the globe, for in some nations, such as Yemen, only 320 000 users are hooked up to the Internet.[12]

For both consumer services and business-to-business relations, the Internet is democratizing global business. It has made it easier for new global retail brands – such as amazon.com – to emerge. The Internet is also helping specialists such as Australia's high sensitivity hearing aids manufacturer Cochlear to reach target customers around the world without having to invest in a distribution network in each country. The ability to reach a worldwide audience economically via the Internet spells success for niche marketers who could never make money by just servicing their niches in the domestic market. The Internet permits customers, especially those in emerging markets, to access global brands at more competitive prices than those offered by exclusive national distributors.[13]

Starting a new business will be much easier, allowing a far greater number of suppliers to enter a market. Small- and medium-sized enterprises, as well as large multinational corporations, will now be full participants in the global marketplace. Businesses in developing countries can now overcome many of the obstacles of infrastructure and transport that limited their economic potential in the past. The global services economy will be a knowledge-based economy and its most precious resource will be information and ideas. Unlike the classical factors of production – land, labour and capital – information and knowledge are not bound to any region or country but are almost infinitely mobile and infinitely capable of expansion.[14] This wide availability, of course, also brings new risks to firms. For example, unlike the past, today one complaint can easily be developed into millions of complaints by e-mail.[15] In consequence, firms are subject to much more scrutiny and customer response on an international level. Overall, these new technologies offer exciting new opportunities to conduct international business.

High technology will also be one of the more volatile and controversial areas of economic activity internationally. Developments in biotechnology are already transforming agriculture, medicine and chemistry. Genetically engineered foods, patient-specific pharmaceuticals, gene therapy and even genetically engineered organs are on the horizon. Innovations such as these will change what we eat, how we treat illness and how we evolve as a civilization.[16] However, scepticism of such technological innovations is rampant. In many instances, people are opposed to such changes due to religious or cultural reasons or simply because they do not want to be exposed to such 'artificial' products. Achieving agreement on what constitutes safe products and procedures, of defining the border between what is natural and what is not, will constitute one of the great areas of debate in the years to come. Firms and their managers must remain keenly aware of popular perceptions and misperceptions and of government regulations in order to remain successful participants in markets.

Even firms and countries that are at the leading edge of technology will find it increasingly difficult to marshal the funds necessary for further advancements. For example, investments in semiconductor technology are measured in billions rather than millions of dollars and do not bring any assurance of success. Not to engage in the race, however, will mean falling behind quickly in all areas of manufacturing when virtually every industrial and consumer product is 'smart' due to its chip technology.

GLOBALIZATION AND TRADE NEGOTIATIONS

Globalization will continue. However, globalization issues will increasingly be understood to go far beyond the economic dimension and be much broader than 'Americanization'. One key question will be whether it is possible to compartmentalize globalization and whether some subcomponents can be adhered to while others are excluded. For example, if one discusses trade relations, must human rights, environmental commitments and conservation of culture necessarily be part of such discussions? Similarly, do open trade relations with the outside require a country to simultaneously fully adhere to a market economy inside the nation? Clearly, there are linkages between all these dimensions, some of them more direct than others. The question is where to draw the boundaries between international collaboration and national sovereignty.

Trade negotiations continue to be fraught with difficulties. The differences between the 148 member nations in the WTO may simply be too great to be bridged in traditional ways. It has been said that nations can be differentiated between those that feed the world, those that fight the world and those that provide the funding for the feeding and fighting. Such a trichotomy, however, seems to be oriented along the problems of yesteryear. From the perspective of national strategy, funding, feeding and fighting are temporary symptomatic actions that reflect the needs of the moment. More long-term may be a differentiation of countries and firms into four categories: those who grow; those who make; those who create; and those who co-ordinate. Each category has very distinct needs, concerns and desires when it comes to trade and investment. For some, the purity of their agricultural production is paramount. Others require a focus on skills and manufacturing employment. Innovators insist on the protection of intellectual property rights while the co-ordinators place major emphasis on free and open communication.

Initially, the discovery of this wide disparity of goals will act as a damper to negotiations and reduce the simplification of trade and investment flows. There will appear to be too much contradiction to achieve closer co-operation, leading to quite substantial delays in any international agreement. However, over time, a better understanding of trade-off capabilities between national or bloc objectives, as well as the pressure emanating from new bilateral and regional negotiations, will reinvigorate the activities of multilateral institutions. To some degree, the search for differences and disagreements will be replaced by the identification of commonalities. The willingness to share burdens and to do so with those resources that are most available in each nation may then provide the forward pedal power of the trade negotiation bicycle.

A key question will be whether nations are willing to abrogate some of their sovereignty even during difficult economic times. An affirmative answer will strengthen the multilateral trade system and enhance the flow of trade. However, if key trading nations resort to the development of insidious non-tariff barriers, unilateral actions and bilateral negotiations, protectionism will increase on a global scale and the volume of international trade is likely to decline. The danger is real. Popular support for international trade agreements appears to be on the wane. The public demonstrations in Cancun during the WTO meetings indicate that there is much ambivalence among individuals and nongovernmental organizations about trade. It is here where international business academics are or should be the guardians who separate fact from fiction in international trade policy discussions. Qualified not by weight of office but by expertise, international business experts are the indirect guarantors of and guides toward free and open markets. Without their input and impact, public apathy and ignorance may well result in missteps in trade policy.[17]

International trade negotiations also will be shaped by restructured composition of global trade. For example, players with exceptionally large productive potential, such as the People's Republic of China, will substantially alter world trade flows. And although governments and firms will be required to change many trading policies and practices as a result, they will also benefit in terms of market opportunities and sourcing alternatives.

Finally, the efforts of governments to achieve self-sufficiency in economic sectors, particularly in agriculture and heavy industries, have ensured the creation of long-term, worldwide oversupply of some commodities and products, many of which historically had been traded widely. As a result, after some period of intense market share competition aided by subsidies and governmental support, a gradual and painful restructuring of these economic sectors will have to take place. This will be particularly true for agricultural cash crops such as wheat, corn and dairy products and industrial sectors such as steel, chemicals and automobiles.

GOVERNMENT POLICY

International trade activity now affects domestic policy more than ever. For example, trade flows can cause major structural shifts in employment. Links between industries spread these effects throughout the economy. For example, fewer domestically produced cars will affect the activities of the steel industry, and shifts in the sourcing of textiles will affect the cotton industry. Global productivity gains and competitive pressures will force many industries to restructure their activities. In such circumstances, industries are likely to ask their governments to help in their restructuring efforts. Often, such assistance includes a built-in tendency toward protectionist action.

Such restructuring is not necessarily negative. For example, since 1900, farm employment in the United States has dropped from more than 40% of the population to less than 3%.[18] Yet, today, the farm industry feeds more than 290 million people in the United States and still produces large surpluses for export. A restructuring of industries can greatly increase productivity and provide new resources for emerging sectors of an economy.

Governments cannot be expected, for the sake of the theoretical ideal of 'free trade', to sit back and watch the effects of deindustrialization on their countries. The most that can be expected from the executive branch and from legislators is that they will permit an open-market orientation subject to the needs of domestic policy. Even an open-market orientation will be maintained only if governments can provide reasonable assurances to their own firms and citizens that the openness applies to foreign markets as well. Therefore, unfair trade practices such as governmental subsidization, dumping and industrial targeting will be examined more closely, and retaliation for such activities is likely to be swift and harsh.

Increasingly, governments will need to co-ordinate policies that affect the international business environment. The development of international indexes and trigger mechanisms, which precipitate government action at predetermined intervention points, will be a useful step in that direction. Yet, for them to be effective, governments will need to muster the political fortitude to implement the policies necessary for co-operation. For example, international monetary co-operation will work in the long term only if domestic fiscal policies are responsive to the achievement of the co-ordinated goals.

At the same time, as the need for collaboration among governments grows, it will become more difficult to achieve a consensus. In the Western world, the time from 1945 to 1990 was characterized by a commonality of purpose. The common defence against the Communist enemy relegated trade relations to second place and provided a bond that encouraged collaboration. With the common threat gone, however, the bonds diminished and the priority of economic performance increased. More often, economic security and national security were seen as competing with each other, rather than as complementary dimensions of national welfare that can operate in parallel.[19]

The response to the attacks of 11 September 2001 has perhaps galvanized a new common sense and allowed a shared vision to emerge. There are five key dimensions to this shared vision:

- *A common sense of vulnerability.* What happened in New York and Washington, DC, can occur at any location around the globe.
- *A common sense of outrage.* The murders did not engender moral ambivalence, at least not among international businesspeople.
- *A renewed global sense of collaboration.* There appears to be a better understanding of the need to work together, to identify mutual goals and to have a vision of a future with substantial commonalities.
- *Politics of common sense.* Rigid claims in cross-national discussions are beginning to yield to more simple and direct questions. In spite of some issue-specific major disagreements, there are indications of an increased willingness to tackle the tough issues – in the international business setting, issues such as agricultural subsidies, dumping regulations, property rights and investment rules.
- *A common set of shared concerns.* Rather than emphasizing all the things that make us different and separate us, such as local concerns, special quirks and home-grown idiosyncrasies, there seems to be a greater concentration on the issues that make us behave alike, bring us together and strengthen the bonds between us.

Over time, perhaps all these commonalities will make life better and collaboration easier.[20]

Policy makers also need a better understanding of the nature of the international trade issues confronting them. Most countries today face both short-term and long-term trade problems. Trade balance issues, for example, are short term in nature, whereas competitiveness issues are much more long term. All too often, however, short-term issues are attacked with long-term trade policy measures and vice versa. In the United States, for example, the desire to 'level the international playing field' with mechanisms such as vigorous implementation of import restrictions or voluntary restraint agreements may serve long-term competitiveness well, but it does little to alleviate the publicly perceived problem of the trade deficit. Similarly, a further opening of Japan's market to foreign corporations will have only a minor immediate effect on that country's trade surplus or the trading partners' deficit. Yet it is the expectation and hope of many in both the public and the private sectors that instantly visible changes will occur.[21] For the sake of the credibility of policy makers, it therefore becomes imperative to identify precisely the nature of the problem and to design and use policy measures that are appropriate for its resolution.

In the years to come, governments will be faced with an accelerating technological race and with emerging problems that seem insurmountable by individual firms alone, such as pollution of the environment and global warming. As market gaps emerge and time becomes crucial, both governments and the private sector will find that even if the private sector knows that a lighthouse is needed, it may still be difficult, time-consuming and perhaps even impossible to build one with private funds alone. As a result, it becomes increasingly important for government to work closely with the business sector to identify market gaps and to devise market-oriented ways of filling them. The international manager in turn will have to spend more time and effort dealing with governments and with macro rather than micro issues.

THE FUTURE OF INTERNATIONAL BUSINESS MANAGEMENT

Global change results in an increase in risk. One short-sighted alternative for risk-averse managers would be the termination of international activities altogether. However, businesses will not achieve long-term success by engaging only in risk-free actions. Further, other factors make the pursuit of international business mandatory.

International markets remain a source of high profits, as a quick look at a list of multinational firms shows.[22] International activities help cushion slack in domestic sales resulting from recessionary or adverse domestic conditions and may be crucial to the very survival of the firm. International markets also provide firms with foreign experience that helps them compete more successfully with foreign firms in the domestic market.

International Planning and Research

Firms must continue to serve customers well to be active participants in the international marketplace. One major change that will come about is that the international manager will need to respond to general governmental concerns to a greater degree when planning a business strategy. Further, societal concern about macro problems needs to be taken into account directly and quickly because societies have come to expect more social responsibility from corporations. Taking on a leadership role regarding social causes may also benefit corporations' bottom lines, because consumers appear more willing than ever to act as significant pressure points for policy changes and to pay for their social concerns. Therefore, reputation management, or the art of building reputation as a corporate asset, is likely to gain prominence in the years ahead as the pressure on corporations to be good corporate citizens grows.[23]

Increased competition in international markets will create a need for more niches in which firms can create a distinct international competence. As a result, increased specialization and segmentation will let firms fill very narrow and specific demands or resolve very specific problems for their international customers. Identifying and filling the niches will be easier in the future because of the greater availability of international research tools and information. The key challenge to global firms will be to build and manage decision-making processes that allow quick responses to multiple changing environmental demands. This capability is important, because firms face a growing need for worldwide coordination and integration of internal activities, such as logistics and operations, while being confronted with the need for greater national differentiation and responsiveness at the customer level.[24]

In spite of the frequent short-term orientation by corporations and investors, companies will need to learn to prepare for long-term horizons. Particularly in an environment of heated competition and technological battles, of large projects and slow payoffs, companies, their stakeholders and governments will need to find avenues that not only permit but also encourage the development of strategic perspectives. Figure 14.4 provides an example of such a long-term view.

Figure 14.4: Long-term planning.

Source: Boeing: www.boeing.com/

Governments both at home and abroad will demand that private business practices not increase public costs and that businesses serve customers equally and non-discriminately. The concept directly counters the desire to serve first the markets that are most profitable and least costly. International executives will therefore be torn in two directions. To provide results acceptable to governments, customers and to the societies they serve, they must walk a fine line, balancing the public and the private good.

International Product Policy

One key issue affecting product planning will be environmental concern. Major growth in public attention paid to the natural environment, environmental pollution and global warming will provide many new product opportunities and affect existing products to a large degree. For example, manufacturers will increasingly be expected to take responsibility for their products from cradle to grave and be intimately involved in product disposal and recycling.

Firms will therefore have to plan for a final stage in the product life cycle, the 'post-mortem' stage, during which further corporate investment and management attention are required, even though the product may have been terminated some time ago.[25]

Although some consumers show a growing interest in truly 'natural' products, even if they are less convenient, consumers in most industrialized nations will require products that are environmentally friendly but at the same time do not require too much compromise on performance and value.

Worldwide introduction of products will occur much more rapidly in the future. Already, international product life cycles have accelerated substantially. Whereas product introduction could previously be spread out over several years, firms now must prepare for product life cycles that can be measured in months or even weeks. As a result, firms must design products and plan their domestic marketing strategies with the international product cycle in mind. Product introduction will grow more complex, more expensive and more risky, yet the rewards to be reaped from a successful product will have to be accumulated more quickly.

Early incorporation of the global dimension into product planning, however, does not point toward increased standardization. On the contrary, companies will have to be ready to deliver more mass customization. Customers are no longer satisfied with simply having a product: they want it to meet their needs and preferences precisely. Mass customization requires working with existing product technology, often in modular form, to create specific product bundles for a particular customer, resulting in tailor-made jeans or a customized car.

Factor endowment advantages have a significant impact on the decisions of international executives. Nations with low production costs will be able to replicate products more quickly and cheaply. Countries such as China, India, Israel and the Philippines offer large pools of skilled people at labour rates much lower than in Europe, Japan or the United States. All this talent also results in a much wider dissemination of technological creativity, a factor that will affect the innovative capability of firms. For example, in 2002, almost half of all the patents in the United States were granted to foreign entities. Table 14.1 provides an overview of US patents granted to foreign inventors.

This indicates that firms need to make non-domestic know-how part of their production strategies or they need to develop consistent comparative advantages in production technology in order to stay ahead of the game. Similarly, workers engaged in the productive process must attempt, through training and skill enhancement, to stay ahead of foreign workers who are willing to charge less for their time. Furthermore, we increasingly see that an organization's ability and willingness to learn and to transfer knowledge is becoming the most critical key to multinational success. Developing the nexus between people and processes is therefore a crucial corporate activity.

An increase will occur in the trend toward strategic alliances or partnering, permitting the formation of collaborative arrangements between firms. These alliances will enable firms to take risks that

State/Country	Totals	State/Country	Totals	State/Country	Totals
Andorra	1	Germany	11 954	Philippines	19
Arab Emirates	6	Greece	22	Poland	13
Argentina	58	Guatemala	5	Portugal	12
Armenia	1	Honduras	2	Romania	4
Australia	991	Hungary	48	Russian Federation	203
Austria	559	Iceland	15	Saint Kitts	2
The Bahamas	13	India	267	Saudi Arabia	10
Barbados	4	Indonesia	147	Singapore	421
Belarus	2	Israel	1108	Slovakia	9
Belgium	801	Italy	1961	Slovenia	16
Bermuda	5	Jamaica	2	South Africa	124
Bolivia	1	Japan	36 340	South Korea	4009
Bosnia and Herzegovina	1	Jordan	1	Spain	358
Brazil	112	Kazakhstan	2	Sri Lanka	15
Bulgaria	1	Kenya	1	Sweden	1824
Canada	3857	Kuwait	8	Switzerland	1532
Cayman Islands	12	Lebanon	2	Syria	2
Chile	13	Liechtenstein	17	Taiwan	6730
China, Hong Kong	589	Lithuania	5	Thailand	61
China, People's Rep.	390	Luxembourg	52	Tunisia	1
Colombia	8	Macau	2	Turkey	18
Costa Rica	8	Malaysia	62	Turks and Caicos	1
Croatia	12	Malta	1	USSR	1
Cuba	9	Marshall Islands	1	Uganda	1
Cyprus	1	Mexico	105	Ukraine	28
Czech Rep.	29	Moldova (Rep)	1	United Kingdom	4197
Czechoslovakia	2	Monaco	21	Uruguay	3
Denmark	559	Netherlands Antilles	3	Uzbekistan	1
Dominican Rep.	1	Netherlands	1681	Venezuela	32
Egypt	5	New Guinea	1	Vietnam	4
Estonia	6	New Zealand	173	British Virgin Islands	3
Fiji	1	Nigeria	4	Yemen	1
Finland	856	Norway	261	Yugoslavia	4
French Polynesia	1	Pakistan	1	Zimbabwe	1
France	4421	Panama	1		
Georgia (Rep.)	5	Peru	1		

Total patents issued in US in 2002	184 428
Total patents issues to US inventors	97 132
Total patents issued to foreign inventors	87 296
Foreign holders as a percentage of total	47.3 %

Source: United States Patent and Trademark Office, Office of Electronic Information Productions/Patent Technology Monitoring Division, Patent Counts by Country/State and Year All Patents, All Types January 1, 1977–December 31, 2002. Washington, DC, 2003, www.uspto.gov

Table 14.1: US patents granted to foreign inventors in 2002.

they could not afford to take alone, facilitate technological advancement and ensure continued international market access. These partners do not need to be large in order to make a major contribution. Depending on the type of product, even small firms can serve as co-ordinating subcontractors and collaborate in product and service development, production and distribution.

On the production management side, security concerns now make it imperative to identify and manage one's dependence on international inputs. Industrial customers, in particular, are often seen as pushing for local sourcing. A domestic source simply provides a greater feeling of comfort.

Some firms also report a new meaning associated with the 'made-in' dimension in country-of-origin labelling. In the past, this dimension was viewed as enhancing products, such as perfumes made in France or cars made in Germany. Lately, the made-in dimension of some countries may create an exclusionary context by making both industrial customers and consumers reject products from specific regions. As a result, negative effects may result from geographic proximity to terrorists, as has been claimed by some about textile imports from Pakistan.

The bottom line still matters. After all, money needs to be made and international business tends to be quite profitable. However, the issue of dependability of supplies is raised at many senior-management meetings and a premium is now associated with having a known and long-term supplier. In the future, foreign suppliers may have to be recommended by existing customers or partners and be able to cope with contingencies before their products are even considered.

International Communications

The advances made in international communications will also have a profound impact on international management. Entire industries are becoming more footloose in their operations; that is, they are less tied to their current location in their interaction with markets. Most affected by communications advances will be members of the services sector. For example, Best Western Hotels in the United States has channelled its entire reservation system through a toll-free number that is being serviced out of the prison system in Utah. Companies could even concentrate their communications activities in other countries. Communications for worldwide operations, for example, could easily be located in Africa or Asia without impairing international corporate activities.

For manufacturers, staff in different countries can not only talk together but also share pictures and data on their computer screens. These simultaneous interactions with different parts of the world will strengthen research and development efforts. Faster knowledge transfer will allow for the concentration of product expertise, increased division of labour and a proliferation of global operations.

Distribution Strategies

Innovative distribution approaches will determine new ways of serving markets. For example, television, through QVC, has already created a shopping mall available in more than 138 million homes worldwide.[26] The use of the Internet offers new distribution alternatives. Self-sustaining consumer distributor relationships emerge through, say, refrigerators that report directly to grocery store computers that they are running low on supplies and require a home delivery billed to the customer's account. Firms that are not part of such a system will simply not be able to have their offer considered for the transaction.

The link to distribution systems will also be crucial to international firms on the business-to-business level. As large retailers develop sophisticated inventory tracking and reordering systems, only the firms able to interact with such systems will remain eligible suppliers. Therefore, firms need to create their own distribution systems that are able to respond to information technology requirements around the globe.

More sophisticated distribution systems will, at the same time, introduce new uncertainties and fragilities into corporate planning. For example, the development of just-in-time delivery systems makes firms more efficient yet, on an international basis, also exposes them to more risk due to distribution interruptions. A strike in a faraway country may therefore be newly significant for a company that depends on the timely delivery of supplies.

Companies have accepted that the international pipeline has slowed down and that customary steps will now take longer in a new security environment. But the structure of the pipeline and the scrutiny given to the materials going through the pipeline have become important.

Firms that had developed elaborate just-in-time delivery systems for their international supplies were severely affected by the border and port closures immediately following the 11 September 2001 attacks. These firms and their service providers continue to be affected by increased security measures. Firms are also focusing more on internal security and the need to demonstrate externally how much more security-oriented they have become. In many instances, government authorities require evidence of threat-reduction efforts to speed shipments along. Also, insurance companies have increased their premiums substantially for firms that are exposed to increased risk.

In the past, cargo security measures concentrated on reducing theft and pilferage from a shipment. Since 11 September, additional measures concentrate on possible undesirable accompaniments to incoming shipments. With this new approach, international cargo security starts well before the shipping even begins. One result – perhaps unintended – of these changes is a better description of shipment content and a more precise assessment of duties and other shipping fees.

Carriers with sophisticated hub-and-spoke systems have discovered that trans-shipments between the different spokes may add to delays because of the time needed to re-scrutinize packages. Although larger 'clean areas' within ports may help reduce this problem, a redesign of distribution systems may lead to fewer hubs and more direct connections.

Firms with a just-in-time system are also exploring alternative management strategies, such as shifting international shipments from air to sea. More dramatically, some firms are considering replacing international shipments with domestic ones, in which truck transport would replace trans-border movement altogether and eliminate the use of vulnerable ports. Future scenarios also accommodate the effects of substantial and long-term interruptions of supplies or operations. Still, any actual move away from existing just-in-time systems is likely to be minor unless new large-scale interruptions occur.

Many new positions have been created in the corporate security field, focusing on new production sites, alternative distribution methods, server mobility and new linkages with customers. In some instances, key customers have been involved in the development of emergency procedures to keep operations going.

In spite of these measures, however, vulnerability to attack continues to be high. For example, 43% of all the maritime containers that arrived in the United States in 2001 came through the ports of Los Angeles and Long Beach. There are no required security standards governing the loading or transport of an inter-modal container. Most are 'sealed' with a 50-cent lead tag. An explosive device in a single container might well gridlock the entire flow and loading systems.[27]

International Pricing

International price competition will become increasingly heated. As their distribution spreads throughout the world, many products will take on commodity characteristics, as semiconductors did in the 1980s. Therefore, small price differentials per unit may become crucial in making an international sale. However, since many new products and technologies will address completely new needs, forward pricing, which distributes development expenses over the planned or anticipated volume of sales, will become increasingly difficult and controversial as demand levels are impossible to predict with any kind of accuracy.

Even for consumer products, price competition will be substantial. Because of the increased dissemination of technology, the firm that introduces a product will no longer be able to justify higher prices for long; domestically produced products will soon be of similar quality. As a result, exchange rate movements may play more significant roles in maintaining the competitiveness of the international firm. Firms can be expected to prevail on their government to manage the country's currency to maintain a favourable exchange rate. Technology also allows much more interaction on pricing between producer and customer. The success of electronic commerce providers such as www.ebay.com or www.priceline.com demonstrates how auctioning and bidding, alone or in competition with others, offers new perspectives on the global price mechanism.

Through subsidization, targeting, government contracts or other hidden forms of support, nations will attempt to stimulate their international competitiveness. Due to the price sensitivity of many products, the international manager will be forced to identify such unfair practices quickly, communicate them to his or her government and insist on either similar benefits or government action to create an internationally level playing field.

At the same time, many firms will work hard to reduce the price sensitivity of their customers. By developing relationships with their markets rather than just carrying out transactions, other dimensions such as loyalty, consistency, the cost of shifting suppliers and responsiveness to client needs may become much more important than price in future competition.

KNOWLEDGE AND INTERNATIONAL BUSINESS

In this section, we introduce the concept of knowledge in international business, including organizational approaches to cross-border knowledge exchanges. One of the generally accepted views of knowledge recognizes that an international manager's knowledge is a constantly evolving process, which leads to outcomes that are enhanced by experiential and theoretical learning. Knowledge can exist at various levels simultaneously. These encompass the knowledge of an individual manager, a group of managers, within an organization and between organizations. There are also two distinct interpretations of knowledge, namely knowledge that you hold as a result of previous learning and knowledge as action. In the literature on international business, the view of knowledge-as-possession is by far prevalent. Recently, the concepts of knowledge-as-possession and knowledge-as-action have been widely introduced into the general and more specific interpretations of international business operations.

In international business, multinational companies are presented as differentiated networks characterized by flows of knowledge, capital and products. The capacity and capability to develop and share knowledge are regarded as fundamental organizational capacities of these companies. Thus international business operations and multinational companies have lately become a focal point of special interest in knowledge creation and transfer. The reasons are as follows. First and foremost, multinational companies operate in diverse cultural contexts, being exposed to a great variety of diverse sources of knowledge that is contextually specific. The specifics of knowledge content stem from diverse and varied customers' wants and needs, competitor features and level of technological attainment. Second, multinational companies generate innovation in a variety of locations. Third, they can combine resources and capabilities spread across their subsidiaries in order to generate and leverage new knowledge.

Thus, knowledge flows in international business operations have become a priority issue for managers and researchers.

A knowledge-based strategy formulation of a multinational company should start with the primary intangible resource: the competence of people. Products, assets and the intangible relations in an international firm are the results of human action, and depend ultimately on people for their continued existence. People are seen to be constantly expanding, existing and creating new knowledge by both tangible means, such as craft, houses, gardens and cars, and intangible corporate associations, ideas and relationships.

Those working in a particular company can use their competencies and capabilities to create value for the organization in two ways: 1) *externally*; and 2) *internally*. For example, internal conversion of knowledge is when the managers within an international manufacturing organization direct the efforts of their employees internally to create tangible goods and intangible structures such as better processes and new product designs. When subsequently managers direct their attention outside the organization, they will not only deliver goods and money but also create intangible structures such as customer relationships, brand awareness, reputation and new customer experiences.

CAREERS IN INTERNATIONAL BUSINESS

By studying this book you have learned about the intricacies, complexities and thrills of international business. Of course, a career in international business is more than jet-set travel between New Delhi, Tokyo, Frankfurt and New York. It is hard work and requires knowledge and expertise. Yet, in spite of the difficulties, international business expertise may well become a key ingredient for corporate advancement. Preparing for such expertise can, however, be fraught with risk as the following Focus on Culture shows.

FOCUS ON

CULTURE   Ensuring Student Safety Abroad

After the terrorist attacks of 11 September 2001, student safety has become a more vivid concern for many universities. International outreach has long been seen as an important element in undergraduate education. Today, universities must spend time and resources to ensure that those international experiences are safe. For example, a generation ago US students primarily studied abroad in Western Europe. Now they are literally scattered around the globe, often in remote and isolated places. More than 154 000 US students are studying abroad for college credit, twice the number a decade ago. Varying degrees of perceived anti-American sentiment worldwide has made university administrators very security conscious.

Kroll, Inc., a New York-based global risk-management company with offices all over the world, has seen its security consulting business for colleges and universities double since 11 September 2001. It is no longer enough simply to warn students not to speak English in loud voices or not to wear clothing with US logos. Today, universities are developing contingency plans for their students studying overseas with planned responses for crises ranging from the breakout of war to students being taken hostage.

Many emergency response strategies include a complete extraction plan should all students studying abroad need to be brought back to the home campus. Before 11 September only about 10% of universities had contingency plans for students studying abroad. Now such plans are standard fare. Also common are pre-departure orientation programmes where students are informed about risky conditions abroad and how those risks vary from site to site. For example, Georgetown University's Office of International Programmes advises students not to visit high-risk areas such as Israel, Zimbabwe or Indonesia while travelling abroad and will not enter into formal agreements to send students to these locations.

For universities like Georgetown, where more than half of the students study abroad, programme choices are critical. High-profile cases of injuries and deaths of students while on study-abroad trips has added to the pressure on administrators to keep students safe. In 1998 a group of students on a study-abroad trip with St. Mary's College of Maryland were gang-raped when the bus they were riding in was attacked by roadway bandits in Guatemala. Several of the students sued the school, alleging negligence on the part of the professors planning the trip and claiming that the school should have been aware of a similar bus attack on a group of tourists just six months earlier. Although St. Mary's officials disputed some of the students' claims they eventually settled the lawsuit for US$195 000, but not before the school had received a lot of bad press.

Sources: www.theyhoya.com/news/012803/news2.cfm, accessed 23 September, 2003; Annie Gowen, 'Caution Tops Syllabus for US Students Abroad: Schools Seek Strategies to Counter Threats', *Washington Post*, 21 June 2003, B1.

To prepare for a career in international management, you should be well versed in a specific functional business area and take summer internships abroad. You should take language courses and travel, not simply for pleasure but to observe business operations abroad and gain a greater appreciation of different peoples and cultures. The following pages provide an overview of further key training and employment opportunities in the international business field.

Further Training

One option for the student on the road to more international involvement is to obtain further in-depth training by enrolling in graduate business school programmes that specialize in international business education. A substantial number of universities around the world specialize in training international managers. According to the Institute of International Education, the number of US students studying for a degree at universities abroad rose to 241 791 students in 2007. At the same time, business and management are the most popular fields of study for the 623 805 international students at American universities.[28] The Erasmus programme in Europe supports co-operation between the universities of 31 countries and has enabled over 1.5 million students to study abroad to date. A review of college catalogues and of materials from groups such as the Academy of International Business will also be useful here.

In addition, as the world becomes more global, more organizations are able to assist students interested in studying abroad or in gathering foreign work experience. For example www.iiepassport.org, www.studyabroad.com, www.overseasjobs.com and www.egide.asso.fr provide rich information about programmes and institutions.

For those ready to enter or rejoin the 'real world', different employment opportunities need to be evaluated.

Employment with a Large Firm

One career alternative in international business is to work for a large multinational corporation. These firms constantly search for personnel to help them in their international operations. Table 14.2 lists web sites that can be useful in obtaining employment internationally.

Many multinational firms, although seeking specialized knowledge such as languages, also expect employees to be firmly grounded in the practice and management of business. Rarely, if ever, will a firm hire a new employee at the starting level and immediately place him or her in a position of international responsibility. Usually, a new employee is expected to become thoroughly familiar with the company's internal operations before being considered for an international position. A manager is sent abroad because the company expects him or her to reflect the corporate spirit, to be tightly wed to the corporate culture and to be able to communicate well with both local and corporate management personnel. In this liaison position, the manager will have to be exceptionally sensitive to both headquarters and local operations. As an intermediary, the expatriate must be empathetic, understanding and yet fully prepared to implement the goals set by headquarters.

AVOTEK Headhunters

www.avotek.com/
Nieuwe Markt 54
6511 XL Nijmegen
Netherlands
Telephone: 31 24 3221367
Fax: 31 24 3240467
e-mail: avotek@tip.nl

Lists web sites and addresses of jobs and agencies worldwide. Offers sale publications and other free reference materials.

Council on International Education Exchanges

www.ciee.org/
7 Custom House St., 3rd Floor
Portland, ME 04101
USA
Telephone: 001 (800) 40-STUDY or 001 (207) 553-7600
Fax: 001 (207) 553-7699
e-mail: info@councilexchanges.org

Paid word and internships overseas for college students and recent graduates. Also offers international volunteer projects, as well as teaching positions.

Datum Online

www.datumeurope.com/
91 Charlotte Street
London W1P 1LB
UK
e-mail: admin@datumeurope.com

Online database providing all the resources to find IT, sales and accountancy jobs across Europe.

Dialogue with Citizens

europa.eu.int/citizens
International Market Directorate General

MARKT A/04, C 107 03/52
European Commission
Rue de la Loi, 200
B-1049 Brussels
Belgium
Telephone: (011) 322 299-5804
Fax: (011) 322 295-6695
e-mail: mail@europe-direct.cec.eu.int

Factsheets on EU citizens' right regarding residence, education, working conditions and social security, rights as a consumer, and ways of enforcing these rights, etc. Easy-to-use guides that give a general outline of EU citizens' rights and the possibilities offered by the European Single Market. A Signpost Service for citizens' practical problems.

Ed-U-Link Services

www.edulink.com
PO BOX 2076
Prescott, AZ 86302
USA
Telephone: 001 (520) 778-5581
Fax: 001 (520) 776-0611
e-mail: info@edulink.com

Provides listings of and assistance in locating teaching jobs abroad.

The Employment Guide's Career Web

www.employmentguide.com
295 Bendix Rd
Virginia Beach, VA 23452
USA
Telephone: (877) 876-4039
e-mail: customerservice@cweb.com

Online employment source with international listings, guides, publications, etc.

Escape Artist.com Inc.

www.escapeartist.com
Suite 832-1245
World Trade Center
Panama
Republic of Panama
Fax: 011 507 317-0139
e-mail: headquarters@escapeartist.net

Web site for US expatriates. Contains links for overseas jobs, living abroad, offshore investing, free magazines, etc.

Euro Jobs

www.eurojobs.com
Heathfield House
303 Tarring Rd
Worthing
West Sussex BN11 5JG
UK
Telephone: 44 (0) 1260 223144
Fax: 44 (0) 1260 223145
e-mail: medialinks@eurojobs.com

Lists vacant jobs all over Europe. Also includes the possibility of submitting CV to recruiters; employment tips and other services.

EURopean Employment Services – EURES

www.europa.eu.int/eures
Employment and Social Affairs Directorate General

Rue de la Loi, 200
B-1049 Brussels
Belgium
Telephone: (011) 322 299-6106
Fax: (011) 322 299-0508 or 295-7609
e-mail: empl-eures@cec.eu.int

Aims to facilitate the free movement of workers within the 17 countries of the European Economic Area. Partners in the network include public employment services, trade unions and employer organizations. The partnership is co-ordinated by the European Commission. For citizens of these 17 countries, provides job listings, background information, links to employment services, and other job-related web sites in Europe.

Expat Network

www.expatnetwork.com
5 Brighton Rd.
Croydon
Surrey CR2 6EA
UK
Telephone: 44 (0) 20 8760 5100

(Continued)

Fax: 44 (0) 20 8760 0469
e-mail: expats@expatnetwork.com

Dedicated to expatriates worldwide, linking to overseas jobs, country profiles, health care, expatriate, gift and book-shop, plus in-depth articles and industry reports on issues that affect expatriates. Over 5000 members. Access is restricted for non-members.

Federation of European Employers (FedEE)

www.fedee.com
Adam House
7–10 Adam Street
The Strand
London WC2 N6AA
UK
Telephone: 44 (0) 207 520 9264
Fax: 44 (0) 1359 269 900
e-mail: fedee@globalnet.co.uk

FedEE's European Personnel Resource Centre is the most comprehensive and up-to-date source of pan-European national pay, employment law, and collective bargaining data on the web.

FlipDog.com

www.flipdog.com
5 Clock Tower Place
Suite 500
Maynard, MA 01754
USA
Telephone: 001 (877) 887-3547
e-mail: info@flipdog.com

Constitutes the Internet's largest job collection. In addition to US coverage, includes approximately 82 000 vacancies in other countries. One of the most comprehensive employment search engines on the Internet.

Hot Jobs.com Ltd.

www.hotjobs.com
406 West 31st St.
New York, NY 10001
USA
Telephone: 001 (212) 699-5300
Fax: 001 (212) 944-8962
e-mail: support@hotjobs.com
Contains international job listings.

Jobpilot

www.jobpilot.co.uk
Brook House
10 Church Terrace
Richmond
Surrey TWL10 6SE
UK
Telephone: 44 (0) 208 614-7800
Fax: 44 (0) 208 948-7322
e-mail: info@jobpilot.co.uk
'Europe's unlimited career market on the Internet'.

Monster.com

www.monster.com
TMP Worldwide Global Headquarters

1633 Broadway
33rd Floor

New York, NY 10019
USA
Telephone: 001 (800) MONSTER or 001 (212) 977-4200
Fax: 001 (212) 956-2142

Global online network for careers and working abroad. Career resources, including message boards and daily chats.

Overseas Jobs.com

www.overseasjobs.com
AboutJobs.com Network
12 Robinson Rd.
Sagamore Beach MA 02562
USA
Telephone: 001 (508) 888-6889
e-mail: info@overseasjobs.com

Job seekers can search the database by keywords or locations and post a CV online for employers to view.

PlanetRecruit.com

www.planetrecruit.com
Planet Recruit
Beaumont House
Kensington Village
Avonmore Road
London, W14 8TS
UK
Telephone: 44 (020) 7000 9980
e-mail: support@planetrecruit.com

One of the world's largest UK and international recruiting networks. Features accounting and finance, administrative and clerical, engineering, graduate and trainee, IT, media, new media and sales, marketing and public relations jobs from about 60 countries.

The Riley Guide

www.rileyguide.com
Margaret F. Dikel
11218 Ashley Drive
Rockville, MD 20852
USA
Telephone: 001 (301) 881-0122
Fax: 001 (301) 984-6390
e-mail: webmaster@rileyguide.com

A directory of employment and career information sources and services on the Internet, providing instruction for job seekers and recruiters on how to use the Internet to their best advantage. Includes a section for US residents on working abroad, including in Europe.

SCI-IVS EUROPE

www.sciint.org
International Secretariat – Antwerpen
St-Jacobsmarkt 82
B-2000 Antwerpen,
Belgium
Tel. 32 3 2265727
Fax: 32 3 2320344
e-mail: info@sciint.org

(Continued)

Through various non-commercial partner organizations worldwide and through SCE international, national and regional branch development, the European branch of SCI participates in the SCI network, which exchanges over 5000 volunteers each year in short-term (2–4 week) international group workcamps and in long-term (3–12 month) volunteer postings in more than 60 countries.

Transitions Abroad Online: Work Abroad

www.transitionsabroad.com
PO Box 745
Bennington, VT 05201
USA
Telephone: 001 (802) 442-4827
Fax: 001 (802) 442-4827
e-mail: info@transitionsabroad.com

Contains articles from its bimonthly magazine; a listing of work abroad resources (including links); and lists of key employers, internship programmes, volunteer programmes, and English-teaching openings.

Upseek.com

www.upseek.com
Telephone: 001 (877) 587-5627
e-mail: salesinfo@upseek.com

A global search engine that empowers job seekers in the online job search market. Provides job opportunities from the top career and corporate sites with some European listings.

Vacation Work Publications

www.vacationwork.co.uk
9 Park End Street
Oxford OX1 HJ
UK
Telephone: 44 (0) 1865 241978
e-mail: vacationwork@vacationwork.co.uk

Lists job openings around the world, in addition to publishing many books on the topic; has an information exchange section and a links section.

WWOOF INTERNATIONAL

www.wwoof.org
PO Box 2675
Lewes BN7 1RB
UK
WWOOF INTERNATIONAL is dedicated to helping those who would like to work as volunteers on organic farms internationally.

Source: European Union www.eurunion.org

Table 14.2: Web sites in gaining international employment.

It is very expensive for companies to send an employee overseas. The annual cost of maintaining a manager overseas is often a multiple of the cost of hiring a local manager. Companies want to be sure that the expenditure is worth the benefit they will receive. Failure not only affects individual careers, but also sets back the business operations of the firm. Therefore, firms increasingly develop training programmes for employees destined to go abroad.

Even if a position opens up in international operations, there is some truth in the saying that the best place to be in international business is on the same floor as the chief executive at headquarters.

Employees of firms that have taken the international route often come back to headquarters to find only a few positions available for them. After spending time in foreign operations, where independence is often high and authority significant, a return to a regular job at home, which sometimes may not even call on the many skills acquired abroad, can turn out to be a difficult and deflating experience. Such encounters lead to some disenchantment with international activities as well as to financial pressures and family problems, all of which may add up to significant executive stress during re-entry.[29] Since family re-entry anxiety is one reason 25% of expatriates quit within one year of their return, companies are increasing the attention paid to the spouses and children of employees. For example, about 15% of Fortune 500 firms offer support for children of employees relocated abroad.[30]

Opportunities for Women in Global Management

As firms become more and more involved in global business activities, the need for skilled global managers is growing. Concurrent with this increase in business activity is the ever growing presence and managerial role of women in international business.

Research conducted during the mid-1980s[31] indicated that women held 3.3% of the overseas positions in US business firms. By 2000, 13% of expatriates in US corporations were women.[32] The reason for the low participation of women in global management roles seems to have been the assumption that because of the subservient roles of women in Japan, Latin America and the Middle East, neither local nor expatriate women would be allowed to succeed as managers. In fact, expatriates are not seen as local women, but rather as 'foreigners who happen to be women', thus solving many of the problems that would be encountered by a local woman manager.

There appear to be some distinct advantages for a woman in a management position overseas. Among them are the advantages of added visibility and increased access to clients. Foreign clients tend to assume that 'expatriate women must be excellent or else their companies would not have sent them'.

It also appears that companies that are larger in terms of sales, assets, income and employees send more women overseas than smaller organizations. Further, the number of women expatriates is not evenly distributed among industry groups. Industry groups that use greater numbers or percentages of women expatriates include banking, electronics, petroleum, publishing, diversified corporations, pharmaceuticals and retailing and apparel.

For the future, it is anticipated that the upward trend previously cited reflects the increased participation of women in global management roles.

Employment with a Small or Medium-Sized Firm

A second alternative is to begin work in a small or medium-sized firm. Very often, such firms have only recently developed an international outlook and the new employee will arrive on the 'ground floor'. Initial involvement will normally be in the export field – evaluating potential foreign customers, preparing quotes and dealing with activities such as shipping and transportation. With a very limited budget, the export manager will only occasionally visit international markets to discuss business strategies with distributors abroad. Most of the work will be done by mail, fax, e-mail or telephone. The hours are often long because of the need, for example, to reach a contact during business hours in Hong Kong. Yet the possibilities for implementing creative business transactions are virtually limitless. It is also gratifying and often rewarding that one's successful contribution will be visible directly through the firm's growing export volume.

Alternatively, international work in a small firm may involve importing; that is, finding low-cost sources that can be substituted for domestically sourced products. Decisions often must be based on limited information and the manager is faced with many uncertainties. Often things do not work out as planned. Shipments are delayed, letters of credit are cancelled and products almost never arrive in exactly the form and shape anticipated. Yet the problems are always new and offer an ongoing challenge.

As a training ground for international activities, there is probably no better starting place than a small or medium-sized firm. Later on, the person with some experience may find work with a trading or export management company, resolving other people's problems and concentrating almost exclusively on the international arena.

Self-Employment

A third alternative is to set up as a consultant or establish a trading firm. Many companies are in need of help for their international business efforts and are prepared to part with a portion of their profits in order to receive it. Yet it requires in-depth knowledge and broad experience to make a major contribution from the outside or to run a trading firm successfully.

Specialized services that might be offered by a consultant include international market research, international strategic planning or, particularly desirable, beginning-to-end assistance for international entry or international negotiations. For an international business expert, the hourly billable rate typically is as high as US$500 for principals and US$150 for staff. Whenever international travel is required, overseas activities are often billed at the daily rate of US$3000 plus expenses. Even at such high rates, solid groundwork must be completed before all the overhead is paid. The advantage of this career option is the opportunity to become a true international entrepreneur. Consultants and those who conduct their own export–import or foreign direct investment activities work at a higher degree of risk than those who are not self-employed, but they have an opportunity for higher rewards.

This concludes the text portion of this book. We hope you have worked with it, learned from it and even enjoyed it. It is important for us also to learn from our customers. Please provide us with feedback, both praise and suggestions for improvement by contacting us at:

- s.t.marinova@bham.ac.uk
- mmarinov@glos.ac.uk

Thank you for being an international business student!

SUMMARY

This final chapter has provided an overview of the environmental changes facing international managers and alternative managerial response to the changes. International business is a complex and difficult activity, and yet it affords many opportunities and challenges. Observing changes and analysing how to best incorporate them in the international business mission is the most important task of the international manager. If the international environment were constant, there would be little challenge to international business. The frequent changes are precisely what make international business so fascinating and often highly profitable for those who are active in the field.

QUESTIONS FOR DISCUSSION

1. For many developing countries, debt repayment and trade are closely linked. What does protectionism mean to them?
2. Should one worry about the fact that the United States is a debtor nation?
3. How would our lives and our society change if imports were banned?
4. Is knowledge important for a multinational company and how can internal and external knowledge contribute to the competitive advantage of an organization?
5. How have security concerns changed the way international firms do business?

INTERNET EXERCISES

1. Using the web site of Living Abroad (www.livingabroad.com), research several international schools that may interest you. What are the most interesting links to other web sites concerning international issues? Why are you particularly interested in them?
2. The web site www.overseasjobs.com provides valuable information for those interested in jobs overseas. What skills do international employers seem to value most? Peruse the job listings and find several jobs in which you might be interested. Also take a look at the profiles of several international companies for whom you may be interested in working. What characteristics do the international firms listed here possess?

TAKE A STAND

It is virtually impossible to be totally protected from terrorism. However, some safety measures can be developed. For example, to reduce the exposure of students to terrorist attacks it helps to keep them all at home. Another reduction of risk can be achieved by not letting them be exposed to anyone outside their familiar groups. Say goodbye to study abroad programmes, and forget about international students and scholars!

FOR DISCUSSION

1. Does such an approach make things better?
2. What do you propose?

PART 6

CASE STUDIES

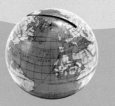

Case Study 1

RENAMING THE VIETNAMESE CATFISH[1]

The US Catfish Industry

The cultivation of water plants and animals for human use started thousands of years ago. Globally, aquaculture's growth has more than doubled in the 1990s (to more than 35 million tonnes a year). To meet the demand for improved quality protein sources, scallops, oysters, salmon and catfish are being raised in controlled environments. Farm-raised fish is of high quality and, unlike ocean-caught fish, is available all year long.

US aquaculture production has grown more than 49% since 1991.[2] Aquaculture is the fastest growing segment of agriculture in the US. Farmed seafood makes up about one third of the seafood consumed in the United States. About two thirds of the shrimp and salmon and almost all of the catfish and trout consumed by Americans are raised in ponds.[3]

Thick-skinned, whiskered, wide-mouthed wild catfish can be found in the wild in channels and rivers of the southern United States. Wild catfish is typically described as pungent, bony and muddy. However, as a result of aquaculture technology, catfish is now an economical farm-raised species with a mild flavour. Catfish are raised in clay-based ponds filled with fresh water pumped from underground wells. They are fed an enriched, high-protein, grain-based food. Their firm, white flesh can convey strong flavours and stands up to a variety of cooking techniques, which makes it suitable for virtually any ethnic cuisine.[4]

Americans consumed about 275 million kilograms of catfish in 2000,[5] most of which came from 14 000 hectares of catfish ponds in the United States, mainly located in Mississippi, Arkansas and Louisiana. The US catfish industry is estimated to sell more than US$4 billion worth of fish product each year. Catfish is especially popular in Southern dishes, but its use has been growing also in the Midwest. Fillets are now available in New York supermarkets and fish stores. One recent poll placed catfish as the country's third favourite seafood, beaten only by shrimp and lobster.[6]

The Issue

The United States is the leading market for Vietnamese catfish (followed by Hong Kong, the European Union and Australia). In 2001, the United States produced 270.5 million kilograms and imported about 3.7 million kilograms of catfish, out of which 90%, about 3.2 million kilograms came from Vietnam. By the end of 2001, prices for US catfish had dropped to 50 cents a pound, about 15 cents below the cost of production and about 30 cents below the price in 2000. US producers blamed the Vietnamese for the falling prices.[7]

Vietnamese catfish exporters and importers in turn blame US producers for dragging prices down. They say that the Americans are mainly at fault for expanding inventories up to 30%, a figure obtained from the National Agricultural Statistics Service (www.usda.gov/nass). Vietnamese fish importers also claim that American catfish growers are to blame for their own difficulties because they sell the domestic fish in only a few states. 'It is the failure to adequately market the product effectively throughout the US,' says Andrew Forman, president of Boston-based Infinity Seafood LLC. According to a report by Consulting Trends International, a California-based consulting firm, the price drop is 'primarily the result of higher domestic catfish inventories in the US, which will depress prices through the end of 2001 and 2002'.

The American catfish industry has almost tripled in size from 1985 to 2001. Hugh Warren, vice president of the Catfish Institute of America, says that this growth is strictly due to the industry's marketing effort of US$50 million. He feels that as importers, the Vietnamese get a free ride.[8] The US industry offers 15 000 jobs that earn US$8 an hour in the poorest parts of America. These jobs are being 'stolen' by cheap Vietnamese imports.[9]

In an attempt to change this situation, American catfish farmers, industry associations and supporting organizations came to Washington, DC to call on officials at the State Department, the Commerce Department, the Food and Drug Administration and Congress (which in July 2000 signed a bilateral agreement with Vietnam to foster free trade) for help. They waged an advertising campaign against their Vietnamese competitors in order to convince the public that Vietnamese catfish is of low quality and raised in dirty waters.[10]

Congressional Reaction

The support from Congress was swift. In December 2001 an amendment was added to an appropriations bill that barred the Food and Drug Administration (FDA) from spending money 'to allow admission of fish or fish products labeled in whole or in part with the term "catfish" unless the fish is from the *Ictaluridae* family'. The senators from the South, who introduced the labelling bill, claimed Vietnamese fish was as different scientifically from catfish 'as cow from a yak'.[11] Supporting a different view, Senator Phil Gramm (R-Tex.) characterized the Vietnamese catfish as follows: 'Not only does it look like a catfish, but it acts like a catfish. And the people who make a living in fish science call it a catfish. Why do we want to call it anything other than a catfish?'[12] This meant that the FDA needed to identify different kinds of catfish.

In January 2002, under Congress' direction, the FDA published 'Guidance for Industry' regulations on how the imported catfish should be labelled. Under the regulation, Flat Whiskered Fish is an acceptable substitute for the Flat Whiskered Catfish; but Katfish or Cat Fish are not. Instead, importers, restaurants and grocery stores will have to use a name such as 'basa', which is one other name to call catfish from the *Pangasius* (*Pangasiidae*) family. US producers were counting on such labels to discourage the sales of imported fish.

About 30% of US seafood restaurants serve Vietnamese catfish, which is slightly milder and softer than the American variety. The amendment and the regulation were not good news for them. As the owner of Piazza's Seafood World, a New Orleans-based importer, put it: 'Nobody in the US owns the word "catfish"'.[13] However, Vietnam is still free to export catfish to the United States, as long as it is called something other than catfish.

When Is a Catfish a Catfish?

In order to identify different kinds of catfish, the FDA sought expert help on the catfish question. Before promulgating its regulation it consulted Dr Carl J. Ferraris of the ichthyology department at the California Academy of Sciences. Dr Ferraris's response was that there was no scientific justification to treat or rename catfish from Vietnam differently those from the United States.[14]

According to US catfish farmers, the only true catfish belongs to the family with the Latin name *Ictaluridae*. The Vietnamese variety is in the family *Panasiidae*, which are 'freshwater catfishes of Africa and southern Asia'. Vietnamese catfish farmers claim that they have created a new agricultural industry, turning their rice and soybean fields into profitable fish farms in the poor regions of the country. By giving up crops, they gave up heavy use of chemical fertilizers and pesticides, which is good for the environment. They also gave up agriculture subsidies at a time when lawmakers wanted to get the government out of farming.[15]

US catfish farmers say their catfish is raised in purified water ponds, which have to be tested by federal agencies and meet the standards of Catfish Institute. The US catfish industry must go through inspections from 17 federal agencies (including Department of Commerce, Food and Drug Administration and Environmental Protection Agency). By contrast, the Vietnamese imports have only to meet FDA approval.[16] The Vietnamese catfish are raised in cages that float in marshes in the Mekong river; some of the senators from the South talk about the possibility of toxins from Vietnam being in that 'dirty' river.[17]

The Issue and the Free Trade

Vietnam's catfish industry provides a useful example of how global co-operation can enhance participation in global business. An Australian importer, for example, taught the Vietnamese how to slice catfish fillet, French researchers worked with a local university on low-cost breeding techniques, and Vietnam's leading catfish exporters depended on American industrial equipment from the United States.[18] However, a stumbling US economy has made American farmers, along with many others in a number of industries, very sensitive to surging imports, and the catfish dispute represents a case of domestic politics alignment against free-market forces.[19] Critics in both Vietnam and the United States say that the catfish issue is an example of protectionism and hypocrisy, undermining the free-trade policies espoused by the United States at the World Trade Organization talks in Doha.

'After spending years encouraging the Vietnamese that open trade is a win-win situation, it would be a shame if immediately after the trade agreement is signed the US shifts to a protectionist "we win, you lose" approach on catfish,' says Virginia Foote, president of the US–Vietnam Trade Council in Washington.[20]

In the ongoing dispute of how to manage global trade, agriculture and its cousin aquaculture are very sensitive issues. On the one side are industrial nations that use farm policy not only to promote their agribusiness overseas but also to protect their markets and farmers at home – European countries have used their agricultural subsidies to defend their countryside from the urban invasion – whereas developing countries try to raise their standard of living by breaking into those markets with less expensive products.

Questions for Discussion

1. Is it fair for the Vietnamese catfish importers to step in and capture market share while the market has been expanded due to the significant efforts and investments of the US industry? How should quality (if quality differences exist) considerations be reconciled?
2. The label ban would probably make consumers pay a higher price than they would have paid otherwise. Is this right?
3. Can any industry in the United States influence lawmakers to make decisions in their favour?

This case was written by Professor Michael R. Czinkota, Georgetown University McDonough School of Business, and graduate student Armen S. Hovhannisyan, Georgetown University School of Foreign Service.

Source: This case was written by Professor Michael R. Czinkota, Georgetown University McDonough School of Business, and graduate student Armen S. Hovhannisyan, Georgetown University School of Foreign Service.

Case Study 2

TURKEY'S KRIZ

> It was only when optimistic Turks started snapping up imports that investors began to doubt that foreign capital inflows would be sufficient to fund both spendthrift consumers and the perennially penurious government.
>
> —'On the Brink Again', *The Economist*,
> 24 February 2001

In February 2001, Turkey's rapidly escalating economic *kriz*, or crisis, forced the devaluation of the Turkish lira (TL). The Turkish government had successfully waged war on the inflationary forces embedded in the country's economy in early 2000, but just as the economy began to boom, pressures on the country's balance of payments and currency rose. The question asked by many analysts in the months following the crisis was whether the crisis had been predictable and what early signs should have been noted by the outside world.

The Balance of Payments Accounts

Figure 1 presents the Turkish balance on current account and financial account between 1993 and 2000 (ending less than two months prior to the devaluation). Several issues are immediately evident:

- Turkey seemingly suffered significant volatility in the balances on these key international accounts. The financial account swung between surplus (1993) to deficit (1994) and back to surplus again (1995–1997). After plummeting in 1998, the financial surplus returned in 1999 and 2000.
- As is typically the case, the current account behaved in a relatively inverse manner to the financial account, running deficits in most of the years shown. But significantly, the deficit on current account grew dramatically in 2000, to more than US$9.8 billion, from a deficit in 1999 of only US$1.4 billion.

Many analysts are quick to point out that the sizeable increase in the current account deficit should have been seen as a danger signal of imminent collapse. Others, however, point out quite correctly that most national economies experience rapid increases in trade and current account deficits during rapid periods of economic growth. And to add weight to the argument, the net surplus on the financial account seemed to indicate a growing confidence in the Turkish economy's outlook by foreign investors.

An examination of the subcomponents of these major account balances is helpful. As illustrated in Table 1, the rapid deterioration of the current account in 2000 was largely the result of a rapid jump in imported goods and merchandise. The goods import bill rose from US$39.8 billion in 1999 to more than US$54.0 billion in 2000, an increase of 36% in one year. At the same time, services trade and current income accounts, both credits and debits subcomponents, showed little change. Unfortunately, the statistics reported to the International Monetary Fund (IMF) provide little in additional detail as to the composition of these rapid imports, their industry or nature, and their financing.

A similar decomposition of the surplus on the Financial Account also allows us to identify where in the various inflows and outflows of capital in Turkey there was a significant change. Table 2 provides this Financial Account decomposition. According to Table 2, the doubling of the Turkish Financial Account surplus in 2000 was largely the result of a massive increase – more than US$7 billion – in 'net other investment'. This was partly the result of significant Turkish bank borrowing on international financial markets – capital acquired outside of Turkey. This is recorded as a net capital inflow. The problem, however, is that eventually the debt will have to be repaid.

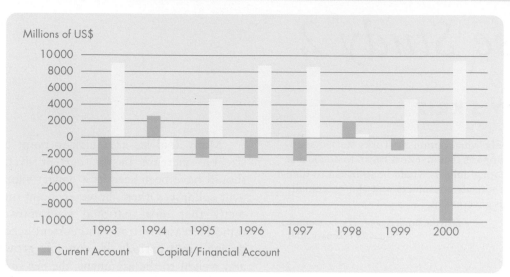

Figure 1: Turkey's balance of payments, 1993–2000.

One very important determinant of these account balances was the telecommunications sector. Throughout 2000, TelSim, the national telecommunications provider in Turkey, imported billions of dollars, worth of equipment from Nokia (Finland) and Motorola (United States). The equipment was purchased on trade credit, meaning that TelSim would repay Nokia and Motorola at a future date for the equipment, primarily from the proceeds of activating the equipment for telecommunications services.

TelSim, however, defaulted on its payments, and Nokia and Motorola were left with billions of dollars in losses.

As illustrated in Figure 3, the Turkish lira's collapse in February 2001 was large and sudden. Although the balance of payments current and financial accounts recorded major swings in their relative values in the year prior to the crisis, the question remained as to the underlying causes of the crisis.

	1998	1999	2000
Goods: exports	31 220	29 325	31 664
Goods: imports	−45 440	−39 768	−54 041
Balance on goods	−14 220	−10 443	−22 377
Services: credit	23 321	16 398	19 484
Services: debit	−9859	−8953	−8149
Balance on services	13 462	7445	11 335
Income: credit	2481	2350	2836
Income: debit	−5466	−5887	−6838
Balance on income	−2985	−3537	−4002
Current transfers: credit	5860	5294	5317
Current transfers: debit	−133	−119	−92
Balance on transfers	5727	5175	5225
Balance on current account	1984	−1360	−9819

Source: International Monetary Fund, *Balance of Payments Statistics Yearbook, 2001*, 913

Table 1: Sub-accounts of the Turkish current account, 1998–2000 (millions of US dollars).

	1998	1999	2000
Net direct investment	573	138	112
Net portfolio investment	−6711	3429	1022
Net other investment	6586	1103	8311
Balance on Financial Account	448	4670	9445

Source: International Monetary Fund, *Balance of Payments Statistics Yearbook, 2001*, 913

Table 2: Sub-accounts of the Turkish financial account, 1998–2000 (millions of US dollars).

Turkish Banking

The Turkish banking system was notoriously corrupt in the latter part of the 1990s. Bank licences, which gave the holder the right to open commercial and investment banking operations in Turkey, were given or sold as political favours by influential members of the Turkish government. These banks, once operational, were free to go to the international marketplace and represent themselves as established and creditable borrowers. And borrow they did.

The crisis was Turkey's worst in decades. Its banks had borrowed billions of dollars at low rates, converted them to lira, and bought high-yielding Turkish government T-bills. The strategy worked until the lira lost 40% of its value in a few days. Interbank interest rates hit 7000%. Unable to pay their dollar debts, most Turkish banks were technically insolvent.[1]

Throughout 1998, 1999 and the first half of 2000, many Turkish banks borrowed large quantities of dollars outside of Turkey. The banks then converted the dollar proceeds into Turkish lira and purchased Turkish government bonds as investments. The motivation was clear: borrowing at low dollar rates and reinvesting in much higher government bond rates created significant profits. These profits would persist as long as the Turkish lira held its value.

But the lira's value was heavily managed by the Turkish government. Because of the relatively high inflation rates suffered throughout 1998 and 1999 (see Figure 2), the Turkish government had pursued a gradual but continual devaluation policy. The managed devaluation, similar to Brazil's under the Real Plan between 1994 and 1999, was not sufficient. The lira was devalued at a rate significantly less than what the inflation differentials called for.

The activities of the banks added fuel to an economy already afire. This investment structure was none other than *uncovered interest arbitrage*. Uncovered interest arbitrage is when an investor borrows in a low-interest rate currency and reinvests in a high-interest rate currency, all the while assuming the exchange rate will not change significantly. If the exchange rate does not change, the investor reaps a sizeable speculative profit. If the exchange rate does change, and the high-interest rate currency falls in value (as most of international financial theory states it should), then the investor may suffer major losses.

This growing industry in interest arbitrage had a series of immediate and eventual impacts on the Turkish financial system:

- The dollar-to-lira conversion in the spot market aided in propping-up the value of the Turkish lira. As seen in Figure 3, the lira was managed in value against the US dollar over time. Although Turkish inflation rates were substantially higher than US dollar inflation, the large quantities of dollars converted into lira artificially boosted the demand for lira, raising its value (or preventing a further devaluation than what inflation would call for).

- The continuing demand for Turkish government bonds – government debt – allowed the government to fund increasing budget deficits at manageable costs. The strong demand by the banks for Turkish securities prevented the yields on government bonds from rising dramatically. It also prevented market forces from signalling to the government the dangers of its growing deficit spending and national debt.

- The growing external debt obligation of the Turkish banks, however, was an expanding threat to the stability of the banking system. Once the

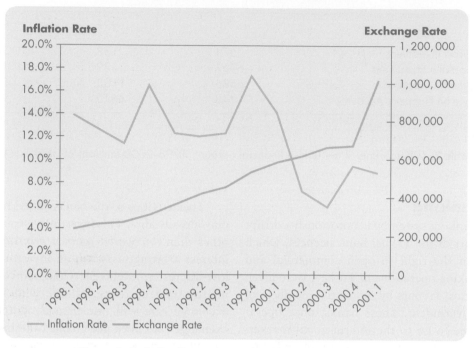

Figure 2: Turkish inflation rate and exchange rate (quarterly).

Source: International Monetary Fund, *International Financial Statistics*, October 2001, 842–843. Copyright 2001 by International Monetary Fund. Reproduced with permission of International Monetary Fund in the format Textbook via Copyright Clearance Center.

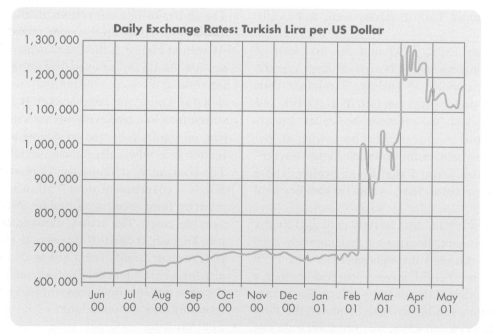

Figure 3: The fall of the Turkish Lira. Time period shown in diagram: 1 June 2000–30 May 2001.

Source: Copyright © 2002 by Prof. Werner Antweiler: University of British Columbia, Vancouver BC, Canada.

obligations came due, and many of the bank debts were *callable,* meaning that the international banks could demand repayment overnight, the rush to exchange lira for dollars for debt service would drive the exchange rate down dramatically.

Turkey had, however, been quite successful in its fight against the ingrained inflationary forces. In the latter half of 2000 the inflation rate had dropped dramatically and interest rates had followed. The resulting economic boom immediately showed itself in a rapid increase in imports and the corresponding current account deficit for the year 2000. As a number of journalists noted, the country's disinflation programme had been a 'victim of its own success'.

Economic Death Spiral

In the autumn of 2000 the Turkish economy was booming, but the country's ability to service its growing international indebtedness was getting perilously close to the edge. In late October a major Turkish bank failed when it could not meet its foreign debt service obligations. As interest rates and inflation rates started spiralling upward once again, the Turkish government turned to the IMF for help. The banking system was saved – at least temporarily – by a US$7.5 billion loan package from the IMF. (Between the autumn of 1999 and the spring of 2001, the IMF committed over US$11 billion to Turkey.) The IMF, as part of its loan conditions, required the government to reduce foreign indebtedness, reconstruct and clean up the Turkish banking system, and undertake a privatization programme for many state-owned industries.

But these extensive measures were much easier said than done. As the economy now slowed, the various government and financial austerity measures were politically unpopular. Turk Telecom, the state-owned fixed-line telecommunications company, offered 33.5% ownership to any foreign or domestic investor. Not a single bid was received. An offer for controlling interest in Turkish Airlines was met by a similar lack of interest by international investors.

In December 2000 the European Union and Turkey engaged in a series of heated and public debates over political and trade relations. Turkey complained that the EU was placing unfair and discriminatory barriers in its way as it attempted to accede to EU membership. The EU responded that many of Turkey's current trade restrictions were not in the spirit of membership. Turkey explained that it was in the midst of an economic crisis, and was only attempting to slow the rapidly growing current account deficit. Tensions escalated.

Turkish Kriz

On 18 February 2001, a public argument erupted between President Ahmet Necdet Sezer and the Prime Minister Bulent Ecevit over the lack of progress in removing corrupt politicians from office. President Sezer complained that the Prime Minister's efforts had been 'half-hearted'. Although the Prime Minister quickly tried to quell international concerns by renewing his commitment to the Turkish disinflation programme and the on-going initiatives to reduce political corruption, the damage was done.

The following day, 19 February, international investors pulled more than US$5 billion of capital out of the country. The Turkish central bank's total foreign exchange reserves, US$20 billion, would be unable to sustain a defence at this rate of capital flight. On 22 February 2001 the Turkish government announced it was floating the lira. As illustrated in Figure 3, the lira's value immediately plummeted from TL685 000/US$ to over TL1 000 000/US$.

In the months that followed, the Turkish lira continued to fall, and many of the country's banks collapsed. Industrial production, which had grown 2% and 1% in the third and fourth quarters of 2000, respectively, fell 20% in the first quarter of 2001.

Turkey's economy has steadily recovered from the severe crisis of 2001. The country's 2004 US$18.6 billion loan agreement with the IMF expired in February the same year and a new follow-on deal saw Turkey get fresh support in the period 2005–2008. In return for the funding, Turkey is expected to keep inflation under control and introduce significant market reforms.

Questions for Discussion

1. Where in the current account would the imported telecommunications equipment be listed? Would this correspond to the increase in magnitude and timing of the financial account?

2. Why do you think that TelSim defaulted on its payments for equipment imports from Nokia and Motorola?

3. Was the Turkish lira's collapse the result of a balance of payments crisis, an inflation crisis, a political crisis or an economic crisis?

4. Describe precisely how the Turkish banks were performing uncovered interest arbitrage. Do you feel this was an inappropriate investment policy?

5. How could the Turkish banks be contributing to financial crisis if they were purchasing Turkish government bonds and helping finance and support their own government?

6. Which do you think is more critical to a country such as Turkey, fighting inflation or fighting a large trade and current account deficit?

7. The report from *Corporate Finance* magazine, although noting the outside possibility of a devaluation, was largely positive regarding Turkey's future in January 2001. What would you have thought?

Case Study 3

GLOBALIZING A SMALL HYDRAULIC FIRM FROM EASTERN EUROPE[1]

In 1989 the Communist regimes in Eastern Europe collapsed. All countries from the former Soviet Bloc system embarked on the road of transition from central planning, based on state ownership of productive assets, to a market-led system. This was a process of unprecedented radical economic, political and social changes. The transition period entailed ownership transformation of all productive assets. The post-communist states launched ambitious privatization programmes trying to find investors who could revive and upgrade the production facilities. There was little experience, limited knowledge and scarce financial resources to carry out a complete system transformation of national economies. Managerial and technological know-how were deficient. Home-grown entrepreneurship was in its infancy.

The Bulgarian government had to face the mammoth task of restructuring the national economy which was until then based almost entirely on state ownership. A Privatization Agency was set up to carry out the transfer of ownership. The Agency had to find investors willing to take ownership of state-owned companies.

Transformation of a Bulgarian Small Enterprise

The industry for the production of hydraulic equipment was relatively new for the Bulgarian economy. It started its existence in the mid-1960s. One of its major companies, Hydroprobivna Technika SP Ltd, was a successor of a small enterprise for hydraulic drilling and punching equipment established in 1987. The firm was in a sub-sector of the Bulgarian machine-building industry with a focus on the production of hydraulic hammers with stroke energy from 80 to 5000 Joules and mass of 70 to 1500 kg. These were mounted on hydraulic excavators or special manipulators.

Although the company managed to produce durable equipment that was welcome in the former Council for Mutual Economic Assistance (CMEA) market during the communist era, the collapse of the internal CMEA trading system created a severe problem for the sales of manufactured goods. The company could satisfy the annual demand for hydraulic hammers in Bulgaria at less than 20% of its production capacity. The initial penetration into international markets beyond the limits of the CMEA system encountered difficulties due to insufficient experience and lack of service networks. The company management did not know what international markets required. A Foreign Trade Agency owned by the state had organized all previous international trading arrangements for them. Hydroprobivna Technika did not have market intelligence and did not know who their customers were and where to find them. The former CMEA international market collapsed, the domestic market shrank and new market opportunities were obscure.

At that turbulent time, the Danish firm, Breakers A/S, that had provided the technological know-how for the establishment of Hydroprobivna Technika, decided that there was a strategic opportunity for a more substantial involvement in a low-cost production base in Bulgaria. The management of Breakers was aware of the technical and technological capabilities of the ailing Bulgarian state-owned enterprise and its highly experienced workforce. Breakers A/S was owned by Lifton Industries Plc, which at the time was based in the United Kingdom. The parent company, prompted by Breakers, decided to acquire the Bulgarian operation.

But there was a problem. At the start of the transition period there was no legal framework allowing for the privatization of state-owned companies. The only possible option was an international joint venture (IJV). It could let Breakers increase its involvement in the management of Hydroprobivna Technika incrementally. It could gain experience in developing relationships with the Bulgarian authorities and make gradual changes in the technology of the Bulgarian company.

Hydra Team Ltd was established as an IJV on 13 May 1992. Its activities included production, R&D and marketing of hydraulic drilling equipment for the Bulgarian and export markets. The fixed capital was 100 000 Bulgarian leva (BGL), around US$110 000 at the exchange rate of the day. Partners of Hydra Team were Breakers A/S and Hydroprobivna Technika SP Ltd, which was still a state-owned company. The shares of the IJV were distributed between the partners with 80% owned by Breakers A/S and 20% by the Bulgarian government. The Danish partner had to invest in developing the technological capabilities of Hydroprobivna Technika, staff training and development, as well as providing market access for its products that were to become a part of Breakers' product portfolio.

The IJV secured the distribution of products manufactured by Hydroprobivna Technika and Breakers on the markets of Bulgaria and Romania under the brands 'Hydra Team' and 'Lifton'. Hydra Team bought the hydraulic equipment produced by Hydroprobivna Technika and sold it through its distribution network in international markets. As the technology of Hydroprobivna Technika was lagging behind world standards, there were significant deficiencies in product design and quality. That caused serious problems in international sales. Nevertheless, both IJV partners were trying to improve performance. Those efforts were actively mediated by the Danish General Manager of the IJV who knew the intricacies of Bulgarian culture and had extensive business networks.

Breakers A/S was a joint-stock company established in 1962 for the development, production and marketing of manual hydraulic instruments and hydraulic stations under the brand name of Lifton. Breakers was a member of the company group Lifton Industries together with Powerfab, a British producer of micro-escalators and Pocal Industries Inc., Pennsylvania, a US small breakers producer.

Following the establishment of the IJV, laws for the privatization of state-owned enterprises were introduced. Breakers A/S, via the parent company Lifton Industries Ltd, announced its willingness to privatize Hydroprobivna Technika in 1992. Its intent was to acquire control over the management and make further investment into technological improvements.

Lifton Industries decided to participate in the privatization of state-owned assets in Bulgaria. Two major opportunities were considered: buying know-how or acquiring a complete factory. The decision was made to give priority to the purchase of production know-how in the form of skills and experience. Hence, the investor's motives were skills and efficiency seeking (at the time of privatization the salaries in Bulgaria were between 25 and 30 times lower than those in the respective companies in Denmark and the United Kingdom).

The motives of the state-owned Hydroprobivna Technika were mainly to improve its technological level, quality standards and gain market share in international markets. There were no other foreign investors willing to participate in this privatization bid. At a certain stage, the Bulgarian Privatization Agency considered other methods of privatization, including privatization through management/employee buy-in. However, Lifton Industries was very persistent and offered the best conditions and opportunities for the technological and marketing development of the company. The Bulgarian Privatization Agency invited several other foreign investors to participate in the bid, but they did not show any interest. A few Bulgarian potential buyers were invited by the Privatization Agency, but their financial capabilities were rather limited.

On 22 October 1993 the Bulgarian Privatization Agency, representing the Bulgarian Government, and Breakers A/S signed a preliminary agreement for the sale of 97% of the shares of Hydroprobivna Technika. The purchase was made via the IJV Hydra Team. The deal amounted to US$350 000 payable in cash within a week from the signing of the contract. The money was provided by Breakers A/S. The buyer undertook the liabilities of Hydroprobivna Technika equivalent to BGL4.8 million. The buyer also undertook the responsibilities not to reduce the number of jobs and to make investments from their own funds to the amount of US$350 000 over three years.

Environmental Characteristics

The instability in the Bulgarian legislation had a negative impact on companies with foreign capital in the first years of transition. Higher taxes were imposed on companies with foreign direct investment. In the early and mid-1990s, the government policy clearly favoured state-owned companies. They were given interest-free credits that were easily accessed even by loss-making firms. Companies with foreign capital were disadvantaged as they were not favoured by the credit system. In 1995, the General Manager of Lifton Hydra Team, Gerhard Hansen, a Danish national who lived and worked in Bulgaria for more than 20 years, said that the Bulgarian government did not like foreign investors very much because they were something new for the Bulgarian business context. However, he believed that knowing the local environment and having patience, persistence and networks of contacts were of utmost importance for the success for any business venture in the country.

The most severe problems were caused by the differences in the content of the legal documents and their enforcement. For example, rules on taxation were interpreted differently by the tax agents when applied to state-owned companies and to firms privatized with foreign direct investment. The Bulgarian Ministry of Finance constantly sent letters to Lifton Hydra Team requiring from them to pay outstanding taxes that were owed to the state by Hydroprobivna Technika before it was privatized. The customs regulations created a lot of difficulties due to slow document processing practices, poor customer service and red tape.

Nevertheless, the managers of Lifton Hydra Team were highly successful in dealing with the fiscal, legislative and regulatory pressures in Bulgaria. The company had a unique position – it was the only player in its industry that had production facilities in the country. It was supported by the local authorities and had good relationships with the government. Moreover, its legal advisers were well informed about the changes in the highly volatile economic and legal environment. The management recognized that there were two problems, which were critical for the success of any business venture in Bulgaria. One was related to the need for fundamental changes in the legal system to make it compatible with EU code law practices and the second one was law enforcement. The General Manager of Lifton Hydra Team was an active member of the Bulgarian International Business Association (BIBA) that was lobbying for more

favourable conditions for companies with foreign investment. They were organizing meetings with government officials and influential members of the legal establishment, lobbying MPs and exchanging information, trying to support foreign investors who needed a particular type of help or advice.

Market Position

The export markets served by Lifton are characterized by demand significantly exceeding supply. Lifton has not faced any substantial competition in Bulgaria. More than 95% of its production in volume terms and almost 99% in value terms has been for export. With the rest of the production output the company has managed to achieve 90–95% domestic market share. There are also imports from German and Swedish companies but they do not have production facilities in the country. Several small producers of hydraulic equipment, based on craftsmanship, have also appeared and disappeared in Bulgaria throughout the 1990s and early 2000s. Such firms have been either in the form of single proprietorships or family-run businesses. Many of them have not survived for long due to a low technological level of production, competition from bigger players and the limitations of the relatively small, stagnated domestic market. Their current market share is estimated to be around 1.5–2.0%.

Lifton Industries work in close co-operation with its major competitors worldwide. The internationalization philosophy adopted by the company is to rely on co-operation rather than on competition. They work together with the largest hydraulic producers in the world on standardizing hydraulic production and technology. Contracts for technical support and comprehensive after-sales service are long term. Relationship management is considered to be of major importance for the international success of the business.

This approach has also been embraced by Lifton Bulgaria. The Bulgarian subsidiary underwent a gradual organizational culture change that was to enforce the values of the parent company. The management have emphasized the importance of gaining and retaining key clients and managing key accounts. Interactions and exchange of information with key customers have been conducted on a regular basis. The sales contracts with major clients are mostly medium to long term. The buying centre develops a portfolio of key accounts, which secures the market positions of the company. The company collaborates with other Bulgarian and foreign manufacturers to improve operations and enhance the quality of parts and components.

Compared with the technological level in the hydraulic industry, the technology applied in Bulgaria before the privatization of the company was outdated and in a poor state of maintenance. Most of the production machines were transferred by Breakers A/S but they could be used only for a limited number of operations. The quality of manufactured products was acceptable for the undersupplied domestic market in terms of durability and exploitation parameters. However, productivity, efficiency and effectiveness were low. Following the acquisition, Breakers A/S introduced new production technology and precise measuring instruments. The technological level of Lifton Bulgaria became better than the average world standard.

Gradually, it launched a broad range of new products, most of which were in the introductory phase of the product life cycle for the Bulgarian and the former CMEA markets. Some of Lifton's new products are also in the introductory phase for world export markets. In the 1990s the company spent approximately 10% of its annual turnover on R&D and new product development.

All functions performed are closely integrated and aim to meet specific customer requirements. A Marketing Department was set up to deal with a diverse customer base, including contractors, paving companies, demolition companies, sewerage companies, municipal authorities, gas, water and electricity boards, telephone and cable television companies, railway companies, wholesalers and retailers selling building materials. Lifton products are used by EU construction firms in Germany, Italy, the United Kingdom, Denmark and Poland, as well as Turkey. Currently, the company aims to penetrate the markets of the Commonwealth of Independent States (CIS), mainly Russia, the Middle East, where Bulgarian production has traditionally been very well positioned, China, Australia and North America. Lifton tools operate under the toughest conditions. Reliability of Lifton's products has gained the trust of companies such as BT, Tele Danmark (a Danish phone company), Danish Municipalities, the Swedish Road Maintenance Organization, Eriksson AB, CSX (a leading American railroad company), Athens Water Board in Greece, the Ministry of Public Works in Thailand, Ankara Municipality in Turkey, Korean Municipalities in South Korea, the United Nations, the National Administration of Roads in Romania, Bulgarian mining, road building and construction companies, Bulgarian Municipalities and United Rentals in the USA.

Representatives of Lifton Bulgaria visit all their major customers twice a year. They aim at developing customer relationships encouraging feedback, suggestions and recommendations for improvements in the range and functional characteristics of products. In 1995 the company started tailoring all products to client needs. Product adaptation has become the norm. All changes are discussed between clients and the company engineers. Lead-engineers work on designing the changes and facilitate their implementation in the production process. In the domestic market, the company also works closely with its customers and has applied a tailor-made approach to the key Bulgarian clients since 1998. After-sales services provide product maintenance after sales. This has become a major source of information for product development.

The objectives of the marketing strategy are associated with the shortage of hydraulic products in view of desirable quantity and variety. By meeting some of the existing demand and offering high quality standards, the company tries to expand its market share in export markets. The objective is to increase the volume of sales in all export markets 5–10 times over the next 10 years. The potential of the Bulgarian market is perceived to be limited despite its rapid growth over the last 8 years. The company has its own distribution network in the domestic market with two regional centres. Market research data on domestic market trends is collected by the company itself; market intelligence for export markets is provided by the parent company.

The major competitive advantage of Lifton Bulgaria in the domestic and export markets is its cost leadership coupled with world-recognized quality of products. Based on the cost advantage, the company charges significantly lower prices than its competitors both in the domestic and international markets.

The assets and capabilities of Lifton Bulgaria have changed considerably post-privatization. According to the contract with the Bulgarian Privatization Agency, Lifton Industries committed itself to investments of US$350 000 over three years. By the end of 1994 the required amount of investment had already been exceeded. By the end of 1997 the number of jobs increased by 20% and the production capabilities of the firm doubled. In the same period, the working capital increased 30 times, considering the inflation of the national currency.

Company Performance

Improved performance based on product innovation, quality assurance and employee input has been rewarded financially. The profit generated per unit of production has become substantially higher than the one for respective hydraulic equipment produced in Denmark and the United Kingdom.

Sales revenue and profit after tax are used to measure and monitor company performance. Using these indicators management make decisions on investment opportunities. In the last few years, the company has invested in product development and new products creation at the rate of 6–8 times more than the average for the hydraulic industry worldwide (calculated on the basis of turnover and net profit).

Recently, market share in international markets was introduced as market-related performance criterion. Company performance is monitored, measured and evaluated relative to objectives that are set in the yearly budget and strategic plans.

Prior to privatization, the company had approximately 65% of the domestic market and its export was exclusively for Romania and the former Soviet Union. To date, export is for countries from the EU, North America, some former CMEA countries, Turkey and the Middle East. Prior to privatization, the amount of export, in absolute terms, was 15 times less than it was in 2000. In the period 1999–2001 the production of Lifton Bulgaria increased by more than 250% and this resulted in a substantial increase of export market share.

The organizational structure has been transformed from inward looking, focused on the production process, to market focused. All employees recognize their role in contributing to creating a satisfied end-customer. The reward structure is based on external market performance and customer satisfaction. Senior management in all functional areas give top priority to creating satisfied customers. The major priorities are regular assessment of customer requirements and satisfaction.

Lifton Industries began to extend production capacity in Lifton Bulgaria in 2000. The production of machine- and manual-hydro-drilling equipment has been transferred from Denmark to Bulgaria. Some €0.7 million were invested in 2001 and 2002 for new machines and equipment. In 2002, Lifton Bulgaria started an ambitious five-year investment programme. The Bulgarian subsidiary became the biggest one in Lifton's system by the end of 2003. The investment made in Lifton Bulgaria amounted to more than US$6 million.

Competitive Environment

Demolition projects are being undertaken all over the world. Demolition work requires companies to use specialized demolition and drilling attachments. The most popular attachments are breakers (with crushers, cutters and pulverizers to finish). There are sizes available for every carrier from a skid steer loader to a large excavator. One can find the most up-to-date attachments produced by Rammer, Lifton, Soosan, Furukawa, Rock Drills, Krupp Berco, Bautechnik, Taeshin, Genesis, Italdem, Indeco and Montabert. There are also more specific tools from Taets (for piles) and Antraquip (for concrete demolition).

A number of industry players such as Atlas Copco, Padley and Venables, and Bosch have been developing the market for hand held breakers for smaller jobs. The design of the smaller demolition tools has largely improved. They are an attractive alternative to the traditional, less precise methods of dismantling. The leading companies in this field are Dimas and Partner.

Aquajet and Conjet have focused their product development on hydro-demolition because it causes less vibration damage to adjacent buildings. Splitting concrete (on bridges, parapets and foundations) with hydraulic splitters dramatically reduces the likelihood of damage to adjacent structures.

The demolition industry is dominated by huge corporations, which invest billions of dollars in R&D, developing carriers and attachments. Among them are Bosch, Bridgestone, Caterpillar, Daewoo, DaimlerChrysler, Deutz, Fiat-Hitachi, Komatsu, Krupp, Liebherr, MichelinScania and Volvo.

The middle-sized companies that compete in the breaker's global market are Antraquip, Case, Darda, Genesis, Gradall, Grasan, Indeco, Passini, Rammer, Padley and Venables, and Svedala (acquired by Sanvik). Lifton Industries was an established medium-sized producer of demolition breakers with a market share of 16.7% in Europe and 7.9% of the demolition attachments market in the world in 2001.

There are quite a few niche players focusing on a particular type of technology or product range, including Aquajet, Atlas Copco, Bobcat, Brokk, Conjet, Dimas, Montabert and Soosan.

Rammer

Rammer, with headquarters in Lahti, Finland, is an integral part of Sandvik Mining and Construction. They operate through a service and sales network on every continent. The backbone of their worldwide network is the authorized local distributors and their dealers. These private companies are close to the customers and provide the service that is expected from the dealer of a leading equipment manufacturer. The company attempts to be local and global at the same time.

Rammer engineering focuses on hydraulic attachments for rock excavation, demolition and recycling. The products are known for their effectiveness and reliability. They feature noise and dust suppression, electronic documentation and remote control.

The product range consists of full lines of hydraulic hammers, cutter-crushers and pulverizers, pedestal boom systems and tools. Rammer was the first to offer heavy-duty rock breaking hammers and a full range of silenced hammers. Rammer (Tamrock) also holds the patent for the Constant Blow Energy operating principle. The company is continuing the tradition of technological advancement with the introduction of a number of new systems and solutions.

Svedala

According to Thomas Older, Svedala Industry's CEO, 'Svedala is one of the very few companies in the world that can bring to bear such a wealth of resources to the customers in the industry sectors we serve. We know that our customers want to buy

systems and they want to buy from a source that is large enough and diverse enough to provide the entire system. They do not want to have to deal with a host of suppliers.'

Svedala develops, manufactures and markets systems for worldwide applications. These systems are used by customers in mining, mineral processing, crushing, screening, bulk materials handling and construction. They mine coal, iron ore, gold and copper. They process food, pulp, waste and a variety of other materials.

Svedala not only serves the construction industry with its aggregate-producing systems, but also with systems to finish concrete and asphalt projects with its world-famous line of rollers, pavers, vibrators and tampers.

Although Svedala is a Swedish-based company, over 90% of its sales are in overseas markets. More than 50% of its sales are outside Europe. The largest single market is North America, accounting for more than a third of overall sales.

Svedala's market strategy has been to build up a worldwide network of local Svedala companies organized to serve the total needs of customers involved in maintaining and expanding infrastructural facilities in both developed and developing countries. The company has done this through numerous acquisitions, as well as by developing markets through its international operations.

As a full-service supplier, Svedala offers a complete spectrum of engineering services including feasibility studies, installation, commissioning and start up. Lifetime onsite customer support involves monitoring of performance to ensure a maximum return on investment for customers.

Svedala has a matrix organizational structure. Each of the country organizations has access to all the business areas of Svedala and its product lines. For instance, an Australian customer needs only to contact the Svedala organization in Australia to get access to any of the products, systems and services offered by the global company.

Case Corporation

Inventor Jerome Increase Case founded Case in Racine, Wisconsin, USA in 1842 to build threshing machines. Later, the company gained global recognition as the first builder of steam engines for agricultural use, eventually becoming the world's largest maker of steam engines.

By 1912, Case had established itself in the construction equipment industry as a manufacturer of road-building equipment such as steam rollers and road graders. The company built its construction equipment business through several acquisitions, starting with American Tractor Corporation in 1957. By the mid-1990s, Case had expanded to become the world's leading manufacturer of light- to medium-sized construction equipment.

Case Construction Equipment is marketed by CNH Global, which was formed in November 1999 through the merger of Case Corporation and New Holland NV. Currently, more than 60 products carry the Case brand, in a product portfolio ranging from compact trenchers and skid steers to the high-power excavators and wheel loaders. The manufacturing and R&D facilities of Case Corporation are found all over the world: in Belgium, France, Germany, Italy, Brazil, the United States, India and the United Kingdom.

Darda Corporation

Darda is a mid-sized company with its headquarters in the Black Forest, Germany, with distributors worldwide. It produces and sells unconventional special tools for the demolition of concrete and rock. In 1967 the hydraulic rock and concrete splitter was invented by the company's founder Helmut Darda. Patents were granted for the quality and uniqueness of the Darda splitters. Darda has taken on the exclusive distributorship for the Swedish Brokk demolition robots in Germany and Austria. The company has a distributor network in Australia, Belgium, Brazil, Canada, China, Germany, Norway, Austria, Poland, Oman, Saudi Arabia, Andorra, Portugal and Sweden.

Genesis

Genesis Equipment & Manufacturing, located in Superior, Wisconsin, USA, entered the world of hydraulic equipment design and manufacture through extraordinary high-quality, optimum performance attachments. Genesis has adopted a new approach to attachment design and manufacture. It is a concept driven by personal attention to customer needs. The company is headquartered in Germany, with distribution and service centres throughout Europe.

Gradall

Gradall, located in Ohio, USA, is recognized as a leader in the manufacture of hydraulic excavators and material handlers. The operating philosophy of Gradall is to meet customer needs by establishing and then maintaining an environment that encourages all employees to pursue improved quality and productivity in the company, its supply base and its distributors.

In the beginning, Gradall produced hydraulic excavators, but by 1982, its product collection grew substantially to include terrain material handlers. In June 1999, Gradall joined forces with JLG Industries, the world's foremost manufacturer, distributor and international marketer of lift equipment. JLG and Gradall are both dedicated to the continuous improvement of products and processes, manufacturing equipment that is the best in its class. The alliance with JLG helped to position Gradall as a powerful player within the construction industry.

Grasan

Grasan was founded in 1970 in Mansfield, Ohio, USA, as a manufacturer of conveying, crushing and screening equipment for coal, aggregates and construction industries. With its 5570-square-metre manufacturing facility and annual sales over US$10 million, Grasan specializes in the design and production of mobile and stationary equipment. The company designs and builds complete crushing, screening, conveying, stacking and feed/storage systems for quarry operations of all types and sizes. In 1985, Grasan led the industry in developing equipment and systems for recycling concrete, asphalt, and construction and demolition debris.

Indeco

Located in Stratford, Connecticut, USA, Indeco offers high-quality demolition attachments in the industry for breaking concrete and rock. Its products include breakers, compactors, stationary boom systems and grapples. In the last 30 years, Indeco specialized in the production of demolition products and attachments for breaking and demolition needs. The company offers a complete line of reliable heavy-duty hydraulic breakers, compactors and grapples engineered to fit each specific brand of excavators, loader-backhoe, skid-steer loader and mini excavators. Indeco specializes in finding the most efficient and effective ways of getting demolition work done in a broad variety of conditions.

Padley and Venables

Padley and Venables (P&V) is the UK's leading manufacturer of high-quality tools for rock drilling, quarrying, mining, tunnelling, construction, civil engineering and demolition industries worldwide. P&V has been established in the marketplace since 1911 and today is one of the world's leading manufacturers of consumables, rock drilling and demolition tools.

Continuous R&D and testing of P&V's wide range of products together with ongoing investment in modern technology reflect the company's commitment to manufacturing tailored products for customers worldwide. All P&V's products are manufactured from materials within a Quality Assurance Management System certified to British Standards and ISO 9002. The company's demolition tools are totally manufactured and processed within the company's factory, using the latest machinery and technology to ensure that the finished products comply with the quality standards expected by its customers.

Aquajet

Aquajet systems started out its life as Svensk Vattenbilningsteknik over 20 years ago. The company is based in Holsbybrunn, southern Sweden. It specializes in the manufacturing of high-pressure water jet equipment. Export accounts for 90% of output and 80% of these are dealt with through selected independent local dealers and distributors. The distributors also provide Aquajet's after-sales service. The product line includes high-pressure power packs – containerized or open skid mounted – computer controlled robots, robotic equipment for industrial applications as well as accessories and equipment for robotic high-pressure jobs. The company also provides engineering, consulting and technical support.

Atlas Copco

Atlas Copco, a leading compressor manufacturer, is a global industrial group headquartered in Stockholm, Sweden. It acquired Chicago Pneumatic India, a pneumatic tool manufacturer. The acquisition increased Atlas Copco's operations, giving it an increase of 80% in pricing power and sales in 2000. The sales of rock drilling equipment showed a significant increase by 24% in 2001 compared to 2000. Rationalization of capacities has brought in sufficient cost-efficiencies and an increase in profitability.

Brokk

Brokk AB is a company, headquartered in Skellefteå, Sweden. It produces lightweight remote controlled demolition machines for working in cramped conditions. The low weight of the machines produced by Brokk makes them easily transportable on a car trailer and flap-down outriggers.

Dimas

Dimas, headquartered in Jönköping, Sweden, is a manufacturer of diamond tools and equipment that came into existence at the beginning of the 1970s. At that time the sawing and drilling industries were in their infancy. The company supplies diamond tools covering dry and wet cutting blades, grinding tools, drill bits and diamond wire for drilling through concrete, stone, brick and asphalt.

Since the early 1980s Dimas has also manufactured sawing and drilling equipment but the emphasis has always been on diamond tools. It acquired Promac, a manufacturer of high-tech and intelligent tools. The move is a part of Dimas' commitment to build a complete product line, which includes a comprehensive range of machines.

Soosan Breakers

This is a South Korean manufacturer of demolishing equipment headquartered in Seoul. It was established in 1984. The company has become technically independent by developing its own product portfolio and has received high recognition for product originality. Soosan has recently obtained an Impact Energy certificate, which solidified the company's position as one of the leaders in production technology.

Latest Developments

In 2004, the sales of Lifton Bulgaria rose by more than 20% compared with the value of sales in 2003 and profit before tax totalled BGL1 million (US$678 000). This growth was largely due to its successful entry into the Australian, Chinese and US markets. In 2004, the turnover of the Bulgarian and Danish Lifton companies amounted to DKr55 million with a total of 141 employees. The Bulgarian company built a reputation for its quality, reliability and trustworthiness working with clients from diverse cultural settings. The co-operative relationships with Breakers A/S flourished over the years and became a successful background for new business agreements. The consolidation in the global hydraulic industry coupled with the EU expansion created new opportunities for business growth, consolidation and internationalization.

In January 2005, the Swedish engineering group Atlas Copco purchased Lifton Bulgaria and Lifton Breakers A/S, Denmark. Included in the acquisition is the right to the Lifton brand. Atlas Copco has an annual turnover of about €5 billion, employs 26 000 people and sells products and services via over 150 sales centres all over the world. The acquired business became part of the Atlas Copco Construction Tools division within the Construction and Mining Technique business area. 'The acquisition expands our product range in the hand-held sector. Lifton is a company with a strong market presence and a wide range of high quality, mainly hand-held hydraulic tools,' says Bjorn Rosengren, Business Area Executive of Atlas Copco

Construction and Mining Technique. Atlas Copco's strategy is to gain market share by expanding existing product range, market penetration and original equipment manufacturing (OEM). In July 2005, Lifton Bulgaria signed a five-year contract for OEM of hydraulic kits for Caterpillar, USA. All products contracted with Caterpillar are developed in Bulgaria based on Caterpillar's standards and are sold under the Caterpillar brand name.

Questions for Discussion

1. Why did Lifton Industries Plc acquire the manufacturing operations of Hydroprobivna Technika? Discuss the privatization motives of Lifton Industries Plc, Hydroprobivna Technika and the Bulgarian government.
2. Discuss the international marketing strategy of Lifton Bulgaria.
3. Do you think that Lifton Bulgaria should have focused on own-brand development to expand its international presence? Discuss the advantages and disadvantages of brand development strategy and OEM strategy for a small company operating in a global undersupplied business-to-business market.

Source: This case was developed by Svetla T. Marinova and Marin A. Marinov. It is intended to be used as a basis for classroom discussion rather than to illustrate either effective or ineffective handling of a business situation. The case cannot be used without the written permission of the authors or reproduced in any way. The authors wish to acknowledge the assistance of the General Managers of Lifton Bulgaria, Mr. Gerhard Hansen and Ms Borjana Manolova, in developing the case. Reproduced with permission.

Case Study 4

COSMETICS FROM POLAND[1]

Dr Irena Eris is an enigmatic entrepreneur and a symbol of business success in Poland. In 1999, the Business Centre Club honoured her with the title Business Woman of the Decade. In 2003 she was recognized for the creation of an internationally competitive Polish brand and in 2004 was placed on the list of the most influential women in Polish history who had turned the course of events, overcome stereotypes and initiated new thinking. In 2005 she received the Economic Award of the President of Poland. Dr Eris was also named the European of 2007, an award given to people who have had outstanding achievements in the field of integration and co-operation of the European nations and states.

It all started in 1982 when Dr Eris, a PhD from the Faculty of Pharmacology at Berlin's Humboldt University, inherited some cash that was the equivalent of six small Fiat cars. With this inheritance she and her husband opened a cottage workshop producing nourishing facial cream in 1983. The first cosmetic products were mixed in a makeshift machine made by a local locksmith friend.

The Polish Cosmetics Market

Poland has long established traditions in the production of cosmetics. Max Faktor born in Łódź, Poland, during the 1870s, became the founder of modern make-up, creating the global Max Factor brand. Helena Rubinstein, a Polish immigrant, is one of the biggest names in facial care. In the Communist Era, Poland was by far the largest cosmetics producer in the former Council for Mutual Economic Assistance (CMEA). The cosmetics of Pollena and Nivea were cherished by women and men of all ages. Poland was also the largest market for cosmetics. About 90% of the cosmetics products had affordable prices to all consumers. Only 5% of the cosmetics represented luxury products, most of them imported. The market was dominated by perfumes (66%), followed by skin care products (25%) and make-up.

At present, the cosmetics industry in Poland employs approximately 19 000 people. It has remained one of the key employers in the volatile labour market. The transition process to a market-led system caused enormous job losses for the Polish workforce. The 'shock therapy' approach to the privatization of state-owned enterprises led to the mushrooming of small cosmetics companies. By the end of 2005, they numbered more than 470. Less than 15% of them employed more than 50 people.

In the last 10 years the production of cosmetics in Poland has experienced steady annual growth (see Figure 1). In 2002 the market was valued at 1.85 billion Polish zloty (PLN). At the end of 2005, it grew to PLN8.7 billion, expanding by 3.1% on its 2004 value. Its growth was primarily fuelled by the country's better economic climate and the Poles' rising buying power. Market size is another factor that attracts cosmetics manufacturers to focus on Poland. With its population of almost 40 million, Poland is the largest market in Central Europe and the eighth largest in the European Union. Its population makes Poland a market larger than the combined markets of all the other 10 accession countries that entered the EU together with Poland in May 2004.

The value of Polish cosmetics exports in 2002 was US$291 million, representing almost 10% growth compared with 2001. More than two-thirds of all exports went to former CMEA markets and about 30% to the European Union member countries. The major importers of Polish cosmetics were Russia (18% of the total value of Polish exports), Hungary (14%), Lithuania (12%), Ukraine (11%), Germany (8%) and the United Kingdom (7%). Avon Cosmetics, Miraculum, Cussons Group, Kolastyna, Ziaja, Dr Irena Eris, Polena Ewa and L'Oréal are the biggest exporters. The main importing countries by 2007 were Germany, with about 23% of total import, France (21%), the United Kingdom (17%), and Italy and Spain with 6% each. French, German and Italian

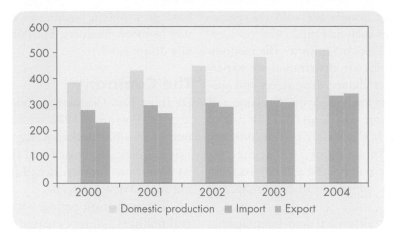

Figure 1: Market size, US$ million.

cosmetics charge a price premium and enjoy high brand recognition.

Cosmetics manufacturers in Poland can be divided into four groups:

- Producers owned by the Pollena conglomerate, purchased by foreign investors (Beiersdorf, Cussons Group and Unilever). They develop and introduce new products in the Polish market and upgrade inherited cosmetics products from the acquired entities.
- Formerly state-owned cosmetics manufacturers, privatized and functioning independently (Pollena Ewa and Miraculum).
- A large group of Polish private cosmetics firms established in the 1980s and 1990s (Inter-Fragrances, Dr Irena Eris Cosmetics Laboratories, Kolastyna, Soraya, Dax Cosmetics, Dermika and Ziaja).
- New factories built by global foreign cosmetics companies (Johnson&Johnson, L'Oréal, Avon and Oriflame).

The strong domestic producers have established positions in the skin and body care product market segment. They control about two-thirds of this market. The market leader in the body care cosmetics is Beiersdorf-Lechia, with almost 30% share, followed by Johnson&Johnson with 8%, Unilever (7%), Kolastyna (6.5%) and Dr Irena Eris (5%). The facial care cosmetics market segment is dominated by Dr Irena Eris with 16%, followed by Ziaja (10%), Oceanic (9%) and Cussons (8%). All foreign facial care brands have positioned themselves in the middle or premium sector of the market. For example, the US Johnson&Johnson dominates the middle sector with 45% market share, while the French Garnier with its brand L'Oréal leads in the premium sector with more than 50% market share. The market pressure coming from foreign brands has pushed most of the Polish facial care brands into the low price mass markets. The self-tanning cosmetics segment is dominated by L'Oréal with 27.5%, Beiersdorf with 25.3% and Dr Irena Eris with 12.2%.

In 2002, the companies with highest sales revenues were Procter & Gamble, Unilever Połska, Henkel Połska, Avon Cosmetics Połska, Cussons Połska, L'Oréal Połska, Beiersdorf-Lechia, Oriflame, Pollena Ewa, Dr Irena Eris, Kolastyna, Forte Sweden and Miraculum.

With a population of 40 million, the eighth largest country in Europe, the cosmetics market in Poland is still growing and is highly competitive. Per capita consumption is about five times lower than the average of the pre-2004 EU member countries. The key competitive factors are price, quality and brand recognition. Packaging and advertising have become increasingly important. Poles tend to be risk averse when choosing everyday cosmetics. They prefer to buy a known traditional brand from a known store. Purchasing decisions are determined by company reputation and brand recognition.

Premium cosmetics brands are sold via specialized networks of stores such as Empik, Galeria Centrum, Ina Center and French Sephora. The medium and low-priced cosmetics are distributed via hypermarket and supermarket chains, drug stores and specialty stores. Companies such as Avon, Oriflame and Amway use direct selling. The largest distributor of cosmetics is Polbita. It is a privately owned company established in 1990. Polbita owns 20% of the cosmetics distribution system in Poland and runs its store chain Drogeria Natura, consisting of more than 330 retail outlets.

Since 1988 almost all global and international cosmetics brands have entered the Polish market. They seek new market development and expansion. The best recognized foreign brands are: Christian Dior, Guerlain, Yves Saint Laurent, Yves Rocher, Yves Saint Rocher, L' Oréal, Laboratories Paris, Lancôme, Paloma Picasso, Guy Laroche, Giorgio Armani, Cacharel, Coty, Elizabeth Arden, Pierre Robert, Colgate Palmolive, Nivea, Jean Pierresand, Vichy Laboratories, Jade, Max Factor, Revlon, Maybelline, Biotherm, Givenchy, Nino Cerruti, Margaret Astor and Rimmel. They have all set up their own exclusive stores and beauty salons. Aggressive advertising, new product development and simultaneous product introduction in Paris and Warsaw reinforce their premium market position. Global companies such as Procter & Gamble and Unilever have also invested heavily in Poland.

The ongoing process of market liberalization and EU enlargement has been favourable for the growing market presence of foreign cosmetics brands in Poland. The variety of products and services has led to much greater consumer choice. This has increased the competitive pressure on Polish brands. They have less financial and market strength to launch aggressive marketing campaigns. Moreover, most of the Polish companies are too small to compete against global multinationals. One manager of a Polish medium-sized cosmetics company, who preferred not to be identified, stated: 'Small and medium-sized cosmetics companies do not have enough market power. I cannot see how they can compete successfully against the multinationals after the EU enlargement. It is unlikely that the Polish government will protect us. It will not provide financial help for consolidation. Foreign giants will have no problem pushing us out of business. There will be more products, but Polish brands will gradually disappear.'

The Company

Dr Irena Eris Cosmetic Laboratories was set up in socialist Poland in 1982 with a monthly production output of 3000 packages. By 1986, the demand for Eris cosmetics increased and the company expanded its operations rapidly. It had increased capacity and introduced new products.

The transition period with its diverse economic and political reforms created new opportunities for business growth. The increased productivity and profitability of the company in the early 1990s led to the launch of a new plant. Dr Eris re-invested most of the company profits in product innovation and new technologies.

Presently, the company employs 350 employees and produces 300 types of products grouped in several product lines. The monthly output is approximately 1 000 000 units. All company cosmetics products meet the quality standards defined by the European Union and the US Food and Drugs Administration. Dr Irena Eris holds ISO 9001 (since 1996) and Environment Management ISO 14 001 (since 2001). Those certificates guarantee that the company's cosmetics are of global quality and their production is environmentally friendly.

Dr Eris has decided to focus on innovative solutions and R&D. The R&D investment in 2004 was 3.4% of the company's turnover. In 2005 it was increased to 4.6%. A large team of dermatologists, allergy specialists, biologists and molecular biologists works on various projects at the company's Centre for Science and Research set up in 2001 (see Figure 2). The Centre is active in the efforts to establish the Polish Platform of the International Agreement for the Development of Alternative Animal Research Methods. R&D is intrinsic for the company's philosophy. It is the core of its strategy to develop scientifically advanced products. They are targeted at consumers who are interested in cosmetics with scientifically advanced functional characteristics.

Scientific research and innovative solutions have become the core in the brand positioning strategy of Dr Irena Eris in the cosmetics market in Poland. The recipes for all products are original

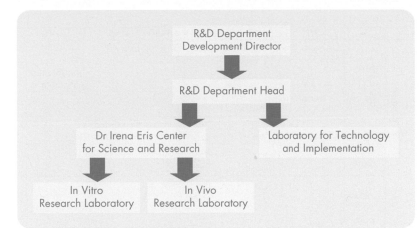

Figure 2: Structure of the R&D department. More details about the research programme can be obtained from: www .drirenaeris.pl/badania/en/badania.php and www.drirenaeris.pl/en/kosmetyki_skladniki.php.

Source: Dr Irena Eris Cosmetics Laboratories.

and based on in-company research. This makes them distinctive and more difficult to copy by competitors. In the mid-1990s, Dr Eris was the first in Europe to propose the use of vitamin K in cosmetics and lately, it was the first company in the world to test and use an innovative complex FitoDHEA + folacin in its products.

Brand Image

The brand image of Dr Irena Eris is built upon respect for people, stressing their individual nature and the importance of co-operation. The brand development strategy reflects the value of interpersonal relationships within the company and with its clients. The brand value of Dr Irena Eris is based on its holistic approach to the individual specific needs and preferences of customers. It offers an individual skin care programme for home use and for use in specialized professional salons and spa hotels. Dr Irena Eris is one of the best known Polish brands. In 2001, market research carried out by Pentor showed that 93% of Poles can recognize it among other cosmetics brands.

The brand has gained international recognition. In 2005 it was nominated for that year's Beauty Awards for the best cosmetics introduced in the UK market. It was also awarded Prix d'Excellence *Marie Claire* for being the most advanced cosmetics brand in the Polish market in 2004, and the Gold Glamour award by the British edition of *Glamour*.

The consumer target groups of Dr Irena Eris span all age groups. These are women who prioritize cosmetic efficiency based on research. They wish to use high-quality products that are modern and pleasant in use. The market segmentation approach of the company is based on four segments (see Figures 3 and 4).

The company targets the economy segment with mass products. The premium segment is reached with innovative products. The dermocosmetics segment is served with health and hygienic products. Specialized products are designed for the professional segment. These segments are reached via 20 000 retail points of sale for widely distributed products and 1000 points of sale for products destined for limited distribution via pharmacies, beauty parlours and centres.

Diversification

The company has diversified in related activities. Following the success of a four-star Spa Hotel, Dr Irena Eris in Krynica Zdrój in Poland, it has invested in a second Spa Hotel Dr Irena Eris Wzgórza Dylewskie in Wysoka Wieś near Ostróda, which was completed in the first half of 2006. The Spa Hotels offer a comprehensive, tailor-made skin treatment and revitalizing programme. Skin treatment is complemented by a range of health improvement packages including exercises, massage, spa therapy and physical activities. The spa

		25–30	30–35	35–40	40–45	45–50	50–55	55+
Women	Face Care	Dr Irena Eris Skin Mood		Dr Irena Eris ReACT!		Dr Irena Eris Fortessimo		Dr Irena Eris Fortessimo Maxima
		Dr Irena Eris SIN SKIN		Dr Irena Eris InCell				
			Dr Irena Eris YOU				Dr Irena Eris NANO ENTRÉE	
	Body Care		Dr Irena Eris BODY ART					
Men	Face and body care		PLATINUM MEN					

Figure 3: Brands and consumer target groups. More information about the products and brands can be found at www.beautyexclusive.com/erisskincare.html.

Source: Dr Irena Eris Cosmetic Laboratories.

hotel concept promotes Dr Eris as a modern lifestyle brand.

Moreover, the brand Dr Irena Eris has been extended to the franchise chain Dr Irena Eris Cosmetic Institutes. There are 22 of them established in the largest Polish cities. Such institutes were opened in Moscow and Bogota, Colombia. By the end of 2007, 12 new institutes were serving clients in Poland and abroad. The institutes offer several basic company treatments based on the Dr Irena Eris Professional Program. The treatments are carried out using preparations from the company's own specialized line of cosmetics. They are exclusively used in beauty parlours (Prosystem). The therapy is complemented by a line of products for subsequent home care (Prosystem home care). The treatments are selected individually and preceded by obligatory skin diagnosis by dermatologists partnering with Dr Irena

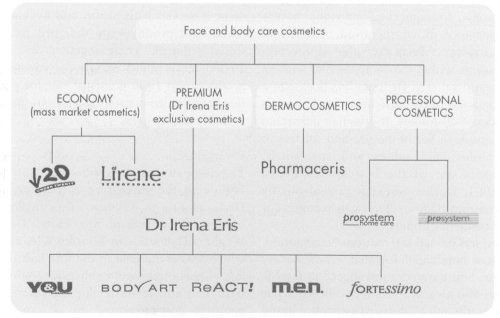

Figure 4: Market segments and company brands.

Source: Dr Irena Eris Cosmetic Laboratories.

Eris Cosmetic Institutes. The personnel of the institutes consist of beauty therapists trained at the company's own training centre.

Marketing Communications

The marketing communications strategy of Dr Irena Eris is consistent with its overall strategic focus on innovative and modern cosmetic solutions. It is the Polish company with the highest advertising expenditure. Advertising and PR activities are carried out in the lead international markets. Advertising and promotional materials are generally standardized but adapted to the local language requirements. The company has strengthened its position in the professional segment through developing close relationships with key business customers and participating in international fairs.

Dr Irena Eris Cosmetic Laboratories is involved in sponsorship and social activities. Every year the company donates products and money to the value of more than PLN500 000 for charitable causes. It is a key contributor to the Always Healthy and Active Club programmes set up to meet the needs of 7 000 000 adult Polish women. The programme aims to increase the knowledge of mature women about health-related issues, and improve their general health and quality of life. In 2001, Dr Eris was awarded the Summa Bonitas award from the foundation Zdążyć z pomocą for its corporate social responsibility (more information at http://www.businessweek.com/magazine/content/04_19/b3882011.htm).

In 2004, the sales volume of Dr Irena Eris Cosmetics Laboratories was PLN97.6 million (€24 million) from domestic and export sales. This was 15% growth compared with the results in 2003. In 2004, after-tax profit was PLN7 million.

Internationalization

Dr Irena Eris has been developing its international presence since the mid-1990s. The company management has recognized the potential benefits of economies of scope and used various sources of information and business support for foreign market entry.

Most of the initial attempts were driven by opportunities based on personal contacts. In 1989 the company started exporting its products. The debut was made in the vast US market. The large Polish community in the US formed a formidable basis for foreign market expansion. Personal relationships and contacts were of foremost importance. Currently, Dr Eris cosmetics are available in over 1000 specialized US salons.

The company was quick to step into the neighbouring German market. An expansion into the former CMEA market strengthened its export revenue.

By 2006, the products of Dr Irena Eris had reached the markets in 24 countries around the globe. They are sold in beauty shops, pharmacies, supermarkets and beauty salons. Major markets are the USA, Lithuania, Russia, the Czech Republic, Hungary, the Slovak Republic, the Ukraine and Germany, but the products may be also purchased in places such as Tasmania, Taiwan and Singapore. In 2004, Dr Irena Eris products were introduced to the UK market, via Boots retailer, and in 2007 to the Irish market. The growth of exports has been substantial and in 2004 the company recorded an increase of international sales by 40%.

Questions for Discussion

1. Do you agree with the statement of the anonymous Polish manager about the future for Polish small and medium-sized cosmetics manufacturers?
2. What should Dr Irena Eris Cosmetics Laboratories do to reinforce its position as market leader in the facial cosmetics segment in the Polish market?
3. Discuss the market entry modes used by Dr Irena Eris Cosmetics Laboratories in its internationalization strategy.

Source: The case was developed by Svetla T. Marinova and Marin A. Marinov. It is intended to be used as a basis for classroom discussion rather than to illustrate either effective or ineffective handling of a business situation. The case cannot be used without the written permission of the authors or reproduced in any way. The authors wish to acknowledge the assistance of Dr Irena Eris and her Personal Assistant Ms. Aleksandra Trzcinska in developing the case. Reproduced with permission.

Case Study 5

GENERAL MOTORS AND AVTOVAZ OF RUSSIA

> To compete on technology, you have to spend on it, but we have nothing to spend. Were there a normal economic situation in the country, people wouldn't be buying these cars.
>
> —Vladimir Kadannikov, Chairman,
> AvtoVAZ of Russia

> There are 42 defects in the average new car from AvtoVAZ, Russia's biggest car marker. And that counts as the good news. When the firm introduced a new model last year, a compact saloon called the VAZ-2110, each car came with 92 defects – all the fun of the space station Mir, as it were, without leaving the ground.
>
> —'Mir On Earth', *The Economist*,
> 21 August 1997

In June 2001, David Herman, President of General Motors (GM) Russia, and his team arrived in Togliatti, Russia, for joint venture negotiations between GM and OAO AvtoVAZ, the largest car producer in Russia. GM and AvtoVAZ had originally signed a memorandum of understanding (MOU) – a non-binding commitment – on 3 March 1999, to pursue a joint venture (JV) in Russia. Now, nearly two years later, Herman had finally received GM's approval to negotiate the detailed structure of the joint venture with AvtoVAZ to produce and sell Chevrolets in the Russian market.

The Russian car market was expected to account for a significant share of global growth over the next decade. Herman was increasingly convinced that if GM did not move decisively and soon, the market opportunity would be lost to other car makers. Ford, for example, was proceeding with a substantial JV in Russia and was scheduled to begin producing the Ford Focus in late 2002 (it was already importing car kits). Fiat of Italy was already in the construction phases of a plant to build 15 000 Fiat Palios per year beginning in late 2002. Daewoo of Korea had started assembly of compact saloon 'kits' in 1998 and was currently selling 15 000 cars a year.

However, Herman also knew that doing business in Russia presented many challenges. The Russian economy, although recovering from the 1998 collapse, remained weak, uncertain and subject to confusing tax laws and government rules. The Russian car industry seemed to reel from one crisis to another. The second largest car producer, GAZ, had been the victim of an unexpected hostile takeover only three months previous. GAZ's troubles had contributed to GM's fears over the actual ownership of AvtoVAZ itself. In addition, AvtoVAZ had been the subject of an aggressive income tax evasion case by Russian tax authorities in the summer of 2000. Finally, from a manufacturing point of view, AvtoVAZ was far from world class. AvtoVAZ averaged 320 worker-hours to build a car, a stark comparison against the 28 hours typical of Western Europe and 17 hours in Japan.

Further complicating the situation was a lack of consensus within different parts of GM about the Russian JV. GM headquarters in Detroit had told Herman to find a third party to share the risk and the investment of a Russian JV. Within Adam Opel, GM's European division, there were questions about the scope and timing of Opel's role. Prior to becoming GM's vice president for the former Soviet Union, Herman had been chairman of Adam Opel. He had been forced out of Opel after growing disagreements with Lou Hughes, vice president of GM's international operations, the unit that oversaw Opel. Hughes wanted Opel to lead the development of three global automotive platforms, whereas Herman wished to keep Opel focused on recovering its once dominant position in Germany and Western Europe. Now, Herman needed Opel's support for the Russian JV and had to convince his former colleagues that the time was right to enter Russia. As he prepared for the upcoming negotiations, Herman knew there were many more battles to be fought both within GM and in Russia.

General Motors Corporation

General Motors Corporation (United States), founded in 1908, was the largest automobile manufacturer in the world. GM employed more than 388 000 people, operated 260 subsidiaries, affiliates and joint ventures, managed operations in more than 50 countries, and closed the year 2000 with US$160 billion in sales and US$4.4 billion in profits.

John F. 'Jack' Smith had been appointed chairman of GM's Board of Directors in January 1996, after spending the previous five years as president and CEO. Taking Jack Smith's place as president and CEO was G. Richard 'Rick' Wagoner, Jr., previously director of strategic and operational leadership within GM. GM's international operations were divided into GM Europe, GM Asia Pacific and GM Latin America, Africa, Middle-East. GM Europe, headquartered in Zurich, Switzerland, provided oversight for GM's various European operations including Opel of Germany and the new initiatives in Russia.

Although the largest car manufacturer in the world, GM's market share had been shrinking. By the end of 2000, GM's global market share (in units) was 13.6%, with the Ford group closing quickly with a 11.9% share, and Volkswagen a close third at 11.5%. Emerging markets, such as that of Russia, represented so-called 'white territories' which were still unclaimed and uncertain markets for the traditional Western car makers.

The Russian Automobile Industry

The Russian automotive industry lagged far behind that of the Western European, North American or Japanese industries. Although the Russian government had made it a clear priority to aid in the industry's modernization and development, inadequate capital, poor infrastructure and deep-seated mismanagement and corruption resulted in out-dated, unreliable and unsafe automobiles.

Nevertheless, the industry was considered to be promising because of the continuing gap between Russian market demand and supply and because of expected future growth in demand. As illustrated in Table 1, between 1991 and 1993 purchases of cars in Russia had grown dramatically. But this growth had been at the expense of domestic producers, because

Russian production	1991	1992	1993	1994	1995	1996	1997	1998	1999
AvtoVAZ	677 280	676 857	660 275	530 876	609 025	684 241	748 826	605 728	717 660
GAZ	69 000	69 001	105 654	118 159	118 673	124 284	124 339	125 398	125 486
AvtoUAZ	52 491	54 317	57 604	53 178	44 880	33 701	51 411	37 932	38 686
Moskovich	104 801	101 870	95 801	67 868	40 600	2929	20 599	38 320	30 112
KamAZ	3114	4483	5190	6118	8638	8935	19 933	19 102	28 004
IzhMash	123 100	56 500	31 314	21 718	12 778	9146	5544	5079	4756
Doninvest	0	0	0	0	321	4062	13 225	4988	9395
Other	14	14	6	7	1	41	3932	3061	1307
Total	1 029 800	963 042	955 844	797 924	834 916	867 339	985 809	839 608	955 406
% change	26.6	26.5	20.7	216.5	4.6	3.9	13.7	214.8	13.8
Russian Exports	411 172	248 032	533 452	143 814	181 487	144 774	120 551	67 913	107 701
% of production	39.9	25.8	55.8	18.0	21.7	16.7	12.2	8.1	11.3
Imports into Russia	26 649	43 477	405 061	97 400	69 214	54 625	42 974	62 718	55 701
% of sales	4.1	5.7	49.0	13.0	9.6	7.0	4.7	7.5	6.2
Auto Sales in Russia	645 277	758 487	827 453	751 510	722 643	777 190	908 232	834 413	903 406
% growth		17.5	9.1	29.2	23.8	7.5	16.9	28.1	8.3

Source: www.just-auto.com, December 2000

Table 1: The Russian car industry, 1991–1999 (units).

imports had garnered most of the increase in sales, largely because of a reduction in car import duties. With the reduction of import duties in 1993, imports surged to 49% of sales and Russian production hit the lowest level of the decade. Domestic producers reacted by increasing their focus on export sales, largely to former CIS countries. Exports ranged between 18% and 56% of all production during the 1991–1995 period.

With the reimposition of import duties in 1994, the import share of the Russian marketplace returned to a level of about 7 to 10%. Domestic production began growing again and fewer Russian-made cars were exported. Unfortunately, just as domestic producers were nearly back to early-1990s production levels, the 1998 financial crisis sent the Russian economy and automotive industry into a tailspin. Domestic production of cars fell nearly 15% in 1998. Car sales in Russia as a whole fell by 8%. The industry, however, experienced a strong resurgence in 1999 and 2000.

Russian automotive manufacturing was highly concentrated, with AvtoVAZ holding a 65% market share in 2000, followed by GAZ with 13% and an assorted collection of what could be called 'boutique producers'.[1] Although foreign producers accounted for less than 2% of all car manufacturing in Russia in 2000, estimates of the influx of used foreign-made cars were upwards of 350 000 units in 2000 alone.

Although much had changed in Russia in the 1990s, much had also remained the same. In the Russian car market, demand greatly exceeded supply. Russians without the right political connections had to wait years for their cars. Cars were still rare, spare parts still difficult to find and crime still rampant. It was still not unusual to remove windscreen wipers from cars for safekeeping when parked on major city streets. Cars had to be paid for in cash, because dealer financing was essentially unheard of as a result of the inability of the Russian financial and banking sector to perform adequate credit checks on individuals or institutions. And once paid for, most Russian-made new cars were full of defects to the point that 'repair' was often required before driving a new car.

AvtoVAZ

It's mind-blowingly huge. The assembly line goes on for a mile and a quarter. Workstation after workstation. No modules being slapped in. It's piece by piece. The hammering is incessant. Hammering the gaskets in, hammering the doors down, hammering the bumpers. On the engine line a man seems to be screwing in pistons by hand and whopping them with a hammer. If there's a robot on the line, we didn't see it. Forget statistical process control.

'Would You Want to Drive a Lada?', *Forbes*, 26 August 1996

AvtoVAZ, originally called 'VAZ' for Volzhsky Avtomobilny Zavod (Volga Auto Factory), was headquartered approximately 1000 kilometres southeast of Moscow in Togliatti, a town named after an Italian communist. The original auto manufacturing facility was a JV (in effect, a pure turnkey operation) with Fiat SpA of Italy. The original contract, signed in 1966, resulted in the first cars being produced in 1970. The cars produced at the factory were distributed under the Lada and Zhiguli brands and for the next 20 years became virtually the only car the average Russian could purchase.

AvtoVAZ employed more than 250 000 people in 1999 (who were paid an average of US$333 per month), and produced 677 700 cars, US$1.9 billion in sales and US$458 million in gross profits. However, the company had a pre-tax loss of US$123 million. AvtoVAZ was publicly listed on the Moscow Stock Exchange. The Togliatti auto plant, with an estimated capacity of 750 000 vehicles per year, was the largest single car assembly facility in the world. It had reached full capacity in 2000. But the company developed only one new car in the 1990s and had spent an estimated US$2 billion doing so.

In the early 1990s, following the era of Perestroika and the introduction of economic reforms, AvtoVAZ began upgrading its technology and increasing its prices. As prices skyrocketed, Russians quickly switched to comparably priced imports of higher quality. As a result, AvtoVAZ suffered continual decreases in market share throughout the 1990s (see Table 1), although it still dominated all other Russian manufacturers.

The financial crisis of August 1998 actually bolstered AvtoVAZ's market position, with the fall of the Russian rouble from Rbl 11/US$ to over

Rbl 25/US$. Imports were now prohibitively expensive for most Russians.

> It's cynical to say, but in the case of a devaluation, the situation at AvtoVAZ would be better. There would be a different effectiveness of export sales, and demand would be different. Seeing that money is losing value, people would buy durable goods in the hopes of saving at least something.
>
> Vladimir Kadannikov, Chairman of the Board,
> AvtoVAZ, May 1998

AvtoVAZ also suffered from tax problems and was called a 'tax deadbeat' by the Russian press. In July 2000, the Russian Tax Police accused AvtoVAZ of tax fraud. The accusations centred on alleged under-reporting of car production by falsifying vehicle identification numbers (VINs). The opening of the criminal case coincided with warnings from the Kremlin that the new administration of President Vladimir Putin would not tolerate continued industry profiteering and manipulation from the country's oligarchs, individuals who had profited greatly from Russia's difficult transition to market capitalism. AvtoVAZ denied the charges and less than one month later, the case was thrown out by the chief prosecutor for tax evasion. A spokesman for the prosecutor's office stated that investigators had found no basis for the allegations against AvtoVAZ executives.

AvtoVAZ Ownership

One of the primary deterrents to foreign investment in Russia had been the relatively lax legal and regulatory structure for corporate governance. Identifying the owners of most major Russian companies was extremely difficult.

Although much about the ownership of AvtoVAZ remained unclear, it was believed that two different management groups controlled the majority of AvtoVAZ shares. One group was led by the current Chairman, Vladimir Kadannikov, and held 33.2% of total shares through an organization he controlled, the All-Russian Automobile Alliance (AVVA). A second group, represented by a Mr Yuri Zukster, controlled 19.2% through a different organization, the Automobile Finance Corporation (AFC). A Russian

investment fund, Russ-Invest, held 5%, with the remaining 42.6% under 'undisclosed' ownership.

AvtoVAZ itself held an 80.8% interest in Kadannikov's AVVA Group, an investment fund. AVVA, in turn, held a 33.2% interest in AvtoVAZ (see Figure 1 for an overview of the complex relationships surrounding AvtoVAZ). AVVA itself was in some way influenced, controlled or owned in part, by one of the most high-profile oligarchs in Russia, Boris Berezovsky.

In 1989, prior to the implementation of President Boris Yelstin's economic reforms, Boris Berezovsky, a mathematician and management-systems consultant to AvtoVAZ, persuaded Vladimir Kadannikov to cooperate in a new car distribution system. Berezovsky formed a car dealer network, LogoVAZ, that was supplied with AvtoVAZ vehicles on consignment. LogoVAZ did not pay for the cars it distributed (termed 're-export' by Berezovsky) until a date significantly after his dealer network sold the cars and received payment themselves. The arrangement proved disastrous for AvtoVAZ and incredibly profitable for Berezovsky. In the years that followed, hyperinflation raged in Russia, and Berezovsky was able to run his expanding network of businesses with AvtoVAZ's cash flow. (Berezovsky has admitted to the arrangement, and its financial benefits to him. He has also pointed out, correctly, that under Russian law he has not broken any laws.) LogoVAZ was also one of the largest car importers in Russia.

In 1994, the Russian government began privatizing many state-owned companies, including AvtoVAZ. Boris Berezovsky, Vladimir Kadannikov and Alexander Voloshin, recently appointed chief of staff for Russian President Vladimir Putin, then formed AVVA. The stated purpose of AVVA was to begin building a strong dealer network for the car industry in Russia. AVVA quickly acquired its 33.2% interest in AvtoVAZ, in addition to many other enterprises. AVVA frequently represented AvtoVAZ's significant international interests around the world.

By 2000, Berezovsky purportedly no longer had formal relations with AVVA, but many observers believed he continued to have a number of informal lines of influence. In December 2000, AVVA surprised many analysts by announcing that it was amending its charter to change its status from an investment fund to a holding company. Auto analysts speculated that

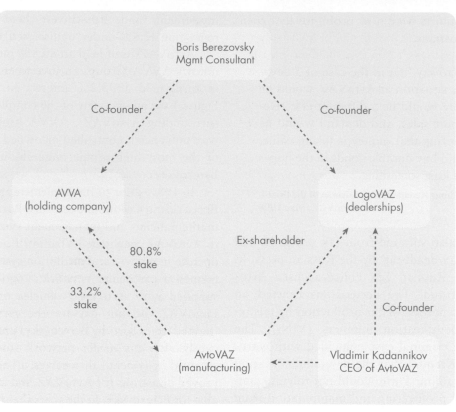

Figure 1: AvtoVAZ's web of influence and ownership.

Source: Adapted from www.just-auto.com.

AVVA was positioning itself to run AvtoVAZ, which had reorganized into divisions (car production, marketing and sales, and research and development).

Share ownership anxiety had intensified in November 2000 when the second largest car manufacturer in Russia, GAZ, had been the victim of a hostile takeover. Beginning in August 2000, Sibirsky Alyuminiy (SibAl) started accumulating shares in GAZ until reaching the 25% plus one share threshold necessary for veto power under Russian law. The exact amount of SibAl ownership in GAZ, however, was unknown, even to GAZ. Current regulations required only the disclosure of the identity and stake of stockholders of 5% equity stake or more. Only direct investors were actually named, and those named were frequently only agents operating on behalf of the true owners. Adding to the confusion was the fact that frequently the 'nominees' named represent multiple groups of ultimate owners. The inadequacy of information about ownership in Russia

was demonstrated by GAZ's inability to actually confirm whether SibAl did indeed have a 25% ownership position.

Rumours surfaced immediately that AvtoVAZ could be next, and the threat could arise from SOK, AvtoVAZ' largest single supplier. Many industry players, however, viewed this as highly unlikely.

'Besides Kadannikov, the brass at AvtoVAZ tend to keep a low profile, but they still rank among Russia's elite executives, and they are independent,' said an official of a foreign supplier in Russia. 'SOK may be powerful with AvtoVAZ, and AvtoVAZ may find SOK highly useful, but I doubt SOK ever could impact AvtoVAZ strategy, and I think SOK ultimately plays by rules set by AvtoVAZ.'

'Domino Theory: AvtoVAZ following
GAZ falling to new owner?', www.just-auto.com,
12 December 2000

Management of AvtoVAZ also felt that they had an additional takeover defence, which strangely enough arose from their history of not paying corporate taxes. In 1997, as part of a settlement with Russian tax authorities on US$2.4 billion in back-taxes, AvtoVAZ gave the Russian tax authorities the right to 50% plus one share of AvtoVAZ if the firm failed – in the future – to make its tax payments. AvtoVAZ management now viewed this as its own version of a 'poison pill'. If the company became the target of a hostile takeover, management could stop paying taxes and the Russian government would take management control, defeating the hostile takeover.[2]

AvtoVAZ Suppliers

Unlike many former Communist enterprises, AvtoVAZ was not vertically integrated. The company depended on a variety of suppliers for components and subassemblies and an assortment of retail distributors. It had little control over its suppliers, and was prohibited by law from retail distribution. In recent years, AvtoVAZ's supplier base had been continually consolidated. The three biggest suppliers to AvtoVAZ were DAAZ, Plastik and Avtopribor (see Table 2), all of which had been purchased by the Samara Window Company (abbreviated as 'SOK' from the Russian name) in the preceding years.[3]

Starting from a relatively small base, SOK had grown from a small glass window factory to a diversified enterprise of roughly US$2 billion sales in 1999, with businesses that included bottled water, building construction, medical equipment, plastic parts and windows, and most recently, AvtoVAZ's largest supplier and retailer. Although SOK officially purchased only 8000 cars per year for distribution from

AvtoVAZ, it was purportedly selling over 40 000 cars per year. The difference was rumoured to be cars assembled by SOK from kits purchased or 'exchanged' with AvtoVAZ. AvtoVAZ, often short of cash, frequently paid taxes, suppliers and management in cars.

Dealerships and Distribution

In the early 1990s hundreds of trading companies were formed around AvtoVAZ. Most trading companies would exchange parts and inputs for cars, straight from the factory, at prices 20–30% below market value. The trading companies then sold the cars themselves, capturing significant profit, while AvtoVAZ waited months for payment of any kind from the trading companies. The practice continued unabated in 1996 and 1997 because most of the trading companies were owned and operated by AvtoVAZ managers. Russian law did not prevent management from pursuing private interests related to their own enterprises.

Crime was also prevalent on the factory floor. Mobsters would purportedly enter the AvtoVAZ factory and take cars directly from the production lines at gun point. Buyers or distributors were charged US$100 for 'protection' at the AvtoVAZ factory gates. To quote one car distributor, 'They were bandits. Nevertheless, they provided a service.' By the autumn of 1997 the intrusion of organized crime became so rampant within AvtoVAZ that Vladimir Kadannikov used Russian troops to clear the plant of thugs.

International Activities

AvtoVAZ was actually a multinational company, with significant international operations in addition to significant export sales.

Supplier	Location	Parts
Avtopribor	Vladimir	Clusters for instrument panels, gauges, speedometers
Avtosvet	Kirzhach	Connectors, exterior and interior lights, reflectors, signals
DAAZ	Dimitrovgrad	Electronics, lights, mouldings, wheels
Osvar	Vyazniki	Exterior and interior lights, reflectors, signals, warning lights
Plastik	Syzran	Foam, plastics, sealants
Syzranselmash	Syzran	Chemicals, headliners, sun visors, window lifters

Source: www.just-auto.com, December 2000

Table 2: AvtoVAZ suppliers owned or controlled by SOK.

	1991	1992	1993	1994	1995	1996	1997	1998	1999
Baltic countries	8392	3895	3325	590	8832	2648	1101	716	487
CIS countries	126 440	42 900	19 644	4491	1601	1074	962	108	331
Elsewhere	269 936	271 763	280 593	196 696	175 161	129 957	94 303	68 689	49 957
Total exports	404 768	318 558	303 562	201 777	185 594	133 679	96 366	69 513	50 775
Total sales	674 884	673 821	656 403	528 845	607 279	680 965	736 000	599 829	677 669
Export (%)	60	47	46	38	31	20	13	12	7

Source: www.just-auto.com, December 2000

Table 3: AvtoVAZ exports.

As illustrated in Table 3, in 1991 AvtoVAZ was exporting more than 125 000 cars per year to the countries of the Soviet state. With the deconstruction of the old Soviet Union, sales plummeted to the now-CIS countries as a result of the proliferation of weak currencies from country to country, as well as the imposition of new import duties at every border to Russia of 30% or more.[4] In the late 1990s, sales were essentially zero. Similarly, sales in the Baltic countries of Latvia, Lithuania and Estonia had also essentially disappeared.

Brazil has been the site of substantial AvtoVAZ activity in the past decade, with starts and stops. AvtoVAZ had originally flooded the Brazilian market in 1990 with imports when the government of Brazil had opened its borders to imports. Despite 85% import duties, deeply discounted Ladas and Nivas sold well. However, in 1995, the Brazilian government excluded AvtoVAZ from a list of select international manufacturers that would be allowed much lower import duties. AvtoVAZ then withdrew from the Brazilian market. In November of 2000, Avto-VAZ concluded the negotiation of an agreement with a Brazilian entrepreneur, Carlos de Moraes, for his company, Abeiva Car Imports, to begin assembly of Nivas in 2001. The target price, 17 000 Brazilian reais, (about US$8900), would hopefully make them affordable for Brazilian farmers.

In the past decade, AvtoVAZ has exported to a variety of European countries as well, including Germany, Portugal, Spain, the United Kingdom and Greece. These sales have typically been small special-order models of the Niva (diesel engines, Peugeot gas engines, etc.). Continued issues surrounding quality and reliability, however, had pushed the company toward an emerging market strategy. It was hoped that low-income markets such as Egypt, Ecuador and Uruguay would reignite the export potential of the company. GM's strategy was based on extreme low prices to successfully penetrate local markets.

Foreign Entry into Russia

GM interest in Russia extended back to the 1970s when Opel had proposed shipping car kits to Moscow for assembly. The plan foundered because of GM concerns about quality control. In 1991, GM renewed its interest in Russia, once again opening talks with a number of potential JV partners. But after more than a decade, few deals had materialized.

In December 1996, GM opened a plant in Ela-buga, Tatarstan, in a JV with Yelaz to assemble Chevrolet Blazers from imported kits (complete knockdown kits, or CKDs). The original plan had been to ramp up production volumes rapidly to 50 000 units a year. But the operation struggled. One problem was the product; the Blazers were two-wheel drive with 2.2-litre engines. The Russian consumer wanted the four-wheel drive version widely sold in the United States, typically powered by a 3-litre engine. A second problem was the origin of the kits. The CKDs were imported from Brazil and most Russians did not have a high degree of respect for Brazilian products.

In September 1998, operations were suspended as a result of the Russian financial crisis. Only 3600 units had been assembled. An attempt was made to restart assembly operations in 1999, this time assembling Opel Vectras, but when it became apparent that the market for a vehicle costing US$20 000 would not succeed in the needed volumes, the JV's assembly operations were closed. GM still had more than 200 Blazers in inventory in January 2001 and was

Foreign manufacturer	Russian partner	Car model	Target price range (US$)	Capacity per year	Expected startup
Daewoo (Korea)	Doninvest	Compact	6000–8000	20 000	1998
BMW (Germany)	Avtotor	523, 528	36 000–53 000	10 000	2000
Renault (France)	City of Moscow	Megane	8500–13 500	100 000	1998
Ford (USA)	Bankirsky	Dom Focus	13 000–15 000	25 000	2002
Fiat (Italy)	GAZ	Palio, Siena	7000–10 000	15 000	2002
GM (USA)	AvtoVAZ	Niva, T3000	7500–10 000	75 000	2002

Table 4: Foreign car producers in Russia.

attempting to close out the last vestiges of the operation.

From 1998 to 2002, there were a number of foreign car producers in various stages of entry into the Russian marketplace, as summarized in Table 4. Daewoo of Korea, which had made major volume achievements in a number of former Eastern Bloc countries such as Poland, had begun assembly of compact saloon kits in 1998, and had quickly reached a sales level in Russia of 15 000 units in 1999. Similarly, Renault of France had followed the kit assembly entry strategy with the Renault Megane in 1998, but had only assembled and sold 1100 units by the end of year 1999.

Others, such as Ford Motor Company of the United States, had announced JVs with Russian manufacturers to build cars in Russia. The Ford Focus, priced on the relatively high side at US$13 000 to US$15 000, was planned for a production launch in late 2002. The facility planned was to produce 25 000 cars per year. The Russian government had given its blessing to the venture by allowing the elimination of import duties on imported inputs as long as the local content of the Focus reached 50% within five years of

start-up (2008 under current plans). Ford was already importing the Focus to begin building a market, but in the early months of 2001, sales were sluggish.

Fiat of Italy was potentially the most formidable competitor. Fiat planned to introduce the Fiat Palio and Fiat Siena into the Russian marketplace through a JV with GAZ in 2002. Although the planned capacity of the plant was only 15 000 cars per year, the Fiat Palio was considered by many experts to be the right product for the market. The critical question was whether Fiat could deliver the Palio to the market at a low enough price. In its negotiations with the Russian government, Fiat announced its intentions to make the Palio a true 'Russian-made' car that would quickly rise to over 70% in local content. If Fiat could indeed achieve this, and there were many who believed that if anyone could it was Fiat, then this would be the true competitive benchmark.

Renewed Interest

For most Russians, price was paramount. The average income levels in Russia prevented car pricing at Western levels. As seen in Table 5, prices over the past few

Price range (US$)	1998		1999	
	Seg (%)	Cum (%)	Seg (%)	Cum (%)
Below 5000	3	3	85	85
5001–10 000	65	68	12	97
10 001–15 000	15	83	1	98
Above 15 000	17	100	2	100

Seg = segment
Cum = cumulative
Source: General Motors

Table 5: Russian car market shares by price.

years had dropped as a result of the 1998 financial crisis. For 2001, analysts estimated that almost the entire market in Russia was for cars priced below US$10 000. Given that the average Russian's salary was about US$100 per month, cars remained out of reach for the average Russian.

In a September 2000 interview, David Herman summarized GM's viewpoint on pricing and positioning:

> We could not make an interesting volume with a base price above US$10 000. Such a vehicle would feature few specifications – ABS and airbags plus a 1.6-litre 16-valve engine. But, if the car costs US$12 000, it is only US$2000 less than certain foreign imports, and this gap may be too small to generate enough sales to justify a factory. We knew we could make a vehicle cheaper with AvtoVAZ, but we need to ensure the price advantage of T3000 imports over competitive models is closer to US$7000 than US$2000.[5]

GM had originally considered the traditional emerging market approach of building complete cars in existing plants and then disassembling them by removing bumpers, wheels and other separable parts, shipping the disassembled 'kit' into Russia, and reassembling with local labour. The disassembly/assembly process allowed the car to be considered domestically produced by Russian authorities, thereby avoiding prohibitive import duties. The market assessment group at GM, however, believed that Russian buyers (as opposed to customs officials) would see through the 'ruse' and consider the cars high-quality imports. But marketing research indicated the opposite: Russians did not want to buy cars reassembled by Russians. The only way they would purchase a Russian-made car was if it was extremely cheap, like the majority of the existing AvtoVAZ and GAZ product lines, which retailed for as little as US$3000 per car. GM, realizing that it could not deliver the reassembled Opel to the Russian marketplace for less than US$15 000 per car, dropped the kit proposal.

GM's marketing research unveiled an additional critical element. Russians would gladly pay an additional US$1000 to US$1500 per car if it had a *Chevrolet* label or badge on it. This piece of research resulted in the original proposal that David

Herman and his staff had been pursuing since early 1999: a two-stage JV investment with AvtoVAZ that would allow GM to both reach price targets and position the firm for expected market growth. In the first stage, GM would co-produce a four-wheel-drive SUV named the Lada Niva II (VAZ-2123). The target price was US$7500 and plant capacity was to be 90 000 cars. The Niva II would be largely Russian-engineered and, therefore GM would avoid many of the development costs associated with the introduction of a totally new vehicle. The Lada Niva I had originally been introduced in 1977 and updated in new models in 1990 and again in 1996. It had been a successful line for AvtoVAZ, averaging 70 000 units per year throughout the 1990s.[6] Since the Niva II was largely Russian-engineered, GM would bring capital and name to the venture.

The second stage of the project would be the construction of a new factory to produce 30 000 Opel Astras (T3000) for the Russian market. Herman's proposal was for AvtoVAZ to use a basic Opel AG vehicle platform as a pre-engineering starting point. Pre-engineering represented about 30% of the development cost of a vehicle. The remaining 70% would be developed by AvtoVAZ's 10 000 engineers and technicians who worked at a much lower cost than Opel's engineers in Germany. Herman's Russian Group estimated that even if GM and AvtoVAZ used AvtoVAZ's factory to build the existing Opel Astra from mostly imported parts and kits from Germany, the resulting price tag would have to fall to between US$12 500 and US$14 000 per car. This was still considered too expensive for substantial economic volumes. Using the Russian engineering approach, the car would be cheaper, but still fall at the higher end of the spectrum, retailing at about US$10 000 per car. As shown in Table 4, this would still put the higher-priced Chevrolet in the lower end of the foreign-made market.

By no means was there consensus within GM and Opel about the viability of the proposed JV. One concern was that as a result of the cash shortage at AvtoVAZ and the slow rate of negotiation progress, in order to build test-models of the new Niva, AvtoVAZ had to use 60% of the old Niva's parts. Although many of the consumers that tested the Niva II ranked it above all other Russian-built cars, the car was rough riding and noisy by Western standards. One Opel engineer from Germany who safety-tested the Niva II and evaluated its performance declared it 'a real car, if primitive'. Heidi McCormack, General Director for GM's Russian operations believed that with some minor engineering adjustments, better materials for the interior construction and a new factory built and operated by GM, the quality of the Niva II would be 'acceptable'.

GM management was pleased that AvtoVAZ appeared willing to contribute the rejuvenated Niva to the JV. 'That's their brand-new baby,' said McCormack. 'It's been shown in autoshows. And here's GM, typical big multinational, saying, "Just give us your best product"'.[7] But in the end, AvtoVAZ's limited access to capital was the driver. Without GM, AvtoVAZ would probably take five years to get the Niva II to market; with GM the time could be cut in half.

Negotiations

Negotiations between AvtoVAZ and GM had taken a number of twists and turns over the years, involving every possible dimension of the project. The JV's market strategy, scope, timing, financing and structure were all under continual debate. GM's team was led by David Herman.

Herman had been appointed VP of General Motors Corporation for the former Soviet Union in 1998. Starting with General Motors Treasury as an attorney in 1973, Herman had extensive international experience, including three years as GM's manager of sales development in the USSR (1976–1979), and other managing director positions in Spain (1979–1982), Chile (1982–1984) and Belgium (1986–1988). These were followed by chief executive positions for GM (Europe) in Switzerland and Saab Automobile. From 1992 to 1998, Herman had been chairman and managing director of Adam Opel AG in Germany. Herman's departure from Opel in Germany was purportedly the result of losing a highly publicized internal battle over the future strategic direction of Opel. Herman had argued that Opel should focus on developing product for the domestic market, while others in the organization argued that Opel should focus on 'filling the pipeline for GM's ambitions in emerging markets'. Many have characterized his new appointment as head of GM's market initiatives in Russia as

a Siberian exile. Herman's parents were Belorussian and he had studied Russian at Harvard. In addition to Russian and English, he was also fluent in German and Spanish.

Market Strategy

Back in Detroit, the JV proposal continued to run into significant opposition. GM President Rick Wagoner continued to question whether the Russian market could actually afford the Opel-based second car, the Opel T3000. Wagoner wondered whether the second phase of the project should not be cut, making the Niva the single product that the JV would produce. This could potentially reduce GM's investment to US$100 million.

A further point of debate concerned export sales. As a result of the 1998 financial crisis in Russia, a number of people inside both GM and AvtoVAZ pushed for a JV that would produce a car designed for both Russian sales and export sales. After 1998 the weaker Russian rouble meant that Russian exports were more competitive. If the product quality was competitive for the targeted markets, there was a belief that Russian cars could be profitably exported. As a result, Herman expanded his activities to include export market development. The working proposal now assumed that one third of all the Chevrolet Nivas produced would be exported. The domestic market continued to be protected with a 30% import duty against foreign-made automobiles, both new and used.

Herman brought AvtoVAZ senior management to the Detroit auto show in the spring of 2000 to meet with GM President Rick Wagoner and Vice Chairman Harry Pearce. The meetings went well. In March 2000, however, GM announced an alliance with Fiat. A key element of the alliance involved GM acquiring 20% of Fiat's automotive business. GM paid US$2.4 billion using GM common stock for the 20% stake, which resulted in Fiat owning 5.1% of GM. In June 2000, GM and Fiat submitted a joint bid for Daewoo, which was part of the bankrupt Daewoo *chaebol* (a Korean term for a conglomerate of many companies clustered around one parent company, which usually hold shares in each other and are often run by one family; similar to the *keiretsu* in Japan). The bid was rejected. Herman returned to Russia, once again slowing negotiations until any possible overlap between GM and Fiat ambitions in Russia were resolved.

Timing

In the summer of 1999, AvtoVAZ had formally announced the creation of a JV with General Motors to produce Opel Astras and the Chevrolet Niva. However, this announcement was not confirmed by GM. Later in 1999, GM's European management, primarily via the Opel division, lobbied heavily within GM to postpone the proposed Chevrolet Niva launch until 2004 to allow a longer period of economic recovery in Russia. Upon learning of this, Kadannikov reportedly told GM to 'keep its money', and that AvtoVAZ would launch the new Niva on its own. The two sides were able to agree on a tentative 2003 launch date.

Financing

In May 2000, Herman's presentation of the JV proposal to Wagoner and Pearce in Detroit hit another roadblock: the proposed US$250 million investment was considered 'too large and too risky for a market as risky as Russia – with a partner as slippery as Avto-VAZ'.[8] Wagoner instructed Herman to find a third party to share the capital investment and the risk, because GM would not risk more than US$100 million itself. Within three months Herman found a third party – the European Bank for Reconstruction and Development (EBRD). EBRD was willing to provide debt and equity. It would lend US$93 million to the venture and invest an additional US$40 million for an equity stake of 17%.[9]

The European Bank for Reconstruction and Development was established in 1991 with the express purpose of fostering the transition to open market-oriented economies and promoting private and entrepreneurial ventures in Eastern Europe and the Commonwealth of Independent States (CIS). As a catalyst of change, the bank seeks to co-finance with firms that are providing foreign direct investment (FDI) in these countries in order to help mobilize domestic capital and reduce the risks associated with FDI. Recent economic reforms and the perceived stability of President Putin's government had convinced the EBRD's senior management that conditions were right.

GM management knew that US$332 million would be insufficient to build a state-of-the-art manufacturing facility. However, given that Avto-VAZ's contributions would include the design, land and production equipment, US$332 million was believed to be sufficient to launch the new Niva. The planned facility would include a car body paint shop, assembly facilities and testing areas. AvtoVAZ would supply the JV with the car-body, engine and transmission, chassis units, interior components and electrical system.

Structure

A continuing point of contention was where the profits of the JV would be created. For example, Avto-VAZ had consistently quoted a price for cement for the proposed plant that was thought to be about 10 times what GM would customarily pay in Germany. Then, just prior to the venture's going before the GM Board for preliminary approval for continued negotiations, AvtoVAZ made a new and surprising demand that GM increase the price the JV would pay AvtoVAZ for Niva parts by 25%. (Vladimir Kadannikov demanded to know where the profits would be, 'in the price of the parts each side supplied to the joint venture or in the venture itself?').[10] When Herman warned them this would scuttle the deal, AvtoVAZ backed off. After heated debate, the two parties now agreed that they would not try to profit from the sale of components to the JV.

The structure for the management team and specific allocation of managerial responsibilities had yet to be determined. Although both sides expected to be actively involved in day-to-day management, GM had already made it clear that management control of the JV was a priority for going forward. GM also wanted to minimize the number of expatriate managers assigned to the venture. AvtoVAZ saw the JV as an opportunity for its managers to gain valuable experience and expected to have significant purchasing, assembly and marketing responsibilities. AvtoVAZ expected GM to develop and support an organizational structure that ensured technology transfer to the JV. AvtoVAZ knew that in China GM had created a technical design centre as a separate JV with its Chinese partner. The specific details as to how GM might be compensated for technology transfer to Russia remained unclear. Finally, the issue of who would control the final documentation for the JV agreement had yet to be agreed.

The JV would be located on the edge of the massive AvtoVAZ complex in Togliatti. It would use one factory building that was partially finished and previously abandoned. The building already housed much equipment in various operational states, including expensive plastic moulding and cutting tools imported from Germany in the early 1990s, which AvtoVAZ had been unable to operate effectively but could not resell.

Progress

Again, primarily out of frustration with the pace of negotiations, AvtoVAZ announced in January 2001 that it would begin small-scale production of a SUV under its own Lada brand. Herman once again was able to intervene. Herman promised GM's Board that AvtoVAZ would actually build no more than a few dozen of the SUVs 'for show'. The two sides also continued to debate whether AvtoVAZ would be allowed to sell the prototypes of the new Niva that AvtoVAZ planned to build (approximately 500). GM was adamant, according to long-standing policy, that these should not find their way to the marketplace. AvtoVAZ countered that this was routine for Russian manufacturers and served as a type of 'test fleet'.

Finally, on 6 February 2001, Herman presented the current proposal to GM's board in Detroit. After heated debate, the board approved the proposal. The possibility of entering a large and developing market, with shared risk and investment, was a rare opportunity to get in early and develop a new local market. According to Rick Wagoner:

> Russia's going to be a very big market.... We'll sell it in former Soviet Union, and eventually export it and because of the cost of material and labour in Russia, we should reach a price point which gives us a decent volume. That will give us a chance to get a network and get started with suppliers and other partners in Russia in a way which I hope will make us amongst the leaders.[11]

David Herman had gained the approval of the General Motors Board to pursue and complete negotiations with AvtoVAZ. The negotiations themselves, however, represented an enormous undertaking, and both GM and AvtoVAZ had many issues yet to be resolved.

Questions for Discussion

1. What are the specific pros and cons of the proposed joint venture from the AvtoVAZ perspective?
2. What are the specific pros and cons of the proposed joint venture from the General Motors perspective?
3. If you were negotiating on the part of AvtoVAZ, what specific issues would have to be resolved (so-called 'walk-away points') before the joint venture would be acceptable?
4. If you were negotiating on the part of General Motors, what specific issues would have to be resolved before the joint venture would be acceptable?

Sources: Copyright © 2002 Thunderbird, The American Graduate School of International Management. All rights reserved. This case was prepared by Professor Michael H. Moffett for the purpose of classroom discussion only, and not to indicate either effective or ineffective management.

Appendix 1

OAO AvtoVAZ profit and loss statement, 1996–1999.

Jan–Oct (in thousands of roubles)	1996	1997	1998	1999
Net sales less VAT	23 697 167	26 255 183	9 533 172	33 834 987
Less cost of goods sold	(18 557 369)	(21 552 999)	(7 650 161)	(25 998 011)
Gross profits	5 139 798	4 702 184	1 883 011	7 836 976
Gross margin	21.7%	17.9%	19.8%	23.2%
Less sales and marketing expenses	(638 739)	(497 540)	(168 381)	(603 170)
Operating income	4 501 059	4 204 644	1 714 630	7 233 806
Operating margin	19.0%	16.0%	18.0%	21.4%
Interest	–	–	–	–
Dividend income	3366	3392	159	8749
Income on asset disposal	3 084 203	23 052 035	2 516 466	4 115 346
Loss on asset disposal	(3 935 990)	(21 718 864)	(3 430 751)	(5 716 732)
Income from core business	3 652 638	5 541 207	800 504	5 641 169
Non-operating income	400 185	372 340	69 415	252 713
Non-operating expenses	(1 136 225)	(1 033 305)	(299 123)	(1 124 448)
Income for period	2 916 598	4 880 242	570 796	4 769 434
Less income tax	(682 556)	(1 166 911)	77 268	(1 112 039)
Disallowable expenses	(409 906)	(7 069 333)	(251 574)	(1 674 947)
Net income	1 824 136	(3 356 002)	396 490	1 982 448
Return on sales (ROS)	7.7%	12.8%	4.2%	5.9%
In US dollars				
Exchange rate (roubles/US$)	5.6	6.0	9.7	24.6
Net sales	4 231 636 964	4 375 863 833	982 801 237	1 375 405 976
Gross profits	917 821 071	783 697 333	194 124 845	318 576 260
Income from core business	652 256 786	923 534 500	82 526 186	229 315 813
Income for period	520 821 071	813 373 667	58 844 948	193 879 431
Net income	325 738 571	(559 333 667)	40 875 258	80 587 317

Source: AvtoVAZ

Appendix 2

AvtoVAZ product prices by city (February 2001, in Russian roubles).

Code	Model	Type	Tolyatti	Moscow	St. Petersburg
21 060	Lada Classic	1976 saloon	84 100	86 500	90 100
2107	Lada Classic	1982 saloon	86 700	91 700	94 400
21 083	Lada Samara	1985 3-door hatch	111 900	117 500	115 800
21 093	Lada Samara	1987 5-door hatch	112 200	119 700	115 800
21 099	Lada Samara	1990 saloon	122 500	132 000	132 600
21 102	Lada 2110	1996 saloon	146 500	150 700	151 700
21 103	Lada 2110	1997 estate	161 100	164 800	162 300
21 110	Lada 2110	1999 5-door hatch	157 200	161 900	168 900
2112	Lada Samara II	2001 3-door hatch	167 300	168 600	168 300
2115	Lada Samara II	1997 sedan	143 000	153 700	149 600
21 213	Lada Niva	1997 SUV	103 500	111 300	111 100

Average (roubles)		126 909	132 582	123 582
Exchange rate (roubles/US$)		30.00	30.00	30.00
Average (US$)		4230	4419	4111

Source: AvtoVAZ

Appendix 3

Russian demographics and economics, 1993–1999.

Actual indicator	1993	1994	1995	1996	1997	1998	1999
Real GDP growth (%)	−8.7	−12.%	−4.1	−3.5	−0.8	−4.9	3.2
GDP per capita (US$)	1135	1868	2348	2910	3056	1900	1260
Consumer price index (% chg)	875	308	198	48	15	28	86
External debt (bill US$)	112.7	119.9	120.4	125.0	123.5	183.6	174.3
Foreign direct investment (bill US$)	n/a	0.5	0.7	0.7	3.8	1.7	0.8
Population (millions)	148.2	148.0	148.1	147.7	147.1	146.5	146.0
Unemployment rate (%)	5.3	7.0	8.3	9.3	10.8	11.9	12.5
Wages (US$/hour)						0.63	0.36
Exchange rate (roubles/US$)	1.2	3.6	4.6	5.6	6.0	9.7	24.6

Source: Economist Intelligence Unit, February 2001

Appendix 4

Foreign car manufacturers and Russian Partners in Russia.

Partner	Model	Manufacturer/price range (US$)/capacity			
		Low	High	Per year	Start-up
Daewoo Doninvest	Compact saloon	6000	8000	20 000	1998 Assembly
BMW Group ZAO Avtotor	523 and 528 models	36 450	53 010	10 000	2000 Assembly
Renault City of Moscow	Clio Symbol Megane	8500 13 500	9000 16 000	100 000 3000	1998 Assembly 2002 Assembly
Ford Motor Co ZAO Bankirsky Dom	Focus	13 000	15 000	25 000	2002 Staged to >50% local in 5 years
Fiat SpA OAO Gaz	Palio Siena	9000 10 000	10 000 11 000	10 000 5000	2002 Production
General Motors OAO AvtoVAZ	New Niva Astra T3000	7500 10 000	10 000 12 000	75 000	2002 Production

Source: Economist Intelligence Unit, February 2001

Appendix 5

EBRD's Commitment to the GM-VAZ Joint Venture, Russia

The EBRD proposes to provide financing for the construction and operation of a factory to manufacture and assemble up to 75 000 Niva vehicles in Togliatti, Russia.

Operation Status: Signed

Business Sector: Motor vehicle manufacturing

Board Review Date: 28 March 2000

Portfolio Classification: Private sector

The Client: General Motors–AvtoVAZ Joint Venture is a closed joint-stock company to be created under Russian law specifically for the purpose of carrying out the project. Once the investment is complete, AvtoVAZ (VAZ) and General Motors (GM) will hold an equal share in the venture. GM is currently the world's top automotive manufacturer with production facilities in 50 countries and 388 000 employees worldwide. VAZ is the largest producer of vehicles in Russia, having sold approximately 705 500 (over 70% of the Russian new car market) in 2000.

Proposed EBRD Finance: The EBRD proposes to provide up to 41% of the financing of the venture in a combination of a loan of US$100 million (108 million euros) and an equity investment of US$40 million (43 million euros). The loan includes interest during the construction phase. Up to US$38 million of the loan may be syndicated after signing to reduce EBRD exposure.

Total Project Cost: US$338 million (365 million euros)

Project Objectives: The construction and operation of a factory to manufacture and assemble up to 75 000 Niva vehicles per annum in Togliatti, Russia.

Expected Transition Impact: The transition impact potential of this transaction stems primarily from the demonstration effects associated with the entrance of a major Western strategic investor into the Russian automotive market. The fact that this investment has two well-known partners who are investing equally in the joint venture adds both to the visibility and the potential of the project. This complex project is one of the largest examples of foreign direct investment in post-crisis Russia in a period when many foreign investors are still adopting a wait and see approach. The use of Russian design and engineering skills together with the introduction of Western technologies, methods and processes and the related development of skills are further key sources of positive demonstration effect, especially given the huge modernization needs of the Russian automotive sector. Other suppliers and client companies will also benefit from technological links or training programs with the joint venture.

Environmental Impact: The project was screened B/1, requiring an audit of the existing facility and an analysis of the impact associated with the joint venture (JV). While typical environmental issues associated with heavy manufacturing are present at the main AvtoVAZ facility, there have been no prior operations at the site of the proposed JV. Potential liabilities arising from historic soil and ground water pollution were addressed as part of the due diligence, and no significant levels of contamination have been identified. The engine for the new Niva will meet Euro II (Russian market) and Euro IV (European market) standards for vehicle emissions. All vehicles will be fitted with catalytic converters. Safety standards for all vehicles will meet EU and GM standards in full. On formation, the JV will adopt GM management and operations systems and GM corporate practices for all aspects of environment, health and safety and will be in compliance with all applicable EU and best international environmental standards.

Case Study 6

GLOBAL TELECOM LEADERS MEET A FAMILY CONGLOMERATE

The mood was jubilant when Motorola announced in September 2000 that it had lent an additional US$700 million to TelSim, a Turkish-based Global System for Mobile Communication (GSM) operator, in support of its efforts to dominate the booming mobile telephone market in this emerging country. The overall agreement was potentially worth US$2 billion for the deployment of a mobile network by vendor financing, and it was considered to be the largest financing deal in telecommunications. Motorola viewed entering Turkey's burgeoning cellular market as an important business objective.

Simultaneously, as the last act of its relationship with TelSim since 1994, Nokia of Espoo, Finland won a three-year deal worth US$900 million in June 2000 with TelSim of Turkey to deliver a full GSM network expansion. After the announcement, Pertti Melamies, Area Vice President, Nokia Networks, confidently stated:

> This deal, the largest to date for Nokia Networks, illustrates our clear leadership in GSM equipment. By 2001, we estimate the number of mobile subscribers in Turkey will be in excess of 15 million.... This provides TelSim the flexibility to be ideally positioned to meet the voice and data capacity, quality of service and cost challenges of continued strong growth in the Turkish market.[1]

These happy days seemed quite distant later in 2001. A sombre looking Christopher Galvin, CEO of Motorola of Schaumburg, Illinois, announced the third straight quarterly loss in 2001: US$1.4 billion – one of the biggest quarterly losses in the history of the company. The stock price fell to US$16.72 in October, from a 52-week high of US$29.81. As disclosed by Motorola, the major cause of the loss was attributed to TelSim with the unpaid US$728 million as the first instalment of its debt.[2] Similarly, Nokia of Finland was unable to collect US$240 million due from TelSim.

The press provided global, intensive coverage of the problem experienced by Motorola and Nokia, and the problem was also brought to the attention of the respective governments. Consequently, the two telecom giants jointly filed a lawsuit on 28 January, 2002, in a New York federal court,[3] driven by fears that TelSim never intended to repay its loans.

In January 2002, Turkish Prime Minister Bulent Ecevit and US President George Bush met in Washington, DC to discuss the legal battle going on between Turkish TelSim and American Motorola.

Importance of the Turkish Market as an Emerging Economy

Advances in wireless technology and a worldwide push toward privatization provided double-digit growth opportunities in the telecommunication sector. The demand was particularly strong in an emerging market. Strategically, Motorola and Nokia were able to position themselves to become the leading suppliers to start-up telecom service companies. One of the emerging markets that drew the attention of the equipment manufacturers was Turkey.

Turkey, straddling Europe and Asia, is one of the leading emerging markets. With a population of more than 65 million, and a liberalized and booming economy and stock market, Turkey had started appearing on everybody's radar screen as a promising market for both trade and investment. Even though privatization was well under way, the state-owned enterprises, along with family owned conglomerates, had played an important role in the economy.

Turkey signed a customs union agreement with the European Union in the late 1990s and liberalized the regulation of foreign direct investment. Accordingly, the leading major family conglomerates such as Koc and Sabanci established numerous joint ventures with foreign companies. Turkey was also one of the countries that encouraged and attracted foreign involvement in the Build–Operate–Transfer (BOT) scheme. Turkey's long established relationship with the Commonwealth of Independent States (CIS) was of particular interest for the international business community. Additionally, Turkey applied for membership in the European Union and the Turkish government was being careful not to jeopardize its standing with the IMF and the EU member countries.

Although three quarters of the population resides in urban areas, agriculture still plays a significant role in the country. It contributes 16% of GDP and employs around 40% of the workforce. Turkey, an upper-middle-income economy, had a per capita GDP (PPP) of US$6700 in 2002.

Inflation has been a problem for the Turkish economy for the past 20 years. In the last of a series of financial crises, in February 2001, the local currency was devalued by about 40%, which immediately hit Turkish firms hard. External shocks, such as the devastating 1999 earthquakes and aftershock of 11 September 2001, have also affected the economy. GDP contracted by 8.5% in 2001. To support the efforts to lower the inflation rate and ease the economy, the IMF provided a US$15.7 billion loan wrapped in a rescue.

The Uzan Conglomerate

TelSim is Turkey's second largest GSM operator and is privately managed by the Uzan family, as an affiliate of Rumeli Holding, with a 66% stake. The Uzans launched TelSim in 1994 in order to reap the benefits of the opportunities in the very promising, yet infant, Turkish telecom industry. TelSim announced that it had two million subscribers by the end of 1999 and its plan for 2000 involved 5.5 million. Even though it failed to meet its targets, TelSim had spectacular growth, with slightly less than five million users by 2000. It was the second private sector company to receive a GSM licence, which will expire in 2023, from the Turkish government. TelSim tried to remain at the forefront of wireless communications and was the first to embark on leading-edge new technologies and services. TelSim's investments in infrastructure, technology and marketing reached US$3 billion by 2001.

The Uzan family appeared as a significant player in the Turkish economy in the late 1980s. As is common in emerging markets, the Uzans' extensive operations in various sectors reported to and were controlled by a family owned holding company, Rumeli Holding. Rumeli Holding operates in many sectors, from cement manufacturing to banking, including broadcasting and print media. The Uzan empire controls at least 137 entities in nine countries[4] and the Uzans' wealth is believed to exceed US$1.6 billion.

The Uzans are one of Turkey's richest, most powerful clans. They are descended from farmers who immigrated to Turkey from Sarajevo around 1910. Family patriarch Kemal Uzan, 70, a civil engineer, was the first to make a mark in business, founding a construction company in 1956. He landed lucrative contracts for soccer stadiums in the 1960s, and dams and hydroelectric power plants in the 1970s and 1980s, thanks in part to a cozy relationship with the Turkish prime minister (and later president) Turgut Ozal. He expanded the business into a banking and media empire. In 1984, Kemal Uzan bought Imar Bank for US$21 million. A year later he founded Adabank, which was managed by his sons, Cem Cengiz and Murat Hakan. Incidentally, Cem Uzan was once Bill Gates' neighbour at the top of the Trump World Tower in New York.[5]

In the past two decades the Uzans have built a small family construction business into a giant private holding company with interests in everything from energy to 'pay TV'. The Uzan family ranked fifth in a published list of Turkish billionaires.

The banks provided Cem Uzan with an entrée into the family enterprises at age 24, after graduating with a degree in business from Pepperdine University. By the time he was 30, he proved his prowess by slyly overcoming Turkish laws preventing private transmission of TV signals: working with Turgut Ozal's son, he rented studios in Germany and beamed the signal via satellite. Cem called it Star TV, which was the first-ever private TV channel in Turkey. It operated illegally for several years, and Ozal's administration not only turned a blind eye but also encouraged it to operate freely and end the state monopoly on TV broadcasts. Then the Uzans pushed Ahmet Ozal out of the partnership and seized power[6] and a year later introduced radio stations; earlier in the year the Star group started a tabloid-style newspaper and called it the *Star Daily*. When the paper was launched, people began to wonder when and if the newspaper would be used like the TV station to extract favours for the Uzan Empire.

Motorola and Nokia are not the only business partners to receive a raw deal as a result of their involvement with the Uzan family. The Uzans have committed similar acts of fraud and deceit against other major domestic and international corporations, including Siemens, Ericsson, Italstrade/Fintecna and many others.

Siemens provided vendor financing to TelSim until early 2000, when TelSim failed to pay a number of outstanding invoices issued by Siemens. The total debt owed to Siemens is in excess of US$25 million. In March 2000, the Uzans demanded that Nokia increase the cash portion of a new loan facility by US$25 million to permit TelSim to pay its debts to Siemens, which Nokia did. The Uzans, however, did not use this money to repay the Siemens debt. Siemens severed its ties with TelSim and filed an enforcement proceeding and a bankruptcy action against TelSim to collect the amounts owed. TelSim countersued on Siemens' collection action, asserting that Siemens had installed faulty equipment and alleging that the company owed TelSim US$50 million.[7] In an act of extortion in connection with the commercial disputes, the Uzans used their Star newspaper companies to launch a series of libellous attacks against Siemens and its current and former chief executive officers, Zafer Incecik and Arnold Hornfeld.

Erikson Telekomunikasyon AS (Ericsson) had entered into a business arrangement with TelSim's chief rival in the Turkish mobile phone industry, Turkcell. In an apparent act of retaliation aimed at Turkcell and Ericsson, Cem Uzan's Star TV twice aired a false 'news' item during a nationally televised football match claiming that Ericsson funnelled money to a terrorist organization.[8]

The Uzan family seemed to be more charitable abroad than it at home. In return for attendance at a lavish dinner in Buckingham Palace, Cem Uzan gave generously to the Prince of Wales Foundation, a charity set up by the heir to the British throne.

Among other ventures, the Uzans formed a political party, The Youth Party, and participated in Turkey's most recent national elections. The Youth Party collected some 7% of the votes cast, a major success for an organization that was formed only five months earlier. Critics commented that Cem Uzan was seeking to enter the Parliament in order to gain immunity from potential prosecution from questionable business matters. The Uzans were not only being prosecuted by US and Finnish courts for fraud against Nokia and Motorola but also by the Turkish courts. It was claimed that he founded the party in order to transfer some of his assets. Cem Uzan has been likened by some to Italy's Prime Minister Silvio Berlusconi, or a younger version of the former US presidential candidate Ross Perot. Italian media mogul Silvio Berlusconi became prime minister only three months after founding his Forza Italia party amid a similar disillusionment in Italian politics. The Uzan empire, like Berlusconi's, also embraces banking and finance enterprises, a soccer team, television and radio stations, and newspapers with a sharp tongue.

Motorola and Nokia: The Western Partners

Motorola is a US-based high-tech company. Founded in 1928, Motorola has always been a manufacturer of consumer electronics products. By 1960, Motorola started expanding globally and by the mid-1970s, its focus shifted to high technology markets in commercial, industrial and government fields.[9] Motorola was the second-largest manufacturer of mobile handsets and a leader in telecom infrastructure equipment. It reported US$26 679 million in net sales, US$2485 million in net earnings (loss) and 97 000[10] employees in the year 2002.[11]

Motorola was the leader in the mobile phones business with a 33% market share; however, its share eroded to 15% between 1999 and 2002. (Nokia became the market leader.) During that time, the company made a series of strategic mistakes. It was late in making the switch from old analogue systems to more reliable digital technology. Then Motorola pushed expensive phones that could access the wireless web instead of the cheaper phones that consumers wanted, a stumble that more nimble and style-conscious competitors such as Nokia used to race ahead. Also, its semiconductors division faced a substantial decline with the economic slowdown during the year 2000–2001. (It laid off 4000 workers in the semiconductor division in February 2001.) The telecommunications infrastructure division saw its fortunes diminish as well. Consequently, in the first five months of 2001, more than 26 000 jobs were cut

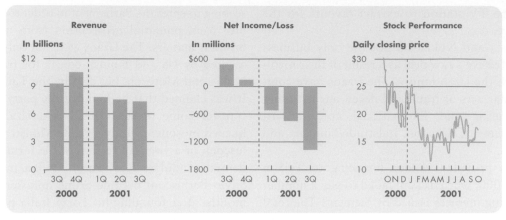

Figure 1: Motorola: by the numbers.

Source: www.marketdata.sungard.com.

and a total of 39 000 were targeted to be cut in 2001 (see Figures 1–4).

Nokia

With a culture nearly 140 years old, Finland-based Nokia is the world's largest mobile phone producer and a global leader in mobile communications. Nokia grew its market share in mobile phones from 19% in 1997 to close to 40% in 2002. Its net sales reached US$30.1 billion in 2002, of which Nokia Mobile Phones group made up around 76%.[12]

During the 1980s and 1990s, Nokia became a major player in telecommunications and consumer electronics in Europe. Nokia acquired companies in Sweden, Germany, France and Switzerland. In the 1980s, Nokia advanced in information technologies, cable and telecommunications fields.

Nokia redefined its corporate goals and focus in the early 1990s and decided to intensify its efforts in business and telecommunications. At the time, Ericsson of Sweden was the biggest competitor in the region and the world. Nokia became very competitive under the administration of CEO Jorma Ollila. Nokia's market share increased dramatically around the globe while Motorola and Ericsson lost market share steadily. Nokia eventually became the number one supplier of mobile phones in the world. Experts agree that Nokia's better understanding of the

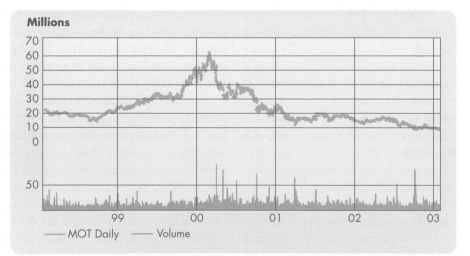

Figure 2: Motorola performance 1999–2003.

Source: www.motorola.com.

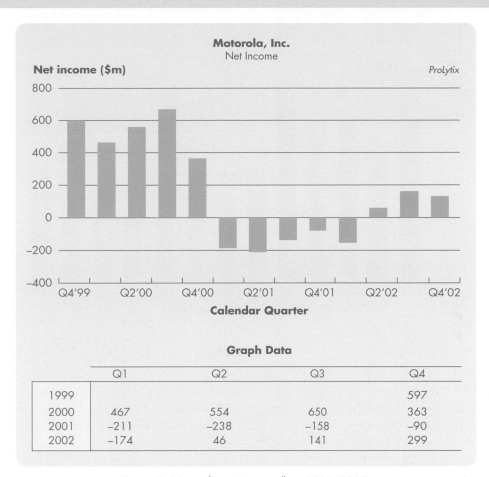

Figure 3: Motorola net income/loss 1999–2002.

Source: www.motorola.com.

consumer market gave them the edge to be more competitive. The phone designs and operating costs were lower at Nokia, which helped their competitiveness at the global scale. The use of mobile phones skyrocketed between 1991 and 2000. The number of phones in use increased from 6 million to 400 million. Overall, in the wireless communications market, Nokia was perceived by the experts to be leaner and more efficient. Today, it is the global sales leader in wireless communications.

The Turkish Telecom Market

Historically, telecom companies were state-owned firms with a monopoly position. Foreign ownership was not allowed. With the advent in wireless technology, an accelerated trend toward privatization and liberalization began to open up the national markets to competition from within and elsewhere. The Turkish telecom industry was one of the first to take advantage of these evolutions in the wireless sector.

Turkey's telecommunication industry is more than a century old. It was one of the founding members of the predecessor organization of the ITU in 1865. A telegraph line was installed in 1847 and the first automatic telephone exchange in the Balkans was installed in Ankara in 1926. At first, the phone service provided by the state-owned PTT was very bad; you could wait half a day for an international call to come through and 15 years for a telephone to be installed in your home. However, by the end of 2001, there were some 18.9 million fixed telephone lines in service, for a teledensity of 28. As of 1998, all Turkey's 36 000 villages had a telephone.[13] Household telephone penetration is estimated at 87% and the digitalization ratio is 88% in switchboards and 97% in transmission.

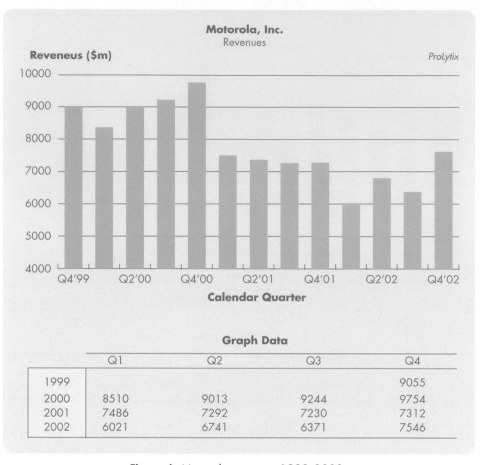

Figure 4: Motorola revenues 1999–2002.

Source: www.motorola.com.

TurkTelekom, the incumbent telecommunication operator, ranks among the biggest telecom providers in emerging Europe. It stands out among developing telecom operators for its high rate of digitalization and significant strength in satellite capacity. This enables it to cover Turkey's remote areas and become an important transit venue for international traffic.

Turkey invested heavily in the 1980s in order to modernize and expand its telecom system. TurkTelekom, a state-owned company, still had the monopoly over land lines. A government plan called for 2.5 million additional lines to be built between 2000 and 2005. Turkey missed out in the 1990s when telecommunications witnessed a record number of mergers, acquisitions and privatizations. In 1992 Morgan Stanley had valued TurkTelekom at between US$18 billion and US$20 billion. Lack of investment, loss of market share to the aggressive cellular companies and

the unpopularity of emerging-market stocks have subsequently almost halved TurkTelecom's market value. At the end of 1997 the government attached a price tag of US$10 billion. In 1990s, there were many international telecom companies interested in the Turkish telecommunications market. These included Telefonica (Spain), SBC Communications (US), Vodafone Airtouch (UK), Mannesmann (Germany), Orange, British Telecom, Telecom Italia, Bezeq (Israel), France Telecom and Deutsche Telekom.

A law was passed requiring Turk telecom to be privatized by Spring 2003 and a regulator, the Telecommunications Authority was set up. In November 2005 the company was finally privatized to Oger Telecom. In May 2008, Turk Telekom completed the fifth largest initial public offering (IPO) in the world by selling the 15% of the government stocks worth 2.4 billion dollars. After the sale of these stocks the

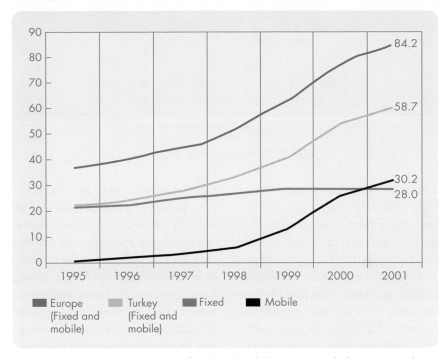

Figure 5: Telephone subscribers (fixed and mobile) per 100 inhabitants in Turkey.
Source: Michael Minges, Turkey ICT Profile, www.itu.int/ITU-D/ict/cs/letters/turkey.html.

new organizational structure comprised: 55% Oger Group, 15% small shareholders and 30% Government of Turkey.

For the wireless communication sector, privatization has long been underway. With two private sector companies already in operation, Turkcell and TelSim, two more companies started operating in the second half of 2001. The market was expanding fast. The number of subscribers was 2.5 million in 1998 and reached 11 million in 2001 (Figure 5). Despite this high growth, the penetration rate was a low 13%, compared to the penetration rates in UK of 23%, France at 29% and Germany at 23%. The number of subscribers was projected to increase to 32 million by 2008, making Turkey one of the five fastest growing wireless markets in Europe.

Turkey's mobile market has grown tremendously. TurkTelekom launched an analogue NMT network in 1986. In 1994, two digital GSM operators, Turkcell and TelSim, launched services in a revenue-sharing arrangement with TurkTelekom. The market leader is Turkcell, with 12 million subscribers. Turkcell shares are traded in IMKB (Istanbul Stock Exchange) and NYSE (New York Stock Exchange); however, a vast

majority belong to Turkish Cukurova Holding, the third largest industrial conglomerate, which also manages the company, and Finnish Sonera, Finland's largest mobile operator. The others in the market, in descending order of number of subscribers, are TelSim, Aria (jointly owned by Turkish Is Bank and TelecomItalia) and Aycell of TurkTelekom. The mobile market was further opened in 2001 when two new GSM 1800 operators introduced service. Aria, owned by TelecomItalia Mobile and Turkish Is Bank, launched in March 2001. In December, TurkTelekom's Aycell began operations.

Official statistics of the Turkish Government claim 16 million Internet users, 21%. There are some 65 ISPs, of which the largest is Superonline, partly owned by Turkcell. TurkTelekom is also active in the market through its national backbone (Turnet), international gateway and dial-up service Ttnet (which features a IP Dial Tone service allowing nationwide Internet access).[14]

There is no Turkish provider of equipment and infrastructure for mobile services. Therefore, Turkish telecom service operators had to rely on external sources. The major equipment and infrastructure

	GSM penetration rate (%)	Number of operators	Population (million)
UK	23	4	59
France	29	3	58
Germany	23	4	82
Turkey	13	4	65

Source: www.tradepartners.gov.uk/text/telecom/turkey/profile/overview.shtml

Table 1: Wireless markets in Europe.

suppliers included Alcatel (France), Ericsson (Sweden), Motorola (US), Nokia (Finland) and Siemens (Germany). Existing equipment and infrastructure provider companies tend to have price and logistics advantages over new entrants. Their long-established relations with the key decision makers and influencers raise the barriers further against entries into the market. In addition, the costs of switching suppliers are high for the service operators. These factors make it quite difficult for latecomers to break into the market as a supplier. Such first-to-market advantages become especially important in the fast growing telecom sector, where the need for new equipment is inevitable (Tables 1 and 2).

TelSim's Foreign Partners and the Default

Motorola and TelSim signed an agreement for the supply and deployment of a third generation (3G) mobile network capable of providing advanced multimedia services, which was worth a total of US$1.9 billion. For Motorola, Turkey was a very promising market. The number of mobile subscribers increased from 1.5 million in 1997 to 8.2 million in 1999. In many countries in Europe, more than half the population owned a mobile phone, while fewer than 10% of Turks did. The Turkish market was also a duopoly, which made the privately held TelSim seem to be a very attractive target for a foreign buyer. To Motorola, TelSim started to look less like a customer and more like a very smart investment bet.

Motorola committed to providing a vendor-financing loan (supplier's credit) to TelSim, to be paid back in instalments. In vendor financing, the supplier company provides the buyer company with loans specifically issued to enable the procurement of its own products/services. There is a rising trend toward vendor financing in order to boost growth and increase market share; however, some consider it quite risky because the borrowers are usually start-ups or growing companies. In the presence of credit-worthy partners, vendor financing is a very wise tactic that can increase sales and help acquire loyal customers. The peak year for vendor financing came in 2000, with US$25 billion to US$30 billion in loans, many of them offered to the fourth or fifth largest carrier in a market.

The promise of a big payday, with a multinational swooping in to drop billions on TelSim, lured Motorola and Nokia into an increasingly tangled relationship with the Uzans. When TelSim asked for more money in September 1999, Motorola executives bit. They agreed to an additional US$215 million loan for equipment and marketing, on the condition that TelSim repay swiftly with new financing guaranteed by a British export–import bank. However, when bankers came to review the company finances, a TelSim employee accused one

Operator	Major owners
Turkcell*	Cukurova Holding 61%, Sonera (Finnish) 39%
TelSim	Rumeli Holding (controlled by the Uzan family)
Aria	Is-Tim (Is Bank of Turkey and TelecomItalia Mobil)
Aycell	TurkTelekom

*Turkcell iletisim Hizmetleri AS.

Table 2: Turkish mobile market leaders.

of them of stealing documents. According to Motorola executives, an irate Hakan Uzan showed up at an Istanbul restaurant where they were dining and refused further access to the company books.[15]

The first instalment to be paid back to Motorola, US$728 million, was due on 30 April 2001. To secure the loan, the deal gave Motorola the option to sell 66% of TelSim shares, which were put up as collateral. Under the original terms of the loan, TelSim would technically default if it failed to pay US$728 million within 30 days of the original payment date.

As part of its ongoing business relations, TelSim signed a similar agreement with Nokia. The deal was worth around US$700 million and the first repayment instalment was US$240 million, in April 2001. The collateral behind the debt was 7.5% of TelSim shares.

When the first payment date arrived, the two telecom giants did not receive any payments. In May 2001, the Uzans claimed that they had liquidity problems after a devaluation of the Turkish lira three months previously.[16] The Uzans argued that the conflict reflects their suppliers' unwillingness to face up to the losses stemming from the global crash in the telecommunications markets, recession in Turkey and the substantial devaluation of the Turkish lira.

In January 2002, Motorola and Nokia jointly sued the family under the RICO Act (Racketeer Influenced and Corrupt Organizations Act, a law often used to indict mobsters) claiming that the Uzans never intended to repay the loans. Their claims were based on the dilution of the collateral: 66% stake of Motorola and 7.5% of Nokia were diluted to 22.5% and 2.5% with a capital increase. The suit was filed in New York because the Uzans had assets in the United States and were listed as residents of the city.[17] It is interesting to note that, in order to win their damages claim under US racketeering legislation, plaintiffs must prove that they were victims of a pattern of behaviour rather than of a simple breach of contract.

The Uzans obtained a Turkish court order saying that the New York lawsuit must be halted. None of the defendants or their lawyers attended the trial in New York. The family has similarly ignored orders entered by a British court, leading to 15-month jail terms being imposed on Kemal Uzan, the family patriarch, and Murat Hakan Uzan and Cem Cengiz Uzan, his two sons. The court also imposed a four-month sentence on Aysegul Akay, their sister. The Uzans have also countered the attack in American and British courts with lawsuits filed in Turkey. They have arranged for criminal charges to be filed against Motorola and Nokia executives, who they say threatened to injure them physically. In a statement printed in the Uzan family owned *Daily Star* newspaper, TelSim said it would seek compensation from both companies for 'unfounded and hurtful' accusations made against it, and would sue Motorola for not fulfilling contracts.

In New York, a judge issued two temporary restraining orders freezing the Uzans' nine residences in New York and US$8 million in funds the family is alleged to have in the United States. He also barred the Uzans from transferring any TelSim assets, took into a depository the stake in the company issued to Standart Telekom and prohibited the family from exercising their voting rights on shares created at a meeting on 4 January 2002. The same judge then revoked the ruling on the 73.5% stake on 15 February, allowing TelSim to remain in Turkish hands for the moment. A similar freezing of Uzan assets occurred in London a few days later.[18]

Following the suit, TelSim denied that the allegations made had any basis, either in law or in fact, and found the suit to be unethical. TelSim said it made numerous attempts to resolve the dispute, which was caused by economic difficulties in Turkey.[19]

Good partnerships are seen as keys to success by foreign investors, especially in nationalistic countries such as Turkey.[20] There are arguments that Motorola chose the wrong partner because the Uzans have been involved in more than 100 criminal and civil cases.[21] Moreover, Turkey's business elite has been virtually united in shunning the Uzans. TUSIAD, the premier businessman's group, refuses to invite any of them to be members.[22] However, Motorola disclosed in early 2002 that the two companies began their relationship in 1994 and there had been no defaults or signs of trouble for about six years. Similarly, Nokia said that TelSim had met its obligations early on.[23]

The Aftermath of the Conflict

The missed first instalments triggered a series of events with significant implications for TelSim, its suppliers, the international business community and the respective governments. The issue became a hot topic between top politicians of the United States and Turkey, and was even discussed by the presidents of each country. The most critical problem is probably the loss of credibility by Turkey and Turkish firms. As stated in *The Economist*: 'Foreigners who want to do business in Turkey will be thinking twice'.[24]

Another impact is expected on global vendor financing. It is expected that such decisions now will be made after deeper investigations and stricter requirements. As a result, growing firms in emerging markets may find fewer finance options.

Motorola and Nokia were blamed for their own wrongdoings. Authorities blamed the two telecom giants for choosing a poor or questionable partner. In recent years, the Uzans have been involved in many disputes ranging from a Polish prosecutor's investigation into losses at their cement works in Nowa Huta to Turkish stock market regulators' long-running battle against irregularities at two publicly traded electricity plants that the Uzans control.

Regardless of the Uzans' questionable business deals in and outside of Turkey, Nokia commented that there was no hint earlier in the dealings with TelSim that difficulties would emerge, and Motorola characterized its pre-default relations with TelSim as on the whole a good one. Another likely error on the part of Motorola and Nokia was the failure to anticipate loopholes in the Turkish legal system. The two companies filed their unusual joint civil action after Rumeli Holding instigated a capital increase diluting TelSim shares held in an escrow account as their collateral for separate loans to Turkey's second cellular operator. During the hearing of the case in New York, Hakan Uzan, the younger brother, said the capital increase was carried out to comply with Turkish company laws.

Motorola and Nokia were also criticized for not taking into account the political and economic risks of doing business in Turkey. Despite the booming economy and an explosive telecommunications market, instability, high inflation, two decades of frequent devaluations and financial crises, uneven income distribution, political failures and distrust for politicians were some of the indicators of a troubled economy.

Questions for Discussion

1. What should Motorola and Nokia have done prior to partnership with the Uzan conglomerate in order potentially to avoid a disastrous relationship? How well informed were they about the Uzans? What criteria should been considered for partner selection? Would better-established conglomerates such as Koc and Sabanci make better partners?

2. Did Motorola and Nokia choose the most appropriate form of partnership with the Uzan family? What should they have done to safeguard their interests?

3. How appropriate was it for Nokia and Motorola to resort to a legal resolution right at the outset? Could they have chosen a different strategy to dispute resolution that would have been more effective in an emerging market situation?

4. What do the plaintiffs aim to gain in court: the money, the prestige or Wall Street's trust? How would the Motorola and Nokia shareholders react?

5. How did the recession in the global economy affect the chain of events? Would the lawsuit still take place during better economic times?

6. How should Western businesspeople better prepare themselves for conducting business in high-growth, yet high-risk, emerging markets? What strategies and guidelines should they follow?

Case Study 7

TOYOTA EUROPE

It was January 2002, and Toyota Motor Europe Manufacturing (TMEM) had a problem. More specifically, Mr Toyoda Shuhei, the new President of TMEM, had a problem. He was on his way to Toyota Motor Company's (Japan) corporate offices outside Tokyo to explain the continuing losses of European manufacturing and sales operations. The CEO of Toyota Motor Company, Mr Hiroshi Okuda, was expecting a proposal from Mr Shuhei to reduce and eventually eliminate the European losses. The situation was intense given that TMEM was the only major Toyota subsidiary suffering losses.

Toyota Motor Company was the number one car manufacturer in Japan, the third largest manufacturer in the world by unit sales (5.5 million units or one vehicle every six seconds), but number eight in sales in Continental Europe. The global car manufacturing industry had been experiencing, like many industries, continued consolidation in recent years as margins were squeezed, economies of scale and scope pursued, and global sales slowed.

Toyota was no different. It had continued to rationalize its manufacturing along regional lines. Toyota had continued to increase the amount of local manufacturing in North America. In 2001, more than 60% of Toyota's North American sales were locally manufactured. But Toyota's European sales were nowhere close to this. Most of Toyota's car and truck manufacturing for Europe was still done in Japan. In 2001 only 26% of the cars sold in Europe were manufactured in Europe (including the UK), the remainder being imported from Japan (see Figure 1).

Toyota Motor Europe sold 634 000 cars in 2000. This was the second largest foreign market for Toyota, second only to North America. TMEM expected significant growth in European sales, and was planning to expand European manufacturing and sales to 800 000 units by 2005. But for fiscal year 2001, the unit reported operating losses of ¥9.897 billion (US$82.5 million at ¥120/US$). TMEM had

three assembly plants in the UK, one plant in Turkey and one plant in Portugal. In November 2000, Toyota Motor Europe announced that it would not generate positive profits for the next two years due to the weakness of the euro.

Toyota had recently introduced a new model to the European market, the Yaris, which was proving very successful. The Yaris, a super-small vehicle with a 1000cc engine, had sold more than 180 000 units in 2000. Although the Yaris had been specifically designed for the European market, the decision had been made early on to manufacture it in Japan.

Currency Exposure

The primary source of the continuing operating losses suffered by TMEM was the falling value of the euro. Over the recent two year period the euro had fallen in value against both the Japanese yen and the British pound. As demonstrated in Figure 1, the cost base for most of the cars sold within the Continental European market was the Japanese yen. Figure 2 illustrates the slide of the euro against the Japanese yen.

As the yen rose against the euro, costs increased significantly when measured in euro-terms. If Toyota wished to preserve its price competitiveness in the European market, it had to absorb most of the exchange rate changes, suffering reduced or negative margins on both completed cars and key subcomponents shipped to its European manufacturing centres. Deciding to manufacture the Yaris in Japan had only exacerbated the problem.

Management Response

Toyota management was not sitting passively by. In 2001 they had started up some assembly operations in Valenciennes, France. Although a relatively small percentage of total European sales as of January 2002, Toyota planned to continue to expand its capacity and capabilities to source about 25% of European sales by 2004. Assembly of the Yaris was

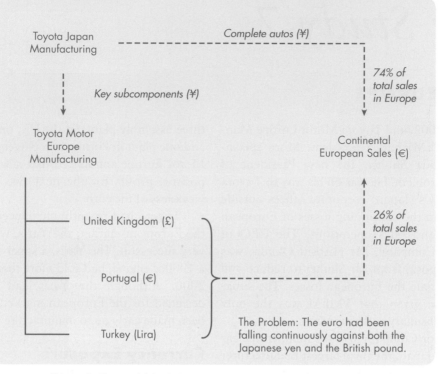

Figure 1: Toyota Motor's European currency operating structure.

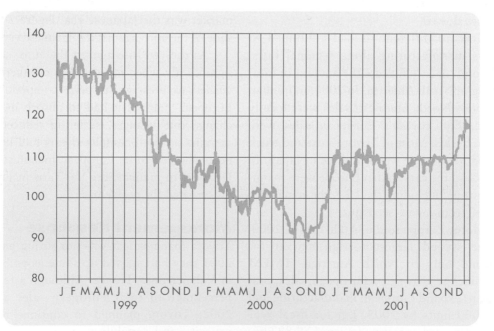

Figure 2: Daily exchange rates: Japanese yen per euro.

Source: © 2003 by Prof. Werner Antweiler, University of British Columbia, Vancouver, BC, Canada.

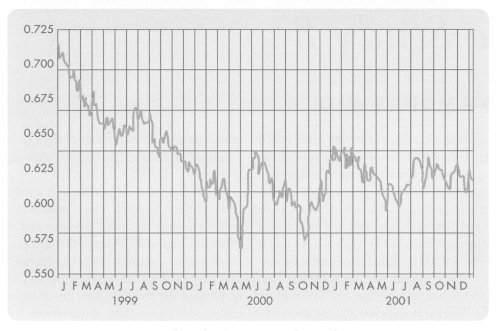

Figure 3: Daily exchange rates: British pounds per euro.

Source: © 2003 by Prof. Werner Antweiler, University of British Columbia, Vancouver, BC, Canada.

scheduled to be moved to Valenciennes in 2002. The continuing problem, however, was that it was an assembly facility, meaning that much of the expensive value-added content of the cars being assembled was still based in either Japan or the United Kingdom.

Mr Shuhei, with the approval of Mr Okuda, had also initiated a local-sourcing and procurement programme for the UK manufacturing operations. TMEM wished to decrease the number of key components imported from Toyota Japan to reduce the currency exposure of the UK unit. But again, the continuing problem of the British pound's value against the euro, as shown in Figure 3, reduced even the effectiveness of this solution.

Questions for Discussion

1. Why do you think Toyota had waited so long to move much of its manufacturing for European sales to Europe?
2. If you were Mr Shuhei, how would you categorize your problems and solutions? What was a short-term and what was a long-term problem?
3. What measures would you recommend Toyota Europe take to resolve the continuing operating losses?

Source: Copyright © 2002 Thunderbird, the American Graduate School of International Management. All rights reserved. This case was prepared by Professor Michael H. Moffett for the purpose of classroom discussion only, and not to indicate either effective or ineffective management.

Case Study 8

WHEN DIAMONDS WEEP

They may be prehistoric pieces of highly compressed carbon, but diamonds play an important role in the world economy. They are found in nature, as opposed to synthetic diamonds, which are produced in laboratories. Mining companies search for deposits deep underground, but natural diamonds are also found along riverbanks enabling anyone with a sieve and a spade to find one. In 2001, global production of natural, rough (meaning uncut and unpolished) diamonds was US$7.8 billion in value and 117 million carats in weight (one carat equals 0.2 g). As shown in Figure 1, in 2006, the top six natural diamond-producing countries accounted for more than 90% of the world's rough diamond supply.

From Mine to Market

Once diamonds have been excavated, they are sorted, by hand, into grades. Although there are thousands of categories and subcategories based on the size, quality, colour and shape of the diamonds, there are two broad categories of diamonds – gem-grade and industrial-grade. Approximately 59% of the 2001 production was of gem-quality. In addition to jewellery, gem quality stones are used for collections, exhibits and decorative art objects. Industrial diamonds, because of their hardness and abrasive qualities, are often used in the medical field, in space programmes and for diamond tools.

After the diamonds have been sorted, they are transported to one of the world's four main diamond trading centres: Antwerp, Belgium, which is the largest; New York; Tel Aviv, Israel; and Mumbai, India. Between 5 and 10 million individual stones pass through the Antwerp trading centre each day. After they have been purchased, the diamonds are sent off to be cut, polished and/or otherwise processed. Five locations currently dominate the diamond-processing industry: India, which is the largest (processing 9 out of every 10 diamonds); Israel; Belgium; Thailand; and New York. Finally, the polished diamonds are sold by

manufacturers, brokers and dealers to importers and wholesalers all over the world, who in turn, sell to retailers.

Global retail sales of diamond jewellery surpassed US$60 billion in 2001. The United States is by far the world's leading diamond importer and market for the gems (see Figure 2). Despite the effects of the 11 September 2001 terrorist attacks, overall US diamond jewellery sales for 2001 amounted to US$26.1 billion, or 44% of the total market, down by only 1% from the previous year. One explanation for the smaller than expected drop was that purchases of engagement rings rose dramatically after the attacks – a trend that continued through 2001.

The total time from extraction to the time at which the diamond is sold to the end consumer is called the 'pipeline' and usually takes about two years.

The De Beers Dynasty

For more than a century, a single company has controlled the diamond industry – De Beers. De Beers was founded in the late nineteenth century by the infamous colonial capitalist Cecil Rhodes after the discovery of the Kimberley diamond fields in South Africa. In its early years, the company produced more than 90% of the world's diamonds. However, rival producers entered the market in the early twentieth century, which challenged De Beers' pre-eminence. Now a privately held company with offices in London and Johannesburg, De Beers currently controls about 60% of the world diamond supply. Furthermore, about two thirds (by value) of the world's annual supply of rough diamonds are sorted and valued through De Beers' subsidiary Diamond Trading Company (DTC).

In addition to the diamonds that De Beers acquires from the 20 mines it operates in South Africa, Namibia and Botswana, De Beers also buys excess diamonds on the market to maintain a stable market price. All the diamonds that De Beers acquires

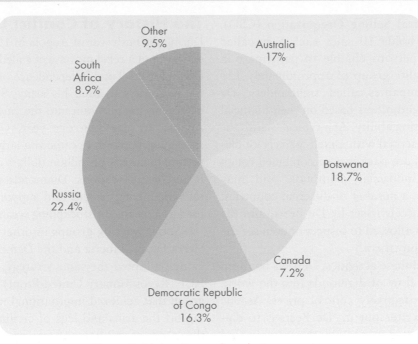

Figure 1: Major diamond-producing countries.

Source: Data taken from Donald W. Olson, 'Diamond, Industrial', *US Geological Survey 2006 Minerals Yearbook*, 2006, http://minerals.usgs.gov/minerals/pubs/commodity/diamond/myb1-2006-diamo.pdf, accessed 9 June 2008.

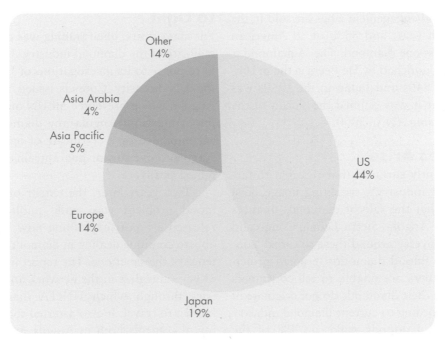

Figure 2: Global retail sales of diamond jewellery.

Source: Adapted from 'Conflict Diamonds', *Global Witness*, p. 3, www.oneworld.org/globalwitness, accessed 28 March 2003.

flow into the Central Selling Organization (CSO). This organization holds 10 sales each year called 'sights'. The only persons eligible to participate in these sales are an elite group of approximately 120 individuals and companies called 'sightholders'. De Beers chooses its sightholders based on their financial stability and marketing ability. At a typical 'sight', the sightholders are presented with mixed 'parcels' of diamonds. The parcels are packages of combined rough gem-quality and industrial diamonds, and may include stones from a number of different countries. The price of the parcels is set by De Beers, and the sightholders are not allowed to inspect or even see the parcels before they buy them.

As a result of all these activities, DeBeers has been able to control the flow of diamonds into the world market and thus, effectively control prices. As one *Washington Post* writer put it, 'De Beers is to diamonds what the Wizard was to Oz: the entity behind the curtain pulling the strings'.[1]

Diamonds have long held a certain mystique. Thanks in large part to De Beers' skilful marketing efforts, diamonds have taken on an aura of rarity and eternity. Prior to the 1930s, diamond rings were rarely given as engagement rings. Today, more than 1.7 million diamond engagement rings are sold in the United States each year, and 85% of all American women own at least one diamond. The 'A diamond is forever' campaign launched by De Beers in the in United States in the 1940s and Japan in the 1960s was such a success that it was dubbed the slogan of the century by *Advertising Age* in 2000.

Controversies Arise

Reports have recently surfaced that threaten to tarnish the diamond industry's sparkling image. The reports revealed that the sale of diamonds finances deadly conflicts in Angola, Sierra Leone, Congo and Liberia. The controversy around these so-called 'conflict diamonds' or 'blood diamonds' erupted principally because retailers are unable to tell consumers with certainty that their diamonds do not originate in conflict areas. According to current diamond industry estimates, conflict diamonds make up 4% of the annual global production of diamonds. However, human rights advocates disagree with that number. They argue that as many as 15% of all diamonds on the market could be conflict diamonds.

The History of Conflict Diamonds

During the bush war of Angola in 1992, Jonas Savimbi was head of a rebel movement called UNITA (National Union for the Total Independence of Angola). Looking for new ways to fund his army, Savimbi decided to extend his organization into the vast diamond fields of Angola. In less than one year, UNITA's diamond-smuggling network became the largest in the world – netting hundreds of million dollars a year, with which it purchased weapons. Diamonds were also a useful tool for buying friends and supporters and could be used as a means for stockpiling wealth.

Soon, warring groups in other countries such as Sierra Leone, Liberia and the Democratic Republic of Congo adopted the same strategy. For example, the RUF (Revolutionary United Front) in Sierra Leone, a group that achieved international notoriety for hacking off the arms and legs of civilians and abducting thousands of children and forcing them to fight as soldiers, has controlled the country's alluvial diamond fields since 1998. Although, the civil war itself has finished, disturbances continue. The RUF developed into a political party in 2003, which existed until 2007.

Investigators Bring Problem to Light

For many years, illicit trading was disregarded by the majority of the diamond industry. However, in 1998, in response to its investigations of UNITA in Angola, the UN Security Council issued sanctions against Angola, which prevented all UN member states from importing from Angola any diamond that was not accompanied by a certificate of origin issued by the Angolan government guaranteeing that it had been mined legally.

Two years later, the extent of the conflict diamond problem was made public when the UN released a report explaining how UNITA had been able to continue dealing in diamonds despite the existence of the sanctions. The report included the names of key smugglers in the network and cities and countries through which UNITA diamonds had been known to travel. It also asserted that a lack of meaningful controls both in Angola and in the Antwerp diamond-trading centre may have actually encouraged the illegal trading activity. The problem in Angola, according to the report, was that virtually anyone in Angola could legally possess, buy or sell diamonds within the country. There were five buying companies officially licensed by the government, but these buying companies employed many subcontractors. Because the subcontracted buyers worked on a commission basis, they had a financial incentive not to care about the origin of the diamonds. So, UNITA diamonds had no trouble finding their way into the official channels. The report also accused the Belgian authorities of failing to establish an effective import identification scheme and also of failing to monitor the activities of suspect brokers, dealers and traders.

Since the report was released, the UN Security Council has imposed additional sanctions on diamond dealing in Liberia and now interdicts diamond trade from the rebel-held areas of Sierra Leone as well. However, only a few countries have enacted laws to implement these sanctions.

In 2002, trade statistics were circulated by several human-rights groups. The data showed that the quantity of diamond imports listed from certain countries on the books in Antwerp did not match the quantity of exports listed for those same countries (see Table 1). Furthermore, countries that did not even have working mines were reported as exporting large quantities of

diamonds. Apparently, the origin of many of the diamonds entering Antwerp had been changed or disguised.

Ties to Terrorist Groups

The issue of conflict diamonds has taken on even greater policy significance after the 11 September 2001 terrorist attacks in the United States. Evidence emerged that diamonds were being used by terrorist organizations, including al Qaeda and Hezbollah, as a channel for transferring wealth around the world. Diamonds do not set off alarms at airports, they can't be sniffed by dogs, they are easy to hide and are highly convertible to cash. According to US and European intelligence officials, diamond dealers working directly with men identified by the FBI as key operatives in the al Qaeda network purchased gems from the RUF rebels in Sierra Leone. The Sierra Leoneans were desperate for cash and were unable to sell directly in the diamond markets of Tel Aviv and Antwerp because of the sanctions. As a result, they sold the diamonds at a deep discount to al Qaeda middle men who smuggled the diamonds into Liberia, Monrovia and other countries where they would

	1994	1995	1996	1997	1998	1999
Official exports from Sierra Leone	30.2	22.0	27.6	10.5	1.8	1.2
Declared Belgian imports from Sierra Leone	106.6	15.3	93.4	114.9	65.8	30.4
Difference	76.4	(6.7)	65.8	104.4	64	29.2
Official exports from Cote d'Ivoire	3.1	2.9	2.4	4	3.6	4.6
Declared Belgian imports from Cote d'Ivoire	93.6	54.2	204.2	119.9	45.3	52.6
Difference	90.5	51.3	201.8	115.9	41.6	48
Official exports from Liberia	No data because of civil war, although no official exports are likely to have occurred				0.8	0.9
Declared Belgian imports from Liberia	283.9	392.4	616.2	329.2	269.9	298.8
Difference	283.9	392.4	616.2	329.2	269.1	297.9
Official exports from Guinea	28.6	34.7	35.5	46.9	40.7	40.2
Declared Belgian imports from Guinea	165.7	26.2	83.6	108.1	116.1	127.1
Difference	137.1	−8.5	48.1	61.2	75.4	86.9
Official exports from Gambia	0	0	0	0	0	0
Declared Belgian imports from Gambia	74.1	14.9	128.1	131.4	103.4	58
Difference	74.1	14.9	128.1	131.4	103.4	58

Source: Ian Smillie, 'The Kimberley Process: The Case For Proper Monitoring', September 2002, www.partnershipafricacanada.org, accessed 28 March 2003

Table 1: Belgian diamond imports compared with exports from certain countries (US$ millions).

eventually sell the diamonds through legitimate channels for huge profits. Although the exact amount is unknown, intelligence officials believe that al Qaeda has reaped millions of dollars in virtually untraceable funds from the illicit sale of diamonds since 1998.

The Kimberley Process

On 5 November 2002, representatives from 52 countries, along with mining executives, diamond dealers and members from advocacy groups, met in Interlaken, Switzerland to sign an agreement that they hoped would eliminate conflict diamonds from international trade. The agreement was called the Kimberley Process and took effect on 1 January 2003.

The Kimberley Process is a United Nations-backed certification plan created to ensure that only legally mined rough diamonds, untainted by conflict, reach established markets around the world. According to the plan, all rough diamonds passing through or into a participating country must be transported in sealed, tamper-proof containers and be accompanied by a government-issued certificate guaranteeing the container's contents and origin. Customs officials in importing countries are required to certify that the containers have not been tampered with and are instructed to seize all diamonds that do not meet the requirements.

The agreement also stipulates that only those countries that subscribe to the new rules will be able to trade legally in rough diamonds. Countries that break the rules will be suspended and their diamond-trading privileges will be revoked. Furthermore, individual diamond traders who disobey the rules will be subject to punishment under the laws of their own countries.

Critics Speak Out

Several advocacy groups have voiced concerns that the Kimberley Process remains open to abuse, and that it will not be enough to stop the flow of conflict diamonds. Many worry that bribery and forgery are inevitable and that corrupt governments officials will render the scheme inoperable. Even those diamonds with certified histories attached may not be trustworthy.

The General Accounting Office (GAO), the investigative arm of the US Congress, also voiced concerns in a 2002 report: [T]he period after rough diamonds enter the first foreign port until the final point of sale is covered by a system of voluntary industry participation and self-regulated monitoring and enforcement. These and other shortcomings provide significant challenges in creating an effective scheme to deter trade in conflict diamonds.[2]

In response to the GAO's statement, the State Department said that it was more important to establish the accountability measures now than to debate how they could be improved. A De Beers spokesperson shared the same sentiments in a 2002 speech in London saying, 'What we have now is certainly not a perfect construct, the system is not absolutely watertight, and there are still a number of outstanding anomalies. It is, however, the best compromise that could be agreed without placing intolerable burdens on the industry.'[3]

The US Response

In late 2002, the US House of Representatives passed the 'Clean Diamond Trade Act', legislation that would have fully implemented the Kimberley Process recommendations in the United States. However, the bill died when the Senate failed to act on it during the same term. In response to the bill's demise, the State Department announced in early 2003 that it would 'work expeditiously with Congress to pass legislation as soon as possible'.[4] Even without the legislation, the US diamond industry started to implement the Kimberley plan in 2003.

In late February of 2003, the WTO Council for Trade in Goods agreed that countries could block trade in conflict diamonds despite the fact that by doing so, they would violate several articles of the GATT, because of 'the extraordinary humanitarian nature of this issue'.[5] Many applauded the announcement as an important step in getting US legislation moving forward.

New Technologies Offer Solutions

Recently, a number of new technologies have emerged which, if adopted by the diamond industry worldwide, could change the way that diamonds are mined, traded and sold. One emerging technology is laser engraving. Lasers make it possible to mark diamonds – either in their rough or cut stage – with a symbol, number or bar code that can help to identify that diamond whenever verification is necessary. Companies that adopt the technology have an interesting marketing opportunity to sell brands of diamonds. Establishing brand awareness and building equity in its name, these companies hope, will add value to the diamond and help increase consumer confidence. Sirius Diamonds, a Vancouver-based cutting and polishing company, now microscopically laser engraves a polar bear logo and an identification number on each gem it processes. Another company, 3Beams Technologies of the United States, is currently working on a system to embed a bar code inside a diamond (as opposed to on its surface), which would make it much more difficult to remove.

Another option is the 'invisible fingerprint' invented by a Canadian security company called Identex. The technology works by electronically placing an invisible information package on each stone. The fingerprint can include any information that the producer desires, such as the mine source and production date. The data can only be read by Identex's own scanners. Unfortunately, once the diamond is cut, the fingerprint will be lost, although it can be reapplied at any time. Clearly, this represents a major drawback to the technology because it can be abused. Nevertheless, the technology's creators believe that it will soon become an industry standard because it is a quick and cost-effective away to analyse a stone. The technology will supplement the security of paper certification, or could eventually replace it, says Identex's president Bob Jennens.

Finally, processes are being developed to read a diamond's internal fingerprint – its unique sparkle and combination of impurities – with a machine called a Laser Raman Spectroscope (LRS). A worldwide database could identify a diamond's origin and track its journey from the mine to end consumer. However, industry expert Martin Irving is not optimistic about the chances that such a database could ever be created. There is also the problem of volume. Currently, nine out of every ten diamonds are polished in India, but there is only one LRS machine in the entire country

Questions for Discussion

1. In light of the conflict diamond issue, would you buy a diamond? Why or why not?
2. Do you think that the Kimberley Process certification plan will help decrease the global trade in conflict diamonds? Why or why not?
3. Why do you think the diamond industry in the United States began implementing the certification scheme even before it had garnered proper legislative support?
4. Should the US limit its importing of diamonds only to those countries that can effectively guarantee (e.g., through laser engravings or digital fingerprints) that they are 'clean' diamonds?

Sources: This case was prepared by Alison M. Hager under the supervision of Professor Michael R. Czinkota of Georgetown University. David Finlayson, 'Preserving diamond's integrity', *Vancouver Sun*, 23 December 2002; 'A crook's best friend', *The Economist*, 4 January 2003; Philip T. Reeker, 'Implementing the Kimberley Process', 2 January 2003, www.diamonds.net, accessed 28 March 2003; Robert R. Fowler, 'Final Report of the UN Panel of Experts on Violations of Security Council Sanctions Against UNITA', (S/2000/203) 10 March 2000; 'Al Qaeda Cash Tied to Diamond Trade', *The Washington Post*, 2 November 2001; 'Conflict and Security; Conflict Diamonds are Forever', *Africa News*, 8 November, 2002; 'US: Blood Diamond Plan Too Soft', *Associated Press Online*, 18 June 2002; Lynne, Duke 'Diamond Trade's Tragic Flaw', *Washington Post*, 29 April 2001; Alan Cowell, '40 Nations in Accord on 'Conflict Diamonds'', *The New York Times*, 6 November 2002; Rory M. O'Ferrall, 'De Beers O'Ferrall Calls Kimberley End of Beginning', 2 December 2002, www.diamonds.net, accessed 28 March 2003; Donald W. Olson, 'Gemstones', US Survey Minerals Yearbook, 2001, http://www.minerals.usgs.gov/minerals/pubs/, accessed 28 March 2003; Donald W. Olson, 'Diamond, Industrial', US Survey Minerals Yearbook, 2001, http://www.minerals. usgs.gov/minerals/pubs/, accessed 28 March 2003; Lucy Jones,, 'Diamond industry rough to regulate; Central African Republic works to monitor gem trade', *The Washington Times*, 22 August 2002; Amarendra Jha, 'Diamond Pact Hits Surat Cutters', *The Times of India*, 28 December 2002; Ian Smillie, 'The Kimberley Process: The Case for Proper Monitoring', Partnership Africa Canada, September 2002, www.partnershipafricacanda.org, accessed 28 March 2003; Jeffrey Sparshott, 'WTO Targets Conflict Diamonds', *The Washington Times*, 1 March 2003; http://www.keyguide.net; www.debeersgroup.com.

Case Study 9

BUILDING A COMPETITIVE ADVANTAGE IN A MATURE INDUSTRY: THE CASE OF GORENJE

Introduction

Gorenje d.d. is a Slovenian multinational company in the household appliance industry. Located in Slovenia, the company annually produces and sells 3.7 million large household appliances in 70 countries. Although it enjoys a strong market presence, most of its sales are realized in Europe, where Gorenje has a 4% market share. Specifically, Gorenje sells 59% of its products in EU countries, 34% in Eastern Europe and only 7% in non-European countries. It sells 75% of its output under its own brand name and in 2007 had a consolidated revenue of €1.270 million: 80% of the revenue is generated from household appliances, 5% from home interior design and 15% from trade and services.

As a multinational firm operating on a smaller scale compared to the most important players in the industry, Gorenje faces many challenges. It operates in a mature industry, where disruptive innovations are less common, and therefore firms focus on gaining cost advantage as well as customizing products to better satisfy customer needs.

Gorenje's Timeline

1950–1960

- The establishment of Gorenje in a tiny village that bears the same name. Initially the company was involved in the manufacture of agricultural machinery and the provision of building materials.
- In 1958 it expanded its operations to the production of solid-fuel cookers.
- This was followed by a relocation to the nearby town of Velenje and the construction of new assembly facilities.

1961–1970

- The company expanded its production to washing machines and refrigerators and become the leading household appliances manufacturer in Yugoslavia.
- In 1961 Gorenje exported for the first time – 200 cookers to Germany.

1971–1980

- Gorenje began to take over other enterprises.
- Its product range extended to the manufacture of kitchen units, ceramics, medical equipment, telecommunications devices, TV sets and other electrical goods.
- The company employed over 20 000 people across Yugoslavia
- First steps were made to establish a distribution and sales network in Germany, Austria, France, Denmark, Australia and Italy.

1981–1990

- A period marked by disinvestment from non-profitable manufacturing and commercial operations and a consequent refocusing on household appliances.
- Export markets expanded to include UK and the USA.

1991–1996

- A thorough restructuring of Gorenje, away from socialist self-management system to a stock exchange listed, fully privatized company operating in a developing market economy.
- Due to the loss of the domestic market caused by the disintegration of Yugoslavia, reorientation towards export markets took place.
- Establishment of companies in Eastern Europe (Czech Republic, Hungary, Poland, Bulgaria and Slovakia).
- Enterprises were re-established in the new states that had arisen from the disintegration of Yugoslavia.

1997–2005

- Gorenje, d.d., became a public company.
- Invested in new products and technology: opening up of new markets, ecologically-sound and cutting-edge technologies.
- Acquisition of Mora Moravia, a.s., cooking appliances producer from Czech Republic.

2006
- Opened a new plant for refrigerators and freezers in Serbia.
- Introduction of the design product lines Gorenje Pininfarina.
- Initiation of a partnership with the top designer Ora Ïto and Gorenje.

2007
- Acquisition of the company Surovina, d.d.
- New designer product line Ora Ïto launched in Istanbul.
- 15% capital increase and additional shares were listed on a prime market of Ljubljana Stock Exchange.

The Household Appliance Industry

The household appliance industry is a mature industry with steady demand. Global demand for major household appliances is expected to grow 3.9% annually through 2009. The industry is highly concentrated and competitive. The main global players are Whirlpool, Electrolux, Matsushita, Haier, BSHG and General Electric. In Europe, four companies (Electrolux, BSHG, Whirlpool and Merloni) hold approximately 60% of the European market and dictate the trends in the industry. The first three are global players that enjoy economies of scale and invest extensively in product innovation and marketing, whereas the Indesit Company (Merloni) is a regional player. All four companies are growing organically as well as through acquisitions. This group of leading firms is followed by a second tier of companies (Gorenje, Candy, Arcelic, Fagor and Miele) that hold market share between 2 and 7%. Whereas the first four of these companies are growing by enlarging their brand portfolio and through acquisitions, Miele focuses on the production and marketing of premium products targeted at high-end consumers. Both groups of incumbent firms are being challenged by Asian low-cost players (e.g., Haier), which are pushing industry prices downwards thus forcing the competition to streamline operations (Table 1).

Although the European household appliance market is mature and highly concentrated, consumer preferences differ substantially among countries for all three important large domestic appliance categories (washers, refrigerators/freezers and stoves/ovens). For example, in Germany customers mainly purchase electric appliances, whereas in France and in Italy customers also purchase gas stoves and ovens (30% of the units sold within the category). Moreover, in France and Great Britain customers mainly buy free-standing refrigerators/freezers (approximately 80% of units sold within the category), whereas German

Strengths		Weaknesses	
Pan-European players	*Regional players*	*Pan-European players*	*Regional players*
• Strong brand awareness	• Flexible production	• Overcapacity	• Mono brand strategy
• Innovative products	• Aggressive regional retailing	• Complex production	• Local production and distribution
• Cost cutting		• Low flexibility	• Limited sales potential
• Market share gains from small players		• Pricing pressure	• Pricing pressures
Opportunities		Threats	
Pan-European players	*Regional players*	*Pan-European players*	*Regional players*
• Restructuring benefits	• Niche products	• Losing market share	• Takeover candidates
• Emerging markets	• Premium pricing	• Asian players	• Losing market share
• Expansion overseas		• Higher imports	• Losing margins
		• Increased retail competition	

Table 1: SWOT analysis for European home appliance companies.

customers also buy built-in or built-under refrigerators/freezers (approximately 45% of units sold within the category, whereas free-standing appliances have a 50% market share). Customer preferences also differ with respect to washing machines. For example, in Germany almost 90% of washing machines sold are front-loading and the remainder are top-loaders. In contrast, in France sales are equally split between the two designs.

In addition to product preferences, European consumers also differ in terms of marketing channel preferences. Specifically, in France a large market share of sales is held by hypermarkets, whereas Spanish and Swedish consumers purchase appliances to a larger extent at specialized retail chains. Belgians and Germans shop at independent outlets, where the focus is on long-term relations. In Eastern Europe not all retail formats are available and consumers are therefore more limited in choice, but many international retail chains are also investing rapidly in all these markets and are already present in most of them.

Finally, the industry stage in the life cycle differs among markets. Specifically, in Western Europe the industry is in the mature stage, whereas in some Eastern European countries the industry is still in the growth stage.

Although the European markets differ, it is possible to identify some major common trends:

- *Product customization:* During purchasing decisions, consumers not only evaluate functional product features, but also base their decisions on product image. Specifically, consumers search for appliances whose image reflects their personality.
- *Changing lifestyles:* In developed countries, the portion of consumers who prepare meals at home has been decreasing. Eating out is especially popular among the younger generation and this has a direct influence on consumer habits. In addition, the percentage of single households has increased dramatically in the last 10 years.
- *Importance of design:* The kitchen has become a central and integral part of the home, a place where family members meet and a place where they spend time with friends. Therefore, design plays an important role not only in the living room, but also in the kitchen.

- *Increased ecological awareness:* Consumers are increasingly considering product characteristics in view of savings in energy and water consumption when purchasing large household appliances. In addition, the EU is implementing directives that require an assessment of all significant environmental aspects of energy-using products and recycling of electronic and electrical waste.
- *Consolidation:* There has been a wave of mergers and acquisitions in the industry. The single biggest event in 2006 was Whirlpool's acquisition of Maytag. The industry is expected to consolidate further in the future.
- *Production move to emerging markets:* European appliance production continues its eastward migration, with manufacturing capacity mushrooming in Poland, Hungary, Serbia, Russia and Turkey.
- *Entry of low-cost Asian companies:* Although the industry is mature and has many barriers to entry, there is a risk of new entrants; mainly low-cost Asian companies (e.g., Haier and Arcelik).

Gorenje's Business Strategy

Gorenje d.d. is a niche household appliance manufacturer that simultaneously pursues low-cost and differentiation strategies. Gorenje tries to achieve lower production costs and reap economies of scale by transferring the production of low-end products to developing countries, a necessary step given the high labour costs in Europe. Gorenje has a production facility for stoves in the Czech Republic and for refrigerators in Serbia. Along with a cost-efficiency strategy, Gorenje also employs a differentiation strategy based on cutting-edge design. Industrial design at Gorenje focuses not only on aesthetic features, but also on functional product features. In line with this strategy, Gorenje has been working in partnerships with renowned designers. For example, Gorenje has developed a premium line of refrigerators with Pinifarina, branded Gorenje Pininfarina.

Gorenje has a centralized R&D function that is divided into three matrix-organized strategic technological units, headed by central locations: stoves and ovens, washers and dryers, and refrigerators and freezers. Gorenje does not engage in basic research, but instead focuses on development activities. Because of this, the company co-operates closely with suppliers and other partners to incorporate new technologies into innovative products. An important role is played by the electronics department, which supports the development of new large home appliances with modern electronic components. Efficiency and effectiveness during the product development and production process are continuously improved by implementing concurrent engineering, the Six Sigma quality management concept, the 20 Keys method and so on.

Gorenje manages a portfolio of four brands – Gorenje, Sidex, Körting and Mora – which represent two-thirds of the company's sales (the remaining third of sales comes from the OEM business) (Figure 1). The principal brand is Gorenje, which aims to become the leading European brand in household appliance design. The core values that support this strategic orientation are a design-driven philosophy, innovation, trend-setting and inspiration. Gorenje is a pan-European brand, meaning that it has a unified identity and positioning among all the European markets. Household appliances that are branded Gorenje target the upper-middle and middle segments. Product quality and pricing are also tailored to the two selected target segments.

In addition to these two segments, the company also targets high-end customers with the premium line Gorenje Pininfarina and the most upscale customers with niche luxury products, such as the *Smart Table* (a dining table with a pop-up refrigerator), the *Gorenje Fridge-Freezer with Swarovski Crystals* (a refrigerator encrusted with 7000 hand-embedded crystals and controlled via a touch-screen mounted on its door) and other premium products. Thus the Gorenje brand has a wide positioning. The main idea is to make a design-driven line of products available to all target segments. In contrast to Gorenje, Sidex, Körting and Mora are regional brands. Whereas Sidex targets low-end segments in countries such as France, Germany and Slovenia, the brands Körting and Mora target the middle – low segments in countries such as Greece, Italy and Germany.

Gorenje's Internationalization Strategy

Gorenje has a wide global market presence (more than 70 countries), although it mainly operates in European markets. In most European markets Gorenje has direct investments, mainly comprising sales branches (e.g., in Russia, Ukraine and China) and subsidiaries (e.g., in EU countries), whereas in non-European markets it uses exporting as a mode of market entry and servicing (e.g., in the US, Canada, Australia, Argentina, Brazil, India, Japan, etc.; see Table 2).

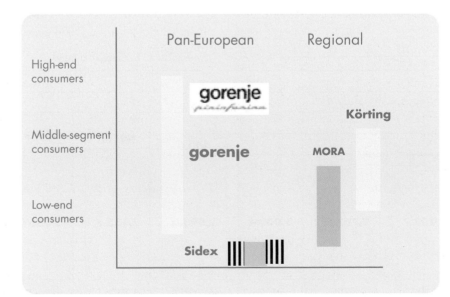

Figure 1: Gorenje branding strategies.

Representative office	Russia (2), Ukraine, Kazakhstan, Greece, China and Kosovo
Sales subsidiary	• EU countries: Austria (2), Germany, United Kingdom, France, Italy, Spain, Belgium, Finland, Sweden, Denmark, Estonia, Latvia, Lithuania, Poland, Slovakia, Hungary, Bulgaria, Romania • Non-EU countries: Norway, Croatia, Bosnia-Herzegovina, Macedonia, Montenegro, Turkey and the United Arab Emirates
Production and sales subsidiary	The Czech Republic and Serbia

Table 2: Gorenje's investments by entry mode.

Although Gorenje has high brand awareness in Europe, its market share varies widely in each European marker (see Figures 2 and 3). It is possible to distinguish three groups of countries:

• Southeastern European countries (such as Slovenia, Croatia, Bosnia, Serbia, etc.), where Gorenje is the market leader. It has established sales subsidiaries in these markets and, in the case of Serbia, also has

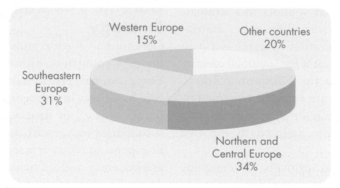

Figure 2: Gorenje large household appliance unit sales by region in 2006.

Note: *Northern and Central Europe* includes Germany, the Netherlands, Austria, Scandinavian countries, the Czech Republic, Slovakia, Hungary and Poland. *Southeastern Europe* includes all former Yugoslav countries and Albania. *Western Europe* includes the UK, Ireland, France, Belgium, Spain, Portugal, Italy, Greece, Cyprus, Turkey and Andorra. *Other countries* include the US, Australia, countries in the Middle East and Far East, Russia, Ukraine, Bulgaria and Romania.

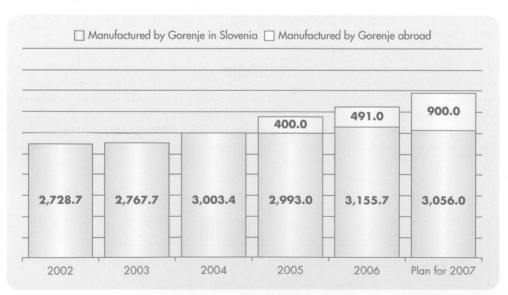

Figure 3: Number of manufactured household appliances by year (in '000s household appliances).

a production subsidiary. Due to its leading market position, the company's marketing activities are oriented towards end consumers.

- Northeastern European countries (such as the Czech Republic, Slovakia, Bulgaria, Scandinavia and the Baltic countries), where Gorenje is among the leading brands. In these countries, it uses a mix of push and pull strategy to increase market penetration.
- Northwestern European countries (Germany, France, the UK, Italy, Spain, Greece, etc.), where Gorenje is one among many players in the industry. In these markets it has sales subsidiaries and engages in marketing activities tailored to intermediaries in order to gain shelf space and increase market presence.

The Future

Gorenje is focused on a balanced utilization of all production capacities and maximizing profit margin as the key criteria of economic performance. It is investing in continued development of new products and services. This has increased its market competitiveness and enabled high-end product placement and higher value added. Business performance has been increasingly based on simultaneously seeking engineering-technological solutions to lower the cost of production and the cost of distribution of existing products. Future growth of business activities is projected in the household appliances division, with the main emphasis placed on appliances with higher margins.

Gorenje has been optimizing the supply chain and seeking alternative and/or new sources of supply in Asia, on other US dollar supply markets and in the countries of Eastern Europe to ensure the price competitiveness of its products. The company has been working on selective implementation of new investment projects with priority given to new products and markets.

Risk management has become more important for the growth of the business due to the highly changeable international business environment. This has been recognized as key for minimizing credit (payment) risks, in particular in the high-risk markets and the markets characterized by lower liquidity.

Discussion Questions

1. Gorenje is an independent company competing in the mature home appliance industry. What are Gorenje's most important sources of competitive advantage?
2. What strategies and tactics could Gorenje implement to compete successfully in this industry in the long run despite its limited financial resources and smaller scale (in comparison to larger multinational companies in this industry)?
3. The company sells both middle/low-end and middle/high-end home appliances (wide price positioning) under the brand name Gorenje. What are the advantages and disadvantages of such a branding strategy?
4. How would you adapt the Gorenje marketing mix strategy for premium products (such as the *Smart Table* and the *Fridge-Freezer with Swarovski Crystals*)?

Source: The case was prepared by Monika Lisjak and Maja Makovec Brenčič. It is intended to be used as a basis for classroom discussion rather than to illustrate either effective or ineffective handling of a business situation. The case cannot be used without the written permission of the authors or reproduced in any way. The authors wish to acknowledge the assistance of Aleksander Uranc, Director of the Marketing Department at Gorenje, in developing the case. *Sources:* Gorenje Annual Report 2005; Gorenje internal data; GfK Group panel data reports, 2004 and 2005; Prasnikar, J. *et al.* (2006) 'An application of the open innovation model in Gorenje d.d.'; Competitiveness, social responsibility and economic growth, Nova Science; Czinkota, M., Ronkainen, I. and Moffett, M. (2002) *International Business,* 6th edition, Harcourt College Publishers, 2002.

Case Study 10

BOLIVIA NATIONALIZES THE OIL AND GAS SECTOR[1]

The time has come, the awaited day, a historic day in which Bolivia retakes absolute control of our natural resources. The looting by the foreign companies has ended.[2]

—Evo Morales, President, Bolivia,
Announcing the Nationalization of Oil and Gas Sector,
on 1 May 2006.

Governments in the region see energy as a commodity they can use to push populist agendas.... From a political point of view, it's a powerful issue to manipulate, but from an industrial point of view, it can do real harm.[3]

—Adriano Pires, Director,
Brazilian Center for Infrastructure Studies,
in May 2006.

These conditions make gas operations practically impossible in Bolivia.[4]

—Jose Sergio Gabrielli, President,
Petroleo Brasileiro SA,[5] on Nationalization,
in May 2006.

The Nationalization Spree

On May Day[6] – 1 May 2006 – Evo Morales Ayma (Morales), President of Bolivia, announced that the oil and gas sector in Bolivia was being nationalized. The announcement was considered significant because Bolivia, with the second largest natural gas resources in South America after Venezuela, played a significant role in the regional gas market. Even as the announcement was being made, the Bolivian army took control of the 56 oil and gas sites in Bolivia, thus completing the process of nationalization. Morales also said that the other natural resources of the country such as mines, forests, etc. would be subsequently nationalized.

Morales gave six months to the foreign companies in the oil and gas sector to renegotiate their existing contracts with the government or leave the country. The companies were also ordered to give up ownership of the oil and gas fields. In addition, all future sales had to be channelled through a state-owned company. Responding to this decree, the foreign companies in Bolivia said they would proceed with caution until the government clarified the terms and conditions of the new contracts.

The announcement also created a stir in the international community. The European Commission[7] said it was worried because the announcement would further push up the already increasing international oil prices. Many European companies, especially those from Spain, had operations in Bolivia. Spain expressed concern over the announcement and said that the step would not be in the best interests of Bolivia. Brazil too expressed deep concern over the announcement. Brazil's President, Luiz Incio Lula da Silva (Lula da Silva) immediately convened a meeting with the CEO of Petroleo Brasileiro SA (Petrobras) and other senior officials from the mines and energy department to discuss the impact of this announcement on Brazil.

The trend of government control over energy resources in South America started in Venezuela, the fifth largest oil exporter in the world, when Hugo Chavez (Chavez), President of Venezuela, imposed heavy taxes and other conditions on foreign companies operating in this sector. Antoine Halff, energy analyst at Fimat International Banque SA,[8] said, 'This is a continuation of the trend toward increasingly aggressive resource nationalization that we have seen across many countries in Latin America, starting in Venezuela. The measure is in line with the populist tone of the new regime in Bolivia; however, how it is carried out in practice still seems somewhat unclear.'[9] It was reported that another South American country, Ecuador, was also considering nationalizing the oil and gas sector.

Some analysts saw the nationalization in Bolivia as an attempt to control vital energy resources against the backdrop of the rising oil and gas prices worldwide and to derive political mileage from it. They felt that this trend of resource nationalization was a disturbing one because it would not only discourage potential investors but could also hamper development of the sector. Gal Luft, Co Director, Institute for the Analysis of Global Security,[10] said, 'This isn't like Saudi Arabia, which over the years has developed know-how to dominate the industry independently. When you cause problems for foreign investors, you cause problems for those who know how to create and develop the industry.'[11]

Oil and Gas Resources in Bolivia

Bolivia, officially known as the Republica de Bolivia (Republic of Bolivia) in Spanish, is a landlocked South American country (see Figure 1(a) for a map of Bolivia and Figure 1(b) for a brief profile of Bolivia). The country is rich in natural resources such as silver, gas, iron, magnesium, etc. As of 2005, the Energy Information Administration (EIA), a US Government energy agency, estimated that Bolivia has the second largest gas reserves in South America. The oil and gas sector had significantly contributed to the Bolivian economy (see Figure 2 for the GDP growth by sectors until 2003). It has also been estimated that Bolivia has 70% of the world's iron and magnesium resources. However, the availability of the resources has in no way been reflected in the country's development and Bolivia is considered one of the poorest and most underdeveloped countries in South America.

Oil Resources

According to the *Oil and Gas Journal*[12] (OGJ), Bolivia had proven resources of 440 million oil barrels[13] as of 2005, a huge rise when compared with the estimated figure of 116 million barrels in 1997. Analysts attributed this rise to the greater exploration and investment by foreign oil companies in Bolivia. The Tarija area in southwestern Bolivia was estimated to contain 80% of the oil reserves. The vast resources of oil allowed Bolivia to meet its oil demand through domestic oil production most of the time without having to resort to imports (see Figure 3 for oil production and consumption figures from 1980 to 2005).

The state-owned oil company, Yacimientos Petroliferos Fiscales Bolivianos (YPFB) controlled the oil assets before the sector was privatized in 1996 (see Figure 4 for the history of oil in Bolivia). After privatization, foreign companies took over control of the oil reserves. YPFB divested itself of its assets but held on to its rights to negotiate and formulate contracts with foreign companies. As of May 2006, Petrobras was the biggest stake-holder in the oil reserves with control over 41% of the reserves. It was followed by Repsol-YPF,[14] which held 35% of the oil reserves. The other foreign companies involved were Total SA[15] (Total), the BG Group[16] and Grupo Pluspetrol.[17]

Gas Resources

OGJ estimated that the proven natural gas reserves of Bolivia were 24.0 trillion cubic feet (TCF) as of 2005.

Figure 1(a): Map of Bolivia.

Source: 'Country profile: Bolivia', www.news.bbc.co.uk, 3 July 2006.

Particulars	Details
Population (July 2006 est.)	8,989,046
Total Area	1,098,580 sq km
Land use (2005)	Arable land: 2.78%
	Permanent crops: 0.19%
	Other: 97.03%
Independence	6 August 1825 (from Spain)
GDP (2005 est.)	US$ 9.657 billion
GDP – real growth rate (2005 est.)	4%
GDP – composition by sector (2005 est.)	Agriculture: 12.6%
	Industry: 35%
	Services: 52.4%
Population below poverty line (2004 est.)	64%
Exports f.o.b. value (2005 est.)	US$ 2.371 billion
Exports – commodities	Natural gas, soybeans and soy products, crude petroleum, zinc ore, tin
Exports – partners (2004)	Brazil 32.1%, US 16.2%, Venezuela 11%, Peru 6.2%, Argentina 5.9%, Colombia 5.4%
Imports f.o.b. value (2005 est.)	US$ 1.845 billion
Imports – commodities	Petroleum products, plastics, paper, aircraft and aircraft parts, prepared foods, automobiles, insecticides, soybeans
Imports – partners (2004)	Brazil 25.8%, Argentina 15.6%, US 13.8%, Peru 6.7%, Chile 5.9%, China 5.7%, Japan 5.6%
External Debt (2005 est.)	US$ 6.43 billion
Foreign Direct Investment (2004)	US$ 271 million

Figure 1(b): Bolivia – a brief profile

Sources: http://www.cia.gov/cia/publications/factbook/geos/bl.html; http://www.pwc.com/images/soacat/highlights_of_ Bolivia_06.pdf.

However, YPFB estimated the proven natural reserves at 26.7 TCF. In the mid-1990s, Bolivia privatized its natural gas sector along with oil and that enabled investment by foreign companies (see Figure 5 for the history of natural gas in Bolivia). After privatization, the exploration of gas increased tremendously and resulted in a 600% increase in proven natural gas reserves since 1997 (see Figure 6 on Bolivia's natural gas reserves). More than 70% of the production of the gas resources was from the Tarija area (see Figure 7 for Bolivia gas production and consumption in Bolivia). The largest natural gas producer in Bolivia was Petrobras followed by Repsol-YPF (see Table 1 for a brief profile of the oil and gas industry in Bolivia).

The Bolivian Gas War

The phrase 'Bolivian gas war' was used to describe an internal conflict in Bolivia on the issue of exploitation of the oil and gas resources by foreign companies. The seeds for the war were said to have been sown when the government decided to eradicate coca crops[18] and to use military force to suppress strikes by labour groups. The war started in early 2003 and peaked in October 2003, when demonstrations and roadblocks by groups of indigenous people[19] and labour groups brought Bolivia to a standstill. The demonstrators were protesting against the fact that the gas and oil resources were being given to foreign companies supported by the US for very low prices without the Bolivian people deriving any tangible benefit from them. They quoted the example of the complete exploitation of Bolivia's once abundant silver mines under Spanish rule without the Bolivians benefiting in any way.

The then ruling coalition government led by President Gonzalo Sanchez de Lozada (Lozada) ordered military action against the protestors and the subsequent crackdown left some 60 protestors dead. After the incident, the coalition government crumbled and Lozada resigned and fled the country. He was

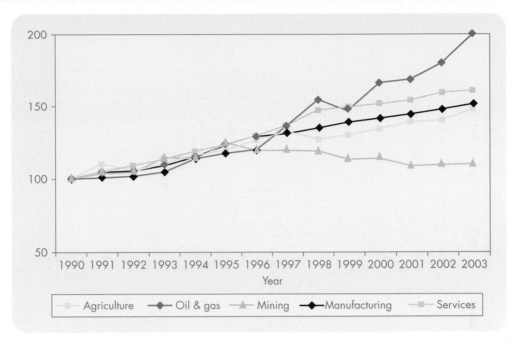

Figure 2: Bolivia GDP growth by sectors 1990–2003.

Source: Elizabeth Zamora, Gaby Candia and Marcelo Lora, 'Economic Growth, Poverty and Institutions: A Case Study of Bolivia', www.gdnet.org, February 2005.

succeeded by the then vice-president Carlos Mesa (Mesa), who conducted a referendum on the issue on 18 July 2004. The referendum had five questions based on which the citizens of Bolivia had to decide and vote (see Table 2 for questions in the referendum).

The five questions, to which the answer had to be either a 'yes' or a 'no', did not include any reference to the key demand of the protestors – the nationalization of the oil and gas sector. A law was also enacted under which every eligible citizen had to participate in the referendum, failing which they would face state

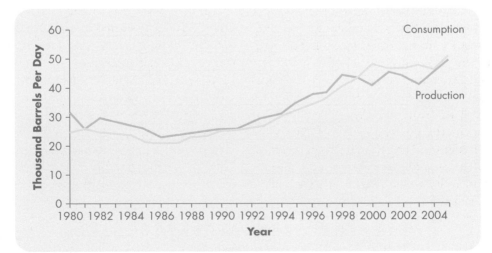

Figure 3: Oil production and consumption in Bolivia: 1980–2005. The production and consumption figures are for the months of January to June in every year.

Source: http://www.eia.doe.gov/emeu/cabs/Bolivia/Oil.html.

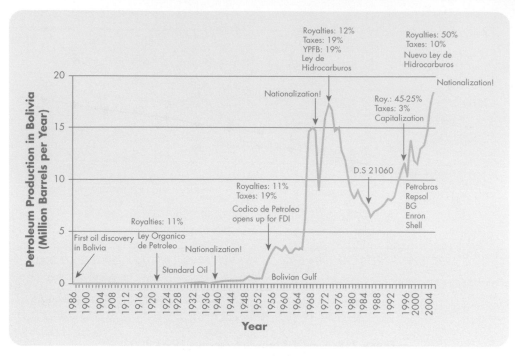

Figure 4: History of oil in Bolivia.

Source: Lykke E. Andersen, 'Natural Gas and Inequality in Bolivia', www.un.org, February 2006.

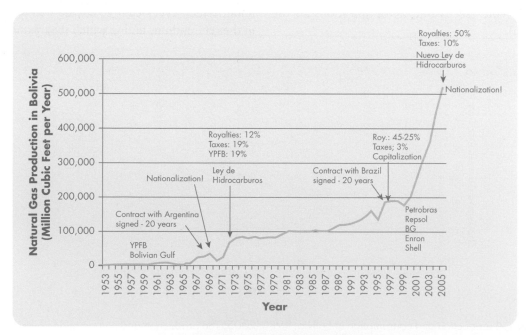

Figure 5: History of natural gas in Bolivia.

Source: Lykke E. Andersen, 'Natural Gas and Inequality in Bolivia', www.un.org, February 2006.

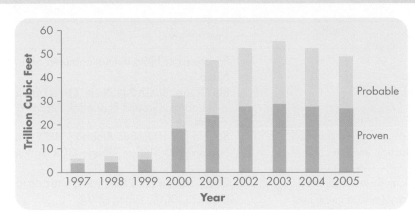

Figure 6: Bolivia's natural gas reserves: 1997–2005.
Source: http://www.eia.doe.gov/emeu/cabs/Bolivia/NaturalGas.html.

action. Protests and demonstrations against the referendum were also barred. A major proportion of the population who participated in the referendum replied 'yes' to all the five questions (see Table 3 for the referendum results), which enabled continuation of the existing policies with no major changes being made.

But the referendum became controversial, because it did not address the key demand, and it was alleged that many voters did not understand the questions properly, because of the way in which they were framed. The referendum also split the protestors with some accepting the results and others denouncing them. The second group charged that the referendum had not been conducted in a fair manner. Protests broke out once again with the protesters demanding

complete nationalization of the oil and gas sector. The blockade of the highways and oilfields by protestors became a regular phenomenon. On 6 March 2005, Mesa offered to resign because the country had become difficult to govern.

However, the Bolivian Congress rejected his offer and the protests intensified. On 17 May 2005, giving in to pressure from the protestors, the Bolivian Congress passed a new gas law, Hydrocarbons Law No. 3058, which replaced the earlier Hydrocarbons Law No. 1689. The new law imposed a 32% tax on the production of the foreign oil companies in addition to the existing 18% and offered wider participation of the indigenous population in the country's law-making body. Under this law, all oil and gas companies operating in Bolivia were given 180 days (from the

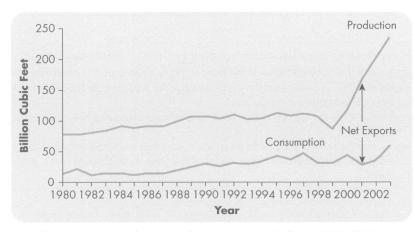

Figure 7: Gas production and consumption in Bolivia: 1980–2003.
Source: http://www.eia.doc.gov/emeu/cabs/Bolivia/NaturalGas.html.

Category	Description
Sector status	Privatized in 1996 but nationalized on 1 May 2006.
Major oil or gas ports	None
Major foreign companies	BG Group, British Petroleum, Orca Petroleum, Perez Companc, Petrobras, Groupa Pluspetrol, Repsol-YPF, Royal Dutch Shell, Total SA.
Major oil fields production (barrels per day)	Sabalo (13 100), San Alberto (7400), Margarita (3600)
Major gas fields production (million cubic feet per day)	Sabalo (385.5), San Alberto (304.6), Vuelta Grande (85.7)
Major refineries capacity (barrels per day)	Cochabamba (27 250), Santa Cruz de la Sierra (20 000)
Major pipelines capacity (million cubic feet per day)	Gasbol (1000), Yabog (230)

Source: Adapted from www.eia.doe.gov

Table 1: Brief profile of the oil and gas sector in Bolivia (figures reported in 2005).

date of this law) to enter into new contracts with YPFB. These new contracts were expected to give more control to YPFB.[20] However, the protests continued on the grounds that there were loopholes in the law that would allow foreign companies to evade tax under certain provisions. The foreign companies expressed concern over the additional tax and said that it would threaten their heavy investment in the Bolivian oil and gas sector.

Due to these protests Mesa once again offered to resign. He said he had done his best to resolve the oil issue and offered an apology for the crisis. In the end he resigned on 6 June 2005, and was succeeded by Eduardo Rodriguez, the chief justice of Supreme Court of Bolivia, who ordered fresh elections in December 2005. The MAS (Movement towards Socialism) party led by Morales won the elections.

The Nationalization

When Morales became President on 22 January 2006, he became the first indigenous native to govern Bolivia for 450 years. He belonged to the 'Aymara' indigenous group. He was actively involved in the Bolivian gas war and used the nationalization of the oil and gas sector as one of the principal planks to contest the December 2005 polls.

On 1 May 2006, the Tarija area in southwestern Bolivia, which contained an estimated 80% of the

No.	Question
Q1	Do you agree that the current Hydrocarbons Law (No. 1689)[43] should be changed?
Q2	Do you agree that the Bolivian State should have rights to hydrocarbons once they reach the ground?[a]
Q3	Do you agree that YFPB (the oil company privatized under Sanchez de Lozada) should be re-established in order to control hydrocarbon production?
Q4	Do you agree that Bolivian gas should be used as a strategic resource to regain useful or sovereign access to the Pacific?
Q5	Do you agree that Bolivian gas should be exported, and that multinationals should pay 50% of projected profits for rights to exploit Bolivian gas, and that the government should invest in health, education, and infrastructure?

Source: http://www.en.wikipedia.org/wiki/Bolivian_gas_referendum%2C_2004
[a]According to a law in Bolivia, once oil or gas was extracted and brought to ground, it would no longer be the national property of the country.

Table 2: Questions in the referendum.

Question	Total Votes	Turnout	Valid Votes	Spoilt*	Blank*	Yes#	No#
1	2,678,449	60.08%	2,064,369	12.10%	10.82%	86.64%	13.36%
2	2,670,213	59.89%	2,075,707	12.51%	9.75%	92.19%	7.81%
3	2,670,215	59.89%	2,054,140	10.73%	12.34%	87.31%	12.69%
4	2,670,039	59.89%	1,926,290	10.72%	17.14%	54.79%	45.21%
5	2,669,213	59.87%	1,910,909	11.72%	16.69%	61.74%	38.26%

Source: Adapted from http://www.en.wikipedia.org/wiki/Bolivian_gas_referendum%2C_2004.
*As a percentage of the total votes
#As a percentage of valid votes

Table 3: Results of the referendum.

country's natural gas reserves, was chosen as the venue for announcing the nationalization decree. Flanked by the key government and military officials, Morales announced the nationalization of the oil of gas sector with the help of presidential supreme decree '28 701' called 'Heroes of Chaco' – in memory of the indigenous Bolivian soldiers who had died in defence of oil reserves in Bolivia's Chaco War with Paraguay in the 1930s. He termed it 'the first nationalization of the 21st century' and a gift to the workers on May Day (see Table 4 for the key points in the nationalization decree).

Another essential point in the decree was that YPFB would be restructured within 60 days in such a way that it would be able to take complete control of the oil and gas production process, which would include exploration, refining and storage (Figure 8 contains the complete text of presidential decree on nationalization). The hardest hit companies due to the nationalization were Petrobras, Respol-YPF and Total, because they operated in two of the largest gas fields in Bolivia, San Alberto and San Antonio.

Petrobras, the biggest investor in Bolivia with approximately US$1.6 billion invested in the country's oil and gas sector, described the government's announcement as a 'unilateral attitude' and said that it would do whatever necessary to protect its interests. The company said it would take steps to maintain the supply of gas to Brazil, more than half of which was imported from Bolivia. It also said that it was freezing all proposed future investments in Bolivia.

Begoña Elices, Director of External Relations, Repsol-YPF said, 'We're worried. There will be a lot of fine print to consider'.[21] The company said that it would send a delegation to Bolivia to discuss its concerns about the nationalization issue. The company also said that, if necessary, it would take legal action to protect its investments. Paul Floren, spokesperson for Total said, 'We have received the Bolivian decree but there's not much we can say as we are still studying it'.[22] The company said that it would adopt a wait-and-see approach before contemplating any action.

Some analysts commented that Morales' nationalization strategy had in fact been framed with an eye

- Complete power to the Bolivian government to set conditions on quantity and prices for internal requirements or exports, commercialization, and to take total control on all aspects oil production and distribution.
- Renegotiation of contracts with all foreign companies within 180 days after nationalization so that they would be in accordance with the oil and gas law number 3058.
- Capture of 51% of the shares from the five private companies that were formed by the division of YPFB in 1996.
- Hike in the tax and royalty from 50 to 82% on companies operating in fields whose registered production average of natural gas (in 2005) was more than 100 million daily cubical feet.
- Audit on investments and taxes on all oil and gas companies (except Petrobras, Respol-YPF and Total) so that their taxes and terms of operations could be reviewed.

Source: Adapted from Gretchen Gordon, 'Bolivia's Nationalization by Decree', www.americas.org, 29 June, 2006

Table 4: Key points in the nationalization decree.

(The text was the English translated version of original decree in Spanish found in the Bolivian Government's official website, www.comunica.gov.bo. The text was translated from Spanish using translate. google.com/)

Article 1

I. In exercise of national sovereignty, obeying the mandate of the Bolivian people as expressed in the binding Referendum of July 18, 2004 and in strict application of constitutional precepts, all oil and gas natural resources of the country are to be nationalized.

The State recovers the property, the possession and the total and absolute control of these resources.

Article 2

I. From May, 2006 on, oil companies that currently carry out activities of production of gas and oil in national territory are obliged to deliver ownership to Petroleum Fields Fiscal Bolivian (YPFB, by its Spanish initials) all production of hydrocarbons.

II. YPFB, in the name of and in representation of the State in full exercise of ownership of all hydrocarbons produced in the country, assumes commercialization, defining the conditions, volumes, and prices both for the domestic market and for exportation and industrialization.

Article 3

I. Those will only be able to continue operating in the country the companies that immediately accept the dispositions of the present Supreme Decree, until in a term nongreater to 180 days from its promulgation, its activity is regularized, by means of contracts that fulfill the legal and constitutional conditions and requirements. At the end of this term, the companies that there are not signed contracts will not be able to continue operating in the country.

II. In order to guarantee the continuity of the production, YPFB, according to directors of the Ministry of Hydrocarbons and Energy, will take to their position the operation from the fields from the companies that refuse to accept or prevent the fulfillment of the arranged thing in the present Supreme Decree.

III. YPFB will not be able to execute contracts of hydrocarbon operation that individually authorized and has not been approved by the Legislative Power in the heat of fulfillment of the mandate of interjection 5 of Article 59 of the Political Constitution of the State,

Article 4

I. During the period of transition, for the fields whose registered production average of natural gas of year 2005 has been superior to the 100 million daily cubical feet, the value of the production will be distributed of the following form: 82% for the State (18% of exemptions and participation, 32% of Direct Tax to Hydrocarbons IDH and 32% through an additional participation for YPFB), and 18% for the companies (that cover costs with operation, amortization of investments and utilities).

II. For the fields whose registered production average of natural gas of year 2005 has been smaller to 100 million daily cubical feet, during the period of transition, the present distribution of the value of the hydrocarbon production will stay.

III. The Ministry of Hydrocarbons and Energy will determine, case by case and by means of audit, the investments made by the companies, as well as their amortizations, costs of operation and yield obtained in each field. The results of the audits will serve as base to YPFB to determine the repayment or definitive participation corresponding to the companies in contracts to be signed according to the established thing in Article 3 of the present Supreme Decree.

Article 5

I. The State takes the control and the direction from the production, transport, hydrocarbon refinement, storage, distribution, commercialization and industrialization in the country.

II. The Ministry of Hydrocarbons and Energy will regulate these activities until new regulations according to Law are approved.

Article 6

I. In application of the terms disposed by Article 6 of the Law of Hydrocarbons, all shares in the capitalized oil companies Chaco SA., Andina SA., and Transredes SA., formerly held by Bolivian citizens that formed part of the Collective Capitalization Fund are transferred without charge to YPFB.

II. So that this transference does not affect payments under BONOSOL, the State guarantees the repayment of the contributions that these companies delivered annually to the Collective Capitalization Fund, as dividends.

III. The shares of the Collective Capitalization Fund that are in the name of the Administrators of Pension Funds in the companies Chaco SA., Andina SA., and Transredes SA., will be transferred to the name of YPFB.

Article 7

I. The state recovers its full participation in the entire productive chain of the hydrocarbon sector.

II. The shares necessary for YPFB to control 50% plus one in the companies Chaco SA., Andina SA., Transredes SA., Petrobras Bolivia refinacion SA., and Compania Logistica de Hidrocarburos de Bolivia SA., are hereby nationalized.

III. YPFB will immediately name its representatives and officials in the respective directorships and will sign new partnership and administrative contracts which guarantee the state control and management of hydrocarbon activities in the country.

Article 8

I. In 60 days, as of the date of promulgation of the present Supreme Decree and within the process of refundación of YPFB, it will be come to its integral reconstruction, turning it a corporative company, is transparent, efficient and with social control.

Article 9

I. In everything what it is not in opposition to the arranged thing in the present Supreme Decree, they will be continued applying to the regulations and effective norms the date, until they are modified according to law.

Figure 8: Complete text of the presidential decree (28 701) on nationalization of oil and gas sector.

on the elections to the Constituent Assembly in Bolivia, scheduled to be held in July 2006. According to them, Morales' rule, which began in January 2006, had not been marked by any major policy or executive decision and he needed a controversial and populist decision to hold sway over the voters.

However, a few other analysts suggested that the nationalization move was in fact a strategy to preserve Bolivian capitalism. Most of the major utility services such as transport, banking, electricity, etc. in Bolivia were privatized. According to these analysts, if Morales failed to win the elections to the Constituent Assembly with a comfortable majority, political instability would once again rear its head in Bolivia, plunging the country into chaos. The Bolivian Gas War had already taken its toll – two presidents had changed within two years – and made Bolivia politically unstable. Therefore, to retain political stability and to attract voters, a nationalization process that didn't actually harm the foreign companies was implemented.

Benefits of Nationalization

The first and foremost benefit to Bolivia from the nationalization of the oil and gas sector was an expected increase in the share of profits of the foreign companies, which could be diverted to state welfare programmes. Nationalization sought to channel the wealth of Bolivia's natural resources for the benefit of the local populace instead of filling the coffers of the foreign companies. After the nationalization, the tax on profit on production was increased from 50 to 82%. Analysts expected that this would result in growth of income to the government of between US$320 million and US$780 million. The two key elements in the renegotiation of the contracts as a part of nationalization were to reclaim important assets by the state owned YPFB, and a greater share of revenues to the Bolivian government.

Nationalization was also expected to generate more jobs to Bolivians because it was alleged that some of the foreign companies were recruiting foreign nationals. Eduardo Gonzalez, a Bolivian citizen, said, 'It's good they want something for us. If Bolivia owns the refinery it means there will be more jobs for Bolivians. Most of the people working in there are foreigners – Brazilians and Peruvians. We should have 100% ownership of it as a resource to help build the country.'[23]

Morales said of the benefits of nationalization, 'For more than 500 years, our resources have been pillaged. This has to end now. What we are looking for . . . are partners – not bosses to exploit our natural resources. Before Bolivia was considered to be a no-man's-land. Now it belongs to its own people, particularly its indigenous peoples. We are about to defend our territory, defend our natural resources. The only way to combat poverty is by recovering our natural resources.'[24]

Apart from the perceived economic benefits and social welfare, nationalization was also expected to increase the pride in Bolivian nationalism. Bolivia had been ruled by Spain in the past. It had also been involved in several wars with neighbouring countries, in the course of which it had lost pieces of land and, most importantly, its access to the sea, thus becoming a landlocked country. Therefore, the Bolivians associated their natural resources with national pride and saw them as an important basis to bargain with the neighbouring countries. Nouriel Roubini, Professor, Economics and International Business, New York University, said, 'There is this kind of historical resentment. Bolivians are giving a slap in the face to Brazilians and Spaniards.'[25]

The Criticism

Some analysts said that Morales had done more harm than good to Bolivia by nationalizing the oil and gas sector. The nationalization had imposed such severe business conditions on the foreign companies that it would make oil and gas exploration and production unprofitable for most of them. Also, foreign companies would have brought in the latest techniques and technologies in exploration and production and that

would have helped in easy location and quality production of oil and gas. Local companies could not hope to match this, Bolivia not being self-reliant in those areas. It was observed that only after the privatization of the sector in 1996 had oil and gas exploration and production grown sharply in Bolivia. Without private participation, active exploration and production would be severely affected in Bolivia, the analysts said.

Another major proposal in nationalization, the takeover of assets and production by the state-owned YPFB, was also heavily criticized. YPFB was perceived as having an inadequate management and infrastructure to handle the responsibility imposed on it. To compound the problem, it required a sizeable investment in it at first to be able to handle the responsibility. Carlos Alberto Lopez, an energy consultant, said, 'YPFB may have the will but it doesn't certainly have the capital or the technology to continue operating the fields in Bolivia without the foreign companies.'[26]

It was also feared that without new investment in the oil and gas sector, Bolivia would be unable to supply gas to Brazil and Argentina as per the original contracts, which would result in loss of revenue to it and a termination of the contracts. Further, lack of investment was also expected to create a shortage of gas on the domestic front for Bolivia and, according to an estimate, it would even necessitate the import of 12 000 barrels of natural gas per day by 2010.[27] James Ferrer, Director, Center for Latin American Issues, George Washington School of Business, said, 'Bolivia doesn't have the money to make major investments to continue developing the natural gas industry on its own. I can't help but believe he's damaging Bolivia's interests . . . by essentially terminating investment opportunities.'[28]

The proposed technical help promised by Chavez for refining and production through the Venezuelan company, Petroleos de Venezuela SA (PDVSA),[29] also came in for criticism. An agreement was expected between PDVSA and YPFB to explore, certify and extract the gas reserves. PDVSA would also train 200 Bolivian engineers and build a gas processing plant and a petrochemical plant. In return, it would get a minority stake in a joint venture with YPFB to carry out the projects. Analysts said PDVSA did not possess the required competence to help YPFB and therefore it was unwise for Bolivia to rely on it. Sophie Aldebert, a Brazil-based gas expert, said, 'There are a lot of questions about the ability of PDVSA in helping Bolivia.'[30]

The nationalization was also expected to lead to a direct confrontation with the largest investor in the oil and gas sector in Bolivia, Petrobras, which had already announced a freeze on all its proposed future investments in Bolivia and criticized the nationalization. Brazil, which imported half of its natural gas needs from Bolivia, was expected to look for other avenues for the import, if Bolivia failed to supply the gas at the agreed quantity levels consistently. Also, Bolivia's foreign earnings would be seriously eroded if it failed to honour the contracts signed with its customers. Andres T. Stepkowski (Stepkowski), a Bolivia-based energy expert with 40 years of experience in South America, said, 'Reliability is a very valuable commodity in the energy market, especially for natural gas which is sold on long-term contracts. If [contracts] aren't honoured, the buyer will turn elsewhere. And that's that.'[31]

The nationalization was also said to have resulted in an imbalance in the regional alliances in South America and in creating a rift among the countries of the alliances. Some analysts opined that nationalization helped to further strengthen the bond of friendship between Morales and Chavez resulting in a change of power equations that led to a curtailment of the role of Brazil, the traditional leader in the politics of the region. Analysts said that because of this friendship, Brazil and Argentina were unable to confront Bolivia directly over the nationalization issue. Morales and Chavez also issued a threat to pull out of the Andean Community[32] if the members signed free trade agreements with the US. This threat was seen by analysts as a step in the opposite direction of progress and economic prosperity in an era of globalization and economic reforms.

After the nationalization was announced, the EU criticized the move and said that it might affect the volatile world energy markets. It said that it would study the nationalization and its effect on those foreign companies that were most likely to be affected. The EU said it should have been contacted before such a decision was taken because some of the foreign companies involved were from Europe. EU chief spokesman, Johannes Laitenberger, said, 'We hope that before the (final) decision is actually taken, any proposal will be discussed...before it is actually adopted.'[33]

The Spanish government also expressed concern over the nationalization in Bolivia, because Repsol-YPF was the biggest player in the oil and gas sector after Petrobras. The Spanish Foreign Ministry said, 'The government hopes that in the 180-day period announced by the Bolivian president for foreign companies to regularize their current contracts, there is authentic negotiation and dialog between the government and the different companies in which each other's interests are respected.'[34]

The decision of Morales to send military troops to take control of the oil and gas fields attracted heavy criticism from foreign investors and industry analysts. Analysts said that there was no need for such an aggressive measure and added that it would portray Bolivia as a totalitarian regime rather than a democratic country. It was estimated that 56 oil and gas fields had been occupied by the military troops with a copy of the presidential decree and banners stating 'Nacionalizado: Propiedad de los Bolivianos' (Nationalized: Property of the Bolivians) being immediately displayed outside the fields. The government justified the use of the military troops on the ground that their presence would deter foreign companies from destroying important documents necessary for the proposed audit and renegotiation of the contracts.

Analysts also criticized the nationalization as an attempt by the Morales government to profit from popular sentiment without showing any concern for the country's long-term future. The nationalization also set the tone for some South American countries, such as Ecuador and Peru, to adopt a similar stance. On 15 May 2006, shortly after Morales' announcement, Ecuador announced that it had cancelled the contract it had with the US oil company Occidental Petroleum Corporation[35] (Occidental) due to a trade dispute. It also said that all Occidental's assets in Ecuador, estimated at around US$1 billion, would be seized. Ecuador also approved a law that would require oil companies to share at least 50% of the profits resulting from oil revenues above standard prices. The law, which most oil companies described as 'unconstitutional', resulted in a confrontation between Ecuador and the US. In the run up to elections in Peru, the contesting parties promised to review the status of the oil and gas sector if they were voted into government.

The Two Summits

On 4 May 2006, a summit was hurriedly organized in Argentina between Lula da Silva, Nestor Kirchner (Argentina's President,), Chavez and Morales to discuss the nationalization in Bolivia. It was essentially organized to allay the fears of Brazil and Argentina, the two largest customers of the Bolivian gas, and to prevent any possible regional crisis. At the end of the summit, the presidents of both Brazil and Argentina promised to respect the right of Bolivia to take sovereign decisions like nationalization, but said that further discussions were needed on gas prices and the issue of production by the foreign companies to prevent a regional crisis.

Lula da Silva said after the summit, 'The important thing is that gas supplies for countries needing them have been guaranteed and that prices will be discussed in the most democratic form possible between all parties involved.'[36] He also suggested that the decision of Petrobras to freeze the proposed investment in Bolivia after nationalization could be reconsidered after further negotiations. He rejected the suggestions that Chavez and Morales were teaming up to increase the prices of oil and gas, a move that would significantly affect the two largest economies in South America, Brazil and Argentina.

According to Chavez there was a necessity to organize the summit to prevent a regional crisis. He said, 'There are those who wish to stoke the tensions. We want to stamp them out.'[37] Chavez used the occasion to denounce the allegations that he, along with the support of Cuba, had provided background help to Morales on nationalization. Morales was widely perceived as being close to Chavez, who was known for his socialistic ideology, and it was believed that his friendship with Chavez had encouraged him to implement the controversial decision of nationalization.

Some analysts opined that the summit clearly indicated that though the harsh clauses in the order of nationalization might appear to be aimed at driving out the foreign companies, at the end of the day Bolivia would try to negotiate them. They said the foreign companies needed Bolivian gas just as Bolivia needed foreign investment and technology. They were of the opinion that measures such as sending in the army to take control of the oil and gas installations were only ploys to dramatize the proposed nationalization in the eyes of the Bolivian public and were not really intended to harm the interest of the foreign companies.

The summit of the EU, Latin America and Caribbean leaders held in Vienna, Austria, in the second week of May 2006 was overshadowed by Bolivia's nationalization decision. The summit was organized to increase the trade and political ties between the respective countries. On the eve of the summit, Morales reiterated that foreign companies would be allowed to recover the investments and make profits but would not be allowed to own the resources. EU leaders appealed to Bolivia and Venezuela to open up their economies to investment saying that such nationalistic policies would damage their economies. Austrian Chancellor, Wolfgang Schuessel, said, 'There are always two possibilities in life: Either you want to open your markets or you don't want to open your markets – it's your choice. But the reality is . . . open market societies are better in their performance than closed, restricted structures.'[38]

Morales met Lula da Silva on the sidelines of the summit and later announced that the differences between Bolivia and Brazil on the nationalization issue had been resolved. Lula da Silva said, 'I told Evo Morales that Brazil needs Bolivian gas and that Bolivia needs to sell its gas to Brazil. The two sides must find the right point of balance, so that Brazil is satisfied and Bolivia is satisfied.'[39] Although the way in which the issue would be resolved was not stated, it was said that the announcement of the patch-up clearly indicated that the proposed nationalization would not be as severe as assumed.

The Road Ahead

According to Alvaro Garcia Linera (Linera), Vice-President of Bolivia and one of the important ideologues of Morales, a road map called 'Andean-Amazonian Capitalism' was required to build a strong Bolivian state that would regulate the growth of the industrial economy and transfer the surpluses to the communities. Linera said it would probably take another half a century to achieve socialism in Bolivia. He said, 'The decolonization of the state and the implementation of a new economic model will pose, from the first day, a left-indigenous government that will begin to initiate a process of irreversible change for the next half century. Andean-Amazonian capitalism is a form that, I believe, is adapted to our reality to improve the possibilities of the emancipation of the worker and community forces in the medium term. For this reason, we conceive of it as a temporary and transitory mechanism.'[40]

In May 2006, Morales had announced that Bolivia's mining industry would also be nationalized in the near future. However, on 2 June, 2006, it was announced that India-based Jindal Steel and Power Ltd had bagged the development rights for 20 billion tonnes of iron ore reserves in the El Mutun region of Bolivia. The value of the deal was estimated at US$2.3 billion. The total iron ore deposits at El Mutun were estimated at 40 billion tonnes, making it one of the largest iron ore reserves in the world.

The nationalization also brought into focus the important factor of a waning US influence in South American politics. Morales who had vowed during the election campaign in the second half of 2005 to be the nightmare of the US, was said to have kept his word by severely criticizing US at every available opportunity, and by forging a close relationship with America's enemies Chavez and Fidel Castro (president of Cuba). Also, the increasing popularity of the leftist politics in the South American countries would be a cause of concern for the US. Larry Birns, an analyst, said, 'The socialism championed by him [Morales] and Chavez is an increasing threat to the United States and its economic model that has dominated for decades. That's what's at stake here. But with the US under-reaction, you'd think the United States is condemned to be an observer.'[41]

Three weeks after the nationalization, US president George W. Bush expressed concern over the erosion of democracy in Bolivia and Venezuela and said that protection of property and human rights was essential for the peace and prosperity of the countries. He commented on the nationalization, 'I will continue to remind people that trade is the best way to help people to be lifted from poverty. We can spend money, and we do in the neighbourhood, but the best way for there to be growth is to encourage commerce and trade and prosperity through the marketplace.'[42]

Questions for Discussion

1. Why does Bolivia engage in Gas War? What goals does the Bolivian government pursue with such a policy?
2. How has the nationalization of the Bolivian oil and gas sector been implemented? What are its consequences for the Bolivian oil and gas supplies to other South American countries?
3. Why is there criticism to the nationalization of the oil and gas sector in Bolivia?

Source: This case was written by Soorya Tejomoortula and Rajiv Fernando, under the direction of Ramalingam Meenakshisundaram, ICFAI Center for Management Research (ICMR). It was compiled from published sources, and is intended to be used as a basis for class discussion rather than to illustrate either effective or ineffective handling of a management situation. ©2006, The ICFAI Center for Management Research. All rights reserved. No part of this publication may be reproduced, stored in a retrieval system, used in a spreadsheet or transmitted in any form or by any means – electronic or mechanical, without permission. Reproduced with permission.

FURTHER READING

Andersen, L.E., 'Natural Gas and Inequality in Bolivia', www.un.org, February 2006.

Benoit, H., 'Morales's Nationalization in Bolivia: Who Got Stabbed?' www.globalresearch.ca, 22 May 2006.

Brand, C., 'Bolivia Dominates EU – Latin American Summit', www.news.yahoo.com, 12 May 2006.

Dangl, B., 'An Overview of Bolivia's Gas War', www.upsidedownworld.org, 2006.

Hudson, S., 'Bolivia Nationalization Further Sidelines US', www.today.reuters.com, 8 May 2006.

Johnson, B., 'Morales' Move Meant to Enhance his Leftist Street Creed', www.sltrib.com, 10 May 2006.

Lakshman, I.A.R., 'Some See Bolivia Strategy Backfiring', www.boston.com, 4 May 2006.

Mignolo, W., 'Nationalization of Natural Gas in Bolivia', www.americas.org, 9 May 2006.

Prada, P., 'Bolivian Nationalizes Oil and Gas Sector', www.nytimes.com, 2 May 2006.

Quiroga, C.A., 'Bolivia: Gas Nationalization Just the Start', http://www.today.reuters.com, 1 May 2006.

Ray, D., 'Leaders Back Bolivia Gas Nationalization', www.businessweek.com, 4 May 2006.

Robinson, M., 'Nationalization Wave Seen Threatening Oil Supplies', www.theglobeandmail. com, 18 May 2006.

Smith, F., 'Bolivia Gas Nationalization Plan Has Risks', www.businessweek.com, 3 May 2006.

Webber, J.R., 'Nationalization of Gas!', www.zmag.org, 4 May 2006.

Zamora, E.,Candia, G. and Lora, M., 'Economic Growth, Poverty and Institutions: A Case Study of Bolivia', www.gdnet.org, February 2005.

Zissis, C., 'Bolivia's Nationalization of Oil and Gas', www.cfr.org, 12 May 2006.

Zuazo, A. and Pearson, N.O., 'Bolivia Turns to Venezuela for Gas Help', www.chron.com, 22 May 2006.

'Bolivia, Brazil Patch up Differences over Nationalization of Gas Industry', www.cbc.ca, 13 May 2006.

'Brazil Criticizes Bolivia for Nationalizing Natural Gas Industry', www.foxnews.com, 10 May 2006.

'Bush Decries 'Erosion of Democracy' in Venezuela, Bolivia', www.news.yahoo.com, 22 May 2006.

'Country Profile: Bolivia', www.news.bbc.co.uk, 3 July 2006.

'Energy in focus for EU-LatAm talks', www.cnn.com, 12 May 2006.

'EU: Bolivia's Nationalization of Gas Fields Could Hurt World Energy Markets', www.thestar. com, 2 May 2006.

'Nationalization - Threat or Promise?' www.minesandcommunities.org, 14 May 2006.

'Take over in Bolivia Jolts Energy Companies', www.iht.com, 2 May 2006.

http://www.cia.gov/cia/publications/factbook/geos/bl.html.

www.comunica.gov.bo.

www.counterpunch.org, 19 July 2004.

www.eia.doe.gov.

www.en.wikipedia.org.

www.oilcrisis.com/bo/.

http://www.pwc.com/images/soacat/highlights_of_Bolivia_06.pdf.

Case Study 11

CORPORATE GOVERNANCE AT BAYERISCHE MOTOREN WERKE (BMW)

Introduction

Bayerische Motoren Werke (BMW) is one of Europe's top car manufacturers. The company's products include motorcycles, cars, software (softlab GmbH) and motorcycling apparel such as leather suits, gloves and boots. Despite poor worldwide economic conditions, BMW had a good year in 2002. The introduction of the Mini (vehicle-brand name) in the US was a hit. BMW also successfully re-launched the Rolls-Royce brand after taking over control of the nameplate from Volkswagen. BMW ended the year 2002 with revenues of US$44 315.8 million and a net income of US$2117.2 million (see Figure 1).

Background Note

In 1913, Karl Rapp opened an aircraft-engine design shop near Munich. He named it Bayerische Motoren Werke (BMW) in 1917. The end of the First World War brought German aircraft production to a halt. BMW shifted to making railway brakes until the 1930s, and introduced its first motorcycle, the R32, in 1923. The company began making cars in 1928 after buying a small-car company Fahrzeugwerke Eisenach.

In 1933, BMW launched a line of larger cars. The company built aircraft engines for Hitler's Luftwaffe in the 1930s and stopped all car and motorcycle production in 1941. Under the period of emergency of Nazism in Germany, BMW operated in occupied countries, built rockets and developed the world's first production jet engine.

With its factories dismantled after the Second World War, BMW survived by making kitchen and garden equipment. In 1948, it introduced a one-cylinder motorcycle, which sold well as cheap transportation in postwar Germany. BMW cars in the 1950s were large and expensive and sold poorly. When motorcycle sales dropped, the company kept itself ticking in the mid-1950s by launching the Isetta, a three-wheeled car.

Herbert Quandt saved BMW in 1959 by acquiring control of the company for US$1 million. Quandt focused on sports saloons and released the first of the 'New Range' of BMWs in 1961.

In the 1970s, BMW's European exports soared, and the company set up a distribution subsidiary in USA. BMW also produced larger cars that crossed the gap with Mercedes-Benz.

Rapid export growth in USA, Asia and Australia continued in the 1980s, but competition from Japanese bikes and poor demand hurt motorcycle sales. The launch of the company's luxury vehicles in 1986 intensified the BMW – Mercedes rivalry. In 1992, BMW outsold Mercedes in Europe for the first time and became the first European car maker to operate a US plant since Volkswagen pulled out in 1988.

BMW teamed with the UK's Rolls-Royce aerospace firm in 1990 to make jet engines for planes that included executive business-travel jets such as the Gulfstream V.

The company bought UK car manufacturer Rover in 1994 and introduced a cheaper vehicle, the four-wheel-drive Discovery. It launched Highlander Land Rover in 1996, to meet the growing demand for 4 × 4 utility vehicles.

BMW offered to buy the luxury Rolls-Royce car unit (including the Bentley) from the UK-based Vickers in 1998, but lost out when Volkswagen countered with a higher offer. Later, BMW bought the Rolls-Royce name for US$66 million from Rolls-Royce PLC, the aerospace company. BMW agreed to let Volkswagen continue producing Rolls-Royce cars until 2003, and the last of the UK-built Rolls was finished on 30 August 2003.

In mid-1998, BMW began cutting jobs at its unprofitable Rover unit. As Rover's plants continued to struggle, BMW's board forced out chairman Brend

	1998	1999	2000	2001	2002	Change in %
Vehicle production	706,426	755,547	834,519	904,335	930,221	2.9
Mini	–	–	–	42,395	160,037	277.5
Motorcycles	60,152	69,157	93,608	100,213	97,553	−2.7
Deliveries to customers						
BMW	699,378	751,272	822,181	880,677	913,225	3.7
Mini	–	–	–	24,980	144,119	476.9
Motorcycles	60,308	65,168	81,263	95,327	103,020	8.1
Workforce at end of year	118,489	114,952	93,624	96,263	101,395	5.3

In euro million	1998 HGB	1999 HGB	2000 HGB	2000 IAS	2001 IAS	2002 IAS	Change in %
Revenues	32,280	34,402	35,356	37,226	38,463	42,282	9.9
Capital expenditure	2,179	2,155	2,138	2,781	3,516	4,042	15.0
Depreciation and amortization	1,859	2,042	2,322	2,435	2,159	2,143	−0.7
Cash flow	2,479	2,807	3,198	3,779	4,202	4,374	4.1
Profit from ordinary activities	1,061	1,111	1,663	2,032	3,242	3,297	1.7
Net profit/loss for the year	462	−2,487	1,026	1,209	1,866	2,020	8.3

Figure 1: BMW group: figures.

Source: Annual Report 2002, BMW.

Pischetsrieder, who had spearheaded the Rover acquisition in 1994. In 2000, BMW sold its Land Rover SUV operations to Ford in a deal worth about US$2.7 billion. Also that year, BMW handed over its Rover Cars operations and MG brand to the Phoenix Consortium, a UK-based group led by former Rover CEO John Towers.

In 2001, BMW launched its Mini brand in the UK. The brand was subsequently launched in other European markets. BMW sent the Mini Cooper to the US in 2002. The following year, BMW took control of the Rolls-Royce brand from Volkswagen.

The Board of Management and Supervisory Board

Like other German companies, BMW has two boards, the Board of Management (BOM) and the Supervisory Board (SB). The BOM manages the group's operations, co-ordinates the group's strategic approach with the SB and, at regular intervals, discusses the current state of strategy implementation with the SB. Transactions of fundamental importance require the approval of the SB.

The provision of sufficient information to the SB is the joint responsibility of the BOM and the SB. The BOM is expected to inform the SB regularly, without delay and in detail, issues important to the group with regard to planning, business development and risk management. The BOM also reports the deviations from previously formulated plans and targets, indicating the reasons for such deviations.

The SB has laid down detailed instructions covering the information and reporting duties of the BOM. As a general rule, in the case of reports required by law, the BOM submits its reports to the SB in writing. Documents required for decisions, in particular the Annual Financial Statements, the Consolidated Financial Statements and the Auditors' Report, are sent to the members of the SB, to the extent possible, before the relevant meeting.

Good corporate governance requires an open discussion both within the boards and between the boards. At the same time, confidentiality is important. When the services of staff members are involved, the members of the two boards are responsible for ensuring that the relevant staff members maintain

Name
Dr Helmut Panke Chairman
Ernst Baumann
Dr Michael Ganal
Dr-Ing. Burkhard Gschel
Stefan Krause
Dr-Ing. Norbert Reithofer
Dr Hagen Lüderitz Executive Director
Dr Dieter Lchelt General Counsel

Figure 2: Board of directors

Source: Annual Report 2002, BMW.

confidentiality. When necessary, the SB meets without the BOM.

In the event of a takeover, the BOM and SB submit a statement of their reasoned position so that the shareholders can make an informed decision on thc offer.

After the announcement of a takeover offer, the BOM do not take any actions outside the ordinary course of business that could prevent the success of the offer without the approval of the General Meeting or the SB. In making their decisions, the BOM and the SB are obliged to act in the best interests of the shareholders and of the enterprise.

In appropriate cases, the BOM convenes an extraordinary General Meeting where shareholders discuss the takeover offer and decide on suitable action.

The BOM and the SB are required to comply with the rules of proper corporate governance. If they violate the due care and diligence expected of conscientious board members, they are liable to BMW for damages.

The provision of loans by BMW or group subsidiaries to members of the BOM and the SB or their relatives requires the approval of the SB.

The BOM and the SB provides information each year in the Annual Report on the group's corporate governance. This includes an explanation of any deviations from the recommendations of the German Corporate Governance Code (GCGC).

Board of Management

Tasks and Responsibilities

The BOM is responsible for independently managing the enterprise, in the enterprise's best interests (see Figure 2). The BOM develops the enterprise's strategy, co-ordinates it with the SB and ensures its implementation. The BOM attempts to ensure that all provisions of law are abided by throughout the group. The BOM also ensures appropriate risk management and risk control throughout the group.

Composition and Compensation

On the basis of various performance criteria, the SB determines the compensation of the members of the BOM. Criteria for determining the appropriateness of compensation are the tasks performed by each member of the BOM, the economic situation, and the performance and outlook of BMW taking into account the competitive environment.

Compensation of the members of the BOM comprises fixed and variable components. Variable compensation includes annually payable components linked to business performance. Compensation of the BOM members is reported in the notes to the Consolidated Financial Statements, the fixed and performance-related components being indicated separately.

Conflicts of Interest

During their period of employment, members of the BOM are subject to comprehensive obligations. Members, in connection with their work, cannot demand or accept from third parties payments or other advantages for themselves or for any other person nor grant unlawful advantages to third parties. No member of the BOM may pursue personal interests in his or her decisions or take advantage of business opportunities intended for the enterprise. All members of the BOM have to disclose promptly conflicts of interest to the SB and inform the other members of the BOM. All transactions between the enterprise and members of the BOM, as well as persons they are close to or companies with which they have a personal association, have to comply with standards customary in the sector. Important transactions require the approval of the SB. Members of the BOM may undertake ancillary activities only after taking the approval of the SB.

The Supervisory Board
Tasks and Responsibilities

The SB advises regularly and supervises the BOM. The SB is also involved in all major strategic decisions (see Figure 3).

The SB appoints the members of the BOM. Together with the BOM, it facilitates long-term succession planning. The SB delegates the preparation of appointments to the BOM to a committee, which also determines the terms and conditions of employment contracts.

For first-time appointments, the maximum possible appointment period of five years is not the general

Name	Credentials
Volker Doppelfeld Chairman	Former Member of the Board of Management of BMW AG **Mandates**** Bayerische Hypo- und Vereinsbank AG D.A.S. Deutsche Automobilschutz Allg Rechtsschutz-Versicherungs AG IWKA AG Bizerba GmbH & Co. KG
Manfred Schoch* Deputy Chairman	Chairman of the Central Works Council
Dr. Hans-Dietrich Winkhaus Deputy Chairman	Former Member of the Board of Henkel KGaA **Mandates**** Degussa-Hüls AG Deutsche Lufthansa AG Deutsche Telekom AG (Chairman) ERGO Versicherungsgruppe AG Schwarz-Pharma AG (Chairman) Henkel KGaA
Ernst Rehmeier* Deputy Chairman	Chairman of the Works Council, Dingolfing
Stefan Quandt Deputy Chairman	Industrial Engineer **Mandates**** CEAG AG DELTON AG (Chairman) Dresdner Bank AG Gerling-Konzern Allgemeine Versicherungs-AG DataCard Corp.
Dr. phil. Karin Benz-Overhage*	Executive Member of the EB of IG Metall **Mandates**** Thyssen Krupp Steel AG (Deputy Chairman)
Ulrich Eckelmann*	Head of the Industry, Technology and Environment section of IG Metall **Mandates**** Thyssen Krupp Automotive AG

Prof. Dr. Bernd Fahrholz	Deputy Chairman of the BOM of Allianz AG and Chairman of the BOM of Dresdner Bank AG
	Mandates**
	Advance Holding AG (Chairman)
	Fresenius Medical Care AG
	HeidelbergCement AG
	Allianz Dresdner Asset Management GmbH
	BNP PARIBAS S.A.
	Dresdner Bank Luxembourg S. A. (Président)
	Dresdner Kleinwort Benson North America Inc.
Hans Glas*	Director of the Dingolfing plant
Konrad Gottinger*	Member of the Works Council, Dingolfing
Arthur L. Kelly	Managing Partner of KEL Enterprises L.P.
	Mandates**
	BASF AG
	DataCard Corp.
	Deere & Company
	HSBC Trinkaus & Burkhardt KGaA
	Northern Trust Corp.
	Snap-on Inc.
Susanne Klatten BSc., MBA	**Mandates****
	ALTANA AG (Deputy Chairman)
	ALTANA Pharma AG
	UnternehmerTUM GmbH
Willibald Löw*	Chairman of the **Landshut**
Prof.Dr. rer. nat. Dr. h.c. mult. Hubert Markl	Professor of Biology
	Mandates**
	Aventis S. A.
	Münchener Rückversicherungs-Gesellschaft AG
	Royal Dutch Petroleum Company/Shell
	Siemens AG
Prof. Dr.-Ing. Dr. h.c. Dr.-Ing. E. h. Joachim Milberg	Former Member of the BOM of BMW AG
	Mandates**
	Allianz Versicherungs-AG
	Royal Dutch Petroleum Company/Shell
	MAN AG
Werner Neugebauer*	Regional Executive Officer of IG Metall Bavaria
	Mandates**
	FAG Kugelfischer Georg Schäfer AG (Deputy Chairman)
Dr.-Ing. Dieter Soltmann	Former general partner of Spaten-Franziskaner-Bräu KGaA
	Mandates**
	Bankhaus Maffei & Co. KGaA
	Deutsche Postbank AG
	Löwenbräu AG (Chairman)

	Müller-Brot AG Münchener Tierpark Hellabrunn AG Bayerische Rundfunkwerbung GmbH
Prof. Dr. Jörgen Strube	Chairman of the BOM of BASF A **Mandates**** Allianz Lebensversicherungs-AG Bertelsmann AG Commerzbank AG Hapag-Lloyd AG Hochtief AG Linde AG
Werner Zierer*	Chairman of the Works Council, Regensburg

*Employee representative.
**Mandates (Membership of other Supervisory Boards and comparable boards with a supervisory function in Germany and abroad).

Figure 3: Supervisory board.

Source: Annual Report 2002, BMW.

rule. A re-appointment prior to one year before the end of the appointment period with a simultaneous termination of the current appointment only takes place under special circumstances. An age limit for members of the BOM is specified. The SB issues Terms of Reference for itself.

The Chairman of the SB co-ordinates work within the SB and chairs all its meetings. The Chairman of the SB also chairs the committees that handled contracts with members of the BOM.

The Chairman of the SB maintains regular contact with the BOM, in particular, with the management. The Chairman of the BOM is expected to inform the Chairman of the SB about important events without delay. The Chairman of the SB then informs the SB and, if required, convenes an extraordinary meeting of the SB.

Formation of Committees

The SB sets up committees with sufficient expertise based on the specific requirements of the Group. Such committees serve to increase the efficiency of the SBs work and the handling of complex issues. The committee chairpersons report regularly to the SB on the work of the committees.

The SB also sets up an Audit Committee (Bilanzausschuss), which handles, in particular, accounting, risk management, auditor independence, the issuing of the audit mandate to the auditor, the determination of auditing focal points and the fee agreement.

Composition and Compensation

Care is taken to ensure that the SB consists, at all times, of members who have the required knowledge, abilities, expertise and experience to complete their tasks properly and who are sufficiently independent. Consideration is also given to international activities of the BMW Group, potential conflicts of interest and the age limit stipulated for members of the SB.

In order to ensure that the SB can supervise and advise the BOM independently, not more than two former members of the BOM can be members of the SB. The SB members cannot hold directorships or similar positions or advisory tasks for companies that are major competitors of BMW.

All members of the SB ensure that they have sufficient time to perform their mandate. If members of the SB are members of the BOM of a listed company, they cannot accept more than four additional SB mandates in listed companies. SB mandates in subsidiaries of the company where the SB member of BMW is a member of the BOM are not included in this maximum number.

The compensation of the members of the SB is specified in the Articles of Association of BMW and takes into account the responsibilities and scope of tasks of the members of the SB as well as the economic situation and performance of the Group. Chairpersonship and deputy chairpersonship of the SB, including chairpersonship of and membership in committees, are taken into account. Members of the SB receive fixed as well as performance-related compensation.

Compensation paid or advantages extended by BMW to the members of the SB for services provided individually, in particular, for advisory or agency services, have to be disclosed. Instances of a member of the SB taking part in less than half of the meetings of the SB in a financial year, also have to be disclosed.

Conflicts of Interest

Each member of the SB is expected to act in the company's interests. The members of the SB cannot pursue personal interests while taking decisions or take advantage of business opportunities intended for the enterprise. Each member of the SB is expected to inform the SB about any conflicts of interest that may result from a consultant or director relationship with clients, suppliers, lenders or other business partners.

The SB is expected to inform the General Meeting of any conflicts of interest that occur and how these are handled. Material conflicts of interest and those that are not merely temporary in nature result in the termination of the mandate of the relevant SB member.

Advisory and other service agreements and contracts for work between BMW and a member of the SB require the SB's approval.

Transparency

The BOM is expected to disclose without delay any new facts which arise within BMW's field of activity and which are not known publicly, if such facts may substantially influence BMW's stock price.

As soon as BMW becomes aware that any party has acquired, exceeded or fell short of 5%, 10%, 25%, 50% or 75% of the voting rights in the company by means of a purchase, sale or any other manner, it discloses this fact without delay.

BMW treats all shareholders equally when it comes to providing information. All new facts made known to financial analysts are also disclosed to the shareholders. The company uses suitable communication media, such as the Internet, to inform shareholders and investors promptly.

Purchase or sale of shares in BMW or derivative instruments relating to BMW by members of the BOM and the SB have to be reported to BMW without delay where the value of the transactions with BMW stock exceeds €25 000 in 30 days. BMW publishes the fact without delay in an appropriate electronic information system or, in a journal generally used to publish statutory stock market information.

The shareholdings, including derivatives, held by individual members of the BOM and the SB are reported in the Notes to the Consolidated Financial Statements where these directly or indirectly exceed 1% of the stock issued by BMW. If the entire holdings of all members of the BOM and SB exceed 1% of the stock issued by BMW, the total amount is disclosed separately for the BOM and the SB.

As part of the group's regular information policy, the dates of essential regular publications (including the Annual Report, interim and quarterly reports, and General Meeting) are published sufficiently in advance in a financial calendar. Information published by BMW about the BMW Group is also accessible via the BMW Group's Internet site.

The Consolidated Financial Statements are drawn up by the BOM and examined by the group auditor and the SB. The Consolidated Financial Statements are made publicly accessible within 90 days of the end of the financial year. Interim reports are made accessible to the public within 45 days of the end of the reporting period.

BMW publishes a list of companies in which it has a shareholding that are not of minor importance to the group. The list includes the name and registered office of each company, the amount of shareholding, the amount of equity and the net profit/loss for the past financial year.

Details of relationships with shareholders considered to be related parties pursuant to the applicable accounting regulations are provided in the Consolidated Financial Statements.

Questions for Discussion

1. How is the corporate governance at BMW organized?

2. Discuss the roles of the Board of Management and Supervisory Board at BMW.

3. Discuss the formation of committees, composition of compensation, conflict of interests and transparency at BMW using the comparative evaluation of corporate governance systems in the US, Germany and Japan presented in the Chapter 13.

FURTHER READING

Edmondson, G., 'Look Who's Building Bimmers', *Business Week Online*, 2 December 2003.

BMW's Shifting Strategy, *Business Week Online*, 9 June 2003.

BMW Annual Report 2002.

www.bmw.com.

www.corporatelibrary.com.

www.hoovers.com.

www.*techlocate.com*.

Case Study 12

DANFOSS' BUSINESS STRATEGY IN CHINA [1]

A key component of our global business strategy is to make China our 'Second Home Market' following Europe by continuing to invest in manufacturing capacity and R&D, and developing a world class technical and sales support team in China.[2]

—Jorgen M. Clausen, CEO and President of Danfoss in 2006.

Here in China, key success parameters for us will be responsiveness, price competitiveness and quality performance through all our activities. This we will obtain through a lean, action-oriented approach with the right degree of co-ordination between relevant functions.[3]

—Claus Toennesen, General Manager, Danfoss (Tianjiin) Limited in 2005.

Introduction

On 1 November 2005, Danfoss China, the wholly owned subsidiary of the Denmark-based Danfoss Group, acquired Zhejiang Haili Electronic Technology Company Limited (also known as Holip).[4] The Danfoss Group is a leading manufacturer of valves and fluid handling components for heating, ventilation and air conditioning equipment, and Holip was a Chinese manufacturer of low-cost frequency converters.[5] This was Danfoss' first acquisition in China since it entered the country in 1994 through a wholly owned subsidiary. The acquisition was important for Danfoss, since the company would now have access to the rapidly growing low-end frequency converters market.

Danfoss retained the Holip brand name and used its own sales network to sell variable frequency converters to the low-end market in China, where the company had no significant presence. Holip was brought under Danfoss Motion Controls Division (see Figure 1 for various divisions of Danfoss). Commenting on the acquisition, Jorgen M. Clausen (Jorgen), President and CEO of the Danfoss Group, said the acquisition ... is in line with Danfoss' growth

ambitions in China in making it our 'Second Home Market.' It will speed up the Danfoss frequency converter business in the Chinese market. Low-cost frequency converters with basic features like those in the Holip range comprise 30% of the Chinese market, which is growing rapidly at 25% annually. Holip variable frequency converters meet the demands in this market, making the acquisition a perfect match for the Danfoss Motion Controls business in China.[6]

Danfoss, which had entered China in 1994, recorded US$120 million in revenues in 2004, a 40% increase from 2003. The company had set a sales target of approximately US$480 million by 2008. Danfoss China had been making losses until 2001, after which the company was broke even and started making profits. The company has a lot at stake in China and plans to make the country its 'second home' after Europe. Danfoss had already invested more than US$100 million in China by 2005 and built a factory in Tianjin Wuqing Development Area (Wuqing). It had shifted some of its manufacturing facilities from Denmark and other regions to China. The Wuqing factory had become the manufacturing hub for Danfoss in the Asia-Pacific region.

Background Note

During the Great Depression[7] in the 1930s, Mads Clausen (Clausen), an engineering graduate, decided to manufacture automatic valves for refrigeration plants in Denmark; at this time, these valves were being imported into Denmark from the US. In 1933, he established Dansk Koleautomatik-og Apparat-Fabrik (Danish Cooling Technology and Apparatus Factory). By 1938, the company (DCTAF) also started producing a number of other products such as ball float valves, thermostats, automatic spring valves, pressure-controlled valves, room thermostats and constant-pressure valves.

In the 1940s, DCTAF expanded its operations in Europe by appointing dealers in Belgium, Norway,

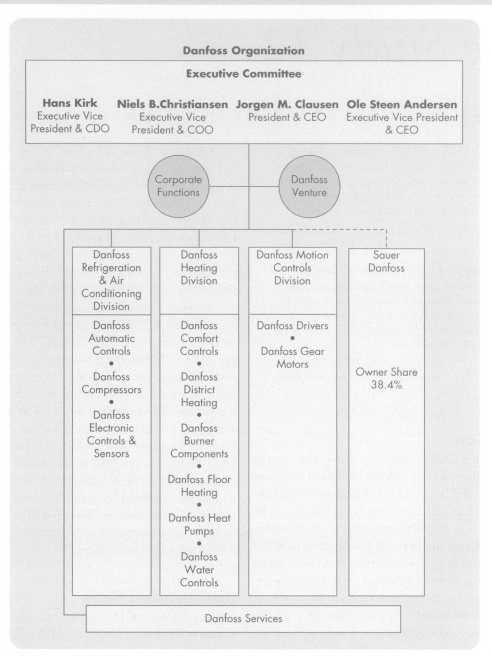

Figure 1: Danfoss organization.

Source: www.danfoss.com.

Sweden, the Netherlands, England, Norway and Spain. In 1946, the company's name was changed to Danfoss for convenience, especially in the international markets. In the same year, a new office with 261 employees was opened in Copenhagen. In 1949, Danfoss established an office in Argentina, its first outside Denmark. In 1950, Danfoss introduced piecework, a system through which the employees were paid on the basis of the quantity produced. By the end of 1953, the number of employees had increased to 2000. Danfoss also started manufacturing compressors and radiator thermostats[8]. In 1955, it launched

	(In million Danish Krone)				
	2005	2004	2003	2002	2001
Net sales	16 416	16 345	15 434	14 923	14 384
Net profit	733	775	744	513	332

Source: www.danfoss.com

Table 1: Danfoss worldwide – financial performance (2001–2005).

its in-house newspaper *Ventilen*. In 1962, Danfoss started its own research department.

After Clausen's death in August 1966, his wife Bitten Clausen took over as the Chairman of the Board. During the 1970s, Danfoss manufactured different types of electronic frequency converters, hydraulic components and flow meters. In the later half of the 1970s, radiator thermostats, which reduced energy consumption, contributed significantly to the company's revenues. In 1980, Danfoss had 9300 employees and its sales turnover was 3.3 billion Danish Krone[9]. By 1985, the sales had increased to 5 billion Danish Krone.

During the 1990s, Danfoss concentrated on producing a range of environment-friendly products such as hydraulic components (Nessie), for which it was awarded the EU Environmental Prize in 1995. In 1996, Jorgen, son of Clausen, was appointed as the President and CEO of the Danfoss Group. In the late 1990s, Danfoss expanded to Estonia and Lithuania, acquired companies and established sales offices in India, Morocco and Greece.

In 2000, Danfoss Fluid Power A/S[10], which manufactured mobile hydraulic products merged with Sauer-Sundstrand Inc. and formed Sauer-Danfoss Inc. Danfoss owned a 38.4% equity stake in the independent Sauer-Danfoss. By 2005, Danfoss had emerged as one of the largest companies in Denmark with an annual turnover of 16.4 million Danish Krone and net profit of 733 million Danish Krone (see Table 1). The company's businesses included a refrigeration and air conditioning division, a heating division and the Danfoss motion controls division.

Danfoss Enters China

Danfoss had been exporting its products to China since 1991 and it had a small share in the Chinese radiator thermostat market. In the early 1990s, the Japanese economy suffered from a severe economic crisis. This made many manufacturers, including Danfoss' customers such as air-conditioning and refrigeration manufacturers, shift their focus to China. The Danfoss board learned that the air-conditioning and refrigeration markets in China were poised for huge growth (see Figure 2 for details of the air conditioning and refrigeration industry in China). Further, China offered huge cost advantages in the form of cheap availability of labour and land. Moreover, the European customers of Danfoss were putting pressure on the company to decrease the prices of expansion valves. All these factors led Danfoss to think seriously of establishing a production facility in China.

Danfoss' initial plan was to produce radiator thermostats and expansion valves by shifting the production of expansion valves from Denmark to China, and to develop China as its global sourcing hub. In May 1994, business and political relations between China and Denmark were fast improving, and Danfoss was given a business licence to establish a wholly owned subsidiary in China. This was not in line with Chinese regulations that required foreign companies to partner with a Chinese company to get a business licence, but Danfoss was looked upon as a special case. In 1994, the parent company set up Danfoss Industries Limited (HK) in Hong Kong, for the marketing and sales of its products in China. In the same year, Danfoss Industries Limited (HK) opened its representative office in Beijing.

Danfoss planned to lease some space before constructing its own manufacturing facility. After a thorough study, Danfoss selected Wuqing for its manufacturing facility because it presented many benefits, such as easy availability of cheap labour and land, proximity to the Chinese capital Beijing, favourable

Starting in the early 1990s, the economic boom in China has increased the disposable income of individuals. This in turn has increased purchases of domestic appliances like refrigerators and air conditioners. The growing popularity of high-rise buildings which house banks, supermarkets, hospitals and restaurants in cities like Shanghai, Beijing and Shenzhen, has also increased the demand for air conditioners and refrigerators significantly.

China opened its market for foreign manufacturers to establish manufacturing facilities in the country during the 1980s. The entry of foreign companies into China picked up pace in the mid-1990s. According to China Refrigeration and Air Conditioning Industry Association (CRAA), the number of air conditioning and refrigeration manufacturers doubled from 217 companies to more than 550 companies between 1990 and 2002. In the recent years, Chinese companies such as Haier, have been expanding their markets to North America, Europe, and other parts of Asia.

The US had been the major exporter of refrigeration and air-conditioning equipment to China – it exported over US$326 million in 2002. After China joined the WTO in December 2001, manufacturers from various countries such as Japan, Singapore, France, UK, Germany, Taiwan, South Korea, Denmark, etc. entered China.

In 2004, more than 26 million refrigerators were sold in the domestic market and about 25 million units were exported. The exports were 52% more than in 2003 and this was due to increased production by foreign companies operating in China. The air conditioning industry in China is expected to stockpile about 30 million units in 2006 due to overproduction (80 million units were manufactured while the demand was only 50 million units in 2005. In 2000, there were about 400 brands in the refrigeration and air-conditioning segment. But by 2003, due to fierce competition, only 150 brands were left, and by 2005 only 33 were left. The top 10 brands including the market leaders – Haier (16.22%), Midea (13.21%) and Gree (9.3%) – accounted for about 75% market share in 2005.

Figure 2: Air-conditioning and refrigeration industry in China. (Compiled from various sources).

local authorities, etc. However, before allowing it to start operations, the Chinese government wanted Danfoss to buy 50 000 sq.m of land in Wuqing immediately. It could use this land for building its manufacturing plant at some time in the future. Danfoss agreed to this, and registered its subsidiary Danfoss (Tianjin) Limited in September 1995 (see Figure 3 for details of Danfoss in China). The company

Figure 3: Danfoss in China.

Source: www.danfoss.com.

started production of thermostats and expansion valves at a leased plant in 1996.

The Initial Years

Danfoss had a tough start in China. Although its own manufacturing facility was inaugurated in July 1997, the company had to continue its operations in the leased plant until 2001. It had problems with its suppliers and its employees and therefore had to focus entirely on its daily operations. Initially, Danfoss could not find suitable suppliers in China and had to procure most of the raw materials required from suppliers in Europe. Language acted as a major barrier, and its many technical specifications often led to confusion among the Chinese suppliers. This resulted in the rejection of many products during testing.

Danfoss also found it difficult to deal with Chinese employees. The management followed the western style of openness and co-operation, which was new to the Chinese employees. They were used to a system that gave importance to individual performance and were not accustomed to working in a group. Hence, they were reluctant to discuss things and did the work as they were ordered to even if they had the knowledge to do it better. The Danfoss management therefore thought they were unco-operative.

On the industry front, the market for radiator thermostats was not growing as fast as expected, although the expansion valves market was promising. Further, the name – Danfoss – was not familiar to many Chinese clients and this restricted the growth in company's revenues. According to Jens M. Jepsen, Head of the Motion Controls Division of Danfoss China, 'The clients were very familiar with some big companies such as Ericsson but they had never heard of Danfoss'.[11] However, Danfoss was confident that its high-quality products and service would do well in China.

In 1998, the production of expansion valves was shifted from Denmark to China. This helped Danfoss reduce its production costs by 40% without affecting the quality of these products. Taking account of the cost advantages, the Danfoss management directed all its manufacturing facilities located globally to procure from its suppliers in China (see Table 2 for Danfoss' manufacturing facilities). Under this initiative, potential suppliers were invited to a seminar in Nordborg, where they could bid for selected components. In 2000, the line components[12] production was also transferred from Denmark to China. In addition, the top management of Danfoss began to consider the possibility of moving most of its production facilities in Europe to China. This idea was not liked by many of the company's stakeholders as well as its production managers in Denmark.

Commenting on this, Claus Toennesen (Toennesen), Production Manager, Danfoss China, said, '[Comparing Danish production costs with Chinese] is really a sensitive subject in the Danfoss Corporation. Eventually, we need to move more production to China in order to fulfil customer wants – it is simply a matter of survival for the company in an increasingly competitive world. However in the short run, it is affecting the working lives of many people in Denmark and they are obviously hesitant.'[13]

The China Strategy

During the early 2000s, Danfoss was registering about 35% annual growth in revenues in China, but was yet to become profitable. The company was still importing a number of products from other countries to cater to the local market and sold them through its

Countries			
Brazil	Finland	Mexico	Sweden
Bulgaria	France	Norway	South Africa
Canada	Germany	Poland	Sweden
China	Great Britain	Russian Federation	Ukraine
Denmark	Italy	Slovenia	

Source: www.danfoss.com

Table 2: Danfoss' manufacturing facilities.

Hong Kong division (as imported goods were not allowed to be sold in China).

However, things changed dramatically after 2001. Toennesen, who was appointed as the General Manager of Danfoss (Tianjiin) Limited in October 2001, managed to convince the company's top management and get permission to move the company's manufacturing operations from the leased premises to its own manufacturing facility. The new factory began production in December 2002. In addition, the factory was also equipped to produce refrigeration and air conditioning products (see Figure 4 for

Refrigeration and A/C	Heating	Motion Controls	Industrial Controls	Water Controls
Compressors	Radiator Thermostats	Frequency Converters	Solenoid Valves	Gate Valves
Electronic Controls	Room Thermostats	Decentral Products	Externally Operated Valves	Non Return Valves and Valves for Regulation
Electronically Operated Valves	Floor Heating Hydronics	Softstarter	Thermostatically Operated Valves	Butterfly Valves
Filter Driers and Sight Glasses	Floor Heating Electrical Climate Controls	Geared Motors	Vacuum Valves	
Line Components	Substations	Motion Control Tool	Coils for Valves	
Liquid Level Controls	Weather Compensators & PI Controllers		Single Pressure Switches	
Pressure and Temperature Regulators	Motorized Control Valves		Dual Pressure Switches	
Sensors and Transmitters for Electronic Controls	Ball Valves		Differential Pressure Switches	
Safety Valves	Pressure/Flow Controllers		Pressure Transmitters	
Solenoid Valves	Temperature Controllers		Pressure Test Valves	
Stop and Regulating Valves	Heat Exchangers		Isolation Valves	
Thermostatic Expansion Valves	Balancing Valves		Temperature Switches	
Thermostats and Pressure Controls	Burner Components		Temperature Sensors	
Water Valves	Heat Meters		Contactors and Motor Starters	
	Solenoid Valves Pressure and Temperature Switches			

Figure 4: Danfoss – product categories in China.

Source: www.danfoss.com.

details of Danfoss China's product categories). Danfoss also started work on expanding the factory to include the production of scroll compressors[14] for air-conditioning units. This facility became operational in mid-2004.

In the air-conditioning business, the Wuqing plant exported most of its air-conditioning products produced in the first year of production because the air-conditioning market had not picked up in China. However, by 2004, its exports came down to 40% of the total production. There were several reasons for this change. The company was able to form alliances with local suppliers and sub-suppliers that increased local procurement to about 60–70%. This helped in manufacturing quality products at a much lower cost, attracting manufacturers such as Gree, China's largest producer of air conditioners. Apart from local players, Danfoss also gained major orders to supply components from global players such as Carrier, York, etc.

In order to improve the skills of its local employees, Human Resources personnel at Danfoss China conducted a series of training sessions and personality development seminars. Since trade unions are not allowed in China, Danfoss arranged an alternative platform where employees were encouraged to talk to the management regarding issues such as working conditions, etc. Meanwhile, the demand for Danfoss' products started growing rapidly as the air conditioner market witnessed a boom. Danfoss also started working on the expansion of the Wuqing factory.

Danfoss benefited from China's entry into the World Trade Organization[15] (WTO) in December 2001, which permitted businesses to sell imported products directly into the Chinese market. This reduced the cost of importing products to China because the imports did not now need to come through Hong Kong. This increased the number of air conditioner and refrigerator manufacturers who established their manufacturing bases in China, which in turn increased the sales of Danfoss products. However, this also attracted several other OEM manufacturers to China.

Another major incident that contributed to Danfoss' improved performance in China occurred in 2003 when Jorgen read an article about a major European manufacturer in a newspaper in early 2003. The article said that the manufacturer was happy with his company recording 40% annual growth in revenues in China, but later found that he was actually losing market share because the market for the same product was growing at 80%. Commenting on this, Jorgen said, 'This made me wonder how successful we really were in China and if we too were being fooled by growth rates that were vastly superior to the ones we were getting in Europe.'[16]

Danfoss conducted a review of all its product markets to assess their growth potential. The review revealed that Danfoss' products were catering mostly to high-end markets and a little bit to the middle markets, totally ignoring the low-end markets. In fact, they did not even know that a low-end market for their products existed. The review showed that the low-end markets offered huge potential to build volumes and Danfoss could increase its market share by 15–20%.

Danfoss also believed that China would emerge as a big market in about 15 years, especially in the refrigeration and freezing appliances business. This growth was imminent as the Chinese government was planning to build a 'cold food chain'[17] with the aim of improving the way food was stored and transported in the country. In China, about 80% of the food was stored and transported to other places without temperature control resulting in 20% of food getting spoilt. With more and more foreign retailers coming to China and events such as the 2008 Olympics in Beijing and 2010 Shanghai World Expo to be held in China, the government wanted to improve its food storage and distribution system (see Figure 5 for details of the cold food chain in China).

All these developments resulted in Danfoss increasing its annual revenue growth target to 50% starting from the year 2004. It also laid down an ambitious plan for China (its 'second home market' after Europe), which was recording slow revenue growth. Elaborating on this, Jorgen said, 'By home market, we mean one where we want to be a market share leader, an aspiration that helps us set a goal for ourselves. Maybe we cannot be #1 in China, but maybe we can be #2 or #3. We certainly don't want to be number 17, because then we will be in trouble later on when the industry consolidates, and we won't have the volumes needed to compete with local Chinese incumbents.'[18]

To cater to the low-end market, Danfoss planned to manufacture products using components manufactured locally and with 'less capital intensive

With the rapid growth of supermarkets and fast-food chains across the major cities in China, the sales of consumer-ready frozen food items like ice-creams, fruits, meat, seafood, etc. have been on the rise. The rising demand requires retailers to keep a stock of these perishable items, while manufacturers are also required to ensure that the items reached retailers without spoilage during transport.

For this, manufacturers need refrigerated vehicles for transportation, while retailers need temperature-controlled storage facilities in their stores. China does not have an adequately developed cold-chain infrastructure and logistics. The facilities available are also very costly, and so only 15% of perishable food items were being handled properly as of 2005. As a rapidly developing nation, and with mega events like 2008 Beijing Olympics approaching, the Chinese government decided that building the infrastructure to handle perishable food items is to be given high priority.

Building a cold food chain cannot be done by an individual company as it involves temperature-controlled warehouses, trucks, local distribution channels and a direct-store delivery system. It requires a group or consortium of companies to work together, support of the government and a proper regulatory framework. In a country like China, where the implementation of communications and IT systems is not extensive, records relating to inventory management, warehouse management and logistics management are by and large recorded on paper. Hence, building efficient IT systems which require huge investments are necessary.

The United States Meat Export Federation (USMEF) launched a 'cold chain project' in Beijing in July 2005. Every year, millions of dollars' worth of items were getting spoiled during transportation from the US to China. USMEF's aim was to build a cold chain system, and then promote the American beef and pork exported to China by emphasizing the safety and quality of the food. According to USMEF, this project would reduce the loss of food items worth millions of dollars during exports.

Another step in this regard was taken by Supply Chain Council by organizing a summit on Cold Chain China Summit on July 12 2006. A number of logistics experts, senior managers in supply chain and logistics departments of various companies, were invited to discuss the challenges involved in building the cold chain system and the best practices for storing and managing temperature-sensitive products in China.

Figure 5: Cold food chain in China. (Compiled from various sources).

techniques', and increase its local procurement from 10 million euros[19] in 2004 to nearly 150 million euros in 2005. This was something that Danfoss engineers had never done before. So, Danfoss decided to develop completely new products by setting up R&D centres for refrigeration, air conditioning and heating in China. Danfoss also planned to distribute these centres across 40 urban localities in China. It would increase its employee strength to 4000 by 2008, and hire a team consisting completely of Chinese managers.

Danfoss was careful to maintain healthy relations with the Chinese government. It invited Chinese officials to visit its factories in Denmark and China, and on occasions such as the opening of a manufacturing facility, officials from Danfoss' top management made it a point to meet Chinese government officials. According to Danfoss, this indicated to the local people and corporates that the government supported the company and its products.

As another step towards making China its second home market, Danfoss purchased another 10 000 sq. m of land beside its Wuqing factory and held the ground breaking ceremony on 14 June 2004, in the presence of government officials and its factory employees. Elaborating on this, Jorgen said, 'It (the opening) is not simply an expansion of our activities and manufacturing facilities in China. More significantly, it is a manifestation of our long-term goal of building our 'Second Home Market' in China.'[20] The construction was completed by June 2005.

Within a year of launching its 'second home' concept, Danfoss felt a change in the attitude of its local employees and customers as they acquired a positive attitude towards the company. Jorgen always told his employees and customers that only he was Danish, whereas the products and technology they bought were all Chinese. He said that they could contribute to employment generation in China by buying

Do your homework: Get your China strategy right.

HR: Find, attract, develop and keep the qualified employees and most important managers necessary for fast growth.

Distribution: It is important to outline and implement the right strategies for how to distribute the products in the huge Chinese market and, if necessary, find and train the right distributors.

Accounts receivable management: Be careful with credits, because there is a higher risk of losses here. The legal system has a lot of problems in China.

Get the products right: Make sure you are competitive, not only in the high-end segment.

Local sourcing and manufacturing: This helps to lower the cost base so you are able to compete with local manufactured products.

Protect your Intellectual Property Rights.

Gunaxi: Build and maintain relationship with the relevant decision makers.

Source: www.danfoss.com

Table 3: Danfoss – eight most important success factors for doing business in China.

Danfoss products. Through its experiences in China, Danfoss formulated eight success factors for doing business in China (shown in Table 3).

The Road Ahead

By mid-2006, although Danfoss had established itself in China, counterfeit products formed a big obstacle to its future growth. A number of local manufacturers copied Danfoss products and sold them under the same name with similar packing. In one such instance, Danfoss was informed of its counterfeit products being sold at very low prices. Danfoss discovered the company that was doing this and reported the matter to the police. The company also started working closely with the local police and government officials to deal with the copycats. However, the company believed that though the problem could be mitigated, it would be difficult to eradicate it completely.

Another problem for Danfoss was that the air-conditioner market in China had become extremely competitive. According to Cai Ying, Information Resource Development Department of the State Information Center (SIC), 'There will be around 25 brands, with a certain sales scale, left in the domestic air-conditioner market in 2006.'[21] At this rate, industry analysts fear that only a few big players would remain in the market, and competition between the OEMs operating in China, such as Danfoss, would increase further.

Danfoss' future plans include improving its market share in China to about 20% by acquiring other companies. The company started negotiations with three Chinese companies in this regard. If the deals are inked, Danfoss will pay for acquiring 60% of the companies' shares at the initial stage, whereas the rest will be paid on the basis of the post-acquisition performance of the company. According to Danfoss, it is very difficult to find suitable partners in China. Moreover, there is a dearth of local talent – people who know English are scarce in China and about 15% of Danfoss employees leave every year. Commenting on this, Carsten Sorensen, President of Danfoss China said, 'It's very hard to hire top people (in this industry) in China and acquisitions are quite difficult because we can't find a suitable Chinese company.'[22]

Questions for Discussion

1. Danfoss had entered China in 1994. What factors motivated Danfoss to enter China? Discuss in detail the problems faced by the company in the initial years and how they were solved.
2. Comment on the 'China Strategy' of Danfoss. Explain how the company went about expanding its operations in China. What are the advantages of establishing a manufacturing facility in China for Danfoss?
3. Danfoss plans to make China its 'second home' after Europe. Discuss the opportunities and threats that Danfoss could face in China in the near future. What should the company do to mitigate the threats?

FURTHER READING

Hoover, W.E. Jr, Making China Your Second Home Market: An Interview with the CEO of Danfoss, www.mckinseyquarterly.com, 2006.

Powell, P., Manufacturers Reach Out to Asian Market, www.achrnews.com, 7 June 2004.

Yan, H., Partner in Success, www.app1.chinadaily.com, 18 September 2003.

Yan, H., Chilling Tales from the China Market, www.shanghai-star.com.cn, 14 April 2006.

Air-conditioning Market Hotting Up, www.china.org.cn, 22 September 2005.

China Cold Chain is Heating Up, www.atkearney.com, 2006.

China's First Conference on Cold Chain Logistics in China Taking Place in Shanghai on July 12, www.prleap.com, 27 March 2006.

China's Transition in Full Swing, www.ari.org, 2002.

Danfoss Acquires Chinese Frequency Converter Company, www.danfoss.com, 3 November 2005.

Danfoss Introduces Innovative Energy Efficient Solutions in China, www.danfoss.com, 20 April 2006.

Internationalization of Sourcing and Knowledge Development: An Organizational Routine Perspective, www.lok.cbs.dk, 2003.

USMEF Cold Chain Project Begins with Two-Day Seminar and Training Course in Beijing, www.usmef.org, 20 July 2005.

Case Study 13

GAZPROM–NAFTOGAZ UKRAINY DISPUTE: BUSINESS OR POLITICS?[1]

I'll remind you that some European countries, members of the European Union, cover 90% of their gas needs with Russian hydrocarbons. Ninety percent! And no one's complained so far'.[2]

—Vladimir Putin, President of the Russian Federation, at an EU[3]–Russia Summit in October 2005.

Why does Turkey pay US$100 per thousand cubic meters, the Baltic countries pay US$110, the Caucasus pays US$100, and Ukraine, which is Russia's closest neighbour, must pay US$230?[4]

—Viktor Yushchenko, President of Ukraine, questioning Gazprom's demand for higher gas prices in December, 2005.

Introduction

On 14 December 2005, the open joint-stock company Gazprom (Gazprom), a state-controlled Russian company with monopoly over gas exports, announced a stiff hike in its gas prices for 2006 for Naftogaz Ukrainy (Naftogaz),[5] the Ukrainian state gas company. Gazprom, which had earlier demanded US$160 per thousand cubic metres (Tcm),[6] hiked the price to US$230 per Tcm and threatened to cut off supplies, from 1 January 2006, if Ukraine did not agree to its new prices. No agreement could be reached with Naftogaz, which had paid US$50 per Tcm of gas in 2005. On 1 January 2006, in the midst of a harsh winter, and the day on which the Russian Federation (Russia) assumed the presidency of G8,[7] Gazprom began to reduce the pressure of gas into the pipeline system meant for Europe that passed through Ukraine. The message was clear – it had decided to go ahead with its threat to cut off gas supplies to Ukraine.

Within hours, more than half-a-dozen countries in Europe reported reduction in the gas supplies received at their terminals (refer to Figure 1 for Gazprom's gas exports to Western Europe and Figure 2 for Russian gas exports to Europe transiting through Ukraine and other countries). By evening, the trading of accusations began. Gazprom claimed that Ukraine[8] was stealing gas meant for Europe that passed through its territory. Ukraine replied that it was only taking 15% of the gas that it was legally entitled to take as transportation charges as well as the gas coming from Turkmenistan through Gazprom's pipelines.[9] Some analysts felt that it was Gazprom that was undersupplying gas to Europe and blaming Ukraine, so as to bring European pressure on Ukraine to agree to its new price for gas.

Gazprom then invited SGS[10] to oversee the amount of gas it was pumping at its stations meant for Europe, passing through Ukraine. Ukraine, however, refused to allow observers to undertake similar inspections. Under the terms of the various treaties that the former Soviet Union[11] had with the European countries, Russia, and thereby Gazprom, was obliged to supply gas up to its former Soviet borders.[12] From there, the European countries took over the responsibility of gas delivery. So even if Ukraine was withholding or illegally siphoning off Russian gas meant for Europe, it was Russia that could be sued, and not Ukraine. On 4 January 2006, Gazprom and Naftogaz announced that they had reached a settlement, wherein RosUkrEnergo,[13] a Swiss registered company, agreed to buy the gas meant for Ukraine from Gazprom at US$230 per Tcm and supply it to Ukraine at US$95 per Tcm after mixing the Central Asian gas bought from Turkmenistan and Uzbekistan at US$60–65 per Tcm. Analysts commented that rather than being a concrete settlement, it was more of a face-saving deal for both Gazprom and Naftogaz.

Background

Gazprom, like many Russian companies, emerged out of the disintegration of the Soviet Union. Under its new President Boris Yeltsin, Russia privatized the state held monopoly departments and factories in order to embrace the market-oriented economic

Country	2000	2001	2002	2003	2004
Germany	34.1	32.6	31.5	29.6	36.1
Italy	21.8	20.2	19.3	19.7	21.6
Turkey	10.2	11.1	11.8	12.8	14.5
France	12.9	11.2	11.4	11.2	13.3
Austria	5.1	4.9	5.2	6.0	6.0
Finland	4.3	4.6	4.6	5.1	5.0

Figure 1: Gazprom's gas exports to Western Europe in Bcm (2000–2004).

Source: http://www.gazprom.com/documents/Statistika%20En.pdf.

reforms and catch up with the West. Gazprom was one of them.[14] But whereas the oil industry was broken up into several fragments and privatized, Gazprom remained a monolith. In spite of its privatization, the state retained a significant stake in the company.

Russia has been using gas ever since 1819, when gas lamps were first used in St Petersburg.[15] With the development of gas and oil industries in the 20th century, gas and oil came to be extensively used in urban and rural areas. In 1948, the Natural Gas Production Head Department was set up at the Ministry of Oil Industry, and this was reorganized into the Head Department of Gas Industry at the Council of Ministers of the USSR in 1956. In 1989, under Mikhail Gorbachev's reform of Perestroika and Glasnost,[16] the state gas concern Gazprom was formed. After the disintegration of the Soviet Union, the Russian Joint stock company Gazprom became the legal successor of this state concern by a Presidential decree. In 1998,

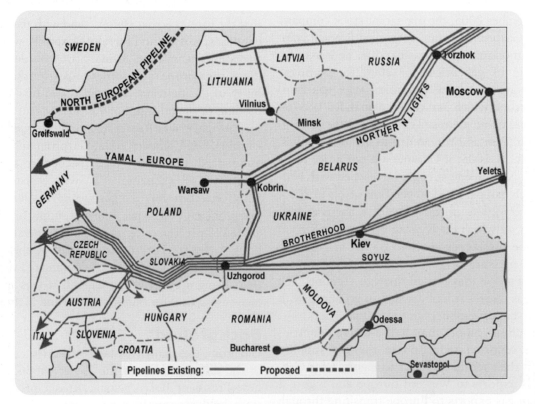

Figure 2: Gas exports to Europe transiting through Ukraine and other countries.

Source: Jonathan Stern, 'The Russian – Ukrainian gas crisis of January 2006', Oxford Institute for Energy Studies.

it was renamed as the Open joint stock company Gazprom.

In 2004, Gazprom was the world's largest gas company engaged in natural gas prospecting, extracting, processing and transportation, as well as gas sales inside and outside Russia. It had reserves of 28 trillion cubic metres of industrial gas, equalling 16% of the world's gas reserves, and produced 545 billion cubic metres (Bcm) of gas. It also owned Russia's Unified Gas Transportation System (UGS), the largest gas transportation system in the world, with over 153 300 km long pipelines and 263 compressor stations along the way. It held stakes in various companies that were engaged in gas exploration, production, refining, transporting and exporting. Its subsidiaries also held stakes in foreign companies that were engaged in the distribution and supply of gas to end consumers.[17] Overall, including the gas supplies from Central Asia and other independent gas producers, the UGS transported 687 Bcm of gas in 2004. Gazprom supplied 292 Bcm of gas for domestic purposes in Russia with the price regulated by the government. It supplied gas to 22.8 million homes, 12 200 industrial facilities and 29 600 boiler houses in 2004[18] (see Figure 3 for Gazprom's production and financial details and Figure 4 for Gazprom's share in Russia's and world's proven gas reserves as of 2004).

Exports to Europe

In the middle of the 1940s, the then Soviet Union began exporting gas on a very small scale to Poland, then under its control, after the end of World War II. Large-scale gas exports began in 1967, with the commissioning of the pipeline 'Druzhba' – meaning 'Friendship' that carried gas from the Soviet Union to Central and East European countries that were under its orbit of influence. Gas exports to these countries were highly subsidized and under favourable terms. Exports to Western Europe began in 1968, when the Soviet Union began shipping gas to Austria's OMV.[19] In the 1970s, the Soviet Union negotiated with the then West Germany for gas supplies. Eventually, gas supplies began to flow to France, Italy and other European countries. Gas exports to the European countries fetched the Soviet Union valuable hard currency and for political reasons, Soviet Union ensured that

Production (Gazprom Group)	Units	2003	2004	(2004/2003)%
Gas reserves increase	Bcm	426.8	378.1	88.6
Condensate and oil production	Million tons	11.0	12.0	109.1
Gas supplies to Russian consumers	Bcm	291.0	292.1	100.4
Gas export to Europe	Bcm	132.9	140.5	105.7
Gas export to CIS countries and Baltic States	Bcm	42.6	52.5	123.2
Trunk pipelines and pipeline branches put into operation	km	1,786.5	1,013.6	56.7
Financials (OAO Gazprom)				
Sales of goods, products, work, services (net of VAT, excise taxes and other obligatory payments)	million roubles	780,613	887,231	113.7
Sales profit	million roubles	207,555	211,593	101.9
Net profit	million roubles	129,671	161,084	124.2
Net assets	million roubles	1,707,213	1,851,961	108.5
Dividends	million roubles	9,469	16,335	172.5
Earnings per share (EPS)	roubles	6.02	6.80	113.0
Net assets per share	roubles	72.1	78.2	108.5
Short-term borrowings	million roubles	275,756	200,355	72.7
Long-term borrowings	million roubles	312,591	459,534	147.0
Capital expenditures (net of VAT)	million roubles	173.70	179.55	103.4

Figure 3: Gazprom's production and financial details.

Source: www.gazprom.ru.

Russia	47,811
Of which Gazprom	28,006
North America	7,526
South America	7,349
Europe	7,834
Africa	13,849
Near and Middle East	71,611
Asia-Oceania	24,656
Total	180,636

Figure 4: World proven natural gas reserves by region as of 1 January 2004.

Source: http://www.gazprom.com/documents/Statistika%20En.pdf.

there was no interruption in its gas supplies to Europe. It attached great importance to building and retaining its credibility as a reliable and stable supplier of gas to Europe.

Gazprom also maintained cordial commercial relations with its European customers. It entered into agreements with various companies to form joint ventures that undertook the task of domestic gas supplies in various countries such as France, Italy, Austria and Greece as well as in most of the former Soviet Republics. Europe was the most important market for Gazprom, and for Europe, Gazprom was the most important supplier, the source of a quarter of its imports. In 2004, Gazprom's exports to Europe were 140.5 Bcm, and to the former Soviet Union republics, 52.5 Bcm. Overall, Gazprom exported gas to 28 countries, the major importers being Germany (36.1 Bcm), Italy (14.5 Bcm), France (13.3 Bcm), Hungary (9.3 Bcm), Ukraine (34.34 Bcm) and Belarus (10.2 Bcm). It earned more than US$18 billion in export revenues in 2004.[20]

Disputes with Ukraine

After the disintegration of the Soviet Union, Russia, the largest republic, became the successor state to the Soviet Union, inheriting all its obligations and entitlements. Russia was not willing to give up its influence over the former republics of the Soviet Union. It agreed to supply gas and oil, and various other things, to the former Soviet Union republics at a highly subsidized rate and under favourable terms. This Russia did to keep the newly independent states from deserting it. It perceived a threat to its power and influence as well as to its security if these countries joined the West and allowed their military bases to be used by other powerful countries. At the same time, Russia made use of the 'destination clauses' in its gas agreements by which the recipients were prohibited from re-exporting subsidized Russian gas to Europe.

The disintegration of the Soviet Union also led to the rise of complex problems between Russia and the newly independent states, especially Ukraine. The Soviet Union's Black Sea Fleet had been headquartered at Sevastopol in Crimea. Crimea had been transferred from the then Russian Soviet Federated Socialist Republic to the then Ukrainian Soviet Socialist Republic in 1954.[21] After the disintegration, Russia refused to recognize the sovereignty of Ukraine over Sevastopol, claiming that it had never been integrated with Ukraine. In 1997, the issue was resolved through a bilateral 'Peace & Friendship' treaty between Russia and Ukraine, which stated that Sevastopol belonged to Ukraine. At the same time, the treaty also set down the terms of a fixed long-term lease agreement of Sevastopol's resources to Russia for maintaining its Black Sea naval headquarters.[22] The assets of the Black Sea Fleet were divided between Russia and Ukraine.

Russia also had other serious problems with Ukraine, such as the control of the nuclear weapons stationed in Ukraine at the time of the disintegration of the Soviet Union. Facilitated by the US, this problem was later resolved peacefully, with Ukraine being given a financial package in exchange for the safe transfer of the nuclear weapons to Russia.

But the biggest irritant to Russia was the fact that Ukraine lay on the way of all of its gas exports to Europe. Ukraine had acquired the rights to gas pipelines in its territory, built by the Soviet Union, without any corresponding obligations. Gazprom, on the other hand, was responsible for gas supplies to Europe up to the former Soviet Union borders. Ukraine, therefore, held virtual monopoly over the transit of Russian gas exports to Europe. There were many disputes regarding the price of Russian gas for Ukraine's domestic consumption, mode of payment for those supplies, and more importantly, the price and mode of payment for the transit of the Russian gas meant for Europe. Ukraine used its monopoly over transit to bargain for extremely low prices for gas imports from Russia. Russia also agreed to pay for the transit of Russian gas to Europe passing through Ukraine's territories.

Ukraine's Naftogaz was made responsible for the purchase and supply of gas for Ukraine's domestic consumption, in addition to its responsibility to oversee the transit of Russian gas through its territory. Ukraine's gas needs were huge, while the domestic production was very little. In 2005, Ukraine's domestic gas consumption was 80 Bcm, out of which only 20 Bcm came from domestic production. For the rest, 36 Bcm was imported from Turkmenistan, 17 Bcm of Gazprom's gas was used as transit fees and the remaining 7 Bcm of gas was bought from Gazprom at US$50 per Tcm.[23] Ukraine therefore was heavily dependent on Russia and Turkmenistan for gas supply to meet its domestic consumption. But it was unable to pay its dues properly.

Several reasons existed for Ukraine's default on payment. There were allegations that one of the main reasons was that many people associated with the Ukrainian government and Naftogaz were siphoning off Russian gas to become rich. Naftogaz could not pay its dues to Gazprom and the debts accumulated year after year. To top it all, it was alleged that Naftogaz had been stealing huge amounts of gas in the 1990s and well into the new millennium too, in order to meet the rising demand for gas, exacerbated by severe winters. This led to serious acrimony between Gazprom and Naftogaz.

Gas Disputes in the 1990s

In 1997, the Asian financial crisis triggered a series of crises all over the world. The financial crisis in Russia the following year led to a steep fall in the value of rouble. The crisis affected neighbouring countries too, especially the former Soviet Union republics. At the same time, there was also a severe slump in gas and oil prices in the world market, leading to a fall in the (foreign exchange) revenues of Gazprom. To add to its woes, there was the non-payment of gas bills in the domestic Russian market.[24] All these forced Gazprom to make its export collections strict and efficient. Accordingly, it pressured Naftogaz to pay up its debts and warned it to stop the illegal withdrawal of gas from its pipelines.

Gazprom hoped its stern warning would stop the siphoning off of Russian gas being exported to Europe. However, contrary to its expectations, the siphoning only seemed to increase. In November 1999 alone, it was alleged that Ukraine had siphoned off 4 Bcm of Russian gas meant for Europe.[25] In response, Gazprom cut off gas supplies to Ukraine, but realized that it did not have much of a control over its gas supplies to Europe, transiting through Ukraine. It therefore decided that any gas illegally taken from the pipelines would be charged at the rate of US$83/Tcm.[26] In mid-2000, the allegations again started, with Gazprom claiming that more than 9 Bcm of gas had been illegally drawn by Ukraine in the first six months.

As the alleged illegal siphoning off of its gas by Naftogaz increased, Gazprom suffered serious erosion in its revenues. Its perception of Ukraine as an unreliable partner led to its seeking alternative sources for its gas exports (Figure 5 shows some of Gazprom's other options). It proposed to build a bypass pipeline through Belarus and Poland that could carry 30 Bcm, with later extensions allowing up to 60 Bcm of gas, to take away as much as 25–50% of gas exports passing through Ukraine. However, analysts said the building of this new pipeline would not increase Gazprom's exports or revenues; instead they could cost Gazprom more than US$1 billion. But Gazprom was of the opinion that with the illegal siphoning off of its gas by Ukraine amounting to huge sums, the pipeline would pay for itself in a few years. Ukraine was also defaulting on its gas bill payments and its gas debts were piling up.

The proposal for a new pipeline set alarm bells ringing in Ukraine and it agreed to a settlement with Gazprom. Meanwhile, a new management took over the responsibility of Gazprom. As Ukraine came to the negotiating table and was willing to co-operate with

Yamal – Europe Gas Pipeline

Russia realized very early that its gas export contract obligations to Europe could be jeopardized by its excessive dependence on intransigent Ukraine for transit. In 1992, it mulled over the idea of building another pipeline to Europe through Belarus.

Accordingly, a new gas pipeline that was supposed to connect its gasfields in Yamal to Europe through Belarus was built. In 1999, the first phase of the Yamal–Europe gas pipeline was commissioned and gas began to be exported through the new pipeline. The initial nominal capacity of the gas pipeline was 30 Bcm per year. As Gazprom had financed the entire project, it took the land that the gas pipelines passed through in Belarus on lease for 99 years.

The Blue Stream Gas Pipeline

On December 15, 1997, Russia and Turkey signed an intergovernmental agreement, under which Gazprom concluded a commercial contract with the Turkish firm 'Botas' to supply 365 Bcm of gas between 2000 and 2025. Accordingly, to implement the agreement and to avoid the involvement of third parties, the parties decided to build an under sea pipeline. The Blue Stream Pipeline Company was formed to build the pipeline. Construction began on February 3, 2000, and was commissioned on December 30, 2002. The Blue Stream Pipeline is 1213 km long with 396 km under the sea. The total cost of the pipeline was $3.4 billion. By 2010, the pipeline is expected to be operating at full capacity, delivering 16 Bcm of gas per year.

The North European Gas Pipeline

The North European Gas Pipeline (NEGP) was a result of Gazprom's desire to eliminate intermediaries in its gas exports to Europe. Accordingly, the NEGP was conceived to carry Russian gas directly to Germany, its largest customer in Europe, by building a pipeline under the Baltic Sea. The Intergovernmental Protocols between Russia and Germany were signed in 2005, just before the German elections, by Vladimir Putin and Gerhard Schroeder. Schroeder stepped down as the German Chancellor after he failed to secure a decisive victory in the elections. Thereafter, Gazprom appointed him to the NEGP board. Construction of the 1200 km long project began on December 9, 2005, and is expected to be completed by 2010. The pipeline is estimated to cost $5 billion. In its initial phase, it was expected to carry 27 Bcm of gas every year. The NEGP had provoked several objections from countries like Ukraine and Poland. They protested that the NEGP would lead to the loss of transit revenues, which they would have otherwise got, had it been laid through their territories. Compiled from various sources.

Figure 5: Gazprom's alternative options for gas exports.

Gazprom on crucial issues, the new Gazprom Chairman, Alexey Miller (Miller), announced that the proposal for a bypass pipeline would be replaced by an 'international consortium' that would operate and refurbish the transit pipelines in Ukraine. Germany, France and Italy showed an interest in participating in such a consortium. But Russia and Ukraine later gave up the plan and focused on bilaterally developing a new pipeline, Bogorodchany-Uzhgorod, to bring additional Central Asian gas (mainly from Turkmenistan) to Ukraine, through Russia, and from there to Europe.

In 2004, Gazprom and Naftogaz reached an agreement that addressed the issues of arrangements for transit of Central Asian gas to Ukraine and the settlement of debts. Naftogaz's debt of US$1.62 billion for the period 1997–2000 was assigned to Vnesheconombank[27], which settled these obligations with Gazprom. Gazprom also made an advance payment of US$1.25 billion to Naftogaz to fix US$1.09/Tcm/100 km as the gas transmission tariff between 2005 and 2009. Gazprom's advance payment to Naftogaz was considered by many analysts as a loan to help Naftogaz pay back its debt. Eural Transgas, the supplier of Central Asian gas to Ukraine, was replaced by a new joint venture RosUkrEnergo to ship mainly Turkmen gas starting from January 2005.[28] RosUkrEnergo had the contract from 2005 to 2028. The agreement stipulated that the treaty would be revised by their respective governments every year. It looked as if all the problems between Russia and Ukraine with regard to gas supplies, payments and transit fees as well as debts had been well settled.

Elections in Ukraine

In the 2004 elections to the Ukrainian Presidency, Prime Minister Viktor Yanukovych (Yanukovych) and ex-Prime Minister Viktor Yushchenko

(Yushchenko) were rival candidates. Prime Minister Yanukovych was supported by the outgoing President Leonid Kuchma and also by Russian President Vladimir Putin (Putin). Yanukovych favoured closer and better ties with his big neighbour Russia. Yushchenko on the contrary, advocated closer ties with the West and with the EU in particular. He was a champion of market-oriented economic reforms.

After two rounds of elections, it was announced that Yanukovych had won the presidential elections. Yushchenko alleged that there had been gross irregularities and took to the streets. There were huge mass protests in the Ukrainian capital city of Kiev. It was called the Orange Revolution, because the protestors used orange coloured ribbons as a sign of their non-violent protests. The Orange Revolution resulted in a third round of elections in which Yushchenko was declared the winner.

Analysts said that the election of a pro-West president was not favourably viewed by Russia. The new government was pro-market oriented and favoured joining the EU and NATO.[29] In a dramatic proposal made in March 2005, Yushchenko asked Gazprom to raise gas transit fees to European levels, which ranged between US$0.9/Tcm/100 km in Belgium to US$4.5/Tcm/100 km in Greece[30] and demanded that the payment be made in cash. Gazprom accepted the proposal enthusiastically but added that its gas prices to Ukraine should also be raised to European levels, which averaged US$230 per Tcm. The mode of payment too should be in cash.[31] Gazprom's demand came as a shock to Ukraine, which had not been able to make its payments to Gazprom, even at gas prices of US$50 per Tcm. Gazprom, however, stuck to the initial Ukrainian proposal and pressed for an increase in gas prices to European levels. Negotiations proved unsuccessful in arriving at a mutually agreeable price.

Meanwhile, another dispute cropped up in May 2005, with regard to the storage of 7.8 Bcm of Gazprom gas in Ukraine.[32] Naftogaz did not make this gas available to Gazprom for deliveries and there were various reports in the media that the gas had been stolen or siphoned off illegally by unknown entities. Later, it was discovered that Naftogaz had sufficient gas reserves to honour its commitment. Gazprom proposed that Naftogaz should either make the gas available for European exports or it would deduct the 7.8 Bcm of gas as payment of its transit fees. The deduction would mean that Naftogaz would receive no gas for the rest of the year. This was an unacceptable situation for Naftogaz and statements from the company suggested that it would use the Gazprom gas meant for Europe to make up for any shortfalls.[33] This led to Gazprom demanding that Naftogaz pay European prices for the 7.8 Bcm of stored gas, because it was meant for Europe. But Ukraine was in no position to do so.

Turn of Events

The issue of increase in gas prices could not be settled and with the negotiations failing to bring about any mutually agreeable price, Gazprom decided to set the price on its own. On 22 November 2005, it announced that from 2006, Naftogaz would have to pay US$160 per Tcm. Ukraine, although agreeing that gas prices should be raised, held that it should be done gradually, because its economy would not be able to withstand such a large price increase in such a short time. It said it would pay US$80 per Tcm but Gazprom stood firm on its demand for US$160 per Tcm. As Naftogaz did not have the wherewithal to pay for current imports at subsidized prices, let alone at increased prices, it refused to comply with Gazprom's new price structure.

Events took an interesting turn on 9 December 2005. In response to Gazprom's demand for higher prices for gas, some Ukrainian officials called for a review of the lease price of US$97 million Russia paid to Ukraine for stationing its Black Sea Fleet in Sevastopol, Crimea.[34] They claimed that the lease price was too low and called for a revaluation of the lease facilities, which they claimed, could be valued as high as US$2 billion. What was interesting was the fact that the call for review came hours after the Ukrainian visit of the US secretary of State, Condoleezza Rice, on 7 December 2005.[35] In response, Russia's ambassador to Ukraine, Viktor Chernomyrdin, dismissed the claims and said there were no legal or any other grounds for revising the 1997 Russia – Ukraine agreement on stationing the Black Sea fleet at Sevastopol.[36]

On 13 December 2005, Gazprom chairman Miller threatened to cut off gas supplies from January 2006, if no agreement was reached. The next day, Gazprom announced that Naftogaz would have to pay the market level prices of US$220–230 per Tcm.

Ukraine protested and said that it was being victimized by Russia for being pro-West. Putin, on being asked about his involvement, replied that he had nothing to do with Gazprom's dealings with Naftogaz and that Gazprom's demand for increased prices was purely an economical one. Gazprom offered to reconsider the prices if Ukraine agreed to a joint venture between Gazprom and Naftogaz, with a stake in Ukraine's pipeline system. Ukraine rejected the offer, because the proposed joint venture would have meant the loss of Ukrainian control over its own pipelines. On 23 December 2005, Ukraine said it would ask the Arbitration Institute of the Stockholm Chamber of Commerce[37] to mediate on the issue.

In a swift and dramatic move, on 29 December 2005, Gazprom announced that it had entered into a deal with Turkmenistan to buy 30 Bcm of its gas at a price of US$65 per Tcm, about half of which was to be delivered in the first quarter of 2006.[38] This came as a surprise to many as it had earlier rejected Turkmenistan's demand to increase the gas prices from US$44 to US$58 per Tcm.[39] As Gazprom did not agree to Turkmenistan's demand for a price hike, Turkmenistan had, in fact, halted gas supplies to Gazprom, in January 2005, citing technical reasons.[40] Analysts believed that this sudden move by Gazprom was to squeeze and scuttle Ukraine's other possible options for gas supplies in the first quarter of 2006. On 30 December, 2005, Putin offered Ukraine a commercial loan of up to US$3.6 billion to help pay for a gas price hike and avoid supplies being cut off. Next day, in a last bid toward conciliation, he offered to order Gazprom to halt the price hike for three months until March, when the Ukrainian parliamentary elections would be over and the severity of winter would also fade away, if Ukraine agreed to market prices. But Ukraine rejected both offers.

Political Aspect

Analysts felt that apart from economic aspects, there were many political aspects to the dispute. Some claimed that the sudden increase in gas prices – more than four times what Ukraine was paying – was the Russian way of punishing Ukraine's newly elected government for pursuing pro-West policies and for deciding to join NATO and the EU. Others alleged that Russia wanted to discredit the government in the parliamentary elections to be held in March 2006. But

some analysts disagreed with the view that Russia was punishing Ukraine. They felt that with Ukraine deciding to leave the Russian orbit of influence and becoming a market-oriented economy to join the EU, Russia's obligation to maintain the Ukrainian economy by supplying heavily subsidized gas was also void. If Ukraine itself wanted to move to a market-oriented economy and be a part of the EU, and demanded a raise in transit prices to European levels for Russian gas going through Ukraine, how could it ask for the continuation of the Russian gas imports at heavily subsidized prices, they asked.[41]

On 1 January 2006, Gazprom cut off Ukraine's gas supplies. Hours later, many European countries reported a drop in their gas pressures and a reduction in gas supplies. By evening, Gazprom alleged that Naftogaz was illegally siphoning off its gas destined for Europe. Naftogaz denied any illegal withdrawal of gas from its pipelines and claimed that it was entitled to receive 15% of the gas passing through its pipelines as transit fee. It also claimed that it was entitled to Turkmen gas, which took 36 hours to reach its borders, which came through Gazprom's pipelines. The next day, Russia said it was sending an extra 95 million cubic metres a day to make up for gas 'stolen' by Ukraine.[42]

The gas dispute between Russia and Ukraine led many European observers to question Russia's credibility as a reliable supplier. Some of them wanted Europe to reduce its dependence on Russia for its gas supplies and to diversify its energy imports. They wanted Europe to explore gas deals with other gas producers, mainly with Algeria and the Middle East. But analysts commented that the diversification of gas supplies was an undertaking with long periods of gestation involving huge costs. And Russia, with its large gas reserves and close proximity to Europe, was a viable option in the short-term as well as long-term. Some analysts felt that the EU and the US had viewed the gas dispute with Russo-phobic perceptions, with most of the media houses favouring Ukraine over Russia.[43] They claimed that Russia and previously the former Soviet Union had always honoured its agreements with Europe.

Ukraine alleged that it was politically being blackmailed by Russia for trying to be a part of NATO and the EU. Gazprom replied that with soaring prices of oil in the international market, it was only fair for the

Belarus	$47
Armenia, Azerbaijan and Georgia	$110
Lithuania, Latvia, Estonia	$120–125
Moldova	$160
Ukraine	$230
Romania	$280
Average EU price	$240

Figure 6: Gazprom's 2006 tariffs per 1000 cubic metres of gas.
Compiled from various sources.

parties to pay reasonable market prices. On being asked why Belarus was still being charged at US$47 per Tcm, it replied that Gazprom had a stake in Beltransgaz that controlled the pipelines of Belarus, and so it was charging Belarus at a concession (see Figure 6 for Gazprom's gas tariffs for 2006).

The Settlement

After a series of negotiations, Gazprom and Naftogaz reached an agreement on 4 January 2006, with the signing of a five-year contract. Under the contract, Gazprom would cease to be a supplier of Russian gas to Naftogaz; instead, RosUkrEnergo would take over the responsibility. Although Gazprom would sell Russian gas to RosUkrEnergo at US$230 per Tcm, RosUkrEnergo would mix it with Central Asian gas and sell it to Naftogaz at US$95 per Tcm. RosUkrEnergo would get 41 Bcm of gas from Turkmenistan, 7 Bcm from Uzbekistan, 8 Bcm from Kazakhstan and 17 Bcm of Russian gas from Gazprom.[44] Naftogaz was also to form a joint venture with RosUkrEnergo for the supply of gas to domestic consumers. On its part, Gazprom agreed to pay Naftogaz a transit fee of US$1.60/Tcm/100 km for gas transit to Europe.[45] Above all, all the transactions between Gazprom and Naftogaz, Gazprom and RosUkrEnergo, and RosUkrEnergo and Naftogaz, were to be in cash.

The agreement, however, left many things unclear. It stipulated that the price of US$95 had been fixed for the first half of 2006, but did not touch the issue of future prices. Many analysts felt that the agreement did not spell out how these arrangements would be profitable to RosUkrEnergo. Moreover, the price at which the Central Asian gas would be made available to RosUkrEnergo in future was a question mark, given the fact that Turkmenistan also wanted to increase its gas prices. Besides, Turkmenistan had already entered into a pact with Gazprom to supply 30 Bcm of gas in 2006. With a flat production of 58 Bcm, analysts wondered how Turkmenistan would be able to make 41 Bcm of gas available to Ukraine. Many felt that the agreement had been drawn up hastily to resolve the crisis, and that further questions and issues were bound to crop up. It was speculated that RosUkrEnergo might be allowed to sell a few Bcm of gas in the European market to make it sustainable. Despite all these doubts, both sides declared that the agreement was successful. Thereafter, gas supplies were restored in full between the two companies.

Outlook

The Gazprom–Naftogaz dispute brought to light the European Union's dependence on Russian gas. With a quarter of the EU's gas consumption needs met by imports from Russia, EU member countries realized the need to diversify their energy imports. Although a part of their gas requirements were met by member countries' domestic production, it had to depend on imports for a major share of its consumption. In terms of imports, Russia accounted for 40%, Algeria 30% and Norway 25%. EU members were also planning to build more storage tanks and increase the capacity of the existing ones to use in times of emergency. The member countries also planned to tap into each others' gas reserves. The EU members also wished to import Liquefied Natural Gas (LNG) from the Middle East in order to reduce its dependency on Russia. But analysts pointed out that energy supply diversification was a long-term strategy and took a long time to bear fruits. Moreover, some of the contracts that Gazprom had with some European gas companies were to last until 2030.

Gazprom also realized that its dependence on Europe for export revenues could seriously affect its growth and sustainability. It therefore ventured into gas deals with various countries, engaging in talks with China, Korea and Japan. These energy hungry countries were eager to tap into the vast resources and reserves of gas and oil in Russia. Gazprom also invested in LNG processing to ship gas in huge tankers to North America by 2010. Such diversification by Gazprom for its exports could have serious implications for EU in future, if the EU failed to secure its gas needs from other sources. In the end, Gazprom's dependence on Europe or any other market would be of little consequence if the Russian domestic gas market could be deregulated and gas prices brought to market level. In such a scenario, analysts felt that the domestic market would itself be able to fuel Gazprom's growth and expansion.

Questions for Discussion

1. What are the major sources of bargaining power of Gazprom?
2. What are the reasons for the disputes with Ukraine? What are the reasons for the current trends and developments?
3. What are the reasons for the current situation with gas supplies from Gazprom to western Europe?

FURTHER READING

Bruce, C., 'Fraternal Friction or Fraternal Fiction? The Gas Factor in Russian-Belarusian Relations', March 2005, http://www.oxfordenergy.org/pdfs/NG8.pdf.

Hill, F. and Fee, F., 'Fueling the Future: The Prospects for Russian Oil and Gas', http://www.demokratizatsiya.org.

Hubert, F. and Ikonnikova, S., 'International Institutions and Russian Gas Exports to Western Europe', http://www.hse.ru/ic6/report16.pdf.

Kupchinsky, R., 'East: Ukraine, Russia Spar Over Turkmen Gas', 20 April 2005, http://www.energybulletin.net/5478.html.

Novak, I., Malynovsky, O. and Kurdelchuk, D., 'Ukraine-Russia: A European Approach to Ukraine's Gas Dilemma', December 2005, http://www.uaba.org/gasdilema.pdf.

Soligo, R. and Jaffe, A.M., 'Market Structure in the New Gas Economy: Is Cartelization Possible?', May 2004, http://www.iis-db.stanford.edu/pubs/20705/Gas_OPEC_final.pdf.

Stern, J., 'Security of European Natural Gas Supplies', July 2002, http://www.chathamhouse.org.uk/pdf/briefing_papers/Sec_of_Euro_Gas_Jul02.pdf.

Stern, J., 'The Russian – Ukrainian Gas Crisis of January 2006', January 2006, http://www.oxford energy.org/pdfs/comment_0106.pdf.

Stern, J., 'Ukraine: EU Neighbourhood Policy and Natural Gas Security', University of Dundee, 2005, http://www.oxfordenergy.org/pdfs/comment_0106.pdf.

Stevens, P., 'Cross-Border Oil and Gas Pipelines: Problems and Prospects', June 2003, www. dundee.ac.uk/cepmlp/main/html/Staff/pstevens_publications.htm.

Twining, D., 'Putin's Power Politics', *The Weekly Standard*, 16 January 2006.

'Beyond Gazprom', 27 December 2005, http://www.forbes.com/columnists/2005/12/23/russian-companies-gazprom-cx_daa_1227angle.html.

'Energy and the new world power play', 1 January 2006, http://www.news.bbc.co.uk/2/hi/europe/4573944.stm.

'Europe Has Left it Too Late to Wrest Back Control from Russia over Gas', 4 January 2006, http://business.timesonline.co.uk/article/0,13130–1969022,00.html.

'Geopolitics of Natural Gas: An Analysis of Prospective Developments in the Natural Gas Trade and Geopolitical Implications', http://www.rice.edu/energy/research/LNG/geopoliticsofLNG.html.

'How Europe Will Save Itself from Russia', 16 January 2006, http://www.kommersant.com/tree.asp?rubric=3&node=39&doc_id=640897.

'Q&A: Ukraine Gas Row', 4 January 2006, http://news.bbc.co.uk/2/hi/business/4569846.stm.

'Russia and the West – Opportunities for a New Partnership', June 2005, http://www.stiftung .koerber.de/bg/recherche/pdf_protokoll/bnd_131_en_text.pdf.

'Russian Natural Gas on Global Markets: Capabilities and Limits', January 2006, http://www.rpi-inc.com/RNGOGMtoc.pdf.

'Sibneft Transfer Deal puts Gazprom Top of the Table', 25 September, 2005, http://www.guardian.co.uk/oil/story/0,1577654,00.html

'The Geopolitics of Natural Gas', March 2005, www.rice.edu/energy/publications/geopoliticsofnaturalgas.html.

'35 Years of Russian Gas Export and Transit', March 2002, http://www.iea.org/Textbase/work/2002/cross_border/MISIULIN.PDF.

'Ukraine Gas Price, Industry Unit Convention, and the Core Issues', 3 January 2006, http://sun-bin.blogspot.com/2006/01/ukraine-gas-price-industry-unit.html.

www.gazprom.ru.

http://www.globalsecurity.org/wmd/library/news/ukraine.

Case Study 14

WAL-MART'S GERMAN MISADVENTURE[1]

I don't think that Wal-Mart did their homework as well as they should have. Germany is Europe's most price-sensitive market. Wal-Mart underestimated the competition, the culture, the legislative environment.

Steve Gotham, Retail Analyst – Verdict Retail Consulting, in October 2002[2]

We screwed up in Germany. Our biggest mistake was putting our name up before we had the service and low prices. People were disappointed.

John Menzer, Head – Wal-Mart International, in December 2001[3]

German Blues

For the world's largest retailing company – Wal-Mart Inc. (Wal-Mart) – the German market was proving difficult to crack. By 2003, even five years after entering Germany, Wal-Mart was making losses. Although Wal-Mart did not reveal these figures, analysts estimated losses of around US$200–300 million per annum in Germany, over the five-year period.

According to analysts, the main reason for Wal-Mart's losses was its failure to understand German culture and the shopping habits of Germans. Although Wal-Mart was famous the world over for its Every Day Low Pricing (EDLP)[4], which turned it into the world's number 1 retailer, it could not make an impact in Europe's most price-sensitive market – Germany. Wal-Mart also ran into a series of problems with German regulatory authorities for its pricing strategies and faced considerable opposition from German suppliers to its centralized distribution system. It had problems with its German workers as well.

However, Wal-Mart was not the only retailer to do badly in Germany in the 1990s. German retailers too faced losses in the period because of the flat economy and rising unemployment. Although Wal-Mart was confident that there would be a turn-around in its fortunes in the German market by late 2003, this opinion was not shared by most independent analysts.

Background Note

In 1962, Sam Walton (Walton) and his brother opened the first Wal-Mart store in Rogers (Arkansas), USA. In the first year of its operations, the store registered sales of over US$1 million. Initially, the Waltons concentrated on opening stores in small towns and introduced innovative concepts such as self-service. By 1967, Wal-Mart had 24 stores with sales of US$12.6 million.

Encouraged by the early success of Wal-Mart, Sam Walton expanded Wal-Mart's operations to Oklahoma and Missouri in 1968. In the following year, Wal-Mart was incorporated as a company under the name Wal-Mart Stores Inc. In 1970, Wal-Mart established its first distribution centre in Bentonville, Arkansas. It floated its first public issue the same year. Wal-Mart continued to grow in the 1970s, benefiting from its highly automated distribution system, which reduced shipping costs and time, and its computerized inventory system, which speeded up the checkout and reordering of stocks. In 1977, Wal-Mart acquired 16 Mohr-Value stores based in Michigan and Illinois. In 1978, it purchased the Hutcheson Shoe Company, and later set up pharmacy, auto service centre and jewellery divisions.

By 1980, Wal-Mart had 276 stores with annual sales of US$1.4 billion. The number of stores increased to 640 with annual sales of US$4.5 billion and profits of over US$200 million by 1984. In the 1980s, strong customer demand in small towns drove the rapid growth of Wal-Mart. Walton said, 'When we arrived in these small towns offering low prices every day, customer satisfaction guaranteed, and hours that were realistic for the way people wanted to shop, we passed right by that old variety of store competition, with its 45% mark ups, limited selection and limited hours.'

In 1988, Walton appointed David Glass (Glass) as CEO of Wal-Mart. Soon after taking over, Glass started Hypermart USA. It was originally a joint

Store name	Description
Wal-Mart stores	Wal-Mart stores are considered the flagship stores of the company offering merchandise in some 36 departments such as apparel, health and beauty aids, household needs, toys, fabrics, jewellery, shoes, etc. These stores operate on the EDLP philosophy.
Sam's Clubs	Sam's Clubs are members-only warehouse clubs, started in 1983. The Clubs act as purchasing agents for their members and offer branded merchandise at 'members only' prices, both for business and personal use. The Clubs operate by selling high volumes of goods at very low profit margins.
Neighborhood markets	Neighborhood Markets are located in markets together with Wal-Mart Supercenters[19]. Neighborhood Markets feature a wide variety of products, including fresh produce, deli foods, fresh meat and dairy items, health and beauty aids, one-hour photo and traditional photo developing services, drive-through pharmacies, stationery and paper goods, pet supplies and household chemicals.
Wal-Mart international	There are international stores of Wal-Mart in nine countries. The Wal-Mart International division oversees day-to-day management of its international stores.
Wal-Mart.com	The e-business venture of Wal-Mart.

Source: www.walmartstores.com

Table 1: Wal-Mart retail divisions.

venture with Cullum Companies (a Dallas-based supermarket chain). In the following year Wal-Mart bought out Cullum's stake in the venture. The Hypermart was a discount store/supermarket chain, which sprawled over 200 000 sq ft. It featured branch banks, fast food outlets, photo developers and playrooms for shoppers' children. This concept was later retooled as Wal-Mart's Supercenters.

In 1990, Wal-Mart acquired McLane Company (a grocer and retail distributor) and launched a new retail format – Bud's Discount City. Sam Walton died in 1992 after a prolonged illness. Under Glass, Wal-Mart continued its impressive growth. In the 1990s, Wal-Mart entered the international markets. In 1999, Wal-Mart was the largest private employer in the US with 1 140 000 Associates[5]. In the same year Cone/Roper Report[6] named Wal-Mart as number 1 Corporate Citizen of America. In 2000, Wal-Mart was ranked 5th in *Fortune* magazine's Global Most Admired All-Stars List. Lee Scott (Scott) became the CEO of the company in 2000. In 2002, Wal-Mart was ranked number 1 in the *Fortune 500* list. It recorded the largest single day sales in the company's history, in 2002, when on the day after Thanksgiving it reported sales of US$1.43 billion. In 2003, Wal-Mart was the world's largest retailer with a total of 4688 stores (3400 stores in the US and 1288 stores in other countries). It reported sales of US$244.5 billion for the year 2003 with a net income of US$8.03 billion.

Business Segments

Wal-Mart has two types of divisions – Retail divisions and Specialty divisions. Retail divisions are further classified into Wal-Mart Stores, Sam's Clubs, Neighborhood Market, International and walmart.com (see Table 1). The specialty division is divided into Tire & Lube Express, Wal-Mart Optical, Wal-Mart Pharmacy, Wal-Mart Vacations and Wal-Mart's Used Fixture Auctions (see Table 2).

Wal-Mart's International Operations

In the early 1990s, Wal-Mart announced that it would go global. It wanted to look for international markets for the following reasons:

- Wal-Mart was facing stiff competition from K-mart[7] and Target[8], which adopted aggressive expansion strategies and started eating into Wal-Mart's market share.
- Wal-Mart also realized that the US population represented only 4% of the world's population and confining itself to the US market would mean missing the opportunity to tap potentially vast markets elsewhere.

Division name	Description
Tire & Lube Express	This division provides a vehicle tyre and oil service to its customers. Started in early 1990s, by 2003 this division had over 1300 stores in 40 states in the US.
Wal-Mart Optical	This division provides optical services to its customers.
Wal-Mart Pharmacy	This division operates pharmacy stores in Wal-Mart stores and also in medical clinics across the US. It employs around 6500 pharmacists.
Wal-Mart Vacations	Wal-Mart Vacations provides customers with travel packages on cruises, holiday packages, car rental and hotel discounts, select theme park tickets and resorts.
Wal-Mart's Used Fixture Auctions	Through this division, Wal-Mart helps customers to resale fixtures for reuse. Auctions are open to the public and held at Wal-Mart locations.

Source: www.walmartstores.com

Table 2: Wal-Mart specialty divisions.

- In the early 1990s, globalization and liberalization opened up new markets and created opportunities for discount stores such as Wal-Mart across the world.

During the first five years of its globalization initiative (1991–1995), Wal-Mart concentrated on Mexico, Canada, Argentina and Brazil, which were close to its home market. It started with Canada and Mexico due to the similarities in people's habits, culture and the business environments in these countries and also because the North American Free Trade Agreement (NAFTA)[9] made it easier for US companies to enter these markets. Wal-Mart's decision to enter Argentina and Brazil was based on the high growth rates of the Latin American markets.

Wal-Mart expanded its international operations through acquisitions, joint ventures, greenfield operations and wholly owned subsidiaries. In 1991, Wal-Mart entered Mexico through a joint venture with Mexican company Cifra, and opened Sam's Clubs in Mexico. Wal-Mart's globalization plans got a boost in 1993, when the Wal-Mart International division was created. In the same year it acquired 122 former Woolco stores from Woolworth in Canada. By 2003, Wal-Mart had a presence in nine countries with 1288 stores, which included 942 discount stores, 238 supercenters, 71 Sam's Clubs and 37 Neighborhood stores (see Table 3 for Wal-Mart's International Presence).

By 2003, Wal-Mart was the largest retailer in Mexico, Argentina, Canada and Puerto Rico, and one of the top three retailers in the UK. In 2003, Wal-Mart's operating income from international operations was US$2.033 billion, 15% higher than in the previous year (see Table 4). However, Wal-Mart was not successful in all the markets it entered. It failed to make an impact in Europe's most price-sensitive market – Germany.

Country	Mode of entry	Year of entry	JV partner/company acquired	No. of stores
Mexico	Joint Venture	1991	Cifra	597
Canada	Acquisition	1994	Woolco Stores	213
Argentina	Greenfield operations	1995	–	11
Brazil	Joint Venture	1995	Lojas Americanas	22
China	Greenfield operations	1996	–	26
South Korea	Acquisition	1998	Makro Stores	15
Germany	Acquisition	1997	Wertkauf and Interspar	94
United Kingdom	Acquisition	2000	Asda	258
Puerto Rico	Wholly owned subsidiary	1993	Wal-Mart Puerto Rico, Inc	52

Compiled from various newspapers and Wal-Mart annual reports

Table 3: Wal-Mart's international presence in 2003.

Fiscal year	Operating Income (in US$ billions)
2003	2.033
2002	1.305
2001	0.949

Source: Wal-Mart 2003 Annual Report

Table 4: Operating income from international operations.

Wal-Mart in Germany

Most American companies entering Europe start with the UK due to the similarities between the US and the UK in culture, language and legal environment. Wal-Mart, however, decided to enter Germany first. Analysts were critical of this decision because the German retailing industry was experiencing slow growth rates and retailers were indulging in price wars, which eroded margins badly. Additionally, Germany had high labour costs, high real estate prices and a very inflexible business environment (see Figure 1).

But Wal-Mart felt it was right to venture into the German market. Ron Tiarks, President, Wal-Mart's German operations said, 'Germany, being the third-largest economy in the world, is very important to us and one obviously that we can't ignore'. *Fortune* wrote in 1999, 'Germany offers Wal-Mart a central base from which it can expand to almost anywhere on the Continent. Wal-Mart clearly wants to be a pan-European player, a goal made more feasible by the euro's promise to ease business across national boundaries.'[10] As Germany was considered a price-sensitive market, analysts felt that Wal-Mart's EDLP philosophy would be successful in the country. German stores usually offered seasonal discounts sales and special sales to increase their sales. With its customer-focused service, it was felt that Wal-Mart would be able gain market share in Germany. However, Wal-Mart faced a number of serious problems in Germany.

Entry Strategy Gone Wrong?

Wal-Mart expanded its presence into Germany through acquisitions. It acquired the 21-hypermarket stores of Wertkauf in 1997. The Wertkauf stores offered both food and general merchandise to the customers. Wal-Mart sources said that Wertkauf stores would provide the necessary footage in the German market. However, as Wertkauf covered only southwestern Germany, it failed to provide the required market penetration to Wal-Mart in Germany. In 1998, Wal-Mart acquired Interspar's 74 hypermarket stores to raise the total number of Wal-Mart stores in Germany to 95.

With the acquisition of Interspar's stores, Wal-Mart became the fourth largest hypermarket retailer in Germany. However, both the Wertkauf and the Interspar stores were not popular with German consumers. A major challenge for Wal-Mart was to change customer perceptions of the stores. Wal-Mart was criticized for acquiring Interspar's stores, because they had made heavy losses and had a poor brand image in the public mind.

Wal-Mart also faced a major problem in trying to integrate the operations of the two companies (Wertkauf and Interspar). John Menzer (Menzer), Head of Wal-Mart International said, 'The challenge of putting the two chains together was more than we thought. We knew Interspar was losing money and we had to turn it around. We had to reconstruct it and lose more money before it could turn around.'[11]

Wal-Mart found out that the store layout and design of Interspar stores did not conform to Wal-Mart's store layout and design worldwide. Interspar stores were of varied sizes and formats and most of the stores were situated in interior areas, where customers opted for general grocery chains. After acquiring Interspar chain stores, Wal-Mart embarked on a renovation programme to bring them to Wal-Mart standards. Wal-Mart reportedly spent around US$150 million to renovate the Interspar stores.

Although acquisitions may not have been the ideal route for Wal-Mart to take in Germany, the company, in fact, had little choice. The German government was refusing new licences for food and grocery retailing, and so if it wanted to enter the German market, Wal-Mart had to go in for acquisitions.

Problems in Operating Environment

Soon after acquiring the stores, Wal-Mart hurried through with their renovation and put its brand name on them to make sure its EDLP message went across. But it was unable to cash in on its EDLP selling point,

As the world's third largest economy, Germany has attracted the attention of the retailers from around the world, such as Marks & Spencer, Toys R Us, for several decades. With a GNP of €2 trillion and population of around 80 million, Germany was rated as one of the biggest retail markets in Europe. In 2002, Germany accounted for 15% of Europe's €2 trillion retail market. The West German retail industry saw tremendous growth rates till the early 1990s. However after the unification of Germany in 1990, the Germany economy went through a tough phase of restructuring, which had an impact on the retailing industry too. The difference between the levels of economic prosperity in West and East Germany pulled down the average growth rates in the German retail industry. By the late 1990s, the German retail industry was growing slowly.

The German retail market was oligopolistic with a few players dominating the industry. In early 2000s, the top ten players accounted for 84% of sales and the top five players in the market garnered around 63% of market share. German consumers reportedly attached more importance to value and price, than customer service. According to analysts, German market was one of the most price-sensitive markets in Europe.

Till the late 1990s, discount stores concentrated only on food and other grocery items; but in the late 1990s, the trend changed and the discount stores moved to non-food items also. For instance, the discount store Aldi emerged as the largest seller of personal computers under its own brand name.

In the early 2000s, with the slowdown in the economy, German retail industry experienced the lowest profit levels of all the developed countries. The profit margin in grocery retailing was just 1.1% in 2002, and in the food segment, it was only 0.5%. Another important feature of the German retailing industry was the domination of family owned enterprises. Most of the retailing enterprises were not listed on stock exchanges.

German retailing industry is highly regulated. Analysts believed that the regulatory environment in Germany hindered the development of retailing in the county. There were many legislations relating to the competition and corporate strategies of retailers. The German government also pursues protectionist policies to support small and medium-scale German retailers. Some of the legislations which affect the retail industry in Germany significantly are summarized below:

- A retailer can operate for a maximum of 80 hours/week. The store working hours are the shortest in Europe. Retailers are not allowed to work on Sundays and holidays. Because of this regulation Wal-Mart was not able to operate its 24/7 convenience stores in Germany.
- Retailers are not allowed to sell below cost for an extended period of time. However, a merchant can discount his goods for a limited period of time.

As regards German consumers, for cultural reasons, they were less friendly and less outgoing compared with American and British consumers. In line with this, in Germany the number of employees per store was low compared to the US and other developed markets.

In order to increase consumer spending, the German government undertook major tax reforms in 2001. This was expected to boost retail sales in the country. However, though government tax reforms boosted consumer spending, it did not benefit retail industry as expenditure took place in the housing, tourism and communications sectors.

During 2003 too, the German retailing industry was expected to have slow growth because of the macroeconomic conditions. The increasing unemployment affected the food retailing sector in the country.

Figure 1: A note on the retailing industry in Germany.

Source: Adapted from various newspaper articles and websites.

chiefly because of the strong competition from German retailers (see Figure 2).

Whenever Wal-Mart lowered its prices on commodities, German retailers such as Aldi, Lidl, Rewe and Edeka also lowered their prices to keep their customers, and so Wal-Mart found it difficult to get a foothold. German retailer Edeka put it plainly, saying, 'The prices Wal-Mart offers are not lower than ours'. In response to Wal-Mart's slashing of prices in 2000, German competitor Real – the hypermarket chain – also decreased prices on around 3000 items. One of the German retailers Rewe even copied Wal-Mart's slogan: 'Jeden Tag Tiefpriese'. In 2000, Wal-Mart also introduced its private label – *Smartprice* – to Germany. However, the German discount retailers had a strong relationship with consumers, and Wal-Mart's private labels were not considered low-priced by the German public.

ALDI: The history of Aldi dates back to the 1940s. In 1946, Theo Abrecht and Karl Abrecht inherited convenience stores from their parents. In 1960, Albrecht Discount Stores began to be called 'Aldi', and there were 300 such stores. In 1961, a hard discount format was formulated by Theo Abrecht and Karl Abrecht. This combined ultra-low prices and high product quality with a very limited product assortment of around 600–700 products with a no-frills shopping experience. In 1962, company was spilt into two independent operations – Aldi Nord (Aldi North) and Aldi Sud (Aldi South). Aldi's northern operations were headed by Theo Abrecht and its southern operations were headed by Karl Abrecht, who operated independently, coordinating major decisions such as suppliers and pricing. The company continued to be known as the Aldi group. By 2002, the Aldi group had around 3741 stores in Germany and had around 2,643 stores internationally. It had a presence in Australia, United Kingdom, United States, France, Denmark, Belgium, Luxembourg, Netherlands, Ireland, Spain and Austria.

METRO AG: Metro AG was formed in 1996 after the merger of Metro Cash & Carry (established in 1964), Kaufhof Holding AG (established in 1879) and Asko Deutsche Kaufhaus AG (established in 1880). With the merger, the Metro AG group became world's third biggest supermarket group, with around 2300 sales outlets, and a distribution network in around 26 countries in the world covering not only European countries but also countries such as China, Turkey, Eastern Europe and Morocco. The Metro group divided its business into five segments: Cash & Carry, under brand name Metro, Makro and Spar (since March 2002); Real (800 hypermarkets) and Extra (supermarkets) in the food sector; Mediamarkt and Saturn selling electronic goods; Praktiker selling home improvement products; and Galeria and Kaufhof, general stores offering consumer goods. More than 40% of Metro AG's turnover was generated from its international stores. For the year 2002, Metro AG reported sales of € 51.5 billion, compared with 2001 sales of €49.5 billion.

EDEKA GROUP: The history of the Edeka group dates back to late 1890s. Edeka group was the brainchild of Friedrich William Raiffeisen and Hermann Schulze Delizsch. Their idea was to set up a purchase association where goods were made available to buyers at low prices. In October 1907, the Edeka Foundation was formed with 23 purchase associations. In the same year, central procurement office called Edeka Center AG was established. Over the years, the group was able to maintain low prices because of its strong relations with its suppliers. Edeka procured goods from regional wholesalers. The Edeka group was made up of a number of independent retailers and co-operative societies. Edeka's product range included organic fruits, vegetables, dairy products and cereals. The food products were marketed under the brand name - Bio Wertkost. The group's brands also included Rio Grande and Mibell. The group also had presence in pharmacy retailing, food processing and wine operations, publishing and banking services.

Figure 2: Profiles of German retailers.

Source: Compiled from various newspapers and company websites.

The lack of strong vendor relations also affected Wal-Mart's operations in Germany. Wal-Mart's success in its home market was mainly due to its efficient supply chain and vendor relations. Unlike in the US, where the company and its suppliers were accustomed to the centralized distribution, in Germany suppliers were not comfortable with the centralized distribution system that Wal-Mart adopted. As in the US, Wal-Mart in Germany also wanted to rely on inputs from suppliers to decide on products assortments. However, in Germany, Wal-Mart's relationship with its suppliers was not mature enough to make this possible. Thus, Wal-Mart ended up trying to sell goods that its customers did not want but which suppliers wanted to push.

Wal-Mart also had a number of inventory problems. Initially Wal-Mart had only one stockroom that stocked all merchandise. The company found it difficult to hire employees for its stockroom due to the low wages it was offering. The shortage of workers delayed the movement of goods leading to excessive stockpiling.

Another operational problem Wal-Mart faced was employee unrest. It was accused of paying low wages and not providing good working conditions. Wal-Mart did not understand the German work culture. As in its US operations, it discouraged employees from forming unions. After acquiring Interspar and Wertkauf, Wal-Mart prohibited members of the work councils of the erstwhile separate companies from meeting each other. The company also rarely consulted the elected representatives of its employees.

Wal-Mart ran into trouble with German unions when it announced employee lay-offs and store closures in 2002 in order to reduce its personnel costs.[12] In addition it also refused to accept the centralized wage-bargaining process[13] in the German retail industry. Because of this, the trade unions organized a walk-out from Wal-Mart stores, which led to bad publicity for the company. Wal-Mart employees also went on a two-day strike in July 2002 demanding negotiation of wage contract by the company.

Problems in External Environment

Wal-Mart faced several problems on the legal front as well. It was accused of breaching various German laws. The company was accused of having violated Section (IV) (2) of 'Act Against Restraints of Competition' (Gesetz gegen Wettbewerbsbeschrankungen or GWB) and Section 335a of the 'Commercial Act' (Handelsgesetzbuch or HGB). Section (IV) (2) of GWB forbids companies 'with superior market power in relation to small and medium-sized competitors' from lowering their prices and engaging in price wars with small companies. Such large companies were allowed to lower prices only after providing justification for the lower prices.

Wal-Mart had lowered the prices of some commodities, namely sugar, milk and margarine, in May 2000. The new prices were reportedly lower than the cost price at which Wal-Mart had bought them. In making this move, Wal-Mart was alleged to have violated Section (IV) (2). In response to Wal-Mart's move, the German retailers Aldi and Lidl also lowered their prices. As the price war continued, the German Federal Cartel Office (FCO) launched an investigation in September 2000. It ordered the retailers to stop selling the commodities below cost price because it would hurt small and medium-size retailers and lead to unfair competition.

In response to the FCO order, Wal-Mart took the case to the Appeals court in Dusseldorf. The Appeals court ruled in favour of Wal-Mart stating that Section (IV) (2) prohibited big players from selling at lower prices, and Wal-Mart could not be considered as a big player in Germany because it did not have a considerable market share or market capitalization. However, the FCO took the case further up to the Supreme Court against the verdict of the Appeals court. In November 2002, the German Supreme Court gave its verdict, declaring that Wal-Mart's selling goods at prices below cost price would result in unfair competition against small and medium-size retailers, and that Wal-Mart should abandon its pricing strategies[14].

Wal-Mart was also hauled up for violating the Commercial Act's Section 335a by not publishing financial data such as balance sheet and profit and loss account statements on its operations in Germany. The trade unions alleged that they were not given access to accounts of the company. In order to gain access to financial information, the trade unions filed a suit against Wal-Mart in the state court. In its verdict the court ruled that Wal-Mart should publish the required financial information; it also fined Wal-Mart senior executives for not providing the required financial information. Wal-Mart sources said that because the company was a limited partnership, it was not mandatory for it to publish financial information under German laws. However, according to the trade unions, under the altered German commercial code, even limited partnership firms were required to publish their financial accounts. In November 2002, Wal-Mart filed a suit in the German Supreme Court against the verdict of the state court asking it to stay state court's decision till the European Court of Justice came out with its decision on disclosure provisions by foreign companies[15].

Cultural Mismatch

Apart from the operational and regulatory problems, Wal-Mart also faced cultural problems in Germany. It found it difficult to integrate the two companies (Wertkauf and Interspar) that it had acquired. The companies had completely different work cultures: Interspar had decentralized operations with independent regional units and Wertkauf was highly centralized with the head office making all decisions. Additionally, Wal-Mart found it difficult to integrate the two companies' cultures with its own.

Employee morale in Wal-Mart Germany was also reported to have been badly affected by the changes in the internal rules and regulations effected by Wal-Mart. The earlier managements of both Interspar and Wertkauf had given their executives liberal expense accounts. But after Wal-Mart's acquisition of the firms, the executives' expense accounts were reduced. For instance, during business trips, they were required to share rooms – which came as a culture shock to the Germans.

Wal-Mart also faced a language problem in Germany. When Wal-Mart entered Germany, the top management who came from the US did not show any inclination to learn German. Within a few weeks, English became the official language of the company in Germany. This resulted in serious communication problems for the German employees. Making English the official language affected employee morale with employees starting to feel like outsiders, and getting increasingly frustrated. The German public also found it difficult to pronounce Wal-Mart's name correctly. They pronounced it as Vawl-Mart.

In Germany, Wal-Mart's world-famous customer service methods fell flat. For example, Wal-Mart's famous Ten-Foot Rule[16] was not implemented in Germany, because German customers did not like strangers interfering with their shopping. Commenting on this, Tiarks said, 'You can't beat those things into your people. They have to be genuine, or the customer sees right through them.' For the same reason, Wal-Mart also did away with the idea of greeters at German stores. In the US, Wal-Mart used to employ greeters at all its stores to welcome customers as they entered. However, in Germany, the company found that customers did not appreciate this idea at all. Apart from this, the German consumers realized that they were the ones who would be paying more because of 'the guy standing at the door' – which is why they did not appreciate it. Finally, Wal-Mart in Germany could not offer loyalty cards[17] because they were banned in Germany.

Future Prospects

Five years after entering the German market, Wal-Mart had still not made a significant impact in the German retail industry. The company reported losses over all the four years up to 2002 in its German operations (see Table 5). It was reported that between 1999–2002 Wal-Mart's sales declined by 5% on average. Increasing costs also pushed up losses for the company. Wal-Mart sources indicated that personnel costs accounted for around 17% of sales; these high costs prompted Wal-Mart to freeze new recruitment. Commenting on the operations in the Germany, Wal-Mart CEO, Scott said, 'We just walked in and said, "We're going to lower prices,

Year	Sales	Operating profit/(loss) (in US$ millions)
1999	2815	(192)
2000	2468	(181)
2001	2506	(164)
2002	2420	(108)

Adapted from www.mventures.com

Table 5: Sales and operating profit in Germany.

we're going to add people to the stores, we're going to remodel the stores because inherently that's correct," and it wasn't. We didn't have the infrastructure to support the kind of things we were doing.'[18]

Although Wal-Mart claimed that sales were picking up, analysts felt otherwise, and said that Wal-Mart in Germany had failed on its customer service promise. Independent studies conducted by some newspapers indicated that Wal-Mart was rated seventh out of the ten major retailers in Germany in terms of overall customer satisfaction (Table 6).

Wal-Mart announced that it would not be looking for further acquisitions in Germany and would concentrate on stabilizing its business in the country. Commenting on the company's plans, Dave Ferguson, Head of European operations, said, 'What we first have to achieve is that the existing stores are operating optimally.'

Retailer name	Rank
Aldi Group	1
Globus	2
Kaufland	3
Lidl	4
Norma	5
Marktkauf	6
Wal-Mart	7
Metro	8
Penny	9
Real	10

Source:www.hicbusiness.org

Table 6: Customer satisfaction ratings of German retailers.

To revive its fortunes in Germany, Wal-Mart announced that it would be focusing on bringing down its capital costs. It announced that instead of opening Wal-Mart supercenters, the company would focus on opening smaller stores in Germany.

In 2006, Wal-Mart pulled out from Germany, acknowledging its inability to compete in the German retail market. Wal-Mart sold its 85 German stores to the rival cash and carry chain Metro incurring a pre-tax loss of about US$1 billion. The only European operation that Wal-Mart now has is ASDA in the UK. Wal-Mart has also conceded defeat in the Korean market. It operates in 13 countries only. By comparison the French Carrefour operates in 29 countries. Apart from operating in China and Japan, Wal-Mart has been best able to adapt its practices to markets with geographical and cultural proximity to the US, such as Mexico and Canada.

Questions for Discussion

1. Wal-Mart started its global operations in the early 1990s when it opened its first international store in Mexico. Analyse the reasons for Wal-Mart's decision to go global.

2. When Wal-Mart announced that it would be entering the German markets, analysts were surprised. Usually, the cultural affinity between the US and the UK leads American companies to target the UK first, before launching onto the European continent. Do you think Wal-Mart's decision to enter the German market was correct? Justify your stand.

3. Even after five years of doing business in Germany, Wal-Mart had failed to make an impact on the German market and had been incurring losses year after year. Analyse the reasons for Wal-Mart's problems in the German market. Do you think the company would be able to improve its performance in Germany?

Source: This case was written by K. Subhadra, under the direction of Sanjib Dutta, ICFAI Center for Management Research (ICMR). It was compiled from published sources, and is intended to be used as a basis for class discussion rather than to illustrate either effective or ineffective handling of a management situation. © 2004, ICFAI Center for Management Research. All rights reserved. No part of this publication may be reproduced, stored in a retrieval system, used in a spreadsheet, or transmitted in any form or by any means, electronic or mechanical, without permission. Reproduced with permission.

FURTHER READING

Dawley, H., Watch out Europe: Here Comes Wal-Mart, *Business Week*, 28 June 1999.

Kahn, J., Wal-Mart Goes Shopping in Europe, *Fortune*, 7 June 1999.

Marino, D., Wal-Mart Steps up German Invasion, www.fool.com, 26 March 2001.

dePommereau, I., Wal-Mart lesson: Smiling service won't win Germans, www.csmonitor.com, 17 October 2002.

Rubin, D., Grumpy German Shoppers Distrust the Wal-Mart Style, www.gaccwa.org, 30 September 2001.

Schmid, J., In Europe, Wal-Mart Pursues a Big Dream, *International Herald Tribune*, 2 October 1998.

Troy, M., Wal-Mart Germany Beefs Up, *Discount Store News*, 4 January 1999.

Troy, M., Wal-Mart Germany's New President Faces Culture, Customer Challenges, *Discount Store News*, 9 February 1998.

Zellener, W., Wal-Mart's Newest Accent is German, *Business Week*, 18 December 1997.

Zellner, W., Schmidt, K.A., Ihlwan, M. and Dawley, H., How Well Does Wal-Mart Travel? *Business Week*, 3 September 2001.

Germany: Stop Bullying Wal-Mart, *Business Week*, 25 September 2000.

Operations Evolve to Offset Doldrums in Deutschland, *DSN Retailing Today*, 5 June 2001.

The first 'real' Wal-Mart is a flop? www.union-network.org, 12 February 2002.

The Wal-Mart Effect, *Business Europe*, 17 May 2000.

Wal-Mart Acquires Interspar Hypermarkets, www.prnewswire.com, 9 December 1998.

Wal-Mart Continues to Lose Money in Germany – Responds through Escalating Price War, www.union-network.org, 29 March 2001.

Wal-Mart in Germany is Not Doing Well, www.union-network.org, 7 March 2000.

Wal-Mart's Low Prices too Low for Germany's Retail Regulators, www.enquirer.com, 9 September 2000.

Wal-Mart Makes Bigger than Expected Losses in Germany, www.union-network.org, 10 March 2000.

www.forbes.com.

www.hicbusiness.org.

www.mventures.com.

www.planetretail.net.

www.walmartstores.com.

www.wilmercutler.com.

GLOSSARY

A

abandoned product ranges The outcome of a firm narrowing its range of products to obtain economies of scale, which provides opportunities for other firms to enter the markets for the abandoned products.

absolute advantage The ability to produce a good or service more efficiently than it can be produced elsewhere.

accounting diversity The range of differences in national accounting practices.

acculturation The process of adjusting and adapting to a specific culture other than one's own.

adaptability screening A selection procedure that usually involves interviewing both the candidate for an overseas assignment and his or her family members to determine how well they are likely to adapt to another culture.

agent A representative or intermediary for the firm that works to develop business and sales strategies and develops contacts.

air shipping/airfreight Transport of goods by air; accounts for less than 1% of the total volume of international shipments, but more than 20% of value.

allocation mentality The tradition of acquiring resources based not on what is needed but on what the plan makes available.

American terms Quoting a currency rate as the US dollar against a country's currency (e.g., US dollars/yen).

analogy A method for estimating market potential from similar products when data for the specific products do not exist.

Andean Community A trade bloc made up of the member states of the South American countries of Bolivia, Colombia, Ecuador and Peru, as well as five associate member countries and two observer countries.

antidumping Laws that many countries use to impose tariffs on foreign imports. They are designed to help domestic industries that are injured by competition from abroad due to imported products being sold at low prices.

antitrust laws Laws that prohibit monopolies, restraint of trade and conspiracies to inhibit competition.

arbitration The procedure for settling a dispute in which an objective third party hears both sides and makes a decision; a procedure for resolving conflict in the international business arena through the use of intermediaries such as representatives of chambers of commerce, trade associations or third-country institutions.

area expertise A knowledge of the basic systems in a particular region or market.

area structure An organizational structure in which geographic divisions are responsible for all manufacturing and marketing in their respective areas.

area studies Training programmes that provide factual preparation prior to an overseas assignment.

arm's length price A price that unrelated parties would have reached.

Asia-Pacific Economic Co-operation (APEC) Made up of 21 member states whose goal is to increase multilateral co-operation in view of the economic rise of the Pacific nations.

autarky Self-sufficiency: a country that is not participating in international trade.

average cost method An accounting principle by which the value of inventory is estimated as the average cost of the items in inventory.

B

back translation The retranslation of text to the original language by a different person than the one who made the first translation.

backward innovation The development of a drastically simplified version of a product.

balance of payments (BOP) A statement of all transactions between one country and the rest of the world during a given period; a record of flows of goods, services and investments across borders.

bank-based regime This regime is characterized with high proportions of financial assets held by banks. Companies obtain most of their external finance from banks. Lending to firms is laden with moral hazard as owner-managers may diminish investment profitability to enjoy private benefits. Bank monitoring helps resolve this problem to a certain extent.

bank draft A financial document drawn against a bank.

barter A direct exchange of goods of approximately equal value, with no money involved.

base salary Salary not including special payments such as allowances paid during overseas assignments.

Baums Commission German Government Panel on Corporate Governance. The Panel has laid the foundation for a comprehensive reform of German company law and has given recommendations for the improvement of corporate management and supervision, transparency and competition.

bearer bond A bond owned officially by whoever is holding it.

Berlin Initiative The Berlin Initiative Group developed the German Code of Corporate Governance (For more detail see http://www.ecgi.org/codes/documents/gccg_e.pdf).

best practice The idea that asserts that there is a technique, method, process, activity, incentive or reward that is more effective at delivering a particular outcome than any other technique, method, process, etc.

bilateral negotiations Negotiations carried out between two nations focusing only on their interests.

bill of lading A contract between an exporter and a carrier indicating that the carrier has accepted responsibility for the goods and will provide transportation in return for payment.

black hole The situation that arises when an international marketer has a low-competence subsidiary – or none at all – in a highly strategic market.

born global Firms that start international activities from their inception, entering oversees markets, penetrating many countries simultaneously.

boycott An organized effort to refrain from conducting business with a particular country of origin or seller of goods or services; used in the international arena for political or economic reasons.

brain drain A migration of professional people from one country to another, usually for the purpose of improving their incomes or living conditions.

Bretton Woods Agreement An agreement reached in 1944 among finance ministers of 45 Western nations to establish a system of fixed exchange rates.

bribery The use of payments or favours to obtain some right or benefit to which the briber has no legal right; a criminal offence in most Western countries but a way of life in many other parts of the world.

Buddhism A religion that extends through Asia from Sri Lanka to Japan and has 334 million followers, emphasizing spiritual attainment rather than worldly goods.

buffer stock Stock of a commodity kept on hand to prevent a shortage in times of unexpected demand; under international commodity and price agreements, the stock controlled by an elected or appointed manager for the purpose of managing the price of the commodity.

bulk service Ocean shipping provided on contract either for individual voyages or for prolonged periods of time.

buy-back A refinement of simple barter with one party supplying technology or equipment that enables the other party to produce goods, which are then used to pay for the technology or equipment that was supplied.

C

Cadbury Report Titled *Financial Aspects of Corporate Governance*, a report of a committee chaired by Adrian Cadbury that sets out recommendations on the arrangement of company boards and accounting systems to mitigate corporate governance risks and failures.

capital account An account in the balance of payments statement that records transactions involving borrowing, lending and investing across borders.

capital budget The financial evaluation of a proposed investment to determine whether the expected returns are sufficient to justify the investment expenses.

capital flight The flow of private funds abroad because investors believe that the return on investment or the safety of capital is not sufficiently ensured in their own countries.

Caribbean Basin Initiative (CBI) Extended trade preferences to Caribbean countries granting them special access to the markets of the United States.

carriage and insurance paid to (CIP) The price quoted by an exporter for shipments not involving waterway transport, including insurance.

carriage paid to (CPT) The price quoted by an exporter for shipments not involving waterway transport, not including insurance.

cartel An association of producers of a particular good, consisting either of private firms or of nations, formed for the purpose of suppressing the market forces affecting prices.

cash management Cash management is the financing of short-term or current assets.

cash pooling Used by multinational firms to centralize individual units' cash flows, resulting in less spending or forgone interest on unnecessary cash balances.

Central American Common Market A trade pact between Costa Rica, El Salvador, Guatemala, Honduras, and Nicaragua, which began in the early 1960s but collapsed in 1969 due to war.

centre of excellence The location of product development outside the home country because of an advantage of skills.

central plan The economic plan for the nation devised by the government of a socialist state; often a five-year plan that stipulated the quantities of goods to be produced.

centralization The concentrating of control and strategic decision making at headquarters.

change agent A person or institution who facilitates change in a firm or in a country.

channel design The length and width of the distribution channel.

Christianity The largest organized world religion with more than 2 billion followers.

code law Law based on a comprehensive set of written statutes.

co-determination A management approach in which employees are represented on supervisory boards to facilitate communication and collaboration between management and labour.

Combined Code on Corporate Governance A set of principles of good corporate governance; provides a code of best practice aimed at companies listed on the London Stock Exchange.

commercial invoice A bill for transported goods that describes the merchandise and its total cost and lists the addresses of the shipper and seller and delivery and payment terms.

Commercial Service A department of the US Department of Commerce that gathers information and assists US business executives in conducting business abroad.

Committee on Foreign Investments in the United States (CFIUS) A federal committee, chaired by the US Treasury, with the responsibility to review major foreign investments to determine whether national security or related concerns are at stake.

commodity price agreement An agreement involving both buyers and sellers to manage the price of a particular commodity, but often only when the price moves outside a predetermined range.

common agricultural policy (CAP) An integrated system of subsidies and rebates applied to agricultural interests in the European Union.

common law Law based on tradition and depending less on written statutes and codes than on precedent and custom – used in the United States.

common market A group of countries that agree to remove all barriers to trade among members, to establish a common trade policy with respect to non-members, and also to allow mobility for factors of production – labour, capital and technology.

communication services Services that are provided in the areas of videotext, home banking and home shopping, among others.

comparative advantage The ability to produce a good or service more cheaply, relative to other goods and services, than is possible in other countries.

competitive advantage The ability to produce a good or service more cheaply than other countries due to favourable factor conditions and demand conditions, strong related and supporting industries, and favourable firm strategy, structure and rivalry conditions.

competitive assessment A research process that consists of matching markets to corporate strengths and providing an analysis of the best potential for specific offerings.

competitive clusters Clusters representing a combination, within a geographical area, of companies, training centres, public and private research centres involved in partnership processes aiming at producing synergies around joint projects that are innovative in nature.

composition of trade The ratio of primary commodities to manufactured goods in a country's trade.

concentration strategy The market expansion policy that involves concentrating on a small number of markets.

confiscation The forceful government seizure of a company without compensation for the assets seized.

Confucianism A code of conduct with 150 million followers throughout Asia, stressing loyalty and relationships.

consulting services Services that are provided in the areas of management expertise on such issues as transportation, logistics and politics.

consumer boycotts are a form of consumer activity representing acts of voluntary abstaining from buying, using or dealing products or services produced by a certain firm or in a certain country as an expression of protest.

container ships Ships designed to carry standardized containers, which greatly facilitate loading and unloading as well as intermodal transfers.

contract manufacturing Outsourcing the actual production of goods so that the corporation can focus on research, development and marketing.

contractual agreement Document that specifies conditions of an exchange and details rights and obligations of involved parties.

contractual hedging A multinational firm's use of contracts to minimize its transaction exposure.

contributor A national subsidiary with a distinctive competence, such as product development.

control The planning, implementation, evaluation and correction of performance to ensure that organizational objectives are controlled.

co-ordinated decentralization Direction of overall corporate strategy by headquarters while granting subsidiaries the freedom to implement strategy within established ranges.

co-ordinated intervention A currency value management method whereby the central banks of the major nations simultaneously intervene in the currency markets, hoping to change a currency's value.

corporate governance The relationship among stakeholders used to determine and control the strategic direction and performance of an organization.

corporate income tax A tax applied to all residual earnings, regardless of what is retained or what is distributed as dividends.

corruption Payments or favours made to officials in return for services.

correspondent banks Banks located in different countries and unrelated by ownership that have a reciprocal agreement to provide services to each other's customers.

cost and freight (CFR) Seller quotes a price for the goods, including the cost of transportation to the named port of debarkation. Cost and choice of insurance are left to the buyer.

cost, insurance and freight (CIF) Seller quotes a price including insurance, all transportation and miscellaneous charges to the point of debarkation from the vessel or aircraft.

cost leadership A pricing tactic where a company offers an identical product or service at a lower cost than the competition.

cost of communication The cost of communicating electronically or by telephone with other locations. These costs have been drastically reduced through the use of fibre-optic cables.

cost of living allowance (COLA) An allowance paid during assignment overseas to enable the employee to maintain the same standard of living as in the home country.

cost-plus method A pricing policy in which there is a full allocation of foreign and domestic costs to the product.

Council Regulation on the Statute for a European Company Contains rules for European Public Companies known as a Societas Europaea (SE).

counterpurchase A refinement of simple barter that unlinks the timing of the two transactions, but still matches the value.

coups d'état A forced change in a country's government, often resulting in attacks on foreign firms and policy changes by the new government.

critical commodities list Governmental information about products that are either particularly sensitive to national security or controlled for other purposes.

Cromme Commission German Government Commission appointed by the German Justice Minister and chaired by Dr Gerhard Cromme. Its purpose was to contribute to the preparation of the German Corporate Governance Code. The Commission produced a draft Code in December 2001 and a final version in February 2002.

cross-marketing activities A reciprocal arrangement whereby each partner provides the other access to its markets for a product.

cross rate Exchange rate quotation that does not include the US dollar as one of the two currencies quoted.

cross-subsidization The use of resources accumulated in one part of the world to fight a competitive battle in another.

cultural assimilator A programme in which trainees for overseas assignments must respond to scenarios of specific situations in a particular country.

cultural convergence Increasing similarity among cultures accelerated by technological advances.

cultural hierarchy represents the subdivision of culture into segments with certain homogeneity. Cultural categorisation is a key to the definition of its specifics and significance.

cultural risk The risk of business blunders, poor customer relations and wasted negotiations that results when firms fail to understand and adapt to the differences between their own and host countries' cultures.

cultural universals Similarities in the total way of life of any group of people.

culture An integrated system of learned behaviour patterns that are characteristic of the members of any society.

culture shock Reactions to the psychological disorientation that most people feel when they move for an extended period of time into a markedly different culture.

cumulative transaction adjustment (CTA) The equity account entry on the consolidated balance sheet of multinational companies that is created to account for the translation of the foreign currency denominated balance sheets of foreign subsidiaries. Its value related to any individual foreign subsidiary only affects the consolidated income of the company upon sale or liquidation of the subsidiary itself.

currency flows The movement of currency from nation to nation, which in turn determine exchange rates.

current account An account in the balance of payments statement that records the results of transactions involving merchandise, services and unilateral transfers between countries.

current transfer A current account on the balance of payments statement that records gifts from the residents of one country to the residents of another.

customer involvement Active participation of customers in the provision of services they consume.

customer service A total corporate effort aimed at customer satisfaction; customer service levels in terms of responsiveness that inventory policies permit for a given situation.

customer structure An organizational structure in which divisions are formed on the basis of customer groups.

customs union Collaboration among trading countries in which members dismantle trade barriers among members and also establish a common trade policy with respect to non-members.

D

data privacy Electronic information security that restricts secondary use of data according to laws and preferences of the subjects.

decentralization The granting of a high degree of autonomy to subsidiaries.

deemed exports Addresses people rather than products, where knowledge transfer could lead to a breach of export restrictions.

delivered duty paid (DDP) Seller delivers the goods, with import duties paid, including inland transportation from import point to the buyer's premises.

delivered duty unpaid (DDU) Only the destination customs duty and taxes are paid by the consignee.

Delphi studies A research tool using a group of experts to rank major future developments.

density Weight-to-volume ratio; often used to determine shipping rates.

deregulation Removal of government interference.

differentiation Takes advantage of the company's real or perceived uniqueness on elements such as design or after-sales service.

direct intervention The process that governments used in the 1970s if they wished to alter the current value of their currency. It was done by simply buying or selling their own currency in the market using their reserves of other major currencies.

direct investment account An account in the balance of payments statement that records investments with an expected maturity of more than one year and an investor's ownership position of at least 10%.

direct involvement Participation by a firm in international business in which the firm works with foreign customers or markets to establish a relationship.

direct quotation A foreign exchange quotation that specifies the amount of home country currency needed to purchase one unit of foreign currency.

direct taxes Taxes applied directly to income.

discriminatory regulations Regulations that impose larger operating costs on foreign service providers than on local competitors, which provide subsidies to local firms only, or that deny competitive opportunities to foreign suppliers.

distributed earnings The proportion of a firm's net income after taxes that is paid out or distributed to the stockholders of the firm.

distributor A representative or intermediary for the firm that purchases products from the firm, takes title and assumes the selling risk.

diversification A market expansion policy characterized by growth in a relatively large number of markets or market segments.

division of labour The premise of modern industrial production where each stage in the production of a good is performed by one individual separately, rather than one individual being responsible for the entire production of the good.

domestication Government demand for partial transfer of ownership and management responsibility from a foreign company to local entities, with or without compensation.

double-entry bookkeeping Accounting methodology where each transaction gives rise to both a debit and a credit of the same currency amount. It is used in the construction of the balance of payments.

dual pricing Price-setting strategy in which the export price and domestic price are differentiated.

dual-use items Goods and services that are useful for both military and civilian purposes.

dumping Selling goods overseas at a price lower than in the exporter's home market, or at a price below the cost of production, or both.

E

East Asia Economic Group (EAEG) Also known as the East Asia Economic Caucus (EAEC). A regional free trade zone proposed in 1990, encompassing the ASEAN member states China, South Korea and Japan.

eclectic Representing a collection of forces or drivers.

eclectic paradigm A theory that provides a three-tiered framework for a company to follow when determining if it is beneficial to pursue foreign direct investment.

e-business/e-commerce The ability to offer goods and services over the web.

economic and monetary union (EMU) The ideal among European leaders that economic integration should move beyond the four freedoms: specifically, it entails (1) closer co-ordination of economic policies to promote exchange rate stability and convergence of inflation rates and growth rates; (2) creation of a European central bank; and (3) replacement of national monetary authorities by the European Central Bank and adoption of the euro as the European currency.

economic exposure The potential change in the value of a firm from unexpected changes in exchange rates; also called 'operating exposure' and 'strategic exposure'.

economic infrastructure The transportation, energy and communication systems in a country.

economic rent The amount of money an owner of a factor of production must receive in order for that owner to rent out that factor of production. Factors of production include labour, capital and land.

economies of scale The increase in efficiency of production as the number of goods being produced increases.

economic security Perception of a business activity as having an effect on a country's financial resources, often used to restrict competition from firms outside the country.

economic union A union among trading countries that has the characteristics of a common market and also harmonizes monetary policies, taxation and government spending, and uses a common currency.

economies of scale Production economies made possible by the output of larger quantities.

education allowance Reimbursement by company for dependent educational expenses incurred while a parent is assigned overseas.

effective tax rate Actual total tax burden after including all applicable tax liabilities and credits.

embargo A governmental action, usually prohibiting trade entirely, for a decidedly adversarial or political rather than economic purpose.

emerging economies Regions of the world that are experiencing rapid development with international significance.

engineering services Services that are provided in the areas of construction, design and engineering.

environmental protection Actions taken by governments to protect the environment and resources of a country.

environmental scanning Obtaining ongoing data about a country.

equity participation Provides incentives to make a loan to a business. Equity participation gives the lender an incentive to make a loan because lenders have a share in the increased equity of the business.

ethnocentrism Tending to regard one's own culture as superior; tending to be home-market oriented.

euro A single currency used by the European Union that replaced all the individual currencies of the participating member states.

Eurobond A bond that is denominated in a currency other than the currency of the country in which the bond is sold.

Eurocurrency A bank deposit in a currency other than the currency of the country where the bank is located; not confined to banks in Europe.

Eurodollars US dollars deposited in banks outside the United States; not confined to banks in Europe.

Euromarkets Money and capital markets in which transactions are denominated in a currency other than that of the place of the transaction; not confined to Europe.

European Monetary System (EMS) An organization formed in 1979 by eight EC members committed to maintaining the values of their currencies within a 2.25% of each other's.

European terms Quoting a currency rate as a country's currency against the US dollar (e.g., yen/US dollars).

European Union An economic union between leading European countries.

exchange controls Controls on the movement of capital in and out of a country, sometimes imposed when the country faces a shortage of foreign currency.

Exchange-Rate Mechanism (ERM) Mechanism for aligning the exchange rates of EU currencies against each other.

expatriate One living in a foreign land; a corporate manager assigned to a location abroad.

experiential knowledge Knowledge acquired through involvement (as opposed to information, which is obtained through communication, research and education).

experimentation A research tool to determine the effects of a variable on an operation.

export complaint systems Allow customers to contact the original supplier of a product in order to enquire about products, make suggestions or present complaints.

export-control system A system designed to deny or at least delay the acquisition of strategically important goods to adversaries; in the United States, based on the Export Administration Act and the Munitions Control Act.

export licence A licence provided by the government that permits the export of sensitive goods or services.

export management companies (EMCs) Domestic firms that specialize in performing international business services as commission representatives or as distributors.

export trading company (ETC) The result of 1982 legislation to improve the export performance of small and medium-sized firms, the export trading company allows businesses to band together to export or offer export services. Additionally, the law permits bank participation in trading companies and relaxes antitrust provisions.

expropriation The government takeover of a company with compensation frequently at a level lower than the investment value of the company's assets.

external economies of scale Lower production costs resulting from the free mobility of factors of production in a common market.

extraterritoriality An exemption from rules and regulations of one country that may challenge the national sovereignty of another; the application of one country's rules and regulations abroad.

ex-works (EXW) Price quotes that apply only at the point of origin; the seller agrees to place the goods at the disposal of the buyer at the specified place on a date or within a fixed period.

F

factor intensities The proportion of capital input to labour input used in the production of a good.

factor mobility The ability to freely move factors of production across borders, as among common market countries.

factor proportions theory Systematic explanation of the source of comparative advantage.

factors of production All inputs into the production process, including capital, labour, land and technology.

factual cultural knowledge Knowledge obtainable from specific country studies published by governments, private companies and universities, and also available in the form of background information from facilitating agencies such as banks, advertising agencies and transportation companies.

field experience Experience acquired in actual rather than laboratory settings; training that exposes a corporate manager to a different cultural environment for a limited amount of time.

FIFO Method of valuation of inventories for accounting purposes, meaning first-in/first-out. The principle rests on the assumption that costs should be charged against revenue in the order in which they occur.

financial incentives Monetary offers intended to motivate; special funding designed to attract foreign direct investors that may take the form of land or building, loans or loan guarantees.

financial infrastructure Facilitating financial agencies in a country; for example, banks.

Financial Reporting Council (FRC) A unified, independent regulator with a mission of promoting confidence in corporate reporting and governance in the United Kingdom.

financing cash flows The cash flows of a firm related to the funding of its operations; debt and equity related cash flows.

fiscal incentives Incentives used to attract foreign direct investment that provide specific tax measures to attract the investor.

fixed exchange rate The government of a country officially declares that its currency is convertible into a fixed amount of some other currency.

flex time A modification of work scheduling that allows workers to determine their own starting and ending times within a broad range of available hours.

floating exchange rate Under this system, the government possesses no responsibility to declare that its currency is convertible into a fixed amount of some other currency; this diminishes the role of official reserves.

focus group A research technique in which representatives of a proposed target audience contribute to market research by participating in an unstructured discussion.

foreign availability The degree to which products similar to those of a firm can be obtained in markets outside the firm's home country; crucial to export determination.

foreign bond Bonds issued in national capital markets by borrowers (private companies or sovereign states) from other countries.

Foreign Corrupt Practices Act A 1977 law making it a crime for US executives of publicly traded firms to bribe a foreign official in order to obtain business.

foreign currency exchange rate The price of one country's currency in terms of another country's currency.

foreign direct investment The establishment or expansion of operations of a firm in a foreign country. Like all investments, it assumes a transfer of capital.

foreign market opportunity analysis Broad-based research to obtain information about the general variables of a target market outside a firm's home country.

foreign market pricing This is the determining of prices by firms in foreign markets when a two-tiered or market-by-market pricing policy is applied.

foreign policy The area of public policy concerned with relationships with other countries.

foreign service premium A financial incentive to accept an assignment overseas, usually paid as a percentage of the base salary.

foreign tax credit Credit applied to home-country tax payments due for taxes paid abroad.

foreign trade zones Special areas where foreign goods may be held or processed without incurring duties and taxes.

Fortress Europe Concern that the integration of the European Union may result in increased restrictions on trade and investment by outsiders.

forward contracts Agreements between firms and banks that permit the firm to sell or buy a specific foreign currency at a future date at a known price.

forward pricing Setting the price of a product based on its anticipated demand before it has been introduced to the market.

forward rates Contracts that provide for two parties to exchange currencies on a future date at an agreed-upon exchange rate.

franchising A form of licensing that allows a distributor or retailer exclusive rights to sell a product or service in a specified area.

Frankfurt Panel on Corporate Governance The Code of Best Practice for German Corporate Governance was drawn up by the Frankfurt Panel on Corporate Governance in July 2000.

free alongside ship (FAS) Exporter quotes a price for the goods, including charges for delivery of the goods alongside a vessel at a port. Seller handles cost of unloading and wharfage; loading, ocean transportation and insurance are left to the buyer.

free carrier (FCA) Applies only at a designated inland shipping point. Seller is responsible for loading goods into the means of transportation; buyer is responsible for all subsequent expenses.

free on board (FOB) Applies only to vessel shipments. Seller quotes a price covering all expenses up to and including delivery of goods on an overseas vessel provided by or for the buyer.

free trade area An area in which all barriers to trade among member countries are removed, although sometimes only for certain goods or services.

Free Trade Area of the Americas (FTAA) A proposed hemispheric trade zone covering all the Americas. Discussions have faltered and there is little chance for a comprehensive trade agreement in the foreseeable future.

freight forwarders Specialists in handling international transportation by contracting with carriers on behalf of shippers.

functional structure An organizational structure in which departments are formed on the basis of functional areas such as production, marketing and finance.

G

gap analysis Analysis of the difference between market potential and actual sales.

generally accepted accounting principles (GAAP) The accounting standards accepted by the accounting profession in each country as required for the preparation of financial statements for external users.

General Agreement on Tariffs and Trade (GATT) An international code of tariffs and trade rules signed by 23 nations in 1947; headquartered in Geneva, Switzerland; now part of the World Trade Organization with 148 members.

General Agreement on Trade in Services (GATS) A legally enforceable pact among WTO participants that covers trade and investments in the services sector.

glasnost The Soviet policy of encouraging the free exchange of ideas and discussion of problems, pluralistic participation in decision making and increased availability of information.

global account management Global customers of a company may be provided with a single point of contact for domestic and international operations and consistent worldwide service.

globalization Trend away from distinct national economic units and toward one huge global market.

glocal Refers to the individual, group, division, unit, organization and community which is willing and able to 'think globally and act locally'.

the Gold Standard A standard for international currencies in which currency values were stated in terms of gold.

goods trade An account of the balance of payments statement that records funds used for merchandise imports and funds obtained from merchandise exports.

government-based regimes Set of rules developed by the central government of a country that regulate ways of doing business in this country.

government regulation Interference in the marketplace by governments.

Greenbury Report A UK government report on corporate governance released in 1995. It addressed a growing concern about the level of director remuneration.

grey market Marketing of products through unauthorized channels.

Gulf Co-operation Council (GCC) Also known as the Co-operation Council for the Arab States of the Gulf (CCASG). A trade bloc involving the six Arab states of the Persian Gulf (Bahrain, Qatar, Kuwait, Oman, Saudi Arabia and the United Arab Emirates) with many social and economic objectives.

H

Hampel Report A UK government report published in 1998, designed to be a revision of the corporate governance system in the UK. The Report aimed to combine, harmonize and clarify the recommendations made by the Cadbury and Greenbury Reports.

hardship allowance A premium paid during an assignment to an overseas area that requires major adaptation.

hedge To counterbalance a present sale or purchase with a sale or purchase for future delivery as a way to minimize loss due to price fluctuations; to make counterbalancing sales or purchases in the international market as protection against adverse movements in the exchange rate.

high-context cultures Cultures in which behavioural and environmental nuances are an important means of conveying information.

Higgs Report Titled *Review of the Role and Effectiveness of Non-Executive Directors*, a report chaired by Derek Higgs reviewing the role and effectiveness of non-executive directors and the audit committee, aiming at improving and strengthening the existing Combined Code on Corporate Governance. It was published in 2003.

Hinduism With 750 million followers, a way of life rather than a religion, with economic and other attainment dictated by the caste into which its followers are born.

housing allowance A premium paid during assignment overseas to provide living quarters.

I

implementer The typical subsidiary role, involving implementing strategy that originates with headquarters.

import substitution A policy for economic growth adopted by many developing countries that involves the systematic encouragement of domestic production of goods formerly imported.

income elasticity of demand A means of describing change in demand in relative response to a change in income.

incoterms International Commerce Terms. Widely accepted terms used in quoting export prices.

indirect involvement Participation by a firm in international business through an intermediary, in which the firm does not deal with foreign customers or firms.

indirect quotation Foreign exchange quotation that specifies the units of foreign currency that could be purchased with one unit of the home currency.

indirect taxes Taxes applied to non-income items, such as value-added taxes, excise taxes, tariffs and so on.

industrial policy A government regulation or law that encourages the ongoing operation of, or investment in, a particular industry.

informal co-operation A form of business partnership not based on contractual arrangements.

information system Can provide the decision maker with basic data for most ongoing decisions.

infrastructure shortages Problems in a country's underlying physical structure, such as transportation, utilities and so on.

input–output analysis A method for estimating market activities and potential that measures the factor inflows into production and the resultant outflow of products.

insurance services Services that are provided in underwriting, risk evaluation and operations.

intangibility The inability to be seen, tasted or touched in a conventional sense; the characteristic of services that most strongly differentiates them from products.

intellectual property right (IPR) Legal right resulting from industrial, scientific, literary or artistic activity.

interbank interest rates The interest rate charged by banks to banks in the major international financial centres.

intermodal movements The transfer of freight from one mode or type of transportation to another.

internal bank A multinational firm's financial management tool that actually acts as a bank to co-ordinate finances among its units.

internal economies of scale Lower production costs resulting from greater production for an enlarged market.

internalization Occurs when a firm establishes its own multinational operation, keeping information that is at the core of its competitiveness within the firm.

international bond Bond issued in domestic capital markets by foreign borrowers (foreign bonds) or issued in the Eurocurrency markets in a currency different from that of the home currency of the borrower (Eurobonds).

international competitiveness The ability of a firm, an industry or a country to compete in the international marketplace at a stable or rising standard of living.

international debt load Total accumulated negative net investment of a nation.

international law The body of rules governing relationships between sovereign states; also certain treaties and agreements respected by a number of countries.

International Monetary Fund (IMF) A specialized agency of the United Nations established in 1944. An international financial institution for dealing with balance of payment problems; the first international monetary authority with at least some degree of power over national authorities.

International Trade Organization (ITO) A forward-looking approach to international trade and investment embodied in the 1948 Havana Charter; due to disagreements among sponsoring nations, its provisions were never ratified.

interpretive cultural knowledge An acquired ability to understand and appreciate the nuances of foreign cultural traits and patterns.

interviews A face-to-face research tool to obtain in-depth information.

intra-company pricing The value assigned on a per unit or per shipment basis to goods transferred from one establishment of an enterprise to another. It may or may not be economically significant. This is not a market price as ownership of the good does not change hands.

intra-industry trade The simultaneous export and import of the same good by a country. It is of interest due to the traditional theory that a country will either export or import a good, but not do both at the same time.

intranet A process that integrates a company's information assets into a single accessible system using Internet-based technologies such as e-mail, news groups and the web.

inventory Materials on hand for use in the production process; also finished goods on hand.

inventory carrying costs The expense of maintaining inventories.

investment income The proportion of net income that is paid back to a parent company.

Islam A religion that has over 1.2 billion followers from the west coast of Africa to the Philippines, as well as in the rest of the world, and is supportive of entrepreneurism but not of exploitation.

J

joint occurrence Occurrence of one or several shifts affecting the business environment in several locations simultaneously.

Joint Research and Development Act A 1984 law that allows both US and overseas firms to participate in joint basic research efforts without fear of US antitrust action.

just-in-time (JIT) inventory Materials scheduled to arrive precisely when they are needed on a production line.

L

lag Paying a debt late to take advantage of exchange rates.

land bridge Transfer of ocean freight on land among various modes of transportation.

Latin American Free Trade Association (LAFTA) A free trade area formed by Mexico and the South American countries in 1961. It was replaced by ALADI in 1980.

Latin American Integration Association (ALADI) A form of regional economic integration involving most of the Latin American countries.

Law of One Price The theory that the relative prices of any single good between countries, expressed in each country's currency, is representative of the proper or appropriate exchange rate value.

lead Paying a debt early to take advantage of exchange rates.

Leontief Paradox The general belief that the United States, as a capital-abundant country, should be exporting capital-intensive products, whereas its exports are labour-intensive.

lesser-developed economy A country that is considered lacking in terms of its economic capabilities, infrastructure and industrial base. The population of a lesser-developed economy often has a relatively low standard of living, due to low incomes and widespread poverty. Such a country has low per capita gross domestic product and relies mainly on agriculture.

LIBOR The London InterBank Offer Rate. The rate of interest charged by top-quality international banks on loans to similar quality banks in London. This interest rate is often used in both domestic and international markets as the rate of interest on loans and other financial agreements.

licensing A firm gives a licence to another firm to produce, package or market its product.

licensing agreement An agreement in which one firm permits another to use its intellectual property in exchange for compensation.

LIFO Method of valuation of inventories for accounting purposes, meaning last-in-first-out. The principle rests on the practice of recording inventory by the 'layer' of the cost at which it was incurred.

liner service Ocean shipping characterized by regularly scheduled passage on established routes.

lingua franca The language habitually used among people of diverse speech to facilitate communication.

lobbyist Typically, a well-connected person or firm that is hired by a business to influence the decision making of policy makers and legislators.

local content Regulations to gain control over foreign investment by ensuring that a large share of the product is locally produced or a larger share of the profit is retained in the country.

location decision A decision concerning the number of facilities to establish and where they should be situated.

logistics platform Vital to a firm's competitive position, it is determined by a location's ease and convenience of market reach under favourable cost circumstances.

low-context cultures Cultures in which most information is conveyed explicitly rather than through behavioural and environmental nuances.

M

Maastricht Treaty The agreement signed in December 1991 in Maastricht, the Netherlands, in which European Community members agreed to a specific timetable and set of necessary conditions to create a single currency for the EU countries.

macroeconomic level Level at which trading relationships affect individual markets.

management contract An international business alternative in which the firm sells its expertise in running a company while avoiding the risk or benefit of ownership.

managerial commitment The desire and drive on the part of management to act on an idea and support it in the long run.

maquiladoras Mexican border plants, with lower labour costs, that make goods and parts or process food for export back to the United States.

marginal cost method This method considers the direct costs of producing and selling goods for export as the floor beneath which prices cannot be set.

market audit A method of estimating market size by adding together local production and imports, with exports subtracted from the total.

market-based regimes Under market-based exchange rate regimes, the characterization of foreign exchange market conditions is important information for domestic monetary policy decisions and impacts the exchange rate.

market-differentiated pricing Price-setting strategy based on demand rather than cost.

market segment Group of customers that share characteristics and behaviours.

market transparency Availability of full disclosure and information about key market factors such as supply, demand, quality, service and prices.

marketing infrastructure Facilitating marketing agencies in a country; for example, market research firms, channel members.

mass customization Working with existing product technology to create specific product bundles, resulting in a customized product for a particular customer.

materials management The timely movement of raw materials, parts and supplies into and through the firm.

matrix structure An organizational structure that uses functional and divisional structures simultaneously.

maximization of shareholder value One of the two alternative objectives of management in private companies (the alternative is *corporate wealth maximization*). The objective of shareholder value maximization is to operate the company in ways that directly reward the equity investors of the company.

media strategy Strategy applied to the selection of media vehicles and the development of a media schedule.

mercantilism Political and economic policy in the seventeenth and early eighteenth centuries aimed at increasing a nation's wealth and power by encouraging the export of goods in return for gold.

microeconomic level Level of business concerns that affect an individual firm or industry.

mininationals Newer companies with sales between US$200 million and US$1 billion that are able to serve the world from a handful of manufacturing bases.

minority participation Participation by a group having less than the number of votes necessary for control.

mixed aid credits Credits at rates composed partially of commercial interest rates and partially of highly subsidized developmental aid interest rates.

mixed structure An organizational structure that combines two or more organizational dimensions; for example, products, areas or functions.

most-favoured nation (MFN) A term describing a GATT clause that calls for member countries to grant other member countries the same most favourable treatment they accord any country concerning imports and exports. In the US, it is now called normal trade relations (NTR).

multidomestic strategy A business strategy where each individual country organization is operated as a profit centre.

multilateral negotiations Trade negotiations among more than two parties; the intricate relationships among trading countries.

multinational corporations (MNCs) Companies that invest in countries around the globe.

N

national security The ability of a nation to protect its internal values from external threats.

national sovereignty The supreme right of nations to determine national policies; freedom from external control.

natural hedging The structuring of a firm's operations so that cash inflows and outflows by currency are matched.

net errors and omissions account Makes sure that the balance of payments actually balances.

net present value (NPV) The sum of the present values of all cash inflows and outflows from an investment project discounted at the cost of capital.

netting Cash flow co-ordination between a corporation's global units so that only one smaller cash transfer must be made.

1992 White Paper A key document developed by the EC Commission to outline the further requirements necessary for a successful integration of the European Union.

non-financial incentives Non-monetary offers intended to motivate; special offers designed to attract foreign direct investors that may take the form of guaranteed government purchases, special protection from competition or improved infrastructure facilities.

non-tariff barriers Barriers to trade, other than tariffs. Examples include buy-domestic campaigns, preferential treatment for domestic bidders and restrictions on market entry of foreign products such as involved inspection procedures.

not-invented-here syndrome (NIH) A defensive, territorial attitude that, if held by managers, can frustrate effective implementation of global strategies.

O

observation A research tool where the subjects' activity and behaviour are scrutinized.

ocean shipping The forwarding of freight by ocean carrier.

official reserves account An account in the balance of payments statement that shows (1) the change in the amount of funds immediately available to a country for making international payments and (2) the borrowing and lending that has taken place between the monetary authorities of different countries either directly or through the International Monetary Fund.

offshore banking The use of banks or bank branches located in low-tax countries, often Caribbean islands, to raise and hold capital for multinational operations.

one-stop logistics Allows shippers to buy all the transportation modes and functional services from a single carrier.

operating cash flows The cash flows arising from the firm's everyday business activities.

operating or service lease A lease that transfers most but not all benefits and costs inherent in the ownership of the property to the lessee. Payments do not fully cover the cost of purchasing the asset or incurring the liability.

operating risk The danger of interference by governments or other groups in one's corporate operations abroad.

opportunity cost The returns forgone on any resource or asset from using it in its next best use. The principle emphasizes that most assets or resources have alternative uses that have real value.

order cycle time The total time that passes between the placement of an order and the receipt of the product.

orientation programme A programme that familiarizes new workers with their roles; the preparation of employees for assignment overseas.

ownership risk The risk inherent in maintaining ownership of property abroad. The exposure of foreign-owned assets to governmental intervention.

P

parallel importation A non-counterfeit product imported from another country without the permission of the intellectual property owner.

Patent Co-operations Treaty (PCT) An agreement that outlines procedures for filing one international patent application rather than individual national applications.

pax Americana An American peace since 1945 that led to increased international business transactions.

pax Romana Two relatively peaceful centuries in the Roman Empire.

pension liabilities The accumulating obligations of employers to fund the retirement or pension plans of employees.

perestroika An attempt to fundamentally reform the Soviet economy by improving the overall technological and industrial base and the quality of life for Soviet citizens through increased availability of food, housing and consumer goods.

perishability Susceptibility to deterioration; the characteristic of services that makes them difficult to store.

physical distribution The movement of finished products from suppliers to customers.

Plaza Agreement An accord reached in 1985 by the Group of Five that held that the major nations should join in a co-ordinated effort to bring down the value of the US dollar.

political risk The risk of loss by an international corporation of assets, earning power or managerial control as a result of political actions by the host country.

political union A group of countries that have common foreign policy and security policy and that share judicial co-operation.

population balance A concern in some countries where the population is being skewed by a preference for male children.

population stabilization An attempt to control rapid increases in population and ensure that economic development exceeds population growth.

portfolio investment account An account in the balance of payments statement that records investments in assets with an original maturity of more than one year and where an investor's ownership position is less than 10%.

portfolio models Tools that have been proposed for use in market and competitive analysis. They typically involve two measures: internal strength and external attractiveness.

ports Harbour towns or cities where ships may take on or discharge cargo; the lack of ports and port services is the greatest constraint in ocean shipping.

positioning The perception by consumers of a firm's product in relation to competitors' products.

preferential policies Government policies that favour certain (usually domestic) firms; for example, the use of national carriers for the transport of government freight even when more economical alternatives exist.

price controls Government regulation of the prices of goods and services.

price escalation The establishing of export prices far in excess of domestic prices – often due to a long distribution channel and frequent markups.

primary data Data obtained directly for a specific research purpose through interviews, focus groups, surveys, observation or experimentation.

private placement The sale of debt securities to private or institutional investors without going through a public issuance like that of a bond issue or equity issue.

privatization A policy of shifting government operations to privately owned enterprises to cut budget costs and ensure more efficient services.

process structure A variation of the functional structure in which departments are formed on the basis of production processes.

product cycle theory A theory that views products as passing through four stages – introduction, growth, maturity, decline – during which the location of production moves from industrialized to lower-cost developing nations.

product differentiation The effort to build unique differences or improvements into products.

product structure An organizational structure in which product divisions are responsible for all manufacturing and marketing.

production possibilities frontier A theoretical method of representing the total productive capabilities of a nation used in the formulation of classical and modern trade theory.

promotional message The content of an advertisement or a publicity release.

protectionistic legislation A trade policy that restricts trade to or from one country to another country.

proxy information Data used as a substitute for more desirable data that are unobtainable.

psychological distance Characterizes the cultural difference between countries affecting the decision-makers' choices of market entry or firms' performance in foreign markets.

punitive tariff A tax on an imported good or service intended to punish a trading partner.

purchasing power parity (PPP) The theory that the price of internationally traded commodities should be the same in every country, and hence the exchange rate between the two currencies of those countries should be the ratio of prices in the two countries.

Q

qualitative information Data that are not amenable to statistical analysis, but provide a better understanding, description or prediction of given situations, behavioural patterns or underlying dimensions.

quality circles Groups of workers who meet regularly to discuss issues related to productivity.

quality of life The standard of living combined with environmental factors, it determines the level of well-being of individuals.

quality of work life Various corporate efforts in the areas of personal and professional development undertaken with the objectives of increasing employee satisfaction and increasing productivity.

quotas Legal restrictions on the import quantity of particular goods, imposed by governments as barriers to trade.

R

reference groups Groups such as the family, co-workers, and professional and trade associations that provide the values and attitudes that influence and shape behaviour, including consumer behaviour.

re-invoicing The policy of buying goods from one unit and selling them to a second unit and re-invoicing the sale to the next unit, to take advantage of favourable exchange rates.

reliability Dependability; the predictability of the outcome of an action. For example, the reliability of arrival time for ocean freight or airfreight.

representative office An office of an international bank established in a foreign country to serve the bank's customers in the area in an advisory capacity; does not take deposits or make loans.

reverse distribution A system responding to the need for product returns that ensures a firm can retrieve a product from the market for subsequent use, recycling or disposal.

roll-on/roll-off (RO-RO) Transportation vessels built to accommodate trucks, which can drive on in one port and drive off at their destinations.

royalty The compensation paid by one firm to another under an agreement.

S

sanction A governmental action, usually consisting of a specific coercive trade measure, that distorts the free flow of trade for an adversarial or political purpose rather than an economic one.

scenario building The identification of crucial variables and determining their effects on different cases or approaches.

sea bridge The transfer of freight among various modes of transportation at sea.

secondary data Data originally collected to serve another purpose than the one in which the researcher is currently interested.

self-management Independent decision making; a high degree of worker involvement in corporate decision making.

self-reference criterion The unconscious reference to one's own cultural values.

sensitivity training Training in human relations that focuses on personal and interpersonal interactions; training that focuses on enhancing an expatriate's flexibility in situations quite different from those at home.

service capacity The maximum level at which a service provider is able to provide services to customers.

service consistency Uniform quality of service.

service heterogeneity The difference from one delivery of a product to another delivery of the same product as a result of the inability to control the production and quality of the process.

services trade The international exchange of personal or professional services, such as financial and banking services, construction and tourism.

set of standard rules Rules developed to help different types of co-operatives create their rules of conducting business in order to comply with the legislation.

shipper's order A negotiable bill of lading that can be bought, sold or traded while the subject goods are still in transit; used for letter of credit transactions.

Single European Act The legislative basis for the European Integration.

Smith Report Report that determines the Corporate Governance Codes and Principles in the United Kingdom in terms of auditing procedures.

Smoot-Hawley Act A 1930 act that raised import duties to the highest rates ever imposed by the United States; designed to promote domestic production, it resulted in the downfall of the world trading system.

social infrastructure The housing, health, educational and other social systems in a country.

social stratification The division of a particular population into classes.

sogo shosha A large Japanese general trading company.

South Asian Association for Regional Co-operation (SAARC) An economic and political organization of eight countries in Southern Asia, comprising India, Pakistan, Bangladesh, Sri Lanka, Maldives, Nepal, Bhutan and Afghanistan.

special economic zones Areas created by a country to attract foreign investors, in which there are no tariffs, substantial tax incentives and low prices for land and labour.

spot rates Contracts that provide for two parties to exchange currencies with delivery in two business days.

standard of living The level of material affluence of a group or nation, measured as a composite of quantities and qualities of goods.

standard worldwide pricing Price-setting strategy based on average unit costs of fixed, variable and export-related costs.

state-owned enterprise A corporate form that has emerged in non-communist countries, primarily for reasons of national security and economic security.

straight bill of lading A non-negotiable bill of lading usually used in prepaid transactions in which the transported goods involved are delivered to a specific individual or company.

strategic alliances A new term for collaboration among firms, often similar to joint ventures.

strategic leader A highly competent firm located in a strategically critical market.

strategic trade policy A government policy aimed at improving the competitive position of a domestic industry and/or domestic firm in the world market.

supply-chain management Results where a series of value-adding activities connect a company's supply side with its demand side.

surveys The use of questionnaires to obtain quantifiable research information.

systems concept A concept of logistics based on the notion that materials-flow activities are so complex that they can be considered only in the context of their interaction.

T

tariffs Taxes on imported goods and services, instituted by governments as a means to raise revenue and as barriers to trade.

tax equalization Reimbursement by the company when an employee in an overseas assignment pays taxes at a higher rate than if he or she were at home.

tax policy A means by which countries may control foreign investors.

teaching services Services that are provided in the areas of training and motivating as well as in teaching of operational, managerial and theoretical issues.

team building A process that enhances the cohesiveness of a department or group by helping members learn how to organize their work and assume responsibility for it.

technology transfer The transfer of systematic knowledge for the manufacture of a product, the application of a process or the rendering of a service.

'tentative US tax' The calculation of US taxes on foreign source incomes to estimate US tax payments.

terrorism Illegal and violent acts toward property and people.

theocracy A legal perspective based on religious practices and interpretations.

total cost concept A decision concept that uses cost as a basis for measurement in order to evaluate and optimize logistical activities.

tourism The economic benefit of money spent in a country or region by travellers from outside the area.

tracking The capability of a shipper to obtain information about the location of the shipment at any time.

trade creation A benefit of economic integration; the benefit to a particular country when a group of countries trade a product freely among themselves but maintain common barriers to trade with non-members.

trade diversion A cost of economic integration; the cost to a particular country when a group of countries trade a product freely among themselves but maintain common barriers to trade with non-members.

trade draft A withdrawal document drawn against a company.

trade-off concept A decision concept that recognizes linkages within the decision system.

trademark Designs and names, often officially registered, by which merchants or manufacturers designate and differentiate their products.

trademark licensing An agreement that allows the licensee to use the licensor's brand identity to market its own products.

trade policy measures Mechanisms used to influence and alter trade relationships.

trade promotion authority The right of the US president to negotiate trade treaties and agreements, with the US Congress' authority to accept or reject, but not amend.

trading blocs Formed by agreements among countries to establish links through movement of goods, services, capital and labour across borders.

tramp service Ocean shipping via irregular routes, scheduled only on demand.

transaction cost theory This foundation of this theory was developed by Ronald Coase in 1932. At its core is this notion: When a firm tries to decide whether to outsource or to produce goods or services on its own, market prices are not the sole factor. There also are considerable transaction costs, search costs, contracting costs and co-ordination costs. Those costs normally determine whether a firm uses internal or external resources for products or services.

transition economies An economy which is changing from a centrally planned economy to a free market.

transaction exposure The potential for currency losses or gains during the time when a firm completes a transaction denominated in a foreign currency.

transfer prices The prices at which a firm sells its products to its own subsidiaries and affiliates.

transfer risk The danger of having one's ability to transfer profits or products in and out of a country inhibited by governmental rules and regulations.

transit time The period between departure and arrival of a carrier.

translation exposure The potential effect of a change in currency values on a firm's financial statements.

transparency A characteristic of an accounting system that implies that companies disclose a great deal of information about accounting practices; more common in Anglo-Saxon countries (UK, USA).

Treaty of Rome The original agreement that established the foundation for the formation of the European Economic Community.

triangular arbitrage The exchange of one currency for a second currency, the second for a third, and the third for the first in order to make a profit.

trigger mechanisms Specific acts or stimuli that set off reactions.

Turnbull Report Titled *Internal Control: Guidance for Directors on the Combined Code*, a report published in 1999 drawn up by a committee chaired by Nigel Turnbull for companies listed on the stock exchange. The report informs directors of their obligations under the Combined Code with regard to keeping good "internal controls" in their companies, or having good audits and checks to ensure the quality of financial reporting and catch any fraud before it becomes a problem.

turnkey operation A specialized form of management contract between a customer and an organization to provide a complete operational system together with the skills needed for unassisted maintenance and operation.

U

undistributed earnings The proportion of a firm's net income after taxes that is retained within the firm for internal purposes.

unsolicited order An unplanned business opportunity that arises as a result of another firm's activities.

unstructured data Information collected for analysis with open-ended questions.

V

value-added tax (VAT) A tax on the value contributed at each stage of the production and distribution process; a tax assessed in most European countries and also common among Latin American countries.

virtual team A team of people who are based at various locations around the world and communicate through intranet and other electronic means to achieve a common goal.

voluntary restraint agreements Trade-restraint agreements resulting in self-imposed restrictions not covered by WTO rules; used to manage or distort trade flows; for example, Japanese restraints on the export of cars to the United States.

W

Webb-Pomerene Act A 1918 statute that excludes from antitrust prosecution US firms co-operating to develop foreign markets.

withholding taxes Taxes applied to the payment of dividends, interest or royalties by firms.

work redesign programmes Programmes that alter jobs to increase both the quality of the work experience and productivity.

work scheduling Preparing schedules of when and how long workers are at the workplace.

working capital management The co-ordination of a firm's current assets (cash, accounts receivable, inventories) and current liabilities (accounts payable, short-term debt).

works council Councils that provide labour with a say in corporate decision making through a representative body that may consist entirely of workers or of a combination of managers and workers.

World Bank An international financial institution created to facilitate trade.

world-class competitors Multinational firms that can compete globally with domestic products.

World Trade Organization (WTO) The institution that supplanted GATT in 1995 to administer international trade and investment accords.

REFERENCES

Chapter 1

1. Source: Based on Richard Baldwin (2006) Globalization: The great unbundling(s), A contribution to the project Globalization Challenges for Europe and Finland organized by the Secretariat of the Economic Council, www.vnk.fi.
2. Paul R. Krugman (1993) 'What Do Undergraduates Need to Know about Trade?', *AEA Papers and Proceedings*, May, 23–26.
3. Margaret P. Doxey (1980) *Economic Sanctions and International Enforcement*, New York: Oxford University Press, p. 10.
4. WTO International Trade Statistics 2002, www.wto.org, accessed 15 July 2003.
5. World Investment Report 2000, United Nations Conference on Trade and Development, New York, 1, 5.
6. UN World Investment Report 2002, www.unctad.org, accessed 20 July 2003.
7. Eugene H. Fram and Riad Ajami (1994) 'Globalization of Markets and Shopping Stress: Cross-Country Comparisons,' *Business Horizons,* January–February, 17–23.
8. *Survey of Current Business*, US Department of Commerce, Washington, DC, January 2002.
9. Foreign Direct Investment in the US, International Economic Accounts, Bureau of Economic Analysis, www.bea.doc.gov, accessed 5 August 2003.
10. Transatlantic Foreign Investment: Confronting Protectionism, Increasing Co-operation, Brussels Forum: Transatlantic Challenges in a Global Era, www.gmfus.org/brusselsforum, accessed 29 December 2006.
11. Michael R. Czinkota and Sarah McCue (2001) *The STAT-USA Companion to International Business,* Economics and Statistics Administration, US Department of Commerce, Washington, DC, 16.
12. OECD, Quarterly National Accounts, Paris, www.oecd.org, 2003.

Chapter 2

1. Adam Smith (1937) *An Inquiry into the Nature and Causes of the Wealth of Nations*, E.P. Dutton & Company, New York, 4–5.
2. Wassily Leontief (1953) 'Domestic Production and Foreign Trade: the American Capital Position Re-Examined', *Proceedings of the American Philosophical Society,* 97(4), as reprinted in Wassily Leontief (1966) *Input-Output Economics*, Oxford University Press, New York, 69–70.
3. In Leontief's own words: 'These figures show that an average million dollars' worth of our exports embodies considerably less capital and somewhat more labor than would be required to replace from domestic production an equivalent amount of our competitive imports. . . . The widely held opinion that – as compared with the rest of the world – the United States' economy is characterized by a relative surplus of capital and a relative shortage of labor proves to be wrong. As a matter of fact, the opposite is true'. Wassily Leontief (1953) 'Domestic Production and Foreign Trade: the American Capital Position Re-Examined', *Proceedings of the American Philosophical Society,* 97(4), 86.
4. If this were true, if would defy one of the basic assumptions of the factor proportions theory, that all products are manufactured with the same technology (and therefore same proportions of labour and capital) across countries. However, continuing studies have found this to be quite possible in our imperfect world.
5. For a detailed description of these theories see Elhanan Helpman and Paul Krugman (1985) *Market Structure and Foreign Trade*, MIT Press, Cambridge, MA.
6. This leads to the obvious debate as to what constitutes a 'different product' and what is simply a cosmetic difference. The most obvious answer is found in the field of marketing: if the consumer believes the products are different, they are different.
7. There are a variety of potential outcomes from external economies of scale. For additional details, see Paul R. Krugman and Maurice Obstfeld (1994) *International Economics: Theory and Policy*, 3rd edition, HarperCollins.
8. Michael E. Porter (1990) 'The Competitive Advantage of Nations', *Harvard Business Review*, March–April, 73–74.
9. Michael E. Porter (1988) 'Clusters and the New Economics of Competition', *Harvard Business Review*, November–December.

Chapter 3

1. 'Rule No. 1: Don't Diss the Locals', *Business Week,* 15 May 1995, 8.
2. Carla Rapoport, 'Nestlé's Brand-Building Machine', *Fortune,* 19 September 1994, 147–156.

3. Alonso Martinez, Ivan De Souza and Fancis Liu (2003) 'Multinationals vs. Multilatinas', *Strategy and Business*, Fall, 56–67.

4. Alfred Kroeber and Clyde Kluckhohn (1985) *Culture: A Critical Review of Concepts and Definitions*, Random House, New York, 11.

5. Geert Hofstede (1984) 'National Cultures Revisited', *Asia-Pacific Journal of Management*, 1(September), 22–24.

6. Robert L. Kohls (1979) *Survival Kit for Overseas Living*, Intercultural Press, Chicago, IL, p. 3.

7. Edward T. Hall (1976) *Beyond Culture*, Anchor Press, Garden City, NY, 15.

8. Gullestrup, H. (2003) *Kulturanalyser – en vej til tværkulturel forståelse? (Cultural Analysis – A Search for a Cross-Cultural Understanding?* Akademisk Forlag, Copenhagen.

9. Marita von Oldenborgh (1996) 'What's Next for India?' *International Business*, January, 44–47; Ravi Vijh (1996) 'Think Global, Act Indian', *Export Today*, June, 27–28.

10. 'The One Where Pooh Goes to Sweden', *The Economist*, 5 April 2003, 59.

11. 'Culture Wars', *The Economist*, 12 September 1998, 97–99.

12. 'Information Minister Aims to Throw Cultural Vulgarians Out of the Game', *The Washington Post*, 2 February 1999, A16.

13. 'Multinational Firms Take Steps to Avert Boycotts Over War', *The Wall Street Journal*, 4 April 2003, A1, A4.

14. George P. Mundak (1945) 'The Common Denominator of Cultures', in *The Science of Man in the World*, Ralph Linton (ed.), Columbia University Press, New York, 123–142.

15. Philip R. Harris and Robert T. Moran (1996) *Managing Cultural Differences*, Gulf, Houston, TX, 201.

16. 'Euroteen Market Grabs U.S. Attention', *Marketing News*, 22 October 2001, 15.

17. David A. Ricks (2000) *Blunders in International Business*, 3rd edition, Blackwell, Malden, MA, 4.

18. David A. Hanni, John K. Ryans and Ivan R. Vernon (1995) 'Coordinating International Advertising: The Goodyear Case Revisited for Latin America', *Journal of International Marketing*, 3(2), 83–98.

19. 'French Snared in Web of English', *The Washington Post*, 27 September 2000, A19; and 'France: Mind Your Language', *The Economist*, 23 March, 1996, 70–71.

20. 'A World Empire by Other Means', *The Economist*, 22 December 2001, 65.

21. Rory Cowan (2000) 'The *e* Does Not Stand for English', *Global Business*, March, L/22.

22. Stephen P. Iverson (2000) 'The Art of Translation', *World Trade*, April, 90–92.

23. Margareta Bowen (1993) 'Business Translation', *Jerome Quarterly*, August–September, 5–9.

24. 'Nokia Veti Pois Mainoskampanjansa', *Uutislehti 100*, 15 June 1998, 5.

25. 'Sticky Issue', *The Economist*, 24 August 2002, 51.

26. Edward T. Hall (1960) 'The Silent Language of Overseas Business', *Harvard Business Review*, **38** (May–June), 87–96.

27. *Statistical Abstract of the United States* (2003), US Government Printing Office, Washington, DC, 868.

28. David McClelland (1961) *The Achieving Society*, Irvington, New York, 90.

29. *World Almanac and the Book of Facts* (2001) Funk & Wagnalls, Mahwah, NJ, 721.

30. 'Out from Under', *Marketing News*, 21 July 2003, 1, 9.

31. 'Islamic Banking: Faith and Creativity', *New York Times*, 8 April 1994, D1, D6.

32. James F. Engel, Roger D. Blackwell and Paul W. Miniard (2001) *Consumer Behavior*, Harcourt, Fort Worth, TX, 381.

33. Douglas McGray, 'Japan's Gross National Cool' (2002) *Foreign Policy*, May/June, 44.

34. Y.H. Wong and Ricky Yee-kwong (1999) 'Relationship Marketing in China: Guanxi, Favoritism and Adaptation', *Journal of Business Ethics*, **22**(2), 107–118.

35. Earl P. Spencer (1995) 'EuroDisney – What Happened?' *Journal of International Marketing*, 3(3), 103–114.

36. Sergey Frank (1992) 'Global Negotiations: Vive Les Differences!' *Sales and Marketing Management*, **144**(May), 64–69.

37. See, for example, Terri Morrison (1994) *Kiss, Bow, or Shake Hands: How to Do Business In Sixty Countries*, Adams Media, Holbrook, MA; or Roger Axtell (1993) *Do's and Taboos Around the World*, John Wiley & Sons, Inc., New York. For holiday observances, see http://www.religioustolerance.org/main_day.htm#cal and http://www.dir.yahoo.com/society_and_culture/holidays_and_observances, accessed 1 September 2003.

38. James A. Gingrich (1999) 'Five Rules for Winning Emerging Market Consumers', *Strategy and Business*, second quarter, 68–76.

39. 'Feng Shui Strikes Chord', available at http://www.money.cnn.com/1999/09/11/life/q_fengshui/; and 'Fung Shui Man Orders Sculpture Out of Hotel', *South China Morning Post*, 27 July 1992, 4.

40. 'US Superstores Find Japanese Are a Hard Sell', *The Wall Street Journal*, 14 February 2000, B1, B4.

41. The results of the Gallup study are available at www.fortune.com.

42. Kenichi Ohmae (1989) 'Managing in a Borderless World', *Harvard Business Review*, **67**(May–June), 152–161.

43. Greg Bathon, 'Eat the Way Your Mama Taught You', *World Trade*, December 2000, 76–77.

44. Peter McGinnis (1993) 'Guanxi or Contract: A Way to Understand and Predict Conflict Between Chinese and Western Senior Managers in China-Based Joint Ventures', in *Multinational Business Management and Internationalization of Business Enterprises*, Daniel E. McCarthy and Stanley J. Hille (eds), Nanjing University Press, Nanjing, China, 345–351.

45. Tim Ambler (1995) 'Reflections in China: Re-Orienting Images of Marketing', *Marketing Management*, **4**(summer), 23–30.

46. Jagdish N. Sheth and S. Prakash Sethi (1977) 'A Theory of Cross-Cultural Buying Behavior', in *Consumer and Industrial Buying Behavior*, Arch G. Woodside, Jagdish N. Sheth and Peter D. Bennett (eds), Elsevier North-Holland, New York, pp. 369–386.

47. Geert Hofstede (1984) *Culture's Consequences: International Differences in Work-Related Values*, Sage Publications, Beverly Hills, CA, Chapter 1.

48. Geert Hofstede and Michael H. Bond (1988) 'The Confucius Connection: From Cultural Roots to Economic Growth', *Organizational Dynamics*, **16**(spring), 4–21.

49. Simcha Ronen and Oded Shenkar (1985) 'Clustering Countries on Attitudinal Dimensions: A Review and Synthesis', *Academy of Management Journal*, **28**(September), 440–452.

50. 'When Will It Fly?' *The Economist*, 9 August 2003, 51.

51. For applications of the framework, see Sudhir H. Kale (1991) 'Culture-Specific Marketing Communications', *International Marketing Review*, 8(2), 18–30; and Sudhir H. Kale (1991) 'Distribution Channel Relationships in Diverse Cultures', *International Marketing Review*, 8(3), 31–45.

52. Jan-Benedict Steenkamp and Frenkel ter Hofstede (1999) 'A Cross-National Investigation into the Individual and National Cultural Antecedents of Consumer Innovativeness', *Journal of Marketing*, **63**(April), 55–69.

53. Hong Cheng and John C. Schweitzer (1996) 'Cultural Values Reflected in Chinese and U.S. Television Commercials', *Journal of Advertising Research*, **36**(May/June), 27–45.

54. 'Building a "Cultural Index" to World Airline Safety', *The Washington Post*, 21 August 1994, A8.

55. 'Exploring Differences in Japan, U.S. Culture', *Advertising Age International*, 18 September 1995, 1–8.

56. James A. Lee (1966) 'Cultural Analysis in Overseas Operations', *Harvard Business Review*, **44**(March–April), 106–114.

57. David Maxwell and Nina Garrett (2002) 'Meeting National Needs', *Change*, May/June, 22–28.

58. W. Chan Kim and R.A. Mauborgne (1987) 'Cross-Cultural Strategies', *Journal of Business Strategy*, 7(Spring), 28–37.

59. Mauricio Lorence (1992) 'Assignment USA: The Japanese Solution', *Sales and Marketing Management*, **144**(October), 60–66.

60. 'Special Interest Group Operations' available at www.samsung.com; and 'Sensitivity Kick', *The Wall Street Journal*, 30 December 1996, 1, 4.

61. Rosalie Tung (1981) 'Selection and Training of Personnel for Overseas Assignments', *Columbia Journal of World Business*, **16**(Spring), 68–78.

62. Simcha Ronen (1989) 'Training the International Assignee', in *Training and Career Development*, I. Goldstein (ed.) Jossey-Bass, San Francisco, 426–440.

63. See for example Johnson & Johnson's credo at http://www.jnj.com/our_company/our_credo/index.htm.

64. 3M examples are adopted from John R. Engen (1994) 'Far Eastern Front', *World Trade*, December, 20–24.

Chapter 4

1. Quoted in Philippe Dollinger (1970) *The German Hansa*, Stanford University Press, Stanford, CA, 49.

2. Robin Renwick (1987) *Economic Sanctions*, Harvard University Press, Cambridge, MA, 11.

3. Margaret P. Doxey (1987) *Economic Sanctions and International Enforcement*, Oxford University Press, New York, 10.

4. George E. Shambaugh (1999) *States, Firms, and Power: Successful Sanctions in United States Foreign Policy*, State University of New York Press, Albany, NY, 202.

5. Gary Clyde Hufbauer, Jeffrey J. Schott and Kimberly Elliott (2003) *Economic Sanctions Reconsidered: History and Current Policy*, 3rd edition, Institute for International Economics, Washington, DC.

6. G. Scott Erickson (1997) 'Export Controls: Marketing Implications of Public Policy Choices', *Journal of Public Policy and Marketing*, **16**(1), 83.

7. Michael R. Czinkota and Erwin Dichtl (1996) 'Export Controls and Global Changes', *der markt*, **35**(3), 148–155.

8. Robert M. Springer, Jr., 'New Export Law an Aid to International Marketers', *Marketing News*, 3 January 1986, 10, 67.

9. Erwin Dichtl, 'Defacto Limits of Export Controls: The Need for International Harmonization', paper presented at the 2nd Annual CiMar Conference, Rio de Janeiro, August 1994.

10. Allen S. Krass (1994) 'The Second Nuclear Era: Nuclear Weapons in a Transformed World', in *World Security: Challenges for a New Century*, 2nd edition, M. Klare and D. Thomas (eds), St. Martin's Press, 85–105.

11. Craig Barrett, President Intel, Speech to the American Management Association, Spring 2002, Phoenix.

12. E.M. Hucko (1993) *Aussenwirtschaftsrecht-Kriegswaffenkontrollrecht, Textsammlung mit Einführung*, 4th edition, Cologne.

13. Michael R. Czinkota (2002), 'From Bowling Alone to Standing Together', *Marketing Management*, March/April, 12–16.

14. Gary Clyde Hufbauer, Jeffrey J. Schott and Barbara Oegg (2001) *Using Sanctions to Fight Terrorism*, Institute for International Economics, Washington DC, 1.

15. http://cornerhouse.icaap.org/briefings/19.html, accessed 15 July 2003.

16. Habib Mohsin and Leon Zurawicki (2002) 'Corruption and Foreign Direct Investment', *Journal of International Business Studies*, **33**(2), 291–307.

17. George Moody (1997) *Grand Corruption: How Business Bribes Damage Developing Countries*, World View Publishing, Oxford, 23.

18. Michael R. Czinkota, Ilkka A. Ronkainen and Bob Donath (2004) *Mastering Global Markets*, Thomson, Cincinnati, 362.

19. Michael G. Harvey (1993) 'A Survey of Corporate Programs for Managing Terrorist Threats', *Journal of International Business Studies*, Third Quarter, 465–478.

20. Harvey J. Iglarsh (1987) 'Terrorism and Corporate Costs', *Terrorism*, **10**, 227–230.

21. G. Hart and W. Rudman (2002), *America Still Unprepared – America Still in Danger*, Council on Foreign Relations, New York, 14.

22. Gary A. Knight, Michael R. Czinkota and Peter W. Liesch (2003) 'Terrorism and the International Firm', Proceedings: Annual meeting of the Academy of International Business, Academy of International Business, Honolulu, HI, 2003.

23. Michael Minor (1988) 'LDCs, TNCs, and Expropriations in the 1980s', *The CYC Reporter*, 53.

24. Shengliang Deng, Pam Townsend, Maurice Robert and Normand Quesnel (1996) 'A Guide to Intellectual Property Rights in Southeast Asia and China', *Business Horizons*, November–December, 43–50.

25. TRIPS, a more detailed overview of the TRIPS agreement, www.wto.org, 1 February 2001.

26. 'Risky Returns', *The Economist*, 25 May 2000, http://www.economist.com.

27. Paul Blustein, 'Kawasaki to Pay Additional Taxes to US', *The Washington Post*, 11 December 1992, D1.

28. http://www.opic.gov, Washington, DC: Overseas Private Investment Corporation, 2 May 2001.

29. Federal News Service, *Hearing of the House Judiciary Committee*, 23 April 1997.

30. Surya Prakash Sinha (1989) *What Is Law? The Differing Theories of Jurisprudence*, Paragon House, New York.

31. Michael R. Czinkota and Jon Woronoff (1991) *Unlocking Japan's Market*, Probus Publishing, Chicago.

32. http://www.tdctrade.com/mktprof/europe/mprussia.htm, accessed 30 June 2003.

33. Timothy P. Blumentritt and Douglas Nigh (2002) 'The Integration of Subsidiary Political Activities in Multinational Corporations', *Journal of International Business Studies*, **33**(1), 57–77.

34. Michael R. Czinkota (2000) 'The Policy Gap in International Marketing', *Journal of International Marketing*, **8**(1), 99–111.

35. Bruce D. Keillor, G. Tomas M. Hult and Deborah Owens (2002) 'An Empirical Investigation of Market Barriers and the Political Activities of Individual Firms', *International Journal of Commerce and Management*, **12**(2), 89–106.

36. Michael R. Czinkota (1991) 'International Information Needs for US Competitiveness', *Business Horizons*, **34**(6) (November/December), 86–91.

37. Najmeh Bozorgmehr and Stefan Wagstyl, 'European Business Sees New Area of Potential', *Financial Times*, 6 February 2002. http://www.ft.com.

38. *International Court of Arbitration: 1999 Statistical Report* (2001), International Chamber of Commerce, Paris.

Chapter 5

1. Rounding errors are solved quite simply with exchange rates. With a few notable exceptions, all active trading takes place using direct quotations on foreign currencies versus the US dollar (€1.1614/$, ¥113.88/$) and for a conventional number of decimal places. These are the base rates that are then used if needed for the calculation of the inverse indirect quotes on the foreign currencies.

2. A currency trader once remarked to the authors that the spot quotes listed on such a screen were no more and no less accurate as the 'true price' than the sticker price on a car in a showroom.

3. Actually, there are a few exceptions. Panama, for example, has used the US dollar for many years.

4. Bearer bonds were issued by the US government up until the early 1980s, when they were discontinued. Even though they were called bearer bonds, a list of bond registration

numbers was still kept and recorded in order to tax investors holding the bearer instruments.

Chapter 6

1. The discussion of economic integration is based on the pioneering work by Bela Balassa (1961) *The Theory of Economic Integration*, Richard D. Irwin, Homewood, IL.

2. 'US, Central American Nations Launch Trade Talks', *The Wall Street Journal*, 9 January 2003, A3.

3. *The European Union: A Guide for Americans* (2002) Delegation of the European Commission to the United States, Washington, DC, ch. 2. See http://www.eurunion.org/infores/euguide/Chapter2.htm.

4. Jacob Viner (1950) *The Customs Union Issue*, Carnegie Endowment for International Peace, New York.

5. 'Japan Seeks Compensation from EU for Post-EU Expansion Tariff Rise', *Jiji Press English News Service*, 1 July 2003, 1.

6. J. Waelbroeck (1980) 'Measuring Degrees of Progress in Economic Integration', in *Economic Integration, Worldwide, Regional, Sectoral*, F. Machlop (ed.), Macmillan, London.

7. 'Argentina Cries Foul as Choice Employers Beat a Path Next Door', *The Wall Street Journal*, 2 May 2000, A1, A8.

8. 'EU-Swiss Trade Opening Up', *World Trade*, September 2000, 20. See also www.secretariat.efta.int.

9. 'The Cancun Challenge', *The Economist*, 6 September 2003, 59–61.

10. EC Commission (1985) *Completing the Internal Market: White Paper from the Commission to the European Council*, EC Commission, Luxembourg.

11. 'A Singular Market', *The Economist*, 22 October 1994, 10–16.

12. Various aspects of the 1992 Common Market are addressed in André Sapir and Alexis Jacquemin (eds) (1990) *The European Internal Market*, Oxford University Press, Oxford, UK.

13. 'Mega Europe', *Business Week*, 25 November 2002, 62.

14. *The European Union: A Guide for Americans* (2002) Delegation of the European Commission to the United States, Washington, DC, ch. 2. See http://www.eurunion.org/infores/euguide/Chapter2.htm

15. Economic growth effects are discussed in Richard Baldwin (1989) 'The Growth Effects of 1992', *Economic Policy*, October, 248–281; or Rudiger Dornbusch, 'Europe 1992: Macroeconomic Implication' (1989) *Brookings Papers on Economic Activity*, **2**, 341–362.

16. John F. Magee, '1992: Moves Americans Must Make', *Harvard Business Review* **67** (May–June): 72–84.

17. 'For US Small Biz, Fertile Soil in Europe', *Business Week*, 1 April 2002, 55–56.

18. 'Summary of the US–Canada Free Trade Agreement' (1988) *Export Today*, **4**(November–December), 57–61.

19. Raymond Ahearn (1997) *Trade and the Americas*, Congressional Research Service, Washington, DC, 3–4.

20. Sidney Weintraub (1997), *NAFTA at Three: A Progress Report*, Center for Strategic and International Studies, Washington, DC, 17–18.

21. 'NAFTA's Do-Gooder Side Deals Disappoint', *The Wall Street Journal*, 15 October, 1997, A19.

22. Hufbauer, G. and Schott, J. (2005) NAFTA Revised, Institute for International Economics, Washington, DC.

23. 'US Trade with Mexico During the Third NAFTA Year', (1997) *International Economic Review*, International Trade Commission, Washington, DC, 11.

24. 'Fox and Bush, for Richer, for Poorer', *The Economist*, 3 February 2001, 37–38.

25. 'Aerospace Suppliers Gravitate to Mexico', *The Wall Street Journal*, 23 January 2002, A17.

26. 'The Latin Market Never Looked so Bueno', *DSN Retailing Today*, 10 June 2002, 125–126.

27. 'Retail Oasis', *Business Mexico*, April 2001, 15.

28. Lara L. Sowinski, 'Maquiladoras', *World Trade*, September 2000, 88–92.

29. 'The Decline of the Maquiladora', *Business Week*, 29 April 2002, 59.

30. NAFTAs Scorecard: So Far, So Good', *Business Week*, 9 July, 2001, 54–56.

31. 'Localizing Production', *Global Commerce*, 20 August 1997, 1.

32. 'Next Stop South', *The Economist*, 25 February 1995, 29–30.

33. 'Latin Trade Pact Poses Political Peril for Bush', *The Wall Street Journal*, 31 December 2002, A4.

34. 'Mexico, EU Sign Free-Trade Agreement', *The Wall Street Journal*, 24 March 2000, A15.

35. 'Trouble in Paradise', *The Economist*, 23 November 2002, 36–37.

36. 'Caribbean Parity Enters the Picture', *World Trade*, July 2000, 46.

37. 'Latin Lesson', *Far Eastern Economic Review*, 4 January 2001, 109.

38. 'The FTAA: Why Is This Giant Trade Pact So Important?' *World Trade*, July 2003, 44; 'The Americas: A Cautious Yes to Pan-American Trade', *The Economist*, 28 April 2001, 35–36.

39. 'Ripping Down the Walls Across the Americas', *Business Week*, 26 December 1994, 78–80; 'Free Trade Pact Looks Promising for Marketers, Advertisers', *Marketing News*, 18 August 2003, 6–7.

40. Emily Thornton, 'Will Japan Rule a New Trade Bloc?', *Fortune*, 5 October 1992, 131–132.

41. Paul Krugman (1992) 'A Global Economy Is Not the Wave of the Future', *Financial Executive*, 8(March/April), 10–13.

42. Michael R. Czinkota and Masaaki Kotabe (1992) 'America's New World Trade Order', *Marketing Management*, 1(summer), 49–56.

43. 'Afrabet Soup', *The Economist*, 10 February 2001, 77.

44. 'Try, Try Again', *The Economist*, 13 July 2002, 41.

45. Eric Friberg, Risto Perttunen, Christian Caspar and Dan Pittard (1988) 'The Challenges of Europe 1992', *The McKinsey Quarterly*, 21(2), 3–15.

46. 'Lean, Mean, European', *The Economist*, 29 April 2000, 5–7.

47. Gianluigi Guido (1991) 'Implementing a Pan-European Marketing Strategy', *Long Range Planning*, 24(5), 23–33.

48. 'TABD Uses Virtual Organization for Trade Lobbying', *Crossborder Monitor*, 2 July 1997, 1.

49. 'OPEC's Joyride Was Great While It Lasted', *Business Week*, 3 June 1996, 52. See also www.opec.org.

50. 'Are We Over a Barrel?' *Time*, 18 December 2000, B6–B11.

51. 'Inside OPEC's Backroom Deal to Keep Oil Supplies Flowing', *The Wall Street Journal*, 29 July 2003, A1, A8.

Chapter 7

1. www.emdirectory.com.

2. J. Gingrich (1999) 'Five Rules for Winning Emerging Market Consumers', *Strategy and Business*, second quarter, 19–33.

3. 'GE Pins Hopes on Emerging Markets', *The Wall Street Journal*, 2 March 2005.

4. J. Gingrich (1999) 'Five Rules for Winning Emerging Market Consumers', *Strategy and Business*, second quarter, 19–33.

5. J. Gingrich (1999) 'Five Rules for Winning Emerging Market Consumers', *Strategy and Business*, second quarter, 19–33.

6. *The World Factbook 2007*, CIA.

7. 'Trend of Brain Drain on Reverse to India: Scientist'. *Indo-Asian News Service*, 25 March 2006.

8. 'Background Note: China'. *US Department of State*, March 2006. http://www.state.gov/r/pa/ei/bgn/18902.htm.

9. A. Yeh, 'New Dawn in a Shared Language', *The Financial Times*, 13 April 2005.

10. 'Background Note: India'. *US Department of State*, December 2005. http://www.state.gov/r/pa/ei/bgn/3454.htm.

11. 'Background Note: China'. *US Department of State*, March 2006. http://www.state.gov/r/pa/ei/bgn/18902.htm.

12. A. Yeh, 'New Dawn in a Shared Language', *The Financial Times*, 13 April 2005.

13. 'Background Note: India'. *US Department of State*, December 2005. http://www.state.gov/r/pa/ei/bgn/3454.htm.

14. 'Background Note: China'. *US Department of State*, March 2006. http://www.state.gov/r/pa/ei/bgn/18902.htm.

15. A. Yeh, 'New Dawn in a Shared Language', *The Financial Times*, 13 April 2005.

16. 'Background Note: India'. *US Department of State*, December 2005. http://www.state.gov/r/pa/ei/bgn/3454.htm.

17. 'Background Note: China'. *US Department of State*, March 2006. http://www.state.gov/r/pa/ei/bgn/18902.htm.

18. 'Manufacturing Employment Data'. *Bureau of Labor Statistics*, February 2006, accessed 15 March 2006.

19. OECD Online Database, document, accessed 20 September 2008.

20. M. Czinkota (2003) 'An Analysis of the Global Position of US Manufacturing'. *Thunderbird International Business Review*, September/October, 505–519.

21. 'Background Note: China'. *US Department of State*, March 2006. http://www.state.gov/r/pa/ei/bgn/18902.htm.

22. A. Yeh, 'New Dawn in a Shared Language', *The Financial Times*, 13 April 2005.

23. Wu Chen, 'View From China: Less Admiration for US Business', *CFO Magazine*, 1 November 2005.

24. 'Background Note: China'. *US Department of State*. March 2006. http://www.state.gov/r/pa/ei/bgn/18902.htm.

25. 'Kremlin Blocks Big Acquisition by Siemens AG', *The Wall Street Journal*, 14 April 2005.

26. 'China Seeks Its Own High-tech Standards', *CNN.com*, 27 May 2004; 'Despite Shelving WAPI, China Stands Firm on Chip Tax', *InfoWorld*, 22 April 2004. http://www.infoworld.com/article/04/04/22/HNshelvingwapi_1.html.

27. 'In Brazil, Thicket of Red Tape Spoils Recipe for Growth', *The Wall Street Journal*, 24 May 2005.

28. 'China's Power Brands', *Business Week,* 8 November 2004, 77–84.

29. 'Background Note: India'. US Department of State, December 2005. http://www.state.gov/r/pa/ei/bgn/13454.htm.

30. 'Background Note: China'. *US Department of State*, March 2006. http://www.state.gov/r/pa/ei/bgn/18902.htm.

31. 'Manufacturing Employment Data'. *Bureau of Labor Statistics*, February 2006, accessed 15 March 2006.

32. OECD Online Database. document, accessed 20 September 2008.

33. M. Czinkota (2003) 'An Analysis of the Global Position of US Manufacturing'. *Thunderbird International Business Review*, September/October, 505–519.

34. Lee, D. 'China's Chopstick Tax Seems Dim to Some' *The Los Angeles Times*, 24 March 2006.

35. 'Background Note: China'. *US Department of State*, March 2006. http://www.state.gov/r/pa/ei/bgn/18902.htm.

36. A. Yeh, 'New Dawn in a Shared Language', *The Financial Times*, 13 April 2005.

37. Wu Chen, 'View From China: Less Admiration for US Business'. *CFO Magazine*, 1 November 2005.

Chapter 8

1. Hartmut Holzmüller and Barbara Stöttinger (1996) 'Structural Modeling of Success Factors in Exporting: Cross-Validation and Further Development of an Export Performance Model', *Journal of International Marketing*, 4(2), 29–55.

2. Brendan J. Gray (1997) 'Profiling Managers to Improve Export Promotion Targeting', *Journal of International Business Studies*, 28(2), 387–420.

3. Taewon Suh, Mueun Bae, and Sumit K. Kundu (2003) 'Antecedents to Smaller Firms' Perceived Cost and Attractiveness in Going Abroad', in *Enhancing Knowledge Development in Marketing*, B. Money and R. Rose (eds), American Marketing Association, Chicago, IL, 2003.

4. S. Tamer Cavusgil (1993) 'Preparing for Export Marketing', *International Trade Forum*, 2, 16–30.

5. Masaaki Kotabe, Srini S. Srinivasan and Preet S. Aulakh (2002) 'Multinationality and Firm Performance: The Moderating Role of R&D and Marketing Capabilities', *Journal of International Business Studies*, 33(1), 79–97.

6. Michael R. Czinkota (1982) *Export Development Strategies*, Praeger, New York, 10.

7. Michael Kutschker and Iris Bäuerle (1997) 'Three Plus One: Multidimensional Strategy of Internationalization', *Management International Review*, 37(2), 103–125.

8. Michael Kutschker, Iris Bäuerle and Stefan Schmid (1997) 'International Evolution, International Episodes, and International Epochs – Implications for Managing Internationalization', *Management International Review*, 2, Special Issue, 101–124.

9. Kent Eriksson, Jan Johanson, Anders Majkgard and D. Deo Sharma (1997) 'Experiential Knowledge and Cost in the Internationalization Process', *Journal of International Business Studies*, 28(2), 337–360.

10. S. Tamer Cavusgil and Shaoming Zou (1994) 'Marketing Strategy–Performance Relationship: An Investigation of the Empirical Link in Export Marketing Ventures', *Journal of Marketing*, 58(1), 1–21.

11. Michael W. Peng (2000) *Business Strategies in Transition Economies*, Sage Publications, Thousand Oaks, 283–284.

12. Andrew McAuley (1999) 'Entrepreneurial Instant Exporters in the Scottish Arts and Crafts Sector', *Journal of International Marketing*, 7(4), 67–82.

13. Vibha Gaba, Yigang Pan and Gerardo R. Ungson (2000) 'Timing of Entry in International Market: An Empirical Study of US Fortune 500 Firms in China', *Journal of International Business Studies*, 31(1), 39–55.

14. Masaaki Kotabe and Michael R. Czinkota (1992) 'State Government Promotion of Manufacturing Exports: A Gap Analysis', *Journal of International Business Studies*, winter, 637–658.

15. Michael R. Czinkota and Michael L. Ursic (1994) 'An Experience Curve Explanation of Export Expansion', in *International Marketing Strategy*, Dryden Press, Fort Worth, 133–141.

16. Carl Arthur Solberg (1997) 'A Framework for Analysis of Strategy Development in Globalizing Markets', *Journal of International Marketing*, 5(1), 9–30.

17. Michael R. Czinkota (2001) 'A National Export Development Policy for New and Growing Businesses', in *Best Practices in International Business*, M. Czinkota and I. Ronkainen (eds), South-Western, Cincinnati, 35–45.

18. Van Miller, Tom Becker and Charles Crespy (1993) 'Contrasting Export Strategies: A Discriminant Analysis Study of Excellent Exporters', *The International Trade Journal*, 7(3), 321–340.

19. O.E. Williamson (1985) *The Economic Institutions of Capitalism*, Free Press, New York.

20. Michael R. Czinkota and Masaaki Kotabe (2000) 'Entering the Japanese Market: A Reassessment of Foreign Firms' Entry and Distribution Strategies', *Industrial Marketing Management*, 29, 483–491.

21. Rajesh Chakrabarti and Barry Scholnick (2002) 'International Expansion of E-Retailers: Where the Amazon Flows', *Thunderbird International Business Review*, 44(1), 85–104.

22. Pieter Pauwels and Paul Matthyssens (1999) 'A Strategy Process Perspective on Export Withdrawal', *Journal of International Marketing*, 7(4), 10–37.

23. Birgit Ch. Ensslinger (2003) 'Born Globals – Begriff und Bedeutung', in *Die Internationalisierung von kleinen und mittleren Unternehmungen*, D. Holtbruegge (ed.), ibidem Verlag, Stuttgart.

24. Øystein Moen and Per Servais (2002) 'Born Global or Gradual Global? Examining the Export Behavior of Small and Medium-Sized Firms', *Journal of International Marketing*, 10(2), 49–72.

25. *Source:* Richard M. Castaldi, Alex F. De Noble and Jeffrey Kantor (1992) 'The Intermediary Service Requirements of Canadian and American Exporters', *International Marketing Review*, **9**(2), 21–40.

26. Michael W. Peng and Anne Y. Ilinitch (1998) 'Export Intermediary Firms: A Note on Export Development Research', *Journal of International Business Studies*, **3**, 609–620.

27. Dong-Sung Cho (1987) *The General Trading Company: Concept and Strategy*, Lexington Books, Lexington, MA, 2.

28. Lee Smith, (1995) 'Does the World's Biggest Company Have a Future?' *Fortune*, 7 August, 125.

29. Yoshi Tsurumi (1980) *Sogo shosha: Engines of Export-Based Growth*, The Institute for Research on Public Policy, Montreal.

30. Atilla Dicle and Ulku Dicle (1992) 'Effects of Government Export Policies on Turkish Export Trading Companies', *International Marketing Review*, **9**(3), 62–76.

31. Vanessa Bachman (2003) Office of Export Trading Companies, US Department of Commerce, Washington, DC, 17 September.

32. Nancy Lloyd Pfahl (1994) 'Using a Partnership Strategy to Establish an International Trade Assistance Program', *Economic Development Review*, winter, 51–59.

33. Donald W. Hackett (1979) 'The International Expansion of US Franchise Systems', in *Multinational Product Management*, Warren J. Keegan and Charles S. Mayer (eds), American Marketing Association, Chicago, 61–81.

34. Global Franchising Statistics, International Franchise Association, Washington, DC, www.franchise.org, accessed 22 September 2003.

35. Nizamettin Aydin and Madhav Kacker (1990) 'International Outlook of US-Based Franchisers', *International Marketing Review*, **7**, 43–53.

36. Thomas Gross and John Neuman, 'Strategic Alliances Vital in Global Marketing', *Marketing News*, 19 June 1989, 1–2. See also www.ti.com.

37. Iris Berdrow and Henry W. Lane (2002) 'International Joint Ventures: Creating Value Through Successful Knowledge Management', *Journal of World Business*, **38**(1), 15–30.

38. 'MD-90 Airliner Unveiled by McDonnell Douglas', *The Washington Post*, 14 February 1993, A4.

39. Jordan D. Lewis (1990) *Partnerships for Profit: Structuring and Managing Strategic Alliances*, The Free Press, New York, 85–87.

40. Joel Bleeke and David Ernst (1995) 'Is Your Strategic Alliance Really a Sale?' *Harvard Business Review*, **73** (January–February), 97–105.

41. Gary Hamel, Yves L. Doz and C.K. Prahalad (1989) 'Collaborate with Your Competitors – and Win', *Harvard Business Review*, **67**(January–February), 133–139.

42. Vern Terpstra and Chwo-Ming J. Yu (1990) 'Piggy-backing: A Quick Road to Internationalization', *International Marketing Review*, **7**, 52–63.

43. Michael Z. Brooke, *Selling Management Services Contracts in International Business*, Holt, Rinehart and Winston, London, 7.

44. Richard W. Wright and Colin S. Russel (1975) 'Joint Ventures in Developing Countries: Realities and Responses', *Columbia Journal of World Business*, **10**(spring), 74–80.

45. Kathryn Rudie Harrigan (1984) 'Joint Ventures and Global Strategies', *Columbia Journal of World Business*, **19**(summer), 7–16.

46. J. Peter Killing (1983) *Strategies for Joint Venture Success*, Praeger, New York, 11–12.

47. www.eads.com, accessed 23 September 2003.

48. Jeremy Main, 'Making Global Alliances Work', *Fortune*, 17 December 1990, 121–126.

49. United Nations (1975) *Guidelines for Foreign Direct Investment*, United Nations, New York, 65–76.

50. Robert E. Spekman, Lynn A. Isabella, Thomas C. MacAvoy and Theodore Forbes III (1996) 'Creating Strategic Alliances Which Endure', *Long Range Planning*, **29**(3), 346–357.

51. 'Airlines Urged to Link with Foreign Carriers', *The Washington Post*, 2 November 1994, F1, F3.

52. Dennis J. Encarnation and Sushil Vachani (1985) 'Foreign Ownership: When Hosts Change the Rules', *Harvard Business Review*, **63**(September–October), 152–160.

53. Richard H. Holton (1980) 'Making International Joint Ventures Work', paper presented at the seminar on the Management of Headquarters/Subsidiary Relationships in Transnational Corporations, Stockholm School of Economics, June 2–4, 1980, p. 4.

54. John M. Mezias (2002) 'How to identify liabilities of foreignness and assess their effects on multinational corporations', *Journal of International Management*, **8**(3), 265–282.

55. Shih-Fen S. Chen and Jean-Francois Hennart (2002) 'Japanese Investors' choice of joint ventures versus wholly owned subsidiaries in the US: The role of market barriers and firm capabilities', *Journal of International Business Studies*, **33**(1), 1–18.

Chapter 9

1. Global Business Policy Council (2000) *Globalization Ledger*, A.T. Kearney, Washington, DC, April, 3; Jane Fraser and Jeremy Oppenheim (1997) 'What's New About Globalization?' *The McKinsey Quarterly*, **2**, 168–179.

2. Jonathan Sprague, 'China's Manufacturing Beachhead', *Fortune*, 28 October 2002, 1192A–J.

3. The section draws heavily from George S. Yip (2002) *Total Global Strategy II*, Prentice Hall, Englewood Cliffs, NJ, Chapters 1 and 2; Jagdish N. Sheth and Atul Parvatiyar (2001) 'The Antecedents and Consequences of Integrated Global Marketing', *International Marketing Review*, 18(1), 16–29; George S. Yip (1989) 'Global Strategy . . . In a World of Nations?' *Sloan Management Review*, 31(fall), 29–41; Susan P. Douglas and C. Samuel Craig (1989) 'Evolution of Global Marketing Strategy: Scale, Scope, and Synergy', *Columbia Journal of World Business*, 24(fall), 47–58; George S. Yip, Pierre M. Loewe and Michael Y. Yoshino (1988) 'How to Take Your Company to the Global Market', *Columbia, Journal of World Business*, 23(winter), 28–40.

4. Ernst Dichter (1962) 'The World Customer', *Harvard Business Review*, 40(July–August), 113–122.

5. Kenichi Ohmae (2001) *The Invisible Continent: Four Strategic Imperatives of the New Economy*, Harper Business, New York, Chapter 1; Kenichi Ohmae (1999) *The Borderless World: Power and Strategy in the Interlinked Economy*, Harper Business, New York, Chapter 1; Kenichi Ohmae (1985) *Triad Power – The Coming Shape of Global Competition*, Free Press, New York, 22–27.

6. Luciano Catoni, Nora Förisdal Larssen, James Nayor and Andrea Zocchi (2002) 'Travel Tips for Retailers', *The McKinsey Quarterly*, 38(3), 88–98.

7. Catherine George and J. Michael Pearson (2002) 'Riding the Pharma Roller Coaster', *The McKinsey Quarterly*, 38(4), 89–98.

8. 'Paper Prices Are Driving Flurry of Industry Mergers', *The Wall Street Journal*, 10 May 2000, B4; 'Finnish Paper Concern to Buy Champion', *The Wall Street Journal*, 18 February 2000, A3, A6.

9. Stuart Crainer (2001) 'And the New Economy Winner is . . . Europe', *Strategy and Business*, 6(second quarter), 40–47.

10. Suzy Wetlaufer (1999) 'Driving Change: An Interview with Ford Motor Company's Jacques Nasser', *Harvard Business Review*, 77(March–April), 76–88.

11. 'Telecommunications', *The Economist*, 4 April 2002, 102.

12. Gary Knight (2002) 'Entrepreneurship and Marketing Strategy: The SME Under Globalization', *Journal of International Marketing*, 8(2), 12–32.

13. 'A Dedicated Enemy of Fashion: Nestle', *The Economist*, 31 August 2002, 51.

14. Jordan D. Lewis (2000) *Trusted Partners: How Companies Build Mutual Trust and Win Together*, The Free Press, New York, 157.

15. Cait Murphy, 'The Hunt for Globalization that Works', *Fortune*, 28 October 2002, 67–72.

16. '3 Big Carmakers to Create Net Site for Buying Parts', *The Washington Post*, 26 February 2000, E1, E8.

17. Myung-Su Chae and John S. Hill (2000) 'Determinants and Benefits of Global Strategic Planning Formality', *International Marketing Review*, 17(6), 538–562.

18. 'Computing's New Shape', *The Economist*, 23 November 2002, 11–12.

19. C. Samuel Craig and Susan P. Douglas (2000) 'Configural Advantage in Global Markets', *Journal of International Marketing*, 8(1), 6–26.

20. Michael E. Porter (1998) *Competitive Strategy*, The Free Press, New York, Chapter 1.

21. 'Europe's Car Makers Expect Tidy Profits', *The Wall Street Journal*, 27 January, 2000, A16.

22. Lori Ioannou, 'It's a Small World After All', *International Business*, February 1994, 82–88.

23. 'Nokia Widens Gap With Its Rivals', *The Wall Street Journal*, 20 August 2002, B6.

24. Michael Porter (1987) *Competitive Advantage*, The Free Press, New York, Chapter 1.

25. Robert M. Grant (2002) *Contemporary Strategy Analysis: Concepts, Techniques, Applications*, Blackwell, Oxford, UK, Chapter 8.

26. George S. Yip (2002) *Total Global Strategy II*, Prentice-Hall, Upper Saddle River, NJ, Chapter 10.

27. The models referred to are GE/McKinsey, Shell International and A. D. Little portfolio models.

28. Yoram Wind and Susan P. Douglas (1981) 'International Portfolio Analysis and Strategy: Challenge of the '80s', *Journal of International Business Studies*, 12(fall), 69–82.

29. 'P&G Puts Nappies to Rest in Australia', *Advertising Age*, 19 September 1994, I-31.

30. 'The Fight for Digital Dominance', *The Economist*, 23 November 2002, 61–62.

31. 'Will Renault Go for Broke in Asia?' *Business Week*, 28 February 2000; and 'Ford, GM Square Off Over Daewoo Motor: The Question is Why?' *The Wall Street Journal*, 14 February 2000, A1, A13.

32. 'Tissue Titans Target Globally with Key Brands', *Advertising Age*, 20 December 1999, 4.

33. Richard Tomlinson, 'Europe's New Computer Game', *Fortune*, 21 February 2000, 219–224.

34. Saeed Samiee and Kendall Roth (1992) 'The Influence of Global Marketing Standardization on Performance', *Journal of Marketing*, 56(April), 1–17.

35. 'Euroteen Market Grabs U.S. Attention', *Marketing News*, 22 October 2001, 15.

36. Aruna Chandra and John K. Ryans, 'Why India Now?' *Marketing Management*, March/April 2002, 43–45.

37. Imad B. Baalbaki and Naresh K. Malhotra (1993) 'Marketing Management Bases for International Market Segmentation: An Alternate Look at the Standardization/Customization Debate', *International Marketing Review*, 10(1), 19–44.

38. Alonso Martinez, Ivan de Souza and Francis Liu (2003) 'Multinationals vs. Multilatinas: Latin America's Great Race', *Strategy and Business*, Fall, 45–58.

39. 'Whirlpool's Platform for Growth', *Financial Times*, 26 March, 1998, 8.

40. 'Shania Reigns', *Time*, 9 December 2002, 80–85.

41. Larry Greenemeier, 'Offshore Outsourcing Grows to Global Proportions', *Information Week*, February 2002, 56–58.

42. 'Philips Electronics to Make China One of Three Big Research Centers', *The Wall Street Journal*, 20 December 2002, B4.

43. W. Chan Kim and R. A. Mauborgne (1988) 'Becoming an Effective Global Competitor', *Journal of Business Strategy*, 8(January–February), 33–37.

44. Gary Hamel and C. K. Prahalad (1985) 'Do You Really Have a Global Strategy?' *Harvard Business Review*, 63(July–August), 75–82.

45. 'Nokia Widens Lead in Wireless Market While Motorola, Ericsson Fall Back', *The Wall Street Journal*, 8 February 2000, B8.

46. Andreas F. Grein, C. Samuel Craig and Hirokazu Takada (2001) 'Integration and Responsiveness: Marketing Strategies of Japanese and European Automobile Manufacturers', *Journal of International Marketing*, 9(2), 19–50.

47. James A. Gingrich, 'Five Rules for Winning Emerging Market Consumers' (1999) *Strategy and Business*, Second Quarter, 19–33.

48. 'Does Globalization Have Staying Power?' *Marketing Management*, March/April 2002, 18–23.

49. Kamran Kashani (1989) 'Beware the Pitfalls of Global Marketing', *Harvard Business Review*, 67(September–October), 91–98.

50. John A. Quelch and Edward J. Hoff (1986) 'Customizing Global Marketing', *Harvard Business Review*, 64(May–June), 59–68; George S. Yip, Pierre M. Loewe and Michael Y. Yoshino (1988) 'How to Take Your Company to the Global Market', *Columbia, Journal of World Business*, 23(winter), 28–40.

51. George S. Yip and Tammy L. Madsen (1996) 'Global Account Management: The New Frontier in Relationship Marketing', *International Marketing Review*, 13(3), 24–42.

52. David B. Montgomery and George S. Yip (2000) 'The Challenge of Global Customer Management', *Marketing Management*, Winter, 22–29.

53. Available at www.whirlpoolcorp.com.

54. John A. Quelch and Helen Bloom (1999) 'Ten Steps to Global Human Resources Strategy', *Strategy and Business*, 4(first quarter), 18–29.

55. Sharon O'Donnell and Insik Jeong (2000) 'Marketing Standardization within Global Industries', *International Marketing Review*, 17(1), 19–33.

56. Lawrence M. Fischer (2002) 'Thought Leader', *Strategy and Business*, 7(fourth quarter), 115–123.

57. Robert J. Flanagan (1999) 'Knowledge Management in the Global Organization in the 21st Century', *HR Magazine*, 44(11), 54–55.

58. Michael Z. Brooke (1986) *International Management: A Review of Strategies and Operations*, Hutchinson, London, 173–174.

59. Jay R. Galbraith (2000) *Designing the Global Corporation*, Jossey-Bass, New York, Chapter 3.

60. William H. Davidson and Philippe Haspeslagh (1982) 'Shaping a Global Product Organization', *Harvard Business Review*, 59(March/April), 69–76.

61. See http://www.loctite.com/about/global_reach.html.

62. See, for example, Samuel Humes (1993) *Managing the Multinational: Confronting the Global–Local Dilemma*, Prentice Hall, London, Chapter 1.

63. Vijay Govindarajan, Anil K. Gupta and C. K. Prahalad (2001) *The Quest for Global Dominance: Transforming Global Presence into Global Competitive Advantage*, Jossey-Bass, New York, Chapters 1 and 2.

64. 'How Goodyear Sharpened Organization and Production for a Tough World Market', *Business International*, 16 January 1989, 11–14.

65. Michael J. Mol (2001) *Ford Mondeo: A Model T World Car?*, Idea Group Publishing, Hershey, PA, 1–21.

66. *3M Annual Report 2000*, 1–3, 15; '3M Restructuring for NAFTA', *Business Latin America*, 19 July 1993, 6–7.

67. Philippe Lasserre (1996) 'Regional Headquarters: The Spearhead for Asia Pacific Markets', *Long Range Planning*, 29(February), 30–37; John D. Daniels (1987) 'Bridging National and Global Marketing Strategies Through Regional Operations', *International Marketing Review*, 4(autumn), 29–44.

68. Daniel Robey, *Designing Organizations: A Macro Perspective*, Richard D. Irwin, Homewood, IL, 327.

69. Christopher A. Bartlett and Sumantra Ghoshal (2002) *Managing Across Borders*, Harvard Business School Press, Cambridge, MA, Chapter 10.

70. See www.philips.com/.

71. Spencer Chin, 'Philips Shores Up the Dike', *EBN*, 14 October 2002, 4.

72. Milton Harris and Artur Raviv (2002), 'Organization Design', *Management Science*, 48(July), 852–865.

73. John P. Workman, Jr., Christian Homburg and Kjell Gruner (1998) 'Marketing Organization: Framework of Dimensions and Determinants', *Journal of Marketing*, 62(July), 21–41; Chuck U. Farley (1995) 'Looking Ahead at the Marketplace: It's Global and It's Changing', Donald R. Lehman and Katherine E. Jocz (eds), *Reflections on the Futures of Marketing*, Marketing Science Institute, Cambridge, MA, 15–35.

74. William Taylor (1990) 'The Logic of Global Business', *Harvard Business Review*, 68(March–April), 91–105.

75. Mohanbir Sawhney (2001) 'Don't Homogenize, Synchronize', *Harvard Business Review*, 79(July–August), 100–108.

76. Ilkka A. Ronkainen (1996) 'Thinking Globally, Implementing Successfully', *International Marketing Review*, 13(3), 4–6.

77. Russell Eisenstat, Nathaniel Foote, Jay Galbraith and Danny Miller (2001) 'Beyond the Business Unit', *The McKinsey Quarterly*, 37(1), 180–195.

78. 'Country Managers', *Business Europe*, 16 October 2002, 3; John A. Quelch and Helen Bloom (1996) 'The Return of the Country Manager', *International Marketing Review*, 13(3), 31–43.

79. Rodman Drake and Lee M. Caudill (1981) 'Management of the Large Multinational: Trends and Future Challenges', *Business Horizons*, 24(May–June), 83–91.

80. Joe Studwell (2002) *The China Dream*, Atlantic Monthly Press, New York, 104–105.

81. Göran Svensson (2001) '"Glocalization" of Business Activities: A "Glocal Strategy" Approach', *Management Decision*, 39(1), 6–13.

82. Christopher A. Bartlett and Sumantra Ghoshal (1990) 'Matrix Management: Not a Structure, a Frame of Mind', *Harvard Business Review*, 68(July–August), 138–145.

83. Carlos Ghosn (2002) 'Saving the Business Without Losing the Company', *Harvard Business Review*, 80(January), 37–45.

84. 'See Jack. See Jack Run Europe', *Fortune*, 27 September 1999, 127–136.

85. Noel Tichy (1999) 'The Teachable Point of View: A Primer', *Harvard Business Review*, 77(March–April), 82–83.

86. 'GE Mentoring Program Turns Underlings into Teachers of the Web', *The Wall Street Journal*, 15 February 2000, B1, B16.

87. Richard Benson-Armer and Tsun-Yan Hsieh (1997) 'Teamwork Across Time and Space'. *The McKinsey Quarterly*, 33(4), 18–27.

88. David A. Griffith and Michael G. Harvey (2001) 'An Intercultural Communication Model for use in Global Interorganizational Networks', *Journal of International Marketing*, 9(3), 87–103.

89. 'Internet Software Poses Big Threat to Notes, IBMs Stake in Lotus', *The Wall Street Journal*, 7 November 1995, A1–5.

90. Ingo Theuerkauf, David Ernst and Amir Mahini (1996) 'Think Local, Organize. . . . ' *International Marketing Review*, 13(3), 7–12.

91. C.K. Prahalad (1999) 'Globalization, Digitization, and the Multinational Enterprise', paper presented at the Annual Meetings of the Academy of International Business, November 1999.

92. James A. Gingrich (1999) 'Five Rules for Winning Emerging Market Consumers', *Strategy & Business*, second quarter, 19–33.

93. Christopher A. Bartlett and Sumantra Ghoshal (1986) 'Tap Your Subsidiaries for Global Reach', *Harvard Business Review*, 64(November–December), 87–94.

94. 'The Zen of Nissan', *Business Week*, 22 July 2002, 46–49.

95. Richard I. Kirkland, Jr., 'Entering a New World of Boundless Competition', *Fortune*, 14 March 1988, 18–22.

96. Michael D. White (1999) 'The Finnish Springboard', *World Trade*, January, 48–49.

97. David A. Aaker and Erich Joachimsthaler (1999) 'The Lure of Global Branding', *Harvard Business Review*, 77(November/December), 137–144.

98. Julian Birkinshaw and Neil Hood (2001) 'Unleash Innovation in Foreign Subsidiaries', *Harvard Business Review*, 79(March), 131–137; Julian Birkinshaw and Nick Fry (1998) 'Subsidiary Initiatives to Develop New Markets', *Sloan Management Review*, 39(spring), 51–61.

99. Vijay Govindarajan and Robert Newton (2000) *Management Control Systems*, McGraw-Hill/Irwin, New York, Chapter 1.

100. Anil Gupta and Vijay Govindarajan (1994) 'Organizing for Knowledge Within MNCs', *International Business Review*, 3(4), 443–457.

101. William G. Ouchi (1997) 'The Relationship Between Organizational Structure and Organizational Control', *Administrative Science Quarterly*, 22(March), 95–112.

102. Laurent Leksell (1981) *Headquarters–Subsidiary Relationships in Multinational Corporations*, Stockholm School of Economics, Stockholm, Sweden, Chapter 5.

103. Henry P. Conn and George S. Yip (1997) 'Global Transfer of Critical Capabilities', *Business Horizons*, **38**(January/February), 22–31.

104. Anant R. Negandhi and Martin Welge (1984) *Beyond Theory Z*, JAI Press, (Greenwich, CT), 16.

105. Richard Pascale, 'Fitting New Employees into the Company Culture', *Fortune*, 28 May 1984, 28–40.

106. Michael R. Czinkota and Ilkka A. Ronkainen (1997) 'International Business and Trade in the Next Decade: Report from a Delphi Study', *Journal of International Business Studies*, **28**(4), 676–694.

107. Tsun-Yuan Hsieh, Johanne La Voie and Robert A. P. Samek (1999) 'Think Global, Hire Local', *The McKinsey Quarterly*, **35**(4), 92–101.

108. R. J. Alsegg (1971) *Control Relationships Between American Corporations and Their European Subsidiaries*, AMA Research Study No. 107, American Management Association, New York, 7.

109. Ron Edwards, Adlina Ahmad and Simon Moss (2002) 'Subsidiary Autonomy: The Case of Multinational Subsidiaries in Malaysia', *Journal of International Business Studies*, **33**(1), 183–191.

110. John J. Dyment (1987) 'Strategies and Management Controls for Global Corporations', *Journal of Business Strategy*, **7**(spring), 20–26.

111. Alfred M. Jaeger (1983) 'The Transfer of Organizational Culture Overseas: An Approach to Control in the Multinational Corporation', *Journal of International Business Studies*, **14**(fall), 91–106.

112. Michael Goold and Andrew Campbell (2002) 'Do You Have a Well-Designed Organization?' *Harvard Business Review*, **80**(March), 117–124.

Chapter 10

1. 'AMA Board Approves New Marketing Definition', *Marketing News*, 1 March 1985, 1.

2. Robert Bartels (1968) 'Are Domestic and International Marketing Dissimilar?' *Journal of Marketing*, **36**(July), 56–61.

3. Pankaj Ghemawat (2001) 'Distance Still Matters: The Hard Reality of Global Expansion', *Harvard Business Review*, **79**(September), 137–147.

4. For one of the best summaries, see Country Monitor (2003), *Indicators of Market Size for 117 Countries*, EIU, New York.

5. Philip Kotler (2003) *Marketing Management: Analysis, Planning and Control*, Prentice Hall, Upper Saddle River, NJ, 146.

6. 'Coke to Test Coffee in Scandinavia', *Advertising Age*, 19 May 2003, 16.

7. Samuel Craig and Susan P. Douglas (2001) 'Conducting Market Research in the Twenty-First Century', *International Marketing Review*, **18**, 80–90.

8. Van R. Wood, John R. Darling and Mark Siders (1999) 'Consumer Desire to Buy and Use Products in International Markets: How to Capture It, How to Sustain It', *International Marketing Review*, **16**(3), 231–242; J.A. Weber (1979) 'Comparing Growth Opportunities in the International Marketplace', *Management International Review*, **19**(winter), 47–54.

9. Igal Ayal and Jehiel Zif (1979) 'Marketing Expansion Strategies in Multinational Marketing', *Journal of Marketing*, **43**(spring), 84–94.

10. Michael Rennie (1993) 'Born Global', *The McKinsey Quarterly*, **4**, 45–52.

11. Carl A. Sohlberg (2002) 'The Perennial Issue of Adaptation or Standardization of International Marketing Communication: Organizational Contingencies and Performance', *Journal of International Marketing*, **10**(3), 1–21.

12. Jean-Noël Kapferer (1998) *Survey Among 210 European Brand Managers*, Euro-RSCG, Paris.

13. Davis Goodman (1998) 'Thinking Export? Think ISO 9000', *Export Today*, August, 48–49.

14. 'Krispy Kreme: Sweet on Britain', *USA Today*, 12 August, 2003, 6A, 7A.

15. Phillip D. White and Edward W. Cundiff (1978) 'Assessing the Quality of Industrial Products', *Journal of Marketing*, **42**(January), 80–86.

16. Johny K. Johansson, Ilkka A. Ronkainen and Michael R. Czinkota (1994) 'Negative Country-of-Origin Effects: The Case of the New Russia', *Journal of International Studies*, **25**(1), 1–21.

17. Philip Kotler and David Gertner (2002) 'Country as Brand, Product, and Beyond: A Place Marketing and Brand Management Perspective', *Journal of Brand Management*, **9** (April), 249–261.

18. Matthew B. Myers and S. Tamer Cavusgil (1996) 'Export Pricing Strategy–Performance Relationship: A Conceptual Framework', *Advances in International Marketing*, **8**, 159–178.

19. www.pcnolan.com, accessed 23 July 2003.

20. Ling-yee Li and Gabriel O. Ogunmokum (2001) 'Effect of Export Financing Resources and Supply-Chain Skills on Export Competitive Advantages: Implications for Superior Export Performance', *Journal of World Business*, **36**(3), 260–279.

21. Perry A. Trunick (1994) 'CLM: Breakthrough of Champions', Council of Logistics Management's 1994 Conference, *Transportation and Distribution*, December.

22. Huan Neng Chiu (1995) 'The Integrated Logistics Management System: A Framework and Case Study', *International Journal of Physical Distribution and Logistics Management*, **6**, 4–22.

23. Elizabeth Canna (1994) 'Russian Supply Chains', *American Shipper*, June, 49–53.

Chapter 11

1. Extremity-stimulus medical appliances are electrically charged sheaths that are fit over the hands, feet or other extremities of the human subject where increased blood flow and nerve tissue regeneration is desired. This is a fictional product.

2. There are, of course, other traditional decision criteria used in capital budgeting, such as the internal rate of return, modified internal rate of return, payback period and so forth. For the sake of simplicity, NPV is used throughout the analysis in this chapter. Under most conditions, NPV is also the most consistent criterion for selecting good projects, as well as selecting among projects.

3. A note of particular irony in this case was that the chief currency trader for Allied-Lyons had authored an article in the UK trade journal *The Treasurer* only a few months before. The article had described the proper methods and strategies for careful corporate foreign currency risk management. He had concluded with the caution to never confuse 'good luck with skilful trading'.

4. *Trade Finance,* May 1992, 13.

5. 'Current Activities of International Organizations in the Field of Barter and Barter-Like Transactions' (1984) *Report of the Secretary General*, United Nations, General Assembly, 4.

6. Jean-François Hennart and Erin Anderson (1993) 'Countertrade and the Minimization of Transaction Costs: An Empirical Examination', *The Journal of Law, Economics, and Organization*, **2**, 307.

7. Jean-François Hennart (1990) 'Some Empirical Dimensions of Countertrade', *Journal of International Business Studies*, **21**(2), second Quarter, 243–270.

8. Abla M. Abdel-Latif and Jeffrey B. Nugent (1994) 'Countertrade as Trade Creation and Trade Diversion', *Contemporary Economic Policy*, **12**(January), 1–10.

9. Jong H. Park (1988) 'Is Countertrade Merely a Passing Phenomenon? Some Public Policy Implications', in *Proceedings of the 1988 Conference*, R. King (ed.), Academy of International Business, Charleston, SC, Southeast Region, 67–71.

10. J.-F. Hennart (1990) 'Some Empirical Dimensions of Countertrade', *Journal of International Business Studies*, **21**(2), 243–270.

11. Rolf Mirus and Bernard Yeung (1993) 'Why Countertrade? An Economic Perspective', *The International Trade Journal*, **7**(4), 409–433.

12. Paul Samuelson (1980) *Economics*, 11th edition, McGraw Hill, New York, 260.

Chapter 12

1. This chapter was initially contributed by Susan C. Ronkainen.

2. 'Of Tactics and Strategy' (2000) *Global Business*, March, 64; www.arthurandersen.com.

3. Richard D. Hays (1974) 'Expatriate Selection: Insuring Success and Avoiding Failure', *Journal of International Business Studies*, **5**(summer), 25–37.

4. 'India's Technology Whizzes Find Passage to Nokia', *The Wall Street Journal*, 1 August 2000, B1; B12; 'Nokia's Secret Code', *Fortune*, 1 May, 2000, 161–174.

5. 'Ford's Brave New World', *The Washington Post*, 16 October 1994, H1, H4.

6. Christopher A. Bartlett and Sumantra Ghoshal (2003) 'What Is a Global Manager?' *Harvard Business Review*, **81**(August), 99–107.

7. 'Waking Up Heineken', *Business Week*, 8 September 2003, 68–72; Jan van Rosmalen (1985) 'Internationalising Heineken: Human Resource Policy in a Growing International Company', *International Management Development*, Summer, 11–13.

8. John A. Quelch and Helen Bloom (1999) 'Ten Steps to a Global Human Resources Strategy', *Strategy and Business*, first quarter, 18–29.

9. Floris Majlers (1992) 'Inside Unilever: The Evolving Transnational Company', *Harvard Business Review*, **70**(September–October), 46–52.

10. Vijay Govindarjan and Anil K. Gupta (2001) 'Building an Effective Global Business Team', *Sloan Management Review*, **42**(summer), 63–72.

11. Randall S. Schuler, Susan E. Jackson, Peter J. Dowling and Denice E. Welch (1991) 'The Formation of an International Joint Venture: Davidson Instrument Panel', in *International Human Resource Management*, Mark Mendenhall and Gary Oddou (eds), PWS–Kent, Boston, pp. 83–96.

12. 'Company & Industry: Ukraine', *Crossborder Monitor*, 23 October 1996, 4; 'Middle Managers in Vietnam', *Business Asia*, 8 May 1995, 3–4.

13. Peter Lorange (1986) 'Human Resource Management in Multinational Cooperative Ventures', *Human Resources Management*, **25**(winter), 133–148.

14. *2002 Global Relocation Trends Survey Report* (2003), GMAC Global Relocation Services, Warren, NJ; available on www.gmacglobalrelocation.com.

15. 'People Who Need People', *The Wall Street Journal*, 25 September 2000, R8.

16. 'For 'Extreme Telecommuters,' Remote Work Means Really Remote', *The Wall Street Journal*, 31 January 2001, B1, B7.

17. Carla Rapoport, 'The Switch Is On in Japan', *Fortune*, 21 May 1990, 144.

18. Anders Edström and Peter Lorange (1985) 'Matching Strategy and Human Resources in Multinational Corporations', *Journal of International Business Studies*, 16(fall), 125–137.

19. Elizabeth Klein (1992) 'The US/Japanese HR Culture Clash', *Personnel Journal*, 71(November), 30–38.

20. Mirjaliisa Charles and Rebecca Marschan-Piekkari (2002) 'Language Training for Enhanced Horizontal Communication: A Challenge for MNCs', *Business Communication Quarterly*, 65(2), 9–30.

21. Rabindra Kanungo and Richard W. Wright (1983) 'A Cross-Cultural Comparative Study of Managerial Job Attitudes', *Journal of International Business Studies*, 14(fall), 115–129.

22. David Ahlstrom, Gary Bruton, and Eunice S. Chan (2001) 'HRM of Foreign Firms in China: The Challenge of Managing Host Country Personnel', *Business Horizons*, 44(May), 57–62.

23. Lester B. Korn, 'How the Next CEO Will Be Different', *Fortune*, 22 May 1990, 157–161.

24. 'The Elusive Euromanager', *The Economist*, 7 November 1993, 83.

25. Jean E. Heller (1980) 'Criteria for Selecting an International Manager', *Personnel*, May–June, 18–22.

26. Robert Rosen (2000) *Global Literacies: Lessons on Business Leadership and National Cultures*, Simon & Schuster, New York.

27. Susan Schneider and Rosalie Tung (2001) 'Introduction to the International Human Resource Management Special Issue', *Journal of World Business*, 36(winter), 341–346.

28. (no authors listed) (1970) *Compensating International Executives*, Business International, New York, 35.

29. Joel Bleeke and David Ernst (1993) *Collaborating to Compete*, John Wiley & Sons, Inc., New York, 179.

30. Lee Smith, 'Japan's Autocratic Managers', *Fortune*, 7 January 1985, 14–23.

31. 'Expat Spouses: It Takes Two', *Financial Times*, 1 March 2002, 35; Margaret A. Schaffer and David A. Harrison (2001) 'Forgotten Partners of International Assignments: Development and Test of a Model of Spouse Adjustment', *Journal of Applied Psychology*, 86(2), 238–252.

32. 'Have Wife, Will Travel', *The Economist*, 16 December 2000, 70.

33. *Runzheimer Reports on Relocation* (1997) Runzheimer International, Rochester, WI, at www.runzheimer.com.

34. 'Global Managing', *The Wall Street Journal Europe*, 10–11 January 1992, 1, 20.

35. Jan Selmer and Alicia Leung (2003) 'Provision and Adequacy of Corporate Support to Male Spouses: An Exploratory Study', *Personnel Review*, 32(1), 9–14.

36. Linda Stroh, Arup Verma and Stacy Valy-Durbin (2000) 'Why Are Women Left at Home: Are They Unwilling to Go on International Assignments?' *Journal of World Business*, 35(fall), 238–245; Nancy J. Adler (1984) 'Expecting International Success: Female Managers Overseas', *Columbia Journal of World Business*, 19(fall), 79–85.

37. J. Stewart Black and Hal B. Gregsen (1999) 'The Right Way to Manage Expats', *Harvard Business Review*, 77(March/April), 52–61; Rosalie Tung (1981) 'Selection and Training of Personnel for Overseas Assignments', *Columbia Journal of World Business*, 16(spring), 68–78.

38. Michael G. Harvey (1997) 'Dual-Career Expatriates: Expectations, Adjustment and Satisfaction with International Relocation', *Journal of International Business Studies*, 28(3), 627–658.

39. L. Robert Kohls (1997) *Survival Kit for Overseas Living*, Intercultural Press, Yarmouth, ME, 62–68.

40. 'Polar Opposites', *Global Business*, August 2000, 24.

41. C. Delia Contreras and Fabio Bravo (2003), 'Should You Accept an International Assignment?' *Chemical Engineering Progress*, August, 67–76.

42. Michael G. Harvey (1993) 'A Survey of Corporate Programs for Managing Terrorist Threats', *Journal of International Business Studies*, 24(3), 465–478.

43. Mary Helen Frederick (1992) 'Keeping Safe', *International Business*, October, 68–69.

44. 'There's No Place Like Home', *Business Week*, 9 October 2001, 35.

45. Nancy Mueller (2000) *Work Worldwide: International Career Strategies for the Adventurous Job Seeker*, John Muir Publications, Berkeley, CA, Chapter 5.

46. Michael G. Harvey (1981) 'The Other Side of Foreign Assignments: Dealing with the Repatriation Dilemma', *Columbia Journal of World Business*, 16(spring), 79–85.

47. Raymond J. Stone (1986) 'Compensation: Pay and Perks for Overseas Executives', *Personnel Journal*, January, 64–69.

48. Karen E. Thuemer (2000) 'Asia Adds Up', *Global Business*, June, 51–55.

49. US Department of State (2003) *Indexes of Living Costs Abroad, Quarters Allowances, and Hardship Differentials*, January, Table 3.

50. 'The Winds of Change Blow Everywhere', *Business Week*, 17 October 1994, 87–88; 'School Days at Work: Firms See Training as Key to Empowerment', *Crossborder Monitor*, 3 August 1994, 1, 7.

51. Industrial Democracy in Europe International Research Group (1981), *Industrial Democracy in Europe*, Clarendon Press, Oxford, UK, Chapter 14; Industrial Democracy in Europe International Research Group (1993) *Industrial Democracy in Europe Revisited*, Oxford University Press, Oxford, UK, Chapter 5.

52. Erna Szabo, Felix C. Brodbeck, Deanne N. Den Hartog and Gerhard Reber (2002) 'The Germanic Europe Cluster: Where Employees Have a Voice', *Journal of World Business*, **37**(spring), 55–67.

53. John Addison (1999) 'Non-Union Representation in Germany', *Journal of Labor Research*, **20**(winter), 73–91.

54. 'EU Works Councils Get Underway', *Crossborder Monitor*, 16 October, 4.

55. 'Labour Disputes', *The Economist*, 22 April 2000, 96.

56. 'MNCs Under Fire to Link Trade with Global Labor Rights', *Crossborder Monitor*, 25 May 1994, 1.

57. 'Labor Strife in Indonesia Spotlights Development Challenge', *Crossborder Monitor*, 25 May 1994, 7.

58. 'Firms Rethink Hostility to Linking Trade, Labor Rights', *The Wall Street Journal*, 2 February 2001, A12.

59. Herman Gadon (1984) 'Making Sense of Quality of Work Life Programs', *Business Horizons*, **27**(January–February), 42–46.

60. 'Jeans Therapy', *The Wall Street Journal*, 20 May 1998, A1, A7.

61. 'Hour by Hour', *Global Business*, November 2000, 25.

62. S. B. Prasad and Y. Kirshna Shetty, *An Introduction to Multinational Management*, Prentice-Hall, Englewood Cliffs, NJ, Appendix 8-A.

63. Jay Mazur (2000) 'Labor's New Internationalism', *Foreign Affairs*, January/February, 79–93.

64. 'Cooperation Worth Copying?' *The Washington Post*, 13 December 1992, H1, H6.

65. 'Detroit Meets a 'Worker Paradise'', *The Wall Street Journal*, 3 March 1999, B1; B4.

Chapter 13

1. This definition of the corporate objective is based on that supported by the International Corporate Governance Network (ICGN), a not-for-profit organization committed to improving global corporate governance practices. Note that this definition of the corporate objective is clearly that of stockholder wealth maximization, defined previously in Chapter 11.

2. 'OECD Principles of Corporate Governance', The Organization for Economic Co-Operation and Development, 1999.

3. For example, in Germany, supervisory board audit committees must include employee representatives. However, according to US law, employees are not independent.

4. This example is borrowed from Frederick D.S. Choi and Richard Levich (1992) 'International Accounting Diversity and Capital Market Decisions', in *Handbook of International Accounting*, Frederick D.S. Choi (ed.), John Wiley & Sons, Inc., Hoboken, NJ.

5. This table and the following associated discussion draws heavily on the excellent study of this subject by Philip R. Peller and Frank J. Schwitter of Arthur Andersen & Company (1992) 'A Summary of Accounting Principle Differences Around the World', in *The Handbook of International Accounting*, Frederick D.S. Choi (ed.), John Wiley & Sons, Inc., Hoboken, NJ, Chapter 4.

6. Disclosure has continued to be one of the largest sources of frustration between countries. The disclosure requirements of the Securities and Exchange Commission (SEC) in the United States for firms – foreign or domestic – in order to issue publicly traded securities are some of the strictest in the world. Many experts in the field have long been convinced that the depth of US disclosure requirements has prevented many foreign firms from issuing securities in the United States. The SEC's approval of Rule 144A, selective secondary market trading of private placements, is an attempt to alleviate some of the pressure on foreign firms from US disclosure.

7. Frederick D.S. Choi and Gerhard G. Mueller (1992) *International Accounting*, 2nd edition, Prentice Hall, Englewood Cliffs, NJ, 262.

8. T.L. Friedman (1999) *The Lexus and the Olive Tree*. Farrar, Straus and Giroux.

Chapter 14

1. William Lazer and Eric H. Shaw (2000) 'Global Marketing Management: At the Dawn of the New Millennium', *Journal of International Marketing*, 8(1), 65–77.

2. The information presented here is based largely on an original Delphi study by Michael R. Czinkota and Ilkka A. Ronkainen using an international panel of experts.

3. Mike Moore, 'Preparations for the Fourth WTO Ministerial Conference', Paris, 9 October, 2001, http://www.wto.org.

4. 'Business and Political Leaders Discuss Digital Divide', *World Economic Forum*, Davos, http://www.wforum.org, 2 February 2001.

5. 'The Corporation and the Public: Open for Inspection', *World Economic Forum*, 27 January 2001, www.wforum.org, 2 February 2001.

6. John Pomfret, 'Chinese Industry Races to Make Global Name for Itself', *The Washington Post*, 23 April 2000, H1.

7. Catherine L. Mann, 'Is the US Trade Deficit Still Sustainable', *Institute for International Economics*, Washington, DC, 1 March 2001.

8. 'US International Transactions; 2nd quarter 2003', http://www.bea.gov, 15 September 2003.

9. UN Population Division, World Urbanized Prospects, www.un.org/esa/population, accessed 10 December 2002.

10. John Lancaster, 'The Desperate Bachelors', *The Washington Post*, 2 December 2002, A1, A17.

11. www.internetworldstats.com, accessed 2 January 2009.

12. www.internetworldstats.com, accessed 2 January 2009.

13. John Ouelch, 'Global Village People', *WorldLink Magazine*, January/February, 1999, www.worldlink.co.uk.

14. Renato Ruggiero, 'The New Frontier', *WorldLink Magazine*, January/February, 1998, www.worldlink.co.uk.

15. Minoru Makihara, Co-Chairman of the Annual Meeting of the World Economic Forum, Davos, 2001, www.wforum.org.

16. Polly Campbell, 'Trend Watch 2001', *The Edward Lowe Report*, January 2001, 1–3.

17. Michael R. Czinkota (2000) 'The Policy Gap in International Marketing', *Journal of International Marketing*, 8(1), 99–111.

18. Labour Force Statistics, 1976–2000, Paris, OECD, 2001.

19. Michael R. Czinkota (1994) 'Rich Neighbors, Poor Relations', *Marketing Management*, spring, 46–52.

20. Michael R. Czinkota, Ilkka A. Ronkainen and Bob Donath (2004) *Mastering Global Markets: Strategies for Today's Trade Globalist*, Thomson, South-Western, Mason, OH.

21. Michael R. Czinkota and Masaaki Kotabe (2000) 'The Role of Japanese Distribution Strategies', *Japanese Distribution Strategy*, M.R. Czinkota and M. Kotabe (eds), Business Press, London, 6–16.

22. Howard Lewis III and David Richardson (2001) *Why Global Commitment Really Matters*, Institute for International Economics, Washington, DC.

23. 'The Corporation and the Public: Open for Inspection', World Economic Forum, www.weforum.org, 2 February 2001.

24. Benn R. Konsynski and Jahangir Karimi (1993) 'On the Design of Global Information Systems', in *Globalization, Technology, and Competition: The Fusion of Computers and Telecommunications in the 1990s*, S. Bradley, J. Hausman and R. Nolan (eds), Harvard Business School Press, Boston, 81–108.

25. Michael R. Czinkota and Masaaki Kotabe (2001) *Marketing Management*, 2nd edition, South-Western College Publishing, Cincinnati, 234–235.

26. Corporate Facts, www.QVC.com, accessed 2 October 2003.

27. Gary Hart and Warren B. Rudman (Stephen E. Flynn, Project Director) (2002) *America Still Unprepared – America Still in Danger*, Council on Foreign Relations, New York.

28. Institute of International Education, *Open Doors*, Internet Document, www.iie.org, 2 January 2009.

29. Michael G. Harvey (1989) 'Repatriation of Corporate Executives: An Empirical Study', *Journal of International Business Studies*, 20(spring), 131–144.

30. Joann S. Lublin, 'To Smooth a Transfer Abroad, a New Focus on Kids', *The Wall Street Journal*, 26 January 1999, B1, B14.

31. Nancy J. Adler (1984) 'Women in International Management: Where are They?' *California Management Review*, 26(4), 78–89.

32. 'US Woman in Global Business Face Glass Borders', *Catalyst Perspective*, November 2000, www.catalystwomen.org.

Case Study 1

1. This case was written by Professor Michael R. Czinkota, Georgetown University McDonough School of Business, and graduate student Armen S. Hovhannisyan, Georgetown University School of Foreign Service.

2. Catfish Institute: www.catfishinstitute.com.

3. Elizabeth Becker, 'Delta Farmers Want Copyright on Catfish', *The New York Times*, 16 January 2002, A1.

4. Meredith Petran, 'Catfish', *Restaurant Business*, New York, 1 February 2000.

5. Margot Cohen and Murray Hiebert, 'Muddying the Waters', *Far Eastern Economic Review*, 6 December 2001.

6. 'The Vietnamese Invade: Catfish in the South', *The Economist*, 6 October 2001.

7. Philip Brasher, 'When is a Catfish Not a Catfish', *Washington Post*, 27 December 2001.

8. James Toedman, 'Fighting Like Cats and Dogs Over Fish; It's US vs. Vietnamese as Trade Battle Goes Global', *Newsday*, 10 March 2002, F2.

9. 'The Vietnamese Invade: Catfish in the South', *The Economist*, 6 October 2001.

10. 'One of these negative advertisements, which ran in the national trade weekly *Supermarket News,* tells us in shrill tones, 'Never trust a catfish with a foreign accent!' This ad characterizes Vietnamese catfish as dirty and goes on to say, 'They've grown up flapping around in Third World rivers and dining on whatever they can get their fins on. . . . Those other guys probably couldn't spell US even if they tried'. Quoted in Senator John McCain's 18 December, 2001 Press Release, http://mccain.senate.gov/catfish.htm.

11. Philip Brasher, 'When is a Catfish Not a Catfish', *Washington Post*, 27 December 2001.

12. Philip Brasher, 'When is a Catfish Not a Catfish', *Washington Post*, 27 December 2001.

13. Margot Cohen and Murray Hiebert, 'Muddying the Waters', *Far Eastern Economic Review*, 6 December 2001.

14. Elizabeth Becker, 'Delta Farmers Want Copyright on Catfish', *The New York Times*, 16 January 2002, A1.

15. Elizabeth Becker, 'Delta Farmers Want Copyright on Catfish', *The New York Times*, 16 January 2002 A1.

16. Tim Brown, 'South and Southeast, Vietnam Embroiled in Catfish Controversy', *Marketing News*, 22 October 2001.

17. 'The Vietnamese Invade: Catfish in the South', *The Economist*, 6 October 2001.

18. 'The Vietnamese Invade: Catfish in the South', *The Economist*, 6 October 2001.

19. James Toedman, 'Fighting Like Cats and Dogs Over Fish; It's US vs. Vietnamese as Trade Battle Goes Global', *Newsday*, 10 March 2002, F2.

20. Margot Cohen and Murray Hiebert, 'Muddying the Waters', *Far Eastern Economic Review*, 6 December 2001.

Case Study 5

1. Other significant Russian car manufacturers included AutoUAX, AZLK, KamAZ, Roslada, SeAZ, IzhMash and Doninvest.

2. The Russian government was not, however, anxious for this series of events to unfold. It would also mean that AvtoVAZ would be entering an 18-month period in which it paid no taxes whatever to the government if the option were exercised by the Tax Police.

3. *Sok* means 'juice' in Russian, but in the car sector in Russia, the English-language joke was that SOK was SOKing-up the supplier industry.

4. AvtoVAZ did attempt to restart CIS sales in 1997 with the introduction of hard-currency contracts. The governments of Uzbekistan, Byelorussia and Ukraine, however, forbid residents from converting local currency into hard currency for the purpose of purchasing cars (in two cases, specifically the product of AvtoVAZ). AvtoVAZ has accused the authorities in these countries of working in conjunction with Daewoo of Korea, which has production facilities in Uzbekistan and the Ukraine, in order to shut them out.

5. 'Exclusive Interview: David Herman on GM's Strategy for Russia, www.just-auto.com, September 2000.

6. One of the primary reasons for the success of the Niva was the poor state of Russian roads. The four-wheel drive Niva handled the pot-holed road infrastructure with relative ease.

7. Gregory L. White, 'Off Road: How the Chevy Name Landed on SUV Using Russian Technology', *Wall Street Journal*, 20 February 2001.

8. Gregory L. White, 'Off Road: How the Chevy Name Landed on SUV Using Russian Technology', *Wall Street Journal*, 20 February 2001.

9. The willingness of EBRD to invest was a bit surprising given that two of its previous investments with Russian automakers, GAZ and KamAZ, had resulted in defaults on EBRD credits. A third venture in which EBRD was still a partner (20% equity), Nizhegorod Motors, a JV between Fiat and GAZ, had delayed its car launch from late 1998 to the first half of 2002.

10. Gregory L. White, 'Off Road: How the Chevy Name Landed on SUV Using Russian Technology', *Wall Street Journal*, 20 February 2001.

11. 'David Herman on GM's Strategy for Russia, www.just-auto.com, September 2000.

Case Study 6

1. www.nokia.com.

2. 'Beware Turks Bearing Phones: A Salutary Tale of Byzantine Borrowing', *The Economist*, 31 January 2002.

3. 'Beware Turks Bearing Phones: A Salutary Tale of Byzantine Borrowing', *The Economist*, 31 January 2002.

4. Matthew Swibel, 'The World Billionaires: Dial 'D' For Dummies', *Forbes*, 18 March 2002.

5. Christopher Bowe, 'Beware Turks Bearing Cell Phones: Motorola and Nokia Sue Turkey's TelSim', *Financial Times*, 2 February 2002.

6. http://www.turkishdailynews.com/old_editions/10_07_99/comment.htm.

7. http://www.techlawjournal.com/courts2002/motorola/20020128.asp.

8. http://www.techlawjournal.com/courts2002/motorola/20020128.asp.

9. http://www.motorola.com/content/0,1037,115-280,00.html.

10. http://premium.hoovers.com/subscribe/co/factsnet.xhtml?COID-11023. http://www.hoovers.com/co/capsule/3/0,2163,11023,00.html.

11. Andrea Petersen, 'Motorola Has Third Straight Quarterly Loss,' *The Wall Street Journal*, 10 October 2001.

12. http://www.nokia.com/nokia/0,8764,72,00.html.

13. Michael Minges, Turkey ICT Profile, http://www.itu.int/ITU-D/ict/cs/letters/turkey.html.

14. Michael Minges, Turkey ICT Profile, http://www.itu.int/ITU-D/ict/cs/letters/turkey.html.

15. Karen Lowry Miller, 'The Stupid Loan Bubble: The story of how Motorola and Nokia lost nearly $3 billion in Turkey opens a window on excesses that still threaten big telecoms,' *Newsweek International*, 28 October 2002.

16. 'Beware Turks Bearing Phones: A Salutary Tale of Byzantine Borrowing', *The Economist*, 31 January 2002.

17. Christopher Bowe, 'Beware Turks Bearing Cell Phones: Motorola and Nokia Sue Turkey's TelSim', *Financial Times*, 2 February 2002.

18. Christopher Bowe, 'Beware Turks Bearing Cell Phones: Motorola and Nokia Sue Turkey's TelSim', *Financial Times*, 2 February 2002.

19. 'Judge's Order Prevents Turkey's Uzan Family From Selling Apartments,' *Wall Street Journal*, 30 January 2002.

20. Leyla Boulton, 'Investment Problems', *The Financial Times*, 26 March 2002.

21. Leyla Boulton, 'Investment Problems', *The Financial Times*, 26 March 2002.

22. Leyla Boulton, 'Investment Problems', *The Financial Times*, 26 March 2002.

23. Shawn Young and Hugh Pope, 'Motorola and Nokia Allege Fraud, Sue Turkish Mobile-Phone Family', *The Wall Street Journal*, 29 January 2002.

24. 'Beware Turks Bearing Phones: A Salutary Tale of Byzantine Borrowing', *The Economist*, 31 January 2002.

Case Study 8

1. Lynne Duke, 'Diamond Trade's Tragic Flaw', *Washington Post*, 29 April 2001.

2. General Accounting Office, Critical Issues Remain in Deferring Conflict Diamond Trade. Washington: Government Printing Office, 2002.

3. http://www.newswire.ca/en/releases/archive/April2003/11/CO362.html.

4. http://www.state.gov/r/pa/prs/ps/wo2/1G275.htm.

5. http://www.wto.org/english/news_e/news03_3/goods_council/_zbfer03_3.htm.

Case Study 10

1. This case was written by Soorya Tejomoortula and Rajiv Fernando, under the direction of Ramalingam Meenakshisundaram, ICFAI Center for Management Research (ICMR). It was compiled from published sources, and is intended to be used as a basis for class discussion rather than to illustrate either effective or ineffective handling of a management situation. © 2006, The ICFAI Center for Management Research. All rights reserved. No part of this publication may be reproduced, stored in a retrieval system, used in a spreadsheet or transmitted in any form or by any means – electronic or mechanical, without permission. Reproduced with permission.

2. Paulo Prada, 'Bolivian Nationalizes Oil and Gas Sector', www.nytimes.com, 2 May 2006.

3. Walter Mignolo, 'Nationalization of Natural Gas in Bolivia', www.americas.org, 9 May 2006.

4. Jeffery R. Webber, 'Nationalization of Gas!', www.zmag.org, 4 May 2006.

5. Petroleo Brasileiro SA, popularly known as Petrobras, is a Brazilian government co-owned oil company. It was established in 1953 and is headquartered in Rio de Janeiro. It is a major oil producer and distributor in Brazil. The company is renowned for developing advanced technology for deep water and ultra-deep water oil production (*source*: http://www.en.wikipedia.org/wiki/Petrobras).

6. May Day, also known as the Labor Day or the International Worker's Day, was instituted to commemorate the social and economic achievements of the international labour movement. It also marks the official sanction of the eight-hour work day on 1 May 1886 in the US after agitation by the trade and labour unions. It is usually celebrated in various parts of the world in the form of rallies and demonstrations (*source*: http://www.en.wikipedia.org/wiki/May_day).

7. The European Commission (EC) is the executive body of the member countries of the European Union. Its main function is to propose and implement legislation and also to act as guardian of the treaties signed by the European Union.

8. Fimat International Banque SA is one of the largest global brokerage companies in the world and is a wholly owned subsidiary of Société Générale Group. It offers services to a vast majority of financial institutions, large global industry players on listed or OTC derivatives, cash products such as fixed income, tangible commodities, forex and equities (*source*: www.fimat.com/fimat/).

9. Carlos Alberto Quiroga, 'Bolivia: Gas Nationalization Just the Start', www.today.reuters.com, 1 May 2006.

10. The Institute for the Analysis of Global Security (IAGS) is a non-profit public educational organization that works on energy security. It seeks to promote public awareness on the impact of energy dependency on the US economy and security. It also develops technological and policy solutions that would help to create an era of energy independence, and increase peace, prosperity and stability in the world (*source*: http://www.iags.org/about.htm).

11. 'Take Over in Bolivia Jolts Energy Companies', www.iht.com, 2 May 2006.

12. *The Oil and Gas Journal*, established in 1902, is one of the world's most widely read weekly publications on the petroleum industry.

13. One barrel contains 42 US gallons or 158.99 litres of oil.

14. Repsol-YPF is Spain's biggest oil company with operations in over 30 countries. The company owns 99% of YPF, Argentina's number one oil company, and hence the name Respol-YPF. It operates five refineries in Spain, four in Latin America and produces chemicals, plastics and polymers. It sells oil under the brands Campsa, Petronor and Repsol at more than 3600 service stations in Spain and has about 3000 stations in Latin America (http://www.en.wikipedia.org/wiki/Repsol-YPF).

15. Total SA is a French oil company. It is one of the biggest oil companies in the world.

16. BG Group is an energy production and distribution company headquartered in London, England.

17. Grupo Pluspetrol is an Argentine oil company established in 1976.

18. Coca refers to a plant that is used to manufacture cocaine, a narcotic drug. Efforts were made to destroy coca plantations in an effort to control and contain the illicit drug trade and cocaine drug abuse. However, it was reported that Bolivia was still one of the largest cultivators of coca in the world (the third-largest after Colombia and Peru) with an estimated 26 500 hectares under cultivation in August 2005 (*source:* www.cia.gov).

19. According to a 2001 census, Bolivia had 39 types of indigenous groups making up 61.8% of the total population. Among them, the important indigenous groups were the Quechua and Aymara.

20. 'Will Recent Nationalizations in Bolivia Give Rise to Claims Under Political Risk Insurance Policies?' www.bilaterals.org, 15 June, 2006.

21. Paulo Prada, 'Bolivian Nationalizes Oil and Gas Sector', www.nytimes.com, 2 May 2006.

22. Simon Romero, 'Bolivia Leaps into a Nationalist Flow', www.iht.com, 3 May 2006.

23. 'Nationalization – Threat or Promise?', www.minesandcommunities.org, 14 May 2006.

24. 'Energy in Focus for EU-LatAm Talks'. www.cnn.com, 12 May, 2006.

25. Carin Zissis, 'Bolivia's Nationalization of Oil and Gas', www.cfr.org, 12 May 2006.

26. Fiona Smith, 'Bolivia Gas Nationalization Plan Has Risks', www.businessweek.com, 3 May 2006.

27. Indira A.R. Lakshmanan, 'Some See Bolivia Strategy Backfiring', www.boston.com, 4 May 2006.

28. Indira A.R. Lakshmanan, 'Some See Bolivia Strategy Backfiring', www.boston.com, 4 May 2006.

29. Established in 1975, Petroleos de Venezuela SA (PDVSA) is a state-owned oil exploration and production Company in Venezuela. It is also a major exporter of petroleum from Venezuela and sells it under the brand name, Citgo, in US.

30. Alvaro Zuazo and Natalie Obiko Pearson, 'Bolivia Turns to Venezuela for Gas Help', www.chron.com, 22 May 2006.

31. Alvaro Zuazo and Natalie Obiko Pearson, 'Bolivia Turns to Venezuela for Gas Help', www.chron.com, 22 May 2006.

32. Andean Community refers to a trade bloc that consists of the following South American countries: Bolivia, Colombia, Ecuador, Peru and Venezuela.

33. 'EU: Bolivia's Nationalization of Gas Fields Could Hurt World Energy Markets', www.thestar.com.my, 2 May 2006.

34. 'Brazil Criticizes Bolivia for Nationalizing Natural Gas Industry', www.foxnews.com, 10 May 2006.

35. Occidental Petroleum Corporation established in 1920 is one of the oil corporations in US. The company is based in Los Angeles and its main activities are exploration, production of petroleum products, coal and phosphates.

36. Debora Ray, 'Leaders Back Bolivia Gas Nationalization', www.businessweek.com, 4 May 2006.

37. Bridget Johnson, 'Morales' Move Meant to Enhance his Leftist Street Cred', www.sltrib.com, 10 May 2006.

38. Constant Brand, 'Bolivia Dominates EU-Latin American Summit', www.news.yahoo.com, 12 May 2006.

39. 'Bolivia, Brazil Patch up Differences over Nationalization of Gas Industry', www.cbc.ca, 13 May 2006.

40. Hector Benoit, 'Morales's Nationalization in Bolivia: Who Got Stabbed?' www.globalresearch.ca, 22 May 2006.

41. Saul Hudson, 'Bolivia Nationalization Further Sidelines US', www.today.reuters.com, 8 May 2006.

42. 'Bush Decries "Erosion of Democracy" in Venezuela, Bolivia', www.news.yahoo.com, 22 May 2006.

43. The Hydrocarbons Law No. 1689 was passed on 30 April 1996. Under this law all hydrocarbon reserves were brought under the control of the state. The right to explore and exploit hydrocarbon fields and market the products would be exercised by the state through YPFB. Any individual or legal entity, whether Bolivian or foreign national, could simultaneously enter into one or more joint venture agreements with YPFB for the exploration, exploitation and marketing of hydrocarbons (*source:* http://www.bolivia.usembassy.gov/english/commercial/hclaw.htm).

Case Study 12

1. This case was written by M. Vinaya Kumar, under the direction of Vivek Gupta, ICFAI Center for Management Research (ICMR). It was compiled from published sources, and is intended to be used as a basis for class discussion rather than to illustrate either effective or ineffective handling of a management situation. © 2006, ICFAI Center for

Management Research. All rights reserved. No part of this publication may be reproduced, stored in a retrieval system, used in a spreadsheet, or transmitted in any form or by any means, electronic or mechanical, without permission. Reproduced with permission.

2. 'Danfoss Introduces Innovative Energy Efficient Solutions in China', www.danfoss.com, 20 April 2006.

3. www.danfoss.com.

4. Holip was founded in 2001 in Haiyan, 100 kilometres from Shanghai. It has about 200 employees engaged in manufacturing and marketing variable frequency converters.

5. A frequency converter is an electronic device that converts alternating current (AC) of one frequency to AC of another frequency (source: www.wikipedia.org).

6. 'Danfoss Acquires Chinese Frequency Converter Company', www.danfoss.com, 3 November 2005.

7. On October 1929, the New York Stock Exchange witnessed a sudden fall in the stock prices and the fall continued for the next three years. By 1932, the value of the stocks was about 20% of what they were in 1929. This ruined many investors and banks and about 11 000 of the total 25 000 US banks were affected. This resulted in low consumer spending which reduced production leading to an overall economy downturn. This is referred to as the Great Depression and it also affected Europe and the colonies of European powers. The depression ended in 1939.

8. Thermostats used to control the temperature of radiators (valves) are called radiator thermostats.

9. On 12 May 2006, US$1 = 5.84 Danish Krone and 1 euro = 7.46 Danish Krone.

10. In 1998, Danfoss hived off its hydraulic products manufacturing division under the name Danfoss Fluid Power A/S. It was separated from Danfoss' core business activities.

11. Hu Yan, 'Partner in Success', www.app1.chinadaily.com, 18 September 2003.

12. Line components for refrigeration and air-conditioning include various product categories such as oil separators, shut-off valves, check valves, filters and strainers.

13. Poul Houman Andersen, Poul Rind Christensen, et al., 'Internationalisation of Sourcing and Knowledge Development: An Organisational Routine Perspective', www.lok.cbs.dk, 2003.

14. Scroll compressors, found in air coolers and refrigerators, pump or compress liquids and gases. They are also called scroll vacuum pumps or scroll pumps.

15. Headquartered in Geneva, Switzerland, the World Trade Organization is an international organization dealing with the rules of trade between nations through the agreements negotiated and signed by the respective member countries.

The main aim of the WTO is to help producers, exporters and importers of goods and services in conducting their businesses (source: www.wto.org).

16. William E. Hoover Jr, 'Making China Your Second Home Market: An Interview with the CEO of Danfoss', www.mckinseyquarterly.com, 2006.

17. Cold chain logistics involves temperature-controlled warehousing, distribution, trucking and direct store delivery. These are supported by refrigeration technologies, and well-trained staff and workforce, which ensure food safety.

18. William E. Hoover Jr., 'Making China Your Second Home Market: An Interview with the CEO of Danfoss', www.mckinseyquarterly.com, 2006.

19. On 12 May 2006, 1 euro = US$1.2767 or 1 US$ = 0.78 326 euro.

20. www.danfoss.com.

21. 'Air-conditioning Market Hotting Up', www.china.org.cn, 22 September 2005.

22. Hu Yan, 'Chilling Tales from the China Market', www.shanghai-star.com.cn, 14 April 2006.

Case Study 13

1. This case was written by Suresh Gujarathi, under the direction of Sanjib Dutta, The ICFAI Center for Management Research (ICMR). It was compiled from published sources, and is intended to be used as a basis for class discussion rather than to illustrate either effective or ineffective handling of a management situation. ©2006, The ICFAI Center for Management Research. All rights reserved. No part of this publication may be reproduced, stored in a retrieval system, used in a spreadsheet, or transmitted in any form or by any means, electronic or mechanical, without permission. Reproduced with permission.

2. Daniel Twining, 'Putin's Power Politics', The Weekly Standard, 16 January 2006.

3. The European Union (EU), an intergovernmental and supranational union of democratic countries, was founded to enhance political, economic and social co-operation.

4. http://blog.kievukraine.info/2005_12_01_kievukrainenewsblog_ archive.html.

5. Naftogaz owns the transit pipelines that carry Russian gas to European countries.

6. On 22 November 2005, Gazprom demanded that Ukraine pay US$160 per Tcm of gas.

7. G8 stands for Group of 8, a group of rich and powerful democratic countries, whose members meet every year to discuss political and economic matters of international importance. Its members are Canada, France, Germany, Italy, Japan, the UK, the US and the Russian Federation.

8. As Gazprom is controlled by the Russian state and Naftogaz by Ukraine, the terms Gazprom and Russia and Naftogaz and Ukraine have been used without any distinction, unless specifically mentioned otherwise.

9. Ukraine also imported gas from Turkmenistan.

10. 'Société Générale de Surveillance' (SGS), based in Switzerland, is the world's leading company in inspection, verification, testing, and certification of materials and products.

11. The disintegration of the Union of Soviet Socialist Republics, usually called the Soviet Union, in 1991, resulted in the birth of 15 newly independent states: Russia, Ukraine, Belarus, Moldova, Latvia, Lithuania, Estonia, Armenia, Azerbaijan, Georgia, Kazakhstan, Kyrgyzstan, Uzbekistan, Tajikistan and Turkmenistan.

12. Most of the agreements that Gazprom had with other gas companies of the former Soviet Union republics and European countries came under the ambit of Inter-governmental Protocols and therefore the state was as much responsible for the gas supplies as the company itself.

13. RosUkrEnergo, a Swiss-registered company formed in 2004, was a 50:50 joint venture between a Gazprom subsidiary and an Austrian-registered company, Centragas, which was managed by an Austrian bank on behalf of undisclosed owners (*source:* http://news.bbc.co.uk/1/hi/business/4569846.stm, 4 January 2006).

14. Gazprom was privatized between 1993 and 1995, under the Russian Privatization law. Even then, in 2004, the Russian state held a non-majority stake of more than 38 % in Gazprom. In 2005, the Russian government paid US$7.12 billion to acquire a majority stake.

15. St Petersburg was the capital of the Russian Empire, prior to the Russian Revolution of 1917.

16. Mikhail Gorbachev was the last General Secretary (1985–1991) and President (1990–1991) of the former Union of Soviet Socialist Republics. His attempts to introduce political and economic reforms through Perestroika (restructuring) and Glasnost (openness) unleashed separatist forces in the republics and ultimately led to the collapse of the Soviet Union. He is also credited with facilitating the end of the Cold War.

17. As of September 2002, Gazprom held 100 % stake in 66 companies, more than 50 % stake in 44 companies and up to 50 % stake in 52 companies.

18. www.gazprom.ru.

19. OMV, founded in 1956, was Austria's largest listed company in 2005 and a leading oil and gas group in Central and East Europe.

20. www.gazprom.ru.

21. 'The Transfer of the Crimea to the Ukraine', http://www.iccrimea.org/historical/crimeatransfer.html.

22. The agreement was to be effective from 1997 to 2017.

23. 'Russia–Ukraine Gas Dispute', http://en.wikipedia.org/wiki/Russia-Ukraine_gas_dispute.

24. Domestic gas prices in Russia are regulated and stipulated by the government and as a result are very low for various political reasons. In 2004, the price of gas in Russia for domestic consumption was US$27 per Tcm.

25. Jonathan Stern, 'Ukraine: EU Neighbourhood Policy and Natural Gas Security', University of Dundee, 2005, http://www.oxfordenergy.org/pdfs/comment_0106.pdf.

26. Jonathan Stern, 'Ukraine: EU Neighbourhood Policy and Natural Gas Security', University of Dundee, 2005, http://www.oxfordenergy.org/pdfs/comment_0106.pdf.

27. Vnesheconombank, founded in 1924, was a specialized state financial institution. It ensured centralized foreign economic operations, serviced sovereign foreign debt, granted loans and issued guarantees on behalf of the Government of the Russian Federation.

28. Jonathan Stern, 'Ukraine: EU Neighbourhood Policy and Natural Gas Security', University of Dundee, 2005, http://www.oxfordenergy.org/pdfs/comment_0106.pdf.

29. North Atlantic Treaty Organization (NATO), established in 1949, is an international organization for collective security headquartered at Brussels in Belgium.

30. Transportation tariffs in the most important transit countries in Western Europe in 2005 were: US$2.5/Tcm/100 km in Germany and US$2.7/Tcm/100 km in Austria.

31. 'On Alexey Miller's Meeting with Ivan Plachkov and Alexey Ivchenko, 28 March 2005', http://www.rustocks.com/index.phtml/Pressreleases/0/74/7338?filter=2005.

32. Large amounts of gas were stored in underground storage facilities as a hedge against the increased demand during severe winters.

33. Jonathan Stern, 'Ukraine: EU Neighbourhood Policy and Natural Gas Security', University of Dundee, 2005, http://www.oxfordenergy.org/pdfs/comment_0106.pdf.

34. 'Ukraine May Raise Rent on Russia's Black Sea Fleet', http://www.globalsecurity.org/wmd/library/news/ukraine/ukraine-051209-rferl01.htm.

35. 'US 'Committed' To Ukraine's Integration With West', http://www.globalsecurity.org/wmd/library/news/ukraine/ukraine-051207-rferl01.htm.

36. 'Russian Officials Dismiss Ukraine's Threat On Sevastopol', http://www.globalsecurity.org/wmd/library/news/russia/2005/russia-051210-rferl01.htm.

37. The Arbitration Institute of the Stockholm Chamber of Commerce, established in 1917, was a leading arbitration institute for the resolution of trade disputes.

38. Jonathan Stern, 'The Russian–Ukrainian Gas Crisis of January 2006', Oxford Institute for Energy Studies, January 2006. http://www.oxfordenergy.org/pdfs/comment_0106.pdf.

39. In 2005, Gazprom bought only 7 Bcm of gas from Turkmenistan.

40. Roman Kupchinsky, 'East: Ukraine, Russia Spar Over Turkmen Gas', 20 April 2005. http://www.energybulletin.net/5478.html.

41. Some Russians argued that if Ukraine wanted to move to a market economy, it should pay market prices for its gas imports. They said that when people go to a petrol station for filling the car, they simply pay the price. They do not bargain or negotiate or haggle over the price.

42. 'Russia Vows to End Gas Shortage', http://news.bbc.co.uk/2/hi/europe/4575726.stm.

43. 'Press Shivers from Gas Woes', http://news.bbc.co.uk/1/hi/world/europe/4578000.stm.

44. Jonathan Stern, 'The Russian–Ukrainian Gas Crisis of January 2006', Oxford Institute for Energy Studies, January 2006, http://www.oxfordenergy.org/pdfs/comment_0106.pdf.

45. 'Wrap: Russia–Ukraine Natural Gas Dispute Settled', http://en.rian.ru/world/20060104/42849487.html.

Case Study 14

1. This case was written by K. Subhadra, under the direction of Sanjib Dutta, ICFAI Center for Management Research (ICMR). It was compiled from published sources, and is intended to be used as a basis for class discussion rather than to illustrate either effective or ineffective handling of a management situation. © 2004, ICFAI Center for Management Research. All rights reserved. No part of this publication may be reproduced, stored in a retrieval system, used in a spreadsheet, or transmitted in any form or by any means, electronic or mechanical, without permission. Reproduced with permission.

2. Isabelle de Pommereau, 'Wal-Mart lesson: Smiling service won't win Germans', www.csmonitor.com, 17 October 2002.

3. Daniel Rubin, 'Grumpy German Shoppers Distrust the Wal-Mart Style', www.gaccwa.org, 30 December 2001.

4. EDLP was a pricing strategy adopted by Wal-Mart to ensure lowest prices among all retail chains on its products.

5. Wal-Mart's employees are called Associates.

6. An annual national survey on philanthropy and corporate citizenship.

7. K-mart is a leading US retailer.

8. Target is one of the leading discount US retail chains.

9. NAFTA, signed in 1993, removed most of the trade and investment barriers between the United States, Canada and Mexico.

10. Jeremy Khan, 'Wal-Mart Goes Shopping in Europe', Fortune, 7 June 1999.

11. 'Operations Evolve to Offset Doldrums in Deutschland', DSN Retailing Today, 5 June 2001.

12. It was reported that Wal-Mart had the highest employee costs among German retailers. The high costs were attributed to heavy recruiting by Wal-Mart anticipating huge business and its misreading of the German retailing environment. For instance, Wal-Mart had to lay off employees who were taken on as greeters as the German public did not take to the idea, and it also had to cut down the number of employees in many stores due to low sales.

13. In a centralized wage bargaining process, the wages across all companies in a particular industry are decided according to the average productivity in the industry.

14. The German Supreme Court felt that Wal-Mart pricing margarine below cost was legal as it was done for only a brief period. However the court was against Wal-Mart's pricing of sugar and milk below cost prices.

15. Many European firms had filed cases against Germany's alterations to its commercial code, which required the firms to publish financial information. The European Court of Justice's decision was still awaited.

16. As per Ten-Foot Rule of the company, whenever an employee comes within 10 feet of a customer, the employee should look up to the customer, greet him/her and ask if s/he needs any help.

17. Loyalty Cards were offered by supermarkets and big retail chains to select loyal customers. The businesses offered special prices for the customers possessing loyalty cards. However, in 2002, many customer groups accused companies of using loyalty cards to track down the purchasing patterns of the customers and started opposing loyalty card schemes.

18. Wendy Zellner, 'How Well Does Wal-Mart Travel?' Business Week, 3 September 2001.

19. Wal-Mart Supercenters were opened in 1988. They combined full grocery lines and general merchandise under one roof, giving customers the opportunity to purchase food and non-food products from a single retail outlet in a one-stop family shopping experience.

INDEX